Ninth Edition

The Theory and Practice of International Relations

WILLIAM CLINTON OLSON

Dean Emeritus, School of International Service
The American University, Washington, D.C.

with

JAMES R. LEE

School of International Service
The American University, Washington, D.C.

Prentice-Hall International, Inc.

© 1994 by Prentice-Hall, Inc.
A Simon & Schuster Company
Englewood Cliffs, New Jersey 07632

Printed in the United States of America

10 9 8 7 6 5 4 3 2 1

ISBN   0-13-098823-5

Prentice-Hall International (UK) Limited, *London*
Prentice-Hall of Australia Pty. Limited, *Sydney*
Prentice-Hall Canada Inc., *Toronto*
Prentice-Hall Hispanoamericana, S.A., *Mexico*
Prentice-Hall of India Private Limited, *New Delhi*
Prentice-Hall of Japan, Inc., *Tokyo*
Simon & Schuster Asia Pte. Ltd., *Singapore*
Editora Prentice-Hall do Brasil, Ltda., *Rio de Janeiro*
Prentice-Hall, Inc., *Englewood Cliffs, New Jersey*

To the memory of Robert Gale Woolbert, master teacher, scholar *extraordinaire*, bibliographer for the Council on Foreign Relations quarterly *Foreign Affairs*, counsellor for the serious student, erudite wit in Latin as well as English, constant friend and coworker in the Foundation for the Advancement of the Social Sciences in Denver, in short, the ultimate role model for a young professional in the struggling "discipline of international relations" (a term which he, a distinguished *historian* would have disdained), this ninth edition is dedicated with love and appreciation.

CONTENTS

PART II   THE TRANSFORMATION OF CLASSICAL THEORY

PREFACE

Changes in the composition of what only a few months ago were termed "satellite" governments, to say nothing of the collapse of the USSR itself, would seem to render any book pretending to explain international relations today out-of-date before it emerges from the printing presses. Then the dramatic implementation of the United Nations security procedure in Kuwait demonstrated the organization's ability to deal effectively with aggression by a strong state against a weak one. No wonder the leader of an even stronger state, whose diplomacy and military might had made possible what President Bush fondly called "the hundred hours' war," felt justified in proclaiming a "new international order."

Yet the fundamentals of the analysis of world developments are not all that transitory. If we have learned anything at all since 1919 and before from the efforts of hundreds of scholars in dozens of countries to create a "scientific study of international relations," it is that even what has recently occurred should fit into paradigms already in place to help us to understand the source and the significance of those events. Fitting recent events into paradigms (both old and new) is what this ninth edition is designed to accomplish.

Though this is a revision of what is called a "previous work," about ninety-five percent (many of them by the growing cadre of outstanding female scholars in the field) of the selections have never before appeared in this series. "Theory," given primary attention in the Introduction, figures prominently throughout the book in recent writings by such intellectual leaders in the field as Steve Smith, Joseph Nye, James N. Rosenau and Richard Rosecrance. The "practice" side of the ledger is now better represented in the writing of such statesmen as Boutros Boutros-Ghali, Andrei Kozyrev, Michel Rocard, and Li Peng. As always, we try never to lose sight of the basic hypothesis of this long-standing text, namely that one cannot understand IR without theoretical grounding just as one cannot understand it without frequent reference to the "real" world, and above all, without seeing the connection between the two. In this inexact science, theory rarely creates nor always reflects practice, but if the discipline is ever to make a significant contribution to the improvement of international society, this linkage must be a strong one. Scholar-statesmen like Zbigniew Brezinski, Carlos Fuentes, Tom Farer, and Mohammed Ayoob reflect and demonstrate that essential linkage.

Earlier prefaces have indicated that "*T AND P*" should be utilized as a "second book" to supplement the assigned text in an introductory course in international relations. Professors from all over the country as well as abroad who have made use of other editions advise me that this is not necessarily so and that this may well be adopted as a textbook, especially for courses somewhat more advanced than the conventional "background of current events" variety. Without trying to mimic a dictionary, we have endeavored to clarify—by usage—such basic concepts and terminology in the discipline as systems theory, sovereignty, balance of power, diplomacy, imperialism, regimes, nation-state, ethnicity, functionalism, ecopolitics, strategy, geopolitics, international political economy, and collective security, to name but a few.

Starting with an introduction devoted mainly to theory, eleven chapters organized into three principal divisions dealing with various aspects of IR follow.

Part One concerns "the new world order"—how will the Clinton Administration pursue Bush's initiative at the conclusion of the Gulf war and how have foreign leaders reacted to the whole idea?

Part Two is concerned with transformations in classical theory in the generally acknowledged basic elements that make up the discipline, or field, of international relations, cast in terms of "players in the game" of world politics—the roles of the state, diplomacy, the "international system," law and institutions, and the new organizing concept of "regime theory."

Part Three is concerned with the competition of values in such problem areas as security and conflict management, environmental issues, trade and the world economy, and democracy and human rights. In each category, an attempt has been made to present different, but responsible, contemporary analyses and viewpoints from many countries, and to avoid any particular "line," be it political, ideological or professional.

Readers should find the carefully chosen quotations that precede the introductory material for each chapter full of useful insights by some of the giants of international thought over a long period of time. Following each introduction will be found a series of "discussion questions," designed both for the student and for the instructor in order to relate the selections and the introduction to one another in a provocative manner.

Finally, over the years since the project was undertaken, many changes have taken place in the way scholars look at international relations. The once standard "state-centric" approach now has many challengers. In a community of discourse in which such expressions as "global village" abound, power is no longer what American idiom might call "the be-all and end-all" in international relations. Perhaps to be more accurate, security is being seen in ways other than military. Without abandoning the essentially classical tradition upon which this series has from the beginning been based, this edition endeavors to be even more sensitive to these emerging areas of security concerns.

Once again, I happily acknowledge what I owe to my dear wife, Betsy. Her direct and indirect support have been more helpful than she can ever realize in half a century of her husband's multifarious efforts at international education, all the way from being a T.A. at Yale and a neophyte professor at the ideal college which is Pomona, to trying to inform Congressmen about foreign affairs, to running a famous study center in Italy, to agonizing over giving foundation grants to the most worthy, to "Deaning" at American and Columbia, to the return again and again to the best of all professions—teaching, and now to full-time writing.

Deep-felt thanks are also due to Professor Barry Hughes in the conceptual stage and to Christopher Laxton in editing. Most importantly, I wish to acknowledge the contributions of a new partner in producing another edition of this old standby, Professor James R. Lee, who is equally at home in government research and the halls of academe, in economics and in politics, and in time-honored analytical principles and the most advanced methodological techniques. He is mainly responsible for chapters two, nine, and ten. Professor Lee's teaching assistant, Kate Bunting, has earned the gratitude of us both in the professional way in which she has assisted with the final production of the manuscript. Christopher Dwyer and Peggy Gill of Faculty Services at the School of International Service have been unfailingly helpful in meeting every request for assistance, often on short notice. And in closing, we all wish to say that the constructive encouragement of the Political Science editor at Prentice Hall, Julia Berrisford, has been particularly valuable to us.

Windmill Creek Farm
Port Royal, Pennsylvania

The Theory and Practice
of
International Relations

INTRODUCTION

NEW INSIGHTS IN INTERNATIONAL RELATIONS THEORY

The French say that if one does not have what one would like, one must be content with what one has got. Resigned, perhaps. But content? A state of dissatisfaction is a goad to research. Scholars in international relations have two good reasons to be dissatisfied: the state of the world and the state of their discipline. If only these two reasons always converged!

Stanley Hoffman, 1977[1]

Are things any better in IR now than they were when these words were written? In terms of theoretical advancement, unquestionably yes. In terms of consensus and clear definition, the wisdom of Quincy Wright, in the best book ever written about the study of IR, is still worth pondering nearly half a century later:

> International relations has only begun to emerge as a recognized discipline treated comprehensively and systematically in textbooks and academic curricula. . . . Some say a discipline exists only in so far as a body of data has been systematized by a

---

[1]"An American Social Science: International Relations," *Daedalus*, Vol. 1, Summer 1977, p. 59. This seminal article, while it seemed to reflect Hoffmann's unawareness of most of what had been accomplished by the idealist school in the inter-war period in the study of IR in the United States in favor of the contributions of European-trained realists from the mid-forties, remains one of the most influential ever written in and about our discipline.

distinctive analytical method. This definition would deny the title to most *academic* disciplines, but at least a discipline implies consciousness by writers that there is a subject with some sort of unity. . . .[2]

The first textbooks on IR as such which began to appear in the early 1920s in fact recognized that consciousness. This broke down in the 1930s, only to reappear in a radically different form in the 1940s and 1950s. Now that the Cold War is over, is it to surface again?

Today, a number of serious writers express serious doubts. Helen Milner is concerned that "in much current thinking, anarchy has been declared to be the fundamental assumption about international politics."[3] She disagrees, but feels this assumption has held back theory in IR. Two thoughtful leaders in the theory field, Yale Ferguson and Richard Mansbach, regret that "unfortunately, even as we urgently need to make sense of this new world of ours, theories of international relations are similarly in a condition of unprecedented disarray,"[4] while Mark Hoffman goes even further in stating that "International Relations as an academic discipline is at a major crossroads."[5] One reason for this, argues Steve Smith, is what he calls a "paradigmatic dominance" by US neo-realists which has "led to the subject strongly reflecting US policy concerns" and "made it very difficult for the subject to evolve on a cross-national, cumulative basis."[6] In other words, it is that IR is not international enough—that it still seems to experience problems in developing legitimacy as an academic discipline.

It is not that progress has not been made. The current cadre of highly trained specialists in theory readily concede that it has, but what is elusive is a third period of consensus (the first being the quest for peace and the second the quest for power, but more of that later). The discipline seems to be going in what John Groom of Canterbury thinks is at least three directions at once: world society approaches, structural analysis, and what he calls "realism resurgent," and observes that

[2]Quincy Wright, *The Study of International Relations* (New York: Appleton-Century-Crofts, 1955), p. 23.

[3]Helen Milner, "The Assumption of Anarchy in International Relations Theory: a Critique," *Review of International Studies*, 17, 1991, p. 67. Professor Milner, a member of the Institute of European Studies at Columbia, is a specialist on international economic cooperation. The *RIS* is probably the best single source of readable IR theory extant in professional periodicals today, the British contingent managing to continue to express profound ideas in plain English in refreshing contrast to the American propensity for obscurantist jargon.

[4]Yale H. Ferguson and Richard W. Mansbach, "Between Celebration and Despair: Constructive Suggestions for Future International Theory," *International Studies Quarterly*, 35, 1991, p. 363.

[5]Mark Hoffman, "Critical Theory and the Inter-Paradigm Debate," *The Study of International Relations: the State of the Art*, ed. by Hugh C. Dyer and Leon Mangasarian (London: Macmillan, 1989), p. 60. An American, Mark Hoffman teaches IR at the London School of Economics and Political Science.

[6]Steve Smith, "Paradigm Dominance in International Relations: the Development of International Relations as a Social Science," *Millenium: Journal of International Studies*, 16, 2, Summer 1987, p. 189. Now a Professor at the University College of Wales in Aberystwyth, Steve Smith has made a signal contribution to the discipline as chair of the editorial board of the Cambridge University Press/British International Studies Association "Cambridge Studies in International Relations" series.

IR comes in many forms. There is Academic IR, which develops theory and coherence, and Instrumental IR, which is concerned with utility. Colonial IR is about the domination of the center and Scientific IR is about method. Reasonable IR valuesprudence and Providential IR relates to conceptual categories. To this we can add Post-modern IR.[7]

Lest the reader conclude, before even getting into the subject, that IR represents as backward a world as politics itself, let it be noted that mathematics has invaded the discipline and there are more keen minds dealing with IR theory in this and other dimensions than ever before. The discipline may be moving in many directions, but it *is* moving. One of the most impressive recent advances, for example, is reflected in Nicholson's seminal new work, *Formal Theories in International Relations,* in which he opens his treatment of the present state of formal and mathematical international relations theory with the observation that this is "a growing field which, though regarded merely as a passing fashion by some, holds great promise."[8] That is both the joy and despair of IR—it's always been that way. But surely IR can no more be sure of where it is going than the reality which it endeavors scientifically to analyze—what in *The Tempest* Shakespeare called "the great globe itself."

While this edition does not pretend to offer any fundamental *theoretical* contribution to the literature, the reader will find a number of selections with keen insights into theory in this complex field by writers who also deal with practice—how things are actually done. This, after all, has always been the *raison d'etre* for this particular series—to bring together what have so often been apart (even miles apart), the experience of the practitioners and the vision of the thinkers about IR. Zbigniew Brzezinski draws on his years of service as National Security advisor to the President to advocate "selective global commitment" by policy-makers, while another former member of the NSC staff, Jessica Tuchman Matthews, feels that the time has come to redefine security. The Secretary-General of the United Nations, Boutros Boutros-Ghali, pleads for greater attention to the problems of Africa, just as a leading environmental scientist in Canada, Peter Sand, forcibly argues the case for collective responsibility in ecology. Several world leaders and diplomats are represented. And so on.

In this introductory chapter, four quite different new insights which concentrate upon the theory of international relations have been chosen. An established thinker opens the discussion. Seyom Brown endeavors to show that, despite the failure of leading experts to "predict" the downfall of the USSR and its

---

[7]William C. Olson and A.J.R. Groom, *International Relations Then and Now: Origins and Trends in Interpretation* (London: HarperCollins Academic/Routledge, 1991), p. 305. This work, which the authors call "the little book" because it deals with such a vast subject in less than 500 pages, traces the development from ancient times of concepts about the relationships between peoples and states. The authors, Olson taking the period up to the 1960s and Groom bringing down to the present, stress the period since a kind of discipline began to emerge toward the end of the first World War, concentrating upon the Anglo-American contribution. It might be noted that until very recently useful additions rarely came from anywhere else!

[8]Michael Nicholson, *Formal Theories in International Relations* (Cambridge: Cambridge University Press, 1989), p. xi.

international system, the basic theoretical predispositions of the discipline remain sound. Nevertheless, in a delightful and provocative expose, he feels compelled to offer five explanations of why the collapse happened. As one of the pioneers in the emerging field of feminist IR theory, Marysia Zalewski brings a fresh perspective which is still struggling for recognition from exponents of the realist-positivist explanation of IR, dominant since World War II and especially the Cold War. With the end of that period, certain paradigms may now be effectively challenged, some of which are institutional as well as philosophical and social. For example, *androcentrism* (male predominance) in parliaments, scientific establishments, security regimes, and universities themselves has fundamentally colored theory. A window of opportunity for a new theoretical breakthrough has suddenly presented itself and Zalewski reviews what she and certain other feminist IR theorists hope to do about it, including the presentation of the paper excerpted in this section at the Atlanta ISA convention in 1992. Another younger writer who is essentially outside the mainstream of IR thought is James R. Lee (a former student of David McLellan at Riverside and a member of Dean Olson's doctoral seminar in IR theory at American, who along with Fred Sonderman of Colorado College formed the original three collaborators in this series). Leading into Part I of the book, which asks how new the "new world order" will be, Lee speculates as to whether anything is changing in the four distinct aspects of the discipline itself. He argues that the "valueless orientation characteristic of the realistic approach" might well now give way to a return to what he calls the kind of "moral stance" in the analysis of and prescriptions for altering and hopefully improving relationships between states and peoples which underlay the very purpose of the study of international relations in the first place, following hard upon the horrors of the first World War. To fill out this opening chapter, we turn to another stalwart in the discipline, James N. Rosenau. In referring to the "1980s puzzle," he breaks new ground once again in presenting a challenging theory concerning not only obvious technological and communications advancement but peoples' basic needs and fundamental values. He concludes that instead of what appears to be turbulence and chaos, there in fact may well be an "underlying set of structures sustained by increasingly skillful citizens eventually adapting to the dynamism of change." Grappling with similar issues in his contribution, Seyom Brown, Wien Professor of International Cooperation at Brandeis, advances five explanations for the collapse of the global rivalry between the USSR and the USA which might serve to show that "our *basic* assumptions about how the world works have not been seriously contradicted by these unanticipated occurrences."

Does any of this represent consensus? Looking back upon the early development of IR, an initial phase produced what William Olson calls the "period of the first consensus," which was the quest for peace.[9] Indeed, preventing war through collective security and international order was the central value upon which the emerging discipline was based. But just as the democracies, for all their commitment to freedom, proved unable to stop the dictators, the consensus

[9]Olson and Groom, *op. cit.*, pp. 56–78.

of the peace-seeking IR specialists collapsed with the League of Nations. The literature of the 1930s, while profound and often moving, was inconsistent, offering little of value to policy-makers in their futile efforts to cope with Hitler. Even as war was breaking out in September 1939, there appeared one of the seminal works in the history of IR, E.H. Carr's *The Twenty Years' Crisis,* blaming academics along with parsons, editorial writers, MPs, and the public in general for misunderstanding the meaning of power.[10] This policy paucity in turn resulted in a new criterion for the study, the analysis of the quest for power.[11] From this second consensus came a long period—roughly corresponding to the Cold War—of what Smith has termed the "paradigm dominance" of the policy-oriented American realists.

Theory is always elusive, indeed, to some students undertaking their studies in this field, even intimidating. It can be very simple: theory tries to explain why what happens, happens in the way it does, in as objective and scientific a way as possible. Whether it actually succeeds in doing that is something else, and when one gets into what the object of science is supposed to be, which is to be able to predict, IR specialists find themselves less certain of themselves than any other of the social scientists. This is because while the State can organize itself internally in a fairly logical manner, based upon existing conditions and smoothly functioning governmental machinery, relations *between* States have never, except for brief periods and for particular purposes, been able to accomplish that. Despite all the talk about such theoretical concepts as "global village" or "international society," the governing theory is still that each State is sovereign.

Leaders of a State may think it is sovereign and whether anyone else likes it or not, they claim in practice that it can do whatever it pleases—or at least what it can get away with—just so it doesn't begin to interfere with the parallel ability of other States to do likewise. Saddam Hussein and his followers and spokesmen, from the mobs of Baghdad to the serene halls of the General Assembly in New York, may represent the most outspokenly articulate exponents of this old idea on the world stage today. But the Oxford-trained Thatcher thought and acted on the basis of the same premises when as "the Iron Lady" of diplomacy she recovered the Falklands from Argentina. Saddam took something that wasn't his, though he claimed it was a province of Iraq, and Thatcher recovered something which was hers, though Argentina claimed Britain had stolen it over a century earlier (actually it was from the colonial hegemony of the day—Spain). The myth of sovereignty has an answer for everything—even Serbia's "ethnic cleansing" of the Moslems of Sarajevo and armed gangs stealing food given by an aroused international community to emaciated Somalian babies.

---

[10]Edward Hallett Carr, *The Twenty-Years' Crisis 1919–1919: an Introduction to the Study of International Relations* (London: Macmillan, 1939). In one of the first and most influential contributions to the realist approach to IR theory which began to emerge with World War II, Carr was severely criticized for appearing to justify the infamous Munich settlement between Chamberlain and Hitler; a second edition appeared in 1946 omitting this section. Before becoming the chief editorialist for the London *Times,* Carr had held the Chair in International Politics at Aberystwyth (the University College of Wales), the first in the discipline, created in 1923.

[11]Olson and Groom, *op. cit.,* pp. 104–29.

While it is stimulating, even at times titillating, to eagerly pore over these latest headlines and watch the sharp explosive images coming in on the TV screen, these alone really provide little in the way of understanding why it is all happening that way. Crisis tumbles upon crisis, but that is just what in high school and college used to be called "Current Events." One thing that made early courses by teachers of international politics unpopular with other professors was their very popularity with students who were fascinated with getting what seemed to be "inside dope" about Mukden, Abyssinia, the Sudetenland, the fall of France, and the Battle of Britain, which Edward R. Murrow described nightly on the family radio, starting with his famous opener, "This—is London." The next morning the IR prof explained it all.

That has all changed now. The generation of the 1960s concluded after watching the killing and the "body count" from Vietnam that neither the U.S. Civil War nor the two World Wars could have happened had there been TV then. Yet this was a period which produced some of the best work in IR theory. Shortly after Wright produced his monumental treatise in 1955 on the development of the study of international relations from the perspective of several different disciplines, Kaplan broke through with his complex *System and Process in International Politics* (1957, unfortunately, a somewhat intimidating book more often criticized than read).[12] The next decade saw two anthologies which successfully endeavored to canvas the best theoretical thinking represented in the work of leading writers of the time, Hoffmann's *Contemporary Theory in International Relations* (1960)[13] and Knorr and Rosenau's *Contending Approaches to International Politics* (1970), the very title revealing the nature of the consensus problem which still plagues—or blesses—the field).[14] These books (if they can be found) are still very much worth reading and indeed adding to serious IR students' private libraries. A different type of treatment appeared at the end of the 1970s, *Contending Theories of International Relations: a Comprehensive Survey* (1981), which was not an anthology but a full-fledged analysis of theory and its various exponents by two penetrating scholars, Dougherty and Pfaltzgraff, the third edition of which marked the end of yet another decade (1990).[15] Light and Groom judge which to be "probably the preeminent general survey of approaches to the study of IR."[16]

Meanwhile literally hundreds of articles, chapters, books, and summaries demonstrate the intellectual vigor of IR. The literary phase of this brief introduction may as well end with a strong recommendation to acquire two more recent anthologies which analyze the literature, "musts" for the serious student,

---

[12]Morton A. Kaplan, *System and Process in International Politics* (New York: John Wiley and Sons, 1957).

[13]Stanley Hoffmann, *Contemporary Theory in Interntional Relations* (Englewood Cliffs, N.J.: Prentice-Hall, Inc., 1960).

[14]Klaus Knorr and James N. Rosenau, eds., *Contending Approaches to International Politics* (Princeton, N.J.: Princeton University Press, 1970).

[15]James E. Dougherty and Robert L. Pfaltzgraff, Jr., *Contending Theories of International Relations: a Comprehensive Survey* (New York: Harper and Row, 1981–1990).

[16]Margot Light and A.J.R. Groom, eds., *International Relations: A Handbook of Current Theory* (Boulder, CO: Lynne Rienner Publishers, Inc., 1985), p. 218.

by Groom with Mitchell in 1978, *International Relations Theory: a Bibliography*,[17] and with Light in 1985, *International Relations: a Handbook of Current Theory*.[18] Two years later in the United States, Patrick Morgan came out with the fourth edition of his provocative, even fun-loving, *Theories and Approaches to International Politics: What Are We to Think?*.[19] Armed with these, one can really attack this burgeoning and exciting subject with enthusiasm and at least a prospect of understanding.

DISCUSSION QUESTIONS

1. How would you define "theory?" Do you find the term or the idea behind it intimidating?
2. Do you agree with Helen Milner's contention that one of the basic—and faulty—"assumptions" among writers on world politics is that this is a world of anarchy? Just what is "anarchy?" What are some of the alternatives?
3. Lee deplores the "value-free" approach to social science in general and IR in particular. If you agree, what values should be introduced into the study of IR? Is "power" a value? Is "peace?" What about "development?" Or "patriotism?"
4. Explain Zalewski's critique of IR theory. How would IR change if the feminist approach were more influential than it has been in the past? Have women leaders in fact been less warlike in office?
5. After having read Rosenau, take another look at the quotation from Stanley Hoffmann which opens this chapter, which he wrote a decade and a half ago. Is the world better off now? Is the study of IR? The world of politics, needless to say, affects IR, but is there any evidence that it works the other way 'round—in other words, does IR make any difference in the so-called "real world"?
6. In what ways, if any, do you think policy-makers can benefit from theory? Can you think of any recent world leader who has exhibited any grasp of theory at all—Mao Tse-tung? Mitterand? Thatcher? Reagan? Cueller de Perez? Gorbachev? What about President Clinton, who actually "majored" in International Relations as an undergraduate at the School of Foreign Service at Georgetown before going to Oxford as a Rhodes Scholar?
7. Which of Brown's five "explanations" do you find the most convincing? The least? Is he too defensive about the failure of the panjandrums of IR to predict the historic events of 1989–91?
8. What's wrong with the "current events" approach to learning about IR?

[17]A.J.R. Groom and C.R. Mitchell, eds., *International Relations Theory: a Bibliography* (London: Frances Pinter Ltd., 1978).

[18]*op. cit.*, fn 16.

[19]Patrick M. Morgan, *Theories and Approaches to International Politics: What Are We to Think?*, 4th ed. New Brunswick and Oxford: Transaction Books, 1987. If the reader doubts our judgement that this is a fun-loving book, let him just note the title of the first chapter: "An Ointment with Many Flies," or the last, "Kant-or-Cant-or Can't?". *Tempus fugit.*

9. Re: the "I" in "IR", should it connote inter-*state* or inter-*nation* relations, or both?
10. What is the principal argument in Rosenau's "relocation of authority" article? Do you agree with it? Why or why not?

1 EXPLAINING THE TRANSFORMATION OF WORLD POLITICS

SEYOM BROWN

Chairman of the Department of Politics and Lawrence A. Wien Professor of International Cooperation, Brandeis University, Waltham, Massachusetts, Seyom Brown is the author of *New Forces, Old Forces and the Future of World Politics* (1988) and other works.

. . . , few statespersons or analysts doubt that the Cold War is over. There is considerable disagreement among academics, however, over the causes of the collapse in 1989–90 of the global rivalry between the United States and the Soviet Union that had polarized world politics for some forty years. Like physicists observing an unanticipated implosion and trying to find in it confirmation of their own particular hypothesis among many contending theories, so we students of political behavior have been able to witness a time-compressed transformation of seemingly stable relationships in world politics, and we are beginning to argue about what this dramatic development in *our* laboratory tells us about the validity of contending theories of international relations and world politics.

Most of us are ready to admit our failure to predict the dramatic developments of 1989 and 1990—the dismantling of the Berlin Wall, the reunification of Germany, the retraction of Soviet control of Eastern Europe, the attempts to install multi-party systems and market-oriented economies throughout the Soviet sphere, the demands for political autonomy by many of the constituent nations of the Soviet Union. Equally, most of us would still like to show that our *basic* assumptions about how the world works have not been seriously contradicted by these unanticipated occurrences, that despite the seeming anomalies, the paradigm or paradigms in which we have come to believe remain essentially intact. Well, let us see.

This contest among alternative explanations is also engaging those with little professional interest in theory, for its outcome has more than academic implications. The reasons that are most widely accepted by scholars, policy-makers, and publics for the momentous changes that have been taking place may well become the basic assumptions underlying the policies that shape the post–Cold War era—just as the accepted explanations for the break-up of the grand alliance that defeated Nazi Germany became the assumptions underpinning interpretations of the Cold War.

Excerpted from *International Journal* XLVI spring 1991, by permission. Copyright © Canadian Institute of International Affairs, Toronto.

EXPLANATION 1: IMPERIAL OVERSTRETCH

The end of the Cold War might be seen as a validation of the leitmotif of the recent best-selling treatise, *The Rise and Fall of the Great Powers,* in which the historian, Paul Kennedy, showed how empires tend to enlarge their spheres of control to the point where their capabilities can no longer sustain their commitments. In attempting to retain control of these spheres, the power of the over-extended imperium to compete with emerging international rivals is weakened and it even experiences a deterioration in its capacity for effective governance at the national core of its domains.[1]

The Kennedy book gave scholarly legitimacy to a view, which was circulating simultaneously in the American policy community during the second administration of Ronald Reagan and in the Kremlin under Mikhail Gorbachev, that the worldwide rivalry of the superpowers was sapping the best of the human and material resources of the two countries and thereby allowing both of them to be overtaken by Japan and the West Europeans. Gorbachev clearly saw the Cold War as the principal obstacle to perestroika. Some of Reagan's economic advisers had also become convinced that their domestic "revolution" was being subverted by the huge budgetary and trade deficits generated by the accelerating arms race. Seen in this light, the personal "chemistry" experienced by Reagan and Gorbachev at their summit meetings was (to coin a phrase) more metafiscal than metaphysical in origin.

Richard Rosecrance, the international relations scholar, advanced a parallel thesis in *The Rise of the Trading State: Commerce and Conquest in the Modern World,*[2] but with a tele-

ological twist: the declining influence of the United States and the Soviet Union in the late Cold War period, relative to the rise in influence of Japan and the countries of Western Europe, signalled a progressive transformation of the world system from one dominated by territorially based and militarily supported rivalries to one in which countries best secure their values through participation in mutually beneficial international commerce. In a hopeful prognosis, Rosecrance looked forward to a gradual abandonment by the Cold War leaders of their obsolescent confrontational rivalry—an adaptation on both sides to the requirements for effectiveness in the evolving trade-dominated world.

Although plausible, *mutual* imperial overstretch as the explanation for the evaporation of Soviet-American global rivalry gives greater credit than warranted to the Reagan administration's perception of a basic contradiction between its activist Cold War policy and the requisites for economic competitiveness against the Japanese and the West Europeans. The Pentagon continued to be victorious in its battle to exempt the defense budget from cutbacks, with Reagan himself the prime champion of the continuation of immensely expensive projects such as the Strategic Defense Initiative and the stealth bomber. By 1987 the president and his foreign policy advisers did come around to crediting Gorbachev with "sincerity" in wanting to call off a new round in the superpower arms race, but they attributed Gorbachev's receptiveness to their success in pricing the Soviet Union out of the competition.

Whether by the middle of the 1980s the United States was, in truth, overstretching its resource base to maintain its pursuit of an all-continents rivalry with the other superpower remains a matter of considerable debate among international relations

[1] Paul Kennedy, *The Rise and Fall of the Great Powers: Economic Change and Military Conflict from 1500 to 2000* (New York: Random House 1987).

[2] Richard Rosecrance, *The Rise of the Trading State: Commerce and Conquest in the Modern World* (New York: Basic Books 1986). Ed. note: This book is reproduced in part as Selection 33 below.

analysts and political economists. (My own belief is that the Gorbachev régime's surprising volte-face in the 1987–90 period on the fundamental issues of the Cold War may have saved the United States from the embarrassing consequences of its otherwise stubborn refusal to recognize that many of its external commitments had indeed outrun the internal wherewithal to sustain them.) It is clear, however, that most of Reagan's foreign policy advisers were still enthusiastic supporters of this imperial policy—some even more than before, now that the Soviet Union was "on the ropes." And when President Bush proclaimed in 1990 that "the Cold War is over," he did so with the proud demeanor of the imperial victor.

EXPLANATION 2: HEGEMONIC PEACE

Official United States views on the end of the Cold War can find congenial scholarly reinforcement in theories that locate the basic cause of system-wide order and relative peace (or disorder and pervasive war) in the presence (or absence) of a dominant great power whose security and well-being depend on the perpetuation of a peaceful international order—a great power with both the material resources and the will to defend that international order. A number of schools of thought which have wide support in the academic discipline of international relations subscribe to this basic explanation.

The most parsimonious variants are extrapolations from the structural realist theory of international politics propounded by Kenneth Waltz.[3] This school holds that the distribution of war-making capabilities at the end of World War II determined the bipolar Cold War rivalry. Hence, once it became clear to the Soviet side in the mid-1980s that it was unable to continue to generate the military capabilities required to stay at least even with the United States side, the Soviet Union rationally chose to opt out of the competition.

More complex, but essentially similar, theories are provided by the hegemony/leadership school, whose progenitors were historians Arnold Toynbee and Ludwig Dehio and political scientists Quincy Wright and A.F.K. Organski, and which was best represented in the 1980s by George Modelski and his associates in a series of publications attempting to explain 'long cycles' of war and peace.[4] The closely related 'hegemonic stability' school rests on concepts developed by an economist, Charles Kindleberger, and elaborated by a political scientist, Robert Gilpin, and it focusses mainly on the role of great powers in sustaining a liberal global economic order.[5]

From the perspective of most of the hegemony theorists, the global conflicts of the twentieth century were brought on by the demise of the Pax Britannica of the nineteenth century and the ensuing contest for world and regional hegemony that collapse precipitated. World War II eliminated Japan, Germany, Britain, and France as serious contenders in this competition, and in consequence the two remaining "super" powers were able to establish hegemony in rival regional spheres of influence while undertaking an all-continents contest for world hegemony. (Between 1945 and 1947, the United States, given the overwhelming economic and military superiority with

[3]Kenneth Waltz, *Theory of International Politics* (Reading MA: Addison-Wesley 1979).

[4]George Modelski, ed, *Exploring Long Cycles* (Boulder CO: Lynne Rienner 1987). See also Joshua S. Goldstein, *Long Cycles: Prosperity and War in the Modern Age* (New Haven, CT: Yale University Press 1988).

[5]The most prominent international politics version of the "hegemonic stability" thesis is Robert Gilpin's *War and Change in World Politics* (New York: Cambridge University Press 1981).

which it emerged from World War II, could have aggressively and decisively assumed the role of global hegemon, but held back, for reasons not adequately explained in the theory.) The Cold War between the United States and the Soviet Union persisted for four decades without exploding into World War III mainly because of mutual fears of the massive destruction that would ensue. Eventually, however (and here I am speculating about how the hegemony/leadership school might explain recent events), the required commitment of resources to prevent the other side from gaining decisive geopolitical superiority sapped the strength of the Soviet Union internally—in some versions the Soviet Union, lacking a sufficiently modernized economy, was never even close to being a fully capable challenger—leaving the United States, at last, the undisputed political-military hegemon in the world, ready to preside over a new era of peace among the great powers.[6] Ronald Reagan happily expresses a popular contemporary American version of the peace-through-hegemony theory in his autobiography:

> I knew that [Gorbachev] . . . had strong motives for wanting to end the arms race. The Soviet economy was a basket case, in part because of the enormous expenditure on arms. He had to know that the quality of

American military technology, after reasserting itself beginning in 1981, was now overwhelmingly superior to his. He had to know we could outspend the Soviets on weapons as long as we wanted to . . . The world was approaching the threshold of a new day. We had a chance to make it a safer, better place for now and the twenty-first century.[7]

The explanation of Marxists and neo-Marxists—there are probably more of these today outside the erstwhile Soviet sphere than within it—for the demise of the Cold War is in many respects remarkably similar to that of the hegemony theorists. They view it, however, as only a pause in the working out of the longer historical dialectic. The temporary winner is not the United States per se, but the advanced corporate capitalism that had become increasingly headquartered in the United States in the twentieth century. The current world ascendancy of advanced capitalism over the ineffective and premature challenge from the Leninists based in relatively backward Russia and the Maoists of underdeveloped China is seen as confirming the prognoses of contemporary neo-Marxist theoreticians, most prominently Immanuel Wallerstein and his disciples. In their view, the historical era in which the core capitalist countries exploit the peripheral societies of the world has yet to play itself out fully, but ultimately the inner contradictions of capitalism will lead to its collapse and supplantation by a successor system.[8] To my knowledge, Wallerstein and those who work with him have not yet published formal scholarly explanations of the apparent end of the Cold War. However, in numerous forums over the past year, reputable scholars of this persuasion

---

[6]It should be noted that Gilpin, for whom the text of hegemony is the success of the dominant great power in presiding over an open global economy, has been less sure of the ability of the United States to sustain the liberal world trading order it imposed following World War II. Now that the principal trading partners of the United States perceive less need for American military help in fending off an aggressive Soviet Union, a durable Pax Americana looks less and less plausible. Rather, Gilpin foresees an era of increasing mercantilist rivalry among the United States, Japan, and the European Community and a stubborn reliance by Third World countries on illiberal protectionist measures—trends he found strongly emergent even before the evaporation of Cold War hostility. See Robert Gilpin, *The Political Economy of International Relations* (Princeton NJ: Princeton University Press 1987).

[7]Ronald Reagan, *An American Life* (New York: Simon and Schuster 1990), 14–15.

[8]Immanuel Wallerstein, ed, *The Politics of the World Economy* (Cambridge: Cambridge University Press 1984).

have argued that the world system is merely experiencing a phoney peace in the long struggle against capitalist domination. They suggest that the situation may yet get worse (through the exploitative absorption of the resources and peoples of Eastern Europe and the Soviet Union into the capitalist periphery) before there is a global regrouping of "progressive" forces. Meanwhile, with the removal of the countervailing power of the Soviet Union, the prospect is for a period of intensified economic, political, and military intervention by the United States and other capitalist powers against recalcitrant elements in the periphery—the war against Iraq on behalf of George Bush's "new world order" being only a harbinger of things to come.[9]

EXPLANATION 3: THE GEIST WHOSE ZEIT HAS COME

The theories of Imperial Overstretch and Hegemonic Peace are manifestly too neat as explanations of the dramatic and still volatile transformation of the Cold War system into the (as yet undefinable) *post*–Cold War system. In giving overwhelming causative weight to changing international distributions of military and economic power (which governing élites calculate and presumably respond to), these theories fail to account for the fact that in Eastern Europe, at least, most of the pressures for fundamental change were generated and nurtured by dissident intellectuals, artists, youth groups, technocratic modernizers, would-be entrepreneurs, and (in Poland) labour leaders. To be sure, it was a series of démarches promulgated at the pinnacle of the Soviet hierarchy, by a new general secretary of the Communist party, that revamped the foreign and domestic priorities of the Soviet Union and gave the green light to reformers throughout the Soviet sphere in Eastern Europe in 1989 and 1990 to establish new "self-determined" political and economic systems; but in initiating these actions, the Gorbachev régime (itself comprising many technocratic modernizers and closet dissidents who had risen to the top of the system) was responding at least as much to "forces from below" as to the changing "global correlation of forces."

Perhaps it is time to turn the philosopher Hegel's grand dialectic of history right side up from the upside down position into which it was turned by Karl Marx; for haven't we been witnessing the global contagion of the culture of freedom—a higher synthesis, as it were, of the ideas of British liberalism, the French Revolution, American democratic capitalism, and their various hybrids? This spirit of the times, or Zeitgeist, simply could not be contained, despite the efforts of the Soviet communists to quarantine the masses behind iron curtains and brick walls and to immunize the party and government élites with "scientific" Marxism-Leninism.

Hegel, of course, has been out of fashion in post–World War II social science, even though the godfather of the field of comparative politics, Max Weber, can appropriately be regarded as a neo-Hegelian. Certainly, contemporary international relations theory, still under the sway of Hans Morgenthau's powerful argument that ideology is merely the handmaiden of tangible power interests,[10] is virtually bereft of works that give determinative weight to cultural

[9]Noam Chomsky, for example, in various public presentations around the Boston area in 1990, vigorously articulated the thesis: Watch out! With the United States no longer inhibited by an anticapitalist superpower opponent, the world is in for its biggest binge of capitalist imperialism yet.

[10]Hans Morgenthau, *Politics among Nations* (New York: Knopf 1948 and subsequent editions).

factors. An exception is the largely over-looked study by the British scholar, Evan Luard, comparing the types of international relationships that have prevailed in seven significantly different historical configurations: the Chinese multistate system of 771–221 B.C.; the Greek city states during the period 510–338 B.C.; Europe during its dynastic period, 1300–1559; the "Age of Religions," 1559–1648; the period from the Peace of Westphalia, 1648, to the French Revolution of 1789; the "Age of Nationalism" from the French revolution to 1914; and, finally, the "Age of Ideology" starting with World War I and persisting through the Cold War.[11] Luard's choice of periods to demarcate and his labelling of their dominant characteristics are certainly open to scholarly challenge; his important contribution is to give norms and ideologies a central

place once again in the explanation of the evolution of world politics, instead of viewing them simply as dependent variables. The obvious impact on world geostrategic relationships of today's spreading Zeitgeist of democratic capitalism would seem to confirm the essential wisdom of Luard's approach.

But the idea of democratic capitalism has been around for a long time and vigorously championed since World War II in opposition to socialism, especially its Marxist version—the other twentieth-century candidate for the Geist Whose Zeit Has Come. We are still left with the question: *Why now?* Why, in the space of less than three years, did the idea of structuring society around a free market economy and an openly competitive pluralist polity suddenly attain explosive popularity in the stronghold of its antithesis?

EXPLANATION 4: GORBACHEV AS GREAT MAN OF HISTORY

Unlike most social scientists, media pundits characteristically have few qualms about attributing momentous historical developments to the genius—constructive or malevolent—of particular personalities. Biography sells better than multivariate analysis. Napoleon Bonaparte brings on the age of the *nation*-state; Lenin makes Marxism a global political force; Franklin Roosevelt saves the United States from socialism; Hitler causes World War II; Stalin causes the Cold War; Gandhi and Nehru bring independence to India; Mao restores greatness to China; Martin Luther King transforms the American south; Margaret Thatcher undoes the British welfare state—that is the stuff of popular history. We professional scholars tend to scoff—perhaps too readily—at *Time* magazine's "Man of the Year" hyperbole (Gorbachev was their "Man of the Decade" for the 1980s).

I am not arguing for a return to the extreme view of that nineteenth-century historian, Thomas Carlyle, who stated that "Universal History, the history of what man has accomplished in this world, is at bottom the History of the Great Men who have worked here." Neither am I willing to embrace Leo Tolstoy's counter that "we need only to penetrate to the essence of any historic event—which lies in the activity of the general mass who take part in it—to be convinced that the will of the historic hero does not control the actions of the mass but is itself continually controlled."[12] The Gorbachev phenomenon is surely a counter to both these views.

Gorbachev's policies and personality are inextricably of the "essence"—as gener-

[11]Evan Luard, *Types of International Society* (New York: Free Press 1976).

[12]The Carlyle and Tolstoy quotes are offered by Dean Keith Simonton in his illuminating study, *Genius, Creativity, and Leadership: Historiometric Inquiries* (Cambridge MA: Harvard University Press 1984), 135, 147.

ators and consequences—of the profound historical transformation we are experiencing. Imagine what the world would be like in 1991 if Yegor Ligachev had succeeded Konstantin Chernenko as general secretary in 1985. Yet, after almost singlehandedly unleashing the creative forces imprisoned in the Soviet sphere of totalitarian polities and command economies, Gorbachev soon found himself caught up in a chaotic stampede towards political decentralization and economic privatization which was swifter and more radical than he could have anticipated or was capable of modulating effectively. In response, in particular to the growing centrifugal pressures threatening to dissolve the Soviet Union into numerous sovereign nations, Gorbachev pulled back, however ambivalently, from some of his earlier concepts of perestroika and glasnost. And there were dire predictions even from within the Gorbachev entourage (witness Eduard Shevardnadze's resignation speech)

that the country—as if doomed to recapitulate Russia's often tragic history—was headed once again towards a dangerous period of oscillation between anarchy and draconian dictatorship.

A sensible stance towards all of this theorizing is provided by the proposition of the psychologist/historian Dean Keith Simonton that the *interaction* of genius and Zeitgeist is a crucial determinant of the drama of history:

> The zeitgeist participates as linear or cyclical trends, as economic or political conditions, and as a backdrop of events that determines the . . . success of a . . . leader. At the same time the impact of the situational context is tempered by such individual attributes as intelligence, morality, leadership qualities . . . and belief structure . . . "Being the right person" is almost as important as "being in the right place at the right time."[13]

EXPLANATION 5: ALL OF THE ABOVE (BUT NONE BY ITSELF)

This is the explanation I come to, not from a wimpy eclecticism, but rather out of a philosophical/analytical conviction, reinforced by observations of the origin, persistence, and (now) decline of the Cold War system,[14] that change or stability can be generated at any level (from micro to macro) in the world polity. Moreover, forces generating such change or stability—as we see in the dramatic contests between radicals, moderate reformers, conservatives, and Stalinists now being played out in the Soviet Union—can come from or be processed through structures and fields not fully encompassed by the political system per se, namely, ethnic, cultural, religious groupings, the economy, and the ecological environment. Developments in any of these fields, even natural developments in the physical universe, can affect—sometimes

profoundly—the conditions of life, the perceptions, and the values of those who construct, operate, and transform the world's political system and subsystems.

I look at the phenomena we are all struggling to explain, particularly the demise of the Cold War, from the assumption that the various systems and subsystems that make up the world polity are open to one another: causes and effects typically move laterally from subsystem to subsystem, but may also move vertically from one level to the next, even leaping over levels. The configuration of each system or subsystem is in some sense unique; and some of them, as a matter of policy, may try to restrict the ex-

[13]*Ibid,* 165.
[14]See, especially, my *New Forces, Old Forces, and the Future of World Politics* (New York: Scott, Foresman/Little, Brown 1988).

tent to which they are open to influence from the other systems. But with the increasing mobility of persons, substances, and information, the *interpenetrability* (let alone simple interdependence) of the various systems that make up the world political system would seem to be a more useful premise on which to build attempts to understand the kind of systemic change we have been experiencing.

If this be heresy to those who worship at the god of theoretical parsimony, so be it.

I receive support for my premise about open systems from the analytic strategy for understanding the turbulence of the contemporary era that the international relations theorist, James Rosenau, has been championing of late. We need, he advises, to conceive of "whole systems and subsystems as the cast of characters at the macro level, that along with individuals at the micro level, act out global dramas." Such a conceptual framework, Rosenau suggests, "facilitates inquiry into the conflicts that divide

collectivities and the efforts they make to bridge the issues that separate them." It establishes a basis "for assessing parameter change and tracing turbulence in a world of interacting systems and subsystems." By their very nature, Rosenau reminds us, "complex systems encompass both wholes and parts. We can begin to understand them only if we employ a method that allows us to move our analytic eyes back and forth between systems and subsystems and thus between collectivities, their subgroups, and the individuals who comprise them."[15]

I agree. For if we insist on neat, impenetrable analytical boundaries, and levels of analysis that must never be fused, we will fail, once again, not only in our attempts at retrospective explanations of past transformations but also in our ability to anticipate profound change in the future.

[15]James N. Rosenau, *Turbulence in World Politics: A Theory of Change and Continuity* (Princeton, NJ: Princeton University Press 1990), 41, 123–4.

2 FEMINIST THEORY AND INTERNATIONAL RELATIONS

MARYSIA ZALEWSKI

Marysia Zalewski has recently been appointed lecturer in the Department of International Politics at the University College of Wales, Aberystwyth. She specializes in the areas of feminist theory, gender, and International Relations theory.

INTRODUCTION

Feminist theory has made rather a late arrival on to the scene of the International Relations academic agenda. Surely, International Relation's most established academics claim, the business of wars, superpower relations and inter-state behavior are in no need of a theory of gender? What's the problem? Perhaps there should be more women teaching International Relations or in foreign policy decision-making communities (but would they push the button?) but surely that is about the extent of the problem?

International Relations has been reluctant to open its doors to the challenge posed by feminism and theories of gender. Long after other social sciences had at least given marginal attention to the presumed gender neutrality of their subjects, International Relations remained stubbornly convinced that gender was a variable which could be ignored. However, the mid-1980s provided a window of opportunity for feminist critical voices to get on the agenda. It is often claimed that the academic study of International Relations is dominated by the United States and this is reflected in the way the discipline develops. That this is the case is evidenced by the dominance of the realist/positivist paradigm which recent critical voices have pitted themselves against. Recent literature on feminist theory and International Relations, at least that emanating from the United states, has tended to assume, almost unchallenged, the dominance of Realism, its positivist credentials being the target of increasing attack since the mid-1980s with post-modernist voices taking a leading role in that attack. It is not surprising, therefore, that many feminists have been drawn towards post-modernism, seeing potential for developing a post-modern feminism, when the only other alternative seems to be Positivism and Realism. There is however a major tension in the acceptance of the tenets of post-modernism

Excerpted by permission of the author and publisher from *From Cold War to Collapse: World Politics in the 1980s,* ed. by Bowker and Brown. Cambridge: Cambridge University Press, 1992. Copyright © Cambridge University Press, 1992. I would like to thank Steve Smith for providing immeasurable support and advice.

into feminist thought, a point which I will return to later.

Given the title of this volume, the fundamental question is, "what does feminist theory have to say about International Relations in general and the changes in world politics in the 1980s in particular?" In order to address this question I want to take a few steps backwards. This chapter originated as a paper at the 1990 British International Studies Conference in Newcastle. Prior to writing the paper I was given to understand that, despite the expertise and experience of the majority of the audience with regard to International Relations, the level of understanding and awareness with regard to feminist theory was somewhat limited (this assumption turned out to be, in the main, correct). Because of this, the paper was structured in such a way as to introduce the uninitiated to feminist theory and its recent arrival on the International Relations academic agenda. In a similar way, I see a major task of this chapter as offering some back-ground to the rising interest in feminist theory and International Relations. The richness and diversity of feminist thought is difficult to overestimate and problems often arise when those uneducated in matters of feminism try to understand the implications of feminist critiques of their subject. In an attempt to go some way to redress the problem of the paucity of feminist knowledge this chapter will introduce the reader to a variety of feminist perspectives presented firstly as a chronological/political typology, highlighting the main strands, and secondly as an epistemological typology.[1] I will then outline and discuss some of the literature on feminist critiques of International Relations. Finally, I will offer an assessment on the impact of feminist theory on International Relations focusing on the main debates; I will then make some concluding remarks regarding what feminist theory has to say about the changes in world politics in the 1980s speculating on the future direction of the feminist critique of International Relations.

FEMINIST THOUGHT

Liberal Feminism

Liberal feminism is perhaps the most long-standing and easily understood and accept-able version of feminism. It is the "add women and stir" variety of feminist thought. As its name suggests liberal feminism takes its philosophical roots from liberalism placing much importance on the primary importance of the individual and the necessity for individual freedom and autonomy. However, as many feminist critics of liberal political and democratic theory have pointed out, traditional theory either does not include women or prescribes women a specific and subordinate role in society.[2] The individual referred to in traditional theory was implicitly and explicitly a male individual. For standard liberal feminism the exclusion of women is an error based on

[1]For those working within feminism, such a brief outline of feminist thought might be perceived as doing an injustice to its vastness and diversity. However, I feel it is necessary to serve as an introduction to the International Relations scholar curious to know what feminism means to the study of International Relations. In the future, I might be tempted to follow Anne Sisson Runyan's and V. Spike Paterson's lead in encouraging readers to "undertake the extensive reading program required to become familiar with feminist theory and praxi" (A. Sisson Runyan and V. Spike Peterson, "The Radical Future to Realism: Feminist Subversions of IR Theory," *Alternatives,* vol. 16, no. 1, 1991, p. 102, note 41).

[2]D. Coole, *Women in Political Theory* (Brighton: Wheatsheaf, 1988); and C. Pateman, "Feminism and Democracy," in G. Duncan (ed.), *Democratic Theory and Practice* (Cambridge: Cambridge University Press, 1983); and C. Pateman, *The Sexual Contract* (Oxford, Basil Blackwell, 1988).

erroneous and misogynist beliefs about women. But this error can be redressed by bringing women back in. Eighteenth and nineteenth-century liberal feminists, such as Mary Wollstonecraft, J. S. Mill and Harriet Taylor Mill, campaigned for rights to equal education and entry into public life as well as the abolition of laws which gave men ownership of their wives. Twentieth-century liberal feminism has carried on the campaign for equal rights with, for example, the suffragette's and suffragist's plea for formal political equality via the vote in the early part of the century, and the Sex Discrimination and the Equal Pay Acts of the mid to late twentieth century. Liberal feminism is currently alive and well and much effort is put into getting women included, especially in traditionally male dominated institutions such as the House of Parliament, the scientific community and institutions of higher education.

Marxist and Socialist Feminism

These two forms of feminist thought are interlinked as they share the same roots—a Marxist materialist analysis; it is material forces which shape and structure social life and individual lives within society, not individuals as separate units. From a traditional Marxist perspective the cause of women's oppression is to be found in the exploitative economic system. What is needed is the elimination of capitalism to liberate women—and of course men. With the demise of capitalism there will be no need for women to sell themselves and their services to maintain their livelihood. A major criticism of this Marxist analysis of women's oppression is that it does not explain the oppression of women in pre-capitalist or socialist societies. It is primarily for this reason that many Marxist feminists have expanded the scope of explanations for women's oppression to include more than

capitalism and exploitative class relations. They attempt to synthesize various explanations for women's oppression using many of the insights of other strands of feminist thought, particularly radical feminism. We can call this strand of feminism socialist feminism.

Socialist feminism makes an explicit commitment to the abolition of both class and gender. Socialist feminists argue that we need to transform not only the ownership of the means of production but also the social system which is dominated by patriarchy. Socialist feminists share the Marxist conception of human nature—people are only really free and fulfilled if there is free productive activity. For Marxists, productive activity is limited to labor and usually that is labor which is paid for in the public sphere. But socialist feminists include other forms of productive activity, specifically the procreative and sexual work done by women in the home. Sexuality and procreation are human activities which are no more biologically determined than any other and are thus capable of social development. Socialist feminism draws upon the insights of the radical feminist analysis of the male control of women's sexuality and reproductive capacities claiming that women's sexuality is developed for men's enjoyment rather than women's. This control of women's sexuality, fertility, and reproduction finds expression in patriarchal laws, policies, and practices throughout the world which limit women's own control within these areas.

Marxist feminists see class as the primary oppressor. Women are exploited both economically and sexually but until the capitalist system is abolished the sexual system of domination will continue as it is necessary to furnish capitalism's needs. Socialist feminists see a worldwide web of domination and oppression but are attempting not to fall into the exclusive universalizing tendencies of either Marxist or radical feminism.

Radical Feminism

Radical feminism emerged alongside the left wing, civil and human rights type movements of the 1960s and 1970s and does not easily fit into preexisting philosophical frameworks. Because radical feminism is so wide-ranging and constantly emerging, I am going to list four of the basic tenets of radical feminist thought and practice just to give an insight into radical feminist ideas.

Firstly, radical feminism takes women as its chief concern and for radical feminism there is a common and universal oppression of women. Obviously, women of different races, classes, and colors will have enormously different experiences of life, but for radical feminism the systematic existence of patriarchy is fundamental, all pervasive, and the root of all other oppressions.

Secondly, male domination and control is not limited to unjust legislation or unequal treatment at school, for example, but it permeates every aspect of life—economic, social, psychological, sexual, political, and personal. Radical feminism asserts that women's lives are not only dominated by men and masculine values at a physical level but also in the way we learn to understand about ourselves, our role and status in society, how we should act, how we should live and what counts as "normal" behavior. Even what counts as acceptable knowledge and ways of explaining events in the world and life generally are shot through with masculine values. Radical feminists claim that masculine ideals and ideas have taken supremacy in the world and have divided the world into categories of good and bad, us and them, superior and inferior. This categorization or bifurcation exists at all levels, and women and "female" characteristics occupy the subordinate position at every stage. For example, the practice of science and its promising student—social science—is premised on objectivity, reason, rationality,

nonemotiveness, coolness—all identified by radical feminists (and others) astypical "masculine" values and attributes which hold a higher place in the hierarchy than do the characteristically "female" opposing traits of subjectivity, emotiveness, and intuition. Radical feminists challenge both this bifurcation and also the inferior value of traditional female characteristics. Radical feminists typically eulogize the traditional womanly virtues such as nurturing and caring and envisage the promotion of a womanculture which encourages and validates these characteristics.

A third distinctive tenet of radical feminism is the aim to redescribe reality—to use different criteria to judge importance, to use a different value system, and to ask different questions. Women's real lives and subjective experiences are to be taken seriously and are to have a high status. A fourth point, common to radical and socialist feminism, is that the personal is the political (and for Enloe the personal is international).[3] The notions that the personal is the political brings into focus that it is not just political and judicial institutions which have oppressed women but private lives and relationships are also oppressive and they should not remain hidden and secret. Separating public and private worlds is another example of the false bifurcation or dichotomy characteristic of male dominated society. In reality, public and private worlds are inextricably linked, and for radical feminism the power that exists in the relationship between men and women, or more specifically between husbands and wives, is the best example of a relationship characterized by dominance and control. Radical feminism is skeptical of existing political theory and practice as it is ineluctably shot through with patriarchal ideology. Radical feminists

---

[3]C. Enloe, *Bananas, Beaches and Bases: Making Feminist Sense of International Politics* (London: Pandora, 1989), p. 195.

want to redescribe the world from a woman's perspective, ask different questions about the world and use different methods of gaining knowledge and understanding of the world.[4]

Liberal, socialist, Marxist and radical feminism are the most common and basic strands of feminist thought but a typology emerging from a more fundamentally epistemological level is being taken up by contemporary feminist theorists of International Relations, especially those in the United States. This way of discussing feminist critiques stems from a fundamental concern about the validity of feminist claims. The recurring hostility and dismissal of many of the claims made by feminists has led to a concern over the epistemological status of feminist theories. From the early 1980s, onwards, many feminist scholars have been involved in comparing feminist epistomologies in an attempt to produce the epistemological basis appropriate for feminist theory. The epistemological typology most commonly used is the three-fold categorization delineated by Sandra Harding.[5] Harding discusses three feminist approaches to traditional theorizing; feminist *empiricism*, feminist *standpoint* and feminist *post-modernism*.

Feminist Empiricism

The feminist method allows for the tendency for human knowers to fall prey to cognitive dissonance. The feminist empiricist is a realist (in philosophical, not International Relations terms)—there is a world out there which (a) can be apprehended and understood using the correct methods correctly and (b) which exists independently of either our senses or our creation of knowledge about it. In short, there is a world out there which we can uncover if we *correctly* use the existing methodological tools inherited from the Enlightenment, i.e., reason, logic, noncontradiction, observation, controlled measuring—all of these being "neutral" procedures. The difference between standard empiricism, or positivism, and feminist empiricism is that the latter claims that there has been an *androcentric* (male centred) bias in conventional empiricism. The standard empiricist researcher would have us believe that the social identity of the inquirer is irrelevant as the scientific method works via falsification and verification. If a researcher is biased in one way or another this will show up when her or his work is tested by another researcher. However the feminist empiricist will discount the latter in two ways. Firstly, it is claimed that the gender of researchers does matter, not necessarily on an individual level but on a larger scale. It is argued that women as a *social group* are more likely to notice androcentric bias than men, as a social group, and therefore more likely to produce unbiased and objective results.[6] Secondly, the feminist empiricist would claim that it is not just at the level of the social identity of the researcher that androcentrism exists but also in the selection of problems to investigate. A powerful form of social control and androcentric bias exists at the level of the identification and definition of what issues to look at. For the feminist empiricist the scientific method is not at fault; it is simply that its methods are used incorrectly. The eradication of androcentric bias is a necessary measure to achieve the goal of objective knowledge, the goal of apprehending the truth about the world.

[4]Readers wanting to learn more about feminist theory would be advised to begin by consulting texts such as, H. Eisenstein, *Contemporary Feminist Thought* (London: Unwin Paperbacks, 1988); A. M. Jagger, *Feminist Politics and Human Nature* (Brighton: Harvester, 1983); and R. Tong, *Feminist Thought: A Comparative Introduction* (London: Unwin Hyman, 1989).

[5]S. Harding, *The Science Question in Feminism* (Milton Keynes, Open University Press, 1986).

[6]*Ibid.*, p. 25.

Feminist Standpoint

The feminist empiricist claim that past knowledge suffers from an androcentric bias does not fit easily with the empiricist belief in the possibility of an unmediated apprehension of the real world. Feminist standpoint theorists provide a way of incorporating this belief as they reject the possibility of an unmediated truth. Instead they rely on a more materialist understanding of social being and consciousness, claiming that knowledge will be affected, and constructed, by the prevailing social, political, ideological and historical setting. However, the concept of truth is not rejected altogether. Indeed, just as the proletariat is able to gain more understanding about the oppressive nature of the capitalist system once a revolutionary consciousness has developed, so can the woman, from a feminist standpoint perspective, see and understand the world more clearly once a feminist consciousness has been developed. Men's dominant position in social life has produced only a partial understanding of life. Women, as the oppressed group, can pierce through these distorted views and develop a more adequate understanding of the world.

Feminist Post-Modernism

Post-modernists reject the idea that there is a real world out there waiting to be discovered. Knowledge and reality are social constructs and any attempt to discipline the world into an homogeneous straitjacket is both futile and a reflection of power structures which will continue to define what is "good" and "right." Post-modernism is the subject of much debate and consternation not least because of its ability to shock, be explosive, and difficult to grasp hold of (precisely its adherent's intention). Jane Flax claims that "post-modernists share at least one common object of attack—the Enlight-

enment" and that despite their many differences post-modernist discourses are all deconstructive and seek to distance us from and make us "skeptical about the ideas concerning truth, knowledge, power, history, self and language that are often taken for granted within and serve as legitimations for contemporary Western culture."[7]

Post-modernists revel in denying privilege (the architect, the philosopher, the author, the composer) and eulogize the nature of difference and plurality. Rather than searching for coherent epistemologies post-modernists engage in rhetoric and conversation. Post-modern feminists typically share the post-modern critique of grand, universalizing narratives and are intent on creating a standpointed, deconstructive but nonprescriptive discourse. . . .

Feminist post-modernism is the subject of much debate within mainstream feminist theorizing and also within the International Relations feminist community. There is not the space here to do justice to the various debates regarding the utility of post-modernism for feminist discourse; what I will do is briefly mention two of the major challenges to the appropriation of the tenets of post-modernism into feminism. Firstly, one of the basic tenets of post-modernist thought is the problematization of the centrality of the subject, both as the exemplar of an ahistorical, transcendental category and as privileged owners of knowledge and authoritative statements about the world. The decentring of the subject has led some critics of post-modernism to argue that this makes any feminist politics impossible as the category of "women" becomes decentered into nonexistence. As Linda Alcoff claims, for many contemporary feminist theorists, the concept of woman has become a prob-

[7] J. Flax, *Thinking Fragments: Psychoanalysis, Feminism and Postmodernism in the Contemporary West* (Berkeley and Los Angeles: University of California Press, 1990), p. 29.

lem.[8] Alcoff argues that this is a problem of primary significance for feminist theory as the concept and category of "woman" has been the necessary point of departure for any feminist theory and feminist politics. The post-modern distaste for subject-centered enquiry and subject-based politics propels post-modernism into gender blindness. Take for example the special issue of *International Studies Quarterly* on "Speaking the Language of Exile: Dissidence in International Studies." The editorship of this mainstream North American International Relations journal was temporarily taken over by two post-modern writers, Richard K. Ashley and R. B. J. Walker. The purpose of the issue was to give a platform to the critical and dissident voices in contemporary International Relations. Not one of the articles in this issue represented feminist concerns. It might be suggested that these "exiles on mainstreet" are as gender insensitive as their neo-Realist colleagues.[9]

This leads on to a second major problem with the conflation of post-modernism and feminism. The post-modernist intention to challenge the power of dominant discourses in an attempt to lead those discourses into disarray is at first glance appealing but we have to ask what will the replacement be? If we are to believe that all is contingent and we have no base on to which we can ground claims to truth, then "power alone will determine the outcome of competing truth claims."[10] Post-modernist discourse does not offer any criteria for choosing among competing explanations and thus has a tendency to lead towards nihilism—an accusation often levelled at the purveyors of post-modernism and to which they seem unable to provide any answer, except perhaps in the words of one post-modernist scholar "what's wrong with nihilism?"[11] Feminists drawn towards the post-positivist nature of post-modernism, but repelled by its gender insensitivity, have been tempted to adopt an eclectic approach, selecting the admirable qualities of post-modernist thought and rejecting the undesirable. However, this "pick 'n' mix" approach misunderstands the epistemological incompatibilities of post-modernism and feminism. Post-modernism is essentially an anti-epistemological and apolitical collection of interpretations whereas feminism is grounded in an emancipatory politics which necessitates some semblance of an epistemological foundation. Feminists within the International Relations community seem to be in a quandary, having to choose between either positivist or post-modern discourse. This, however, is not the only choice, a point to which I will return later.

CONCLUSIONS

Feminist critiques have been included as part of the "third debate" of the "post-positivist" challenge to International Relations.[12] Along with critical theory and post-

[8]L. Alcoff, "Cultural Feminism versus Post-Structuralism: The Identity Crisis in Feminist Theory," *Signs: Journal of Women in Culture and Society,* vol. 13, no. 3, 1988, p. 405.

[9]I am grateful to Steve Smith for suggesting the phrase "exile on main street" (he acknowledges prior use of the phrase by the Rolling Stones, circa 1971).

[10]J. Flax, "Postmodernism and Gender Relations in Feminist Theory," *Signs: Journal of Women in Culture and Society,* vol. 12, no. 4, 1987, p. 625.

[11]Some would claim that post-modernism is not necessarily nihilistic (see Sisson Runyan and Peterson, p. 102 note 35). However, this is not an uncontentious claim, see the exchange between Hawkesworth and Hekman in *Signs: Journal of Women in Culture and Society,* vol. 15, no. 2.

[12]Y. Lapid, "The Third Debate: On the Prospects of International Theory in a Post-Positivist Era," *International Studies Quarterly,* vol. 33, no. 3, 1989, pp. 235–54.

modernism, feminist theory is seen to be part of the challenge to the hegemony of realist, positivist discourse. A useful way to analyze the current directions and trends within the arena of feminist theory and International Relations is to highlight some of the common themes and questions that have emerged.

a. Reworking of core concepts: can we use existing concepts and theories? Is there theoretical space to "bring women in"?
b. Would it make any difference if women were equally represented in the International Relations community?
c. Does it matter that women and men (to a large extent) inhabit different words in terms of experience and expectations?
d. Why is it that women's experience is marginalized and does not appear to be really significant? Why don't women count?
e. Should we concentrate on how international policies and processes vary in their effects on women and men? And perhaps more crucially what are the implications of such an investigation?
f. Are International Relations theories inherently "male biased"?
g. Should feminist discourse be added on to International Relations or should International Relations accommodate itself to the demands of feminism?

These are some of the questions being raised by feminists within International Relations. That these questions are given some thought, and that this essay is included in this volume, indicates that issues of feminism and gender are having some impact on mainstream International Relations, although it still remains very much at the margins. However, I should make it clear that it

is not an easy task to apply one disparate and large body of theory to another. For example, there is a tendency to be asked to give a "feminist" answer to, or perspective on, an issue already outlined and defined as worthy of investigation by the existing creators of the discipline. This is like asking a committed Marxist to run a factory more successfully than its capitalist owner. Both would have completely differing views as to what constitutes success. It is of course possible at some level to supply a number of feminist perspectives to issues already identified as important by the discipline such as defense of national sovereignty. But this is more complicated than it sounds, as it entails taking into account a whole area conventionally defined as invisible or as part of the private realm and therefore out of the scope of conventional political analysis. A key task of feminist analysis is to extend the scope of the agenda rather than answering questions about what is already on the agenda.

What does feminist theory do to International Relations? If I were to conform to a conventional understanding of the changes in world politics in the 1980s, what would feminist theory have to offer?[13] Liberal feminism has much to offer by highlighting the neglect of women in traditional theory and practice and redressing that error. International Relations hardly deserves its self-appointed label of international if women are left out. But the liberal emphasis on "including women in" tends to accept the traditionally defined agenda, which imposes a veto on what is and what is not a legitimate area of study for scholars of International Relations. Radical and socialist/Marxist feminism, particularly if utilizing a specifically standpoint epistemology, provides a basis for extending the existing agenda. From

[13]Here I would include, for example, the changes in Eastern Europe, the Gulf War, and the breakup of the Soviet bloc.

these perspectives the assertion is made that women's voices and lives *are* important and not secondary. If we recall Halliday's comment that taking gender into consideration might lead in conventional terms to "unacceptable conclusions" this should lead us to ask, "what are these unacceptable conclusions and why would they be unacceptable"?[14] Halliday discusses women and nationalism and the place of women's rights in the formulation of inter-state relations. National independence is a key concept in International Relations theory and a key value on the international agenda. Given the value put on independence and the murky history of imperialism, the concept is accepted, if not totally uncritically, as a "good thing." But what are the specific effects on women? Often nationalism signals a return to traditional subordinate roles for women, maintaining male control over women's lives, hardly a gender neutral effect. Similarly, in the case of women's human rights it does not seem to matter that Western governments continue to support regimes in which women are relegated to the status of a subspecies without even formal political equality. Similarly, we take no notice that the international spread of prenatal diagnostic technology is being abused in countries such as China and India to abort female fetuses on the grounds that they are the "wrong" sex. We in the West are very insistent that our distaste of racial apartheid is known about but gender apartheid is too easily accepted as either a private or cultural affair. If the implications of considering issues of gender lead to unacceptable conclusions, if the cost appears to be too high, we must ask ourselves the questions, "how much do we care about the injustices of gender?" and "how much do women count?"

However, we should be very wary of uncritically adopting the notion of rework-

ing core concepts from a "feminist" perspective. It is of vital importance that concepts, of, more accurately, defending concepts such as sovereignty and nationalism, should be analyzed in detail with regards to the differing effects they have on men and women. Similarly, we should stop and ask ourselves the question "if we are so concerned about human rights why do violations of women appear to be a private or a cultural issue?" An obvious example is the genital mutilation of approximately 80 million women worldwide. However, we should take care when reconceptualization implies using stereotypical feminine traits. This concentration on women's ways of knowing, whether deemed to be socially constructed or not, skirts dangerously close to essentialism and probably also serves to retain the perception that feminism is for women only. Instead it is much more illuminating to widen the perception of power in the way Cynthia Enloe does. The use of power to smooth the workings of international politics is much more widespread than conventional International Relations analyses would have us believe.

The contribution of post-modern feminism is harder to gauge. Post-modernism is the subject of much debate in feminist circles both inside and outside the International Relations community. I was a discussant (along with V. Spike Peterson) on a feminist theory panel at the 1991 International Studies Association Conference in Vancouver, commenting on papers given by Christine Sylvester and Gecta Chowdry. One of my abiding memories from that panel, and the other feminist/gender panels (apart from them being paradigmatic examples of interesting and stimulating conference sessions), was the overwhelming desire to maintain and create a distance from the intellectual straitjacket of Realist discourse. It is hard to convey to those outside the discipline of International Relations just how dominant Realism is. Indeed, its critics, as

---

[14]Halliday, "Hidden from International Relations," p. 423.

well as its purveyors, tend to reify Realism, adding to its hegemonic status.[15] The urgent need to displace realist, positivist discourse has led many feminists to climb aboard the post-modernist bandwagon with its alleged commitment to the rebuttal of tyrannical truth claims. Indeed, given the choice between positivist realism and the promise of a reflexive, anti-foundationalist post-modernism, I confess I too would probably veer towards the latter. However, it is not as simple, or as clear, as that.

The dichotomy between positivist and post-modernist discourse gives the impression that there are only two alternatives. I would suggest that critical theory, following Sandra Whitworth and Mark Hoffman, offers the possibility of a third alternative.[16] There is not the space here to develop this perspective in any detail but I will outline some basic features. A feminist critical theory would regard the problematization of gender as its starting point. It is not committed to the discovery of one single truth and its political stance is emancipatory and normative but not prescriptive. This model makes a specific connection between knowledge and interests and thus crucial initial questions to be asked are: "Whose interests and served by defining the study and practice of International Relations in certain ways?" "Whose interests are consistently served by accepting the claim that private lives are not the proper sites of academic research?" A critical feminism would examine the silences in International Relations and ferret out the implicit and explicit assumptions about women and their "nature" and "roles." Research into the gendered im-

plications of these findings would call into question the "givenness" or "naturalness" of the world International Relations is trying to explain.

A critical feminist theory would look at the changes in world politics in the 1980s and come up with some interesting conclusions. The "democratization" of Eastern Europe has been seen by many in the West and the East as a change for the better. Of course this is a somewhat simplistic understanding of the enormous changes that are occurring but nevertheless there is some consensus that democratization is at least better than that which existed before. But if we look more closely at the gender specific effects of democratization we are left with a different picture. Romania may now have relaxed its draconian abortion and contraception laws but in the 1990 Romanian election campaign there was a move away from suggesting women should be given political responsibility. Women now hold only 3.5 percent of parliamentary seats. In Czechoslovakia the figure is 6 percent and in Hungary 7 percent. The East is indeed following the example of the West, but is this necessarily a good thing as far as women are concerned?

The changes in Eastern Europe have also opened the way for the importation of traditionally Western styles of entertainment for men. The use of women as sex objects, particularly via pornography and beauty contests, is finding a large market in the East. The American monthly *Playboy* sold out its first Hungarian language edition within days and Poland's news stands are full of pornographic material. Poland's acceptance of the use of women as objects of sexual desire sits uneasily next to Lech Walesa's current moves to ban abortion completely. And in both Czechoslovakia and Poland there is a growing (male) consensus that one way to solve the economic plight of working men is to send women home. A

[15]As Sisson Runyan and Peterson do in their article, "The Radical Future of Realism," p. 71.
[16]Whitworth, "Gender in the Inter-Paradigm Debate;" and Mark Hoffman, "Critical Theory and the Inter-Paradigm Debate," *Millennium*, vol. 16, no. 2, 1987, pp. 231–49; and Mark Hoffman, "Conversations on Critical International Relations Theory," *Millennium*, vol. 17, no. 1, 1988, pp. 91–5.

feminist may well turn round and look at the changes in Eastern Europe and comment "the more things change, the more they stay the same, at least for women."

There are many feminist critiques of International Relations, each with varying weaknesses and strengths. Liberal feminist attempts to "include women in" and Marxist/socialist attempts to make us aware of the gendered consequences of the policies and practices of a capitalist, racist and patriarchal world system are invaluable counters to the partial perspective of current International Relations research. The radical feminist insistence that women's real lives and experiences are of vital importance is also a necessary antidote to an International Relations heavily concerned with the activities of men. It might be regarded as somewhat churlish to imply that certain feminist perspectives are more useful than others, as each perspective has valuable contributions to make. However, the importance of the political imperatives of feminism urges me to suggest that a critical feminist theory will provide even further insights into the gender blindness of International Relations.

Critical feminism does not ask us to include women and their issues on the agenda because we are already there. This perspective will not take the existing agenda as a given but will ask what is left out by defining the agenda in such a way. A critical feminist perspective will endeavour not to fall into the trap of prescribing what is important in women's lives or to women but will draw attention to policies and practices which exploit women or which limit their autonomy. A critical feminist approach will

illuminate the connections between interests served and knowledge created by International Relations research, but without falling into the functionalist trap of equating interests served with first and final causes. This critical feminist approach will take the problematization of gender insensitive credentials of other critical approaches. This perspective makes us question the very gender neutrality of the subject, its assumptions and approaches, the crucial point being that the gendered assumptions embedded within International Relations produced distorted and partial knowledge. This should make us think long and hard about what International Relations is and especially about the version of it that we define as the subject of International Relations. Disciplines create boundaries, and these boundaries have powerful effects on what a subject defines as its agenda. In International Relations, these boundaries, like those in all the other social sciences, have long ignored gender questions: raising these questions now may appear political or biased, or simply as against common sense. The problem for International Relations is that it is one of the last social sciences to face up to the possibility that its cherished concepts and agenda may not be gender neutral. This silence is now so loud that it screams. We should not be afraid to acknowledge that feminism is a subversive strategy as implied by Anne Sisson Runyan and V. Spike Peterson. However, when the notion of subversion is stripped to its derisory connotations, applied to it by defenders of the status quo, subversive strategies provide a foundation from which to emancipate and liberate.

3 THE NEW WORLD ORDER AND STUDY OF INTERNATIONAL RELATIONS: HAS ANYTHING CHANGED?

JAMES R. LEE

James Lee is an associate professor in the School of International Service at The American University in Washington, D.C.

I. HISTORY AND THE STUDY OF IR

History has played a key role in the emergence and development of intellectual disciplines, particularly with respect to the social sciences. Many arguably believe that sociology was the first social science discipline or organized field of scientific enquiry. Sociology grew as a field of study to "cure" the many social problems associated with massive urbanization in the nineteenth century. (In fact, Durkheim's seminal sociological study was on the subject of suicide.) Economics developed in a similar manner: industrialization in the nineteenth century magnified the importance of economic trends in the lives of individuals, making resource allocation problems more difficult. Thus, history tends to mold theory and supply appropriate theoretical paradigms for social science theories. These theories are not immutable and do change over time as history unveils itself. For example, as prevailing economic theories crumbled with the Depression of the 1930s, John Maynard Keynes came forward to put economic theory "back together again" with neo-classical economic theory.

By the same token, around 1900, IR became prominent as a discipline because of the growing importance of international behavior both to the individual and to the state (particularly with respect to war). That is to say: the degree to which our world shrank increased the compulsion to learn more about one's neighbors. Further, the danger that we would destroy one another made it imperative that common ground be found. The formal study of IR was thus a child of necessity: human survival.[1]

Raymond Aron, the French theorist, believed that "troubled times encourage meditation" and that the growth of IR as a subject matter for investigation was a response to troubled times. It coincided with the increasing problems of today's world where, especially at the end of each World War, there was a greater need to know and understand the reality of international relations to avoid the cataclysmic conflict which marked the first half of the twentieth century.

The development of IR as an orga-

[1] This evolution is described in great detail by William C. Olson and A.J.R. Groom in *International Relations Then and Now: Origins and Trends in Interpretation* (London: Harper Collins Academic, 1991), Chapter IV.

nized intellectual activity is perhaps a century old. But the examination of IR by scholars is much older. It is said that Thucydides was the first scholar of IR. Writing twenty-four centuries ago, Thucydides focused on the role of Athens and Sparta in the Pelopennisian War to explain the factors motivating decision-makers to choose between conflict and cooperation. History has long had an impact on the study of IR as the following two examples illustrate.

First, technology had a great impact on the founding of IR as a field of study. The modern development of IR coincides with the "Contemporary Era" of modern world history, around the time of the second Industrial Revolution (late nineteenth century).[2] Many have identified significant technological changes which took place in and around the late nineteenth century. It is clear that something of historical significance took place around this time and that around this time IR began to congeal as a field of study.[3]

Why was this period so important? The second Industrial Revolution dramatically shrank the world through technological advances in transportation and communications, thus increasing the likelihood of relations between peoples and ergo the need to study them. In other words, several critical technological leaps made international relations much more possible. These leaps might include the development of the internal combustion engine, the airplane, Marconi's creation of the wireless transmit-

ter, and Bell's invention of the telephone. Is there evidence of a new world consciousness resulting from these inventions? Perhaps so. In 1896 the first World's Fair was held and shortly thereafter the first worldwide Olympics.

Insofar as IR was being created as a formal field of study in the wake of these technological advances, it was quite impressionable. The first World War, because of its close timing to the onset of the birth of the study of IR, therefore made a great imprint on it. In the early stages of IR's development, optimism engendered by the League of Nations' "outlawing" of war under the Kellog-Briand Agreement after the War led IR researchers to embrace an idealist orientation to research. A single belief attracted most of the idealist scholars—the belief that the establishment of a strong international organization would resolve the perplexing issues of international relations and therefore lead to the end of the types of conflict just witnessed. If this sounds familiar, it is because many felt in 1919 that the postwar aftermath also held the promise of a new world order(NWO).

The scholarship of the early interwar period was so optimistic that the field took on an engineering-like persona. Simply solving the technical and procedural problems of establishing a world government, it was thought, would bring peace. Consequently, research tended to focus exclusively on international law and the constitutional and procedural difficulties of international institutions. However, by 1939 historical and practical realities overtook this optimistic approach. The political turmoil in Europe and the Far East in the 1930s, the rise of dictators, and the impotence of the League of Nations in the face of these events contributed to a feeling of despair and cynicism. Hans Morgenthau and realism became the focus of IR research.

It is clear that history has had a tre-

[2]These terms are used by Geoffrey Barraclough in *An Introduction to Contemporary History* (reprint edition, Harmondsworth, Middlesex, England: Penguin Books Ltd., 1984).

[3]See William C. Olson, "International Politics: 1919–1969," in Brian Porter *The Abersytwyth Papers* (London: Oxford University Press, 1972). Many point to Paul Reinsch's *World Politics at the End of the Nineteenth Century as Influenced by the Oriental Situation* (New York: Macmillan, 1900) as the first book on IR as a discipline.

mendous pull on the direction of the study in IR, via changes in technology and new events in international affairs. Whether the NWO will be more like the idealist 1920s or the realist 1950s is of course impossible to say. With hope, we have initially looked in the idealistic direction. Perhaps recent technological advances in "compunications" (the combining of the computer with telecommunications) will promote the idealist direction. In either event, the forces of technology and events seem to augur significant changes for the study of IR in the years ahead.

The next few years will offer a Renaissance for IR. For one it will offer the field the opportunity to move from narrowly defined security interests of a largely military nature and more towards the multidisciplinary type of field envisioned by Quincy Wright.[4] More importantly, it may be an opportunity for the study of IR to have a greater effect on the conduct of international affairs than ever before in history.

2. IS IR A DISCIPLINE?

Many inside and outside of the field of IR do not regard the study of IR as a separate discipline similar to other social sciences such as economics or sociology. This fact naturally says a lot about the state of theory in the field, which on the whole lacks a large degree of consensus. To understand the debate, a short discussion about disciplines of intellectual activity is required.

A discipline is a set of methods governing the examination of certain behavior and theories about the behavior that are thought to be true. In the social sciences this behavior usually applies to a particular aspect of the human condition, whether it be centered on culture (anthropology), resource allocation (economics), or how the mind works (psychology). By ordering and closing a system of thought, disciples (researchers) can establish rules conducting methods for deriving knowledge. Out of these rules may come findings based on agreed-upon confidence, subsequently leading researchers to propose "laws" about behavior. In sum, whereas any individual intellectual undertaking can be said to *have* discipline, a recognized field of study generally *sets* discipline.

If IR is a discipline, it is easily the most different type of social science. Unlike sociology, economics, psychology, or anthro-

pology IR does not concern itself with examining some type of behavior—such the relation of human beings to the physical world in geography—but concerns itself rather with the nature and characteristics of large-scale social organizations.

This particular focus makes a significant difference in what is studied in IR. Other social science disciplines examine behavior across levels of organization in society, meaning that economists look at economic behavior at the world level, the state level as well as at the household level. IR, on the other hand, focuses on the behavior of other social sciences related to a single dimension in a hierarchy of authority: the world dimension. In other words, if we use psychological tools to study Stalin and understand how he thought, we in IR do so not because we have a primary interest in the study of psychology, but of an interest in Stalin's impact on relations between nations.

To have discipline implies intrasubjectivity between a group of researchers: a rigor based on concordant world views regarding essential tenets of behavior. What can be regarded as indicators of concur-

[4]Quincy Wright, *The Study of International Relations* (New York: Appleton-Century-Crofts, 1955).

rence necessary for a discipline? Certainly a core group of concepts which are known and used by researchers in explaining behavior is one sign. Another is a set of manuscripts which relate in some way to one another and perhaps journals and periodicals which focus solely on that subject.

Some would divide the necessary criteria for establishing a discipline into two discrete parts: identifiable intellectual and social characteristics. Intellectual characteristics include a distinct subject-matter, agreed-upon models, unique concepts, specialized vocabulary, and standardized methods. Social characteristics include a number of teachers and students and a separate university department status.

By these criteria IR meets the intellectual and social criteria required of a discipline only marginally well. Concepts abound (power, conflict, etc.) and surely the vocabulary of IR has become specialized. But "agreed upon" models do not exist and many like Hedley Bull repudiate the idea that there is any international model with a real world counterpart; rather, anarchy rules. Part of the problem is that the very definition of a model varies widely among IR researchers. Sadly, there is often no basis even for comparison.

Most social sciences would, however, have a difficult time meeting any strict criteria for judging a discipline. It is doubtful that one could say there are any *agreed-upon* models of economics, for example. To the contrary, there are *several* agreed-upon models. That is precisely the problem. As for teachers and students, separate IR departments do exist at many colleges and universities around the world. The bulk of IR scholars nonetheless remain within departments of Political Science. The technological revolution of today and the NWO both suggest reasons to believe a leap in the amount of international activity may occur. Over time, IR will become more closely recognized as a discipline distinct from political science because there will be more and more students learning about IR and more teachers teaching it.

3. WHAT IS THE UNIT OF ANALYSIS?

IR focuses on inter-nation relations. Or does it? The nation-state is not a universal concept, but a peculiar political institution evolving out of the traditions of Western European liberalism. The nation is closely tied to a particular people who share, among many things, a common language, culture, and history. The state is on the other hand an institution (according to David Easton) that directs the authoritative allocation of values and, over time, has become the preeminent entity for political organization in the world. In Europe, the nation and the state were fairly well matched in terms of geographic boundaries. Therefore, it was probably no more than a matter of custom to call the field IR since it was "invented" by Europeans, when in fact it was not the nation that was the focus of interest, but rather the state. Outside of Europe, the state and the nation were quite different entities and therefore the very idea of the nation-state was something quite different. These were nation*s*-states: that is, they were collections of nations unified under the umbrella of a single political organization. The difference for them is revealed in the state-building process. In these latter entities, building was often limited by long-standing cultural and ethnic differences.

Simply because IR researchers focus on the state does not mean that our subject should be defined by the fact that some type of behavior or activity crosses state borders.

After all, borders are often arbitrary and changing and most of the things that happen to cross these boundaries are of little importance. Rather, we are interested in large-scale social organizations that coalesce at the world level. Often, these forces are organized in the form of sovereign states. But IR researchers also study other large-scale social organizations, such as nongovernmental organizations (ideologies or religions) or international organizations (multilateral or bilateral). In our field, this point is no more poignantly apparent than by simply looking at our most frequent areas of research. There is more written about the foreign affairs of the United Fruit Company or about Islam than there is about the foreign affairs of Botswana or Bolivia.

If we could somehow chart on a graph these large-scale social entities of concern to the study of IR over time, the trends would reveal a declining importance of the state as an instrument of large-scale social organization in the world and a rise of other types of organization (nongovernmental and international). This is no doubt the result of a shrinking world and a higher level of aggregation in world behavior than ever before.

Both the size and viability of the state have changed over time. Athens and Sparta were no more than city-states when they existed twenty-four centuries ago. Two centuries ago, states (empires) were much larger on average than today and states have steadily declined in size since then. Recent events only amplify this trend towards downsizing the state. The fact that the state changes in this way is somewhat vexing for the scholar. How can the IR scholar compare the behavior of Athens in the Peloppenissian War with that of the United States in the Cold War? In the first case, this involved less than a million people in a localized area. The latter involved billions of people spread across the planet.

The state's ability to control the lives of the people in it has fallen as communications and transportation worldwide have grown, as John Herz noted quite some time ago. This has led to a rise in nonstate actors as key determinants of IR behavior as borders have become much more permeable. This permeability is said to be a contributing factor to the fall of the communist system which required a rigid control of information.

As the state dims in importance and international bodies such as the United Nations or the European Community continue to expand in dominion, the focus of the study of IR will move from one which is subsystem dominant to one more systemic in nature. Perhaps the approach will more resemble Political Science than IR, in that it will study governance in an organization as opposed to relations between independent entities. This will probably work until relations between peoples on differing planets need to be understood. Then what?

4. WHY STUDY IR?

An early intent of IR scholars and their research, especially in the 1920s, was to promote cooperation between peoples of the world and to find ways to avoid international conflict. This essential purpose was diverted by history with the onset of World War Two and the Cold War. Because of the nature of these struggles, IR focused via the works of Hans Morgenthau on the realistic role of power in IR. These two periods did however provide IR with some degree of intellectual direction, in what William C.

Olsen and A.J.R. Groom call the "quest for peace" and the "quest for power."[5]

What will be the period of the third consensus? There is good reason to believe the focus will finally aim at achieving some kind of world order. Why this time? Simply put, because it has never been more imperative to do so. However, in order to define an order it may be necessary to redefine the state, especially vis-a-vis other levels of analysis of international behavior.[6] Specifically, the "quest for order" will need to examine how the state-based system can work more effectively with international organizations and individuals, representing the opposite ends of an organizational spectrum, to bring about prosperity and avoid conflict.

CONCLUSION

The paper has touched on four aspects of the New World Order and its impact on the study of IR. First, one can expect a substantial impact because of the mix of historical and technological forces at hand. Second, the field will grow and more resemble a separate discipline of study and, in the process, become even more independent from political science. Third, the focus on security concerns in study on the state will decline and the multi-disciplinarity of the field will increase. Finally, the need to make more explicit links to other levels of analysis will be needed both in theory and in practice. The potential for a Renaissance in IR exists. It is, however, more like an opportunity than an outcome.

[5]William C. Olson and A.J.R. Groom, *International Relations: Then and Now: Origins and Trends in Interpretation* (London: Harper Collins Academic, 1991).

[6]The levels of analysis in IR are discussed in many places including in Norman J. Padelford, George A. Lincolnn, and Lee D. Olvey, *The Dynamics of International Politics* (Macmillan and Collier Macmillan: New York and London, 1976), p. 34.

4 THE RELOCATION OF AUTHORITY IN A SHRINKING WORLD

We playwrights, who have to cram a whole human life or an entire historical era into a two-hour play, can scarcely understand this rapidity [of change] ourselves. And if it gives us trouble, think of the trouble it must give political scientists, who have less experience with the realm of the improbable.

Vaclav Havel[1]

It is difficult to quarrel with the widespread interpretation that much of the change sweeping through world politics has its roots in the policies pursued by Mikhail Gorbachev since 1985. Surely the dismantling of the Berlin Wall and the advent of noncommunist regimes in Poland, Hungary, and Czechoslovakia can, to a large degree, be traced to perestroika, glasnost, and the unwillingness of the Soviets to come to the defense of their beleaguered Communist colleagues to their west. And surely the wars in Afghanistan, Angola, and Cambodia were, to a large degree, brought to an end because the Kremlin withdrew its support for them.

But analyses that rest primarily on the Gorbachev or Soviet factor can be profoundly misleading. They run the risk of overlooking some fundamental political dynamics if they do not take the next step and ask why the changes in eastern Europe and elsewhere came so quickly, so thoroughly, and so peacefully? Why did not the governments of the Soviet bloc retain their established controls and steer the pace of change? Why were the 1989 processes of spontaneous coalescence of great numbers of Poles, Czechs, Hungarians, East Germans, Bulgarians, and Romanians around actions and goals that would enlarge their voice in the affairs of their countries so similar to the upheavals that occurred within the previous few years in Sri Lanka, Soviet Georgia, Armenia, and Estonia, South Korea, Algeria, Haiti, Taiwan, Mexico, Ethiopia, Singapore, Tibet, Argentina, India, the Philippines, the West Bank and Gaza Strip, Chile, Burma, Panama, China, the Sudan, and Yugoslavia? Why, in short, has the lurch toward change and accommodation unfolded on a global scale, and, equally important, why did so many historic breakpoints occur in and among so many countries in such a short span of time?

[1]From an address to the United States Congress, as reported by the *Los Angeles Times*, Feb. 22, 1990, p. A8.

Reprinted by permission from the author and from *Comparative Politics*, 24, April 1992, pp. 253–272. Copyright © The City University of New York, 1992.

THE 1980s PUZZLE

Taken together, these questions highlight what might be called the 1980s puzzle—the perplexing globalization of patterns wherein the loci of authority were relocated and restructured. Whatever may be the proper solution of this puzzle, its pervasiveness suggests that today's turbulence is too extensive to be explained solely by the impact of Mr. Gorbachev. Viewed from a more encompassing perspective, his contribution and the transformations underway in the Soviet Union are not so much sources of change as they are agents of change, dynamics that have fomented and channeled shifting patterns to be sure, but only because prior dynamics were operating to make it possible for the Gorbachev factor to have an impact. The late 1980s would not have unfolded as they did without the Soviet Union's pulling back from the Cold War, but neither would they have occurred if individuals and publics had not been ready to seize the openings, challenge the authorities, and press their demands.

Nor is it sufficient to look for a solution to the puzzle solely in the pressures for political expression that are generated by economic circumstances. Both the rich and the poor have evidenced a readiness to coalesce and claim authority for themselves. Part of the explanation might be found in the processes of rapid economic development, for example in such countries as Taiwan, South Korea, and China, but this is hardly a central piece of the puzzle inasmuch as there are too many poor countries or regions, such as Romania, Burma, Tibet, and Soviet Georgia, where historic breakpoints occurred but where movement into the stages of economic development that foster mushrooming demands for political autonomy has yet to occur.

Similarly, it can hardly be said that widespread nationalism lies at the heart of

the explanation. Ethnic loyalties were a factor in such places as Sri Lanka, Estonia, and the West Bank, but again there are a number of situations where authority crises were sustained by other than nationalistic fervor.

Nor can it be said that the solution of the puzzle lies in the lure of democratic institutions. To be sure, as illustrated by the placing of a replica of the Statue of Liberty in Tiananmen Square and the singing of "We Shall Overcome" in Wenceslas Square, the demand for such institutions, or at least for political autonomy and self-governance, has been global in scope. Except for Iran, none of the upheavals of the 1980s involved a clamor to follow and support a single leader or an authoritarian ideology. Nevertheless, the notion that this period of turbulence has been sustained by global aspirations for more democracy also falls short of an adequate explanation. It fails to account for the timing of the upheavals, for the surfacing of such aspirations in the 1980s. If the desire for democracy has fueled the convergence of peoples in the central squares of diverse cities, why were the same squares empty in the 1970s? Why did they not fill up in the 1960s? The answer, again, must be that prior dynamics were at work. Important and heartwarming as the mushrooming of prodemocracy forces throughout the world has been, they too are agents of change, the products of even more fundamental sources that culminated in a single historical moment.[2]

Theoretically, of course, it is possible that the pervasive pattern is mere coincidence, that separate circumstances in each situation gave rise to the appearance of an overall pattern but that in fact the 1980s

[2]For a cogent discussion of the complexity of the prodemocracy movements, see Dankwart A. Rustow, "Democracy: A Global Revolution?," *Foreign Affairs,* 69 (Fall 1990), 75–91.

were marked only by a series of country-specific and issue-specific episodes. Again, however, the argument is flawed. It suffers not only in the face of empirical indicators of causal chains wherein more than a few of the various challenges to authority were linked to each other, but it also falters when confronted with the extremely low probability of numerous historic breakpoints unfolding *simultaneously* (or within a very short time frame) in diverse, widely separated countries in the absence of any overall sources that are operative on every continent.

Beyond the situation-specific pieces of the puzzle, in other words, must lie global dynamics that are the better part of the explanation. The ensuing inquiry identifies five such dynamics that have quickened the pace of world politics, rendered it ever more tumultuous, and facilitated the impact of the Gorbachev factor and other immediate stimuli at work on the world scene. All of these dynamics are global in scope, and they can all be said to have culminated, converged, and interacted in the late 1980s in such a way as to facilitate a break with historic patterns. In effect, the discussion suggests, the world is *not* now passing through a transition to some new form of world order, but rather that it has already undergone such a transition and is, today, well ensconced in a new order.

Stated summarily, one of the five global dynamics involves the shift from an industrial to a postindustrial order and focuses on the dynamics of technology, particularly on those technologies associated with the microelectronic revolution that have made social, economic, and political distances so much shorter, the movement of ideas, pictures, currencies, and information so much faster, and thus the interdependence of people and events so much greater. A second is the emergence of issues, such as atmospheric pollution, terrorism, the drug trade, currency crises, and AIDS, that are

the direct products of new technologies or the world's greater interdependence and are distinguished from traditional political issues by virtue of being transnational rather than national or local in scope. A third dynamic is the authority crises that stem from the reduced capacity of states and governments to provide satisfactory solutions to the major issues on their political agendas, partly because the new issues are not wholly within their jurisdiction, partly because the old issues are also increasingly intertwined with significant international components (for example, agricultural markets and labor productivity), and partly because the compliance of their citizenries can no longer be taken for granted. Fourth, with the weakening of whole systems such as states, subsystems have acquired a correspondingly greater coherence and effectiveness, thereby fostering tendencies toward decentralization (what I call "subgroupism") at all organizational levels that are in stark contrast to the centralizing tendencies (such as nationalism) of earlier decades and that are in deep tension with the centralizing tendencies (transnationalism) of the present fostered by the new interdependence issues and the globalization of national economies. Finally, there is the feedback of the consequences of all the foregoing for the skills and orientations of the world's adults who comprise the groups, states, and other collectivities that have had to cope with the new issues of interdependence and adjust to the new technologies of the postindustrial order: with their analytic skills enlarged and their orientations toward authority more self-conscious, today's persons-in-the-street are no longer as uninvolved, ignorant, and manipulable with respect to world affairs as were their forebears.

The solution of the 1980s puzzle, in short, is subtle. It is not based on a single-cause model. Nor does it presume that the micro changes preceded the others in time.

On the contrary, all of them are seen as being initially responses to the technological upheavals that underlay the ever-growing interdependencies of economic, political, and social life. Once the microlevel shifts began, however, alterations in the status of states, governments, and subgroups were bound to follow a people became receptive to the decentralizing consequences inherent in their growing capacity to locate their own interests more clearly in the flow of events.

A BIFURCATIONIST PERSPECTIVE

Before elaborating on the key dynamics that underlie this renewal and redirection, let us note briefly what they have produced if one looks beyond the agents of change on the current scene and employs instead a more encompassing perspective. At the core of the new order as redefined criteria of political legitimacy and a relocation of authority that have transformed the capacities of governments and the conduct of public life. Put most succinctly (and for reasons adduced later), just as legitimacy is increasingly linked to the performance of officials rather than to traditional habits of compliance, so has authority been relocated in the direction of those political entities most able to perform effectively. This relocation has thus evolved in two directions, "upward" toward transnational organizations and "downward" toward subnational groups, with the result that national governments are decreasingly competent to address and resolve major issues confronting their societies.

If the new order is a response to the need for structures that accommodate both the powerful centralizing and decentralizing forces unleashed by the dynamics of technology, and if it is founded on transformed processes whereby legitimacy and authority are generated and sustained, its form consists of an ungainly, asymmetrical set of global structures that accord a lesser (though not trivial) role to the state-centric system and a greater (though not overpowering) role to a newly emerged multicentric system. The states that have dominated politics for more than three centuries, in other words, have given way to a bifurcated system in which actors in the state-centric world compete, cooperate, interact, or otherwise coexist with counterparts in a multicentric world comprised of a vast array of diverse transnational, national, and subnational actors. These two worlds of world politics—what I call the "bifurcated" global system[3]—are ungainly in the sense that they lack the hierarchical arrangements to which practitioners of politics have long been accustomed. The strong still tend to prevail over the weak in the state-centric world, but such a hierarchy is not so salient in the multicentric world or in the interaction of the two worlds. Instead, viewed from a bifurcationist perspective, authority and legitimacy are so widely dispersed within, among, and outside states as to mute—and in some instances even to erase—hierarchical distinctions. In effect, the pluralistic tendencies of world politics are too powerful to sustain the symmetry of the historic pecking order.

This is not to argue that states are headed for oblivion. Although decreasingly effective, national governments are still in place, still willing and able to exercise police powers on behalf of their perceived authority, still ready to abide by the norms and practices of the state system, and still needed to perform key tasks of governance. Because public order still needs to be maintained, because economies still need a mod-

[3]James N. Rosenau, "Patterned Chaos in Global Life: Structure and Process in the Two Worlds of World Politics," *International Political Science Review,* 9 (October 1988), 357–394.

icum of management, because justice still needs to be dispensed, because systemwide laws still need to be framed and administered, because the resources necessary to carry out these tasks still need to be generated—because there is still a need, in other words, for polities that attend to the demands of societies—there is no reason to anticipate a diminution in the competence of states and their international system to the point where they are irrelevant actors on the world stage.

So it is not the sovereignty or the jurisdiction of states that is problematic, but rather the exclusivity and the scope of their competence that has changed. Due to the dynamics noted below, they and their governments have undergone a narrowing of the range within which their authority and

legitimacy are operative. Today they are confronted with the new interdependence issues that can be addressed only through cooperation with other international actors and, consequently, a narrowing of the range of their effective authority. And today they are also increasingly subject to divisiveness among subgroup factions at home that further limits their ability to resolve problems and realize goals.

In sum, to adhere to a bifurcationist perspective is not to highlight the uncertainties and ambiguities that presently pervade world politics. It is, rather, an integrated framework which allows for the examination of changes that are expressive of a world transformed by the relocation of political authority and the redefinition of political legitimacy.[4]

A NOTE ON HISTORICAL COMPARISONS

Notwithstanding the inclusion of qualifiers which stress that history is the product of multiple causes, the foregoing analysis has proven so capable of generating outright rejection that it is helpful to pause and focus on the two prime bases for dismissing the assessment that the interactive impact of the five dynamics, and especially the new sources of "people power," have transformed global structures and quickened the pace of historical change. One ground for rejection concerns the Gorbachev factor. The other focuses on the notion that the upheavals of the late 1980s do not represent a new configuration of historical forces. Both lines of reasoning spring from a presumption that the fundamental foundations of world politics remain unaltered, that the commotions in public squares and the signs of global bifurcation will subside and be followed by a resurgent interstate system and a resumption of the traditional practices through which it manages world affairs.

The analysis presented here makes no pretense at "proving" that this reasoning is false, but it does offer an alternative interpretation that, we hope, calls into question the presumption that modern history remains on course.

To suggest that the Gorbachev factor is only one of several interactive sources of the 1980s puzzle is rejected by some analysts on the grounds that it excessively complicates what was essentially a simple and longstanding process of interstate politics. Gorbachev's withdrawal of Soviet support for East European and other Communist regimes, it is argued, was sufficient to bring about the upheavals that brought an end to the Cold War. To add other factors to this explanation is to abandon the principle of parsimony: why cite the impact of technol-

---

[4]For a full elaboration of the bifurcationist approach see James N. Rosenau, *Turbulence in World Politics: A Theory of Change and Continuity* (Princeton: Princeton University Press, 1990).

ogy, the consequences of new interdependence issues, the advent of authority crises, and the greater competence of subgroups and citizens when the withdrawal of Soviet support explains so much of what happened? The answer is equally direct: the Gorbachev factor is, to repeat, a central dimension of the upheavals, but it leaves enough unexplained to warrant abandoning parsimony in search of a fuller account. The Gorbachev factor may be sufficient for eastern Europe, but its explanatory power does not extend to Turkey, where the government was forced to rethink its plans to build a power plant on the Aegean coast when "tens of thousands of people in Izmer formed a human chain along the sea front in one of the biggest demonstrations in Turkey in recent years."[5] Nor does it extend to Albania, which has recently been the scene of collective actions by disgruntled citizens even though Albania has never been dependent on Soviet support. Similarly, as previously noted, the Gorbachev factor surely does not serve as an adequate explanation of developments in Burma, the Ivory Coast, Nepal, the West Bank, and a host of other countries that also lacked a Soviet presence even as people power reversed long-standing patterns. Events in other parts of the world may indeed have been fostered by attempts to emulate developments in eastern Europe, but the breadth and depth of the spread to situations where there had been no previous Soviet support surely indicates the presence of additional historical dynamics.

As for the contention that the upheavals of the 1980s are hardly unique, that other periods of modern history (notably the American and French revolutions of the late eighteenth century and the surge of collective actions in Europe in 1848) have also witnessed the impact of people power, that the AIDS epidemic is comparable to the impact of the plague in Europe in the fourteenth century, and that many other parallels can be drawn between the present and the past, it is questionable whether the impact of change has ever been so global, so rapid, or so structurally consequential in the past as it is in the present. Today's transformations are worldwide in scope, reaching into every remote corner of all the continents; their pace involves breathtaking rapidity that could not have been matched in the preelectronic eras of the past; and their results have involved the restructuring of whole societies as well as the bifurcation of global politics. Involved, in other words, are differences in kind rather than simply in degree. The scope, pace, and consequences of change today may be so much greater than seemingly similar developments in the past that the dynamism for further transformations may not yet have run its course. As one observer puts it, "we are moving . . . from a stable past into a dynamic future, through the kind of change a materials physicist might call a change of phase."[6] Accordingly, to say that the profundity of these changes is no different from those of earlier eras is to risk ignoring unnecessarily the possible emergence of new structures and processes of world history. One might even say that the recitation of past parallels is a substitute for undertaking fresh analysis, for reexamining core premises about the nature of global politics.

Stated differently, the ensuing decades may indeed prove the bifurcation model to be erroneous. States and their governments could regain their status as unchallenged sovereign authorities. The interstate system could prove resilient and gain control over the interdependence issues and the multicentric world, thereby rendering the bifur-

---

[5]*Wall Street Journal Europe,* May 8, 1990, p. 3.

[6]Crawford Robb, "The Historical Process—A New Perspective," *Futures* (February 1987), 74.

cation of global politics into a temporary period of history, a mere prelude to the restoration of the centuries-long international pecking order. If such developments occur, then the analysis presented here will have been falsified. On the other hand, if such developments do not occur, if citizenries do not turn quiescent and the tides of change continue to subvert the old order and relocate authority along bifurcated lines, then the ensuing discussion can not be easily rejected.

AUTHORITY, LEGITIMACY, AND COERCION

Given a readiness to suspend historical comparisons, it ought not be surprising that states are no longer as competent as they once were. If the exercise of authority, the viability of legitimacy, and the use of coercion are understood as variable rather than static processes, it does not seem so momentous to acknowledge that states have weakened sufficiently to be rivaled by another system of global actors. The fact that states have long been seen as sources of authority and legitimacy that entitle them to employ coercion does not negate the possibility of authority and legitimacy being relocated and the right to engage in coercive action thereby being redefined. Indeed, despite the continuities of history, authority, legitimacy, and coercion have always been susceptible to change, to moving across a wide continuum that ranges from the evocation of automatic compliance at one extreme to obstinate defiance at the other. Put differently, to speak of the relocation of authority is to refer to shifts in the locus of initiatives and responses in control relationships. In the present period the expansion of skills among citizens has led to more and more initiatives emanating from their ranks and to public agencies being increasingly placed in the role of complying, modifying, or otherwise responding to the demands made from the private sector.

The processes whereby authority and legitimacy are created, sustained, undermined, and relocated are the subject of a vast literature that need not detain us here.

It is sufficient to recognize that no collectivity could persist for long without having authority as a legal basis for the conduct of its leaders and the maintenance of its hierarchical structures. It is through the exercise of authority that decisions are made and implemented and the coherence of collectivities thereby preserved. If a collectivity lacked authority relations, if its members felt entitled to do as they pleased, goals could not be framed, and energies could not be concerted; there could be no collective action, and the collectivity would soon lose its identity as a social system distinct from its environment. Authority relationships, in other words, are those patterns of a collectivity wherein some of its members are accorded the right, or take the initiative, to make decisions, set rules, allocate resources, and formulate policies for the rest of the members, who in turn comply with, modify, reject, or otherwise respond to the decisions, rules, and policies.[7]

In many collectivities, authority relations are formally incorporated into their interaction patterns through constitutions,

[7]For extended discussions of authority relationships in and between collectivities, see James S. Coleman, "Authority Systems," *Public Opinion Quarterly*, 44 (Summer 1980), 143–163; Richard E. Flathman, *The Practice of Political Authority: Authority and the Authoritative* (Chicago: University of Chicago Press, 1980); Myron J. Aronoff, ed., *The Frailty of Authority* (New Brunswick: Transaction Books, 1986); and Oran R. Young, *Compliance and Public Authority: A Theory with International Applications* (Baltimore: The Johns Hopkins University Press, 1979).

bylaws, statutes, and judicial decisions. Yet it would be erroneous to limit the concept of authority relations to formal structures in which the source of authority can be documented. The exercise of authority also occurs in informal settings, in decisions that evoke compliance even though the right or initiative to make them has not been stated in legal form. As one observed has said, "the smallest microunit of modern political action systems is authority to make a new decision in a manner that may become binding (at least through its consequences) on another."[8] Authority relations are thus to be found wherever people undertake collective tasks—in families, classrooms, religious groups, unions, athletic teams, business firms, revolutionary movements, terrorist organizations, and a host of other social formations beside governmental entities.

There are various reasons why people accord legitimacy to the acts of authorities and comply with their orders. One is fear of the coercive consequences of noncompliance; another is an understanding that collective coherence and action serve their needs and goals; a third is the expectation that others will also comply.[9] Mostly, however, compliance is a matter of habit: repeated instances of compliance become deeply ingrained as a response when certain procedures are followed and certain kinds of pronouncements are issued. The longer authority has been in place, the greater is the legitimacy that attaches to it, and thus the more deep-seated are the habits of compliance it evokes. Under these stable conditions, authorized actions and policies are

simply accepted unquestioningly by those toward whom they are directed. The compliance may be preceded by argument, bargaining, and delay, and the actions and policies may thus be moderated, but in the end the habit of compliance will normally prevail as the relational outcome.

For several centuries, the highest authority has been lodged in states. Their sovereignty, which accords them the final say in disputes among their members or in the conduct of relations with actors abroad, has entitled them to take authoritative actions which have traditionally been considered legitimate and beyond questioning. Both the citizens of a state and actors external to it have accepted its acts and policies as decisive. Accordingly, its citizens have long been habituated to complying with them, and citizens of other states abroad have long acknowledged that they are not entitled to interfere in the processes whereby the acts and policies are framed and implemented.

In short, the historic pattern has been one in which the authority of officials is simply taken for granted and not challenged. One did what one was told—pay taxes, submit to a military draft, abide by regulations—irrespective of how well or poorly the authorities carried out their tasks. If the authorities used coercion, then it was a legitimate interpretation of their responsibilities and not subject to objection. Under these conditions when compliance was essentially habitual, political learning was minimal. Imbued with values that mandated acceptance of whatever was required by those in authority, people did not ponder the propriety of a course of action or doubt whether the actors were entitled to undertake such actions. They simply did as they were instructed and thus compliance fed back to reinforce the perceptions officials had of their own legitimacy.

Is authority thus a "possession" that leaders bring to bear in their control rela-

[8]Dean R. Gerstein, "To Unpack Micro and Macro: Link Small with Large and Part with Whole," in Jeffrey C. Alexander, Bernhard Giesen, Richard Munch, and Neil J. Smelser, eds., *The Micro-Macro Link* (Berkeley: University of California Press, 1987), p. 103.

[9]For a cogent discussion of this point, see Kenneth J. Arrow, *The Limits of Organization* (New York: W. W. Norton, 1974), ch. 4.

tionships? Is it a capability, like weapons, on which they rely to obtain compliance? These questions seem best answered in the negative. Unlike weapons, authority is not tangible or fixed in time and space. Often, to be sure, its nature and limits are spelled out in documents, and for some observers these pieces of paper are the authority itself. In practice, however, the exercise of authority depends on the intangible bases on which it is accepted by those toward whom it is directed. Written words that do not evoke widespread compliance are not authority, even if they have long served as authorizing instruments. The written words can be altered by statute or other legal means in an attempt to enlarge or diminish the authority of leaders, but such changes take on meaning only as they evoke correspondingly different responses from those toward whom they are directed. Clearly, then, authority pertains to relational and not to possessional phenomena. It is enhanced, dissipated, or otherwise altered only by virtue of variations in the responses of those whose compliance is sought. As one astute observer has put it:

> Authority is another name for the willingness and capacity of individuals to submit to the necessities of cooperative systems. Authority arises from the technological and social limitations of cooperative systems on the one hand, and of individuals on the other. Hence the status of authority in a society is the measure both of the development of individuals and of the technological and social conditions of the society.[10]

It follows that substantial alterations in "the development of individuals" are bound to have consequences for the location and structure of authority relations: the more refined their analytic skills become, the greater the uncertainties that accompany the relocation of authority are likely to be. And it also follows that as "the technological and social conditions" of the world become increasingly complex and overwhelming, so are issues and problems likely to seem increasingly beyond the control of national governments and international organizations, thus intensifying the decentralizing tendencies that relocate authority in less encompassing collectivities. In the words of one anonymous observer, "it may be that authority—the power to take responsibility—can at this point be recovered only on a local level, and that this is why local politics has acquired new significance."[11]

Much the same can be said about the nature of legitimacy. Although the rules and procedures for exercising control may be codified and cited as the "authority" for policies pursued, legitimacy does not automatically attach to the actions that follow. When the right to take such actions is unchallenged by the membership, the decisions, rules, and policies that flow from its exercise are said to possess legitimacy. Like authority, therefore, legitimacy is rooted in relational phenomena. The two are, so to speak, different sides of the same coin: authority attaches to the actions of leaders, and legitimacy is the acceptance attached to the actions by the membership.

Clearly, then, the readiness of a membership to accept and abide by the decisions of its leaders is not a static feature of political systems. It may remain fixed for long periods, but it can vary. The variability can range from highly integrated relationships, in which the membership habitually and automatically complies with the leadership's decisions, to those in which the degree of compliance is in doubt. Between these extremes the habits of compliance may give

---

[10]Chester I. Barnard, *The Functions of the Executive* (Cambridge, Mass.: Harvard University Press, 1938), p. 134.

[11]"The Talk of the Town," *The New Yorker*, Oct. 9, 1989, p. 37.

way, progressively, to reflection over, skepticism of, anguish about, and eventually resistance to the decisions.

Authority relations can undergo change if diverse forces at work within or external to a polity alter its value priorities and thereby erode the readiness of its members to comply habitually with the leaders' directives. Sometimes the erosion reaches the point where leaders are inclined to resort to coercion to implement their policies. But the use of force is normally a last resort for any political leadership. Leaders know that, even if the force they employ is overwhelming and likely to produce effective control, the costs of its application are likely to be much higher than if they used other, less

violent control techniques. While they may feel they have no choice, that the dangers of public disarray are so great as to justify calling out the police or army, they know that taking such steps is likely to erode the habits of compliance still further and bring on a full-blown crisis of authority.

Thus it is that, just as leaders are tempted to resort to coercion in moments of crisis, they might be tempted to hold off, to dally and temporize, in the hope that through negotiations and threats the situation will ameliorate, disorder will diminish, and authority will somehow be restored without a shot being fired. And so it is, too, that often this temporizing encourages the other parties to escalate their demands.

THE SKILL REVOLUTION

Of course, the bifurcated structures of world politics and the relocation of authority and legitimacy are more than just the context within which present-day turbulence unfolds. They are also integral parts of the turbulence in the sense that the new macro structures and loci of authority feed back as sources of the underlying micro dynamics that are impelling citizens to protest, publics to coalesce, and leaders to yield. It is, obviously, much easier to anticipate success through collective action if states have already been revealed as sharing the global stage with other types of collectivities and if authority has already been perceived as susceptible to relocation.

As previously indicated, perhaps the most profound and pervasive of the dynamics that both underlie and respond to the new, bifurcated global order involves the skills through which individuals comprehend and react to the world around them. Due largely to the advent of powerful new technologies for generating, circulating, sifting, depicting, and storing information, people in every corner of the world are in-

creasingly capable of locating themselves in the course of events, of discerning their own interests in an ever more interdependent and complex world, of tracing complex scenarios in which their micro actions can have macro collective outcomes, of appreciating that sometimes their interests are best served through collective outcomes which enhance their subgroups and that sometimes they are better served by outcomes which reinforce their whole systems, of learning that today's actions can be the source of future problems, of grasping that long-standing habits of compliance are susceptible to transformation, of perceiving the discrepancy between official interpretations and the scenes depicted on their television screens, of emotionally monitoring the moods and orientations of their fellow citizens, and of adapting to rather than denying the presence of fundamental changes. For want of a better term, I summarize these diverse enlarged capacities by referring to them as "expanded analytic and emotional skills." Such an expansion is a prime dynamic in world affairs because it feeds on itself, leading people everywhere to participate ever more effectively and extensively in the course of events and the consolidation of the bifurcated global structures.

The stimuli to global expansion of the foregoing skills are remarkable. From the data on education to those on travel, from the statistics on the distribution of television sets to those pertaining to computers, from the vast proliferation of the world's communications system to the increasing number of situations (such as fuel shortages, traffic jams, and polluted horizons) that describe innocent micro actions producing noxious macro outcomes, mentally competent adults today are literally bombarded with experiences that seem bound to enlarge their analytic and emotional skills. Consider, for example, the global communications system. One assessment yielded a world with 550 million telephones, 600 million television sets, over 1.5 billion radios, several million communicating personal computers, facsimile and telex machines, millions of mobile radio units, over 100 civilian and military communications satellites, over 100 submarine cable links, thousands of microwave towers, millions and millions of cable and copper wires in twisted pairs to cities around the world, and so on. Every day between 5 and 10 billion telephone conversations flow through the global electronic machine.[12]

These statistics, of course, depict only the bare outlines of the global system at single points in time several years ago. Given the continuous dynamism of electronic technologies, doubtless they already understate the current channels through which information flows around the world.[13] Indeed, the stimuli to expanded analytic skills become all the more impressive if traced in a decadal context. In the case of television, for example, between 1965 and 1985 the number of transmitters at least doubled in every region of the world, and the number of receiving sets at least tripled; at the global level, the increase was sevenfold for transmitters and more than threefold for receivers.[14]

That such changes are likely to alter the context within which people conduct their daily lives and relate to the world around them is perhaps more incisively evident in the fact that in the twenty-nine years between 1960 and 1989, when the last two presidential elections in Brazil were held, the proportion of households with television sets rose from 5 to 72 percent.[15] Or consider the implications of the fact that people everywhere are now frequently exposed to visual images of heads of state talking and acting in response to the crises of the moment. So, too, they have seen riots in Pretoria, a wall being dismantled in Berlin, a space shuttle exploding after launch, a government toppled in Prague, a war in the Persian Gulf, a massacre in Beijing, a revolution in Romania, election fraud in Manila, an embassy surrounded in Teheran, a hijacked airliner, to mention but the more obvious examples from the recent past. Nor is the opportunity to observe such scenes confined just to urban areas. From peasants in remote Andean villages to herdsmen in

---

[12]The data summarized here are from Richard R. Calino, "International Communications: Coping with Disasters and Crises in the Electronic Village," remarks before the Annenberg Schools of Communications, Washington, D.C., October 10, 1986, p. 1.

[13]The completion of the first fiber-optic telephone cable across the Atlantic, for example, vastly increased the number of transatlantic phone calls that can be placed simultaneously. The three existing copper cables, along with satellites, carry a total of 20,000 conversations, whereas the fiber-optic cable carries 40,000. Put even more impressively, a single optical fiber can sustain more than 8,000 conversations simultaneously, whereas the figure for copper wire is forty-eight. Calvin Sims, "On New Cable, More Calls to Europe Possible," *New York Times*, Dec. 14, 1988, p. 1.

[14]UNESCO, *Statistical Yearbook* (Paris: 1987), pp. 6.21–6.22.

[15]"Bursting Brazil: Its Growth since the 1960 Election," *New York Times*, Nov. 15, 1989, p. A10.

Mongolia, people in all parts of the world are experiencing a spectacular expansion in their horizons of observability.[16]

While the impact of television as a stimulus to learning is global in scope, much the same can be said about those parts of the world where the computer has become a part of daily routines. In a vast array of jobs people are now found sitting in front of computer terminals and using them to deal with the problems of production, supply, distribution, and consumption.[17] The transformation of the industrial order into its postindustrial successor involves a transition from a reliance on action-centered skills, in which workers use their brains to coordinate their bodies, to a dependence on intellective skills, in which they use their brains to coordinate observations, concepts, and patterns.[18] Accordingly,

> as information technology restructures the work situation, it abstracts thought from action. Absorption, immediacy, and organic responsiveness are superseded by distance, coolness, and remoteness. Such distance brings an opportunity for reflection. . . . As [a] worker from [a pulp mill] summed it up, "Sitting in this room and just thinking has become part of my job. It's the technology that lets me do these

things." The thinking this operator refers to is of a different quality from the thinking that attended the display of action-centered skills. It combines abstraction, explicit inference, and procedural reasoning.[19]

The study from which this quotation comes was organized around observations of pulp mill operators, bankers, and clerical employees, all of whom were employed by firms in the process of computerizing their production operations and business routines. The patterns found were consistent across the different situations; they involved a transition frequently described "in the same words: 'It's a thinking job now'; 'You must use your brain, not your hands,'; 'The job is more mental, it takes place in your head.'" In effect, "the terrain of effort had shifted, not from muscles to brain, but from the complete sensual involvement of the worker's physical presence to an involvement that depended more exclusively upon the worker's quality of mind."[20]

To the extent that today's citizens are thus ensconced in a world of the split screens, zoom lens, and instant replays of television and the graphics, spread sheets, data bases, and search-and-revise routines of computers, it is difficult to imagine that the capacities they bring to politics remain unaffected. If nothing else—and there is probably a great deal more—their ability to discern how they can contribute to collective action seems bound to be enhanced.

But the argument that people are increasingly skillful with respect to public affairs is not confined to the changes wrought by the microelectronic revolution alone. Education has also undergone phenomenal growth in the same period. In all parts of the world and for males and females at all levels, from the primary school through the university, the student population has stead-

---

[16]See, for example, Bradley Graham, "Prime Time in the Andes," *Washington Post National Weekly Edition,* Mar. 21–27, 1988, p. 19, and Christopher S. Wren, "TV (and with It the World) Comes to the Grasslands of Inner Mongolia," *New York Times,* Nov. 14, 1984, p. 4.

[17]Despite the notion that the education, government, and entertainment fields account for a preponderance of those who work regularly with computers, "the most important single fact to emerge" from a study of the "information workforce" is that some 80 percent of this new labor pool consists of people "who collect, arrange, coordinate, monitor and disseminate information about activities taking place within the economy." Anthony Smith, "Telecommunications and the Fading of the Industrial Age," *Political Quarterly,* 54 (April-June 1983), 131.

[18]The differences between action-centered and intellective skills is developed in Shoshana Zuboff, *In the Age of the Smart Machine: The Future of Work and Power* (New York: Basic Books, 1988), pp. 75–76.

[19]Ibid., p. 75.
[20]Ibid., pp. 185, 188.

ily risen from 1960 through 1985,[21] and as a result more and more people have been exposed to the special kind of analysis that sets the classroom aside from other settings. For those who teach it is not always clear that the analytic skills of students are capable of being enlarged, but the data depicting high correlations along this line are so consistent under so many different circumstances that it is difficult to reject the idea that education matters insofar as the skills and orientations of citizens are concerned.[22] And the fact that the pronounced expansion occurred in educational enrollments during the same years in which the bifurcation of world politics gathered momentum supports the interpretation that our time is witness to the emergence of ever more analytically skillful and emotionally competent citizens.

Nor does the combination of the microelectronic and educational explosions fully account for the stimuli which may lead individuals to expand their analytic skills. Besides broadcasters and educators who intentionally seek to affect citizens, there is, so to speak, life itself, those routines embedded in the more encompassing process wherein the greater complexity and interdependence of communities and countries are compelling people to cope with a mounting volume of cross-cutting messages and overlapping problems. The impulse to thrust heads in the sand may be as great as ever, but the ability of individuals to keep their heads covered with the sand seems bound to decline as the rising tide of global interdependence erodes the beaches.

Put less metaphorically, greater interdependence and faster communications

have placed heavier emphasis on the micro sources of macro outcomes and made people more aware of themselves as participants in global scenarios. While the life of communities has always been founded on such processes, never before has the transformation of individual behaviors into collective problems seemed so poignantly evident. There are numerous occasions each day when citizens of the industrial world are made conscious of themselves as links in causal chains. From the traffic jams in which they get caught to the boycotts they are asked to join, from the water shortages they are asked to alleviate to the tax revolts in which they can participate, from the workers' rallies in Poland to the urban mobs in Iran which they have seen on live television, today's citizens have had ample firsthand exposure to the links between individual and collective behavior.[23] Similarly, when they start their automobiles, turn on their air conditioners, or buy their groceries, many may have a fleeting thought that these simple acts are among the worldwide processes that contribute to pollution (or clean air), oil shortages (or gluts), and famines (or surpluses).

Likewise, in this era when national economies are so clearly and intricately woven into shifts in the global economy, people can hardly be oblivious to the once remote sequences whereby global capital flows and banking practices culminate in threats to their savings, jobs, and ability to travel. Reports of volatile exchange rates

---

[21]UNESCO, *Statistical Yearbook*, pp. 2.32–2.33.

[22]For comparative data that demonstrate the impact of education upon the political activities of citizens, see Sidney Verba, Norman H. Nie, and Jae-on Kim, *Participation and Political Equality: A Seven-Nation Comparison* (New York: Cambridge University Press, 1978), p. 67.

[23]The pervasiveness of the personalization of these links between individual and collective action was captured well in a recent full-page advertisement signed by 691 individuals affiliated with one company who stressed that "We're Picking UP nearly 3,500 Pieces of Litter a Week. . . . On our way to work or on our way home we're picking up a candy wrapper, an empty soda can, a crumpled paper bag, whatever, and throwing it in the nearest trash can. What a difference if thousands more would do the same! So join us. Start a program in your company. Together we can shine up the Big Apple." *New York Times*, Sept. 22, 1989, p. A17.

among the world's currencies are constant reminders of the extent to which one's economic well-being depends on decisions made in distant places.

Another noteworthy aspect of the complexity in which individuals find themselves today derives from the wide-ranging movement of people around the world as a consequence of expanded business and professional travel, tourism, programs for study abroad, and the flight of refugees. People today are participants in more extensive and numerous social networks than was the case for earlier generations. Many of them have become "boundary spanners," individuals who move freely around the world, interpreting its configurations and uncertainties for those who do not travel widely. Recent figures on travel beyond contiguous countries are staggering: some 400 million people are estimated to have engaged in such travel in 1988 (thus leading tourism revenues in that year to rank third among all export industries and to represent 25 percent of international trade in services[24]), and the number has been growing at an annual rate of 5 to 7 percent.[25]

In sum, the stimuli to expanded competence on the part of citizenries are numerous and powerful. If one asks what the advent of extensive foreign travel, instantaneous communications, and information

retrieval—of satellites bringing pictures of ongoing events into homes everywhere and of computers storing, processing, and disseminating information heretofore unknown and ungatherable—may be doing to individuals as actors on the global stage, the answer seems inescapable that such stimuli have an enormous, if not always desirable, potential for shaping how people perceive, comprehend, judge, enter, avoid, or otherwise interact with the world beyond their workplace and home. Most notable perhaps, the new electronic technologies have so greatly collapsed the time in which organizations and movements can be mobilized that the competence of citizens feeds on itself, in the sense that they can virtually "see" their skills and orientations being cumulated into larger aggregates that have consequence for the course of events. No longer does the translation of commitment into action await word brought by stagecoach that like-minded citizens are banding together or that leaders discern an opportunity for effective participation. Today, events and the words about them are, in effect, simultaneous occurrences. Unlike any prior time in history, therefore, citizens are now able to intrude themselves readily into a situation anywhere in the world, because information about its latest twists and turns is immediately at hand.

SPONTANEOUS AUTHORITY

To trace numerous stimuli to expanded analytic and emotional skills is not, of course, to demonstrate that in fact such an expansion

has occurred. To discern that people are more able than ever to "see" how micro actions can aggregate to macro outcomes and thus to intrude themselves into the course of events is not to show that they seize the opportunities to do so. Indeed, many observers are inclined to be skeptical that a relocation of authority sustained by a skill revolution has occurred. Yes, they would argue, regimes have been toppled in eastern

[24]Louis J. D'Amore, "Tourism—The World's Peace Industry," in L. J. D'Amore and J. Jafari, eds., *Tourism—A Vital Force for Peace* (Montreal: First Global Conference, 1988), p. 7.

[25]Louis J. D'Amore, "Tourism: A Vital Force for Peace," *The Futurist* (May-June 1988), 27.

Europe, and yes, the streets of Rangoon, Beijing, Seoul, Manila, and elsewhere have been jammed with people giving voice to their demands. But such events have occurred before in history, only to be followed by publics retreating back to quiescence as the challenged authority structures get modified or reconstituted. Face it, the skeptics would conclude, the record of history well justifies positing citizens everywhere as remote from and uninformed about world affairs, as simplistic, as incapable of learning, as rabble, as masses that are normally passive but that can be easily manipulated and/or mobilized by state officials or opposition leaders.

But such reasoning is belied by the spontaneity of virtually all the uprisings of the 1980s, beginning in Kwangju, Korea, at the very start of the decade and running through the upheaval in Bucharest, Romania, at the very end of the decade.[26] This more recent history traces a record of citizens everywhere judging the performance of officials as unacceptable and then relocating authority in the direction of themselves.[27] In one case, Estonia, the history

even includes a rally attended by one-third of the entire country.[28]

As the upheavals gathered momentum, to be sure, new organizations came into being—or old ones took advantage of the upheaval—and undertook mobilizing and leadership tasks that extended and enriched the aggregative dynamics.[29] Change could not have come to Poland without Solidarity as a macro whole that gave voice and direction to the micro parts. Conversely, where the initial micro stirrings were not followed by organizational coherence—as was the case in Burma and China—the change processes have yet to culminate. Nevertheless, the fact that so many of the uprisings were marked by spontaneity amounts to cogent evidence that the analytic and emotional skills of people have expanded, that they seize upon as well as "see" the opportunities to contribute to collective

[26]Nor did the spread of spontaneous uprisings come to an end with the closing of the decade. It continued apace in 1990 in Kuwait, Mongolia, Nepal, Albania, the Ivory Coast, and several other countries of sub-Saharan Africa. See, for example, Youssef M. Ibrahim, "An Affluent Kuwait Joins an Arab Trend toward Democracy," *New York Times,* Mar. 11, 1990, p. 1; Nicholas D. Kristof, "Calls for Reform Widen in Mongolia," *New York Times,* Mar. 11, 1990, p. 10; and Kenneth B. Noble, "Clashes and Unrest Grow Fiercer in Ivory Coast," *New York Times,* Mar. 3, 1990, p. 3.

[27]Although the analysis focuses on how more competent citizens are intruding themselves into politics through collective actions that converge upon the public squares of the world, it must be stressed that such highly visible activities are not the only form of mass behavior to which their enhanced skills can contribute. The same capabilities can also underlie a readiness to avoid collective action in situations where restraint seems more appropriate to the accomplishment of desired outcomes. Consider, for example, this account of the mass restraint exercised in Lithuania during a key period of its drive

for independence from the Soviet Union. "In Vilnius, the public's self-control has been phenomenal . . . . Television suggested that the people were constantly on the streets, changing national songs and weeping with joy under their tricolor. Lithuanians, however, are economical with political gestures. When the moment is right, they will turn out by the hundreds of thousands, but for the most part they have behaved as if an attempt to break out of the Soviet Union was a monthly routine." Neal Ascherson, "The Trial of Lithuania," *The New York Review,* Apr. 26, 1990, p. 3.

[28]David K. Shipler, "Symbols of Sovereignty," *The New Yorker,* Sept. 18, 1989, p. 52.

[29]Interestingly, the question of whether the spontaneous actions of citizens preceded or followed organizational effort can be of political as well as analytic concern. It became a central issue in Romania during the early days following that country's revolution, with spokespersons for small parties that emerged in opposition to the new, postrevolution ruling group—the Council for National Salvation—complaining that the council had been in existence for some six months and was thus manipulating its perpetuation in power. The council, on the other hand, was quick to assert that this was not the case, that the revolution had been unplanned and instantaneous. As the prime minister at the time, Petre Roman, put it, "we had no contact. It was spontaneous. The [popular] Front was created on the spot." Cf. *New York Times,* Jan. 3, 1990, p. 1.

The Relocation of Authority in a Shrinking World **49**

outcomes. Hundreds of thousands—and in some instances millions—of people do not suddenly converge in the same city square for the same purposes by chance. Either they are organized to do so or, in the absence of any coordinated mobilization, they do so because they have the skills which enable them to sense the urgency and virtue of converging. Since most of the uprisings of the 1980s originated well before organizations could be formed or activated, the spontaneity of the participants says a great deal about their analytic and emotional skills. Consider Tiananmen Square. The coalescence of prodemocracy forces there in May 1989 "happened with startling, and seemingly inexplicable swiftness,"[30] so much so that "without weapons, without communications other than *xiaodao xiaoxi*, or grapevine, without transportation other than bicycles, and trucks borrowed from farmers and work units, without even any agreement on what they are demonstrating for—except the right to demonstrate—the students and those protecting them are blocking a modern, well-equipped army."[31]

Similar accounts of leaderless uprisings elsewhere in the world during this period can readily be cited,[32] but Tiananmen Square serves as a quintessential case because it was the site of more than 1 million people converging on the same place at the same time without being mobilized by experienced leaders and an effective organizational hierarchy. Such a large scale captures well the likelihood that citizens have undergone an expansion in their analytic skills and a restructuring of their orientations toward authority and legitimacy that are irre-

versibly transforming the conduct of politics. How else to explain the extraordinary convergence of humanity? How else to account for the systematic controlling of intersections, the blocking of streets, the clearing of passageways, the procuring of trucks, and the distribution of limited resources? These developments did not occur randomly. They did not happen because people suddenly discovered they were possessed of courage. They did not happen because seasoned leaders used a well defined organizational network to get out their memberships. They did not happen because a national figure used a television platform to exhort a normally quiescent public into taking action. No, they happened because, in an environment enriched by pictures of "people power" that succeeded elsewhere in the world and of *xiaodao xiaoxi* supplementing televised scenes depicting the unfolding situation "downtown," numerous individuals had the wherewithal to assess their priorities, to set aside their long-standing compliance habits, to link the authority of top leaders to their performances as well as to the traditional prerogatives of their offices, to construct a scenario which allowed for indecision on the part of the authorities, to discern that this hesitancy enhanced the probability of micro actions leading to macro outcomes, to sense that enough of their fellow citizens were engaging in similar reasoning to insure further the conversion of micro sentiments into corresponding macro responses, and then to participate in the proceedings by assessing where they might best fit in the collective endeavor.

It might be argued that, while Tiananmen Square exemplifies the capacity of citizens to converge spontaneously as a collective force, it is hardly a reflection of relocated authority because the Chinese regime reasserted its dominance by a resort to force. Such an argument, however, falters in the face of two considerations. One is

[30]Nicholas D. Kristof, "China Erupts . . . The Reasons Why," *New York Times Magazine,* June 4, 1989, p. 28.
[31]Fred C. Shapiro, "Letter from Beijing," *The New Yorker,* June 5, 1989, p. 73.
[32]See, for example, Robert Pear, "Burmese Revolt Seen as Spontaneous," *New York Times,* Sept. 10, 1988, p. 3, and Flora Lewis, "The Czechs Start Over," *New York Times,* Dec. 17, 1989.

that, despite the Chinese regime's crack-down, provincial and local Communist Party leaders throughout the country subsequently ignored directives from Beijing and pursued their own policies.[33] Second, spontaneous mass demonstrations resulted in a relocation of authority in many other countries. This account of the 1980 events that culminated in the acquisition of legitimacy by Solidarity in Poland serves as a good summarizing example of how micro spontaneity has preceded and fostered the macro coherence through which authority has undergone relocation.

> For a moment, [the leaders were caught by surprise. They] were not so much leaders as followers of a process of social combustion that raced forward spontaneously and uncontrollably: first came the mass movement; then came the demands and the negotiations. . . . Suddenly, there was a power in society where none was supposed to be. . . . Right in the heart of a totalitarian system, under which people are supposed to be at their most helpless, Solidarity gave the world one of the most startling demonstrations of the power of the people that it has ever seen.[34]

If expanded analytic and emotional skills explain the spontaneous origins of new authority structures, it remains to account for how the skills get tapped and enable great numbers of people to coalesce into a potent political force. Such convergences are easy to comprehend when organizational channels or the mass media provide information on their scheduling and progress. But what about the many situations in recent years when the organizational networks and media were controlled by those who wished to prevent mass rallies and such rallies occurred nonetheless? How do hundreds of thousands of analytically skillful people manage to concert their energies without the aid of an established organizational network or the assistance of extensive television or radio coverage?

Although tempting, it is not sufficient to respond to these questions by stressing that such convergences somehow "just happen." Obviously, systematic factors must be operative, factors that are less manifest than organizational cadres and the mass media but that nonetheless tap into the expanded skills of citizens in such a way as to guide, if not to coordinate, their actions. Three such factors, all of them independent of whether the mass media are controlled so as to provide people with distorted information (as is presently the case in Burma, China, the West Bank, and South Africa), can be identified. One of them involves the emotional skills of individuals, which operate as either supplements to or substitutes for analytic skills in the following way.

> . . . the structures of the social world, especially as centered on the networks upholding property and authority, involve continuous monitoring by individuals of each other's group loyalties. Since the social world can involve quite a few lines of authority and sets of coalitions, the task of monitoring them can be extremely complex. How is this possible, given people's inherently limited cognitive capacities? The solution must be that negotiations are carried out implicitly, on a different level than the use of consciously manipulated verbal symbols. I propose that the mechanism is *emotional* rather than cognitive. Individuals monitor others' attitudes toward social coalitions, and hence toward the degree of support for routines, by feeling the amount of confidence and enthusiasm there is toward certain leaders and activities, or the amount of fear of being at-

[33]Nicholas D. Kristof, "In China, Too, Centrifugal Forces Are Growing Stronger," *New York Times*, Aug. 26, 1990.

[34]"Notes and Comments," *The New Yorker*, Oct. 20, 1986, p. 35.

tacked by a strong coalition, or the amount of contempt for a weak one. These emotional energies are transmitted by contagion among members of a group, in flows which operate very much like the set of negotiations which produces prices within a market.[35]

The other two factors that account for the remarkable timing whereby thousands of citizens converge under the adverse conditions of controlled and distorted mass media involve the energy of activists. Neither the analytic skills nor the emotional antennae of citizens are sufficient to initiate actions that get aggregated into collective pressures and outcomes. For this to happen, word of the aggregative processes must spread, and it is here where the activists in the population become agents of communication, either through uncoordinated but cumulative behavior or through ad hoc, informal organizational networks. The former type of activism is illustrated by *xiaodao xiaoxi,* the grapevine sustained through word-of-mouth that was no less central to the upheavals in eastern Europe as it was to the developments in Tiananmen Square. In East Germany, for example: "Doctors called mechanics. Mechanics called construction workers. Construction workers called nurses. Nurses called doctors. Neighbors called neighbors. This is how the demonstrations came to life in Frankfurt, Plauen, Dresden, and, above all, Leipzig."[36]

Somewhere between word-of-mouth and the mass media lie the hastily formed, temporary, and rudimentary organizations of activists whose commitments lead them to create alternative channels of communications for distributing schedules, tasks, and

ideas. An account of the events leading to the fall of the Communist regime in Czechoslovakia provides a good insight into these preorganizational dynamics. Faced with a "conservative official press" that prevented them from getting "their word out to the working people," the students who began the translation of micro impulses into macro outcomes "overnight . . . created their own 'mass media' on the streets."

> They covered the walls of the city's subway system, bus windows, escalator railings, shop windows, and street lamps with information on demonstrations and strikes and with posters saying: "Workers Join Us For Freedom!" "Students Against Violence Ask For Your Help!" and "Strike for Democracy." . . . These days virtually every public place in Prague is crowded with people reading notices, looking at pictures of the Friday night clashes and signing declarations. . . .[37]

It is useful to stress that such accounts of spontaneous actions by citizens are offered as evidence, not of a sudden lurch toward goodness on the part of humankind, but of relocated authority, of decentralizing tendencies having combined with newly refined skills of citizenship to produce a greater readiness to become involved in collective action. Let us be clear on this point. The thesis advanced here is not founded on an idealism which posits that people become more humane, intelligent, tolerant, and cooperative as a consequence of a more information-enriched environment. Nor does it spring from a naiveté which presumes that more exposure to education and closer proximity through television to events unfolding in far-off places are encouraging individuals to be less selfish and more civic-minded. The point is, rather,

[35]Randall Collins, "On the Micro Foundations of Macrosociology," *American Journal of Sociology,* 86 (March 1981), 944 (italics in original).

[36]David Binder, "At Confessional East Berlin Congress, 'An Absolute Break' with Stalinism," *New York Times,* Dec. 18, 1989, p. A8.

[37]Esther B. Fein, "Student's Ask Workers' Aid in Czech Rally," *New York Times,* Nov. 24, 1989, p. A16.

that while the attitudes and priorities of publics may not differ from those held in the past, their skills in employing, articulating, directing, and implementing their attitudes and priorities have undergone a major transformation.

FUTURE SCENARIOS

Although the evidence of expanded analytic skills fostering a relocation of authority on a global scale is not conclusive, it is surely sufficient to pose the question of what such transformations might imply for politics in the future. If it is the case, that is, that the world's adult population has acquired greater capacities for relating to the course of events, does this mean that the decentralizing tendencies are likely to persist to the point where public order and governmental policymaking become increasingly fragile and chaotic? It might. Conceivably, more upheavals lie ahead as people become increasingly accustomed to having their narrow self-interests served and their collective demands met. Or, possibly, a period of relative tranquility lies ahead as people become increasingly aware that their collective actions have led to nonextremist accommodations that are worth preserving.

Much of one's assessment of these contrasting scenarios depends on one's understanding of the values that are likely to accompany greater analytic and emotional skills. Such skills are, in themselves, neutral. They can foster a greater readiness to advance the well-being and dignity of groups, or they can heighten inclinations to serve greedy aims and promote the well-being of special interests. There is no necessary correlation between being more skillful and more altruistic or selfish.

But if their emotional skills enable individuals to sense more accurately whether altruism or self-interest predominates among their neighbors and in the society at large, then one of these tendencies is likely to be in the ascendancy for long stretches of time as people reinforce each other's leanings. This means that the tendencies toward decentralization that predominate at present and that have led subsystems throughout the world to press for greater autonomy within their more encompassing systems—as the Croatians have done in Yugoslavia, the Tamils in Sri Lanka, and factions within the PLO—are likely to persist and even intensify into ever greater fragmentation in authority relations at all levels of governance. It seems doubtful, for example, to expect that the decentralizing tendencies presently at work in the Soviet world will come to a halt if and when the nationalisms of eastern Europe and the U.S.S.R. achieve satisfaction. The analytic skills which, for example, lead Lithuanians to see value in their own autonomy may well lead to further fragmentation that pits various groups of Lithuanians against each other. As one observer of post-Ceausescu Romania commented about the absence of democratic experience in that country: "If anything, I worry about excessive pluralism. The peoples of Eastern Europe, after forty years, are going to enjoy, even glory in, diversity for awhile."[38]

Yet there may be one respect in which the greater analytic and emotional skills are not neutral. It is at least plausible that, the more skillful people are, in identifying their self-interests and relating them to the public arena, the greater will be their flexibility to appreciate when the tendencies toward decentralization and centralization become

[38]Stephen Szabo, quoted in Robert C. Toth, "Barren Trees Sported Pears, and Ceausescu Fell," *Los Angeles Times*, Dec. 27, 1989, p. A12.

excessive and threatening. If this is so, if publics and their leaders are increasingly capable of reversing course, of perceiving that they collectively possess the competence to revise the priorities they attach to their system and subsystem loyalties, then the future is very likely to be episodic and turbulent, with periods of narrow self-interests being ascendant at one point in time, only to yield to the predominance of broad community interests at the next moment when the defects of the existing priorities become increasingly evident.

Traces of these cyclical fluctuations, in which global tendencies toward centralization foster countertendencies toward decentralization and vice versa, are readily discernible. The readiness of Polish workers to follow the lead of Lech Walesa and other leaders of Solidarity to reverse course at their moment of triumph and replace their subsystemic union goals with those of Poland as a whole system is a classic instance of analytic skills fostering, or at least permitting, reordered priorities. And similar traces of an emergent recognition that subsystem successes pose system-level problems are also evident in Czechoslovakia, South Africa, Germany, and western Europe. The predominant trend still appears to be a decentralizing one, and it is reinforced by a worldwide momentum in the direction of free market economies and their encouragement of individual enterprise, but signs of a new cycle can be cited by those who see a global need to focus on collective problems.

Furthermore, if such cycles lie ahead, their management poses no great challenge from a bifurcationist perspective. The bifurcated worlds of world politics are well suited to cope with the repercussions that follow as one stage of the cycle runs its course and gives way to the next. The structures of the state-centric world are amply capable of absorbing and redirecting the tendencies toward centralization and the need for collective approaches to the new interdependence issues, even as the structures of the multicentric world can readily accommodate and channel the tendencies toward decentralization and the need for subgroup solutions to old independence issues.

In sum, the appearance may be one of chaos and turbulence, but the reality is likely to be one of an underlying set of structures sustained by increasingly skillful citizens eventually adapting to the dynamism of change. Doubtless, excesses will occur in the form of stifling centralization and paralyzing decentralization, but analytically competent people can not undo their new skills and revert to old habits. They may yield to repressive measures for a while, and they may selfishly champion their own self-interests for a while, but they can not ignore what they have experienced or quell their newly acquired propensities toward learning.

CHAPTER ONE

THE OLD ORDER
AND THE NEW ORDER

From Stettin in the Baltic to Trieste in the Adriatic, an iron curtain has descended across the Continent [but] if we adhere faithfully to the Charter of the United Nations . . . the highroads of the future will be clear, not only for us but for all, not only for our time, but for a century to come.

Winston S. Churchill, "The Sinews of Peace,"
Fulton, Missouri, 5 March 1946.[1]

Today, as an old order passes, the new world is more free but less stable. Communism's collapse has called forth old animosities and new dangers. Clearly America must continue to lead the world we did so much to make.

William Jefferson Clinton
Inaugural address, January 20, 1993[2]

It was President Bush who began to speak of a "new international order" at what was thought to be a successful conclusion of the gulf war. President Clinton speaks of "continuity" in foreign policy. The first question one even mildly interested in world affairs is apt to ask is, "What's a new order?" Simplistic as this

[1]Reproduced in full in David Cannadine, ed., *Blood, Toil, Tears, and Sweat,* (Boston: Houghton Mifflin Co., 1989), pp. 296–308.
[2]Reproduced in full, *Washington Post* January 21, 1993, p. A27.

may sound, it is in fact a profound question, for one answer is that a new order merely describes a new day, today, which is different from yesterday, therefore new and in the present instance very different. The bipolar world of the Cold War which has dominated politics on the planet for forty-five years is gone. So without anybody doing anything, we have a new world order—a simple statement of an obvious fact, nothing necessarily to celebrate nor to deplore. It just *is*.

The other answer, and the one that intrigues even the well-informed, was that something new was about to be tried, an attempt to build a new and presumably better world which would significantly change the lives of men and women the world over. Could it be that the new order of the one is the old order of the other? In other words, that this new order, enunciated after the Cold War was over, was actually an implementation of what Churchill had hoped for but was frustrated by deadlock between the superpowers in the United Nations until the Security Council endorsed "Desert Storm."

From another perspective, the two leaders share the same, older order, the Western nation-state system which emerged from conferees who drew up the peace ending the Thirty Years' War in 1648. It was in his *Leviathan,* published just three years after the Treaty of Westphalia, that Thomas Hobbes wrote his famous lines about the "state of nature"

> The condition of man . . . is a condition of war or everyone against everyone. . . . No arts, no letters, no society; and which is worst of all, continual fear and danger of violent death; and the life of man, solitary, poor, nasty, brutish, and short.[3]

The system which was supposed to replace such an orderless world is generally agreed to have marked the emergence of the Western nation-state system which has dominated world affairs ever since. Westphalia was where the "old order" which for over three hundred years dominated international relations began, with the end of a long and debilitating war which affected all of Europe.

For a model of some of the basic criteria by which to judge "order," it is still useful to go even further into the roots of inter-state relations, it was in 413 B.C. that Thucydides wrote in his *The History of the Peloponnesian War* that

> . . . in our public acts we keep strictly within the control of law. We acknowledge the restraint of reverence; we are obedient to whomsoever is set in authority, and to the laws, more especially those which offer protection to the oppressed and whose transgression brings admitted shame.[4]

But Thucydides was a realist. His celebrated "Melian debate" (reproduced later in the chapter on diplomacy) analyzing how a weak power responded to a vital threat from a bigger one, remains one of the classics of international literature. What was new about the Westphalian order was not the ideal criteria of Thucydides, but the marriage of ethnicity and legitimacy, that is, the nation-

[3]*Leviathan*, Part I, Chapter 13, cited in John A. Vasquez, *Classics of International Relations*, (Englewood Cliffs, N.J.: Prentice-Hall, Inc., 1986), p. 204.
[4]*The History of the Peloponnesian War*, cited in John Bartlett, *Familiar Quotations*, Fifteenth edition, ed. by Emily Morison Beck (Boston: Little, Brown and Co., 1980), p. 80, 15.

state. Its operating principle was a system with a balance of power among states of varying sizes and resources each of which regarded itself as sovereign, that is, able to make its own decisions without subservience (legally at least) to any other state. There was no overarching body to which any could appeal. Intrigue, even deceit was a commonplace. It was still a game of each against all. From time to time alliances were broken or rearranged, and occasionally an attempt was made to establish some kind of order through such diplomatic gatherings as the Congress of Vienna, which marked the end of the Napoleonic wars. Basically, these arrangements were designed, not to create a system of equal rights and justice, but to certify and continue the new configuration of power produced by the war. It was that old order which Woodrow Wilson wanted to replace and, until his own people rejected his concept for a formalized world order in the form of the League of Nations, thought he had done so, only to die a broken man with a broken dream.

So, which "old order" is being replaced? Or are none of them being replaced, but just played out with a new set of players, or old players with new roles? There are of course other ways of interpreting the term "the old order," and it may be that its only function is inferential, that is, one can hardly speak of a "new order" without some reference to what it is supposed to be replacing. Were we about to witness a radical U.S. initiative toward world government? Most unlikely. Or did Bush's vision of a NWO signal a kind of *Pax Americana*— what would make the U.S. what IR specialists would call a "hegemon"—an all-powerful last superpower holding sway over any who might challenge it, with the Gulf War the model for the immediate application of massive, high-tech power against anyone who dares challenge it. If so, the President of the United States could hardly be expected to telegraph such an unpopular and, to others, threatening posture. But as one well-known security analyst, Earl Ravenal of Georgetown, has pointed out,

> . . . a Bush-type world order requires a Bush-sized defense budget. If we don't want that defense budget, we have to consider adjusting American foreign policy to a rather different kind of world: a much more fragmented international system, with a dozen and a half regional powers playing various autonomous roles, and most of them not particularly subject to American dictates or desires.[5]

Perhaps what Bush had in mind was, simply, nothing at all. No plans were made, no contingencies met, to bring about such a change.

But what of the new President? During the period of the transition between his election in November to his assumption of office on January 20, 1993, Gov. Clinton's public utterances concentrated upon internal issues, particularly the economy. Though his domestic emphasis continued to be upon "change", he consistently stressed "continuity" in international relations, essentially supporting President Bush's efforts in Bosnia, Somalia and notably the Gulf. The refer-

---

[5]Earl Ravenal, "Defense—You Get What You Pay For," *The Wall Street Journal,* August 11, 1992, p. 7. Professor Ravenal teaches at the School of Foreign Service, from which Bill Clinton graduated on his way to becoming a Rhodes Scholar at Oxford.

ences below from his uncharacteristically brief Presidential inaugural address come as close as he had to that point to any "new international order." Doubts that anything really new is being created had already led Joseph Nye to ask, "What New World Order?" at a time when leading experts in other places were expressing themselves with everything from skepticism to hope, such as the holder of the Montague Burton Chair at Oxford, Adam Roberts, in *International Affairs,* or Denice Artaud, senior research fellow of the National Center for Scientific Research in Paris in her panel piece in *Diplomatic History,* or the Foreign Minister of Brazil, Francisco Rezek, in a Yugoslav IR journal, or two British authorities musing about "Africa in a New World Order."[6] What they were all asking was, to borrow Walter Mondale's famous question to Gary Hart in the 1980 presidential primary, "Where's the beef?"

The second chapter in this section will concentrate upon foreign reactions and excerpt statements from four world leaders—the Foreign Minister of Russia, the Secretary-General of the United Nations, the Premier of China, and a leading Mexican writer—on the American President's "new world order." One thing he obviously had in mind in reinventing the term as early as October 1990 in his UN address was to celebrate replacing the old order of the Cold War. That tense period can be said to have begun shortly after WWII had ended, with Stalin's chilling warning that the scientifically correct and predictable clash of historical forces would inevitably result (just as it would have had the Soviet Union and the West not just been victorious allies against Hitler) in a series of terrible wars between capitalism and communism. According to the Marxist formula, the Communists were bound to be victorious—ultimately and inevitably.

This speech inspired—if that is the proper term—Churchill's celebrated "Iron Curtain" address at little Westminster College in Fulton, Missouri, a fragment of which opens this chapter. In turn came the Marshall Plan, a new kind of "club" to which the Russians were invited, but declined, forcing even their new satellite, Czechoslovakia, to cancel its participation in the Paris conference which set in motion the recovery of Europe. Along with the United Nations, the Marshall Plan was to have been the foundation of the "new world order" growing out of the defeat of fascism. Mr. Bush's "Framework for Peace", one had every right to assume, was to be the foundation of the "new world order" growing out of the twin defeats of Communism and Saddam Hussein, an order already tested in the effective implementation, as Churchill had hoped and predicted at Fulton, of the United Nations Charter.

Indeed, within a year another world leader, now rejected in his own country, as had been Churchill, was to go even further in calling for steps toward world government. But this time the world paid little need to this other far-

---

[6]Adam Roberts, "A New Age in International Relations," *International Affairs,* 67, 5, 1991, pp. 509–525; Denise Artaud, "The End of the Cold War: a Skeptical View," *Diplomatic History,* 16, 2, Spring 1992, pp. 256–61; Francisco Resek, "A New International Order," *Review of International Affairs* (Belgrade), March 20, 1991, pp. 1–2; and Lionel Cliffe and David Seddon, in *Review of African Political Economy,* 50, 1991, pp. 3–11. This is just a sampling of a shower of questioning articles which appeared in leading journals in the weeks after the "Framework of Peace" address.

reaching address at Fulton, Missouri (excerpted in Chapter Five), this one by a mere Russian citizen, Mikhail Gorbachev, his vision unmatched by his power. A few weeks before, at the peak of his powers, George Bush had proudly proclaimed that "this is a victory for every country in the coalition, and for the United Nations," and, the President confidently told Congress, "A victory for unprecedented international cooperation and diplomacy. . . ."[7]

These words seemed to open up the exciting possibility of a welcome and timely "sea change" in world politics. The Soviet Union was gone and Communism defeated (at least outside China and Cuba) and a quick "100-hours War" against the invader of Kuwait had been dramatically won. Perhaps most importantly the United Nations system actually worked, having been an absolutely essential ingredient in what appeared at the time to have been a decisive defeat in the Gulf of the latest disturber of the peace. All this prompted the President of the United States, at the moment of his greatest triumph (and standing in the public opinion polls), to proclaim a "new international order." But what did that mean? Theoretically, there are three possible ways of looking at or interpreting the possible meaning of an open "new international order": a new system, new configurations of old systems, and genuine implementation of the existing system.

The *first* possibility might portend an entirely new method of structuring the relationships of states. Balance of power politics would be a thing of the past, which is what Woodrow Wilson had in mind in a similar dramatic period seventy years earlier after the first World War had been won and his unprecedented plan for a League of Nations seemed about to be realized. And not only President Wilson. As Frederick L. Schuman made clear in the first of the great IR textbooks of the inter-war period, the League of Nations should not be regarded as "the creation of a single man or of a single generation of men, but was the culmination of a long process of practical and theoretical preparations for the building of an enduring structure of cooperation between states."[8] Nothing like that seems to be taking place today. Where are the peace societies, the advisers, the demonstrators, the implementors for Bush's new order? This time it really did appear to be one man's idea (though one suspects his National Security advisor, a three-star General with an MA in IR from Columbia, had a hand in it.) While whatever was to take the place of the pre-1991 order *could* take the form of a peace-loving era of friendly cooperation, it could also mean a world empire, chaos, yet another alliance, or anything else, just so it was different from what

---

[7]*Vital Speeches of the Day, LVII*, 12, April 1, 1991, pp. 354–6. March 6, 1991 to a joint session of Congress.

[8]Frederick L. Schuman, *International Politics*, (New York and London, McGraw-Hill 1933), p. 251. For an in-depth treatment of this entire period see William C. Olson and A.J.R. Groom *International Relations Then and Now: Origins and Trends in Interpretation*, (London: HarpersCollins, 1991) Chapter 4, "The period of the first consensus: the quest for peace," a hopeful era of peace-planning through collective security which lasted from the waning days of the first World War to the disillusionment brought on by depression, fascism, and the collapse of the "League system." The "consensus" referred to is one of two which characterized the formative years of the discipline of International Relations, the second being what the authors term "the pursuit of power," or the realist phase following World War II. The current phase encompasses neo-realism, structuralism, and the global society approach, possibly among others; "consensus" is hard to identify.

had prevailed before. In his article in this chapter, Ted Galen Carpenter applies the counter-expression "new world disorder" to what we are about to experience, but just what form the President had in mind was unclear. Presumably, it would have to have some theoretical base, however rudimentary and however ideological, rather than systematic theory. Would America be a new hegemon? The President didn't say.

A *second* possibility is that the idea might merely contemplate essentially the existing "world order" but with an altered configuration of power among the participating States. Some states are stronger, some are weaker and may even disappear in their old form. In any balance of power, if that term is meant to describe any existing hierarchy of states, the relative power of the participants is shifting all the time. In other words, a "new" order occurs whenever the fundamental power ratio changes, which is what happened in 1989 through 1991, when the Cold War and the bipolar system which had dominated world politics since 1946 came to an end. In this "new" world order, all that would be new is that a unipolar system would replace the old bipolar one, but not with "the one remaining superpower," as it likes to call itself, being able to or even wanting to dominate. It may be worth describing here the sensation caused in Washington by the publication of Paul Kennedy's book, *The Rise and Fall of The Great Powers*, especially the section entitled, "The United States: The Problem of Number One in Relative Decline." What he actually did was to apply to the United States a theory based upon a long period of history—that all power is relative—concluding that

> even when it declines to occupy its "natural" share of the world's wealth and power, a long time into the future, the United States will still be a very significant Power in a multipolar world, simply because of its size . . . [but] that the economic and productive power balances are no longer as favorably tilted in the United States' direction as in 1945.[9]

Today, the United States once more has more power than anyone else, but this raises two other questions: 1) what is the theoretical basis for the maintenance of such a high level of preparedness, other than what both Clinton and Bush describe as "a very dangerous world out there," and 2) is anyone applying the other great theoretical lesson of Kennedy's treatise, which is that the underlying support for Great Power status is a strong economy, and that those powers of the past whose leaders have ignored this elementary truth have placed their states in decline.

Classical balance of theory dictates that the "others" would tend to coalesce to deny the strongest power any capability to dominate, if not by the use or threat of quantifiable force in being, then by diplomacy, economic policy, and political

---

[9]*The Rise and Fall of the Great Powers: Economic Change and Military Conflict from 1500 to 2000*, (New York: Random House, Vintage Books ed., 1989), pp. 534–5. In frequent TV and other appearances in the ensuing weeks, Professor Kennedy tried over and over again to explain just what he meant by "relative," but so offended were many self-styled patriots that they never seemed to grasp this elementary point.

resistance. That, theoretically, would be the second possible meaning of a "new international order," which is, in essence, the old order reconstituted. Breathing life into the Charter would turn out to have been little more than a rhetorical and therapeutic exercise. Indeed, the President's words had no sooner hit the wire services than some were noting that just because it was new it might not be better, that change need not mean improvement, and even that in the relative certainty of the old Cold War days "maybe we were better off." Yet, whatever one's reservations of either a practical or a theoretical nature, the new order of Mr. Bush would find the U.S. "number one."

Finally, a *third* theoretical interpretation is one of making the order established with the creation of the United Nations and its Security Council actually work as its founders had intended in the first place. The debilitating use of the veto which had characterized many peacekeeping endeavors for forty-five years, making it impossible for the organization to do its job, would give way to unanimity among the veto-possessing powers in the face of any serious threat to the peace. The Undersecretary General for Political Affairs of the United Nations argued for years before and since his retirement that that workable system is already here, right before our eyes, and all we have to do is use it.[10] In other words, the "new" order is really the "old" order produced by the second World War, but rarely allowed to work; the only other time it did work on a major international security scale was in the Korean War, but that success was only made possible by the fluke of the Russians having walked out of the Security Council just before a crucial vote was to be taken which their veto could have— and most certainly would have—killed. The first test was Kuwait, and the UN system passed with flying colors. The next was Bosnia-Herzegovina. But the region around Sarajevo held no oil, so it was difficult for the Powers to identify what is known as "a vital national interest."

In time, history will probably resemble the second of these theoretical alternatives, that is, more of the same, with more power here, less power there. Instead of a new international order, the world witnessed the implementation of the old order established after the last fundamental reconfiguration of forces. That followed the defeat of Nazi Germany and militaristic Japan in 1945 and the second attempt (the first, the League of Nations, failed in the face of fascist aggression in Africa and Japanese aggression in Asia in the 1930s) to enable the international community effectively to deal with a disturber. In contrast to Korea in 1950, the absence of a Russian veto made possible the Security Council vote of the five veto-possessing states in taking action against Iraq. This raises yet another factor, however, and that is the behavior of the Chinese delegation in that instance and whether its cooperation, obviously somewhat reserved if not reluctant, constituted a true portent of a new international order in which united United Nations action could be counted upon, or whether—next time—the Chinese would assume the old negative veto-wielding role of another Communist state. Being haunted by this prospect may go a long way toward explaining Bush's consistent wooing of Beijing, knowing as he does as former Ambassador

---

[10]Brian Urquhart, whose article on the office of the Secretary-General is excerpted in Chapter Six.

to the UN, that China can block any new order based upon this hypothesis very easily, anytime it wishes to exercise its veto power in the Security Council.

Americans are fond of saying that "there is now only one superpower," but how "super" is the United States? Much has been written in recent years, even before the Cold War had clearly come to an end, about the decline of America. Such terms as "decline" and even "super" have no meaning in the world of politics except a comparative meaning; if "super" means no one else possesses as much power as the United States in terms of wealth, resources, forces-in-being, military infrastructure, especially in combination, then clearly no other state can compete. If the United States is to take the lead in turning an existing international security organization into a permanently-effective agency for keeping the peace, then it needs to act with something faster than the usual glacial speed of diplomacy if it is to get it in place before another super-power emerges. Most probably that would be China, but it could also be a unified Europe, though speculation about Germany or Japan is hardly more credible in superpower, that is, intercontinental, terms than India or Brazil. All need to be locked into any newly implemented order insofar as that is conceivable in a world which is still made up of sovereign states, each with the right and the determination to govern its own affairs, domestic or foreign.

So much for theory. What about practice? If something intentional (rather than merely derivative) is in fact becoming a reality, what will it look like? The elements are both plain and simple:

1. any threat to the peace in the form of aggression by one state against another would be met with force at once based upon a Security Council resolution;
2. members of the Security Council, or at least the five permanent members, would be expected to provide either military and naval forces, financial support, or both in making the authorized action effective against the aggressor;
3. after such effective action, the disturber of the peace would be expected— forced if necessary—to comply with all implementing resolutions of the Security Council.

This worked partially in the Gulf War, and could have completely had not the President, unilaterally and apparently without the advice of his security advisors, decided to make it a "100-hour war", because, it was said, "he liked the symmetry of it."[11] Security Council resolutions had been almost unanimous, with all the veto-possessing states in line as a result of frantic maneuvering by the U.S. delegation at the UN headquarters in New York. But the multinational forces deployed in the desert were largely American, as was the command structure, and the President acted unilaterally in suddenly ending the fighting, the argument being that the war's objective, which was to get Iraq out of Kuwait, had

---

[11]See William C. Olson, "The U.S. Congress: an Independent Force in World Politics?", *International Affairs*, 67, 3, July 1991, esp. "the great Gulf debate," pp. 557–560, excerpted on pp. 146–160.

been achieved. Never, stated Brent Scowcroft repeatedly in public fora, had the objective been to destroy Saddam's regime itself. As a result Saddam was not defeated in the field but only badly crippled, so that within a year and a half, responsible analysts were arguing that he had actually "won." Creation of a "new international order," even of the derivative old order variety, had to start all over again, which is probably why a new President has been wary of even using that expression.

DISCUSSION QUESTIONS

1. In what sense do you feel there is a "new world order" today? Would President Clinton agree?
2. If you were to draw up your own blueprint for a new world order, what would it look like? What possibilities do you see for Mikhail Gorbachev's world government proposal coming about in your lifetime? What are the principal obstacles which might prevent it? How might they be overcome?
3. Why does the Frenchwoman, Denise Artaud, say she is dubious about the end of the Cold War? How does this differ from Barnard's doubts about "victory?"
4. In his article, Professor Nye asserts that the "new world order has begun. It is messy, evolving and not susceptible to simple formulation or manipulation." Isn't he really describing the old world order? Or what Carpenter calls "world disorder?"
5. How useful is it for students of international relations today, thinking about tomorrow, to wade through historical treatments like that of Professor Rosecrance? Wasn't Henry Ford right when he said that "history is bunk?"
6. Make the argument that the Cold War wasn't all that bad and that the world is less secure now than it was when there was a sort of balance between two superpowers and their allies. Now, provide the convincing argument against that view—if you can.
7. Who was Thomas Hobbes? Thucydides? Woodrow Wilson? Why are they important when discussing new orders?
8. In your view, which of Clinton's "five steps" represent a radically new order and which are a continuation of the old?

5 A FIVE-STEP AGENDA FOR A NEW WORLD

WILLIAM JEFFERSON CLINTON

Forty-second President of The United States, Clinton was trained in international relations at the School of Foreign Service at Georgetown University before going to Oxford as a Rhodes Scholar.

Excerpts from President Clinton's address at The American University on February 26, 1993.

Twice before in this century, history has asked the United States and other great powers to provide leadership for a world ravaged by war. After World War I, that call went unheeded. Britain was too weakened to lead the world to reconstruction; the United States was too unwilling. The great powers together turned inward, as violent, totalitarian power emerged. We raised trade barriers. We sought to humiliate, rather than rehabilitate, the vanquished. And the result was instability, inflation, then depression, and ultimately, a second world war. After the second war, we refused to let history repeat itself. Led by a great American president, Harry Truman—a man of very common roots but uncommon vision—we drew together with other western powers to reshape a new era.

Yet, across America, I hear people raising central questions about our place and our prospects in this new world we have done so much to make. In a new global economy still recovering from the after-effects of the cold war, a prosperous America is not only good for Americans. As the prime minister of Great Britain reminded me of just a couple of days ago, it is absolutely essential for the prosperity of the rest of the world. Washington can no longer remain caught in the death grip of gridlock, governed by an outmoded ideology that says change is to be resisted, the status quo is to be preserved. Like King Canute ordering the tide to recede, we cannot do that.

And so, my fellow Americans, I submit to you that we stand at the third great moment of decision in the 20th century. Will we repeat the mistakes of the 1920s and the 1930s by turning inward? Or will we repeat the successes of the 1940s and the 1950s by reaching outward and improving ourselves as well? I say that if we set a new direction at home, we *can* set a new direction for the world as well. . . .

I believe there are five steps we can and must take to set a new direction at home and to help create a new direction for the world.

First, we simply have to get our own economic house in order. I have outlined a new national economic strategy that will give America the new direction we require

Excerpted from *American Scene*, March 12, 1993, pp. III–VI. © 1993 The American University, Washington, D.C.

to meet our challenges. It seeks to do what no generation of Americans has ever been called upon to do before: to increase investment in our productive future and to reduce our deficit at the same time. We must do both. A plan that only plays down the deficit without investing in those things that make us more productive will not make us stronger. A plan that only invests more money without bringing down the deficit will weaken the fabric of our overall economy such that even educated and productive people cannot succeed in it. It is more difficult to do both. The challenges are more bracing. You have to cut more out of spending and raise more other taxes, but it is essential that we do both: invest so that we can compete, bring down the debt so that we can compete. . . .

Second, it is time for us to make trade a priority element of American security. For too long, debates over trade have been dominated by voices from the extremes. One says government should build walls to protect firms from competition. Another says government should do nothing in the face of foreign competition no matter what the dimension and shape of that competition is, no matter what the consequences are in terms of job losses, trade dislocations, or crushed incomes.

Neither view takes on the hard work of creating a more open trading system that enables us and our trading partners to prosper. Neither steps up to the task of empowering our workers to compete or of ensuring that there is some compact of shared responsibility regarding trade's impact on our people, or of guaranteeing a continuous flow of investment into emerging areas of new technology which will create the high-wage jobs of the 21st century.

Our administration is now developing a comprehensive trade policy that will step up to those challenges, and I want to describe the principles upon which it will rest.

It will not be a policy of blame but one of responsibility. It will say to our trading partners that we value their business, but none of us should expect something for nothing. We will continue to welcome foreign products and services into our markets but insist that our products and services be able to enter theirs on equal terms.

We will welcome foreign investment in our businesses, knowing that with it come new ideas as well as capital, new technologies, new management techniques, and new opportunities for us to learn from one another and grow. But as we welcome that investment, we insist that our investors should be equally welcomed in other countries.

We welcome the subsidiaries of foreign companies on our soil. We appreciate the jobs they create and the products and services they bring, but we do insist simply that they pay the same taxes on the same income that our companies do for doing the same business. . . .

And there must be a continuing quest by business and labor and, yes, by government, for higher and higher and higher levels of productivity. Too many of the chains that have hobbled us in world trade have been made in America.

Our trade policy will also bypass the distracting debates over whether efforts should be multilateral, regional, bilateral, unilateral. The fact is that each of these efforts has its place. Certainly we need to seek to open other nations' markets and to establish clear and enforceable rules on which to expand trade. That is why I am committed to a prompt and successful completion of the Uruguay Round of the GATT talks. . . .

Third, it is time for us to do our best to exercise leadership among the major financial powers to improve our coordination on behalf of global economic growth. At a time when capital is mobile and highly fungible, we simply cannot afford to work at cross-purposes with the other major industrial democracies. Our major partners must work harder and more closely with us to reduce interest rates, stimulate investment, reduce structural barriers to trade, and to restore robust global growth. And we must look at new institutions we use to chart our way in the global economy and ask whether they are serving our interests in this new world or whether we need to modify them or create others. . . .

Fourthly, we need to promote the steady expansion of growth in the developing world—not only because it's in our interest, but because it will help them as well. These nations are a rapidly expanding market for our products. Some 3 million American jobs flow from exports to the developing world. Indeed, because of unilateral actions taken by Mexico over the last few years, the volume of our trade has increased dramatically and our trade deficit has disappeared.

Our ability to protect the global environment and our ability to combat the flow of illegal narcotics also rest in large measure on the relationships we develop commercially with the developing world. . . .

These efforts will reap us dividends of trade, friendship and peace.

The final step we must take, my fellow Americans, is toward the success of democracy in Russia and in the world's other new democracies. The perils facing Russia and other former Soviet republics are especially acute and especially important to our future. For the reductions in our defense spending that are an important part of our economic program over the long run here at home are only tenable as long as Russia and the other nuclear republics pose a diminishing threat to our security and to the security of our allies and the democracies throughout the world.

Most worrisome is Russia's precarious economic condition. If the economic reforms begun by President Yeltsin are abandoned, if hyperinflation cannot be stemmed, the world will suffer. . . .

If we are willing to spend trillions of dollars to ensure communism's defeat in the cold war, surely we should be willing to invest a tiny fraction of that to support democracy's success where communism failed. To be sure, the former Soviet republics, and especially Russia, must be willing to assume most of the hard work and high cost of the reconstruction process, but then again remember that the Marshall Plan itself financed only a small fraction of postwar investments in Europe. It was a magnet, a beginning, a confidence-building measure, a way of starting a process that turned out to produce an economic miracle. . . .

These five steps constitute an agenda for American action and a global economy. As such, they constitute an agenda for our own prosperity as well. Some may wish we could pursue our own domestic effort strictly through domestic policies, as we have understood them in the past.

But in this global economy there is no such thing as a purely domestic policy. . . .

Look now at our immigrant nation, and think of the world toward which we are tending. Look at how diverse and multiethnic and multilingual we are, in a world in which the ability to communicate with all kinds of people from all over the world and to understand them will be critical. Look at our civic habits of tolerance and respect. They are not perfect in our own eyes. . . . It's ingrained in the soul of Americans. It's no accident that our nation has steadily expanded the frontiers of democracy, of religious tolerance, of racial justice, of equality for all people, of environmental protection and technology and, indeed, the cosmos itself. For it is our nature to reach out, and reaching out has served not only ourselves but the world as well. Now, together, it is time for us to reach out again toward tomorrow's economy, toward a better future, toward a better direction, toward securing for you, the students at American University, the American dream. Thank you very much.

6 *THE END OF THE COLD WAR: A SKEPTICAL VIEW*

DENISE ARTAUD

Senior Research Fellow at The National Center of Scientific Research in France, Dr. Artaud writes frequently on Franco-American relations while teaching at the Institut d'Etudes Politiques.

Less than two years after the fall of the Berlin Wall, which led almost automatically to the reunification of Germany, one thing is certain: The division of Europe, for forty-five years the symbol of the Cold War, has come to an end. Beyond this not much can be said. Because of the swift succession of events, the most enticing assumptions about the future very quickly lose their credibility. This has been true of recent predictions by Paul Kennedy and Francis Fukuyama. Kennedy argues that "imperial overstretch" has led to a relative decline of American power and hence to a shift in the balance of global economic power. To his way of thinking, the United States should seek to redress the balance by reducing its excessive overseas commitments, spending less on defense, and devoting more of its resources to social and educational programs and to industrial investments.[1] In an essay published in June 1990, Fukuyama presented an even bolder assessment of the past and prescription for the future. He asserted that the demise of fascism and Marxism-Leninism had brought about "the end of history," a growing "Common Marketization" of international relations, and a diminution of the likelihood of large-scale conflict between states.[2] Subsequent developments have not been kind to these prescriptions.

In the wake of the Gulf War and the demise of the Soviet Union, the situation appears more complicated than either Kennedy or Fukuyama anticipated. The United States has obviously emerged as the only superpower, a development that challenges the credibility of the declinist theory. Moreover, a number of countries—Pakistan, India, Israel, Argentina, and Brazil, to name a few—are now capable of equipping themselves with nuclear armaments or of purchasing sophisticated long-range missiles. These nations could pose a real threat to the security of their neighbors, not to mention the interests of the major powers. Until arms sales are controlled more effectively,

[1] Paul Kennedy, *The Rise and Fall of the Great Powers: Economic Change and Military Conflict from 1500 to 2000* (New York, 1987).

[2] Francis Fukuyama, "The End of History?" *The National Interest* 16 (Summer 1989): 18.

war is not likely to be eradicated. What is more, it may be premature to envision a new era of cooperation between American policymakers and the new leadership of the former Soviet Union, a development supposedly presaged by Soviet-American collaboration in the Gulf crisis. Even during that crisis, it should be remembered, the media often hinted that the Soviets were not complying fully with the UN embargo against Iraq. Under these circumstances, perhaps it would be better to await the opening of archives in Moscow before jumping to the conclusion that the two sides had perfectly identical goals, as was suggested at the time by Eduard Shevardnadze.[3]

The Gulf crisis, the danger of nuclear proliferation, and other developments thus raise doubts about a New World Order of everlasting peace, and also about the real unthinkability of a return of East-West tensions. Despite the recent celebrations over the end of the Cold War, will we one day lament "the end of the end of the Cold War"? This proposition may appear so paradoxical as to preclude discussion. But it remains to be seen if Russia's challenge to the West is truly over, or for that matter the challenges raised by Marxism or some other brand of authoritarianism. Beyond these issues, moreover, we must ask about the future of European unification and of American leadership.

To the question of whether the challenge of Marxism is a thing of the past, the obvious answer is "yes," if one considers only the economic aspects of Marxism. *Perestroika* was triggered by the bankrupt state of the Soviet economy, and market economics is now the name of the game not only in countries newly freed from communism but throughout the world. In France, for example, the Socialist government seeks

to promote private investments, although it does not command a majority in Parliament and therefore depends on the tacit agreement of the Communist party in order to carry out its policies. The privatization of state-owned firms is also making considerable headway in Latin America, where the seduction of Marxism had combined with a mercantilist tradition to produce large public sectors (so large that in some cases the percentage of GNP generated through the public sector was higher than in most of the Eastern European countries). The pope himself, in *Centesimus Annus*, his latest encyclical, no longer puts capitalism and Marxism on an equal basis, and has openly pronounced himself in favor of market economics and free enterprise.[4]

On the other hand, even in late 1991 there was still much reluctance in what used to be the Soviet Union to adopt all of the reforms that are essential to a liberal order. The difficulties stemmed in part from the fact that Marxism has always been more than an economic system. It has been a form of totalitarianism, which, unlike democracy, is beyond the reach of law. It has also been a revolutionary praxis that gave its supporters a useful tool in wielding power and acquiring privileges long-embodied in the *nomenklatura*. Marxism created a society based not on merit and competence but on growing bureaucratization and ideological loss of faith, a society where initiative and responsibility did not exist, where values and virtues were corrupted. In this way, Marxism contributed to family breakups, declining health conditions, galloping alcoholism, and the proliferation of gangs. In effect, to quote a French scholar, Marxism-Leninism brought about "a general decapitalization" of Soviet society. More to the point, it set in motion a swift and irreversible process that blocked the creation of values as well as

---

[3]Eduard Shevardnadze, *L'avenir s'écrit Liberté* (Paris, 1991).

[4]*Centesimus Annus* (Vatican City, 1991).

products, of knowledge and know-how, of information of all sorts, and of modernity.[5]

In other words, the difficulties with which the former Soviet Union is now struggling stem from the bankrupt state not only of its economy but also of its society and political system. Assuredly, there are liberal elements that can help in solving many problems, but they are loosely structured and have little grassroots support, especially outside of the large cities. They must also deal with former Communist party members who have not renounced their ideology and who continue to exercise a degree of influence in certain quarters of the armed forces and the military-industrial complex. To be sure, Boris Yeltsin's success may be one step forward on the road to democracy. We should not overlook the authoritarianism of the Russian president, however, or the fact that he cannot rely on a well-developed and democratic political or party structure to thwart the advocates of authoritarianism who are surely waiting in the wings. Nor should we forget that Russia and the other republics still possess substantial conventional and nuclear weapons and that these still remain a potential threat to peace in general and to the global interests of the West in particular.

Regarding the potential threat to Western interests around the world, it might be instructive to remind ourselves of the Soviet Union's foreign policy in the last year of its existence. Although many commentators celebrated the "new thinking" of policymakers in Moscow, the reality was not quite so rosy. The Soviets, it is true, did reduce their aid to Vietnam and Laos and apparently terminated their assistance to several African countries, including Ethiopia, Angola, and Mozambique. They also hammered out a rapprochement with Israel and stopped meddling in the Angolan civil war. At the same time, however, the Soviets managed to maintain their economic aid to Cuba, sent spare parts to the Sandinista-controlled Nicaraguan army, and continued to prop up Afghanistan's Communist government. As these commitments demonstrate, even Moscow's own precarious economic situation did not prevent it from supporting client states whose policies deviated in large measure from the "new thinking" propounded by Shevardnadze. Clearly there existed a sharp contrast between the swift retreat that Soviet leaders were forced to accept in Eastern Europe and Moscow's efforts to retain some links to its clients in the Third World. This contrast, as Charles Fairbanks noted at the time, conjured up the image of a doughnut-shaped empire with a hole in the middle.[6] Fairbanks may have exaggerated the extent to which the Soviet Union still wielded power overseas. But he was right to warn that Moscow continued to pose a threat at the end of the Cold War, a warning that might also apply one day to Russia and some of the other republics of the former Soviet Union. However weakened, they have interests of their own and retain substantial real and potential military power.

Even in Europe it is legitimate to ask if the strategic retreat that moved the Soviet frontier from the Oder River to Brest Litovsk marks the start of a postimperial era in Eastern Europe. German reunification is a fait accompli, and it is unlikely that the former Soviet Union will regain its sway over Poland, Hungary, or Czechoslovakia. The situation in the Balkans is less stable or predictable, as evinced by what happened in Yugoslavia. In 1914 the Sarajevo incident was the spark that ignited World War I. Is it

---

[5] Illios Yannakakis, foreword to Thierry Mallerer and Murielle Delaporte, *L'Armée rouge face à la Perestroika* (Brussels, 1991), xviii.

[6] Charles H. Fairbanks, Jr., "Gorbachev's Global Doughnut," *The National Interest* 19 (Spring 1990): 21–33.

possible that at some time in the future the struggle between different national or ethnic groups might lead to regional conflict? Is it possible that such a struggle might encourage the Russians to extend their influence into the Balkans? Or perhaps the Germans will become diplomatically more aggressive, as they have been in the Yugoslav case. And if so, will Germany's initiatives reveal serious differences with France or within the European Community—differences that the Russians could play upon?

This leads to the issue of European unity, for only a united Europe can countervail potential problems. On an economic level, hopes for European unity have been high in the last few years, because of the transition to a single European market in 1993. Recent talks on monetary union made progress, although there is still evidence of British reservations that could spell trouble in the future. Talks between the EC and Japan also provide evidence of differences between the British, who see the post-1992 European Community as a genuinely open market, and the French, who prefer a more regulated economy. On a political level, the community has even greater problems. During the Gulf crisis, despite its GNP, the size of its population, and its military forces, the EC proved unable to reach a common decision on overseas intervention, and François Mitterrand's diplomatic initiatives failed to conceal the fact that the community had to seek shelter under American foreign policy. Things could not have been otherwise, because the EC has no truly democratic and efficient institutions. In most cases, the Council of Ministers must make its decisions by unanimous vote. The Brussels bureaucracy is largely an irresponsible technocracy. The Strasbourg Parliament, which has no real links to its constituents, is more concerned with ideology than with solving practical problems and more prone to increase the burden of community expenses without much concern for the taxpayers.

Another reason why the EC is stalled is that many see it as only an interim solution before real reorganization of the Continent following the collapse of the Berlin Wall and the Warsaw Pact. In effect, the geographical space held by the EC seems small when compared to the cultural legacy of Ancient Rome, Christendom, and the Enlightenment. Because Europe is too imbued with its spiritual heritage to be only a technocratic entity, some are inclined to object to a community born of the Treaty of Rome and to call instead for "a Europe based on hope," in the words of Georges Bidault, a Europe that might encompass not only a reunited Germany but also Poland and all of the countries of the former Austro-Hungarian Empire.[7] Indeed, all of those countries share a common heritage of rationality, humanism, skepticism, and tolerance.

On the other hand, while the cultural and educational life of Central Europe still sports many intellectuals, it has been dreadfully weakened by forty years of communism. It is no wonder under these circumstances that the churches represent the strongest element in Central Europe and that religious conviction played such an important part in the political revolution of 1989. The political revolution was preceded by a moral and cultural revolution, one of whose ignition points was the "most fantastic pilgrimage in the history of contemporary Europe"—the visit of the newly elected pope, John Paul II, to his homeland in March 1979. The church also helped to shape the "Velvet Revolution" in Czechoslovakia and in the late, unlamented, German Democratic Republic, where the Lutheran *Evangelischekirche* provided an organizing

---

[7]Quoted in Alain-Gérard Selma, "L'Europe des rendez-vous manqués," *Politique Internationale* 51 (Spring 1991): 331–32.

ground for civic opposition to the Communist regime throughout the 1980s. This opposition first formed around the issue of conscientious objection to conscription and took its inspiration from the life and death of the theologian Dietrich Bonhoeffer, a martyr to Nazi tyranny. The Catholic Church also retained its force in those countries. It emerged, in the words of James Kurth, as "the most significant multi-national institution operating in Central Europe,"[8] and was a powerful force in Germany as well, although after reunification the number of German Catholics dropped from 50 to 40 percent of the population.

Religious forces are likely to become a leading factor in the political life of the new Europe and may even serve as a basis for democracy, which, as suggested above, decays unless nourished by the politically sensible and morally virtuous behavior of its citizens. To quote Plato: "The best is for everyone to be ruled by a wise and godlike power, if possible seated in his own heart; if not, let it act upon him from without." In other words, if the state is to be denied control of economic and social life (contrary to what existed in the whole of Soviet Europe), each citizen must accept a check on his or her passions so as not to encroach on the freedom of others. Along that path, religion is no doubt one of the best guides, as the Pole Adam Michinik, a former Communist, declared as early as 1979.[9]

The buoyant religious forces currently at work and the related evolution of Catholic social doctrine lead some to think that Europe will be able to chart a middle course between American capitalism and Communist statism. Such a trend would point to a major victory for the Christian Democratic parties, especially for the CDU in Germany. Should the Social Democrats emerge victorious at the polls, however, the results will not be significantly different. Their platform remains moderate: They adhere to the principles of civil society, social-market economy, and electoral democracy. Outside of Central Europe, notably in France, socialism is very different. It still bears the mark of the Marxist tradition and remains bent on state intervention. It is also nonreligious and even deeply anticlerical. Thus, when François Mitterrand in his October 1989 Valladolid speech implored the Central European countries not to sacrifice their Socialist inspiration to their hatred of the Soviet system, the project he meant to promote was worlds apart from those of Helmut Kohl, Lech Walesa, or Vaclav Havel. In other words, no single project comparable to that of the American Founding Fathers has yet taken shape in the Old World. Hence the pessimism of someone like Ralph Dahrendorf, for whom Europe "will always be a patchwork of languages and cultures in everyday life, politics and the economy."[10]

---

[8]James Kurth, "The Shape of the New World Order," *The National Interest* 24 (Summer 1991): 7.

[9]Adam Michinik, *L'Eglise et la gauche: le dialogue polonais* (Paris, 1979).

[10]Ralph Dahrendorf, *Réflexions sur la révolution en Europe, 1989–1990* (Paris, 1991), 137.

7 WHAT NEW WORLD ORDER?

Joseph S. Nye, Jr.

Joseph S. Nye, Jr., author of Bound To Lead: The Changing Nature of American Power, serves as head of the newly-constituted National Intelligence Council in the Clinton Administration.

The 1991 Persian Gulf War was, according to President Bush, about "more than one small country; it is a big idea; a new world order," with "new ways of working with other nations . . . peaceful settlement of disputes, solidarity against aggression, reduced and controlled arsenals and just treatment of all peoples." Not long after the war, however, the flow of White House words about a new world order slowed to a trickle.

Like Woodrow Wilson's fourteen points or Franklin Roosevelt's four freedoms, George Bush's grand rhetoric expressed the larger goals important for public support when a liberal democratic state goes to war. But after the war, when reality intruded, grand schemes turned into a liability. People were led to compare the war's imperfect outcome with an impossible ideal. The proper standard for judgment should have been what the world would look like if Saddam Hussein had been left in possession of Kuwait. The victory lost its lustre because of an unfair comparison that the president inadvertently encouraged, and recession shifted the political agenda to the domestic economy. The White House thus decided to lower the rhetorical volume.

II

The administration faces a deeper problem than mere political tactics. The world has changed more rapidly in the past two years than at any time since 1945. It is difficult to keep one's conceptual footing within such fundamental shifts in politics. Familiar concepts fail to fit a new reality. It is worth recalling that it took Americans several years to adjust to the last great shift in the late 1940s. But the Bush administration, famous for eschewing "the vision thing," added to the confusion because it had never really thought through what it meant by the concept it launched. Neither the administration nor its critics were clear about the fact that the term "world order" is used in two very different ways in discussions of world politics.

Realists, in the tradition of Richard Nixon and Henry Kissinger, see international politics occurring among sovereign states balancing each others' power. World order is the product of a stable distribution of power among the major states. Liberals, in the tradition of Woodrow Wilson and Jimmy Carter, look at relations among peoples as well as states. They see order arising from broad values like democracy and human rights, as well as from international law and institutions such as the United Nations.

The problem for the Bush administration was that it thought and acted like Nixon, but borrowed the rhetoric of Wilson and Carter. Both aspects of order are relevant to the current world situation, but the administration has not sorted out the relation between them.

From the realist perspective there is definitely a new world order, but it did not begin with the Gulf War. Since order has little to do with justice, but a lot to do with the distribution of power among states, realists date the new world order from the collapse of the Soviet empire in eastern Europe in the autumn of 1989. The rapid decline of the Soviet Union caused the end of the old bipolar order that had persisted for nearly half a century.

The old world order provided a stability of sorts. The Cold War exacerbated a number of Third World conflicts, but economic conflicts among the United States, Europe and Japan were dampened by common concerns about the Soviet military threat. Bitter ethnic divisions were kept under a tight lid by the Soviet presence in eastern Europe. A number of Third World conflicts were averted or shortened when the superpowers feared that their clients might drag them too close to the nuclear abyss. The various Arab-Israeli wars, for example, were brief. In fact some experts believe that a stronger Soviet Union would never have allowed its Iraqi client to invade Kuwait. If so Kuwait can be counted as the victim rather than the cause of the new world order.

Some analysts see the collapse of the Cold War as the victory of liberal capitalism and the end of the large ideological cleavages that drove the great international conflicts of this century. There is no single competitor to liberal capitalism as an overarching ideology. Rather than the end of history, the post-Cold War world is witnessing a return of history in the diversity of sources of international conflict. Liberal capitalism has many competitors, albeit fragmented ones. Examples include the indigenous neo-Maoism of Peru's Shining Path guerrilla movement, the many variants of Islamic fundamentalism and the rise of ethnic nationalism.

This does not mean that the new world politics will be "back to the future."[1] There is an enormous difference between the democratically tamed and institutionally harnessed nationalisms of western Europe and the revival in eastern Europe of untamed nationalisms whose ancient animosities were never resolved in the institutional structure of state communism and the Soviet empire.

Moreover national boundaries will be more permeable than in the past. Nationalism and transnationalism will be contending forces in the new world politics. Large transnational corporations distribute economic production according to global strategies. Transnational technological changes in communications and transportation are making the world smaller. Diplomacy occurs in real time; both George Bush and Saddam Hussein watched Cable News Network for the latest reports. Human rights violations and mass suffering in distant parts of the globe are brought home by television. Although

---

[1]See John Mearsheimer, "Back to the Future: Instability in Europe After the Cold War," *International Security*, Summer 1990.

Marshall McLuhan argued that modern communications would produce a "global village," his metaphor was misleading because a global political identity remains feeble. In fact nationalism is becoming stronger in most of the world, not weaker. Instead of one global village there are villages around the globe more aware of each other. That, in turn, increases the opportunities for conflict.

Not all transnational forces are benign any more than all nationalisms are malign. Transnational drug trade, terrorism, the spread of AIDS and global warming are cases in point. With time, technology spreads across borders, and the technologies of weapons of mass destruction are now more than a half century old. The collapse of the Soviet Union removes two of the factors that slowed the spread of nuclear weapons in the old world order: tight Soviet technological controls and influence over its client states. The United States cannot escape from these transnational problems, and few of them are susceptible to unilateral solutions. Like other countries in the new world order, the United States will be caught in the dialogue between the national and the transnational.

III

The United States will need power to influence others in regard to both transnational and traditional concerns. If the old world order has collapsed, what will be the new distribution of power? Over the past few years of dramatic change, different observers have claimed to discern five alternatives.

Return to bipolarity. Before the failure of the August coup and the final collapse of the Soviet Union, some argued that a newly repressive Soviet or Russian regime would create a harsh international climate and a return to the Cold War. But even if the coup had succeeded, it would not have restored bipolarity. The decline of the Soviet Union stemmed in large part from overcentralization. Stalin's system was unable to cope with the Third Industrial Revolution, in which flexible use of information is the key to successful economic growth. The return of the centralizers might have created a nasty international climate, but rather than restoring Soviet strength, recentralization would have continued the long-term decline of the Soviet economy. The same would be true for a centralizing Russian dictatorship.

Multipolarity. This is a popular cliché that drips easily from the pens of editorialists, but if used to imply an historical analogy with the nineteenth century it is highly misleading, for the old order rested on a balance of five roughly equal great powers while today's great powers are far from equally balanced. Russia will continue to suffer from economic weakness, and its reform is a question of decades, not years. China is a developing country and, despite favorable growth, will remain so well into the next century. Europe is the equal of the United States in population, economy and human resources. Even after the December 1991 summit at Maastricht, however, Europe lacks the political unity necessary to act as a single global power.

Japan is well endowed with economic and technological strength, but its portfolio of power resources is limited in the hard military area as well as in the cultural and ideological appeal that provides soft power. Japan would have to make major changes in its attitudes toward military power as well as in its ethnocentricity before it would be a challenger on the scale of the United States.

Three economic blocs. Those who devalue military power argue that Europe and Japan will be superpowers in a world of restrictive economic blocs. An Asian bloc will form around the yen, a western hemisphere bloc around the dollar and a European bloc (including remnants of the former Soviet Union) will cluster around the European Currency Unit (according to optimists) or the deutsche mark (in the view of pessimists). Others foresee a European versus a Pacific bloc.[2]

There are three problems with this vision. First, it runs counter to the thrust of global technological trends. While regional trade will certainly grow, many firms would not want to be limited to one-third of the global market and would resist restrictive regionalism. Second, restrictive regional blocs run against nationalistic concerns of some of the lesser states that need a global system to protect themselves against domination by their large neighbors. Japan's Asian neighbors do not want to be locked up in a yen bloc with Japan. There will continue to be a constituency for a broader international trade system.

Most important, however, this vision is too dismissive of security concerns. With large nuclear neighbors in turmoil, both Europe and Japan want to keep their American insurance policies against uncertainty. The second Russian revolution is still in its early years, and China faces a generational transition. It is difficult to imagine the United States continuing its security guarantees in the context of trade wars. The end of the Cold War was not marked by European and Japanese calls for withdrawal of American troops. European and Japanese security concerns are likely to set limits on how restrictive the economic blocs become.

Unipolar hegemony. According to Charles Krauthammer, the Gulf War marked the beginning of a Pax Americana in which the world will acquiesce in a benign American hegemony.[3] The premise is correct that the collapse of the Soviet Union left the world with only one superpower, but the hegemonic conclusion does not follow. For one thing the world economy is tripolar and has been since the 1970s. Europe, Japan and the United States account for two-thirds of the world's product. In economics, at least, the United States cannot exercise hegemony.

Hegemony is also unlikely because of the diffusion of power through transnational interdependence. To cite a few examples: private actors in global capital markets constrain the way interest rates can be used to manage the American economy; the transnational spread of technology increases the destructive capacities of otherwise poor and weak states; and a number of issues on the international agenda—drug trade, AIDS, migration, global warming—have deep societal roots in more than one country and flow across borders largely outside of governmental control. Since military means are not very effective in coping with such problems, no great power, the United States included, will be able to solve them alone.

Multilevel interdependence. No single hierarchy describes adequately a world politics with multiple structures. The distribution of power in world politics has become like a layer cake. The top military layer is largely unipolar, for there is no other military power comparable to the United States. The economic middle layer is tripolar and has been for two decades. The bottom layer of

[3]Charles Krauthammer, "The Unipolar Moment," in *Rethinking American Security: Beyond Cold War to New World Order*, Graham T. Allison and Gregory F. Treverton, eds., New York: Norton, 1992.

[2]Jacques Attali, *Lignes d'Horizon*, Paris: Foyard, 1990.

transnational interdependence shows a diffusion of power.

None of this complexity would matter if military power were as fungible as money and could determine the outcomes in all areas. In describing Europe before 1914, the British historian A.J.P. Taylor wrote that the test of a great power was the *ability* to prevail in war. But military prowess is a poor predictor of the outcomes in the economic and transnational layers of current world politics. The United States is better placed with a more diversified portfolio of power resources than any other country, but the new world order will not be an era of American hegemony. We must be wary of the prison of old concepts.

The world order after the Cold War is sui generis, and we overly constrain our understanding by trying to force it into the procrustean bed of traditional metaphors with their mechanical polarities. Power is becoming more multidimensional, structures more complex and states themselves more permeable. This added complexity means that world order must rest on more than the traditional military balance of power alone. The problems encountered by the Bush administration at the end of the Gulf War are

illustrative. The traditional approach of balancing Iran and Iraq was clearly not enough, and U.N. resolutions 687 and 688 (which dealt with Iraq's weapons and refugees) went deep into areas of national sovereignty.

The realist view of world order, resting on a balance of military power, is necessary but not sufficient, because it does not take into account the long-term societal changes that have been slowly moving the world away from the Westphalian system. In 1648, after thirty years of tearing each other apart over religion, the European states agreed in the Treaty of Westphalia that the ruler, in effect, would determine the religion of a state regardless of popular preference. Order was based on the sovereignty of states, not the sovereignty of peoples.

The mechanical balance of states was slowly eroded over the ensuing centuries by the growth of nationalism and democratic participation, but the norms of state sovereignty persist. Now the rapid growth in transnational communications, migration and economic interdependence is accelerating the erosion of that classical conception and increasing the gap between norm and reality.

IV

This evolution makes more relevant the liberal conception of a world society of peoples as well as states, and of order resting on values and institutions as well as military power. Liberal views that were once regarded as hopelessly utopian, such as Immanuel Kant's plea for a peaceful league of democracies, seem less far-fetched now that political scientists report virtually no cases of democracies going to war with each other. Current debates over the effects of German reunification, for example, pit against each

other realists who see western Europe going back to the troubled balance of power, and liberals who fault such analysis for neglecting the fact that unlike 1870, 1914, or 1939, the new Germany is democratic and deeply enmeshed with its western neighbors through the institutions of the European Community. Moreover the interactions between democratic politics and international institutions reinforce each other.

Of course the game is still open in post-Cold War Europe, and Europe is very different from other parts of the world such as the Middle East, where traditional views of the balance of military power are still the core of wisdom. But the experience of Europe (and the democratic market economies more generally) suggests that in at least parts of this hybrid world, conceptions of divisible and transferable sovereignty may play an increasing part in a new world order. The complex practices of the European Community are a case in point.

These liberal conceptions of order are not entirely new. The Cold War order had norms and institutions, but they played a limited role. During World War II Roosevelt, Stalin, and Churchill agreed to a United Nations that assumed a multipolar distribution of power. The U.N. Security Council would enforce the doctrine of collective security and nonaggression against smaller states while the five great powers were protected by their vetos.

Even this abbreviated version of Woodrow Wilson's institutional approach to order was hobbled, however, by the rise of bipolarity. The superpowers vetoed each other's initiatives, and the organization was reduced to the more modest role of stationing peacekeepers to observe ceasefires rather than repelling aggressors. The one exception, the U.N. role in the Korean War, proved the rule; it was made possible only by a temporary Soviet boycott of the Security Council in June 1950. When the decline of Soviet power led to Moscow's new policy of cooperation with Washington in applying the U.N. doctrine of collective security against Baghdad, it was less the arrival of a new world order than the reappearance of an aspect of the liberal institutional order that was supposed to have come into effect in 1945.

But just as the Gulf War resurrected one aspect of the liberal approach to world order, it also exposed an important weakness in the liberal conception. The doctrine of collective security enshrined in the U.N. Charter is state-centric, applicable when borders are crossed but not when force is used against peoples within a state.

Liberals try to escape this problem by appealing to the principles of democracy and self-determination. Let peoples within states vote on whether they want to be protected behind borders of their own. But self-determination is not as simple as it sounds. Who decides what self will determine? Take Ireland, for example. If Irish people voted within the existing political boundaries, Ulster would have a Protestant majority, but if the Irish voted within the geographical boundaries of the island, Ulster would be encompassed within a Catholic majority. Whoever has the power to determine the boundaries of the vote has the power to determine the outcome.

A similar problem plagues Yugoslavia. It seemed clear that relatively homogeneous Slovenia should be allowed to vote on self-determination, but a similar vote in Croatia turns Serbs in some districts into a minority who then demand a vote on secession from an independent Croatia. It is not surprising that issues of secession are more often determined by bullets than ballots.

Nor are these rare examples. Less than 10 percent of the 170 states in today's world are ethnically homogeneous. Only half have one ethnic group that accounts for as much as 75 percent of their population. Most of the republics of the former Soviet Union have significant minorities and many have disputed borders. Africa is a continent of a thousand ethnic and linguistic peoples squeezed within and across some forty-odd states. Once such states are called into question, it is difficult to see where the process ends. In such a world, federalism, local autonomy, and international surveillance of minority rights hold some promise, but a policy of unqualified support for national self-determination would turn into a principle of enormous world disorder.

V

How then is it possible to preserve some order in traditional terms of the balance of power among sovereign states, while also moving toward international institutions that promote "justice among peoples?"

International institutions are gradually evolving in just such a post-Westphalian direction. Already in 1945, articles 55 and 56 of the U.N. Charter pledged states to collective responsibility for observance of human rights and fundamental freedoms. Even before the recent Security Council resolutions authorizing postwar interventions in Iraq, U.N. recommendations of sanctions against apartheid in South Africa set a precedent for not being strictly limited by the charter's statements about sovereignty. In Europe the 1975 Helsinki Accords codified human rights. Violations can be referred to the European Conference on Security and Cooperation or the Council of Europe. International law is gradually evolving. In 1965 the American Law Institute defined international law as "rules and principles . . . dealing with the conduct of states and international organizations." More recently the institute's lawyers added the revealing words, "as well as some of their relations with persons." Individual and minority rights are increasingly treated as more than just national concerns.

Of course in many, perhaps most, parts of the world such principles are flouted and violations go unpunished. To mount an armed multilateral intervention to right all such wrongs would be another source of enormous disorder. But we should not think of intervention solely in military terms. Intervention is a matter of degree, with actions ranging from statements and limited economic measures at the low end of the spectrum to full-fledged invasions at the high end. The U.N. Security Council and regional organizations may decide on limited nonmilitary interventions. Multilateral infringements of sovereignty will gradually increase without suddenly disrupting the distribution of power among states.

On a larger scale the Security Council can act under chapter seven of the U.N. Charter if it determines that internal violence or development of weapons of mass destruction are likely to spill over into a more general threat to the peace in a region. Such definitions are somewhat elastic— witness the imposition of sanctions against Rhodesia in the 1960s. The reasons for multilateral intervention will gradually expand over time. Although Iraq was a special case because of its blatant aggression, Security Council resolutions 687 and 688 may create a precedent for other situations where mistreatment of minorities threatens relations with neighbors or where a country is developing weapons of mass destruction in violation of its obligations under the Nonproliferation Treaty.

In other instances groups of states may act on a regional basis to deal with internal fighting, as Nigeria and others did by sending troops to Liberia under the framework of the Economic Community of West African States. In Yugoslavia the European Community employed the threat of economic sanctions as well as observer missions in an effort to limit the violence. In Haiti members of the Organization of American States imposed economic sanctions in response to the overthrow of a democratically elected government. None of the efforts was fully successful, but each involved intervention in what are usually considered domestic affairs.

It may also be possible to enhance U.N. capabilities for independent actions in cases where the permanent members do not have a direct interest. The gains for collective security from the Gulf War would be squandered, for example, if there were no international response to a Rwandan invasion of Uganda or a Libyan incursion into Chad. A U.N. rapid deployment force of 60,000 troops formed from earmarked brigades from a dozen countries could cope with a number of such contingencies as determined by the Security Council.

Such a fighting force, as contrasted to traditional peacekeeping forces, could be formed around a professional core of 5,000 U.N. soldiers. They would need frequent joint exercises to develop common command and operational procedures. The U.S. involvement could be limited to logistical and air support and, of course, the right to help control its activities through the Security Council and the military staff committee. Many details need to be worked out, but an idea that would have been silly or utopian during the Cold War suddenly becomes worth detailed practical examination in the aftermath of the Cold War and Gulf War.

Such imperfect principles and institutions will leave much room for domestic violence and injustice among peoples. Yugoslavia is an immediate example, and it will not be alone. But the moral horrors will be less than if policymakers were to try either to right all wrongs by force or, alternatively, to return to the unmodified Westphalian system. Among the staunchest defenders of the old system are the poorly integrated postcolonial states whose elites fear that new doctrines of multilateral intervention by the United Nations will infringe their sovereignty. The transition to a liberal vision of a new world order is occurring, but not smoothly. Liberals must realize that the evolution beyond Westphalia is a matter of decades and centuries, while realists must recognize that the traditional definitions of power and order in purely military terms miss the changes that are occurring in a world of transnational communications and instant information.

VI

What is the American national interest in promoting a new world order? As election-year rhetoric asks, why not put America first? The country faces a number of serious domestic problems. The net savings rate has dropped from about 7.5 percent of gross national product in the 1970s to about 4.5 percent today. The federal budget deficit eats up about half of net private savings. The educational system is not producing a high enough level of skills for continuing progress in an information-age economy. In terms of high school dropouts the United States is wasting a quarter of its human resources compared to 5 percent for Japan. There is a need for investment in public infrastructure. Clearly we need to do more at home.

But Americans should beware of a false debate between domestic and foreign needs. In a world of transnational interdependence the distinction between domestic and foreign policy becomes blurred. The real choice that Americans face is not between domestic and foreign policy, but between consumption and investment. President Bush has said that the United States has the will but not the wallet. The opposite is closer to the mark. The United States spends about 31 percent of gross national product on government at all levels, while most European countries spend closer to 40 percent. The United States is a rich country that acts poor. America's U.N. dues are a relative pittance, and many countries see our failure to pay them as proof of our hypocrisy about a new world order. Similarly

Europeans cite our low levels of aid and question our seriousness and relevance to stability in postcommunist eastern Europe. The American economy could support a few more percentage points of gross national product to invest at home while helping to maintain international order.

But why spend anything on international order? The simple answer is that in a world of transnational interdependence, international disorder can hurt, influence, or disturb the majority of people living in the United States. A nuclear weapon sold or stolen from a former Soviet republic could be brought into the United States in the hold of a freighter or the cargo bay of a commercial airliner. Chaos in a Middle Eastern country can sustain terrorists who threaten American travelers abroad. A Caribbean country's inability to control drugs or disease could mean larger flows of both across our borders. Release of ozone-depleting chemicals overseas can contribute to a rise in skin cancer in the United States. With more than 10 percent of U.S. gross national product exported, American jobs depend upon international economic conditions. And even though not a direct threat to U.S. security, the human rights violations brought home to Americans by transnational communications are discomforting. If the rest of the world is mired in chaos, and governments are too weak to deal with their parts of a transnational problem, the U.S. government will not be able to solve such problems alone or influence them to reduce the damage done to Americans.

In addition, even after the Cold War the United States has geopolitical interests in international stability. The United States has a continuing interest that no hostile power control the continent of Europe or that European turmoil draw us in under adverse circumstances, as happened twice before in this century. While such events now have a much lower probability and thus can

be met with a much reduced investment, a wise foreign policy still takes out insurance against low probability events. Given the uncertainties in the aftermath of the Soviet collapse, an American security presence, even at greatly reduced troop levels, has a reassuring effect as European integration proceeds. The United States has an interest in a stable and prosperous western Europe that gradually draws the eastern part of the continent toward pluralism and democracy. The primary role will rest with the Europeans, but if the United States were to divorce itself from the process, we might find the future geopolitical situation far less stable.

The United States also has geopolitical and economic interests in the Pacific. The United States is the only country with both economic and military power resources in the region, and its continued presence is desired by Asian powers who do not want Japan to remilitarize. Japan's current political consensus is opposed to such a military role, and Japanese leaders realize it would be destabilizing in the region. With a relatively small but symbolically important military presence the United States can help to provide reassurance in the region, while encouraging Japan to invest its economic power not in military force but in international institutions and to help share the lead in dealing with transnational issues.

In realist terms the United States will remain the world's largest power well into the next century. Economists have long noted that if the largest consumer of a collective good, such as order, does not take the lead in organizing its production, there is little likelihood that the good will be produced by others. That was the situation in the 1920s when the United States refused to join the League of Nations or cooperate in preserving the stability of the international economy. Isolationism in the 1920s came back to haunt and hurt Americans a decade later. There is even less room for neo-isolationism today.

Why not simply leave the task of world order to the United Nations? Because the United Nations is the sum of its member nations and the United States is by far the largest member. Large scale U.N. efforts like the repulse of Iraq will continue to require the participation of the world's largest power.

The United States correctly wants to avoid the role of world policeman. The way to steer a middle path between bearing too much and too little of the international burden is to renew the American commitment to multilateral institutions that fell into abeyance in the 1980s. The use of multilateral institutions, while sometimes constraining, also helps share the burden that the American people do not want to bear alone. Multilateralism also limits the resentments and balances the behavior of other nations that can lead them to resist American wishes and make it harder for Americans to achieve national interests.

While the Bush administration failed in its policies toward Iraq before and at the end of the Gulf War, its actions in organizing the multilateral coalition that expelled Iraq from Kuwait fit the national interest in a new world order. The administration combined both the hard power of military might and the soft power of using institutions to co-opt others to share the burden. Without the U.N. resolutions it might have been impossible for the Saudis to accept troops and for others to send troops. Nor is it likely that the United States could have persuaded others to foot nearly the entire bill for the war. Had there been no response to Iraq's aggression and violation of its obligations under the Nonproliferation Treaty, the post-Cold War order would be far more dangerous.

In short the new world order has begun. It is messy, evolving, and not susceptible to simple formulation or manipulation. Russia and China face uncertain futures. Regional bullies will seek weapons of mass destruction. Protectionist pressure may increase. The United States will have to combine both traditional power and liberal institutional approaches if it is to pursue effectively its national interest. We want to promote liberal democracy and human rights where we can do so without causing chaos. The reason is obvious: liberal democratic governments are less likely to threaten us over time. We will need to maintain our alliances and a balance of power in the short run, while simultaneously working to promote democratic values, human rights, and institutions for the long run. To do less is to have only a fraction of a foreign policy.

8 THE NEW WORLD DISORDER

TED GALEN CARPENTER

Ted Galen Carpenter is director of foreign policy studies at the Cato Institute.

Since the collapse of the Soviet empire, American officials have been scrambling for alternative rationales for U.S. interventionism in a post-Cold War world. They have exhibited an astounding degree of creativity in formulating new missions, but two have emerged as leading candidates: preserving international "stability," and leading a worldwide movement for democracy. These two objectives would seem to be inconsistent if not fundamentally incompatible, but both have two features in common: each would entangle the United States in a morass of regional, local, and even internecine conflicts throughout the world; and more often than not, each would involve the United States in conflicts that have little or no relevance to America's own vital security interests. Washington would become either the social worker or the policeman of the planet—or, in a worst case scenario, it would seek to play both roles. If either interventionist faction has its way, rather than a peace dividend, the end of the Cold War will bring a de facto peace penalty. The United States will find itself with even more politi-cal and military burdens than it endured throughout the Cold War. . . .

For the Bush administration the goal of global stability has become the post-Cold War equivalent of the search for the Holy Grail. It was entirely in character that the president justified the Persian Gulf war on the basis of world-order objectives. Portraying Saddam Hussein as a modern-day Adolf Hitler, Bush asserted that a vigorous, un-compromising response to Iraq's invasion of Kuwait was essential to deter other potential aggressors. Even more central to the president's world view was his insistence that the United States must lead the effort to en-force collective security. America's mission in the post-Cold War era, according to Bush, should be nothing less than to protect the "sovereignty of nations" and the rule of in-ternational law. That is the essence of his concept of a "new world order."

The administration's commitment to stability, as well as its respect for national sovereignty, is somewhat selective, however. Washington displayed little reluctance about interfering in the internal affairs of Panama

Excerpted by permission from *Foreign Policy,* 84 (Fall 1991), pp. 24–39. © 1992 Carnegie Endowment for International Peace.

and overthrowing the government in December 1989 when that step served other U.S. objectives. Administration leaders responded to allegations of inconsistency and hypocrisy by contending that interference was justified because it advanced the cause of democracy. The invasion, U.S. policymakers noted, helped install the Panamanian government that had been duly elected in May 1989 but had been prevented from taking office by dictator Manuel Antonio Noriega's armed thugs.

Through selectivity in criteria, the adherents of stability are able to make a tacit alliance possible with the more ardent advocates of an American campaign for global democracy. But it is an uneasy alliance. A variety of journalists, pundits, and think tank scholars have advanced their own version of a new world order—a post-Cold War mission for America that is reminiscent of the grandiose objectives outlined by President Woodrow Wilson in his Fourteen Points. They are less concerned about stability in the international system than with bringing the blessings of political democracy to all countries. Indeed, most of them are quite willing to risk or sometimes even create instability to make democracy universal. . . .

WORLD HEGEMON

Both forms of interventionism are based explicitly or implicitly on the belief that with the decline of the Soviet Union, the United States is the sole remaining superpower and can order events in the world without fear of effective opposition. The most extensive and sophisticated exposition of the thesis of renewed U.S. dominance comes from columnist Charles Krauthammer. In his view, "The immediate post-Cold War world is not multipolar. It is unipolar. The center of world power is the unchallenged superpower, the United States, attended by its Western allies." His choice of the word "attended" is especially revealing, for Krauthammer and those who subscribe to his view see other Western powers, even such economic dynamos as Germany and Japan, as little more than servants to carry out the directives of the American empire. According to Krauthammer, "America's preeminence is based on the fact that it is the only country with the military, diplomatic, political and economic assets to be a decisive player in any conflict in whatever part of the world it chooses to involve itself." The United States can, if it has the will, freely employ that multidimensional power, "unashamedly laying down the rules of world order and being prepared to enforce them."

Even if Krauthammer is correct that at present the international system is unipolar—and he is far too quick to dismiss the significance of other players—there is little in the history of international relations to suggest that such a phenomenon could be sustained for a significant length of time. Indeed, historically, second-echelon powers typically coalesce to counterbalance the power of a would-be hegemon. That tendency is reinforced when the strongest state acts in an overbearing manner. Attempting to specify and execute its own definition of a new world order would seem to be precisely the kind of conduct that would accelerate the efforts of other countries to balance Washington's power. Predictably, such pretensions have already provoked apprehension and hostility among political and intellectual elites in nations as diverse as France, India, and Japan.

Even Krauthammer concedes that a unipolar system will not last more than a few decades. His estimate will probably prove to be unduly optimistic—especially if the United States adopts the intrusive global agenda that he recommends. The refusal of Germany and Japan to provide more than diplomatic and financial support (and the latter only under intense U.S. pressure) for Washington's Persian Gulf operation indicates that other powers will seek to pursue their own policy agendas. Those agendas will not always coincide with Washington's. That point was also emphasized when the Soviet Union offered its peace initiative on the eve of the ground offensive in the Persian Gulf war. Moscow was clearly concerned about the impending destruction of a long-time client and the prospect of a large U.S. military and political presence in a region so close to the Soviet Union. Both the concern and the policy response were typical of a government attempting to blunt the influence of a more powerful rival.

Such actions suggest that in future crises other members of the international community are not going to remain in awe of U.S. power and automatically defer to Washington's wishes. Nor have such acts of independence been confined to the Gulf episode. Bonn displayed a striking degree of initiative and independence to advance the process of German reunification. Chancellor Helmut Kohl's original proposal for reunification was presented following only minimal consultation with Washington; indeed, it annoyed the United States and several Western allies at the time. The Kohl-Gorbachev agreement in July 1990 that confirmed Soviet acceptance of reunification and established a timetable for the withdrawal of Soviet forces from eastern Germany was almost ostentatiously a bilateral German-Soviet affair. U.S. participation occurred only on the margins.

That episode illustrates a more general phenomenon in U.S.-European relations. National Security Adviser Brent Scowcroft notes that while Washington is calling for an expanded mission for NATO, the West European countries act increasingly through the European Community and tend to pre-

sent the United States with previously developed positions, which he concedes then become very difficult to negotiate. The desire of the European powers to form a common front on security issues—and adopt positions distinct from those of the United States—may still be at an embryonic stage, but the trend is apparent.

If such independent initiatives are already evident during the initial phase of the power vacuum created by the decline of the USSR (when the relative influence of the United States has increased), they are certain to proliferate as China, France, Germany, Japan, and other major powers find opportunities to implement their own agendas. The concept of a unipolar moment is little more than a mirage that will soon vanish.

Any well-conceived foreign policy must take into account probable domestic and international constraints and dangers. Unless they have a direct connection to the nation's vital security interests, it is not enough that goals be objectively worthwhile—even such generally desirable ones as stability and democracy. The crucial issue is whether a country's goals are attainable, and equally important, whether they are attainable at an acceptable level of risk and cost. That is what Walter Lippmann meant when he referred to the "solvency" of a country's foreign policy.

This assessment of risk and cost is especially important for the government of a free society. The lives, freedoms, and financial resources of the American people are not—or at least should not be—available for whatever use suits the whims of national political leaders. The U.S. government has a fiduciary responsibility to protect the security and liberties of the American people. It does not have a writ to implement the political elite's conception of good deeds internationally any more than it has a writ to do so domestically.

As policy goals, both global stability and global democracy fail the basic tests of solvency that must govern an effective foreign policy. It is not that the realization of such goals is undesirable. The world would undoubtedly be a better place if all countries settled their differences by peaceful means rather than by resorting to military force. It would likewise be a better place if the remaining communist regimes, as well as the assortment of military dictators, one-party states, and feudal autocracies that dominate the Third World, gave way to freely elected governments with limited powers. But it is unlikely that either objective is attainable at any reasonable cost, and it is even less likely that a hyperactivist U.S. role can bring about such utopias. It is far more probable that an American attempt to do so will entangle the United States in a multitude of conflicts that will cause a hemorrhage of lives and wealth.

Both interventionist factions typically evade the issue of solvency. Instead, they contend that exertions of the "national will" and periodic demonstrations of American resolve will suffice. Bush's response to a journalist's question after the February 27 cessation of hostilities in the Gulf War is revealing on that score. Asked whether U.S. forces might have to be used in similar efforts in the future, Bush responded:

> No, I think because of what's happened we won't have to use U.S. forces around the world. I think when we say something that is objectively correct, like don't take over a neighbor or you're going to bear some responsibility, people are going to listen. Because I think out of all this will be a new-found, let's put it this way: a reestablished credibility for the United States of America. So I look at it the opposite. I say that what our troops have done over there will not only enhance the peace but reduce the risk that their successors have to go into battle some place.

This response begs the question of what happens if a future expansionist power is not deterred. And there is reason to question the deterrent effect of the Gulf operation. The relative lack of U.S. casualties in the war would appear to make it easier to mobilize public support for the next interventionist enterprise. But several atypical factors converged to sustain domestic and international support for a massive U.S. intervention against Iraq.

First and foremost was the issue of oil. Several economists and oil experts debunked the notion that Iraq's takeover of Kuwait—or even a subsequent domination of Saudi Arabia—would give Baghdad a "stranglehold" on the economies of the West. But however compelling their arguments were, most members of the public and Congress continued to believe the erroneous alarmist scenarios. The oil issue would not be a major factor if an act of aggression occurs outside the Middle East. Nor would concern about the safety of Israel, which motivated some proponents of intervention.

The egregious nature of Saddam Hussein's conduct was also crucial in generating support for Washington's hard-line policy. Not only was the effort to eliminate Kuwait as an independent country, thereby erasing a member of the United Nations, unprecedented in the postwar world; but Hussein repeatedly managed to play the role of the quintessential villain. His seizure of Western hostages, his blustering threats to use chemical weapons, and, after the war began, his parading of allied prisoners of war all reinforced Bush's allegation that Hussein was a new Hitler who had to be stopped.

It cannot be assumed that the leaders of other expansionist powers will be so clumsy and inept. Moreover, the next "aggressor" is more likely to subvert a weaker neighbor rather than launch a blatant cross-border blitzkrieg. (Indeed, that is what Syria has done over the last 16 years in Lebanon—with considerable success.) A more subtle absorption of a neighboring state would confront new world order practitioners with a far more ambiguous situation and make it difficult to rally support for coercive measures on moral grounds. That problem would be compounded if the leaders of an expansionist power are alert to the subtleties of public relations and cultivate Western public opinion instead of resorting to crude threats.

It is also possible that future expansionist powers will learn some pertinent military lessons from Iraq's experience. For example, if an act of aggression does trigger a U.S. intervention, it seems unlikely that an adversary will remain as passive as Iraq did while the United States builds up massive forces on the border. That strategy obviously did not pay off for Baghdad. The logical response would be to hit the initial U.S. forces as hard as possible—before they gain a decisive edge in the theater of operations. That consideration alone makes it questionable whether officials can guarantee that subsequent interventions will be as low-cost to the United States in terms of lives and dollars. And if the next intervention proves significantly more difficult and bloody, the Vietnam syndrome will make a rapid reappearance.

A sustainable strategy cannot be built merely on the expectation that an occasional show of massive force will enable the United States to pursue global order or global democracy without having to undertake frequent interventions. That approach comes perilously close to a policy based on an elaborate bluff. The military victory in the Gulf does not alter the fact that such a vast deployment placed serious strains on American society. One such application of national power may have turned out to be a popular venture, but a second or third or fourth intervention in the name of the new world order could become rather tiresome—especially if the unique factors that sustained the campaign against Iraq are absent. The issue of solvency cannot be evaded, particularly since the post-Cold War world is likely to have more than a few trouble spots.

AFTER EMPIRES

The international system has always been characterized by instability and there is little evidence that the future will be markedly different. Indeed, the ebbing of the Cold War may produce an upsurge of regional political turbulence. Although both superpowers engaged in subversion and other mischief, they also acted at times to restrain some of their clients when the danger existed that a local conflict might lead to a superpower confrontation. That was particularly true in the volatile Middle East. Moscow's ability to impose such limitations is now virtually gone, and even Washington's ability has diminished—although that decline is less obvious. Regional powers now have far greater latitude to pursue their own policy agendas. Struggles between status quo and revisionist powers are nothing new, and forcible territorial adjustments have been the norm in international affairs for centuries. Iraq's invasion of Kuwait was an omen of a post-Cold War world characterized by a proliferation of local or regional conflicts. Iraq is not the first country, nor will it be the last, to expand its territory or seek to exploit regional power vacuums.

Many parts of the world are still dealing with the legacy of the colonial era. Throughout the Middle East, sub-Saharan Africa, South Asia, and other regions, the European imperial powers carved out colonies without reference to ethnic, linguistic, or economic factors. In some cases, ancient enemies were grouped together in a single political jurisdiction; in other cases, ancient cultures were arbitrarily bisected. When the colonies received their independence, those problems were not rectified, or in such cases as the partition of the Indian subcontinent between predominantly Hindu India and predominantly Muslim Pakistan, were resolved imperfectly.

It is unrealistic to assume that boundaries imposed by long-defunct colonial masters must be regarded by the victims as equitable and immutable. Iraq's territorial claims on Kuwait, for example, long predate the rise of Saddam Hussein; they have existed since the early 1920s when the British established boundaries that preserved London's Kuwaiti protectorate and deliberately limited Iraq's access to the Persian Gulf. Baghdad's failure to enforce its claim in the Gulf war does not mean that the claim will vanish. A more likely scenario is that it will be added to the long list of festering Arab grievances.

Instability per se in distant regions does not threaten America's security. There is no longer any challenge from a would-be hegemonic power such as Nazi Germany or the Soviet Union. During the Cold War, it at least could be argued that what appeared to be minor regional conflicts had larger implications since they typically involved surrogates of the rival superpower. In a starkly bipolar world—one without geopolitical peripheries—a plausible case could be made that a victory by a Soviet client state meant a gain in power for Moscow and a corresponding defeat for the U.S.-led "free world." That thesis greatly oversimplified a complex geopolitical environment even at the height of the Cold War; but with the decline of the Soviet threat and the utter improbability that any other serious hegemonic challenger will emerge in the foreseeable future, it has now lost whatever credibility it may once have had.

In a post-Cold War world there are likely to be numerous quarrels that ought to be irrelevant to the United States. Interfering in such imbroglios in an effort to maintain stability poses far greater dangers than the remote possibility that a limited conflict might spiral out of control and ultimately threaten America's well-being. The observation of defense analyst Earl Ravenal that alliances and other security commitments are "transmission belts for war," converting minor local or regional struggles into potentially lethal entanglements for the United States, applies with special force to U.S.-led collective security enterprises in a post-Cold War setting. If Bush is sincere about his concept of a new world order—if it was not merely a façade to conceal a U.S.-led military campaign in an oil-rich region for mundane power motives—then it must apply everywhere. A serious effort to implement Bush's new world order could easily entangle the United States in a host of obscure conflicts.

There are similar dangers in an American-led crusade for global democracy. Proponents look to the U.S. interventions in Grenada and Panama as models of how Washington can oust dictatorial regimes and replace them with democratic governments. But the situations in Grenada and Panama were atypical. Both countries were tiny and geographically situated where the United States could bring its military power to bear with minimum effort and maximum effectiveness, and neither target regime had much legitimacy with its own population. Those conditions would rarely apply in other cases where the United States might decide to intervene. It is pertinent to recall that at the same time Washington achieved its much-touted success in Grenada, it endured a spectacular failure to promote democracy in Lebanon. That unsuccessful effort cost more than 250 American lives. Long before the Lebanon episode, the United States experienced the far more disastrous failure at democratic nation building in South Vietnam, an effort that cost more than 58,000 American lives and $140 billion. What the democracy crusaders do not comprehend is that there are far more potential Lebanons and Vietnams than Grenadas—and that it is not easy to tell them apart in advance.

Some of the more aggressive exporters of democracy, intoxicated by the U.S. military victory in the Gulf War, have urged the United States to help establish a democratic regime in Iraq. Yet viable democracies are virtually unknown in the Middle East and Iraq itself has few democratic traditions—hardly a promising environment for such an experiment. Moreover, those who assume that democratic regimes will inevitably be pro-Western are likely to be disappointed. When Jordan and Algeria loosened the restraints on political activities and held elections with at least a modicum of freedom and competition in 1989 and 1990, a surge of support ensued for the Muslim Brotherhood, the Islamic Salvation Front, and other radical factions. The victorious groups were heavily imbued with Islamic fundamentalism, were strongly anti-Western, and tended to favor Iraq in the Gulf War. Given the enthusiasm of Iraq's Shiite majority for the revolution engineered by their co-religionists in neighboring Iran, a similar process of radicalization could take place in Iraq.

Finally, there is the danger that goals of international order or democratic revolution will be used as façades to conceal less-savory objectives. In the Cold War, U.S. policymakers frequently stressed a commitment to freedom, democracy, and national self-determination when U.S. actions actually undermined those values. It was not a commitment to democracy or a respect for national self-determination that led to U.S.-orchestrated coups against the elected governments of Iran in 1953 and Guatemala in 1954, or the repeated efforts to undermine Chile's elected government in the early 1970s.

It was not a love of freedom that caused Washington to support such Third World dictators as the shah of Iran, Anastasio Somoza Debayle, Park Chung Hee, and Ferdinand Marcos. Washington may have had economic or strategic reasons for its actions, but the officially cited motives were little more than hypocritical propaganda. . . .

The misuse of democratic rhetoric is indicative of a more subtle problem with the global democracy thesis. Proponents are often more concerned about electoral mechanics than about the underlying principles concerning governmental power. But while competitive elections and majority rule are important features of a political system, they are not sufficient for creating and sustaining a free society. Frightened or malicious majorities can oppress unpopular minorities just as dictatorial oligarchies can, as America's own history demonstrates. Pacifists, socialists, and German-Americans who saw their rights systematically violated during World War I found little solace in the fact that the United States was a bona fide democracy. The incarceration of Japanese-Americans in World War II was no less odious because U.S. elections were held as scheduled throughout the war. Black Americans who had their most basic constitutional rights brutally violated for decades while the judiciary looked the other way could take little comfort in the trappings of U.S. democracy. Unless strict limits are also placed on the power of the political state, a proliferation of democratic regimes will not necessarily translate into a great expansion of human freedom. Unfortunately, that is a distinction that seems to elude many proponents of a global democracy crusade.

DIPLOMACY BY EXAMPLE

Instead of embarking on quixotic crusades for global stability or global democracy, the United States should use the end of the Cold War as an opportunity to adopt a less interventionist role. America can encourage greater respect for international law and the peaceful resolution of disputes through its diplomacy and by setting a good example. But while a greater degree of international order is desirable, it is not crucial to America's own security and well-being. Likewise, the promotion of democracy is a worthwhile but not essential objective, and America's role should be confined to the power of example. The impact of the U.S. model can be potent. Many of the demonstrators in the streets of East European cities and in Tiananmen Square looked to the American system for inspiration. But the source of that inspiration was America's reputation as a haven for the values of limited government and inalienable rights, not Washington's $300 billion-a-year military budget and its network of global military bases. Nearly two centuries ago, John Quincy Adams said that America "is the well-wisher to the freedom and independence of all. She is the champion and vindicator only of her own." That distinction should still guide U.S. foreign policy.

It is especially important that the use of American military power be reserved for the defense of *vital* American security interests. And vital interests must not be defined in the casual, promiscuous manner that they were throughout the Cold War. To be a threat to a vital interest, a development should have a direct, immediate, and substantial connection with America's physical survival, political independence, or domestic freedoms.

Two qualifications to that statement are in order. First, the definition of vital security interests is not exclusively geographical. In general the more distant an unpleasant development the less likely it is to be germane to U.S. security concerns, but America should not fall into the trap of drawing arbitrary lines in the sand. Given the nature of modern weaponry, even dis-

tant threats can sometimes be serious ones. Conversely, some events in the immediate international neighborhood may be no more than annoyances. More important than geography is the convergence of two characteristics in another state: extensive military capabilities—especially the acquisition of weapons of mass destruction and long-range delivery systems—and the unmistakable manifestation of hostile intent toward the United States. Both factors are essential. A regime may be intensely anti-American; but if it does not possess a first-class military force, any threat it could pose will be marginal. Similarly, there is no reason for undue alarm even if another country has a considerable amount of military power, provided it has maintained a consistent record of friendly relations.

Second, an emphasis on vital security interests does not mean that the United States must wait until bombs are falling on American cities before responding to a threat. U.S. leaders have an obligation to monitor the international geo-political environment and assess whether an emerging threat may soon pose a lethal danger, and if it does, to take steps to neutralize it. At the same time, a reasonably specific concept of security interests should discourage policymakers from assuming that every adverse development—no matter how minor, geographically remote, or tangential to core American concerns—requires a response from the United States.

Focusing on vital interests creates the foundation for a policy of strategic independence, which would explicitly avoid military or political entanglements for international "milieu" objectives, whether for global stability or global democracy. American resources, and especially American lives, are too precious to risk on such unattainable, utopian goals.

CHAPTER TWO

IMAGES OF REALITY: WHICH NEW WORLD ORDER?

Our defense is not in armaments, nor in science, nor in going underground. Our defense is in law and order.

Albert Einstein, 1964

During the last three decades and over the eight editions of *The Theory and Practice of International Relations,* no historical event has had more importance to the field of IR than the disintegration of the Soviet Union. It ended a forty-year struggle known as the Cold War and peacefully altered the international landscape as much as other historical watersheds such as World Wars I and II and the defeat of Napoleon at Waterloo. Even though many speak hopefully of a new way of doing things, there are also strong indications that old ways are simply reemerging. From a historian's perspective, the one power world of today is merely a reversion to the British-dominated system of the seventeenth and eighteenth centuries. Or is it that simple?

It is said that a New World Order (NWO) now exists. This does not mean that there is a new system of international relations: The NWO still relies on the sovereign state system that has been in place since the Treaty of Westphalia in 1648. The NWO born about 1991 belongs to a class of historical events that suggest significant changes in the structure of power relations in the world. In the future, this NWO (the collapse of the Soviet Union) will probably be included along with other epochs such as the NWO's born in 1815, 1918, and 1945.

What then is a NWO? At its core, a NWO suggests first that the rankings of the major state actors have significantly changed and therefore the distribution of power in the world has also changed. Perhaps more importantly, not only have the rankings changed but some states have vanished from the order and new ones have been added to it. Consider all that has occurred in the last few years: (1) the Soviet Union is gone and replaced by 15 new states (a sort of American Revolution in reverse), (2) client states of the old Soviet Union ranging from Albania to Zambia have almost universally replaced socialist governments with ones more oriented towards western-style systems, (3) Germany has reunified and Korea may soon do the same, and (4) Eritrea will leave Ethiopia, Czechs and Slovaks have agreed on a "Velvet Divorce" to follow-up their "Velvet Revolution," and Yugoslavia is fragmenting into at least five new states.

All agree that something has changed in the world but the meaning and interpretation differs broadly across the globe. In Einstein's terms, the various relative perspectives on recent events can give radically differing viewpoints on what has occurred. In the United States, there is a feeling of pride at winning the Cold War and relief that the Soviet Union was exhausted by struggle. In Europe, there is a sense of opportunity of regaining power lost and reassuming a larger role in world affairs. In China, there is the same sense of opportunity, mixed with isolation as the number of Communist states dwindle. In Russia there is confusion. On the one hand, they lost the Cold War; on the other, they won their struggle for freedom. For most of the developing world, in Asia, Africa, and Latin America, there is none of this optimism about the future.

For the developing world, little has changed in the NWO. First of all, the rankings of these states stayed the same or became worse: They were at the bottom before and are at the bottom now. Moreover, whatever meager help these countries could expect for development is now lessened by the need to spur development in the former Soviet Union. The logic here is quite simple: it is far better to feed hungry peoples who possess nuclear weapons than it is to feed hungry peoples without them.

If the world (the practice) of IR is now somehow different because of this latest watershed era, then the ideas (the theories) that explain it must evolve as well. This of course is not a new idea. Real historical currents always seem to provide direction to the intellectual ships upon it and this is especially true in IR. As a result, however, the type of research preponderant to a particular period in IR is exceptionally time-bound and obliged to change as the international land-scapes change. Hans Morgenthau (a realist) would surely have been less recognized if he was born twenty years earlier when idealism dominated IR theory.

What kind of world is likely under the NWO and therefore what should we study to understand it? Only the vaguest of responses is possible at this early stage of development in the NWO, but Morton Kaplan's work on system theory and IR may provide some guidelines. Kaplan described a number of configurations of power that have existed and might exist in IR and they can be used as a basis for conjecture about the possible structures that might be seen in the NWO. Kaplan identified six configurations of power:[1]

- the balance-of-power (Europe in the eighteenth century),
- the tight bi-polar (the 1950s Cold War),
- the loose bi-polar (the 1980s Cold War),
- the hierarchical (Britain in the 17th Century),
- the unit veto (weapons of annihilation), and
- the universal (world government).

Kaplan's theory was that when significant changes occurred in the structure and behavior in the international system, disequilibrium characterized by violent conflict was the result. Bringing the system back in balance sometimes would require that the system configuration change from one type to another. Because the system behaves as a servo-mechanism (much like the thermostat in one's house), conflict actually is an adjustment device which allows for system change. What behavior does Kaplan regard as key to assessing system stability and therefore the likelihood of conflict? Five characteristics are said to be most important: essential rules, transformation rules, actor classifications, capabilities, and information.

Out of Kaplan's prototypical list, what are some likely configurations that may emerge in the NWO? The answer is none of them. Rather, what may emerge will be a hybrid that is more complex than any of the individual six systems types. This then suggests that what we ought to study in IR is systems theory and learn how to connect the varied strands that will make up the NWO.

The dominant role of the United States in any vision of the NWO suggests a *hierarchical* system, at least to a certain extent.[2] This probably would be a more benign type of hierarchy compared to what Kaplan had in mind, but nonetheless a hierarchy. A hierarchical system may well occur in conjunction with a *universal* system (for example, a world government), where the United States may well be the first among equals in some type of global framework or super-United Nations or super-NATO. The mix of configurations might also differ according to the dimension of analysis. It may well be a hierarchical system along the military dimension of power (with the United States at the top) but a balance-of-power system along the economic dimension (the United States, Japan, and Europe together at the top).

The *universal* system, representing a world government model, will probably also be more prominent in the NWO. Therefore it is appropriate here to

---

[1]Morton Kaplan, *System and Process in International Relations* (New York: Wiley, 1957). Actually, Kaplan called these configurations "systems" in his work but most IR scholars have come to the conclusion either that he meant this in a more literal sense or else that he was plain wrong. In fact, these were not differing systems but differing configurations of a realist interpretation based on state-based actors.

[2]Paul Kennedy's *The Rise and Fall of Great Powers* suggests that the degree of hierarchy will inevitably lead to its own diminishment via "overreach."

include an article by Boutros Boutros-Ghali, the current head of the United Nations. Admittedly it is hard to separate the idealism of the idea of world government from its realistic implications but the continued development of international frameworks is seemingly inevitable in a shrinking world. In another of the articles that follows Carlos Fuentes gives a Latin perspective on universalism which embraces the ideals set forth some 200 years ago by three Americans—James Madison, Alexander Hamilton, and John Jay—in *The Federalist Papers*. Fuentes argues that these writings, specifically with respect to factionalism, give the basis from which to create governments capable of dealing with multinational societies. This type of government necessarily needs to be based on principles of check and balance. It is especially needed in Latin America, he argues, because of the intense racial and ethnic differences that exist there.

The *unit veto* system also seems a historical possibility, if one assumes that the proliferation of nuclear weapons is probably irreversible. Obviously some part of the unit veto system is already in place. The MAD doctrine (Mutual Assured Destruction) was a unit veto system between the United States and the USSR, and France's "Force de Frappe" represents a similar entity. Even Israel can be said to have a unit veto position. Israel's possession of nuclear weapons, along with a superb air force, constrained the policy choices available to the USSR in Mideast politics. Even Israel could have launched a devastating attack on a superpower such as the USSR.

The *balance of power* system could certainly reemerge in a world that seems to be fragmenting into regional blocs. The United States will clearly be a power and no doubt Russia will be one as well. The European Community (the EC), in some form, will also be a power but forever constrained by remnants of nationalism. Japan is an economic power, China may well be one. It is possible that India, a nuclear power, may some day become a great power. Brazil could as well become great and some think Nigeria may.

What seems least likely is a reemergence of the failed *bipolar* system (both tight and loose) that has marked the conduct of IR for the last half century. The black and white world of the Cold War era will no doubt be replaced with shades of distinction in the NWO and greater fluidity in the alliances between the actors.

Perhaps history can give some counsel as to the likely behavior types possible in the NWO. What is the likely stability in this system? One approach might be to look at other NWOs to determine stability in differing systems. Today's situation is similar to the NWO's that followed World War I (Wilson's 14 Point NWO) and World War II (Truman's Doctrine NWO). In retrospect, the attempts at maintaining peace in these other two instances met with far differing outcomes. The post-World War I NWO failed to keep the peace, while the post-World War II NWO did to a large extent succeed.

Quincy Wright in *The Study of War* noted that the number of relative deaths (as a percentage) from international violence on a long-term basis had been on the rise since the 1600s. However, the last fifty years have, by historical standards, been relatively peaceful in comparison to the last few centuries. Many scholars and pundits alike are warning that "we will miss the Cold War" precisely because of its stability. For one, the system changed without substantial bloodshed. Secondly, it avoided large-scale conflict. Finally, it was able to dampen regional conflict because of the development of client states. Regional conflict did occur (Iran-Iraq), as did proxy wars (Vietnam, Afghanistan), but the second half of this century (so far) has avoided the two catastrophic wars that marked the first half.

Why the difference? Was it the case that the League of Nations, born out of the aftermath of World War I, was unable to prevent large-scale conflict (and may have actually abetted it) while the United Nations (between 1945 and 1990) did? Unlikely. With the veto power in the United Nations the power structures were de facto limited. Rather, the real power in the post-1945 system was in the hands of the collective security organizations of the two great powers (NATO and the Warsaw Pact). The explanation may well be that bilateral collective security arrangements may be more stable than multilateral arrangements. Another characteristic of the system might be its dimension of behavior. In another chapter of this book Richard Rosecrance advances the idea that the territorial wars that have thus far characterized the international system are being replaced or challenged by a system based more on economics. Increasingly, he asserts, the dimension of conflict and cooperation in the world will be measured more and more on an economic basis. This basis will also extend the area and degree of impact of economic factors.

Boutros Boutros-Ghali presents the case that the NWO will transform a world based on an East-West schism to one where the differences will fall along North-South lines. In the process of creating the NWO, the iron curtain will disappear and be replaced by an economic curtain. The enclosed article by Li Peng, premier of China, acknowledges the importance of political economy in the NWO. These principles include a new economic order to lessen the gap between the rich and poor and a recognition of human rights and fundamental freedoms that include economic rights.

At the same time, the likelihood of armed global conflict seems lessened and nuclear weapons are actually being destroyed by the great powers rather than being created. Efforts at stemming nuclear proliferation are working to some degree and even the hands on the famous "Doomsday" clock have been set back from 11:59. The United Nations has, in some cases, recently acted like it can be more effective in solving the world's problems. One can be optimistic and believe that there will continue to be a decline in international violence worldwide and more international cooperation in political matters between states.[3]

The promise of a fading toll of needless deaths from international violence reveals the hidden needless deaths resulting from economic conflict in the world—precisely the area where the next battlefield is said to lie. In comparison to deaths from political conflict, far more people have died from various types of economic conflict or deprivation over the last fifty years. If these people were amassed into an army, it would easily be the largest on the planet. For example,

---

[3]The seminal book in this area remains Quincy Wright's *A Study of War*. He provides some interesting data on death from war over the centuries, with the total rising progressively from the seventeenth century on.

millions of people have died in the Horn of Africa alone (Somalia, Ethiopia, and the Sudan) due to a combination of political and economic factors. Malaria alone has killed far more people since 1945 than has war.

The threat that a growing world population (see Chapter 11) will increase this level of economic conflict and in the process lead to tremendous social upheaval is quite real. Therefore, the real threat to any NWO and its stability seems less likely to lie in political conflict between states than it is in the economic breakdown of states as the cornerstones of a system that has lasted since the Treaty of Westphalia in 1648. We are already witnessing a fragmentation in state authority.

The reason for the fragmentation is simply because states have been so successful in creating political organization and therefore grown so large. However, the ability to manage a large system is becoming more difficult. At the same time, the control of the system itself is fading under the impact of the world trading system. "A trading system may also exact a certain social or governmental cost."[4] Economic market penetration allowed by a world trading system inevitably leads to an increased penetration of political and social markets. Further, economic interdependence causes a lessening in the ability to control one's economic policies. To some extent, the development of greater international "trade" disciplines inevitably acts to undermine "territorial" disciplines, to use Richard Rosecrance's concepts. Andrei Kozyrev, Russia's foreign minister, writes an enclosed article about a NWO where economics take precedence over territorial control. But he believes that the loss of economic sovereignty will to some extent enhance the process of democratization or at least act as a required check to abnormal behavior.

Lester Brown is to the point on the issue: "National economic sovereignty is sacrificed in many ways. Membership in the General Agreement on Tariffs and Trade brings with it certain obligations regarding national behavior in international trade relationships." Brown attributes this change in behavior to the growing interdependence of the world. "What we have been witnessing has been a willingness of nations, by the exercise of their sovereign rights, to recognize that the national interest can no longer be pursued in isolation but is dependent on cooperative action with other nations. This necessarily involves some limitation on national freedom of action in deference to the common good."[5]

Growing economic trade may well lead to the reformulation of states into regional economic units with political representation. It is, for example, said that residents of Seattle and Vancouver have more in common with one another than either does with the federal governments in Washington, D.C. and Ottawa. By the same token, the States of Sarawak and Sabah show outright animosity towards the government in Kuala Lumpur. California threatens to break up into three separate units and Canada into at least two. States will endure, but the ease

[4]Rosecrance, p. 39. Furthermore, he adds that "The operations of the multilateral corporations and movements of funds from country to country are thus in one sense a derogation from democracy, for democratic electorates no longer have the means of controlling their own fates."
[5]Lester R. Brown, *World Without Borders* (New York, Vintage Books, 1973), p. 187.

with which borders can be redrawn *without* violence may dramatically increase in the near future.

The exact shape of the NWO is obviously unclear because historically we are still in transition from one type of system configuration to another. We have already witnessed significant change. Further, events and trends suggest that the function of the state and its social contract with its citizens may change dramatically in the near future. What does all this portend? Perhaps there will be more "world" and less "order" in the New World Order.

DISCUSSION QUESTIONS

1. Discuss the difference between the New World Order and a New World System. Give examples of each throughout history.
2. Can states be ranked in order on the basis of an attribute we in IR refer to as power? In order to rank, it is necessary to measure power. What are the elements of power and how would an indicator of power be constructed?
3. How do differing areas of the world react to the news that a New World Order exists?
4. What is the relation between power and war? Given what world leaders say about the New World Order, and the causes of war, what is the likely course for conflict over the next decade?
5. Discuss sovereignty issues that may arise in the twenty-first century regarding rights and properties in the oceans, Antarctica, space and on other celestial bodies. Will the rule of sovereignty of the principle of the commons prevail?
6. Describe the difference between perceived and actual power and how a large gap between the two can lead to war.
7. The world is witnessing two contradictory trends. One trend is pushing the world towards greater integration (economic) and the other towards greater disintegration (political). Where and why are these trends emerging?
8. What are the limits to sovereignty in a world that is becoming economically interdependent? What are the limits to individual freedoms in such a world?
9. Are there universal human rights or are they time- and situation-specific? Is that part of the NWO?
10. Can the United Nations form the basis from which to keep peace between sovereign states?

9 LATIN AMERICA'S ALTERNATIVE: AN IBERO-AMERICAN FOUNDATION

CARLOS FUENTES

A leading Mexican writer and diplomatist, Carlos Fuentes holds the Robert F. Kennedy Chair of Latin American Studies at Harvard. He was educated at the University of Mexico and the *Institut of Hautes Etudes Internationales* in Geneva.

The paradox is this: If economic rationality tells us that the next century will be the age of global integration of the world's national economies, cultural "irrationality" steps in to inform us that it will also be the century of ethnic demands and revived nationalisms.

How can you quicken the step toward global integration if you have Ukranians and Lithuanians, Georgians and Armenians, Moldavians and Azerbaijanis yapping at your heels, denying the very principle of a worldwide integration of productive forces?

This is where political and cultural imagination must join together to ask: Can we conciliate global economic demands with the resurrection of these nationalistic claims?

THE FEDERALIST IMAGINATION

Both reason and imagination tell us that the name of the solution, that point where you can balance the demands of integration and those of the nationalities, is federalism. My hope is that we shall witness a reevaluation of the federalist theme as a compromise between three equally real forces: the region and the world, passing through the nation.

To this end, the North American book, *The Federalist Papers,* written by Hamilton, Madison and Jay, should be distributed in the millions. Although 200 years old, it may hold the secret to making the new world order work.

The applicability of their eighty-five essays is, of course, neither universal, nor restricted to conditions in 1787. Madison addressed the human tendency toward factionalism. While clearly understanding that its causes were difficult to uproot, he proposed to control its effects. How? Through a seeming paradox: a strong national government but controlled by checks and balances, separation of powers and federal diffusion of power. "You must first enable the government to control the governed; and in the next place oblige it to control itself."

Reprinted by permission from *New Perspectives Quarterly,* Winter 1991, pp. 15–17, © New Perspectives Quarterly, Los Angeles, CA, 1991.

A FEDERAL REPUBLIC OF LATIN AMERICA?

Thanks to *The Federalist Papers,* thirteen factious little colonies of the English New World became a great modern nation. As the United States, Canada, and Mexico today are designing a North American free-trade area, one wonders about the fate of the Ibero-American republics to the south of the United States. Do they pose problems comparable to those we are seeing in the Balkans, Central and Eastern Europe—not to mention Ireland and the Basque country, Brittany and Quebec?

The world change has caught Latin America in a vicious crisis—political, social, economic—with scant resources with which to make ourselves actively present in the new, multipolar order substituting the dead bipolar structure. Yet our contemporary crisis has made us realize that one thing stands on its own feet in the midst of our political and economic failures. And this is our cultural continuity; the multiracial and pluralistic culture we have created during the past 500 years. Contrary to current revindications in Europe and Asia, cultural demands in Latin America do not disrupt the national or even the global rationalities. They reinforce them.

If in Eurasia the problem is the conciliation of international integration with ethnic demands through a new federalist regime, in Latin America the problem is to conciliate economic growth with social justice through, again, a democratic federalism.

Latin America has a peculiar advantage over other areas of today's world. Our national cultures coincide with the physical limits of each one of our nations, even as our larger cultural boundaries embrace the Iberian peninsula, Spain, and Portugal, and through them Europe; and even as our internal diversification includes the Indian and black cultures.

The important thing is that no local separatisms menace our national unity or our neighbor's territorial integrity. Our culture, precisely because it is so varied—European, Indian, black—does not propose religious fundamentalisms or ethnic intolerance. As the Venezuelan author Arturo Uslar Pietri puts it, even when we are purely white in Latin America (and whites are a minority) we are Indian and we are black. Our culture cannot be understood without all three components. We are mestizo: a mixture of tastes, mores, memories, and accents.

What we do bear is profound social injustice. But because the national cultures are contained within the national boundaries, it is up to each of us to solve this problem through local politics. It is here that the federalist idea is quite relevant for Latin America.

Traditionally, we have been ruled from the center and from the top. Today, the emergence of new civil societies from Mexico to Argentina, proposes rule from the bottom and from the outskirts of society. To conciliate both movements is the mission of Latin American democracy. Whether in Salinas' Mexico, Fujimori's Peru, or Collar's Brazil, we are trying to "extend the republic," as Madison put it.

LIFE AFTER DEBT

After the fall of the Berlin Wall, it was widely believed that international resources previously earmarked for Latin America would now quickly shift to Central Europe and the USSR. This has not happened. The magnitude of the Eastern European crisis has given us all pause: nationalisms, separatisms, ethnic revolts and a fifty-year backwardness in all aspects of economic life, from deteriorating infrastructures to wholesale ecocide.

All of this is making us realize that the problems of Eurasia, from the Elbe to the Pacific, require a major international effort, comparable to the Marshall Plan. Massive new public investment is needed to boost communications, education, housing and a clean environment. The private sector doesn't invest in such matters.

In most of these respects, Latin America is more modern and developed. Comparatively, we have a better basis for attracting investment than Poland, Romania, or even Czechoslovakia. As the dust of the critical eighties settles down, we can judge our mistakes but also our successes in historical perspective.

Beginning with the Battle in Uruguay, the Popular Front in Chile, or Lazaro Cardenas in Mexico, the national state did create infrastructure, education, health, and opportunities for the private sector throughout Latin America.

Of course, the state did become bloated. The private sector did become lazy and overprotected. Debt cut everyone's wings.

But, as a result of our historical commitments, there is life after debt. Even as Latin America organizes her democratic existence and reforms her economic life, she has a great contribution to make to international relations. The end of the Cold War creates a new international context that demands cooperation, but refuses intervention. Few regions in the world have a greater experience in diplomatic negotiation than Latin America as a result of our difficult dealings with our powerful northern neighbor. This has created a cultural tradition that stresses peaceful solution of controversies, diplomacy, and adherence to international laws and treaties.

If the federalist spirit becomes successfully ingrained at the national level in Latin America, it can perhaps then play a role in uniting our republics in response to collective external challenges.

The free-trading zone in this continent, starting with Mexico in North America but extending south to Chile and Argentina, would seem to be the first stage, even if the time needed to achieve it is lengthier than expected.

But we should not become fixated on "an initiative of the Americas." Europe and the Pacific are equally important. Indeed, might a Federal Ibero-America be the bridge between Europe and the Pacific?

Exactly 100 years ago, the Cuban patriot Jose Marti warned: "If we want to assure freedom, we must balance trade. A people who want to die trade with only one country. A people who want salvation trade with more than one."

10 THE MARGINALIZATION OF AFRICA

Boutros Boutros-Ghali

Before being elected Secretary-general of the United Nations, Boutros Boutros-Ghali was deputy prime minister for foreign affairs of the Arab Republic of Egypt.

In his Windhoek speech of March 1990, during Namibia's independence celebrations, President Hosni Mubarak of Egypt voiced Africa's concerns in the following words: "While we welcome the rapprochement between East and West and the dismantling of the iron curtain, we hope that a new curtain between North and South shall not be erected. We also hope that this new rapprochement between the two superpowers shall not lead to the marginalization of Africa." The issue of an iron curtain between North and South raises a number of questions. For example, where exactly will this curtain be? How will it be erected? What structure will it have? What consequences will it have for the rich and poor countries?

Let us assume that the new curtain will be established along a discontinuous line separating the Third World from the rich countries. We can trace this hypothetical line around the earth: It cuts across the Pacific Ocean, separates the Soviet Union from China, and runs between Australia and Indonesia. It becomes more obvious as it divides the rich northern and poor southern shores of the Mediterranean. The curtain also falls between the rich and poor shores of the Caribbean, separating the United States from northern South America, Central America, and the Caribbean islands, dividing what Yves Lacoste called the American Mediterranean.

In these two zones, the demographic contrast is most obvious. In the North, the populations of rich countries experience slow growth, whereas the populations in the countries of the South grow exponentially. The countries of North Africa—Mauritania, Morocco, Algeria, Tunisia, Egypt, and Libya—have at present a population of 120 million. Over the next twenty-five years, their population will reach an estimated 200 million.

I

Migration from poor to rich countries in these two zones is already an important problem, and it will continue to be so in the future. Latin Americans migrate to the United States, while Arabs, Turks, and Africans choose to go to Europe. Even if Europe and the United States institute new barriers to control the inflow, critical questions remain as to how such measures will be implemented. How will these rich regions discourage the excess population, now building up on the southern shores of the Mediterranean and the Caribbean, from reaching Europe and the United States without at the same time reinforcing the structure of the new iron curtain? In those two zones of North-South interaction, men and women, through radio, television, and cinema, hear and see for themselves the extent to which their living conditions differ from those of their rich neighbors. Proximity in this case can only exacerbate differences.

The European and North American societies offer the developing countries a special political attraction in their espousal of democracy and their respect for fundamental liberties, conditions that are either weak or nonexistent in developing societies. In addition, it is in the zones of the Mediterranean and Caribbean that colonialism has left its most important mark; the legacy of subjugation and humiliation does not facilitate dialogue. A part of these poorer populations, particularly the political elites, has not forgotten the colonial oppression under which it frequently suffered. Zionist colonialism is there to remind the Arab and Muslim people that military and religious imperialism still exists, if in a different guise.

In addition, whereas communism has lost all influence in the North-South equation, and countries such as Cuba, Nicaragua, Ethiopia, and Angola now constitute lingering phenomena on their way to extinction, the fundamentalist terrorist or anarchist movements in the Third World remain as divisive elements separating North and South. If the Shining Path in Peru or the Medellín cartel in Colombia manage to take power in their respective countries, the elites in these countries will probably take refuge in the United States, just as the Cuban elite escaped the revolution in their country and settled in the United States, where they have transformed Miami into a Hispanic city. Also, if the fundamentalist wave that swept the Shah of Iran from power and replaced him with Ayatollah Khomeini is exported to Arab countries such as Algeria or Tunisia, it is quite possible that it would spread to neighboring countries such as Libya, Egypt, and Jordan. Again, the westernized elites and professional classes can be expected to seek refuge in Europe. If Europe refuses to receive such refugees, the iron curtain will be reinforced. If, on the other hand, Europe does receive these new immigrants, the xenophobic tendencies that exist in Europe will become stronger. The result will be the indirect reinforcement of the iron curtain. Thus, regardless of the attitudes adopted by the United States or Europe, the results will be the same and have destabilizing consequences for North-South relations. The consequences for the Mediterranean, however, will be far more serious than those for the Caribbean.

To begin with, the hinterland of the Mediterranean is the Sahara, the world's largest desert. The Caribbean countries, on the other hand, are in close proximity to large nations with significant economic resources and potential, such as Brazil and Argentina. The surplus population from the Mediterranean's southern shore can go only to Europe, but in the case of the Caribbean it can head either north to the United States or south to the potentially rich countries in Latin America.

Also, the littoral nations of the Caribbean Sea obtained their independence at the turn of the nineteenth century, but the majority of countries bordering the southern shores of the Mediterranean gained theirs only during the second half of the twentieth century. The longer period of independence and the political maturity that comes with it should facilitate dialogue with the rich countries.

Finally, the southern shores of the Mediterranean are largely inhabited by Muslim Arabs, whereas the Caribbean is inhabited by Catholic Hispanics and Protestants. This cultural difference between the immigrants and the host countries of the Mediterranean makes assimilation difficult. Whereas European countries have a lower propensity to assimilate and integrate immigrants from the South, the United States experiences much less difficulty in this regard, as it has been a melting pot for different nationalities and races for more than two hundred years. This comparative analysis leads to the conclusion that the new curtain to separate South from North along the Mediterranean will be far more solid than the one separating South and North in the Caribbean.

II

We can visualize several iron curtains, each with a separate structure, depending on the region in question and the forces at play. All of them, however, will be less solid than the one separating Africa from Europe. Our concern relates to Africa's relations with the rich countries of the North.

In order to better understand the structure of the new iron curtain, we should add to its geopolitical considerations, which we have just discussed, the following six international developments that relate to the rapprochement between East and West.

First, international relations will once again be dominated by Euro-centrism. The demise of colonial empires in the wake of the Second World War and the onset of decolonization should have led to the marginalization of the South and the periphery. The Cold War put a brake on this process. American intervention in Korea and Vietnam, Soviet assistance to Egypt in the building of the Aswan High Dam, Soviet military bases in Aden, U.S. bases in Somalia, Cuban assistance to the MPLA in Angola, and American aid to Savimbi's UNITA are examples of military and economic assistance that was guided by the imperatives of the Cold War. As the Cold War is coming to an end, the U.S. and the sovereign states of the former USSR will have a diminished interest in the developing countries, in spite of the importance of oil and raw materials. This, however, will not lessen the strategic importance the great powers attach to developing countries.

Second, we are also witnessing a revival of the "prodigal son" phenomenon, represented by the return of the countries of Central and Eastern Europe to the larger family of the West. This phenomenon has become, and will continue to be, such a focus of international interest that it practically leaves no place for the Third World or Africa, except where humanitarian aid is concerned.

Third, the process of marginalization is taking place concurrently with the erosion of aid to Africa, whose countries have grown increasingly poor since the inception of the independence process three decades ago. Not only will American, European, and Japanese aid diminish, but aid from Eastern European countries also will be drastically reduced. Technicians from Eastern European countries who assisted African governments already have been recalled. The number of scholarships has diminished, and financial assistance is shrinking; the process of marginalization is now being accelerated as the result of actions by both East and West.

Fourth, the international economy is moving toward liberalization, but a market economy can benefit Africa only if the continent possesses an adequate economic infrastructure and the political institutions required to sustain such an economic model. The countries of Eastern Europe are in a better position to satisfy these requirements and offer better opportunities for foreign investment.

Fifth, manpower in Eastern Europe, which is better qualified than that in Africa, can become assimilated more easily into Western European society. Moreover, on account of cultural and historical similarities, it will provoke less hostile sentiments than Arab and African workers.

And sixth, the West is imposing new conditions on aid to African countries. A democracy based on a multiparty system with a respect for human rights has become an essential requirement for recipients. Such were the conclusions of the Franco-African Summit held at La Baule in June 1990. It is certain, however, that the vast majority of African countries will face enormous political and institutional difficulties in establishing a Western-style democracy that does not correspond to their socio-economic realities.

It can be said, therefore, that the new international configuration superimposing itself on geopolitical realities will contribute to building a new iron curtain between North and South. This iron curtain will, in turn, be reinforced as a result of the gap between the standards of living in the rich and poor countries. In the final analysis, the iron curtain that separated North from South Korea and Eastern from Western Europe was ideological in nature. The new iron curtain that will separate South from North will be an economic and technological one. It will be reproduced automatically every time the North realizes a new stage of progress in the areas of technology, automation, data processing, or genetics.

III

What then can the South and Africa do now to face this new challenge? In May 1988 the Organization of African Unity (OAU), meeting in Addis Ababa, adopted a resolution aimed at sensitizing Third World public opinion to the importance of changes taking place in the international system. Resolution CM 1153, adopted at the initiative of Egypt, invited the nonaligned movement to evaluate the process of détente between the superpowers and to undertake a reevaluation of the international situation and its impact on the Third World.

The adoption of this resolution by the Twenty-fifth OAU Summit that May became the point of departure for an ambitious public relations campaign designed to sensitize and mobilize international public opinion in favor of the Third World and Africa in particular. We shall examine briefly, in chronological order, the actions actually taken by Africa in support of the campaign.

First, on 13 July 1989, during the bicentennial celebrations of the French Revolution, the presidents of Egypt, Tanzania, and Venezuela and the prime minister of India expressed to French president François Mitterand, the chairman of the Group of Seven, their hope that action would be taken as soon as possible toward convening a North-South summit meeting on the economy and environment. Mitterand expressed his appreciation for the initiative, which he described as coinciding with his continuous efforts to relaunch the North-South dialogue.

A few days later, the fifth session of the OAU Ministerial Council, meeting in Addis Ababa, adopted resolution CM 1219. The council:

> Welcomed the initiative taken by the Presidents of Egypt, Tanzania, and Venezuela and the Prime Minister of India towards starting a new process of regular consultations at the summit level between developing and developed countries on the issues of the international economy and the environment;
>
> Considered that such an initiative favors a more fruitful North-South dialogue and encouraged its proponents to pursue their efforts towards the materialization of their idea;
>
> Recommended that the Conference of the Heads of State and Government give a mandate to its Chairman to undertake the necessary initiating so that Africa may make its contribution towards relaunching a North-South dialogue as envisaged in the Paris initiative.

During the nonaligned summit conference held in Belgrade in September 1989, the rapprochement between East and West—and its impact on relations between North and South—was the principal theme of the debates. The main concern of the delegations became how to revitalize nonalignment in view of the end of the Cold War and colonialism. The July initiative of the Group of Four (Egypt, Tanzania, Venezuela, and India) was approved, and Yugoslavia, as chairman of the nonaligned movement, became part of the group. This Group of Five was given a mandate to pursue its goals. In another development, Peru proposed the formation of a new group of fifteen states to meet at head-of-state or government level to promote South-South cooperation. The Group of Fifteen, which included the Group of Five and ten other states, comprised five African, six Latin American, and three Asian states and Yugoslavia.

The two groups, while complementary, have different missions. The Group of Five is to maintain contact with the Group of Seven, the major industrialized countries, with the purpose of preparing for a North-South summit conference. The Group of Fifteen, on the other hand, is to promote South-South cooperation, which is a prerequisite for the establishment of an equitable North-South dialogue. Both groups operate within the framework of the nonaligned movement and the UN Group of Seventy-seven (less-developed countries).

The personal representatives of the heads of state of the Group of Five were to meet with the Group of Seven in Paris and New York in 1989 and 1990, respectively. Unfortunately, the meetings did not materialize, due to the strong opposition of the United States and Great Britain. They have categorically refused to hold a new international North-South conference along the lines of the Cancún Summit.

At the beginning of June 1990, in Kuala Lumpur, at the first summit meeting of the Group of Fifteen, the Group of Five held a working session to affirm its intention to continue its mission in spite of the opposition of the Group of Seven. The Group of Fifteen, on the other hand, held a series of meetings of the personal representatives of the heads of state or government in November 1989 and in January, March, and May 1990. The Kuala Lumpur Summit adopted a thirty-five-paragraph statement that reviewed the international economic situation. It proposed forming a follow-up committee composed of Malaysia, Senegal, and Venezuela; holding a ministerial meeting in Caracas in August 1990; and planning a second summit in Caracas in June 1991.

Finally at Addis Ababa, in July 1990, the Twenty-seventh OAU Summit adopted a program of action titled "Declaration on the Political and Socio-economic Situation in Africa and the Radical Changes Presently Taking Place in the World."

While it may be too early to appraise these efforts of developing countries, one should not underestimate such efforts, which aim at mobilizing Third World solidarity in forestalling the erection of a new iron curtain.

IV

The foregoing analysis points to the fact that, while the international situation has evolved from a climate of confrontation to one of cooperation between East and West, Africa has not been able to achieve sufficient progress in its quest for economic development. This lack of progress exists despite various initiatives adopted, such as the Lagos Plan of Action in 1980, the preparatory program for the economic rehabilitation of Africa in 1985, and the common African position on the question of foreign debt in 1987. On the contrary, the majority of Africa's infrastructures and means of production have deteriorated over the years. The external debt, which amounted to $50 billion in 1980, reached $275 billion in 1990. The number of least-developed African states increased in the past decade from twenty-one to twenty-eight.

What then has been the response of African countries to this situation? First of all, the majority of countries are engaged, at considerable social and political cost, in structural-adjustment programs in cooperation with international monetary and financial institutions. Unfortunately this process, which is based on short-term measures, is inadequate to address the difficulties facing the economies of African countries.

Second, the creditors, encouraged by the political changes in Eastern Europe, wish to impose new conditions of a political nature on assistance to Africa. Their argument is that economic development requires both political participation by the population and consolidation of democratic institutions, as if Africa cannot judge for itself the kind of democratic system best suited to its conditions and needs!

And third, there is a conviction in Africa that South-South cooperation can facilitate its economic rehabilitation and that collective African action should aim at relaunching North-South dialogue and cooperation.

If I have devoted much time and space to the conferences and meetings I had the privilege to attend, and in which Egypt played a leading role, it is to demonstrate that Africa and the Third World are aware indeed that the crisis threatening their future contributes to their marginalization. At first the countries of the Third World tried to make their voices heard. Now they are trying to establish a common platform at regional and intraregional levels within the framework of existing institutions and through new groups that are trying to revitalize such institutions. The outcome of such efforts, however, depends on the response of the rich countries of the North.

V

What then is the attitude of the industrial North toward the plight of the Third World? Does it share the views of developing countries that the crisis is due to the continued fall in prices of raw materials exported from Africa? Or is the reason the astronomical rise in the prices of manufactured goods? Is it the ever-increasing burden of foreign debt, or is it the outflow of financial resources from Africa? In brief, do the rich countries share the view that they are primarily responsible for transforming the present inequitable international system? And, in fact, will the new system that could result from the East-West rapprochement be less equitable than the present one?

The response of the industrialized countries, which I have gathered from both official statements and my meetings with high officials in Europe, the United States, Japan, and the Soviet Union, is summarized below.

The rich countries affirm at the outset that aid given to Eastern Europe will not affect the levels of aid provided to Africa. Paragraph 48 of the Final Declaration of the July 1990 Houston summit of the Group of Seven stipulates:

> We reiterate that our commitment to the developing world will not be weakened by the support of reforming countries in Central and Eastern Europe. The poorest of the developing nations must remain the focus of special attention. The International Development Association replenishment of SDR [special drawing rights—a unit of currency value used by the IMF] 11,600 million, agreed to last December, will provide needed resources for these countries, and makes the incorporation of environmental concerns into development lending. It is our intention to take a constructive part in the Paris Conference on the least-developed countries in September.

Yet the response to problems of the Third World can also be less categorical. I came across it in both the West and the Soviet Union. It is maintained that the superpowers give priority to ending the Cold War and to sponsoring disarmament and the transfor-

mation of Central and Eastern Europe at the expense of developing countries. Then, it is argued, not only will priority be accorded to developing countries, but cooperation between the superpowers and other industrial countries will augment development aid to devise new forms of assistance.

Response to the Third World also moves along ideological lines. There will be no expansion of aid to developing countries unless they adopt a market economy and an open democratic political system that guarantees the efficient functioning of such an economy. In addition, birthrates have to be lowered in certain countries.

For proponents of an international conference on Africa's external debt, there is a less-than-enthusiastic response from the industrial North. Such a conference, which would seek to persuade international public opinion of the gravity of the economic situation in Africa and the African debt problem, is said by the creditor countries to be superfluous, since they claim that they and the international financial institutions are already well aware of Africa's problems. Further, it is argued, there is no single remedy for the debt problem, a position confirmed at the Houston summit conference. Paragraph 57 of the meeting's Final Declaration stipulates:

> The adoption by debtor nations of strong economic reform programmes with the IMF and the World Bank remains at the heart of the debt strategy, and a prerequisite for debt and debt service reduction within commercial bank financing packages. It is vital that debtor countries adopt measures to mobilize savings and to encourage new investment flows and the repatriation of flight capital to help sustain their recovery. In this connection, the recent U.S. Enterprise for the Americas initiative to support investment reform and the environment in Latin America needs to be given careful consideration by finance ministers.

There is also a response from the North to a proposal for a new North-South international conference. Although Canada, France, and Italy have supported the holding of such a conference on a regular basis, it seems unlikely that it will materialize, due to the opposition of the United States, Great Britain, and, to a lesser extent, Germany and Japan. Such a position is not without its own logic. Opposition is based on the fact that international institutions, such as the World Bank and IMF, already exist to oversee North-South cooperation. In addition, the specialized agencies of the UN currently provide the necessary technical assistance in their respective fields of competence. Why should a new organ, which risks being politicized, be created? it is asked. It would be better, it is argued, to reinforce and revitalize existing international institutions that have demonstrated their usefulness.

On the other hand, the Group of Five argues that existing international institutions have not performed well and have only managed to devise short-term solutions. These institutions were created almost half a century ago and are not adapting to new sociopolitical realities. Finally, the marginalization of the Third World, and particularly Africa, calls for a collective awareness and new actions that can emanate only from a new concept of dialogue and interaction between North and South.

The rich countries, in their response, enumerate the practical actions they have taken to help developing countries: across-the-board rescheduling of foreign debts; extension of debt-servicing periods; reduction of debts; cancellation of official debts to the poorest countries; reduction of debt servicing of lower-middle-income countries; and provision of new financial and technical aid. In brief, these nations maintain that innovations have been already introduced to tackle the foreign-debt problem facing developing countries. They have done so, they argue, to forestall the transformation of the discontinuous line separating North and South into a veritable iron curtain.

VI

In conclusion, the rich countries of the North believe that the institutions they created almost half a century ago are capable of producing solutions to the North-South predicament. They nonetheless acknowledge that improvements can be made in the machineries of such institutions.

The major industrialized nations maintain that the problem is not urgent; they attach priority to disarmament and European issues. The crisis in the Third World, they say, can wait. In this respect, it is interesting to note that the problems of developing countries were mentioned after those of Eastern Europe and the Soviet Union in the Houston summit declaration of 1990. In addition, the summit did not propose a single initiative to solve the crisis in the Third World or the foreign-debt problem. The only strategy proposed by the rich countries was for the indebted, developing countries to adopt stringent reform programs and to reach agreements with the IMF and World Bank. They also advocate a new, miraculous remedy, the introduction of political pluralism along Western European lines. Such a prospect risks being ineffective not only because Africa has no democratic traditions and continues to be dominated by tribalism, but because democracy cannot take root unless certain minimal institutions and an adequate living standard exist.

During the 1960s, the African states became a theater of heroic struggle that mobilized local elites in a quest to overthrow colonial power. The objective was to install new governments espousing the ideals and aspirations of liberty, economic development, and social justice. Thirty years later, the new African state is far from fulfilling this early promise. The results have been disappointing for those states that adopted a capitalist mode of development—Côte d'Ivoire, Nigeria, and Zaire—and for those that opted for the Socialist path of development—Angola, Guinea, and Tanzania. This performance, combined with the rapprochement between East and West, has resulted in less interest in Africa on the part of the rich countries. If there has been any dialogue at all between Africa and the industrialized countries, it has been a dialogue of the deaf.

I have attempted to present the two sides of the argument. On the one hand, the rich countries continue to hope to resolve the problems of the Third World—debt, drought, desertification, and so forth—by obsolete aid methods within the framework of existing international institutions. On the other hand, the Third World remains attached to utopias such as the New International Economic Order and the African Common Market by the year 2000, which aim at changing the established order. Nonetheless, I remain convinced that the situation is not without hope. The experience of the past four decades allows us to extract three principal lessons.

First, there exists no simple remedy that can miraculously remove the obstacles to development in African countries. Many years of assiduous work are required within a new framework of North-South cooperation before Africa starts to feel the impact of change.

Second, by virtue of their size and geographic location, the vast majority of African countries will remain economically unviable if they do not cooperate with one another, particularly with their neighbors. Such regional cooperation and integration is a prerequisite for their economic development. Foreign aid must be directed to promote subregional and regional cooperation. Until now, foreign aid has been essentially bilateral. Rich countries are facing the greatest of difficulties in ridding themselves of this attitude. Bilateral aid accentuates micronationalism and leads to duplication and waste. Assistance from the North becomes diffuse by concentrating on unrealistic projects that satisfy only the immediate needs of local authorities, without any regard for the macroeconomic needs of Africa.

Third, unforeseen events, such as military confrontations, political tensions, and natural disasters, interfere with the sound functioning of the current aid policies of the North. It is important, therefore, to envisage mechanisms that ensure a rapid and effective response to such events, coupled with immediate and discrete diplomatic action to resolve inter-African disputes.

The collapse of Marxist regimes poses a new challenge to the liberal political system and market-economy model, which have come to represent the only frame of policy reference. The model, however, has not been able to find a solution to the development problems of Africa. In addition, this model, during the entire period of the Cold War, was unable to contain the process of the marginalization of Africa that, as stated at the outset of this article, has already commenced. Can this model now be successful in the post-Cold War era?

If we wish to avoid great cataclysms, the rich should accept being less rich so that the poor will become less poor. Changes of such a nature on a global level require a different spirit, a new attitude, and a willingness to reconsider one's position. Such is the price that must be paid to ensure the survival of humanity.

11 *"THE CHINESE VIEW OF A NEW WORLD ORDER"*

Li Peng

The present-day world is at a vital turning point. The old structure has come to an end while a new one has yet to take shape. The world is moving in a direction of multipolarization. World peace, national stability, economic development are the aspirations shared by the people everywhere. The tense face-off of the two major military blocs in Europe which lasted for nearly half a century is no longer in place. Some regional hot-spots have either been, or are in the process of being, removed. The international situation has eased to some extent. However, factors threatening world peace and causing international tension have not been removed completely. While some old contradictions and confrontations have disappeared, new ones have cropped up, rendering our world neither tranquil nor peaceful. The Middle East question remains unresolved after the Gulf War. And the peace talks between the Arab countries and Israel are likely to be a long and difficult process. In some European countries, conflicts of differing intensities or even wars have broken out as a result of ethnic strifes. No one can say for sure that similar conflicts and wars will not take place in other parts of Europe. What deserves the close attention of the international community is that the developing countries whose population constitutes the overwhelming majority of the world's total are finding themselves in an increasingly difficult position. The gap between the North and South continues to widen, with the rich countries becoming richer and the poor poorer. Such a state of affairs, if allowed to continue, will eventually lead to fresh disturbances or even new regional conflicts. The start realities show that the questions of peace and development, the two principal themes of the present-day world, remain to be solved.

In contrast to a turbulent Europe, the Asia-Pacific region enjoys relative stability. The signing of the Paris agreements have laid the foundation for the final settlement of the Cambodian conflict. Following their simultaneous participation in the United Nations, the North and South of Korean have signed the protocol on mutual nonaggression and the joint declaration on the de-

This reading is a speech given at the United Nations on January 31, 1992 by the Premier of China, Li Peng, "Chinese Views on a New World Order," *Beijing Review,* 17 Feb. 1992; 35, 7; 12–14. © *Beijing Review.*

nuclearization of the Korean Peninsula. The situation on the peninsula is moving towards relaxation and stability. Quite a few countries in the Asia-Pacific region have enjoyed a rather high economic growth rate thanks to political stability at home. This region has now become a dynamic and promising region in world economic development. A stable and economically prosperous China not only is in the fundamental interests of the Chinese people, but also constitutes an important factor making for peace and stability in the Asia-Pacific region and the world as a whole. Over the past decade or more, China has firmly implemented the policy of reform and opening to the outside world initiated by Comrade Deng Xiaoping, which has brought enormous changes to the country. Right now, China enjoys political stability, social tranquility, ethnic harmony, and a sustained economic growth. With full confidence, the Chinese people are advancing on the road of building socialism with Chinese characteristics. As a developing country with a huge population, China knows full well that its modernization will take a considerably longer period of time. The attainment of this goal requires two indispensable conditions, namely, an environment of prolonged peace and stability internationally and prolonged political stability at home. China pursues an independent foreign policy of peace. It always maintains that differences in social system, ideology, cultural tradition, and religious belief should not be an obstacle to establishing and developing normal relations between states. China is ready to develop friendly relations with all countries on the basis of *the Five Principles of Peaceful Coexistence*. It will never become a threat to any country or any region in the world. China is of the view that no country should seek hegemony or practice power politics. This should be made a principle to be observed universally in international relations. China does not seek a sphere of influence for itself. It does not seek hegemony now, and will not seek hegemony in future when it grows stronger. The past few years saw further strengthening and development of the friendly and good-neighbourly relations between China and its surrounding countries, which is the result of the concerted efforts by China and those countries. This, in our view, not only serves the common interests of both China and those countries, but also contributes to peace and development of the region and the world as a whole.

In order to win a genuine peace in the world and create a favourable environment for development for the people in all countries, the international community is focusing more and more on the subject of what new international order should be established. In our view, such basic principles as sovereign equality of member states and noninterference in their internal affairs, as enshrined in the Charter of the United Nations, should be observed by all its members without exception. In compliance with the spirit of the Charter and the established norms governing international relations, and in light of the changes in the international situation, the Chinese Government wishes to share with the governments of other countries some of its basic views concerning the establishment of a new international order that will be stable, rational, just, and conducive to world peace and development. These basic views are:

The new international order should be established on the basis of the principles of mutual respect for sovereignty and territorial integrity, mutual nonaggression, noninterference in each other's internal affairs, equality, and mutual benefit and peaceful coexistence. The core of these principles is noninterference in each other's internal affairs. The people and governments of various countries are entitled to adopt the social system and ideology of their own choice in light of their national conditions.

Countries, big or small, strong or weak, rich or poor, are all entitled to participate in world affairs as equal members of international community and make their own contributions to world peace and development.

The new international order should include a new economic order. As the ever-widening gap between the North and the South and the continued sharpening of their contradictions have become a destabilizing factor in international life, the establishment of a just and rational new international economic order based on equality, mutual benefit, and providing for appropriate handling of the debt burden has become ever more urgent and crucial.

Human rights and fundamental freedoms of the entire mankind should be universally respected. Human rights covers many aspects. They include not only civil and political rights, but also economic, social, and cultural rights. As far as the large numbers of developing countries are concerned, the rights to independence, subsistence, and development are of paramount importance. In essence, the issue of human rights falls within the sovereignty of each country. A country's human rights situation should not be judged in total disregard of its history and national conditions. It is neither appropriate nor workable to demand that all countries measure up to the human rights criteria or models of one or a small number of countries. China values human rights and stands ready to engage in discussion and cooperation with other countries on an equal footing on the question of human rights on the basis of mutual understanding, mutual respect, and seeking consensus while reserving differences. However, it is opposed to interference in the internal affairs of other countries using the human rights issue as an excuse.

Effective disarmament and arms control should be achieved in a fair, reasonable, comprehensive, and balanced manner. Efforts should be stepped up to attain complete prohibition and thorough destruction of nuclear and chemical weapons at an early date and to ban the development of space weapons. Countries in possession of the largest nuclear and conventional arsenals should take the lead in the discharge of their special responsibilities for disarmament. All nuclear-weapon states should undertake not to be the first to use nuclear weapons, or to use or threaten to use such weapons against nonnuclear-weapon states or nuclear-free zones. The nuclear weapons of the disintegrated Soviet Union should be placed under effective control. As the disarmament issue bears on national security of all states, it should be discussed and addressed with their participation.

The United Nations should uphold justice and play a more active role in maintaining world peace and promoting development, as well as in helping establish a new international order. As most UN member states belong to the developing world, it is only reasonable for people to expect that the organization will do more in defending the rights and interests of the developing countries.

In recent years, the United Nations has played an important role in maintaining world peace and security, accelerating settlement of regional conflicts and promoting economic and social development of various countries. In so doing, the United Nations has enhanced its prestige and that of its Security Council and increased people's confidence in the organization. While affirming this, we must also be aware that the drastic and profound changes in the international situation have led to the reemergence of numerous contradictions previously hidden from public eye, adding to instability in the pursuit of peace and development in the world. It is in this sense that the responsibility of the United Nations and its Security Council has become heavier and the challenges facing them more formidable.

China is ready to cooperate with all other members of the Security Council, discuss issues of common interest to the international community, and exchange views with them as equals in the spirit of seeking common ground while reserving differences so as to expand areas of consensus. China sincerely hopes that the United Nations and its Security Council will play a still more active and constructive role in international affairs. Now, we have a newly elected UN Secretary-General, Dr. Ghali. China supports the work of the Secretary-General and wishes to pledge full cooperation. We are confident that in discharging his duties, the Secretary-General will receive extensive support from the developing countries and the international community at large.

It is our hope that this meeting will have a positive impact on the maintenance of world peace and security and play an important role in helping establish the new international order and defend the rights and interests of the developing countries, thus making a contribution to the progress of humanity.

12 RUSSIA: A CHANCE FOR SURVIVAL

ANDREI KOZYREV

Foreign Minister of Russia since 1991, Andrei V. Kozyrev was born in Brussels and educated at the Moscow State Institute of International Relations before being listed a "worker."

I.

Much of the explanation of the Soviet phenomenon must necessarily be historical. In taking that approach we might conceivably focus only on the last phase of Soviet history and agree with Zbigniew Brzezinski, who said that the crisis of authority in the Kremlin and the perception of the historical collapse of communism have finally brought about a disintegration of the Soviet empire.[1] That, however, would be too facile an explanation. After all the USSR did not materialize out of thin air; it came in the wake of the former Russian Empire and bore many of its birthmarks. It will be long before many of those blemishes cease to affect the fate of those countries that have now inherited the expanses of the former USSR.

The birth and expansion of the Russian Empire had been greatly influenced by an eminently messianic belief in the special mission of tsarist Russia as heir to the global vision of a Third Rome. Totalitarian trends in ideology and political attitudes are still besetting Russia even as it seeks to assert political pluralism. Imperial Russia, even though appearing a priori as a typical colonial empire, was clearly distinct from such maritime powers as Britain or France and the hinterland Austrian Empire. For all its expansionism the Russian Empire did little to improve the well-being of the Russian people at the expense of others. As a celebrated Russian historian, Vassily Kluchevsky, aptly put it, Imperial Russia was a "bloated state of emaciated people." Furthermore the Russian Empire boasted no metropolis as such.

Western colonization, following as it did a clear-cut pattern between metropolis and colonies, was driven by a search for new markets, sources of raw materials, and labor. Colonization made societies more open to the world around them, albeit through sometimes ruthless methods. Russia, by contrast, constantly concerned with protecting its boundaries, was drifting eastward and

[1]Zbigniew Brzezinski, "Selective Global Commitment," *Foreign Affairs*, Fall 1991, p. 3. Excerpted in Selection 31.

stretching its territory outward to fend off outside risks to its historical center. Finally, whereas Western colonization proceeded amid bourgeois revolutions that spelled an end to feudal stagnation, Russian colonization only served to strengthen absolutism. Russian history might be likened to a mammoth cauldron set over a low fire, which boils so slowly that people forget to let the steam escape in time, leading inevitably to a gigantic explosion. An important stage in the process began with Peter the Great, whose reforms were firmly and cruelly imposed from above. Peter propelled the upper crust of Russia into western Europe, turning Petersburg into a northern Palmyra, a shining city among the most precious jewels of European culture. That splendor, however, concealed illiteracy and barbaric squalor just a few miles away.

When a tidal wave of revolution swept across western Europe in the nineteenth century and civic societies took shape, Russia continued its slow-paced search for its own "special place" in an attempt to perpetuate its archaic statehood. No wonder that the utopian Marxist ideas that made their way into Russia from the West acquired wild and most extravagant features. After the old empire collapsed in 1917, the peoples of Russia stood a good chance of improving their lot. The absence of both a classical metropolis in the Russian Empire and severe ethnic repression (everyone seemed to live an equally miserable life) offered good opportunities for engaging all the newly liberated nations, free from mutual hatred, in a common search for a better democratic future for their crumbling country. Theoretically the 1922 treaty that formed the USSR provided a legal foundation for establishing a civilized commonwealth of free nations based on principles of equality.

II.

The fate of democracy in Russia will be determined to a great extent on the economic front. Russia's democratic government is based on mass popular support. However many of those who voted for the present leaders regarded them as individuals capable of rapidly ensuring "social justice" and of transforming into everyday life old myths about the possibility of egalitarian, universal well-being.

Our people have to understand that we can no longer live without measures carried out by the government to introduce a free-market economy, privatization, and liberalization of the entire economy. They must understand the fairness of the diagnosis pronounced by the government regarding the crippled economic organism it inherited. They must understand the political courage of the Russian leadership that decided to carry through extremely unpopular, but realistic, measures to save the country. At any rate critics do not suggest other prescriptions, except for a return to centralized planning, which spells death for the economy.

Assuring the people of real support in this difficult period means much more than providing assistance in its traditional sense. Assistance is not support for people "returning" to a normal economy based on common sense. Russians do not know such an economy. They have lost all historical memory of it after several generations of a totalitarian distribution system.

Looking at assistance in historical terms, the American scholar John Lewis Gaddis perceives yet another important aspect. He notes that of critical importance is not the size, as such, of this assistance but its timeliness, its accurate "targeting" and its coverage in the mass media.[2] This psychological aspect is particularly important in today's Russia, because at stake is helping the entire nation to learn to live a new life, helping it save for the world economy its largest and currently most promising part, which was once artificially cut off from the rest of the world.

The concept of assistance is undergoing fundamental change. Now it is not only humanitarian assistance but first and foremost "target" support for the primary driving forces of the reform: specific program mechanisms to liberate the economy and the emerging strata of businessmen. The way is open for mutually advantageous interaction at a key stage of forming a truly international free market.

This perspective, which focuses on the twenty-first century, should be kept in view when determining, without delay, concrete questions of translating into practice the favorable external background against which Russia is making the transition to democracy. Such practical implementation is called upon to consolidate the positive and mutually attractive character of Russia's current opening to the rest of the world.

We are undertaking concrete steps toward this aim by exploring an area that for decades has been a "diplomatic virgin land" for us. We are joining the International Monetary Fund, the World Bank, and the General Agreement on Tariffs and Trade; becoming more active in the European Bank; establishing in deeds rather than

words an interaction with the Group of Seven industrial nations, the European Community, the Organization for Economic Cooperation and Development, regional banks and economic cooperation forums in Asia and the Pacific and other regions. We have a lot to learn. But rest assured, we are learning fast.

In turn this will help establish Russia as a reliable partner in the community of civilized states. History has witnessed many times how the domestic problems of Russia made that state a dangerous and unpredictable participant in international affairs. However, with the transition to democracy in politics and the economy, our internal life and its driving-belts become understandable to the surrounding world.

No doubt Russia will not cease to be a great power. But it will be a normal great power. Its national interests will be a priority. But these will be interests understandable to democratic countries, and Russia will be defending them through interaction with partners, not through confrontation. In economic matters, too, once on its own feet and later, after acquiring a weight commensurate with its potential in world trade, Russia will be a serious economic competitor to many but, at the same time, an honest partner complying with the established rules of the game in world markets.

The "supertask" of Russian diplomacy in all areas is to make the utmost, concrete contribution to the improvement of the everyday life of Russian citizens.

III.

As far as Russia is concerned, we see our goals—disarmament and limitation of the arms race—in terms of releasing as many

resources as possible and creating the most favorable conditions for the implementation of our socioeconomic reforms. It is our desire to work for further deep cuts in strategic offensive arms and conventional armaments, for a "zero" solution to the tactical

[2]John Lewis Gaddis, "Toward the Post-Cold War World," *Foreign Affairs,* Spring 1991, p. 115.

nuclear weapons problem, complete elimination of chemical weapons and for winding down nuclear tests.

In addition to making a traditional quantitative disarmament more radical, above all nuclear disarmament, the emphasis in the security area is being shifted to confidence-building measures in the nuclear field, to nonproliferation in its broadest interpretation and to defense conversion. Promotion of demilitarization in both societies, without which the world's democratic trend would inevitably ebb, is becoming the pivot for Russo-American partnership in military affairs. A switch from words to deeds in carrying out specific joint ventures in conversion would give real impetus to cooperative investments, which in the long run should become the main channel for Russo-American economic interaction.

How does democratic Russia's course toward rapprochement with the West and NATO, as well as its overall position on arms control issues, differ from the policy of "new thinking"? That policy initiated by Gorbachev and Shevardnadze has accomplished a great deal and started what the world press called "breakthroughs" in limiting strategic offensive and conventional armaments, as well as in other areas. To be sure, those were breakthroughs but ones measured by old standards—those of the Cold War.

It is not the fault but the misfortune of the architects and makers of "new thinking" that those policies could be nothing more than a substantially liberalized modification of the earlier Soviet foreign policy course. Granted, "new thinking" in the world arena ran ahead of attempts at reform undertaken within the country, particularly in the beginning. Some individual concessions were occasionally won from the military-industrial complex on specific issues to be negotiated with the West. But those concessions had to be paid for, and the price was, objectively speaking, susceptible to pressure from the

military-industrial complex in other foreign policy matters—and not only in secondary but fundamental ones. So even when agreement was extracted from the military for considerable reductions in the horrendous stockpiles of armaments, it never proved possible to obtain its consent on the main point—on changing the very attitude toward the United States and the West as a whole. Despite everything that attitude continued in fact to draw on the old ideology. And the old power structure called the "center" was too bound by that ideology to be able to change the situation.

Now in the leadership of Russia we have people who are free from commitments and debts to the communist past, who have completely and unequivocally broken away from communism. The only burden from the past that weighs heavily on them is the dire economic situation, not at all some kind of ideological nostalgia. These new leaders simply cannot think, for instance, of NATO as Russia's adversary.

Let me make a qualification: This is the firm position of those who make up the government of Russia today, but not yet the mentality of the entire society, particularly in its managerial apparatus and in the corridors of the military-industrial complex. Pressure from those quarters on the Russian leadership will continue, and reliable guarantees of irreversibility in this regard are yet to emerge.

But the main point holds: The first-ever president legally elected by the people and a team of his like-minded associates are resolved to create such guarantees through radical democratic market-oriented reforms that already are under way. These reforms are aimed at improving the life of the people today, at their return from a through-the-looking-glass existence to a normal life and to the provision of well-being for themselves, their children, and grandchildren. These reforms offer, in the view of the government, the only path to prosperity in

Russia as a great (but normal!) Eurasian power in all its aspects—European, Asian, Siberian, and Far Eastern—a power that in its domestic life and foreign policy refutes the pessimistic prophecy of Rudyard Kipling that East and West will never meet.

The geopolitical location and historical role of Russia as a bridge between West and East predetermine its active "Eastern policy." Here I would limit myself to mentioning the Asian and Pacific region, an area characterized by a uniquely dynamic development. Among our priorities is to finalize the normalization of relations with Japan on the basis of a peace treaty, including a solution to the territorial issue. We see good prospects for relations with China as well. It is in our interests to have an economically strong China, posing no threat to Russia. On a broader scale all this should help achieve a balanced interrelationship in the "rectangle" comprising Russia, the United States, Japan and China, thus contributing to greater stability and cooperation in Asia and the Pacific.

CHAPTER THREE

THE PLAYERS:
THE CHANGING ROLE
OF THE STATE

All the world's a stage and all the men and women merely players. They have made their exits and their entrances and one man in his time plays many parts. . . . then a soldier, full of strange paths . . . jealous in honor, sudden and quick in quarrel, seeking the bubble reputation, even in the cannon's mouth. And then the justice . . . a world too wide for his shrunken shank.

William Shakespeare,
As You Like It,
II. vii, 39

In a penetrating analysis of certain myths about the principal player in international affairs, Inis Claude once noted that the special task of the analyst of international relations is understanding the external behavior of states and their relationships with one another, tending to focus more attention on

> . . . the forest rather than the trees. Forests consist, however, of trees, and those of us who devote our attention to the multistate system, the global network of states, will be well advised to seek an accurate understanding of the parts that constitute the whole.[1]

The state may remain the source of highest loyalty in international society, but it is constantly undergoing change. Even giant multinational states like the USSR disappear, just as some of the oldest and most stable nations in western Europe have recently endeavored to coalesce into something bigger. Yet the basic unit in international relations still remains the national state, that is, the state based upon the nation, despite spectacular shifts as well as routine adjustments in the configuration of world politics in recent years. Many of the most significant changes have been *within* states, as Ramesh Thakur amply demonstrates in his

[1]Inis Claude, "Myths about the State," *Review of International Studies*, 12, 1986, p. 1, based upon the second E.H. Carr Memorial lecture delivered at the University College in Wales at Aberystwyth.

treatment of what has been happening to social values and political power in India. Other countries which endeavor to encompass more than one ethnic grouping seem to be experiencing increasing trouble, Iraq with its Kurds, the collapsing experiments in Yugoslavia and Czechoslovakia, and the breakup of the former sixteen-unit Union of Soviet Socialist Republics being the most striking examples. New states, such as Croatia and Slovenia, seem suddenly to emerge from nowhere, when in fact they—as nations—have existed for a very long time indeed.

Recognition of the state as the most fundamental entity does not imply, however, that the nation-state in its relationships to others is the sole factor to be observed by anyone seriously endeavoring to make sense out of global politics. Seyom Brown has even coined a new term for the world system as it is now emerging: "polyarchy,"[2] indicating that there are now many centers of power competing for men's loyalties. It can hardly be denied that movements such Shi'ite fundamentalism, the "Greens" and the Irish Republican Army, as well as institutions such as the Catholic Church, labor unions, and multilateral corporations—and literally hundreds of others—all take part in and to some degree alter the process of international relations. Arnold Wolfers understood transnational forces long before most other experts.[3] Since his time, the "level-of-analysis" has become one of the most intriguing aspects of international relations.[4]

Concentrating upon the state does not render the other elements irrelevant, for the nation-state remains the central entity simply because at this stage of human history it lies at the core of power and human loyalty, with all the symbols and emotions which go with it, though increasingly, what are called "nonstate actors," affect how states interact. Fascinating and important in themselves as all these other foci may be, it is their impact upon inter-state relations which makes them significant for the student of IR.

To understand the basic unit in world politics in its present form, one must make some crucial distinctions. The first of these is between the concepts "nation" and "state" and how they combine to form the basis of our study and concern. A noted Greek scholar, Theodore Couloumbis, joins with his American counterpart, James Wolfe, in an excerpt from their internationally used introductory text to differentiate between these key expressions and to show their intimate and indeed crucial connection in IR. The term "nation" is essentially an ethnic one. It is based upon a common heritage, language, culture, and most importantly, a deep sense of identity among the people who make up a nation. To an American, or an Irishman, or a Basque is a source of pride. "State" is a legal and territorial expression, involving a population politically organized un-

---

[2]Seyom Brown, *New Forces, Old Forces, and the Future of World Politics,* Glenview, Ill.: Scott, Foresman and Co., 1988, *passim.*

[3]Arnold Wolfers, "Actors in International Politics," in W.T.R. Fox, *Theoretical Aspects of International Relations,* excerpted in several editions of this book, most recently in the eighth, pp. 31–34.

[4]J. David Singer, "The 'Levels-of-Analysis' Problem in International Relations," in *The International System: Theoretical Essays,* special issue of *World Politics,* XIV, 1, October 1961, pp. 77–92.

der one government in one place with sovereign rights, even though it may have possessions elsewhere. It is different from "nation" in that it may or may not elicit loyalty; a state may contain more than one nation, just as the nation may extend beyond the borders of one state. All Irishmen do not reside in the same state. The Basques are but part of the Spanish state. The Soviet Union *was* for more than seventy years a state made up of many nations, "sovereign" over all its peoples, even if it could not in the end command their loyalty, as the Latvians, Azerbaijanis, Georgians and many others demonstrated. What is not yet clear is whether its successor, the "Commonwealth of Independent State" (CIS) is itself a state, that is, sovereign in the generally-understood sense of that term. Marshall Goldman, in his article in this chapter, wonders how much of a chance democracy really has, unless there emerges a thriving middle class, in a land dominated by tsars and commissars for so long.

It is the combination of the two characteristics of statehood and nationalism which give the basic unit its peculiar strength and relevance in the international system in which we live today. This has not always been so, nor is it likely to remain so, but for our present purposes it is the heart of the matter. Governments come and go; states may normally be expected to go on more or less indefinitely, even though (as in the recent case of Mynamar's changing its name from Burma or Ceylon earlier becoming Sri Lanka and now even changing to Shri Lanka) they may decide to call themselves something different. "Government" refers to the manner and structure whereby the state conducts its affairs, both internally and externally. The state possesses "sovereignty," that quality which enables it the freedom to act, to do whatever its spokesmen want it to do, without any interference from any other state nor indeed from any international body. This is a legal concept with the most fundamental political implications for the way states behave. Its "government," (or "administration" as Americans prefer to call it under their separation of powers doctrine), lasts only so long as the country's voters or, in the case of authoritarian states, its revolutionaries, allow it to continue "in office."

Normally, analysts of international affairs can depend upon the continued existence of a given state as being politically viable with infinitely more assurance than they can upon the ability of a given body of politicians to "stay in power," firmly enough in control of the state's administrative machinery to stay there. The old saying, "The King is dead; long live the King" reminds us of the continuity of the state; today most monarchies are gone, but the states which they controlled (France, notably) still exist under a different form of government. In some states, like Argentina in recent decades, it is big news when the transfer of power from one party to the next is a peaceful one. The absorbing interest which this political process affords, including the occasional total breakdown which results from civil strife or a losing war, is one of the many things which make the study of IR so intriguing—and puzzling.

Yet another distinction contrasts the way in which a state organizes itself for purposes of domestic order and the way it conducts its foreign affairs. The sociology of politics shows us that the old, easy distinction between what is domestic and what is foreign is less easy to make than it used to be.[5] This is one reason that the U.S. Congress seems to act almost as an independent actor in world affairs, every piece of legislation now apparently containing implications for both realms. Comparatively, there are nearly as many varieties of national structure as there are states themselves. There are federal states and unitary ones, dynastic states and republican states, democratic ones and authoritarian regimes, totalitarian governments which control practically everything their citizens do and those which perform very limited functions. It is the outward focus of the state, its ability to effectively conduct foreign affairs, to formulate and pursue national interests, and to enter into binding engagements with other states, that concern those who would understand international relations. The novel way in which the United States conducts its foreign relations provides the special focus of William Olson, formerly Chief of the research arm of Congress. Written just after Bush's great success in the "Desert Storm" operation, his contribution to this chapter endeavors to delineate a "derivative theory" of U.S. foreign policy-making in a system that has for most of the post-WWII era been called "divided government." Now that one party controls both branches, the White House and Congress may prove more cooperative. Time will tell.

The ethnic component of the nation-state, as we have seen, is an essential ingredient of the present system in which nations generally are organized into states. The so-called "ethnic cleansing" policy of the Serbs against the Bosnians is fortunately atypical, though in many, if not most states, there are what might be thought of as "nations within nations," ethnic groups which find it difficult to accept the dominance of others, as was painfully the case in Transylvania, where the old communist Ceauscescu Romanian government seemed determined to wipe out the Hungarians who lived there, just as early in this century Armenians living in Turkey were nearly destroyed by the dominant ethnic group in control. Many new states were based upon artificial entities created in the last century in faraway colonial capitals in their rivalry to carve up Africa, usually encompassing two, three, or even more tribes or linguistic-cultural entities which spilled over into the next-door colony. In Asian societies, such as India or Indonesia, where numerous overlapping ethnic or religious groups have coexisted for centuries, the efforts of central governments to exert greater control over people's lives tend to make such groups more conscious of one another as rivals for scarce resources, stimulating communal tension and even civil strife. Minority nationalism has led to the separation of Bangladesh from Pakistan and the unsuccessful attempt of Biafra to break away from Nigeria. Border wars between Ethiopia and Somalia, India and Pakistan, and between Cambodia and Vietnam are examples of unsettled relationships between nationalism and government. Nor is "the West" exempt from ethnic strife; less extreme examples are Belgium and

[5]See Hidemi Suganami, *Domestic Analogies in International Relations*. Cambridge: Cambridge University Press, 1990. This is another of CUP's "Studies in International Relations" series with the British International Studies Association, of which the author is one of the [least important] founding members.

Canada. The worst recent case is, needless to say, Serbian "ethnic cleansing" against the Muslim population in Bosnia.

These conditions markedly contribute to the instability of the modern era, not only because of the threat to order, but with dangerous and costly implications for international security. One of the great dilemmas is that some governments still lack the means of establishing their authority peacefully, either because their legitimacy is questioned by a significant body of public opinion, as in Panama, or because they cannot meet economic needs fast enough to allay fear and suspicion existing between competing groups within the country, as in Mozambique (which after years of experimentation and division recently abandoned Marxism). Both cases had invited foreign intervention in some form or other. A precise definition of the nation-state may seem difficult to make, though in fact, it should not be difficult if we get back to fundamentals.

To summarize then, what are the attributes one attaches to this basic unit, the nation-state? First of all, it must possess a territorial base; it must be somewhere on the map. The dimensions of that base are irrelevant; Luxembourg is just as much a state as Brazil. This physical quality implies that the nation-state is defined, that it is circumscribed, and that presiding over the territory there is a government with complete jurisdiction.

This is its second attribute—government. To govern a people means to meet their fundamental social needs, to protect them from outside threat, to deal with authority with other entities on their behalf, and to abide by its international obligations. It is this last aspect of government which is of more interest to the analyst of international relations than the actual form of government which may be in power in a given nation-state at a given time. In the effective conduct of foreign relations the loyalty and support of the population is a key ingredient, which doesn't necessarily mean that the society is democratic nor that its definition of that term resembles that of others elsewhere in the world.

A third attribute is obviously that the nation-state have a population; governments-in-exile, however admirable or deserving of authority, lack this attribute and can seldom regain it without the active assistance of friendly regimes. As in the case of territory, the size of the population is unimportant in this context; "ministates" such as Tuvalu or Malta with a few thousand people are just as "qualified" as China, with over a billion.

This leads to the fourth attribute—sovereignty—to which we have already alluded. It is both a legal and a political concept, harking back to the days when the nation-state emerged after the Treaty of Westphalia ended the Thirty Years' War. Kings and other *sovereigns* spoke for the state, but about all that is left now of that habit is the word itself. It has to do with the *right* to govern and to represent. It is enshrined in the Charter of the United Nations, in the expression "sovereign equality," which in pure power terms is an obvious absurdity. But from the middle of the seventeenth century on, individual security, diplomacy, international law, war, commerce, the development of culture and indeed of civilization itself have been influenced in their form and content by the dominance of the nation-state. Now extended around the globe, it is *the* fundamental principle of politics. Just before World War I, there were only sixty-three sovereign states in the world; on the eve of World War II, the number had increased to seventy. Now it is nearly 170, most of them possessing United Nations membership. Subnational movements may produce even more states as larger states break up, but at the same time, states may join together, as did Tanganyika and Zanzibar to form Tanzania and, more recently, the two Germanys. "1992" symbolizes what *may* eventuate in a massive and economically powerful new state of Europe, with over a third of a billion people; could it possibly be called a "nation-state?" Nation-states sometimes disappear, only to reemerge later, as in the case of Poland.

If there is a fundamental new trend in world politics and economics, it is that the clear distinction between nation-states is breaking down without destroying the integrity of the system which binds them together. There are two primary indicators of this breakdown. One is the increasing ability of groups and even of individuals within states to influence and even to alter the course of the policies of governments toward one another, sometimes against the will of their masters. The other is, as we shall see in greater detail in Chapter Seven, that transnational forces are assuming greater influence, so much that some serious analysts feel that they constitute the basis of a new system, one not based upon the nation-state at all any more.

During the long period in which the present system afforded at least the stronger states an opportunity to develop in comparative peace and prosperity, the nation-state performed a timely and generally useful function. With the coming of the twenty-first century, however, certain trends which have already begun to undermine the principle of territorial impenetrability are bound to become more pronounced. These trends reflect the difficulties inherent in the application of the principle of self-determination which glorified nationalism as early as the Paris Peace Conference after the first World War,[6] the development of techniques and instruments of ideological penetration, an expansion of economic interdependence, the accelerated proliferation of weapons of mass destruction, the communication revolution (combined with the literacy revolution), and in the increasing alarm over what is happening to the entire global ecosystem. Will the logic of all this result in the replacement of the allegiance to the nation-state as the core value in world politics? Viewing with alarm does not, in itself, produce any viable alternative.

For the moment, an order of sorts (which we endeavor to describe in Chapter Six) based upon the nation-state as it faces its counterparts all over the world continues, in its often frightening and contradictory way, to survive if not to flourish. Hence, before we can embark upon any attempt to understand the *system*, we have had first to give our attention to the imperfect sovereign "players" or "actors," along with what have come to be known as "nonstate actors," whose interplay makes the system what it is today. We shall now turn to the traditional ways in which they relate to one another known as "diplomacy."

---

[6]On the Paris Peace conference and how it altered the way diplomacy has been conducted ever since, see especially Harold Nicolson, *Peacemaking 1919*, New York: Grosset and Dunlap, 1965; "of all branches of human endeavour," he wrote, "diplomacy is the most protean." p. 3.

DISCUSSION QUESTIONS

1. Is "pursuit of the national interest" a vain quest, since it is really only a justification of what a nation's leaders are trying to do anyway in their foreign as well as domestic politics? Or is it really the ultimate and honorable value in foreign affairs after all?

2. How can two nations both achieve their vital interests if each wants the same thing in the same place at the same time? Might Rosenau's new ideas help resolve this dilemma?

3. Do you feel that the "Westphalian" era of the nation-state as the central reality of world politics is coming to an end?

4. Is the "national interest" essentially the same as the "public interest" but at the international level? Are they both merely a collection of "special interests" or do they have a unique quality—the whole being greater than the sum of its parts?

5. How do the dangers and problems posed by multiethnic societies help one to understand the stresses and violence many countries are experiencing? Is Bosnia an exception or a harbinger of the future?

6. Couloumbis and Wolfe emphasize the distinction between the nation (nationalism) and the state (government). Why have so many Third World governments been obliged to *create* a sense of nationhood and patriotism among their people?

7. Many say that nationalism is a threat to peace. Yet patriotism is usually greatly admired. How do you account for this apparent contradiction?

8. From what the several writers say, do you expect an early end to the nation-state system? If so, what do you see as an alternative? If not, do you think that "wars and rumors of wars" will continue to plague the human race indefinitely?

9. What impresses you most about the U.S. foreign policy-making mechanism described by Olson? Does the election of Clinton invalidate his model, or is it "built into the system?" Should the United States change its Constitution?

13 THE NATION-STATE, SOVEREIGNTY, AND NATIONALISM

THEODORE A. COULOUMBIS AND JAMES H. WOLFE

Co-authors of one of the most popular IR texts, Professors Wolfe of the University of Southern Mississippi and Couloumbis of the University of Athens in Greece are both active in the international IR academic community.

It is certain that the greatest miracles in virtue have been produced by patriotism: This fine and lively feeling, which gives to the force of self-love all the beauty of virtue, lends it an energy which, without disfiguring it, makes it the most heroic of all passions.

Jean Jacques Rousseau

In politics individuals normally do not act alone, but in connection with social groupings. Historically, the political world has been divided in terms of "we" versus "they," the latter being referred to as barbarians, foreigners, outsiders, or, more often, simply the "enemy."[1] Most of us belong to a large number of groups that reflect our work, political views, religious beliefs, and lifestyles. But there is one group that pervades all others: the nation-state. National stereotypes are powerful images, and their use can induce emotional and physiological reactions, such as the primordial "fight-or-flight" syndrome. An investigation of nationalism, both as a pattern of learned group behavior and as a political institution called the nation-state, is fundamental to an understanding of global politics. . . .

Ethnically, nation-states can be either homogeneous or heterogeneous. Most nation-states fall into the latter category. Heterogeneous nation-states encompass a number of ethnic groups that possess either an actualized or an incipient sense of nationhood. Characteristic examples of such states are Brazil, Canada, Great Britain, India, Indonesia, Lebanon, Nigeria, Peru, the Soviet Union, Switzerland, and the United States. Expert studies have indicated that there is indeed a great disparity between ethnic and political boundaries throughout the world. Walker Connor, in an important article published in 1972, found that out of 132 nation-states included in his study only 12 (9.1 percent) could have been described as being ethnically homogeneous.[2] Twenty-five more nation-states (18.9 percent) contained an overwhelmingly large ethnic group accounting for over 90 percent of those states' population. In 25 additional nation-states Connor found that the majority ethnic group accounted for 75 to 89 percent of their population. However, he found that in 31 states (23.5 percent of his sample) the majority ethnic element represented only between 50 and 74 percent of their population. Finally, in 39 states (29.5 percent of his sample) the most populous ethnic group did not manage to reach even the 50 percent level of the total population. Connor found, further, that a multiplicity of ethnic groups were in-

Excerpted from *International Relations* (Footnotes have been renumbered)

deed living together (whether in peace or in conflict) within a large number of modern nation-states. In some cases, states included within their boundaries hundreds of diverse ethnic groups, while in 53 states out of 132 the population comprised five or more distinct and significant ethnic groups.

Since the study of international relations focuses primarily on the relations between nation-states, it is necessary to analyze in some depth the social and ethnic composition of these relatively persistent units of political action. Even if we were to assume that nation-states are transitory phenomena gradually being replaced by nonstate actors, contemporary reality is such that most individuals look to their respective nation-states for protection, identity, and direction. . . .

THE RISE OF MODERN FORMS OF NATIONALISM

Seventeenth-century England is usually presented as the first modern nation-state in which nationalism and its related concept of patriotism became coequal with the idea of individual liberties and popular participation in public affairs.[3] The American Revolution (1776) and the French Revolution (1789) are landmarks in the development of heterogeneous nationalism (in the United States) and homogeneous nationalism (in France). The United States was the result of the unification of former British colonies that had fought against their metropolis to obtain political rights, tolerance of religious diversity, and individual liberties. The Declaration of Independence proclaimed a brand of nationalism based on the perpetuation of a system of liberal ideas and a pluralist and secular way of life. Certain "truths" were held to be self-evident, "that all men are created equal, that they are endowed by their Creator with certain inalienable rights, that among these are life, liberty, and the pursuit of happiness." Given the subsequent ethnic and religious diversity of Americans, the coming of the patriotic slogan *e pluribus unum* is not surprising.

French nationalism was more vigorous, romantic, and ethnically homogeneous than the verbally restrained Anglo-Saxon versions, but equally expansionist. Maximilien Robespierre (1758–94), one of the masterminds of the French Revolution, exemplified the French spirit with these words of self-sacrifice: "I am French, I am one of thy [France's] representatives. . . . Oh sublime people! Accept the sacrifices of my whole being. Happy is the man who is born in your midst; happier is he who can die for your happiness."[4] Napoleon Bonaparte transformed patriotic and nationalist sentiments such as these into an expansionist ideology. The institution of mass conscription called for deep and tangible involvement of citizens in the life of the nation-state. Napoleon's "citizen armies" carried him to victory after victory throughout Europe and the Middle East. Eventually, he was defeated by the very forces of nationalism he had helped awaken.

A third variation of nationalism is associated with the North American frontier of the eighteenth and nineteenth centuries and with the political unification of Germany (1864–71). Some of the proponents of this brand of nationalism likened the state to a living organism passing through the phases of birth, adolescence, maturity, and finally old age. Often, they claimed a domi-

[3]Hans Kohn, *Nationalism: Its Meaning in History,* rev. ed. (Princeton, N.J.: Van Nostrand, 1965), p. 17.

[4]Quoted in *ibid.,* p. 27.

nant role for their nation because of its presumed superior biological heritage [5] Others saw the nation-state as inspired by a divine idea and charged it with a unique historical mission.[6] Whatever the nuances of interpretation, a central idea unites what came to be known as the organic school: the state must expand or die; the conquest of living space (*Lebensraum*) is therefore vital. Germany in the 1933–45 period, under the totalitarian rule of Adolf Hitler, epitomized an extreme and reckless version of organic nationalism. Benito Mussolini (1883–1945), the *Duce* of Fascist Italy, expressed the organic view of the nation-state most graphically:

> Fascism is an historical conception, in which man is what he is only insofar as he works with the spiritual process in which he finds himself, in the family or social group, in the nation and in the history in which all nations collaborate. . . . Outside history man is nothing. Consequently Fascism is opposed to all the individualistic abstractions of a materialistic nature like those of the eighteenth century; . . . Against individualism, the Fascist conception is for the State; and it is for the individual insofar as he coincides with the State, which is the conscience and universal will of man in his historical existence. . . . The nation as the State is an ethical reality which exists and lives insofar as it develops. To arrest its development is to kill it. . . . Thus [the State] can be likened to the human will which

knows no limits to its development and realizes itself in testing its own limitlessness.[7]

The organic and mystical conception of the nation-state was built substantially on the philosophical foundations provided by Georg Wilhelm Friedrich Hegel (1770–1831), the German philosopher.[8] Hegel viewed the history of human civilization as a succession of national cultures. For him, the national state was the highest form of political unit, the embodiment of political power. The *Volksgeist*, the genius and the spirit of a nation, imbued the nation with the qualities of a huge, collective, living, and growing organism. The parts of this organism (such as individuals, groups, regions, and political parties) were to be subordinated to the whole. A lack of such subordination would result in anarchy and chaos. True freedom could be found only within the strict disciplinary lines of the nation-state. The state (as a government) thus emerged as the embodiment of a nation's will and destiny. Finally, the state was seen as having no higher duty than to preserve and strengthen itself.

According to this conception, individuals are best understood as "means" of the state, their value to be measured in terms of their contribution to the survival of the state organism. History is seen as proceeding according to organic laws that are beyond the control of individuals. Thus, concluded Hegel, true political genius could be found among those persons who knew how to identify with higher principles such as the survival, growth, and prosperity of their nation-states.

[5] A widely read treatise on so-called biological nationalism is Joseph Arthur de Gobineau, *The Inequality of Human Races,* trans. Adrian Collins (New York: Putnam, 1915). Gobineau ascribed to the Nordic peoples of Europe a decisive role in history. See also Michael D. Biddiss, ed., *Gobineau: Selected Political Writings* (London: Cape, 1970).

[6] See Georg Wilhelm Friedrich Hegel, *Political Writings,* trans. T. M. Knox (Oxford: Clarendon Press, 1964), and *Philosophy of History,* 2nd ed., rev. and trans. J. Sibree (New York: Collier, 1905).

[7] Quoted in Michael Oakeshott, *The Social and Political Doctrines of Contemporary Europe* (London: Cambridge University Press, 1939), pp. 165–68.

[8] This brief discussion of Hegelian thought derives in large part from the interpretation of George H. Sabine, *A History of Political Theory,* 3rd ed. rev. (New York: Holt, Rinehart & Winston, 1961), pp. 620–67.

It was in the spirit of organic nationalism that a Japanese petty officer, having chosen to die as a kamikaze pilot, could write these words to his dearest ones on October 28, 1944:

> Dear Parents:
>
> Please congratulate me. I have been given a splendid opportunity to die. This is my last day. The destiny of our homeland hinges on the decisive battle in the seas to the south where I shall fall like a blossom from a radiant cherry tree.
>
> I shall be a shield for His Majestey and die cleanly along with my squadron leader and other friends. I wish that I could be born seven times, each time to smite the enemy.
>
> How I appreciate this chance to die like a man! I am grateful from the depths of my heart to the parents who have reared me with their constant prayers and tender love. And I am grateful as well to my squadron leader and superior officers who have looked after me as if I were their own son and given me such careful training.
>
> Thank you, my parents, for the twenty-three years during which you have cared for me and inspired me. I hope that my present deed will in some small way repay what you have done for me. Think well of me and know that your Isao died for our country. This is my last wish, and there is nothing else that I desire.[9]

NATIONAL SOVEREIGNTY

A major characteristic of the nation-state is sovereignty. In the literature of international relations, sovereignty has been defined as supreme state authority subject to no external limitations. The French philosopher Jean Bodin (1530–96) is associated with the earliest clear definition of this concept. Bodin was concerned with the fragmentation and sectionalism that had led to frequent civil wars and chaos in France. His main object, therefore, was to strengthen the position of the monarch as the source of order and unity throughout France. Writing in 1586, Bodin defined the state as "a lawful government of several households, and their uncommon posessions, with sovereign power."[10] Citizenship became the subjection of an individual to the sovereign.

Sovereignty was defined as "supreme power over citizens and subjects unrestrained by law."[11] Thus, the king was given the right to *make, interpret, and execute law unrestrained by all human authority.* He was subject only to the laws of God and to fundamental natural laws such as those requiring the keeping of agreements and respect for private property.

Thomas Hobbes (1588–1679), the famous British political philosopher, elaborated on the concept of sovereignty, subtly shifting its emphasis from the person of the king to the abstraction called government or state.[12] During the turbulent years from 1640 to 1651 in England, which were marked by factionalism and bloodshed, Hobbes wrote with the purpose of strengthening the authority of the king and of absolute government. Hobbes felt that if humans remained in a state of nature (i.e., prior to being orga-

[9]Quoted in Rikihei Inoguchi, Tadashi Nakajima, and Roger Pineau, *The Divine Wind: Japan's Kamikaze Force in World War II* (Annapolis, Md.: United States Naval Institute, 1958). Quoted with permission of the editors.

[10]Sabine, *History of Political Theory,* p. 402.

[11]*Ibid.,* p. 405.

[12]See *ibid.,* pp. 455–76.

nized politically), leading a "solitary, poor, nasty, brutish, and short" life, bloody and uncontrollable conflict would be inevitable. Thus, in order to limit conflict and to preserve the collectivity, it was necessary to concentrate all social authority in the sovereign. The sovereign, a "mortal God" on earth, was equated with the state, which in turn was equated with the government. For sovereignty to shift to its third and contemporary phase, ultimate authority had to be transferred symbolically from the government to the people inhabiting the nation-state.

The French Revolution (1789) epitomizes the symbolic transfer of sovereignty from the king and the government to the people. Since it has proved difficult, however, for the people as a totality to rule in other than small-town settings, sovereignty has remained substantially in the hands of governments who rule in the name of their people. In such states, there is an implicit understanding that the people will scrutinize governmental actions and as a last resort will revolt should their government betray its implicit contract with them.

A helpful distinction should be made between *internal* and *external* sovereignty. *Internal sovereignty* concerns the supreme and lawful authority of the state over its citizens. *External sovereignty,* on the other hand, refers to the recognition by all states of the independence, territorial integrity, and inviolability of each state as represented by its government. The Dutch jurist Hugo Grotius (1583–1645), reputed to be the father of international law, defined *sovereignty* as "that power whose acts are not subject to the control of another." For Grotius, sovereignty was manifested when a state, in dealing with its internal affairs, remained free from the control of all other states. Thus defined, sovereignty has become the cornerstone of the modern international system, where power and authority remain consciously divided and decentralized.

In the final analysis, sovereignty is the ability of a nation-state, through its government, to be master in its house, to have control over its domestic affairs, and in its foreign affairs to have the options of entering or leaving alliances, of going to war or remaining neutral so as to best defend its interests. In practice, however, we find that certain countries have been "more sovereign" than others: some of the great powers enjoy the substance as well as the letter of sovereignty, whereas smaller countries, especially if they are strategically located, are penetrated quite often by the great powers and can be called "sovereign" only in a relatively unauthentic sense of the word.

This discussion of sovereignty brings us to the provocative arguments of John Herz, a thoughtful scholar of international relations, regarding the rise of nation-states and nationalism.[13] Herz maintains that the nation-state is the kind of political unit that, given the nature of available weapons systems, is best designed to keep a territory "impermeable" and to protect its inhabitants. He feels that throughout history the unit which has afforded the best protection and security to human beings has also become the basic political unit. People, according to Herz, tend to recognize in the long run the authority, any authority, which possesses the power of *protection.*[14]

So, in Herz's view, technology and weaponry (both defensive and offensive) are directly responsible for the type of political organization of the international system. Herz maintains convincingly that the death of the feudal system and the walled city-state as units of political autonomy came only after the invention of gunpowder by the German monk Berthold Schwarz (who

[13]See John H. Herz, "The Rise and Demise of the Territorial State," in *International Politics and Foreign Policy,* ed. James N. Rosenau (New York: Free Press, 1961), pp. 80–86.
[14]*Ibid.,* p. 81.

was also the maker of the first powder gun, used at Ghent in 1314). Gunpowder, according to Herz, was responsible for the transition from feudalism to territorial states. This transition resulted in the neutralization of castles in the interior of territorial states and the construction of elaborate fortifications along the states' borders. Once nation-states, as fundamental units of protection, had been forged, the resulting ease of economic and social interaction within them and the relative isolation of their populations from neighboring states helped solidify the different cultures, institutions, and linguistic and religious patterns of behavior that we identify with nation-states today.

According to Herz, international law from the sixteenth century on increasingly legitimized national territoriality. Each nation-state (and especially its ruling elite) was jealous of its independence and wished to maintain its political and military "impermeability." Therefore, we find that early international law focused on the delimiting of national territorial jurisdiction in order to help legitimize and safeguard the independence and sovereignty—in short, the impermeability—of nation-states. War, recognized as well as sanitized by international law, remained the ultimate means of settling disputes among sovereign territorial states whenever peaceful methods of settlement failed to bear fruit. Once established, sovereign authorities sought to perfect and strengthen their administrative control over their subjects. For their part, the people sought and in many instances gained access to the political process, either through electoral participation or through the indirect method of representation. Political democracy, especially as manifested in the extension of the franchise, became the hallmark of the conversion of the state from a dynastic to a participatory entity.

In international as well as in domestic affairs, governments have tried to endow their actions with an aura of legitimacy. Consequently, by adhering to treaties and to customary international law, different ruling elites found that they could benefit mutually. Over time, the development of a nation-state system founded upon an acceptable balance of power gave impetus to the renaissance of the international law of which Grotius was a leading spokesman. The formalization of diplomatic procedure, the establishment of collective defense systems through alliances, and the acceptance of the principle of sovereignty and its corollary of nonintervention in the domestic affairs of other states—all of these were developments that strengthened the hand of nation-state builders. But in the case of ideologically or ethnically fragmented societies, coercive means such as subversion and war were often employed to overthrow legitimate governments. Without a firm basis in a stable political community, sovereignty often proved to be an illusion.

The modern doctrine of popular sovereignty has transferred the source of absolute power from the monarch to the "people." But this transfer of power does not mean necessarily that individual citizens become more able to check the transgressions of expanding administrative states. Indeed, the popularization of sovereignty gave rise to the ideology of mass nationalism, which equates the fate of the citizenry with that of its political leadership. Mass conscription for either military or industrial service, government control of the mass media for the purpose of propagandizing foreign-policy objectives, and the centralization of educational systems to ensure an uninterrupted process of political socialization combined to spread the fever of nationalism that produced the major conflicts of the twentieth century.

CHALLENGES TO NATIONALISM

The biological and mystical conception of nationalism possesses the formidable weapon of assuring its adherents that they alone have a world historical mission to fulfill and that, by implication, their actions in world politics must be just. A typical but certainly not exclusive representative of this point of view was Senator Albert J. Beveridge, who in 1900, while arguing for the annexation of the Philippine Islands by the United States, asserted that the American nation had been chosen to "lead in the regeneration of the world. This is the divine mission of America, and it holds for us all the profit, all the glory, all the happiness possible to man. We are trustees of the world's progress, guardians of its righteous peace."[15]

Nationalism grew steadily in the last 200 years to reinforce the identification of the individual with the state. The process of political socialization, carried out by the family, schools, and peer groups, taught the citizen the inescapable lesson that loyalty to the state fulfills not only an ideological but also a pragmatic purpose. For it is the state that, in return for obedience to its laws, provides innumerable concrete services. Thus, citizen allegiance and government efficiency in the performance of its functions are mutually supportive.

The rise of modern states that were based on a strong nationalistic sentiment was a logical historical response to the industrial revolution. But in the present-day postindustrial international setting, the idealized notion of the nation-state is coming under increasing attack from three quarters: the advance of military technology, the rise of supranational organizations, and the growing role of transnational ideological,

religious, functional, and political movements. In the 1950s, many analysts pointed out the increasing military vulnerability of the state. Principal among these was John Herz, who wrote of the "demise" of the state, arguing that it was no longer capable of protecting its citizens in the event of a three-dimensional modern war involving nuclear, psychological, and economic weapons. Herz foresaw the transformation of the international system into a condition dominated by conflicting regional alliances. Some years later, seeing the impact of decolonization, Herz gradually abandoned his notion of the demise of the state.[16] Yet, as long as the economic and military viability of many of the new states remains in question, the image of a bipolar or tripolar international system retains some validity. In a future time, George Orwell's dreary *1984* scenario may indeed materialize, and our earth may be dominated by the three superpowers of Oceania, Eurasia, and Eastasia.[17]

Assuming that the hallmark of national sovereignty is the rigorous application of the doctrine of nonintervention in the affairs of one state by another, the development of supranational organizations poses the second problem for the future of presumably impermeable nation-states. Among the democracies of the West, notably those of Europe, supranational collaboration to achieve shared goals in the fields of economic development, health, and education is proceeding swiftly. Member states of supranational organizations with policy-making and policy-implementing powers, such as the European Community and the Nordic

[15]U.S. Congress, Senate, Senator Albert J. Beveridge, 56th Cong., January 9, 1900, *Congressional Record*, 33:711.

[16]See Herz, "Rise and Demise of the Territorial State," and "The Territorial State Revisited: Reflections on the Future of the Nation-State," in *International Politics and Foreign Policy*, ed. James N. Rosenau, 2nd ed., rev. (New York: Free Press, 1969), pp. 80–89.
[17]George Orwell, *1984* (New York: A. M. Heath, 1949).

Council, employ the argument (or perhaps the rationalization) that their sovereignty remains unaffected because they have delegated governmental authority to the international civil servants who staff the executive bodies of these organizations. In a legal sense this argument merits respect, but the politics of interdependence have eroded the absolutist quality of the concept of sovereignty and are likely to create rivals for the nation-state as the sole focus of political loyalty.

Transnational ideological/political movements of the twentieth century, such as fascism and communism, present a third formidable challenge to nationalism. The "New Order" or the German National Socialists led by Adolf Hitler (1889–1945) castigated the liberal nineteenth-century version of the nation-state and called for the formation of a hierarchical European system dominated by what Hitler considered a biologically select race committed to an ideology of purity and power. In accordance with this objective, the Elite Guard (SS) of the Nazi movement organized non-German units throughout occupied Europe and sought to use them as a basis for a new Praetorian state whose military despotism would sound the death knell of the conventional European national communities.[18] The outcome of the Nazi assault on the traditional European nation-states was a cataclysmic war from which humankind has yet to recover materially, and from which it may never completely recover spiritually.

Marxism—from a very different angle—also sought to challenge the nation-state and nationalism. In the *Communist Manifesto* (1848) Karl Marx and Friedrich Engels rejected nationalism, viewing it as an instrument of the bourgeois class to divide worker across national frontiers. Although

[18]See George Stein, *The Waffen SS: Hitler's Elite Guard at War, 1939–1945* (Ithaca, N.Y.: Cornell University Press, 1966).

Joseph Stalin (1879–1953) modified this ideological doctrine by making Soviet policy in 1928 a policy of "socialism in one country" and also by appealing to the historic force of Russian nationalism during the great war with Germany, orthodox Marxists continue to this day to treat the nation-state as a "category of history" that is designed to serve the interests of capitalism and that is doomed to disappearance once working classes everywhere rise to power.

On the tactical level, however, revolutionary communist movements have readily espoused the cause of nationalism and have sought to align themselves with anticolonial forces in the Third World. For instance, the support of a coalition of nationalist forces such as the Popular Movement for the Liberation of Angola (MPLA) had been an integral part of Soviet policy. Demands for political self-determination in Eastern Europe, on the other hand, tend to receive a markedly different response. Ruling Eastern European Communist parties subscribe, rather, to the doctrine of "proletarian solidarity" and accept an obligation to combat presumed counterrevolutionary tendencies within their bloc. Under the leadership of the Soviet Union, the members of the Warsaw Pact (with the exception of Romania) occupied Czechoslovakia in 1968 in order to limit revisionist Czech liberalism and by extension Czech nationalism.

The Polish events of 1980–81 reflected yet another powerful example of the gradual fusion between nationalism and communism. The attempt of Polish workers, peasants, and students (supported by the powerful Roman Catholic Church of Poland) was obviously aimed toward the objective of attaining communism with a "Polish face."

In 1976, on the occasion of the Twenty-Fifth Congress of the Communist Party of the Soviet Union (CPSU) and at a subsequent meeting of European Communist leaders in East Berlin, the hard line of "proletarian solidarity" was softened somewhat, much to the satisfaction of the leaders of Communist parties in France, Italy, and Spain, who assert that their parties must formulate policies reflecting the diversity of their national settings rather than blanket guidance from Moscow. Moreover, national communism is still in evidence in Eastern Europe: Hungarian history books continue to refer to Hungary's border with Romania as a historical injustice, and Romanian scholars continue to remind their readers of some Romanian provinces that were lost to the Soviet Union in 1945. When confronted with nationalist fervor in the form of unresolved frontier disputes, the plea of "proletarian solidarity" begins to weaken in appeal.

Despite the threat of multidimensional warfare, the rise of supranational organizations, the challenge of expansionist fascism, and the partial success of communism as a transnational political movement, nationalism remains a vibrant force in world affairs and a solid point of entry into the web of motives surrounding foreign-policy decision making. . . .

14 INDIA AFTER NONALIGNMENT

Ramesh Thakur is Professor of International Relations and Director of Asian Studies at the University of Otago in New Zealand.

India has cut a sorry figure in recent times. It is ailing internally, wracked by political turmoil, social ferment, and economic stagnation. By the end of 1989, after five years in power, the Rajiv Gandhi government had achieved the dubious distinction of being on bad terms with all its neighbors. The successor minority National Front government (1989–90), led by V. P. Singh, managed to destroy Indian society more effectively than any enemy could have dared to hope, by pitting Indian against Indian. And the following transitory government of Chandra Shekhar floundered and flip-flopped embarrassingly in trying to respond to the Persian Gulf crisis. In the process it succeeded in alienating both Baghdad and Washington without winning any friends.

Not many outsiders would shed tears at the sight of a friendless and forlorn India. Indians might receive more sympathy if, instead of forever blaming others, they accepted responsibility for the consequences of their own actions in both domestic and foreign policy. A good beginning would be to recognize that the new revolutionary international times present India with a stark choice. It can persist with an inward-looking policy that marginalizes the country and slides it inexorably into increasing international irrelevance. Or it can take a good hard look at itself and at other former developing countries that have achieved success essentially by dint of their own efforts, and then chart a radically new passage to a brighter India.

It is for India to choose between the comforting familiarity of the old order with its corollary of economic incoherence and international insignificance, or the challenge of exploiting the opportunities opening up in the new world order. The latter choice would entail abandoning the bunker mentality induced by forty years of the Cold War.[1]

[1]Prem Shankar Jha, "Risk of Swimming against the Tide," *Hindu Weekly*, Feb. 9, 1991, p. 9.

II

A growing and vibrant economy for India requires a radical reorientation of policy away from controls imposed by a heavily interventionist state. Four decades of state-guided development have given India slow growth, rising unemployment, and growing dependence on imported capital goods and technology. In international economic exchanges India's policy failures are reflected in a falling share of world exports, a depreciating currency, and an inability to export sophisticated manufactures.

The catalyst for a new economic philosophy for India must be the realization that planned economic development has proven unable to improve its citizens' living standards and similarly unable to maintain global competition with the Western system of market economics. India's new economic order will have to rest on three planks: deregulation, liberalization and reduction in government expenditures in defense spending, salaries, and subsidies. The combination of democratic populism and bureaucratic elitism has given India the worst of both worlds and anchored it firmly to a Third World status. To lift itself out of the Third World and into the ranks of the First, India needs to establish international investor credibility by unleashing market forces and behaving in a fiscally responsible manner at home.

There was some justification for the philosophy of economic development adopted by India at independence. Keynesian interventionism had triumphed against the adversities of the Great Depression, and the Marshall Plan had reinforced faith in the visible hand of government. India's economy grew three times as fast in the 1950s and 1960s as during the British Raj, and faster than the rate of British growth during its comparable stage of development in the eighteenth and nineteenth centuries. The

public sector was instrumental in transforming an exploited plantation economy into a vibrant and diversified industrial power in remarkably short time.

More recent results, however, include economic stagnation, structural rigidity, and backwardness, desperate infusions of international capital to stave off defaults and the persistence of poverty and inequality. Although market forces were allowed to play a greater role in India in the 1980s, the country still has a substantially regulated economy. By 1991, years of budgetary indiscipline by successive governments had brought India's economy to the brink. Before the International Monetary Fund (IMF) came to the rescue with an emergency transfusion of capital, foreign exchange reserves had fallen in January 1991 to a mere two weeks' worth of imports. Persistent current account deficits saw foreign debt climb to more than $70 billion, with a third of export earnings going to debt servicing. For the 1991–92 fiscal year the budget deficit is projected to equal almost 8.5 percent of gross domestic product.[2]

The government of P. V. Narasimha Rao, which came to power after the assassination of Rajiv Gandhi during elections in May 1991, announced liberalization measures and a new industrial policy that by Indian standards were quite radical. With an eye to standard-bearers of the socialist tradition within the Congress Party, the prime minister denied that he was jettisoning the public sector entirely, that the policy represented a departure from Nehruvian socialism, or that it was externally dictated. The reforms, however, are neither as rapid nor as extensive as the situation requires.

In launching the new economic pol-

[2]Figures from *The Economist*, March 9, 1991, p. 20. The July 1991 budget set a target of reducing the fiscal deficit to 6.5 percent of GDP.

icy the Rao government emphasized the need to shed any inferiority complex and squeamishness in seeking inflows of foreign capital for investment. The balance-of-payments crisis of 1991, coupled with the dramatic worldwide trend toward market reforms, convinced many Indians that their country had little alternative to modernizing its industrial and export structure and entering the world economy. At a time when other countries were actively pursuing the infusion of new technology, India's tightly regulated regime perpetuated a noncompetitive environment. Like their former Soviet colleagues, Indian planners were mesmerized by investment targets rather than efficiencies. The collapse of the centrally planned economies of eastern Europe and the Soviet Union—which took one-fourth of India's exports—has made the international economic environment even frostier for India.

It is time therefore to jettison socialist slogans, to dethrone the state from the commanding heights of the economy, to let loose the price mechanism among the sheltered world of Indian businesses and to subject the Indian economy to the competitive pressures of market forces at home and abroad. The state could provide the indispensable legal context for a stable market, and the private sector could provide the growth and jobs.

If the stifling regulatory regime could be lifted and the dead hand of the state removed, India could then exploit its superb base for rapid and substantial industrial expansion. The country has an enormous pool of sophisticated scientists and technicians and an untapped reservoir of entrepreneurial talent. The policies of self-reliance followed by Jawaharlal Nehru and his successors have provided India with the capacity to grow quickly. The future could yet be vibrant and dynamic, if free market policies are given a chance. If they are, then outsiders would do well to remember that India is bigger than the established (Taiwan, Hong Kong, South Korea, and Singapore) and emerging (Malaysia, Thailand, and Indonesia) dragons of northeast and southeast Asia combined. . . .

III

If the Kashmir dispute could be resolved, India's regional role would acquire enhanced credibility. India has a national outlook in economic terms, but it has an international outlook in political terms. It has long sought a global leadership role; nonalignment was a foreign policy strategy to this end. But India lacks a coherent strategy for an integrated regional role.

India's neighbors have tended to view it as overarmed, overweening, and hegemonical. Anxious to project itself on the world stage, India has appeared irritated at regional obstacles in its path to the status of a world power. In a remarkable tribute to a fatally flawed foreign policy, India finds itself without a network of useful friendships in its own region. Commentators contrast India's supercilious attitude to regional neighbors with Indonesia's finesse in handling smaller neighbors in southeast Asia. Similarly, India's potential lies first and foremost in its neighborhood, but instead of realizing this potential India has frightened all its neighbors.

Indian foreign policy has been similarly myopic in neglecting friendships in the Middle East. Efforts to counter Pakistan's influence among the Islamic countries of the Arab world have failed to bear fruit— India's only real friend in the Middle East has been Iraq. Similarly the one genuine friendship with a southeast Asian country, namely Vietnam, was no less of a diplomatic liability in the 1980s.

Of greater bilateral, regional, and international import is the India-China relationship. If in India's relations with Pakistan there is much that unites them, India and China have little in common except a long and disputed border. On the Kashmir dispute the Indian case is strong, and the Pakistani case stronger still. On the Sino-Indian border dispute, the Indian case may be weak, but the Chinese case is still weaker. Since the 1962 war, three obstacles have inhibited normalization of China-India relations: the Soviet factor, Tibet, and the border dispute.

With the collapse of communism and the dissolution of the Soviet Union, the Soviet factor has been transformed from an impediment into a spur to improving Sino-Indian relations. The end of the Cold War and the simultaneous improvement of Moscow's relations with Beijing and Washington dissipates the geostrategic community of interest between India and Russia and threatens to leave India internationally isolated. Delhi's own hesitant probes toward a rapprochement with Beijing used to arouse suspicion and unease in Moscow; they now produce smiles of encouragement. China in turn has become more receptive to Indian overtures, for the closeness of the Russian relationship is no longer viewed as a threat to Chinese security interests. . . .

China's negotiating position is based on the premise that there is a genuine territorial dispute arising out of conflicting interpretations of the authenticity of British Indian claims in the era of imperialism. The benefits to India of a broad compromise are obvious. A settled border with China would facilitate the stabilization of the troubled northeastern region in India's domestic politics and reduce opportunities for mischief in its external relations with Bhutan and Nepal. It would also ease the task of securing Pakistani agreement to convert the line of control in Kashmir into an international border, thereby resolving India's most serious foreign policy problem. . . .

IV

Since the Second World War the most successful bilateral relationships for India and the Soviet Union had been with each other.[3] Relations between Moscow and Delhi had been dynamic, stable, and resilient. The dissolution of the Soviet Union, however, raises important questions.

The Soviet breakup destroyed India's most important source of defense supplies, took away a major export market, left India more vulnerable to hostile resolutions at the United Nations, introduced fresh instabilities in its northern neighborhood, and brought new competitors for foreign aid. The net result is to make links with the West more attractive to India. For example, a high-level U.S. military delegation held talks with Indian counterparts in Delhi in January 1992 and agreed to programs of reciprocal training and participation in regional conferences and seminars.

Efforts will nonetheless continue to preserve friendly ties with the Commonwealth of Independent States. Indian Foreign Minister Madhav Singh Solanki visited Russia last November. India and Russia finalized a new friendship treaty on January 15, 1992, and signed memoranda of under-

[3]See Ramesh Thakur and Carlyle A. Thayer, *Soviet Relations with India and Vietnam*, Delhi, London, and New York: Oxford University Press, Macmillan and St. Martin's Press, 1992.

standing on trade and supplies of defense and power generation equipment. President Boris Yeltsin has agreed to visit India, and Delhi agreed to grant 32 billion rupees of credit to Russia to pay for Indian goods as well as 150 million rupees in humanitarian assistance. India has also moved aggressively to establish political ties (the twelve Commonwealth states were granted formal recognition by India on December 16, 1991), military contracts (Ukrainian enterprises are fulfilling long-term agreements between Delhi and Moscow), and economic agreements (a joint venture for building personal computers in Uzbekistan) with the newly independent republics. Last November the Indian deputy commerce minister said that rupee settlements in India's trade with the Commonwealth states would terminate in 1994–95. After that date India intends to build its economic relations with the sovereign republics on principles of a market economy.

The intimacy of the Indo-Soviet relationship has historically been based on conjunctions of military, economic, and political interests. Moscow showed itself receptive to India's desire for self-reliance. Licensed production enabled India to develop its own arms industry to the point of being about two-thirds self-sufficient.

Yet the Indo-Soviet military relationship was not cost-free for either country. The ready availability of Soviet weaponry actually inhibited development of an indigenous arms industry; successive governments took the easy Soviet option instead of the cost-ineffective path to arms autarky. The sale of arms to India under bilateral repayment arrangements also exacted a significant opportunity cost on the Soviet Union in the form of hard-currency earnings foregone. Arms transfers lead to dependencies; they also create networks of commitments and interests that tie the prestige and credibility of the donor to the fate of client

regimes. Recipients can initiate wars without advance clearance from superpower patrons. For the latter to then withhold support is to risk losing years of investment in the client regime and losing influence globally as a reliable patron.

During the 1991 Gulf War Moscow failed to come to the assistance of a Third World client; it was prepared to stand on the sidelines and watch the Iraqi military machine be destroyed. One of the major attractions of receiving weapons from the Soviet Union had been its reliability as a defense supplier, particularly when the war had broken out. National security policymakers in Delhi will need to assess the implications of Soviet behavior in the Gulf War for the other major recipients of Soviet weapons and adjust patterns of sourcing defense supplies accordingly.

The Indo-Soviet economic relationship, too, has been transformed. From an Indian perspective the Soviet economic link opened up direct trade contacts with the USSR, secured goods and industrial raw materials against rupee payments, enabled imports to be used as a means of increasing the range of exports, stabilized prices of traditional exports, facilitated the expansion of nontraditional exports and permitted the purchase of military equipment without the payment of hard currency and against trade surpluses. Externally it helped achieve the goals of export diversification in both goods and markets while conserving scarce foreign exchange reserves. . . .

Both India and Russia are struggling to achieve economic success by means of a mixed but market-oriented liberalizing economy functioning within a multiethnic, multiparty competitive federal democracy. And because the new Russian government has established good working relations with both China and the United States, India too can seek to improve bilateral relations with those countries without fear of potentially damaging consequences for its relationship with the former Soviet State.

The United States, Europe, and Japan are now better placed than Russia to assist India. In the past a strategic friendship with the Soviet Union that did not incur a strate-gic enmity with the United States gave India the best of both worlds. Now Delhi must deal with the breakup of the Soviet Union and the resulting emergence of an essentially new world order.

V

Indians are unclear about what the "new world order" means in practice. Some worry that it could even be a cloak for a more intolerable Pax Americana: the eagle spreading its wings. Indians were impressed that the Gulf War was prosecuted through the United Nations, but they are not entirely confident that this will always be the model for U.S. military intervention abroad. Before the Gulf War the new world order was to have encompassed a series of interlocking global partnerships: between America, on the one hand, and a united Germany-led Europe and Japan, on the other. The lack-luster performance of Germany and Japan in the gulf crisis, however, raised questions about their role.

India could be even more worried about the prospect of the United States and Russia colluding to impose a joint hegemonism upon the rest of the world. The Gulf War showed that when Washington and Moscow find common ground, New Delhi must either go along or risk being isolated. That war suggested two policy lessons for India: that Russian support for friends and allies can no longer be taken for granted, and that America can mobilize impressive diplomatic resources as well as being an unchallengeable economic and military power. Prudence suggests therefore that countries with strong ties to Russia would be well-advised to undertake discreet bridge-building with the United States.

Discretion has not always been a strong suit of those in charge of Indian for-eign policy. The sacrosanct status of non-alignment, with an attendant dose of anti-Americanism, was apparent during the Gulf War. The Shekhar government initially permitted refueling the U.S. aircraft in Bombay on their way to the gulf, provoking a storm of protest about violating India's non-aligned credentials, and the permission was rescinded. After the 1991 general election the Rao government took note of India's own economic woes, of even worse Soviet economic ills, the dissolution of the Soviet grip on eastern Europe, the Soviet Union's breakup, and America's enhanced global importance—and concluded that a major improvement in Indo-American relations was required.

The end of the Cold War means an end to rival client regimes by the two super-powers in various parts of the world. This should induce greater caution in both India and Pakistan, and encourage bilateral con-flict management. It also puts both coun-tries under greater international scrutiny in regard to their nuclear programs. Simul-taneously, both countries will become com-petitors in the search for infusions of for-eign capital and technology. The emergence of a number of impoverished Common-wealth and east European states has meant that there are more and more countries competing for a finite pool of foreign aid. The enhanced leverage of aid donors in the post-Cold War era should produce reduc-tions in Indian and Pakistani defense bud-gets, greater attention to market-driven economic programs, and hopefully even wider appreciation of complementary interests.

The late 1980s had already witnessed an improvement of the political climate between India and the United States. The reinterpretation of India's role in south Asia was helped by U.S. perceptions of Rajiv Gandhi as being more liberal in his economic policy, and by a reassessment of India as an independent power that could be a force for stability in a troubled region. Thus the United States openly approved India's role in Sri Lanka and the Maldives, and Washington's approval was noted with satisfaction in Delhi. A Defense Department official was quoted as saying that the United States had advised Pakistan on the inadvisability of supporting Kashmiri militants.[4] Indeed U.S. and Soviet interests in Kashmir merged on two crucial points in the 1990 crisis: Both agreed on the need to preserve the peace and on the wisdom of a bilateral settlement of problems between India and Pakistan.

The end of the Cold War will have another odd impact on the foundations of Indo-U.S. relations. Analysts as well as officials underestimated the extent to which there was a doctrinal underpinning to the cool relations between Delhi and Washington. For more than four decades, a policy of containment helped to sustain an unprecedented interventionalist approach to world affairs by the United States. The end of the Cold War may not necessarily see America return to its traditional isolationism, but containment will no longer provide the ideo-

logical underpinning for its global policy. Active involvement in international relations will need to be pursued on some other basis. On the other side, nonalignment in India's foreign policy was the doctrinal antidote to the U.S. policy of containment. The end of the Cold War means that nonalignment joins containment in fading into obsolescence.

Thus, whatever new principle underpins Indian foreign policy, the prospect of America and India being at odds over doctrine are considerably diminished. If India turns toward regionalism, the other major international trend in recent times, it would also bring Indian foreign policy into harmony with the new principles of U.S. foreign policy. . . .

Nonalignment, like the policy of containment, is in a state of terminal fatigue and irrelevance. The alternative, however, does not force India into the role of supplicant. The Gulf War demonstrated America's dominance in international affairs, but it also showed the limits to the exercise of unilateral power by America. Political and economic realities have brought about strategic retrenchments all around the world, a call for greater burden-sharing and the promotion of regional management of regional conflicts. What Washington seeks is not global hegemony but global and regional stability resting on interlocking balances of power. In a new world order there could be a reciprocal underpinning of a global order centered on America and a south Asian balance based on India.

VI

In a memorable speech ushering in India's independence, Jawaharlal Nehru said: "A moment comes, which comes but rarely in

history, when we step out from the old to the new, when an age ends."[5] The age of the

[5]Jawaharlal Nehru, *India's Foreign Policy: Selected Speeches*, New Delhi: Government of India, Publications Division, 1961, p. 13.

[4]*The New York Times*, June 17, 1990.

Cold War has ended. Will India remain a prisoner of the past? Or will the times bring forth a leader bold and visionary enough to break the ideological straitjacket insulating Indian domestic and foreign policy from the freshness and vitality flowing across Europe?

Perhaps only a sense of shock can infuse India with the necessary urgency to change to a radically more productive domestic policy and a dramatically more cooperative policy in its bilateral, regional, and international relations. The socialist legacies of the Nehru era are anachronistic impediments to India's realizing its full potential as a major and dynamic economic power. The conflict with Pakistan is an unnecessary nuisance, that with China a major handicap. Friendship with Russia is a wasting asset if not backed by corrective economic and diplomatic surgery. Claims to leadership of the Third World and the nonaligned movement substituted the mesmerism of numbers at the United Nations for the real world of political, military, and economic clout. It was a status bereft of a useful network of operational relationships.

Nothing better illustrated the bankruptcy of Indian foreign policy than its confused responses to the gulf crisis. It could hardly have been in the country's interest to find itself bracketed with Cuba and Yemen in the Security Council. In allowing sympathy for Saddam Hussein and antipathy toward America to guide policy, Delhi adopted a course of action that was blind and self-defeating. Had Iraq succeeded, the consequences for India and other Third World countries would have been far more calamitous than for America and the industrialized world. Instead of helping to shape the new world order, India risked being shunned as an outcast.

India has generally seen itself as a world power in the making, and conducted its regional and international relations on this basis. The result has been insignificance abroad, suspicion in the region, and turbulence at home. It would be better advised to reverse the process. Stability and prosperity at home and in the region will enhance its international status and give credibility to its claims to global leadership.

India needs American capital and technology; the United States could exploit the vast Indian market potential with a consumer ethic and infrastructure well poised to take off at speed. Given its size and resources an India firmly integrated into the world financial markets would be a major boost to international capitalism. And for too long have India and America allowed transient irritants to undermine an underlying harmony of interests between the two pluralist and federal democracies. The world's most powerful and most populous democracies should be allies, not antagonists.

15 CAN DEMOCRACY TAKE ROOT WHERE TSARS AND SOVIETS RULED?

MARSHALL I. GOLDMAN

Marshall I. Goldman ('80) is professor of Soviet economics at Wellesley College, associate director of the Russian Research Center at Harvard and author of *What Went Wrong With Perestroika*.

Whatever the shortcomings of Mikhail Gorbachev's economic reforms, there is general agreement that his political reforms were remarkably successful. The failure of economic reform is what gave rise to the coup, but the success of the Gorbachev political reforms was reflected by the fact that the people in Moscow and in several other cities refused to obey the illegally issued orders of the would-be usurpers. This was a historic, if not unique, event in Russian history.

Standing in their midst during those heady moments, I found it impossible not to be moved. As they gathered by the hundreds of thousands, there was no doubt that the Muscovites I was watching were fully aware of the first-time nature of their efforts. Not only did they stand up to the tanks and soldiers, but they did it without finding it necessary to take undemocratic measures to suppress the insurrection. All too often, that is what the Russian people have done in the past. This time, however, under the impetus of the recent reforms, a growing number of Soviets lost their historic sense of fear and intimidation by the state. This awareness, in itself, sparked a new feeling of camaraderie, pride, and even a hope for the future in that momentous August week.

To the outsider watching and celebrating these new achievements and shouting and marching along with the crowd, it was a time of euphoria, something that a hardened Kremlinologist like me never expected to see. Added to the euphoria was the sense that by refusing to allow the plotters to shove Gorbachev and Boris Yeltsin out of their posts without resort to the necessary legal procedures, the people in the streets had come to appreciate some of the subtle niceties of democracy. For decades, Western observers despaired of the fact that the Soviet people really did not understand what democracy involved. All too often, it seemed, democracy to a Russian meant only jazz, rock, sunglasses, fancy automobiles, and a VCR. However, by risking their lives to defend Yeltsin and his victory in a fair and square popular election, it was clear that for many Muscovites and many others throughout the country, democracy had come to mean more than materialism.

Unfortunately, the euphoria soon evap-

Excerpted by permission from *Cosmos. A Journal of Emerging Issues.* Vol. 2, No. 1, pp. 38–41. © Cosmos Club, Washington, D.C., 1992.

orated, especially when, instead of improving, economic conditions deteriorated even more, and the political after-effect wrought chaos and anarchy. . . . Against such a background, what are the chances that democracy may yet take hold in what was once the Soviet Union, the place now called the Commonwealth of Independent States (CIS)?

What made the August coup unique is, unfortunately, what diminishes the prospects for democracy; CIS, in all its parts, has had no sustained exposure or success with democracy. Except for the few months when the Provisional Government of Alexander Kerensky attempted to administer the country, the Soviet people have only known tsars or general secretaries. There were for a brief interval before World War I, to be sure, provincial governmental bodies called *zemstvos,* and they were given more and more responsibility for the administration of local affairs. But they never fully opened themselves to the processes of democracy associated with secret-ballot elections, universal suffrage, controls over taxation and expenditures, and safeguards against abuses of political executive power.

Whatever potential the *zemstvos* might have had, the Bolshevik revolution put an abrupt end to all such experimentation. For almost seventy years since, the Soviet people endured a process euphemistically called "democratic centralism"; it might more suitably have been called "the original political sin." In theory, it was argued that the Bolshevik revolution and the overturn of the "bourgeois" Provisional Government was the population's way of saying it had endured enough of noncommunist governments. Their revolution was, the communists insisted, a mandate on behalf of communism and the Bolshevik leadership. Henceforth, they proclaimed, there would be no further need for elections; the "original" leaders were, in effect, authorized permanently to select their successors and subordinates.

To those of us brought up in the tradition of Western democracy, with an insistence on frequent and recurring elections to monitor changes in the mood of the electorate, this is hard to understand. But in the context of Russia's historical experience, it was not incongruent. The historian Edward Keenan, for example, argued in his *Russian Political Culture* that Russia's geophysical location all but necessitates a more collective form of government; such a northern climate requires a collective effort. Thus individual farmsteading of the sort that typifies our country would be too dangerous in Russia, according to Keenan. Moreover, given the crossroads nature of the territory, Russia has been the battlefield for one series after another of invading and marauding armies. This helps to explain the people's willingness—even eagerness—in the past, for strong leaders who could assure them of both order and bread, and what seems to be their historic preference for stability rather than turnover in leadership and change. . . .

Given the predominance of totalitarian regimes and what seems to be public acquiescence or at least the absence of public reaction to such abuse of governments, it is hard to avoid the conclusion that the people of CIS have generally been comfortable with the government they have had. Until recently at least, there were few protests and relatively few protesters. In other words, they got the government they deserved. That may be unfair to those few dissidents who did speak out in the Khrushchev and Brezhnev eras (there were almost none who survived the Stalinist regime), but the very limited nature of their protests serves to make the point.

It may well be that given the cultural geography of CIS, it was too much to expect that its people could ever create a viable democracy. Even if the CIS were more favorably situated, it would still need institutional changes in order to set in motion the kinds of pressure underlying the evolution of democracy in other societies.

Admittedly, there is no simple transformation that would insure the formation of a viable democracy overnight. To an economist, however, it seems essential that before CIS or its constituent parts can be transformed into an enduring democracy, a middle class must be created. It is the middle class, in fact, that has been a bulwark against the onset of communism in the West. That is not to say the existence of a middle class is a foolproof guarantee against totalitarianism, but it certainly helps. Indeed, the collapse of the middle class, or the threat to its existence in the past, has often been associated with the onset of inflation and depression. That, in turn, is a fairly sure indicator that an antidemocratic regime is not far off. That was the case of Germany in the late 1920s.

There has been considerable debate about why communism only made inroads in nonindustrial countries like Russia, China, Cuba, and Vietnam. Marx, after all, had envisaged that it would come instead to countries that had already industrialized. The proletariat, he assumed, would be most attracted to communism, and not the peasants. What Marx neglected, however, was that an industrialized country would have not only a substantial proletariat, but also a substantial middle class—a bourgeoisie, as he liked to describe it. Unfortunately for Marx, the bourgeoisie were usually very much opposed to communism. Moreover, the proletariat was often as not more interested in ascending into the ranks of the bourgeoisie than it was in revolution. By contrast, in developing countries like nineteenth-century Russia, there was not only a small proletariat, but a small middle class, and thus not much of a force for resistance to revolution.

If it is to act as an effective barrier against the onset of communism, however, the middle class must represent something more than just a group with greater wealth and income than that available to the proletariat. The income involved must not derive from the state sector. That implies the existence of private ownership and property, not only of consumer goods, but also of services and means of production. In addition, the right to hire and fire must reside with the private owners of property and not with the state. In other words, there must be pluralism of ownership. Of course, if there is undue concentration of property in the hands of a single owner or family or consortium, the middle class may well lose its independence; it makes little difference, after all, if ownership is held by the state or a small group of private individuals. The trick is that there should be many alternative decision-makers in the society.

The existence of alternative decision-makers makes it possible for critics to criticize without immediate fear of retaliation, or job or income loss in case the state decides to take revenge. No one is ever perfectly immune from some pressure from the state. As long as there are taxes and government contracts, immunity will be impossible. But in most capitalist countries, the majority of the middle class does not live in fear that outspoken criticism of the state will jeopardize their jobs or their livelihood. Only in that way is there likely to be open debate and resistance to economic, political, and social upheaval and the depreciation of democratic rights that such anarchy brings.

Unfortunately, creating the conditions for an independent middle class in today's CIS of the sort just described will not be easy, but there are some promising signs. For example, private property ownership is now allowed by law. From only 900 private and family farms in the Russian Republic as of July 1, 1990, the number grew to about 34,700 a year and a half later, on November 1, 1991. There was also a rapid growth of corporate and private businesses. As of October 1991, approximately 7.5 million people worked in nonstate or cooperative and private firms, and about 12 million people worked in factories that were leased from state enterprises, according to an authoritative Soviet economic source. Despite relatively rapid growth and promises of more to come as the republics begin to move towards privatization, the private and cooperative sectors remain a small fraction of the total economy, not much more than 5 percent. This means that the independent middle class also remains a small percentage of the overall population.

Even more troubling is the fact that the bulk of the new entrepreneurial class is regarded as unsavory by the population as a whole. This is a consequence of the fact that most independent economic activity operates on the fringes of legality or what passed as legality in the old Soviet Union. It is partly because the laws are not precisely spelled out and because those few nonstate entrepreneurs tend to make large profits, which, in turn, attract the Soviet "mafia." These indigenous groups of racketeers control or harass almost all private and cooperative restaurants in the major cities, as well as nonstate trucking in Moscow. The "mafia" also has a major influence on retailing and is rumored to play an important role in the 600 or so commodity and stock exchanges that have sprung up across Russia. Admittedly, many American entrepreneurs have equally shady origins, be they slave traders, robber barons, or stock manipulators, but their Russian counterparts seem even more disreputable, and hardly a group to inspire confidence from the general public.

CHECKS AND BALANCES

Nor is the absence of a middle class the only missing prerequisite for democracy. There seems to be too little understanding of the critical underpinnings needed for democracy. Certainly, under Gorbachev, totalitarian controls largely disappeared. In their place, many of the traditional institutional characteristics associated with democracy were introduced. For example, as part of *glasnost,* Gorbachev encouraged freedom of the press and the flourishing of open discussion in the Soviet Union, including television, that often takes a bolder form than is seen even in the United States. Similarly, as part of what Gorbachev called democratization, there were secret-ballot elections that had more than one candidate.

As impressive as such innovations have been, the are so far only superficial improvements. Unfortunately, the roots of democracy are still very thin. For example, neither Gorbachev nor Yeltsin understands or did anything to introduce the concept of checks and balances. There has been very little discussion about the need to restrict the power prerogatives of the executive branch. There is recognition that there should be a legislative branch and that secret elections should be used to select its members. Yeltsin has championed that form of behavior. But rarely has the Supreme Soviet or its counterparts been used to rein in or countermand the activities of the leaders. Normally, the Supreme Soviets are forums for debate but little action. One of the few instances where an executive decree was countermanded was in the fall of 1991, when Boris Yeltsin declared a state of emergency in Chechen Ingursh, which had declared independence. Until the Russian Supreme Soviet intervened, Yeltsin was prepared to use troops to suppress the Chechen Ingursh population.

In most instances, however, there seems to be little understanding that it is the legislative branch that should decide the magnitude of the taxes people should pay and the expenditures the state should authorize. After several days of debate in December of 1990, for example, the Congress of the People's Deputies of the Soviet Union adjourned without taking any notable action. The next day, on his own, Gorbachev announced that he had decreed the imposition of a nationwide sales tax. Because of public protest, he was forced to revoke the decree a few weeks later, but the reversal was due to public opposition to the tax, not because his actions were deemed to be unconstitutional.

The lack of experience with checks and balances is compounded by the absence of an independently based and well-respected judiciary. The purges under Stalin ruined whatever credibility the courts might have had. It is no wonder there is little understanding of the notion that there should be three equal branches of government: the legislative, the executive, and the judiciary. That also explains the failure to appreciate the importance and role of checks and balances. In the circumstances, there is nothing to prevent arbitrary acts, such as the temporary closing down of newspapers, like *Pravda,* after the coup. There is no effective court system to appeal the actions of the Chief Executive, in that case Yeltsin. Similarly, if there had been a court system that was equal in power to the executive branch, the collapse of the Soviet Union might have been avoided.

While the CIS is far more democratic than the Soviet Union once was, so far the trappings of democracy are not always accompanied by the philosophical anchors that help to insure that democracy will endure. Given a serious collapse of the economy, it may be that no society can sustain its democracy. But the chances are even slimmer when there is no middle class to fight for the status quo and no system of checks and balances to prevent abuses of power.

Memory is not enough. Chinese intellectuals swore that after the Cultural Revolution, they would never again stand for a return of the cult of personality. Russian intellectuals have made similar declarations. But as noble as such sentiments may be, they will not be able to withstand a grab for power by strong leaders. There must be basic institutional changes to prevent abuses and the assumption of too much power by any segment of the government. Given the absence of democratic traditions anywhere in the independent republics, it is not enough to hope that good intentions will prevail.

16 THE U.S. CONGRESS: AN INDEPENDENT FORCE IN WORLD POLITICS?

WILLIAM C. OLSON

Currently working on an intellectual history of the study of IR in the U.S. for Cambridge University Press, Dean Olson headed the School of International Service at the American University. He has lectured in over 25 countries on the legislative impact upon U.S. foreign policy.

Everybody has seen, and critics without number have said, that our form of national government is singular, possessing a character altogether its own; but there is abundant evidence that very few have seen just wherein it differs most essentially from the other governments of the world.[1]

The essential difference from other systems of government that President Wilson referred to was that responsibility for the governance of the United States is centered neither in a parliament nor in a leader, but shared between two institutions, the presidential or Executive branch and the congressional or Legislative one. For most of the country's history, except for treaties, tariffs, and an occasional declaration of war, foreign affairs were generally understood to be the prerogative of the Executive. What congressmen thought or did mattered little to the outside world. What Susan Hammond has called "the Congressional" War of 1812, the refusal to ratify the Versailles Treaty or to join the League of Nations, and the passage of neutrality legislation in reaction to President Roosevelt's desire to "quarantine the aggressors" in Europe in 1937–9 were rare exceptions to this rule.

The era of bipartisan cooperation after the Second World War was seen as an expression of a new national consensus in favor of ending isolationism and embarkation upon a new international order. Truman and Acheson, Democratic President and Secretary of State, worked effectively with such Republican leaders as Senator Vandenberg and Representative Herter to bring about a revolution in American foreign policy. While Congress provided the money for policy implementation and thus effectively assumed a critical role in international affairs, few saw it as having an equal role in the determination of policy.

By the 1970s that had changed. Congress, reacting against having been drawn into a losing war in Vietnam, overrode President Nixon's veto of its new War Powers Act, which restricted the President's ability to perform his role as Commander-in-Chief. In so doing it set a new precedent. Power over foreign affairs was now to be shared. This article will examine the way in which foreign policy is now made in the United

[1]Woodrow Wilson, 7 Oct. 1884, in the preface to *Congressional Government* (New York: Meridian edn, 1956, first publ. 1885).

States and will try to assess how the separation of powers between President and Congress strengthens or weakens the nation's place in the world.[2]

THE SEPARATION OF POWERS, AND WAR POWERS

NonAmericans watching the extraordinary concentration of national attention given to the debate over authorization to go to war in the Gulf on January 11 and 12 must have wondered how each side of the controversy over the role of Congress in taking the country into war could feel so strongly that it was right and the other side wrong. Which one was right?

The answer is that they both were. The constitution of the United States divides responsibility in the realm of foreign affairs in such a way that the Executive and the Legislative branches base their claims upon different provisions. Article One, defining the powers of Congress, lists numerous foreign affairs responsibilities, among them the power to declare war, and this buttresses the view that the founding fathers meant Congress to play an important role. Article Two, on the powers of the Executive, designates the President as the "Commander-in-Chief" and states that "He shall have Power, by and with the Advice and Consent of the Senate, to make Treaties, provided two-thirds of the Senators present concur." This last provision is ambiguous in defining the critical Legislative decision-making function in foreign affairs, the treaty power.

The Gulf War debate was one of two in the postwar era addressing the separation of powers in such a fundamental way, the other being the Vietnam-era debate over the War Powers Act. Under the terms of that act, which became law when Congress overrode Nixon's veto in November 1973, the President may not commit U.S. forces into a potential conflict situation unless Congress explicitly authorizes combat in advance or ratifies it within a sixty-day period after it commences, failing which he has to terminate their deployment. "The fundamental problem," a leading Foreign Relations Committee staffer and an academic authority on Congress and foreign policy agree, "is that the War Powers Resolution does not contain any sanctions against a President who does not comply."[3] In fact presidents have cooperated, in the sense that their performance has been consistent with the requirements of the act without their conceding that it must be. In turn, since it makes the laws and provides the funds, Congress has generally acted so as not to make an issue of it. It hardly needs arguments, because it has the power.

On the Executive side, there is a temptation to make whatever interpretation of the applicability of the law the President considers he needs at any given moment. Thus fortified, presidents generally have felt that they can make their own judgement about when and in what way they must comply with War Powers. Even more basic is the conviction shared by all presidents, regardless of party, that the act is unconstitutional anyway, even though the occasion has yet to arise when the Supreme Court has made

[2]In the preparation of this article the author would like to thank Peter M. Olson, Diplomatic Associate at the School of Foreign Service at Georgetown University, Susan Hammond, of the Center for Congressional and Presidential Studies, American University, Washington, DC, and Phil Williams of the Graduate School of Public and International Affairs, Pittsburgh University.

[3]Pat Holt and Cecil V. Crabb, Jr., *Invitation to Struggle* (Washington, DC: Congressional Quarterly, 2nd edn, 1984), p. 151.

any ruling on the issue. They can also use the precedent of the "Executive agreement" for skirting the treaty powers provisions, as notably demonstrated by Roosevelt to a beleaguered Britain in the "destroyer deal" of 1940. Attempts have been made to provide similarly greater powers for Congress over treaties as well in order to impose Legislative control over these "Executive agreements," in keeping with the theory behind War Powers. Drafts for a "Treaty Powers Act" have been under consideration by the Foreign Relations Committee from time to time for nearly forty years, the idea being to subject all agreements with foreign powers to the process whereby treaties are approved. As even its proponents agree, this would be a gargantuan task. Limited success was reflected in the form of a requirement under the Case Amendment of 1972 that all agreements be transmitted to Congress— not just the Senate—but without necessity for approval before they can take effect. An early effort at all this is described in the hearings on this bill, designed "to help preserve the separation of powers and to further the Constitutional prerogatives of Congress by providing for Congressional review of Executive Agreements."[4] Not much changed.

What was to change as a result of Vietnam was the conventional wisdom that the President is supreme in foreign policy. This was now the conventional wisdom only in the White House and the State Department, where the view was that Congress had asserted itself into a process where it does not, and was never intended to, belong. The view on Capitol Hill was that congressional power had been reasserted to the level that the framers of the constitution intended and the good of the American Republic re-

quires. On this view, the right and obligation to play an active role in foreign policy-making had, until Vietnam, been neglected by a Congress too willing to allow whoever occupied the Oval Office, mortal like anyone else, to determine the course of the nation's direction in international relations. Congress felt it should make its own judgement as to what was the national interest at any given time. Henceforth, foreign policy was to be codetermined. In other words, the true significance for international relations of War Powers was not legal, based upon erudite interpretations of its specific provisions, but political. What Congress did was to make a political statement, pure and simple.

Had President Bush and his Republican colleagues succeeded in taking over the Senate in the 1992 elections by tarring the Democrats with the brush of appeasement for failing sufficiently to support the Gulf War, an end to the constraints of War Powers might have been within Bush's grasp. Two factors militate against this scenario, however. First, no one believed the Republicans could take the House of Representatives as well. Second, there is no guarantee that the Republican legislators are prepared to abandon the added influence over foreign affairs that War Powers has given them too. It was Democrats who were most critical of President Johnson's foreign policies in Asia and the Caribbean, just as the fight against Nixon preceding the passage of War Powers was led by Senator Javits and other Republican members of the Foreign Relations Committee. Codetermination seems here to stay.

Given these strengthened capabilities, what does Congress actually do in carrying out its responsibility in foreign affairs?

---

[4]U.S. Congress, Senate Committee on the Judiciary, Subcommittee on Separation of Powers, "Congressional Oversight of Executive Agreements": *Hear-* *ings,* 92nd Congress, 2nd session on S. 3475 (Washington, DC: U.S. Government Printing Office, 1972).

THE CONGRESSIONAL FOREIGN POLICY ROLES

Congress's most basic foreign policy function is the obligation literally to pay the bills for United States foreign involvement. This necessitates a lengthy dual process whereby the House and the Senate, moving through an elaborate committee structure leading to floor debate in each body, first authorize the expenditure of funds for a particular department or program and then appropriate money to implement it. Because so many subcommittees—as many as sixty-seven in the 99th Congress, 1979–80, for example—are involved, their judgements are usually about specific features of foreign policy rather than about the policy itself. Funding responsibility rests with the appropriations committees.

A second function grows out of this: to monitor or oversee the behavior of federal agencies operating abroad to ascertain whether they are actually carrying out the program approved: in practical terms, whether they are spending the money as the legislators intended. This function too involves committee and subcommittee hearings, and also "hands-on" investigations which have been known to take chairmen, aides, and even full committees to the far corners of the earth. The viability of this mandate has been enormously enhanced by the increased numbers and growing competence of congressional staffs.

A third function is politically to legitimize the policies of the Executive by passing legislation which details the specifics to carry out long-term decisions. This support ranges from passing treaties, to nonbinding resolutions passed with impressive majorities at times of crisis or emergency to demonstrate national concern (as in the case of emergency relief to the victims of Saddam Hussein), to the provision of funds to carry out costly new commitments (such as for-eign aid) when the administration asks the country to make a fundamental change in direction.

A fourth function might be called "representation," a two-way street which can produce a Burkean dilemma. What if what the voters at home demand—as with tariff protection against Japanese automobile imports—is something that the congressman genuinely feels runs counter to the national interest? He is supposed to reflect their views in the way he speaks and votes, and goes to exceptional lengths to make sure they are aware of his determination to do so. Needless to say, the advice of divergent elements in the member's constituency may prove contradictory. The Mexican free trade bill is a telling example, especially for the Democrats, since their labor constituents are against it and their Hispanics for it, a circumstance of which Republican White House strategists were well aware when they proposed the bill to Congress with much fanfare at the border. This is why many congressmen fly to their district (in their home state) nearly every weekend just to keep in touch, and this in turn is where what Senator Fulbright used to regard as the educational responsibility of the member of Congress comes into play: to reveal, explain, and justify his vote or intention to vote in order to bring his constituents around to his point of view. In the case of the Panama Canal Treaty in 1977, for example, several succeeded in persuading initially hostile constituents of the desirability of the treaty; others voted for it anyway hoping that emotions would cool by the next election day. If the member fails, the voters may send someone else to Washington to represent them. This process separates the politician, who adapts his point of view to theirs in order to survive, from the statesman.

The fifth and traditionally the principal foreign policy function of Congress is to stand behind the President. That this has come into question in the last 20–25 years is the reason why an article assessing the impact of Congress upon U.S. foreign policy is not redundant. During the Versailles Treaty fight in 1919, the entire world became aware of the negative power of Congress, but this was a rare event. Normally presidents could rely upon ultimate backing from the Hill on foreign policy matters, no matter how intense or bitter the debates preceding a vote may have been. They could count on this support because foreign affairs were external to the concerns of most people most of the time, and because the people and Congress entrusted their leadership to the White House. Because international affairs were based upon the relations of sovereign states, there was neither need nor advantage, as there was in domestic politics, for individual politicians to sound off with a divided voice on foreign affairs. Sensitive to and guided by the opinions of the voters "back home," members of Congress tended to back their President regardless of party. This attitude prevailed into the 1960s even after vigorous debates on such issues as the 1951 Bricker Amendment (which opposed treaties being "the law of the land"), continued U.S. troop commitment to Europe in the 1950s and 1960s, and the ill-starred Gulf of Tonkin Resolution of 1964 (which gave President Johnson a free hand in southeast Asia).

Then came Vietnam and Nixon. In the January 1991 Gulf debate, it took the fear of an acute diplomatic embarrassment—the fear that the United States might be the only power not to support the American President's bold initiative, perhaps leading to the collapse of the international coalition and therefore policy against Saddam Hussein— to guarantee congressional support. In no other system could such a dilemma have arisen. Foreign policy consensus is no longer assured.

Congress's foreign policy role can also be seen in terms of its three basic postures: those of enabler, negator, and initiator. The first two are traditional and essentially reactive to Executive leadership in foreign affairs, though expressive of a certain degree of independence; the third is different. First, Congress serves as enabler, by acquiescence or with enthusiasm permitting the Executive to carry out its intentions in international relations. Second, it performs as negator, by obstruction or negligence prohibiting or inhibiting the President from putting into effect what he regards as being in the national interest. In its third and more positive role, the "first branch," as Congress likes to think of itself for historical and constitutional reasons,[5] often acts as initiator, coming up with innovative ideas or substituting its own policy for that of the Executive. A penetrating analysis of the legislative course of the Trade Reform Act of 1974 shows how, even though the final version enjoyed wide support, the Jackson–Vanik amendment tying most favored-nation status to Soviet willingness to let Jews emigrate "continued to disrupt the progress of the bill." When in the midst of all this the Yom Kippur War broke out in October 1973, the Secretary of State "immediately engaged in an intensive, personal Middle East mediation effort" fearing that the amendment "would undercut his efforts to work with Moscow for a cease-fire."[6]

Congress performed a policy-setting function in the human rights field not only towards the Soviet Union, but from about the same time in Central America and South

[5]See, for example, Alfred de Grazia *et al.*, *Congress: The First Branch of Government* (Washington, DC: American Enterprise Institute for Public Policy Research, 1966).

[6]See I. M. Destler, *Making Foreign Economic Policy* (Washington, DC: Brookings, 1980), pp. 164–7.

Africa as well. Congressional interference is one reason why the U.S. diplomatic norm is becoming less open and tending more and more towards direct presidential–foreign ministerial contact on politically sensitive issues, rather than proceeding through more public channels. Despite this and other devices, however, the enabler/negator/initiator triad from time to time takes center stage as part of the script for what irritated administrations have on occasion called "535 Secretaries of State."

Congress's ability to perform foreign policy functions effectively has been fundamentally altered by the communications revolution. Significant steps have been taken to overcome what was once so serious a communications gap in relation to a gigantic federal bureaucracy with speed and depth in its sources that it was difficult to argue that the congressional role could be a legitimate or useful one. A number of these stand out. The technological revolution allows every congressional office instant access to data from almost anywhere in town. Second, a revolution has occurred in congressional sophistication, brought about by the attraction to legislative work of top graduates from the best universities as well as experts who come over to Congress from the government bureaucracy. Third, the Freedom of Information Act, resulting from the Church Special Intelligence Committee investigation in the mid-1970s, has all but destroyed the frequently used Executive argument that "If you knew what we know but cannot tell you you'd have to agree with us." Fourth, Congress has become more vigorous in exercising its power of oversight as a result

of loss of Executive credibility—as over the Iran–Contra affair—which has forced it to provide more information. Finally, there is an enhanced flow of information from the lobbies, well-financed and informed, if biased. The problem for congressmen now tends to be having too much information and not enough staff to digest, analyze, and present it to the member in time for it to be useful to him in debate and voting.

There are matters of diplomatic delicacy or strategic secrecy that everyone agrees must be withheld—at least from everyone except members of the Intelligence Committees. The fact that Congress has this access to restricted information for a few of its own renders most of the rest more willing to concede that some restriction of knowledge is acceptable. Others, like Senator William Borah, the isolationist Chairman of the Foreign Relations Committee who said in July, 1939, that his own sources had categorically assured him that there would be no war in Europe, continue to rely upon their own sources, often ideological in nature. What has changed from the early federalist period, however, is that the old Executive argument—that it has a special right to knowledge about foreign affairs which it may not, "in the national interest," share with the Legislative branch—is simply no longer accepted. Today there is not only lively competition for knowledge, but keen differences on how it should be used. And members of Congress are just as able to define "the national interest" in any way they want as the president and his men. Everyone feels he has a right to get in on the act.

POWER AND INFLUENCE IN CONGRESS: FRAGMENTATION, FEDERALISM

The fragmentation of the foreign policy process in Congress through the multitudinous committees and subcommittees can make it

hard to determine where power over foreign policy is actually located. It is a dynamic process, in that the composition, function, power, and even existence of subcommittees can change every second year from Congress to Congress, depending upon everything from the emergence of new realities with which old forms had proved ill-equipped to deal (the creation of the Committee on Science and Technology is a good example) to personal ambition to play a significant foreign policy role (of which the Senate Judiciary Subcommittee on Refugees is a striking example). It is also a federal system, in that the source of political power for a member of Congress is not the party, but the state or its several "districts" whence he comes and to which he owes his first loyalty.

A small number of congressional committees are charged with recommending, monitoring, and in general making judgements about the overall foreign policy of the United States—the Committee on Foreign Relations in the Senate and the Committee on Foreign Affairs in the House; the two Armed Services committees, the two subcommittees on Foreign Operations of the Appropriations committees, and the two Intelligence committees. Of these, the money power lies in Appropriations, especially in the subcommittees dealing with overseas activity. The ultimate policy responsibility lies in Foreign Relations. Other committees, such as Commerce or Agriculture, make narrower recommendations but must obviously take overall policy into account.

The committee process is best seen not as a matter of certain committees being important while others are not, but as a continuum in which a few committees devote more of their attention to international questions, with those at the other end doing so only occasionally or within a scope limited by special mandate. Practically all the committees get involved at one time or another.

The committees derive their place in the foreign policy process not from a contest for political power—there is often so little direct electoral payoff that the extraordinary expansion of congressional interest and activity cannot be explained in this way—but from jurisdiction and oversight. Each committee and subcommittee has an inescapable responsibility to monitor or oversee the work of the federal agencies over which it has jurisdiction. In other words, the principal source of congressional involvement in foreign policy is the expansion of Executive activities—foreign aid, bases, drug control, fisheries, fiscal support—into all parts of the world through many of the administration's departments and agencies. Congress has no choice but to monitor these activities, whether it wants to or not and whether it does it well or not. John Montgomery has shown how:

> congressional attacks on foreign aid have repeatedly forced the agencies involved to reorganize, just when they were achieving self-confidence and beginning to support the research to generate further improvements. Foreign aid suffers from an irresistible, popular tendency to pull up the plant to see if its roots are growing.[7]

The basic task for an oversight committee is to see that "its" agencies spend the resources it makes available as it intended. There are few Executive powers that do not require sanction in the form of the power that money provides, and the Executive cannot get Congress out of the process without getting out of it itself, starting with the involvement of federal departments in some aspect or other of international affairs.

Here is another two-way street. Each Cabinet department has an office of congressional relations or legislative liaison to respond to congressional enquiries. At the State Department, instantaneous responses to calls from Capitol Hill sometimes seem to take priority over everything else. What is a legitimate basis for Executive complaint is

[7]John Montgomery, *Foreign Aid in International Politics* (Englewood Cliffs, N.J.: Prentice-Hall, 1967), p. 87.

when several subcommittees get involved in overseeing the same activity at the same time. In large part because of the collapse of party structure and discipline, as well as post-Watergate reforms in congressional procedures, there is no longer a central monitoring mechanism or switching-yard such as the office of the Speaker which can always determine who gets what enquiries or which controls the movement of the many trains operating on the government's sometimes crowded tracks. Delays and collisions sometimes occur, and they are not always accidents. Often a political action committee or a politically independent congressman or senator needs to justify some hearings or even the existence of a subcommittee. A code word for jurisdiction is "turf."

The power of individuals, especially in a system where there are no backbenchers as there are in the British system, can be crucial in open foreign policy debates as well as behind the scenes. However, merely being chair or ranking minority member of a key committee chairmanship does not automatically give one influence over policy in general. The current chairman of the Senate Foreign Relations Committee is seldom cited as an authority, though his career started in the Foreign Service; nor is the ranking Republican on the Committee, who would presumably take the chair were his party to take over the Senate in the 1992 elections.[8]

Nor does power derive from party position. In the American system the political parties exercise little power except locally and during the presidential elections every four years. In the House of Commons, by contrast, an MP needing policy guidance or information need only call upon Smith Square or Transport House to get what party headquarters thinks he or she requires. In the House of Commons, everyone knows who makes policy and who expresses it from the front benches. In Congress, foreign policy exponents are located all over the place, the strength of their influence depending upon many factors, ranging from articulate opposition, to acknowledged competence on a given topic, to simply a certain degree of popular credibility on TV talk shows, which in the best instances constitute a superb example of the member's educational capability on timely issues.

Congress has always been made up not only *of* states, but of people *from* states and districts, and that is where power remains. With its roots in the relative independence of the original thirteen colonies, the federalism of the American system of government explains why foreign policy utterances by politicians of the same party but from different regions can be radically different on certain issues. Quantitatively, the redistribution of seats from northeastern states to southern and especially western ones as a result of the 1990 census is bound to have an effect on policy. Qualitatively, as the ethnic composition also changes, new voters from Asia and Latin America are becoming more influential, especially as they are well-organized and quite openly lobbying for political power.

THE LOBBIES

While the pro-Israel lobbies represent the most talked about and probably the most effective external force in changing the course of U.S. foreign policy, the primary lobbyist is the President himself. . . .

For many years, commercial enter-

---

[8]This is Jesse Helms (Republican, North Carolina), who with others has expressed reservations about the ab-

sence of language on abortion in the UN Convention on the Rights of the Child, passed by the Gen-

prises such as multinational corporations have exerted what many regard as undue influence on congress members in pursuit of special interests. Fundamentalist and other religious groups are increasingly powerful on such issues as abortion through international agencies. Dozens of patriotic groups presume to best serve the national interest, but almost all lobbyists base part of their justification at least on the assertion that they promote the greater good. But there can be little doubt that by the use of pressure of various kinds—from bribes or, far more often, information or the promise to deliver or withhold votes—foreign interest lobbyists have affected policy in their favour.

The open offer of campaign funds is the fundamental concept and characteristic activity of the political action committee, a relatively recent phenomenon which in theory represents an organized interest and in practice operates primarily on behalf of the politician in Congress in order to keep him there, but which often has sources of income and influence extending far beyond his own particular base. The PACs prepare briefs, provide information not otherwise available, seek funds, draft legislation, explain pros and cons, show the connection between what they want and the needs or capabilities of the member's district, and in general "try to be helpful." In terms of effect, however, "the mere presence of these groups, and the mere fact that they are organized with the intent of persuasion, does not guarantee that they are penetrating the policy formation process."[9] In setting its

own agenda for judging foreign policy, in taking its own initiatives and making its own assessments, Congress often makes use of cues provided by lobbyists. Their causes profit from the exercise of negative power, particularly when Congress imposes its own priorities on how the Executive is allowed to spend on foreign affairs. Lobbyists are often also cautionary, implying that the congressman will pay a political price for doing X, Y, or Z.

Slowly, almost imperceptibly, foreign embassies also came to understand not only that Congress represents something of a new phenomenon in international relations, but that it might be influenced to their country's advantage. Ironic as it may seem now, two friendly congressmen achieved an unfortunate success in 1977–1978 on behalf of Somoza's Nicaragua in persuading a key committee to omit it from a list of countries to be denied foreign aid because of dismal human rights records. An impressive recent example was Britain's ambassador Nicholas Henderson, who in 1982 walked from office to office on Capitol Hill on behalf of Prime Minister Thatcher's Falklands War policy at a time when the American UN ambassador was tilting the other way. It was nip and tuck.

How may the effectiveness of the foreign affairs lobbies be gauged? Do the lobbies account for a substantial element of congressional divergence from Executive wishes? To assess this question, the basic social phenomenon to recognize is identity politics. The basic political device is what might be called constituency foreign policy-making. This takes many directions and dimensions. Not only are there a number of identifiable ethnic lobbies and other kinds of "issues" or "cause" groups, but there are longer-standing functional pressure groups as well—trade, labor, manufacturing, agriculture—which recognize the international impact upon the U.S. econ-

eral Assembly in 1989 and signed by 135 heads of state but not, because of his objections, by the United States, even though it was instrumental in drafting the document. Three leading Republican senators have urged Bush to sign: *Washington Post.* 19 Apr. 1991, p. A21.

[9]Charles Kegley Jr. and Edward Wittkopf, *American Foreign Policy: Pattern and Process* (New York: St Martin's Press, 1979), p. 197.

omy. They express themselves daily by wire and letter, in meetings at home "back in the district," and in the corridors of the Senate and House office buildings where the key committees hold their hearings, whose powerful chairmen (rarely chairwomen) hold sway over constituent-filled chambers. Lobbies which reflect and thrive upon identity— whether Irish-American, Cuban-American, Polish-American, Greek-American, Italian-American, and the now-revivified Lithuanian-American—all base their strength upon blocs of voters who still identify with the nations of their fathers' origins. African-Americans identify with the anti-apartheid movement in South Africa. Many other nations are regarded as "endangered species" which somehow must be saved by the American taxpayer. This is especially true where the melting-pot is no longer melting, that is, where entire sections of cities call themselves things like "Little Vietnam" or "the *barrio*." What Joseph Nye has called "the openness of American culture to various ethnicities"[10] enables lobbies to represent and express a certain degree of anxiety about the welfare and indeed even the future of foreign societies which, they feel, can significantly be affected, perhaps even determined, by congressional action.

Money is not the only currency involved; votes are ultimately what count to the politician who introduces legislation assisting countries whose welfare would be difficult to sustain as a "vital national interest." Some of this has from time to time driven administration spokesmen to the point of exasperation; generally, however, occupants of the White House have come to adjust in anticipation to this kind of foreign interest pressure, and even to acknowledge its potential utility in keeping them there for yet another term.

These are essentially behind-the-scenes aspects of congressional foreign policy behavior. What of the issues that attract public attention?

THE GREAT GULF DEBATE

Many foreign policy issues are on the congressional agenda—foreign aid, narcotics control, promotion of democracy, trade policy, Eastern Europe, terrorism, to name a few.[11] In recent months, however, one stands out in terms of the power of congress. It was the constitutional crisis that did not quite happen.

The invasion of Kuwait took place just as the congressional election campaigns at home in the districts were getting under way in August. The President's immediate action in terms of what he called a "new international order" based upon Second World War lessons drew instantaneous and almost universal support. His step-by-step mobilization of United Nations support was acknowledged to be masterful. There was simply nothing to argue about, at least on the world stage. But when the Commander-in-Chief, right after the congressional elections, suddenly doubled the number of U.S. troops in the Saudi desert in order to assume an offensive posture, rumblings of dissent began. While there was broad public consensus on *defending* Saudi Arabia and applying sanctions against Iraq, the question of actually going to war had not been on the table at the time of the congressional campaign. Some were asking how restoring an

[10]J. S. Nye Jr., "Soft power," *Foreign Policy* No. 80, Fall 1990, p. 170.
[11]For a systematic treatment, see Larry Q. Nowels and Ellen C. Collier, "Foreign Policy Budget: Priorities for the 102nd Congress," *CRS Issue Brief*, updated 28 Feb. 1991.

emir served the cause of democracy. Many others, including members of Congress, said that the real issue was not NIO (new international order) but OIL.

Some argued that Congress should immediately have challenged Bush; others argued for a special session of Congress after Christmas to strengthen his hand in diplomacy. By January the issues had become resolutions. Though the President did not initially feel he needed to demonstrate that he had the support of Congress, he changed his mind and on January 8 issued an unusually blunt appeal to Congress to approve a resolution authorizing the use of "all necessary means" to drive Iraq out of Kuwait.

In response, two principal resolutions were presented to the Senate and the House. The one in the House offered the President authorization, but only if Congress had concluded that further efforts at a peaceful solution, notably continuing the embargo, would not work. Despite the large Democratic majority in the House, this lost by a considerable margin. Then a bill authorizing the use of force passed easily in the House and narrowly in the Senate (52–47, with nine Democrats supporting Bush and two Republicans defecting, so that the shift of any three of these would presumably have produced a constitutional dilemma). The level of debate was extraordinary in its insight, knowledge, conviction, and sincerity, an intellectual and philosophical high point in Congress's foreign policy history. Many concentrated upon strategy and long-term consequences; others, like Senator Joseph Biden, chairman of the Judiciary Committee, stressed the constitutional dimension:

> We are here today because our Constitution . . . commands the Congress to decide the gravest question any country faces: Should it go to war? Let there be no mistake about it, Mr. President, this is a question which the Congress—and only the Congress—can answer. . . . The meaning of the Constitution in this case is clear, direct, and indisputable.[12]

The sober level of debate continued during consideration of the second measure, a bipartisan bill authorizing the use of force immediately after the deadline, sponsored by minority leader Robert Michel of the House and Stephen Solarz, a Democrat who chaired the Asian and Pacific Affairs Subcommittee of the House Foreign Affairs Committee. This was regarded as fulfilling the congressional role under the constitution, though members on both sides of the issue regarded it as a virtual declaration of war even if the language stressed that this was "pursuant to the United Nations Security Council Resolution 678 (1990) in order to achieve implementation" of the several other UN resolutions.

While there were obviously strategic and diplomatic issues under discussion in this great debate, who had the authority in the grave instance of going to war? A senior administration official was quoted as saying, "we don't like the notion that the President is afraid to go to Congress because he fears he will lose . . . we need to put that notion to rest."[13] Much was at stake. To put it in the starkest terms, had the President failed to get the authorization to go to war he sought, observers seemed convinced that, armed with the arguments of White House lawyers and fearful of an unravelling of the coalition of states he had woven together, he would have gone ahead anyway, having already claimed that he had all the authority he required. In addition to that, three days after the vote, a close aide said, "given who George Bush is, he made the intellectual de-

---

[12]*Congressional Record: Senate,* 10 Jan. 1991, pp. S 119–20.

[13]*Washington Post,* 9 Jan. 1991, p. A16.

cision quite easily that this was something worth going to war over. This week the abstract of August turned into the reality of January, but there was always an inevitability about this."[14] This prospect angered many, who felt that they were being manipulated, forced to go along when they had serious and essentially nonpartisan reasons for not doing so yet. To have withheld approval would certainly have produced a constitutional crisis on who controls going to war, the last thing needed at that point where diplomacy had produced an international consensus.[15] In the words of the Speaker of the House, addressing those colleagues who felt they must support the Commander-in-Chief in a time of crisis:

> Do not do it under the notion that you merely hand him another diplomatic tool, another quiver of economic leverage or in-

ternational leverage . . . this nation's leadership is best expressed in this body and in the other body and in the coalition of constitutional consent . . .[16]

Ultimately, Congress had to take some action, if only to vindicate its constitutional war powers. The President's tactical concession of the utility of such action may prove in the end to have strengthened the ability of future congresses to insist upon a similar involvement in the use of force in other crises.

Once the vote was taken, the constitutional debate was over. With the ground war brief and brilliant, for a time the euphoria seemed deafening (particularly from Republican politicians taunting Democrats who had voted for more time) and the issue of the wisdom and indeed even the necessity of war brushed aside. . . .

THE DIVISION OF LABOR

What might be called the "old model" of the American foreign policy process, discernible since the early days of the Republic, though not necessarily what the founding fathers had in mind, can be seen as consisting of four stages in the process whereby the President's programs, based upon his goals, were presented to Congress for that form of approval known as funding. This model, which held up to the years of Vietnam, is summarized in Figure 1.

In the first stage, the initiation of policy towards the outside world was always an Executive responsibility. It was up to the President to indicate where he wanted to go

in international affairs, and up to his principal advisers to figure out how to get there. Once they agreed on this, he forwarded those of his programs requiring funds or other legislative authorization to each house of the Congress, where the second stage—deliberation—began.

This was essentially a legislative responsibility, in terms of both procedure and power. Spokesmen for the Executive had to submit the specifics of what they were asking for to the legislators, to answer questions about them, to defend them against inevitable and often contrived attack, and to weather storms of perhaps weeks of give-and-take before the legislators made up their minds on what to approve, amend, or disapprove. Until they did so, nothing happened: at least, nothing requiring money.

[14]*Washington Post,* 16 Jan. 1991, p. A1.
[15]No such constitutional crisis took place over either Korea (a UN "police action") or the gradual entrapment in Vietnam, but there was neither divided government nor the War Powers Act to contend with then.

[16]*The New York Times,* 13 Jan. 1991, p. 10.

FIGURE 1	THE OLD DIVISION OF LABOR TO 1973
Stage	*Responsibility*
Initiation	*Executive*
Deliberation	*Legislative*
Implementation	*Executive*
Evaluation	*Executive* (constant), *Legislative* (periodic)

As head of state, the President could spend all the time he wanted making speeches, issuing threats, meeting with foreign dignitaries, promising results, and enunciating lofty principles; as Commander-in-Chief he could deploy forces at will. But he could not spend money until Congress went through its elaborate procedures to make it available to him. This stage was emphatically legislative.

The third phase was implementation. This could be called the conduct of foreign policy, obviously and exclusively an Executive responsibility involving the entire panoply of activity usually subsumed under the over-arching term "diplomacy." There was no place for politicians, whose job was finished once they gave their approval, however modified by their constructive judgement or narrow-minded stinginess.[17] Even when "conference diplomacy," particularly in the new international organizations, emerged as a new form of international relations, Congress was ignored—to President Wilson's eventual sorrow when it rejected U.S. membership of the League of Nations. The day-by-day conduct of foreign policy was now in the hands of ambassadors appointed by the President; broad policy matters were the concern of the Secretary of State.

The fourth and final phase, review, could also be called evaluation or judgement. It was both an Executive and a Legis-

lative responsibility, though in fundamentally different ways. For the Executive, this phase is a constant process, most easily characterized by assessment of the responses of foreign governments to U.S. actions or policy. As in foreign ministries everywhere, review takes place all the time as crises occur and methods of dealing with them are tried and, when found wanting, altered on the spot, daily and even hourly. Foreign policy was conducted in this essentially responsive way for much of American history. People in the embassies who did the implementation were always being reconsidered by somebody, but that somebody was always within the diplomatic establishment. Legislative review also took place, not as a constant process but sporadically, only during considerations of authorization and appropriation bills, except for the relatively few members of the committees on Foreign Relations in the Senate and on Foreign Affairs in the House of Representatives.[18]

[17]A persistent problem for U.S. career diplomats has been "bible-belt" or midwestern and southern congressmen's disapproval of what they called the "whiskey budget" (for diplomatic entertaining). This is one reason why choice U.S. ambassadorial jobs have gone to wealthy party supporters.

[18]The balance of power in this old model operated only on one axis, between the two branches, Executive and Legislative. As between the two houses it hardly operated at all until Mar. 1941, when the Lend-Lease Act was passed. From that point on a new balance began to emerge, based upon the money power of the House under Section 7 of Article One and the treaty power of the Senate under Section 2 of Article Two. After the war, in the course of considering foreign aid legislation, the House of Representatives began to perceive the power it could now exercise in foreign affairs through new committee channels. (One of the best-informed subcommittee chairmen ever to wield a gavel was Representative Otto Passman (Democrat, Louisiana) of the House Appropriations Committee, who was basically opposed to the entire concept of foreign aid. For years he was arguably the single most effective negative force in American foreign policy.) To exercise it by denying funds for exercising the military dimension

FIGURE 2   THE NEW BALANCE

Stage	Responsibility
Initation	*Executive*, but often *Legislative* in terms of new ideas, perspectives on long-term objectives, program proposals, even draft legislation
Deliberation	*Legislative*, but more *Executive* time required for deeper and wider-ranging hearings involving more subcommittees, with administration testimony more defensive and thorough
Implementation	*Executive*, but with more frequent on-the-spot staff investigation and "junkets" by committees and individual *Legislative* members
Evaluation	Both, but no longer merely periodic on the part of congressional experts, and more careful attention to *Legislative* reaction on the part of State, Defense, the security community

After War Powers, congressional involvement in foreign affairs expanded for additional reasons besides the effective new precedent. The communications revolution not only between Congress and the world outside but between Congress and the district meant that people organizing against the War back home were demanding results. With improved transportation, visitations by committee delegations or staff to foreign posts came to be accepted as an essential feature of the monitoring process and deepened the legislators' sensitivity to what was going on abroad. Yet another element was the improvement of media coverage of events overseas and of news in general, often with a tone of skepticism and public distrust as this revealed wrongdoing or questionable judgements. Concern made both the voter and the spokesmen on the Hill better informed and more articulate. TV brought the war into voters' living rooms; to this day, many in the military are convinced

*

What is one to conclude from all this? First, while Congress cannot be regarded as anything resembling another sovereign state

that the media, through public opinion and thence to Congress, lost a war which could have been won.

While members tended to rely most heavily on a few trustworthy old cronies from the district back home to gather information and interpret it as best they could, now the members vote themselves increased office support funds to hire experts from the media, universities, thinktanks, industry, retired diplomats, and military specialists to serve as foreign policy aides. They can draw more heavily upon an expanded Congressional Research Service, a more diligent monitoring service in the form of the General Accounting Office, and, if appropriate, the staffs of committees on which they serve. All this has fundamentally altered the model. There is now Legislative involvement at all four stages of the process, even if the essential division of responsibility remains (see Figure 2).

among actors on the international stage, it certainly at times behaves independently from the administration. As far as foreign affairs is concerned, this last is only part of the government. Laws are made and monies

---

of foreign policy would occur only later. Partly as a result, yet another balance emerged, that between the public and its elected leaders, because the intended role of the House had from the beginning been to be close to the people, to reflect its views,

and thus to change as public opinion changed. Not so to change was to risk losing one's seat. This was a major factor in bringing the Vietnam War to such an ignominious end.

provided by Congress. Lobbyists, be they foreign, ethnic, or constituent, focus their insistent efforts on Capitol Hill offices in often successfully influencing U.S. policy.

Second, policy differences between the two branches become more acute when one party controls the White House and the other one or both of the legislative houses, a configuration which has occurred so often since the Second World War as to have become almost the norm. This seems likely to continue for some time to come. Even gaining domination of both branches (which would mean taking control of both Legislative houses) would guarantee the dominant party only partial and probably temporary control of the foreign policy process. Media concentration upon heads of state and foreign offices should not obscure this reality in analyzing what the only remaining superpower does or does not do.

Third, Congress has gradually acquired not only the access to but the competence to make use of information crucial to making foreign policy judgements. Unfortunately, some of the most troublesome lawmakers can be the best informed.

Fourth, the proliferation of foreign affairs responsibility throughout its committee and subcommittee structure means that Congress cannot and will not develop any coherent independent policy of its own. In other words, its impact in the future, while certainly highly responsible when it needs to be, will tend to be fractured, negative, and contradictory. Ironically, this may constitute the principal hope for any new administration to seize and hold the high ground, and hence the key to its own lobbying strategy on Capitol Hill.

Is U.S. foreign policy hence strengthened or weakened? Executive spokesmen invariably complain that congressional interference renders policy-making more cumbersome and policy implementation all but impossible. All the old arguments about secrecy, competence, speed of reaction to crisis, comprehensive planning, and interagency collaboration are still in place. Congressionalists respond that the United States' foreign policy, buttressed by broader knowledge, is demonstrably stronger than before the House and Senate became so intimately engaged in its formulation. In the face of ever-increasing international demands, national unity now rests upon a firmer foundation. Any administration needs to be checked from time to time, as the Bay of Pigs, Vietnam/Watergate and Iran-Contra amply demonstrate. Experience, especially in a Senate which is a continuing body only a third of whose members are up for election at the same time, but also in the House with its seasoned chairmen and knowledgeable staffs, does not come and go every four or eight years. Stability and continuity are assured. If Congress plays politics based upon campaign contributions, administrations tend to base foreign policy decisions upon "how it will play in Peoria," that is, with the folks back home.

Foreign affairs has long since ceased to be the exclusive preserve of an elite protected from the democratic process.

CHAPTER FOUR

THE METHOD:
THE EVOLUTION
OF DIPLOMATIC THEORY

Diplomacy is the management of international relations by negotiation; the method by which these relations are adjusted and managed by ambassadors and envoys; the business or art of the diplomatist.

Oxford English Dictionary

In his essay on the theoretical foundations of diplomatic method, Sir Harold Nicolson observed that the first principle firmly established in diplomacy was that of immunity, since "it must soon have been realized that no negotiation could reach a satisfactory conclusion if the emissaries of either party were murdered on arrival."[1] The world has come a long way since then, but elementary principles still apply, which is why we have included the celebrated Melian dialogue or debate in this chapter. It reflects one of the earliest recorded, protracted exchanges between adversaries, told by a close observer, Thucydides.

As the seasoned diplomatist and former Prime Minister of France, Michel Rocard, argues "international commitments, like all commitments, are not to be taken lightly."[2] The sanctity of commitments has been a cornerstone of diplomacy since earliest times. When commitments are broken, and especially when they are expected to be broken, man descends back into the law of the jungle. Wherever people have existed in separate tribes or other groupings they have needed some means of communicating and regulating their needs and anxieties toward other such conglomerates, whether they were clans, nations, kingdoms,

---

[1]*The Evolution of Diplomatic Method*, (London: Constable and Co., Ltd., 1954), p. 2.
[2]"Europe and the United States," *Critical Issues*, 1992, 2, (New York: Council on Foreign Relations, 1992), p. 37.

or rude empires. Long before the emergence of the modern international system in the absence of common councils among states, the practice developed of establishing more or less permanent legations in each other's courts as a channel of information and negotiation. As Barry Hughes shows in this contribution, this is still central to the process.

Because the ambassador was the personal representative of the ruler or monarch, he enjoyed all the privileges and immunities which would normally be extended to the monarch, say Elizabeth I, were she herself to appear in person. Diplomacy gained its unique status from the special needs that sovereigns had for keeping in regular touch with one another and resolving their differences if their relations were not to break down to their mutual disadvantage. In 1486, Lorenzo de' Medici penned a letter to one of his diplomatic envoys in which he wrote, "now we see what some have long understood, that the Pope and Doge of Genoa have been playing a game, and as regards the Venetians we have an idea that if our words had been heard and remembered, these matters would have a better ending."[3]

Even though the term "diplomacy" is sometimes used interchangeably with "foreign policy" (as in, "Israeli diplomacy seeks security with its neighbors"), there is an important distinction between the determination of policy and how it is implemented. Foreign policy is what a head of state and his advisers decide should be done to serve the country's long-term interests and achieve its immediate national goals; diplomacy, including negotiation, is among the methods or techniques used whereby envoys carry out that policy abroad. Buttressed with information coming in from all over the world minute-by-minute, the Department of State is charged with providing the president with the information and advice necessary for him to determine what that policy should be. Conversely, the Department relays decisions and instructions for their execution to ambassadors serving in foreign capitals. (In the early days of the Republic it often took six months for a letter written with a quill pen to arrive by sea and stagecoach at its destination.) Ambassadors in turn are expected to discuss the implications of these decisions with governments to which they are accredited and within an international organization where they interrelate with delegations of many other states.

Communications technology and multilateral diplomacy have radically altered the nature of diplomacy, particularly the speed with which interchange can and must take place. "The cables" are the lifeblood of the body diplomatic, whose mandate is to carry out the instructions given. Ambassador Charles E. ("Chip") Bohlen once recalled that when he joined the Foreign Service he was told to "observe, analyze, and report" but, "above all, don't get involved."[4] A diplomat's primary task is to respond responsibly and quickly to what he or she has been asked to do, and certainly not to try to serve the interest of the country to which assigned. Another veteran diplomat, David Newsom, has described how

[3]Moorhead Wright III, ed. *The Theory and Practice of the Balance of Power, 1486–1918*, (London: J. M. Dent and Sons, Ltd., 1975), p. 1.

[4]Quoted in *Toward a Modern Diplomacy* (Washington: American Foreign Service Association, 1968), p. 4.

this constant association with foreigners can lead to uninformed, unfair attacks upon a diplomat's very integrity.[5] In fact, effective ambassadors, many of whom are now women, make significant personal contributions to international understanding, depending upon how well they interpret their instructions as well as concerns expressed to them by their hosts. Opposition opinion and trends in what the people themselves are doing constitute vital elements of their reports back home.

While diplomacy may take the form of an actual visit of a head of one state to the capital of another, this rarely constitutes either the substance of policy nor the process whereby the government formulates policy, although it may influence that process. Note the use of the word "conduct" in the following definition by the standard authority (at least of the "old" diplomacy), Sir Ernest Satow, when he wrote that diplomacy is "the application of intelligence and tact to the conduct of official relations between the governments of independent states."[6]

Diplomacy is the closest direct, acceptable, and regular contact in international relations. Policy is formation and direction; diplomacy is communication and implementation—the lubricant of the foreign policy machinery. Traditionally, its form derives from the nature of the state system itself. In the absence of a common forum, such as an international parliament, states were obliged to regulate their contacts directly. For hundreds of years, foreign policy was seen as the exclusive province of the monarch's inner circle, and the preoccupation of its implementers were war, sovereignty, territory, and the advancement of the personal and dynastic ambitions of rulers. Ambassadors were dispatched to win over sometimes skeptical foreigners to their superiors' point of view. As relations became more complex, they were obliged to become knowledgeable about the state to which they had been sent, skilled not only in advancing their sovereign's interests there but in interpreting what was going on in the other sovereign's mind, the better for the sovereign to gain or to forge understandings to their mutual advantage. Being adept at bargaining was essential. Classical diplomacy was more of an art than a science; in theory at least, it sought to mitigate and reduce conflicts by means of persuasion, compromise, and adjustment. It was a diplomacy rooted in the community of interest of a small group of leaders who spoke the same language, catered as often to one another as their own people, and played to one another's strengths and weaknesses. As Kenneth Thompson, one of the keenest nongovernmental observers of the diplomatic process, has pointed out,

> Patience was a watchword; negotiations and talks would be initiated, broken off, discontinued temporarily, and reopened again by professionals in whose lexicon there was no substitute for "diplomacy."[7]

---

[5]The Oscar Iden lecture, School of Foreign Service, Georgetown University, November 18, 1988, published in part as part of the eighth edition of this book under the title, "The Diplomatic Image," pp. 84–90.

[6]*Guide to Diplomatic Practice*, (London: Longmans, 1917), cited by Sir Harold Nicolson, *Diplomacy*, (London: Oxford University Press, 1950), p. 50.

[7]*Christian Ethics and the Dilemmas of Foreign Policy* (Durham: Duke University Press, 1959), pp. 81–82.

By the twentieth century, particularly after the public conscience has been aroused by the sacrifices of World War I, the old diplomacy was discredited and a "new diplomacy" emerged. It had two unprecedented characteristics: It was sensitive to popular attitudes and it often took place in conferences rather than in the confines of foreign offices. For these reasons it has often been called "open diplomacy,"* an opprobrious and even contradictory term to professionals. Since that time, diplomacy has become a highly organized modern enterprise, with large staffs not only in the foreign secretariat, but in each capital where at least the Great Powers endeavor to pursue their interests, which are more often than not economic in nature. Indeed, many business and industrial leaders argue that the Ambassador to an important commercial state should be, first and foremost, a sort of trade representative. Now there are, in addition to the conventional military/naval attachés, cultural, commercial, labor, and even scientific attachés, and the total staff (many of them foreign nationals engaged in everything from filing to sweeping marble floors) may in a major post such as Rome number over 1,000 people, most of whom never heard of diplomatic theory. It is the *practice* of diplomacy, which as William Macomber writes, reveals the kind of difficulties encountered from within the system by those who are trying to implement high-level policy in what might be thought of as low-level situations, where "the application of about 80 percent of their effort to about 20 percent of their target" represents one of the diplomats' persistent problems.[8]

In the old days, the outcome of negotiations was likely to have little effect upon the people at home unless it led to war or the sacrifice of territory to avoid or end a war. But today there are endless problems that can only be addressed in conjunction with other nations, and they are not problems that can easily be neglected nor their solutions postponed, however much politicians may prefer to pursue more popular themes. Yet many issues—nuclear arms control, removal of barriers to commerce, regulation of air travel, combating terrorism, economic development—are less a matter of disagreement over the existence of a problem than one of finding solutions to difficult common problems that defy solution on a purely national level. It took the so-called Group of Seven economic giants years to recognize the significance of the environmental pollution problem about which so many scientists had warned for a long time. Late in his administration, President Bush was severely criticized by most of the rest of the world represented at the Rio "environmental summit" of over a hundred countries for failing to sufficiently recognize the seriousness of the pollution problem. Vice President (then Senator) Gore led the U.S. Senatorial delegation. This reaction stood out in stark contrast to his signal success in making the United Nations system work in bringing about concerted action as it was originally

---

*The term is usually attributed to Woodrow Wilson, who in his "Fourteen Points" speech to Congress early in 1918 advocated as point #1 "open covenants of peace, openly arrived at." Later, cynics claimed that the idea had become "open covenants, secretly arrived at."

[8]William B. Macomber, *The Angels Game: A Handbook of Modern Diplomacy* (New York: Stein and Day, 1975).

intended to do through his and his advisers' superb diplomacy throughout the Gulf crisis in 1991.[9]

Negotiators must approach their task with a problem-solving orientation rather than with a desire to win points at someone else's expense and must be prepared to reflect changes that take place as they go along in their own government's position. In this sense, much of modern negotiation is an extension of the national bureaucratic policy and bargaining process to an international plane. Thus the problem is not in the quality of the people doing the negotiating but in the archaic and cumbersome system itself. Nearly three centuries ago, the great French statesman, François de Calliers, counselled that;

> the good diplomatist must have an observed mind, a gift of application which rejects being diverted by pleasures or frivolous amusements, a sound judgement which takes for granted the measure of things as they are, and which goes straight to the goal by the shortest and most natural paths without wandering into meaningless refinements and subtleties.[10]

While there is no denying that today's envoy possesses much less freedom of action than did those in de Calliers' day, these qualities are just as relevant as they were then.

Nations often send their spokesmen to the table with important differences in style as well as motive. They are not "on the same wave length" as their counterparts, as was shown exasperatingly at the long and drawn-out talks at Panmunjom which ended the Korean war. During the early years following the Bolshevik revolution, Lenin made no secret of his deep conviction that all relations with capitalist countries were to be conducted on the presumption that friendly or even normal relations were impossible between completely opposing ideological systems, one of which was historically destined in time to triumph over the other. Governments constantly under public pressure for quick results are prone to accept illusory or even meaningless concessions from the other side. What is common to both sides is a determination to serve the national interest as each sees it, and the great question is how mutual self-interest can be achieved. The task of diplomacy is quietly to show the way, and today's up-to-the-minute diplomat could well go back to his copy of Callieres for guidance on how to do it. The system doesn't work by itself.

Much is made today of a "new world order," an expression used in a quite different sense after the demise of another enemy forty-five years earlier by a statesman both revered and maligned in his time, Dean Acheson. "Before the present century was two decades old," he wrote in *Power and Diplomacy*, "the system which had provided an international order since Waterloo was mortally

---

[9]The President was not as inconsistent as this would make it seem; in both cases he interpreted the *national* interest in terms of the short-term economic interest of his constituencies, in the Gulf case, oil, and in the Rio case, the cost to manufacturers of pollution controls. But this is politics, not diplomacy.

[10]*On Negotiating with Princes*, 1716.

stricken [and] twenty years later, it had disappeared altogether."[11] What replaced it was the Cold War. Now that too has "disappeared altogether." Some may regret that in light of awesome new complications. Rather than looking back nostalgically, the challenge of diplomacy is to now produce another new international order that will work this time. Prime Minister Rocard brings theory and practice together in asking the tough questions in his article:

> What attitude should we adopt in the face of this evolution? In what way will international relations change? In what way will states and statesmen have to adjust their patterns of thought and action? The way in which we deal with these questions will determine the contours of the planet in which our children will live.[12]

Note that he was using the term "international relations" in its political, not academic, sense, mentioning "statesmen" but not scholars. But the same questions—and answers—apply to both of the IR communities.

DISCUSSION QUESTIONS

1. When does one use the term "diplomacy?" Is this any different from the term "foreign policy?" Or the term "international relations?" Is Rocard's usage too broad?
2. What do you think of the argument that we really don't need diplomats anymore because everything can be handled from the Foreign Office by phone, FAX, cable, or even a quick jet flight to any troublespot in the world?
3. Does Professor Hughes' essay make you more eager or less so to enter a diplomatic career? Why do diplomats have less authority now than they did in, say, de' Medici's time?
4. The UN Charter gives a veto to China in the Security Council. Do you think the United States can expect Beijing to again refrain from using it should another Gulf crisis arise? How many concessions, in trade especially, should Washington give in order to assure such cooperation again?
5. From a traditional viewpoint, one could hardly go further back in time than the Melian dialogue. But does one learn anything about present-day inter-state relations from such a debate? What about the threat by the Serbs against the citizens of Sarajevo? Would the "Cold Warriors"—on either side—have had anything to learn from the Athenians and Melians?
6. One of the oldest quips in international discourse is that a diplomat is someone sent abroad to lie for his country. Is this fair? Or is it just realistic?
7. How would you argue against the proposition that diplomacy is too elitist? Can it be democratic? Should it be?

---

[11](New York: Atheneum, 1962), p. 3.
[12]*op. cit.,* p. 26.

17 *THE MELIAN DEBATE*

THUCYDIDES

Unlike most historians, Thucydides, recorded his interpretations of events as they were taking place in the hope that they would be helpful to the Greece of the time. Most of his *History of the Peloponnesian War* represents a detailed and sophisticated military account by an ex-general, but the fifth book is a masterpiece of diplomatic writing, as instructive today as when it was written, almost 25 centuries ago. Spokesmen for mighty Athens try to explain to the weaker Melian plenipotentiaries why they should surrender without a fight; they explain why they have no intention of doing so even though they are perfectly aware of the probable consequences.

[416 B.C.] **84.** The next summer went Alcibiades to Argos with twenty galleys and took thence the suspected Argives and such as seemed to savour of the Lacedaemonian faction, to the number of three hundred, and put them into the nearest of the islands subject to the Athenian state.

The Athenians made war also against the isle of Melos, with thirty galleys of their own, six of Chios, and two of Lesbos. Wherein were of their own twelve hundred men of arms, three hundred archers, and twenty archers on horseback; and of their confederates and islanders, about fifteen hundred men of arms. The Melians are a colony of the Lacedaemonians, and therefore refused to be subject, as the rest of the islands were, unto the Athenians, but rested at the first neutral; and afterwards, when the Athenians put them to it by wasting of their land, they entered into open war.

Now the Athenian commanders, Cleomedes, the son of Lycomedes, and Tisias, the son of Tisimachus, being encamped upon their land with these forces, before they would hurt the same sent ambassadors to deal with them first by way of conference. These ambassadors the Melians refused to bring before the multitude, but commanded them to deliver their message before the magistrates and the few; and they accordingly said as followeth:

85. *Athenians.* "Since we may not speak to the multitude, for fear lest when they hear our persuasive and unanswerable arguments all at once in a continued oration, they should chance to be seduced (for we know that this is the scope of your bringing us to audience before the few), make surer yet that point, you that sit here; answer you also to every particular, not in a set speech, but presently interrupting us whensoever anything shall be said by us which shall seem unto you to be otherwise. And first answer us whether you like this motion or not?"

86. Whereunto the council of the Melians answered: "The equity of a leisurely debate is not to be found fault withal; but this preparation of war, not future but already here present, seemeth not to agree with the same. For we see that you are come to be judges of the conference, and that the issue of it, if we be superior in argument and therefore yield not, is likely to bring us war, and if we yield, servitude."

87. *Ath.* "Nay, if you be come together

The Peloponnesian War, fifth book, the Thomas Hobbes translation. Adapted from John A. Vasquez, *Classics of International Relations* (Englewood Cliffs, N.J.: Prentice Hall, 1986).

to reckon up suspicions of what may be, or to any other purpose than to take advice upon what is present and before your eyes, how to save your city from destruction, let us give over. But if this be the point, let us speak to it."

88. *Melians.* "It is reason, and pardonable for men in our cases, to turn both their words and thoughts upon divers things. Howsoever, this consultation being held only upon the point of our safety, we are content, if you think good, to go on with the course you have propounded."

89. *Ath.* "As we therefore will not, for our parts, with fair pretences, as that having defeated the Medes, our reign is therefore lawful, or that we come against you for injury done, make a long discourse without being believed; so would we have you also not expect to prevail by saying either that you therefore took not our parts because you were a colony of the Lacedaemonians or that you have done us no injury. But out of those things which we both of us do really think, let us go through with that which is feasible, both you and we knowing that in human disputation justice is then only agreed on when the necessity is equal; whereas they that have odds of power exact as much as they can, and the weak yield to such conditions as they can get."

90. *Mel.* "Well then (seeing you put the point of profit in the place of justice), we hold it profitable for ourselves not to overthrow a general profit to all men, which is this: that men in danger, if they plead reason and equity, nay, though somewhat without the strict compass of justice, yet it ought ever to do them good. And the same most of all concerneth you, forasmuch as you shall else give an example unto others of the greatest revenge that can be taken if you chance to miscarry."

91. *Ath.* "As for us, though our dominion should cease, yet we fear not the sequel. For not they that command, as do the Lacedaemonians, are cruel to those that are vanquished by them (yet we have nothing to do now with the Lacedaemonians), but such as having been in subjection have assaulted those that commanded them and gotten the victory. But let the danger of that be to ourselves. In the meantime we tell you this: that we are here now both to enlarge our own dominion and also to confer about the saving of your city. For we would have dominion over you without oppressing you, and preserve you to the profit of us both."

92. *Mel.* "But how can it be profitable for us to serve, though it be so for you to command?"

93. *Ath.* "Because you, by obeying, shall save yourselves from extremity; and we, not destroying you, shall reap profit by you."

94. *Mel.* "But will you not accept that we remain quiet and be your friends (whereas before we were your enemies), and take part with neither?"

95. *Ath.* "No. For your enmity doth not so much hurt us as your friendship will be an argument of our weakness and your hatred of our power amongst those we have rule over."

96. *Mel.* "Why? Do your subjects measure equity so, as to put those that never had to do with you, and themselves, who for the most part have been your own colonies, and some of them after revolt conquered, into one and the same consideration?"

97. *Ath.* "Why not? For they think they have reason on their side, both the one sort and the other, and that such as are subdued are subdued by force, and such as are forborne are so through our fear. So that by subduing you, besides the extending of our dominion over so many more subjects, we shall assure it the more over those we had before, especially being masters of the sea, and you islanders, and weaker (except you can get the victory) than others whom we have subdued already."

98. *Mel.* "Do you think then, that there is no assurance in that which we propounded? For here again (since driving us from the plea of equity you persuade us to submit to your profit), when we have shewed you what is good for us, we must endeavour to draw you to the same, as far forth as it shall be good for you also. As many therefore as now are neutral, what do you but make them your enemies, when, beholding these your proceedings, they look that hereafter you will also turn your arms upon them? And what is this, but to make greater the enemies you have already, and to make others your enemies, each against their wills, that would not else have been so?"

99. *Ath.* "We do not think that they shall be ever the more our enemies, who inhabiting anywhere in the continent, will be long ere they so much as keep guard upon their liberty against us. But islanders unsubdued, as you be, or islanders offended with the necessity of subjection which they are already in, these may indeed, by unadvised courses, put both themselves and us into apparent danger."

100. *Mel.* "If you then to retain your command, and your vassals to get loose from you, will undergo the utmost of danger, would it not in us, that be already free, be great baseness and cowardice if we should not encounter anything whatsoever rather than suffer ourselves to be brought into bondage?"

101. *Ath.* "No, if you advise rightly. For you have not in hand a match of valour upon equal terms, wherein to forfeit your honour, but rather a consultation upon your safety that you resist not such as be so far your overmatches."

102. *Mel.* "But we know that, in matter of war, the event is sometimes otherwise than according to the difference of number in sides; and that if we yield presently, all our hope is lost; whereas if we hold out, we have yet a hope to keep ourselves up."

103. *Ath.* "Hope, the comfort of danger, when such use it as have to spare, though it hurt them, yet it destroys them not. But to such as set their rest upon it (for it is a thing by nature prodigal), it at once by failing maketh itself known; and known, leaveth no place for future caution. Which let not be your own case, you that are but weak and have no more but this one stake. Nor be you like unto many men, who, though they may presently save themselves by human means, will yet, when upon pressure of the enemy their most apparent hopes fail them, betake themselves to blind ones, as divination, oracles, and other such things which with hopes destroy men."

104. *Mel.* "We think it, you well know, a hard matter for us to combat your power and fortune, unless we might do it on equal terms. Nevertheless we believe that, for fortune, we shall be nothing inferior, as having the gods on our side, because we stand innocent against men unjust; and for power, what is wanting in us will be supplied by our league with the Lacedaemonians, who are of necessity obliged, if for no other cause, yet for consanguinity's sake and for their own honour, to defend us. So that we are confident, not altogether so much without reason as you think."

105. *Ath.* "As for the favour of the gods, we expect to have it as well as you; for we neither do nor required anything contrary to what mankind hath decreed, either concerning the worship of the gods or concerning themselves. For of the gods we think according to the common opinion; and of men, that for certain by necessity of nature they will everywhere reign over such as they be too strong for. Neither did we make this law nor are we the first that use it made; but as we found it, and shall leave it to posterity for ever, so also we use it, knowing that you likewise, and others that should have the same power which we have, would do the same. So that forasmuch as toucheth the favour of the gods, we have in reason no fear of being inferior. And as for the opinion you have of the Lacedaemonians, in that you believe they will help you for their own honour, we bless your innocent minds, but affect not your folly. For the Lacedaemonians, though in respect of themselves and the constitutions of their own country they are wont for the most part to be generous; yet in respect of others, though much might be alleged, yet the shortest way one might say it all thus: that most apparently of all men, they hold for honourable that which pleaseth, and for just that which profiteth. And such an opinion maketh nothing for your now absurd means of safety."

106. *Mel.* "Nay, for this same opinion of theirs, we now the rather believe that they will not betray their own colony, the Melians, and thereby become perfidious to such of the Grecians as be their friends and beneficial to such as be their enemies."

107. *Ath.* "You think not, then, that what is profitable must be also safe, and that which is just and honourable must be performed with danger, which commonly the Lacedaemonians are least willing of all men to undergo [for others]."

108. *Mel.* "But we suppose that they will undertake danger for us rather than for any other; and that they think that we will be more assured unto them than unto any other, because for action, we lie near to Peloponneus, and for affection, are more faithful than others for our nearness of kin."

109. *Ath.* "The security of such as are at war consisteth not in the good will of those that are called to their aid, but in the power of those means they excel in. And this the Lacedaemonians themselves use to consider more than any; and therefore, out of diffidence in their own forces, they take many of their confederates with them, though to an expedition but against their neighbours. Wherefore it is not likely, we

being masters of the sea, that they will ever pass over into an island."

110. *Mel.* "Yea, but they may have others to send; and the Cretic sea is wide, wherein to take another is harder for him that is master of it than it is for him that will steal by to save himself. And if this course fail, they may turn their arms against your own territory or those of your confederates not invaded by Brasidas. And then you shall have to trouble yourselves no more about a territory that you have nothing to do withal, but about your own and your confederates."

111. *Ath.* "Let them take which course of these they will that you also may find by experience and not be ignorant that the Athenians never yet gave over siege for fear of any diversion upon others. But we observe that, whereas you said you would consult of your safety, you have not yet in all this discourse said anything which a man relying on could hope to be preserved by; the strongest arguments you use are but future hopes; and your present power is too short to defend you against the forces already arranged against you. You shall therefore take very absurd counsel, unless, excluding us, you make amongst yourselves some more discreet conclusion; for [when you are by yourselves], you will no more set your thoughts upon shame, which, when dishonour and danger stand before men's eyes, for the most part undoeth them. For many, when they have foreseen into what dangers they were entering, have nevertheless been so overcome by that forcible word dishonour that that which is but called dishonour hath caused them to fall willingly into immediate calamities, and so to draw upon themselves really, by their own madness, a greater dishonour than could have befallen them by fortune. Which you, if you deliberate wisely, will take heed of, and not think shame to submit to a most potent city, and that upon so reasonable conditions as of league and of enjoying your own under tribute; and seeing choice is given you of war or safety, do not out of peevishness take the worse. For such do take the best course who, though they give no way to their equals, yet do fairly accommodate to their superiors, and toward their inferiors use moderation. Consider of it, therefore, whilst we stand off; and have often in your mind that you deliberate of your country, which is to be happy or miserable in and by this one consultation."

112. So the Athenians went aside from the conference; and the Melians, after they had decreed the very same things which before they had spoken, made answer unto them in this manner: "Men of Athens, our resolution is no other than what you have heard before; nor will we, in a small portion of time, overthrow that liberty in which our city hath remained for the space of seven hundred years since it was first founded. But trusting to the fortune by which the gods have preserved it hitherto and unto the help of men, that is, of the Lacedaemonians, we will do our best to maintain the same. But this we offer: to be your friends, enemies to neither side, and you to depart out of our land, after agreement such as we shall both think fit."

113. Thus the Melians answered. To which the Athenians, the conference being already broken off, replied thus: "You are the only men, as it seemeth to us, by this consultation, that think future things more certain than things seen, and behold things doubtful, through desire to have them true, as if they were already come to pass. As you attribute and trust the most unto the Lacedaemonians, and to fortune and hopes, so will you be the most deceived."

114. This said, the Athenian ambassadors departed to their camp. And the commanders, seeing that the Melians stood out, fell presently to the war, and dividing the work among the several cities, encompassed the city of the Melians with a wall. The Athenians afterward left some forces of their own and of their confederates for a guard both by sea and land, and with the greatest part of their army went home. The rest that were left besieged the place.

115. About the same time the Argives, making a road into Phliasia, lost about eighty of their men by ambush laid for them by the men of Phlius and the outlaws of their own city. And the Athenians that lay in Pylus fetched in thither a great booty from the Lacedaemonians. Notwithstanding which, the Lacedaemonians did not war upon them [as] renouncing the peace, but gave leave by edict only to any of their people that would to take booties reciprocally in the territory of the Athenians. The Corinthians also made war upon the Athenians; but it was for certain controversies of their own, and the rest of Peloponnesus stirred not.

The Melians also took that part of the wall of the Athenians, by an assault in the night, which looked towards the market place, and having slain the men that guarded it, brought into the town both corn and other provision, whatsoever they could buy for money, and so returned and lay still. And the Athenians from thenceforth kept better watch. And so this summer ended.

116. The winter following, the Lacedaemonians being about to enter with their army into the territory of the Argives, when they perceived that the sacrifices which they made on the border for their passage were not acceptable returned. And the Argives, having some of their own city in suspicion in regard of this design of the Lacedaemonians, apprehended some of them and some escaped.

About the same time the Melians took another part of the wall of the Athenians, they that kept the siege being then not many. But this done there came afterwards some fresh forces from Athens, under the conduct of Philocrates, the son of Demeas. And the town being now strongly besieged, there being also within some that practised to have it given up, they yielded themselves to the discretion of the Athenians, who slew all the men of military age, made slaves of the women and children, and inhabited the place with a colony sent thither afterwards of five hundred men of their own.

18 THE OPPORTUNITY FOR DIPLOMACY

MICHEL ROCARD

M. Rocard, Prime Minister of France from 1988 to 1991, is an alumnus of the Ecole Nationale d'Administration and the Institute d'Etudes Politiques in Paris. In November 1991 he delivered the Leffingwell lectures at The Council on Foreign Relations in New York, from which the following is taken.

Future relations between the United States and the new Europe will take place in a new and constantly evolving international context. There has been considerable upheaval over the world in the last two years: National minorities have asserted themselves; the free market economy has imposed its values; dictatorships have crumbled; democratic values have triumphed. At the same time, however, the problem of under-development in the Third World and the former communist countries of Eastern Europe has grown worse.

What attitude should we adopt in the face of this evolution? In what way will international relations change? In what way will states and statesmen have to adjust their patterns of thought and action? The way in which we deal with these questions will determine the contours of the planet on which our children will live.

For almost fifty years we have lived in a bipolar world, its equilibrium based on the threat of nuclear holocaust—an unacceptable situation if ever there was one. Yet, now that we have come to the end of that particular tunnel, some people are worried about the future. Confident in the balance of terror that has given us peace since 1945, many people are afraid of the unknown and of what tomorrow will bring. And it is true—you need only watch the news every day—that the disintegration of the Eastern bloc is such a brutal process that it threatens to run completely out of control.

What a short-sighted attitude this is! How can anybody imagine that the enthusiasm of newbound freedom can be contained? How can anybody think that it will happen without pain and difficulty? How can anybody deny the need for radical changes in many countries, where the urgency of the situation is so well illustrated by the sorry state of the former communist societies? Do they think that words alone can alter the pace of history?

I welcome the disappearance of a world divided into opposing poles, and I rejoice, without reservation, at the fall of the "wall of shame," which for thirty years sym-

Excerpted from Michel Rocard, "Europe and the United States," *Critical Issues,* (New York: Council on Foreign Relation Press, 1992), 2. Reprinted by permission Copyright © 1992.

bolized the division of Europe. Along with hundreds of millions of men, women, and children who have finally found their freedom, I prefer to turn my back on the sadness of the past and put all my conviction and all my energy at the service of a promising future.

Today's world is above all a world of hope; we may finally have a chance to lay the foundations of a truly global community. Of course, there are no miracle recipes, no ready-made solutions. Even in developed countries resources are limited. Yet it is essential that we act now by being conscious of the link between national situations and the evolution of the world as a whole.

It is futile to imagine that we can build cocoons inside national boundaries protected from outside influences—pockets of prosperity in a world of misery. We must have a collective view of the organization and the running of the world community. We must banish selfishness and short-sighted nationalism and place our imagination and generosity at the service of the global community. . . .

The leaders of the Third World bear a heavy burden of responsibility today for their irresponsibility of yesterday—even if it is true that the South was a choice arena for limited wars in which the two superpowers attempted to extend their spheres of influence; even if it is true that colonial exploitation was perpetuated through the activities of transnational corporations whose decisions were not always in the interests of the states concerned; and even if it is true that the organization of world trade has made little allowance for Third World countries, despite years of international negotiations.

Paralyzed in its peacekeeping role by the opposition between the two major powers, the United Nations could have become the ideal forum for a true North-South dialogue. Unfortunately, the UN became the scene of sometimes violent confrontations regarding the demands of developing countries for compensation for the damage done by colonialism and the continued exploitation of their resources, which still largely eluded them.

The long negotiations from 1973–74 onward to define a more equitable "international economic order" were meant to establish an initial form of planetary solidarity. Dialogue soon fell on deaf ears, however, the communist countries remaining silent, hiding their inability to provide any economic aid or any new ideas behind a genuine sympathy for the "just cause of the anti-imperialist fighters." I partially believed in that struggle myself, for I could not be satisfied by the attitude of most of the leaders of the rich countries in rejecting the demands of the Third World outright under the pretext that some of them were excessive. There was a mood of revolt among our friends in the South, and revolt is often pure.

The failure of the "global negotiations" was due largely to the almost theological defense of the principle of noninterference, which was part and parcel of the South-North and East-West confrontations. International diplomacy, which was not in a position to generate original practices or concepts that would provide a basis for solutions to tackle the different problems of the world, was left partly paralyzed until a very recent date.

The world is gradually recognizing the superiority of the market economy, with each state defining appropriate regulations to achieve sustainable economic development. The collapse of Marxism convinced most nondeveloped countries, in the South and in the North, that democracy and the rule of law must go hand in hand with economic liberty if each is to be fully effective. The Berlin Wall fell under the pressure of a population eager for democracy, but they also expected this democracy to improve their standard of living. The movement has spread, and is developing today in Africa and Asia. The few remaining bastions of dictatorship are under siege.

THE PARADOX OF LIBERTY

Democracy is a gift of itself—a truth too many citizens in the wealthy countries tend to forget—and its link with prosperity is fully justified, for there can be no sustainable development without democracy. Dictatorship implies withdrawal into a shell, while in our increasingly complex societies the formation of wealth involves the free movement and exchange of information, goods, and people. Building democracy, however, will be a slow process, strewn with obstacles and convulsions.

The sudden collapse of the authoritarian regimes in the South and in the East, with their state-controlled economies, has left a wake of economic disorganization and social disruption, which, at least initially, translates into negative growth rates and a general drop in living standards. For this reason, there is serious risk in the countries undergoing democratization that hopes and expectations will give way to disappointment and, perhaps, to the rejection of the values of liberty and democracy. Today those values are associated with the aspiration to a better life, but they may become synonymous with misery and inequality if their benefits do not rapidly become apparent to all. The international community must therefore mobilize quickly to prevent a minority of speculators and profiteers from emerging as the only beneficiaries of the newfound freedom symbolized by the right to vote and the market economy.

THE ENVIRONMENT

The world environment is seriously threatened today by human activities, and major technological hazards are increasing. Just think of the Chernobyl disaster, the depletion of the ozone layer, and the dramatic warming of the climate! Think of the accidental or intentional pollutions that have become commonplace in our societies—so much so that they barely make news anymore. What about the degradation of arable land through overexploitation in the Northern Hemisphere, and the terrifying desertification that threatens certain countries in the South? Last, but not least, what about the massive urban development spreading everywhere—disorderly, excessive, uncontrolled, perhaps even uncontrollable?

These are challenges from which there is no escape, unless we want to contemplate the downfall of humanity. The very life of our planet is at stake. It is urgent that we organize a concerted response to these environmental problems on a worldwide level, followed up by resolute action. Only the commitment of world authorities can help to produce binding conditions and establish effective follow-up mechanisms. Public opinion, however, plays a vital role in promoting awareness among governments of their responsibilities in this field. Nongovernmental organizations also have a major contribution to make to research and action. . . .

The political concept of human rights

is rooted in a reaction against human misery in our civilization, which has led us to imagine the conditions of a more just and peaceful world. The recognition and promotion of the rights of the individual have become an objective and an active principle of life in modern society at the national level and in the community of nations.

Since the end of World War II and the Universal Declaration of 1948, a considerable normative effort has been made: Over sixty national instruments concerning human rights have been adopted. In reality, however, two worlds exist where human rights are concerned: an ideal, theoretical world—the fruit of negotiations and compromise patiently elaborated by diplomats and jurists—and a real world of passions and hatred, violence and oppression, misery and ignorance.

Let us be humble enough to admit that it was not the pacts of the United Nations that toppled the Berlin Wall or thwarted the Soviet coup! Nor was the long-awaited reunification of Germany the result of international negotiations: It was the people of Berlin who pulled down the wall that divided their families and all of Europe. In Warsaw, Budapest, Prague, or Bucharest, it was the people who toppled communism and its reign of repression and oppression. In Moscow, the military coup in August 1991—a farce from another era—failed because the people of Moscow resisted. Statesmen took note, and the law followed.

These undeniably positive events, which express the will of the people, do not mean that all codification should be stopped, but we must reconcile thought and action, law and reality, the norm and its enforcement. If the law eludes the real world and real life, the old demons of barbarism and lawlessness will rear their ugly heads. We must find the ways and means for dialogue to take place before tragedies occur. We must pay more heed to those who act. We must recognize the new actors on the international scene, as they have defined and imposed themselves, often against all odds, and we must draw up new, more operational concepts.

THE RIGHT TO INTERFERE

In the Soviet Union liberty appeared in the guise of a simple world: *glasnost*—transparency. This was no coincidence. There is a natural tendency for power—all forms of power and those who exert it—to be opaque. It is so easy for the experts to believe that they know best what others need to make them happy. We must combat opacity, which prevents us from hearing, from seeing, from knowing, and which comforts us in the fact that we do nothing to change what should be changed.

Opacity can even be found in the abundance of information in our highly media-conscious societies. We know and then we forget, because we learn something else. We can no longer put up with this constant oscillation between momentary indignation and recurrent amnesia. We must codify the right to assistance for peoples in danger, the right to intervene in the affairs of the world.

For more than twenty years, courageous men and women have been travelling the world bringing succor and assistance to people in distress. Defying taboos, leaping over borders, and forcing the hand of governments and international organizations, they brought to our attention the misery that still reigns in the world. "It was forbidden, but we did not know that," they would say, "so we just did it." They were doctors and they had a duty to sick people wherever they might be.

Today the UN has recognized the right to humanitarian assistance, and the law is in the process of codification. Last spring, thanks to this newly emerging law, over 1 million Kurds received the benefits of a humanitarian operation of exceptional magnitude. In Cambodia, the UN will govern the country for one year on behalf of the whole international community. Our conscience as human beings commands us to carry on the fight.

Once the right to intervene on humanitarian grounds is established, we shall have to develop and implement a right to intervene on democratic grounds to guarantee that human rights are respected everywhere. On the strength of the preamble to the San Francisco Charter, which begins with these marvelous words: "We, peoples of the United Nations . . . ," no tyrant must ever again be able to count on our silence or our inaction. Because all people have a right to dignity, to well-being, and to fulfillment, and because all children have a right to live.

ORGANIZING THE PLANET

Because of the spread of democracy and the market economy across the world, for the first time we have hope of achieving an international consensus on the ways and means of setting a true development process in motion in the countries of the South and the East. This gradual ideological unification places the wealthier nations under an obligation to increase and improve their aid programs, which, unfortunately, will be necessary for many years to come.

The structural adjustment policies necessary for economic revival in the underdeveloped countries almost always lead to fewer jobs in the public sector and to a decrease in public spending. The social cost is therefore terrible in countries where public structures are the origin of a considerable proportion of the income distributed. The Third World countries already know this, and have lived with it for over a decade now. The number of people living in a state of poverty could multiply dangerously, particularly in urban areas, with serious consequences for the younger generation in particular. The needs the governments will have to cater to will increase, while the budgetary resources available decrease.

It is vital, therefore, that the wealthier countries maintain and increase their financial support for many years to come. Absolute priority must be given to the debt problem and also, however difficult it may be, to opening up the markets of the more developed countries. To increase the efficacy of cooperation programs and ensure that the benefits go directly to the populations concerned, we must systematically encourage projects involving the citizens themselves and the associations they form. As a general rule, we must increase the number of microprojects designed specifically to cater to the needs of small communities.

In the Third World, the emergence of authentic democratic trends must encourage us to promote human rights and democratic parties and organizations. Assistance in the building of true states of law, where transparency and economic liberty are guaranteed, has become a priority. In short, the wealthy, democratic peoples of the world must consider those peoples emerging from oppressive regimes as adult peoples, free to decide for themselves, and as equal partners in the international system. Our aim should be a better spread of the burden and a fairer distribution of the benefits of the progress achieved by mankind.

There are too many bodies, organizations, and institutions in the world today responsible for community reflection and action. This calls for a change in the way the community of nations functions and for a reform of the existing organizations. There comes a time when "too many cooks spoil the broth," causing unnecessary waste and red tape, but above all diluting responsibilities.

It has become imperative that we group everything we can under a few major functions—political, economic, humanitarian, and cultural—and that we restore to the UN its essential role in the functioning of the international community. At the same time, we must reinforce the capacity for initiative and action that the UN recovered in recent years under the authority of its exceptional former secretary general, Javier Pérez de Cuéllar. This will entail a reform of the organization and its main decision-making bodies.

It is also time for states and statesmen to assume responsibility for their actions. International commitments, like all commitments, are not to be taken lightly. We must therefore accustom ourselves to signing binding legal documents that provide explicitly for follow-up, control, and even sanctionary measures. Only at this price will we restore the credibility and efficacy of structures for dialogue and cooperation on which increasing demands will be made.

In tomorrow's world, we will have to look beyond the political and economic structures of the present, which developed in conditions that are not necessarily relevant today. Our living spaces will probably be broader than our present states, offering us, perhaps, new frames of reference in which to develop solutions to the difficult problems raised by international migration. Nothing can stanch the flow of men and women driven by misery towards the poles of wealth that the developed nations represent in their eyes. We must seek to channel and organize the flow rather than attempting to oppose it.

We can no more envisage the state outside its international context than we can the individual outside his or her social context. That is why it is futile to dwell on the economic viability of the states born of the disintegration of the Soviet Union, a question which would only be pertinent if the state were the only relevant entity. The fact is that these states, at least on an economic level, can only be elements of larger spaces. Indeed, this seems to be the path they are determined to follow. In this respect, there is no real contradiction between the assertion by ever-smaller minorities of their national identities and the increasing globalization and unification of the world market.

The right of peoples to self-determination will no doubt experience new applications in the coming years, but without leading to the juxtaposition of microentities too small to be managed. An increasing number of larger structures—unions, federations, agreements, and multi- and supranational organizations—should accommodate all the pieces of the planetary puzzle. The move should be towards the definition of political spaces based not on the state or the economic unit—which may be larger or smaller—but on the freedom of people to move and to settle.

Regional communities are already emerging based on concrete interdependence and solidarities in or around which freedom of circulation is being organized. I am thinking, of course, of an example I consider as a model: the EC, an area where free circulation and integration go hand in hand, even if it remains to be decided how much of the European continent it will eventually cover. Other examples are the common Latin American market or the community of Pacific states which are gradually being formed.

The originality of the new North American market lies in the fact that it comprises two highly industrialized nations and one developing state. This remarkable initiative will perhaps provide the first concrete case of gradual integration, in a single space, of peoples with very different cultures and very unequal levels of development, but whose material and human resources are highly complementary.

The spaces of tomorrow will be spaces of liberty for all people.

* * *

If the developments I have attempted to outline here are to materialize without conflict, politicians will have to shake off political, economic, and philosophical ideas inherited from the nineteenth century. Imagination and flexibility must prevail over a blind determination to extend absolute and rigid models to the whole planet. This is a grand ambition indeed. It calls for no less than a complete, global overhaul of international relations and the progressive constitution of an embryo of collective government for world affairs. It is, however, a reasonable ambition, and it must be the basis of our action if we wish to preserve the right—and this is the crux of the matter—the right of future generations all over the world to live in harmony on a healthy, hospitable planet.

19 *THE FUNCTIONS OF DIPLOMACY*

Barry C. Hughes

Barry Hughes teaches international relations at the Graduate School of International Studies at The University of Denver.

Diplomacy involves three activities: representation, reporting, and negotiation. The first two, representation and reporting, center on the conveyance and acquisition of information, of which rational policy-making and implementation require large volumes.

REPRESENTATION

It is important to governments that other states adequately understand their policy concerns and objectives. For instance, one factor contributing to the invasion of South Korea by North Korean forces on June 25, 1950 may well have been inadequate communication by the United States of its commitment to defend South Korea from attack. On January 12, 1950, Secretary of State Dean Acheson gave a speech to the National Press Club in Washington in which he identified the defense perimeter of the Untied States in terms of a line from the Aleutians to Japan to the Ryukyus (islands of southwest Japan) to the Philippines (Dougherty and Pfaltzgraff 1986, 80). Although South Korea was not specifically excluded, it was not included. During his presidential campaign, Dwight Eisenhower subsequently argued that this definition virtually invited the attack. The United States has since been more careful not to omit any strategic interest from its public pronouncements.

States regularly attempt to clarify their policy positions in a variety of ways. One approach in the United States is the statement by presidents of doctrines. The Monroe Doctrine (1823) declared the Western hemisphere off-limits to European powers. The Truman Doctrine (1947) enunciated an intent to support any country resisting Communist pressure. The Carter Doctrine (1980) declared during the Iranian hostage crisis that the Persian Gulf was part of U.S. vital interests. In similar fashion, the Brezhnev Doctrine, formulated with the Soviet invasion of Czechoslovakia in 1967, stated that the Soviets would protect socialism, wherever it exists. On issues of special

Excerpted by permission from *Change and Continuity in World Politics,* 3d ed. Englewood Cliffs, NJ: Prentice-Hall, 1991, pp. 92–97. (Footnotes have been renumbered.)

importance governments also periodically issue "white papers," which generally review a policy problem and state official positions. On a day-to-day basis, foreign ministers routinely brief diplomats from other countries about their policy objectives and intent.

Although states normally wish to communicate clearly, and rely on skilled diplomats to avoid miscommunication, countries also deliberately obfuscate and conceal. With respect to the scope of concerns and intensity of interest, states commonly overstate them to avoid the kind of problem the United States had in Korea. The routine proclamation that a government would "view with serious concern" a particular action by another government deliberately creates some ambiguity about the actual extent of concern and potential counteraction. Similarly, countries may be unwilling to divulge information about their military capabilities. This can sometimes deter action by creating fear of greater retaliation than is actually possible.

Thus governments play a cat-and-mouse game with one another seeking to inform, misinform, and obfuscate. Still another twist is *disinformation* including the propagation of forged documents supposedly originating with one's opponent and intended to discredit that opponent. The Soviet Union once used this technique frequently. For instance, one Soviet forgery of a letter, supposedly from the American undersecretary of state to the ambassador in Greece, suggested that the United States was willing to support a military coup in Greece, if necessary to maintain its military bases there (Holsti 1988, 211–12). The purpose of the letter was to cause an intense anti–American reaction in Greece.

Propaganda, although tainted by frequent inclusion of untruths, is another form of representation. Diplomatic representation focuses on other governments, whereas propaganda frequently targets foreign populations. The United States Information Agency staffs more than one hundred libraries and information centers abroad. It has its own global radio network, the Voice of America. In addition Radio Marti broadcasts specifically for Cuba, as TV Marti began to do in 1990. Similarly, the Soviets have organized hundreds of "friendship societies" around the world. They operate Radio Moscow and Radio Peace and Progress. The British Broadcast Corporation maintains a World Service that has a well-deserved reputation for accuracy and a large global audience. Israel similarly relies on an array of organizations and individuals to communicate its message to the U.S. government and public.

REPORTING

Gathering intelligence and providing it to decision makers is a central activity of diplomats and foreign diplomatic missions. When the Iranian radicals labeled the American embassy in Teheran a "Den of Spies," they were in a most general sense correct. All embassies seek information on the objectives and interests of the states in which they are located. Much of the information search is open and, as we discussed earlier, the host country facilitates it. Because much information given freely omits or even obfuscates important details concerning intent and capabilities, however, states supplement it with clandestinely obtained knowledge.

Historically, the most important clandestine tool was human espionage. The advent of sophisticated electronic eavesdropping extended abilities dramatically. The

United States and the Soviet Union monitor conversations around the world. American evidence in 1988 that Libya was building a chemical weapons factory came in part from overhearing a telephone conversation between Libyan and German scientists.

The sophistication of electronic measures complicates the relationships between embassies and the host governments. The United States and the USSR have built and seek to open new embassies in Moscow and Washington, respectively. The United States found that surveillance equipment so permeated the structure of its new embassy in Moscow that it could never be secure. The United States had sought similarly to infiltrate electronically the new Soviet embassy in Washington, but apparently had less success because the Soviets completed its construction under much stricter controls. To complicate matters, the new Soviet embassy sits on a high point within Washington, so that modern electronic equipment can monitor communication in the heart of the U.S. capital. The United States refuses to let the Soviets occupy their new Washington embassy until they jointly resolve problems in Moscow; that could take many years.

The distinction between diplomat and spy is thus fuzzy at times. In addition governments around the world maintain extensive intelligence operations without the cloak of diplomatic function. Among the most famous or notorious are the Soviet Commissariat for State Security (KGB), the American Central Intelligence Agency (CIA), the Israeli Mossad, and the British MI-6. The bulk of the budgets for such organizations support a range of electronic and human intelligence gathering. Electronic intelligence gathering and protection of communication has become such a large-scale activity that the U.S. Department of Defense also maintains a huge National Security Agency (NSA) devoted solely to it.[1] Electronic intelligence using reconnaissance satellites, spy ships, special aircraft, and ground stations fall into its domain. The outside world may know less about the NSA than about the CIA. The public notoriety of the intelligence organizations comes, however, from their convert actions. The CIA, the KGB, and the services of other states support clandestine psychological, political, military, and economic activities.

NEGOTIATION

The third diplomatic activity, and the one we most often associate with diplomats, is negotiation. Obviously, an important function of negotiation is to reach agreement among two or more countries on issues in which they have partly overlapping, but also competing interests. Each side seeks to attain agreement as close to its own position as possible and skill of diplomats plays an important role. For instance, diplomats seek to conceal their minimally acceptable position or *resistance point* so as to achieve more. It is partly for this reason that the quotation from Sir Henry Wotton, an English official

(1568–1639) is so popular. He defined a diplomat as "an honest man sent abroad to lie for the good of the country" (Van Dinh 1987, 3).

Negotiation most often involves the iterative narrowing of the gap between initial positions—it is hoped in a movement toward the zone of overlap defined by the minimally acceptable positions. In some

[1]The U.S. signals intelligence program may employ 65,000 people, and the Soviets may use five times that many. For instance, the USSR monitors large portions of global FAX traffic (*The Christian Science Monitor*, November 21, 1989, 6).

cases skillful diplomacy even seeks to lower minimums and to create a zone of overlap where none initially existed.[2] For instance, Henry Kissinger flew repeatedly in 1947 between Aswan, Jerusalem, and Damascus and was able to accomplish a lowering of acceptable minimums, so as to secure an agreement among Egypt, Israel, and Syria that defused the military situation remaining from the 1973 Mideast War (Stoessinger 1976, 190–200). His technique became known as *shuttle diplomacy*. President Jimmy Carter accomplished the same feat in 1978, when he brought Egyptian President Sadat and Israeli Prime Minister Begin to Camp David (the U.S. presidential retreat) and shuttled between their cabins until an agreement was obtained.

Diplomacy, however, is often a "velvet glove" that conceals the iron hand of power. Weaker powers must frequently make concessions at the table to avoid losses in a test of power. Because powerful states normally prevail in negotiations, states seek to "negotiate from strength." In Vietnam and in Afghanistan, the United States and the USSR found themselves forced eventually to negotiate from considerable weakness (specifically, an obvious lack of will to continue fighting) and both obtained settlements that did little more than cloak their decisions to unilaterally withdraw. The close relationship between diplomacy and force gives rise to a combination that Craig and George (1983) called *coercive diplomacy*. For instance, the British threatened the use of force against Argentina in the early states of the 1982 Falklands-Malvinas dispute, and moved almost in slow motion to apply force, as a part of their search for a diplomatic settlement. The United States justified its bombing of North Vietnam in terms of forc-

ing the Vietnamese to the negotiating table. As these examples illustrate, coercive diplomacy is not always successful.

Negotiation also sometimes has functions other than the apparent one of attaining agreement. It may have a propaganda function. Both superpowers periodically put forward arms control proposals that appeared sincere, but that were patently unacceptable to the other side and that sought only to convey a peace-loving image to publics around the world. Soviet calls over many years for general and complete disarmament fell into this category. Another function is to stall for time in the hope that the external power balance will shift in one's favor.[3] At the beginning of the Vietnam War negotiations in 1969, interminable debates centered on the shape of the negotiating table. Although reflecting some substantive disagreement (notably the identification and status of parties to the negotiation), the delays represented fundamentally the desire of the parties to seek resolution in the battlefield rather than the conference room. They finally obtained an agreement in 1973, when the United States wanted out of the war.

Negotiating styles differ considerably across time and by country. In the nineteenth century, diplomats commonly conducted discussions covertly and even kept important mutual defense treaties secret. This *old diplomacy* had some advantages. Practitioners could conduct it in a somewhat genteel atmosphere, unconstrained by the passions of public opinion. The contribution of secret treaties to the spread of World War I (by committing states to actions of which other states were unaware), and the democratization of government in the twentieth century, brought a new, public diplomacy. With few exceptions, like the secrete

---

[2]Druckman and Hopmann (1989) review the literature and practice of negotiation and conclude that we must relax the assumptions by the realist model of bilateral, unitary, rational, and symmetrical actors.

[3]Negotiation may also simply placate domestic forces or attempt to divide an opposing alliance (Jensen 1988b, 10).

dispatch of diplomats by Bush to China in 1989, diplomats conduct the *new diplomacy* quite openly. Although sessions took place behind closed doors, the press regularly reported progress in the Intermediate Nuclear Forces and Strategic Arms Reduction Talks negotiations between the United States and the USSR during 1987–90.

Bargaining styles also differ across countries:

Sir Harold Nicolson, a renowned British diplomat argued on the basis of his long experience that the bargaining styles of a country's diplomats reflect major cultural values of their society. He contrasted the "shopkeeper" style of British diplomats—one that is generally pragmatic and based on the assumption that compromise is the only possible reason for outcome of bargaining—with the style of the totalitarian governments, particularly Soviet Russia in the 1920s and during the height of the cold war, and Nazi Germany in the 1930s. The diplomats of these regimes were known for rigidity in bargaining positions; extensive use of diplomatic forums for propaganda displays; coarseness of language; a strategy of trying to wear down opponents by harangues; interminable wrangling over minute procedural points; constant repetition of slogans and clichés; and, most important, the view that agreements were tactical maneuvers only, to be broken or violated whenever it was to one's advantage (to quote Lenin, "Agreements are like pie crusts: They are made to be broken."). (Holsti 1988, 183)[4]

Although ideology underlies much difference in style, power differentials contribute to the explanation. More powerful states can afford "sincere" and "pragmatic" styles aimed at finalizing agreements. Less powerful states are more likely to bluster and posture, and to rely on tactics to wear down the other side. As the Soviets gained military parity with the West, their negotiating style also evolved toward that of the West.[5]

---

[4]Indicating that national characterizations can be dangerous, Barnet (1984) says Lenin was actually quoting an old British proverb.

[5]There remain important differences. Jensen says Soviet negotiators still exhibit insecurity and paranoia in dealing with the West. Former U.S. START negotiator Edward Rowny stresses that the Soviets have greater patience: "The Russians play chess; we play video games. They like the well-thought through results of step-by-step reasoning; we like the instant results of electronic games" (Jensen 1988b, 16).

CHAPTER FIVE

THE GAME: CHARACTERISTICS OF THE SYSTEM

The term "balance of power" is notorious for the numerous meanings that may be attached to it, the tendency of those who use it to shift from one to another and the uncritical reverence which statements about it are likely to command.

Hedley Bull,
The Anarchical Society (1977)[1]

Though the Cold War may be over, the international system is obviously still reflective of power politics. Hence, to understand and to operate effectively within it requires an understanding of the nature of power. In this chapter, that system is described by a philosopher and a political scientist, Martin Hollis and Steve Smith, who bring their respective disciplines together in an unusual and original manner. Because of its vision about the possible future of the international system, it is felt that some attention should be given to the second Fulton, Missouri address (noted in Chapter One), in which citizen Mikhail Gorbachev reflects upon his unique experience as a world leader and comes up with some novel proposals. From an entirely different perspective we include a distinguished academician's assessment of the future of the international system; Barry Buzan, one of the keenest British observers of the evolving constellation of states, shows what security patterns now emerging will dominate the next century.

Before reading what they and a most perceptive exponent of the Third World viewpoint, Mohammed Ayoob, have to offer, it might be well to review the nature of the system which dominated politics for the past forty-five years and is

[1]Hedley Bull, *The Anarchical Society.* (New York: Columbia University Press, 1977), excerpted in the 8th edition of this book, p. 151.

indeed still with us more than many people would like to concede. A bipolar "balance of powder," with all its faults and confusions, has been the principal characteristic of this era. The ways in which the ability of a state to achieve what it wants, while all the other states are trying to do the same thing, plays itself out is what the late W.T.R. Fox termed "the balancing process."[2] Some students of international politics maintain that all human behavior, including the behavior of actors on the world stage, is characterized by a power drive. Bertrand Russell, for example, took the view that of all the desires of humankind, the chief are for power and glory, but noted that some human desires, unlike those of animals, are incapable of complete satisfaction.[3] The power drive is neither unlimited nor omnipresent, even though the concept of power may provide a particularly effective organizing focus for analyzing relations among individuals and groups, including the sometimes gigantic and always complex groupings whose interaction is the subject matter of the study of international relations. Even Machiavelli, whose book *The Prince*[4] still symbolizes the power approach as well as anything ever written, recognized that there are other values or drives in the minds of those who have to determine the course of events. A wide range of objectives, anxieties, and assumptions guide those responsible for determining action in foreign policy. While considerations of power cannot be said to be a conscious priority in each and every situation demanding a decision, much depends upon how power is defined. While Russell postulated that power was the production of intended results, Harold Lasswell thought it was the *ability* to produce intended results. If it is equated with physical force alone, many international relationships simply cannot be explained by sole reference to relative possession of military strength. But if "power" implies not only a military but also a psychological, economic, and even moral ability to influence or control, then one wonders whether it has not lost any precise or analytical meaning. Power, however defined, is not only an immediate means, but a long-range foreign objective in itself—"power for power's sake." It ranks high in many states' "shopping bag" of things to be acquired, indeed *demanded,* from the international community. In this chapter Mohammed Ayoob, in an arresting analysis of what he calls the "security problematic," applies this with telling insight to the demands of third world decision-makers. While the so-called Great Powers have been rendered increasingly impotent because of the force and frequency of these demands, they actually demonstrate their power by being the only ones capable of meeting the demands. Whether they actually choose to do so is a matter of decision. The choice of goals and policies are also conditioned by the

[2]For a tantalizing glimpse into the profound thought of this wise, brilliant but relatively less-then-richly-productive scholar and teacher, see W.T.R. Fox's *Theoretical Aspects of International Relations,* (Notre Dame: University of Notre Dame Press, 1967). He gave most of his intellectual energy to his grateful students, of whom the author was one.

[3]See especially *Power: a New Social Analysis.* (New York: W. W. Norton, 1938).

[4]Niccolo Machiavelli, *The Prince* (1532). According to Theodore Francis Jones, professor of European History at New York University, "in spite of his bad reputation, Machiavelli was a zealous Italian patriot, trying to find the surest way to expel the foreigners and unify Italy." *A Guide to Historical Literature,* (New York: Peter Smith, 1949), p. 686. He adds that the best annotated edition is *Il principe.* ed. by L. Arthur Burd, with an introduction by Lord Acton, Oxford, 1891.

capabilities and leverage a country has at its disposal. No one state is likely to be able to achieve all of its aims; sooner or later, its decision-makers will have to make choices.

The reason that power traditionally looms so large in the analysis of IR is that sovereignty places a premium upon the state's being able to provide "security." This has become a key word. Only a "superpower" can provide the budgets, the sophisticated equipment, the leadership, and the logistics to conduct war on an inter-continental scale. Yet even the one remaining superpower—the United States—is insecure, despite a huge land base framed by mighty oceans, a large and skilled population, and a gigantic industrial infrastructure. What may soon be demonstrated is that there are *no* superpowers left at all, probably not through a collapse of the one remaining, but by a shift of its priorities to other values. National power is not only the product of a state's will and determination to acquire military forces appropriate to its situation and the threat-value of its neighbors.

Before the inexorable demands of the Cold War brought about its collapse as a viable system, the determined will of Soviet leadership and the capacity for stoic endurance of the people over which it ruled enabled the country not only to recover from a devastating war against Hitler but to acquire the military trappings of a nuclear superpower. Although Communist China also possesses a large territory, an enormous population, and (at least until recently) a relatively progressive totalitarian regime, it still has far to go before achieving superpower status. Nonetheless, it would be difficult to overcome in any serious military encounter, partly because of its sheer will to survive and partly (as India learned to its dismay when it was invaded by China) because of a well-organized army. On the other hand, neither Japan nor the countries of Western Europe possess the will to compete on an intercontinental scale despite their highly advanced technology, skilled populations without peer, and remarkable leadership capability. Superpower status has eluded both of them even with the reduction of the USSR to a dubious CIS status and the combined unwillingness and inability of the United States to finance large-scale expenditures for international programs. Indeed, an unexpected outcome of the demise of the Cold War is a perceptible slowing down of the integrative momentum which was on the verge of producing what might in time have become an economic (if not a military) superpower—the European community.

Critics argue that the balance of power is nothing but a succession of imbalances which finally lead to war because states and their leaders want, not equilibrium, but superiority.[5] This propensity for power not only arouses suspicion and distrust, but as Professor Ayoob explains it creates a dilemma for the leaders of countries which figure little in the balancing process, who argue that the very idea of *balance* implies two rival blocs. This makes war more likely, if not inevitable, because each side is bound to regard any loss or defeat of one of its

---

[5]For an authoritative guide to "opinions of and interpretations on" the balance of power as a principle, refer to the index in F.H. Hinsley, *Power and the Pursuit of Peace: Theory and Practice in the Relations of States*, (Cambridge: Cambridge University Press, 1967), pp. 392–393.

allies as threatening the security of the entire alliance, as occurred in 1914. Compromise becomes more difficult, especially if the protagonists both feel that concession would be seen as a diplomatic defeat or an unacceptable sign of weakness. The balancing process may generate an arms spiral as each side feels the other is attempting to gain in weapons capability. The Strategic Arms Limitation Treaty (SALT II) was rejected precisely for this reason, the view in Congress being that the proposed agreement would work unequally to the advantage of the USSR, even though Administration experts denied that this would actually be the case. None of this works to the advantage of developing countries whose leaders struggle to find a place in the system.

The balance of power, Hedley Bull once said, favors the Great Powers at the expense of the small.[6] This would go to the point of partitioning or even devouring them (as in the case of Poland at the end of the eighteenth century or at the end of the second World War when it was divided and then occupied as a buffer against aggression from capitalist or fascist forces). In the Western Hemisphere, American efforts to overthrow the government of Panama, capturing its President in the process and bringing him back to a Florida jail, were justified as being necessary to protect national security. At the same time Moscow sent troops into neighboring Afghanistan to forestall an unfavorable reversal of its influence in that country. In neither case was the superpower ultimately successful (though one must concede that in world politics, "ultimately" is a long time).

The greatest challenge to any balance of power occurs not on the periphery but when a particular participant in the balance seems determined to upset the existing equilibrium, come what may. Having become the dominant land power on the continent after defeating France in 1870, the Kaiser (after he dropped Bismarck and his restraints) appeared intent upon building a navy capable of challenging Britain's power on the high seas as well. In the face of Germany's intentions and growing power, Britain felt compelled to abandon a particularly effective form of the balance of power through "splendid isolation" from the alliance structures of Europe, preferring to come in to restore the balance by, as Churchill once put it, "supporting the weaker side on the continent." An *entente* with France was undertaken in 1904, strengthened in 1907, threatened in 1911, and finally faced with war in 1914. A generation later, Britain proved again too weak to maintain the balance, and war followed in 1939. Traditionally, war has been the ultimate means whereby the balance has been maintained or restored once lost. Peace, whatever the claims of its advocates, is never the basic, however desirable, object of a balance of power policy.

In the aftermath of World War II, the balance of power took on a bipolar form, with only two Powers possessing the means and the apparent will to threaten one another. Even though the impossibility of an accommodation instead of a balance was due to ideology, the only hope for the weaker Asian and Western states for maintaining their own security was through allying themselves with one of the two superpowers. Thus Western European joined an alliance

[6]Bull, *op. cit.*, p. 150.

with the United States, and Communist China allied itself with the Soviet Union, the so-called Warsaw Pact being an alliance in name only, based as it was on a virtual postwar occupation by the Red Army. When by the 1960s global tensions had eased, tensions within each bloc came to the surface. With the defection of China from the Communist bloc and of France partially from the NATO bloc, and with the evident inability of the two superpowers to dictate to their partners in all matters, there emerged what was called (perhaps inaccurately and certainly prematurely) a "multipolar balance." For awhile, at the height the period of *detente,* the Nixon administration was said even to promote the idea of a five-power balance: the United States, the Soviet Union, China, Western Europe, and Japan. More realistically, for a time the normalization of American relations with Beijing gained for Washington a margin for diplomatic maneuvering *vis-a-vis* the Soviet Union characteristic of a three-power balance, neither Japan nor Western Europe being able or willing to play that game. But that game is over.

Toward the so-called "third world," efforts by both protagonists, and later China, to use every technique of favor and influence—economic assistance, military equipment, support for "client" states against domestic and regional foes—to secure an advantageous alignment came all to little avail and at tremendous cost. Instead, they grouped together the target states in the Group of 77 non-aligned countries (actually now over 100) which appears to constitute a bloc of its own, although neither in terms of intent nor of capability has that Group any chance of becoming one in the balance of power sense. China has tried to place itself at the head of this Third World bloc, but few small states have demonstrated much interest in following that lead. To the extent that the global balance was dependent upon the stability of regional balances, the United States found itself at an increasingly perplexing disadvantage. The elites of regional states are far more intent upon making use of outside influence to perpetuate their own existence that they are in serving the interests of big powers, however much help they can get from them. This is simply another reason why the East-West balance was so inherently unstable, at least as a governing theory. As Ayoob explains, it also placed the Third World countries in a difficult dilemma—to try to compete from positions of relative weakness or to accept a permanently subordinate place in the international system.

It is the skill and finesse with which military capability is employed in diplomacy, more than the use or threat of crude military power, that determines the outcome of struggles in faraway places around the globe. Hollis and Smith show how this reality is an essential ingredient of the international system as they understand and explain it. Many of the shifts in the postwar balance have come about through changes in ideological and social alignments within a country with very limited influence from the outside. Just as American military power could have done little to prevent the outcome of the civil war that brought Mao Tse-tung to power, Moscow was equally ineffective in an opposite manner; indeed, its sometimes clumsy efforts to gain influence had more do to with China's shift to the West than anything the U.S. was able to accomplish through exercise of its military strength. Sadat reoriented Egypt's foreign policy independently of the

United States, much to the latter's advantage, not through its effort on a military level but through a quiet diplomatic presence.[7]

Castro's enmity toward the United States was a consequence of a century of American intervention of one kind or another in Cuban affairs, sealed by the abortive Bay of Pigs invasion. All of this suggests that the operationalization of the balance of power in the Third World presents unique obstacles and limitations which neither superpower has ever entirely appreciated. To be sure, in dealing with the Third World the Kremlin has many times altered its ideological line, just as Washington has recast its rhetoric, but the implications of trying to manage relations with the countries which make up the Third World in traditional balance-of-power terms has not been fully grasped. Both powers have suffered reverses by seeking to establish proAmerican (as in the Baghdad Pact) or proSoviet (as in Egypt) balance-of-power arrangements with local regimes whose people and interests were opposed to any such connection. An obsessive effort to integrate every part of the world into the global balance of power is both costly and counterproductive, especially when so much of the effort neglects the underlying needs of the weaker states for economic and social development.

The need for balance in the Third World—the Middle East excepted—may be considerably overrated. Knowledge of other countries' political dynamics and the integrity of diplomats in reporting these dynamics may be more vital to success than a mechanistic version of a military balance. For a time, in the aftermath of the Cuban missile crisis, it appeared that the two superpowers might be engaged in a process of stabilizing the nuclear balance of power. Philip Brenner has revealed in a recent survey of correspondence between Kennedy and Khrushchev in *Problems of Communism* how close the world then was to nuclear war.[8] Mutual suspicion tended to be confirmed as a result of two factors which provided obstacles to meeting the preconditions for agreement. The first was that technological advances take place so rapidly that concessions based upon the technology at any particular moment are regarded as potentially too dangerous. Second, the assymetry that existed can plausibly be seen by the one side as masking the worst possible intentions of the other. Neither was prepared to take a chance on the good will of the other. The value consensus that existed as among the elites of the Great Powers in the heyday of the balance of power in the seventeenth to the nineteenth centuries has been replaced by value systems which have almost nothing in common.

All of this simply illustrates the complexity of the balance of power, both as a concept and as a description of reality at any given time, which any serious student of international relations should try to master as an analytical tool, if not necessarily as a philosophical principle.

---

[7]In his memoirs as National Security Adviser, Zbigniew Brzezinski draws attention to how the "willingness" to compromise was conveyed more by mood, by gestures, than by words" by the late Prime Minister of Egypt, Anwar Sadat, in his contacts with U.S. envoys. *Power and Principle*, (New York: Farrar, Straus, Giroux, 1983), p. 238.

[8]Philip Brenner, "Kennedy and Khruschev on Cuba," *Problems of Communism*, XLI, Spring. 1992, pp. 24–27.

DISCUSSION QUESTIONS

1. Review the new pattern, Barry Buzan postulates for the future. Do any of these seem implausible, given what we have learned about how the system has worked in the present century?
2. Why is the balance of power such an ambiguous idea? How would you define "power" in that construct?
3. In putting forth what he calls a "security problematic" for the Third World, how does Mohammed Ayoob describe the motives and methods of the first and second worlds? Is there a "Second World" now? Which countries now make up the "First World?"
4. Why have Third World combatants felt the effects of wars more keenly than the Western states involved?
5. Do you find the case for the contemporary relevance of the balance of power convincing? What are some counterarguments?
6. Were you a representative negotiating on behalf of the United States in trying to convince the Russians that it is to their advantage to allow the Americans to help them dismantle the missiles still aimed at America, how would you make the case? What are the main points you would anticipate being made against your proposition?
7. At the Vancouver Summit in April 1993, what were the *balance of power* considerations which Presidents Yeltsin and Clinton both had to take account of as they talked?

20 *THE INTERNATIONAL SYSTEM*

MARTIN HOLLIS AND STEVE SMITH

Martin Hollis is Professor of Philosophy at the University of East Anglia, where he is currently pro-vice-chancellor. He has published a number of major books focusing on the philosophy of the social sciences, and is a Fellow of the British Academy.

Steve Smith is Professor of International Politics at the University of Wales, Aberystwyth. He has published widely in the area of international theory and foreign policy analysis. He is Series Editor of the Cambridge University Press Series "Studies in International Relations" and is currently vice-president of the International Studies Association.

Realism has always inclined toward structural explanation, but has not always embraced it with the thoroughgoing fervor of Neo-Realists like Kenneth Waltz.[1] We shall start by tracing the development of Realist ideas of structure and then refine the case for a purely structural theory like Waltz's.

The international system seems a clear example of the sort of social order long of interest to political theorists, namely, an anarchical grouping of self-interested units who cooperate only in so far as it suits them. As such, it stands in marked contrast to the structure found in domestic society, where the constituent units have a body above them to act as law-giver and law-enforcer. The *anarchic* international system contrasts with the *hierarchical* domestic system. At first sight this should mean a weak set of structural international determinants, as opposed to the more obviously coercive hierarchical domestic system. After all, the international system seems only the sum of interactions among the constituent units. It

has no separate organizations or bodies outranking state sovereignty.

Accordingly, much early work in International Relations used the concept of society rather than that of system. International relations seemed well suited to the theory of the social contract in one or other of its main traditional forms. One form comes down to us from Thomas Hobbes's *Leviathan,* published in 1651 in the wake of the English Civil War, and embodies a "conflict" model of society. The other inspired by John Locke's *Second Treatise on Civil Government* (1690), offers a "consensus" model. Both models have their attractions.[2]

Hobbes thought that human beings were competitive by nature and that their natural state—the "state of nature"—was one marked by a war of all against all, with "the life of man solitary, poor, nasty, brutish and short." The basic problem, therefore, is how a commonwealth can arise and flourish. Hobbes's answer was that even ruthlessly

[1]K. Waltz, *Theory of International Politics* (Reading, Mass.: Addison-Wesley, 1979).

[2]T. Hobbes, *Leviathan* [1651] (Glasgow: Fontana, 1983); see especially ch. 13, J. Locke, *Two Treatises of Government* [1690] (Cambridge: Cambridge University Press, 1967).

self-interested individuals will make a social contract, provided that it creates a "power to keep all in awe." This power would need to be a limited central government with a complete but narrow monopoly of coercive authority—"Covenants without the sword are but vain breath." Then each citizen would obey because the government could guarantee that others would obey also, and all could enjoy "commodious living." This model appeals to Realists in International Relations because its Rational Actor assumptions include the self-interested motivation which Realists ascribe to nation states.

Locke took a less harsh view of human nature and so thought cooperation more natural and less fragile. Indeed, civil society so plainly offered benefits to all that the reader sometimes wonders why government is necessary. Locke's answer is the one enshrined in the American constitution, which was drawn up by people influenced by his writings. It allows for a more tolerant and pluralistic style of government than does Hobbes, and, in International Relations, appealed especially to Idealists. If peace, rather than war, is the natural state, then harmonious international relations should not need a world government armed with the sword.

Both versions of social contract theory work "bottom-up," thinking of society as a group of individuals, and of its institutions, its rules and norms, as having emerged by mutual consent from anarchy. One standard objection to such an account of domestic politics is that the "state of nature" envisaged as a starting point is surely a historical fiction and, moreover, one which could inspire a social contract only among individuals who *already* had the practice of making contracts. This objection does not apply to an International Relations version where the individuals are nation states, which do indeed already understand contracts and where an international "civil society" is ap-

parently in the process of emerging before our very eyes. Accordingly, there has been a powerful group of scholars who think in social contract terms and define international society not as a determining structure or system but as a network of norms and rules governing a society of states.[3]

One might object that what has been emerging before our very eyes, especially since 1945, is as likely to be several societies as just one. The objection would be that the "society" of the Western state does not extend across the entire system. The Third World is essentially omitted from the practices and understandings of the developed world. There is no single international society, if by society one means an integrated grouping with a common identity and a common way of seeing the world. But it is more to our purpose to note the existence of "bottom-up" theories in order to contrast them with the theories of the international system which work "top-down" by maintaining that state behavior is caused by structural factors. This contrast has interesting parallels in other social sciences. In economics there is an argument between those who think of market forces as a system, which dictates the behavior of firms, and their opponents who insist that the internal organization of firms affects what happens in the market. In sociology, social structures are seen by some as determinants of social life and by others as groups of institutions thrown up by social interaction. In general, a "top-down" approach has the attraction that, if it works, the social scientist need not worry about what goes on inside the units of the system because they are bound to conform to the demands of the system. This

---

[3]See for example, H. Butterfield and M. Wight (eds.), *Diplomatic Investigations* (London: Allen and Unwin, 1966); M. Donelan (ed.), *The Reason of States* (London: Allen and Unwin, 1978); J. Mayall (ed.), *The Community of States* (London: Allen and Unwin, 1982).

attraction has been strong in International Relations too.

How, then, has the international system been treated in the main theories of international relations? As we have seen, both Idealism and Realism had a place for the system, even though the two theories actually relied much more on other factors to explain international behavior. For the Idealists, the system obtrudes in so far as war is blamed on misunderstanding and misperception. Improving the system was a necessary condition for eliminating war. This view resulted in a very specific role for the League of Nations and for "men of peace." The very subject of International Relations had to be reoriented so as to assist the better working of the international system. However, beneath the surface in Idealist thought was a liberal view of human nature, which, by assuming rationality, downplayed the role of the international system. Conflict was avoidable, and its causes could be found in the domestic settings of states. The international system was involved in the causes of conflict only in exacerbating misunderstanding. There was nothing intrinsically conflict-inducing in the international system. International society was, therefore, not something that needed structural reform if war were to be avoided. War had other sources, and the international system needed attention only to ensure that it allowed the process of mediation to function smoothly. This reflects a very specific view of human nature, and implies a very limited role for systemic causes in international relations.

But, of course, the events of the late 1930s were a powerful reminder that war is not only the result of misunderstanding. That called for a less complacent view of the international system. At the very least, it implied that the system had to be so arranged as to allow for collective security. The system looked as if it might encourage war by its structure, if not cause it. This seemed to be a central message of Realism, with its stress on the need for means to ensure national security. Yet, in the early versions of the Realist case, attention was concentrated on the nature of human beings as the source of conflict in the world. This was certainly the lesson that Morgenthau drew from the events of the 1930s. For Realists, the international system was important because its anarchical structure required that, to avoid war, the mechanisms of diplomacy, international law, and the balance of power operated effectively. It was therefore imperative that states' leaders understood the power-maximizing tendencies of individuals. This not only required a conception of morality between states different from that which applied within societies (since different structures were operating), but also implied that the system somehow operated by the ebbs and flows of the power of states. For Morgenthau, it was the centrality of power that allowed scientific precision to be used in explaining international relations. The theory was a *power-politics* model, and the anarchical structure of the international system was central in explaining how power politics operated.

The nature of the international system determined the basic foreign policy orientations of any particular state, and, Morgenthau held, whether a state followed a policy of *status quo, imperialism,* or *prestige* depended on its location in the international power structure. This, as we saw in Chapter 2, allowed Morgenthau to claim that the personal motives and values of decision-makers were irrelevant to any explanation of the policies of their states. From this angle, Realism looks very deterministic, leaving little room for the individual decision-makers to act. Yet this is only part of the Realist picture, since, as with Idealism, the central theoretical mechanism at work was again human nature. For Morgenthau, it was the nature of individuals that was the final source of explanations of international relations. The international system was not important as a *cause* of state behavior; at most it provided conditions in which human nature could cause war. But this was not how critics saw Realism at the time, and many of the early critiques condemned its failure to deal with the particular motives and values of the individual decision-makers. The Behavioralism of the 1950s explicitly rejected the determinism of Realism and tried to move away from a "billiard ball" conception of international relations in which power was the only motive force.

Yet the Behavioralist critique in fact sharpened the issue of the importance of the systems level, precisely because it sought to be explicit about how theories of behavior were to be built. Two examples are especially interesting. One is the work of Kenneth Waltz on the causes of war.[4] In his widely cited 1959 monograph, *Man, the State and War,* he outlines three levels at which we might explain the occurrence of war. The first is that of the nature of individuals, and essentially assumes that human nature is fixed, and is either evil or at any rate selfish. The second traces war to the character of some kinds of states, and postulates that there would be no war in an international system composed only of a pacific type of state. The third sees war as the result of the structure of the international system, with the central cause being the anarchical structure of the system.

All three levels have received attention in the literature of International Relations over the years, and Waltz's concern is partly to identify the arguments applying on each level. But his aim is also to offer a view as to why war in general (as distinct from specific wars) occurs. He therefore introduces the system itself as a causal factor in a very explicit way: "Wars occur because there is nothing to prevent them," he writes.[5] The point is to show that, although the first two levels may explain the reasons for any specific war, without the third level there can be no general understanding of why war happens. In Waltz, the framework within which other causes operate is the *structure* of the international system. Given the sovereignty of the constituent units of international society (states), and the consequent absence of any authority above the separate states, states are their own umpires. The anarchical structure of the system imposes on all states a security dilemma, whereby they have to ensure their own security without increasing the fears of other states in the system. These factors, claims Waltz, are systemic, and are not reducible to the motives, beliefs, values, or capabilities of the units that comprise the system. To explain international relations, then, we must theorize at the level of the international system.

Waltz was the first to discuss openly the notion that there were a number of levels at which international relations could be explained, but his was very much the voice of a theorist. The notion really took hold in earnest with our second example. This is the work of one of the leading Behavioralist scholars, Morton Kaplan, who, in his 1957 book, *System and Process in International Politics,*[6] proposed that the new science of international relations be built on a systems approach. This would proceed by constructing deductive models of the international system, and then examining history for examples of them. Systems would obey two sets of rules: a set of characteristic behavioral rules that were necessary for the system to stay in equilibrium; and a set of transformation

---

[4]K. Waltz, *Man, the State and War* (New York: Columbia University Press, 1959).

[5]Ibid. p. 232.

[6]M. Kaplan, *System and Process in International Politics* (New York: Wiley, 1957).

rules, dealing with how a system might change to another type of system. Kaplan outlined six of these systems, and insisted that there was no need to identify the nation states involved, since what happened in the system determined the rules of the system and hence the behavior of the units. It is easy to imagine how this type of thinking fitted well with the quantitative approach to the subject. For several years systems theory was all the rage in the discipline.

These two statements of the need to adopt a systems approach were accompanied by many other attempts to explain the nature of international relations by referring to factors outside the individual nation state. Haas, for example, looked at the impact of international integration on the policies of states.[7] Herz wrote of the effects of the development of nuclear weapons on the freedom of action of the superpowers.[8] Rosecrance was concerned to show how international and domestic factors could combine to explain different periods of world history.[9] Masters claimed to discern a powerful analogy between the nature of international and primitive political systems.[10]

THE "LEVEL-OF-ANALYSIS" PROBLEM

This is the moment to say more about the "level-of-analysis" problem, which [is a] use ful way to organize the themes of the book. In his celebrated 1961 article, David Singer contended that throughout the social sciences analysis proceeds on two levels, that of the unit and that of the system.[11] He argued that International Relations had, with the exception of the work of Waltz and Kaplan, largely failed to take the systems level seriously. The bulk of his article dealt with the advantages and disadvantages of each level for purposes of description, explanation, and prediction.

Two central conclusions emerged. First, each level introduces bias into the explanations it provides. The unit or state level exaggerates the differences among states, and underestimates the impact of the system on the actions of states; the systems level assumes that states are more homogeneous than they are and overestimates the impact of the system on the behavior of the units. Secondly, and more radically, the two levels cannot be combined to arrive at one overall explanation of international relations. This was, said Singer, for the same reason that the two most popular map projections, the Mercator and the Polar Gnomonic, could not be combined to give one accurate map of the world. The reason was that each overemphasized some parts of the world and under-represented others, because it is impossible to represent accurately a three-dimensional globe on a two-dimensional surface. For a Positivist like Singer this was especially problematic, since he hoped that a progressive theory of international relations would emerge from the cumulative growth of data. He was concerned that unless the level of analysis were recognized, researchers would not realize that data generated at one level could not simply be combined with data from another level. The biases involved at the two levels would, like the two map projections, make it

[7] See E. Haas, *The Uniting of Europe* (Stanford: Stanford University Press, 1958).
[8] J. Herz, *International Politics in the Atomic Age* (New York: Columbia University Press, 1959).
[9] R. Rosecrance, *Action and Reaction in World Politics* (Boston: Little, Brown, 1963).
[10] R. Masters, "World Politics as a Primitive Political System," *World Politics*, 1964, 16, pp. 595–619.
[11] J. D. Singer, "The Level-of-Analysis Problem in International Relations," in K. Knoor and S. Verba (eds.), *The International System: Theoretical Essays* (Princeton: Princeton University Press, 1961), pp. 77–92.

impossible to construct an accurate overall picture of international relations. More problematic still was the tendency for researchers to shift unawares between levels of analysis in the middle of a study.

For Singer, then, there could be no overarching theory which explained how system-level and unit-level factors interacted to produce state behavior. He also declared that the state level, so popular among historians concerned with the specifics, could offer explanations only as long as it made crucial assumptions. The most important of these was that state behavior could be explained by reference to individual decisions without worrying about the source of the perceptions which informed the decisions.

This assumption needed correcting, since the perceptions of decision-makers were themselves caused, and the international system was an influential source of these perceptions.

Singer's article located the issue of the impact of systemic factors within the Behavioralist mainstream. The system could explain aspects of state behavior (with the actor always assumed to be the state) which could not be explained at the state level. Taken together, the work of Waltz, Kaplan, and Singer firmly established the notion that the international system was a distinct level of analysis, over and above the sum of intended and unintended consequences of state activity.

MULTIPOLARITY AND BIPOLARITY

But this was still far from developing a theory of the impact of the system on the behavior of its constituent units, despite lengthy debates about the effects of different polar configurations of the system. By the mid-1960s the key topic was not the importance of anarchy, but whether the postwar stability in superpower relations was due to the fact that the international system was bipolar in character. This had been a theme in the work of both Morgenthau (who had argued for the stabilizing qualities of multipolarity) and Kaplan (who had also argued that multipolarity was more stable), but this conventional wisdom was being challenged. Once again, this view became associated with the writings of Waltz, who argued that the bipolar structure of the international system was the reason for the absence of great power conflict since 1945.[12]

The debate about the rival merits of multipolarity and bipolarity involved alternative accounts of systemic influences and how they work. There emerged from it a much more thorough and powerful analysis of what is involved in systemic theorizing. The point of departure is to see the international system as so strongly determining the behavior of states that there is no need to consider what goes on within them. The motives and beliefs of individual decision-makers drop out of account, as do the ideologies and political processes within the states, to be replaced by the workings of the international political system with its power structure or hierarchy. Power is still the crucial variable, the attempt to maximize it being what drives actions and its distribution being what determines the interactions of states.

Treating the internal setting of states as exogenous to explanation means casting aside much of what seems to divide states from one another. Was not the Cold War about ideology? Does it not matter what Gorbachev thinks? Are not the British Labour Party's views on defense important?

[12]K. Waltz, "The Stability of a Bipolar World," *Daedalus,* 1964, 93, pp. 881–909.

The critical implication of the systemic account is that these factors cannot be understood except within a context that is external to all states, namely, the international system. There are two main aspects of the system that we need to discuss in order to indicate what a systems account looks like. These are anarchy and polarity.

The concept of international anarchy most commonly used in international relations is a Hobbesian one. It refers to the fact that there is no body above the state; states are the only bodies in international society with sovereignty. States are judges in their own causes, with their location within a situation of anarchy imposing a security dilemma on them. This means no prospect of completely enforceable international law, or of a universal moral code to guide the actions of leaders. Might may not always be right, but unless it is met with equal might it may well prevail. There is no escape from this anarchical setting, and the attempts that states make to get out of some of its worst consequences account for the patterns of arms racing and alliances. Anarchy can only be mitigated, not transcended. As long as the structure of the system remains anarchical, states must continue to ensure their own defenses, and force, or the threat of it, will continue to be a possible outcome of any international interactions.

The second key systemic characteristic is the polar structure of the system. By polar structure we mean the number of independent great powers and their interrelationships. The most common subdivision is into multipolar and bipolar systems, with the former having at least five roughly equal great powers, and the latter having only two. The number of great powers is usually measured by seeing where a natural gap occurs in a hierarchy calculated from military and, to a lesser extent, economic indicators. There has been much debate as to whether

multipolarity or bipolarity is the more stable, in terms of how each maintains equilibrium in the system. The critical question is why the postwar system has stayed stable, and, in particular, whether and how nuclear weapons have helped the maintenance of peace between the great powers.

An answer pitched at the state level, and one favored by most historians, would address itself to the internal workings of the two superpowers and the history of their changing relationship since 1945. A systemic account, by contrast, points to the fact of bipolarity and to how bipolarity stays stable. A simple contrast between bipolarity and multipolarity on this score might be that, whereas multipolarity stays multipolar by the workings of the balance-of-power mechanism, bipolar stability works through a balance of terror. Similarly, the role of alliances is very different in the two systems. In multipolarity, alliances are flexible and are made between approximate equals with no country able to dominate the alliance. In bipolarity, alliances seem to be held together by an ideological glue, and are hierarchical, with each dominated by one superpower. The resulting pattern of international relations in each of the two systems is also distinctive. In multipolarity, alliances are constantly shifting, with ideology playing no role in determining membership; wars are fought when the balance-of-power mechanism breaks down, with the aim of reestablishing that balance after the war. By contrast, in bipolar systems alliances do not shift and ideological differences seem to be at the very root of the division of the world. Yet wars are not fought between the superpowers, or between their main allies. As John Herz has remarked, "absolute power equals absolute impotence,"[13] since, in a bipolar system marked by constant pressure

---

[13]Herz, *International Politics in the Atomic Age*, p. 22.

and crisis, any war would be an all-out affair of complete mutual destruction.

This sketch serves to show how systemic accounts can talk of the nature of international relations without having to identify the states involved. How very unlike the attitude of the national leaders—and, indeed, the media! So, let us be absolutely explicit: It does not matter who the two superpowers have been since 1945. Even two powers with similar ideologies would have been antagonists. Had they been the United Kingdom and the United States, or China and the Soviet Union, the systems perspective argues that the basic nature of international relations would have been the same. The systems perspective also implies that the invention of nuclear weapons has only strengthened the bipolar nature of the postwar order, and not created it. A bipolar world without nuclear weapons would be much the same as one with nuclear weapons. Similar reasoning causes systems theorists to worry about a multipolar world with nuclear weapons, since the logic of multipolarity suggests that short wars will be fought to redress the balance of power, even if they are short *nuclear* wars. . . .

CONCLUSION

Even the most rigorous and forceful attempt at a wholly systemic account of international relations cannot dispense with all unit-level causes. We have found three broad reasons why the units must be credited with contributing to the behavior of the system. The first—inconclusive but suggestive—is that international power cannot easily be conceived by analogy with natural force, as if the military and economic power of the U.S. were like the mass of a large planet. This point is inconclusive because power is both a resource to be used by agents, which means that they have to know how to use it, and a structural feature, the importance of which does not depend on its being used or even being directly perceived by the actors. Secondly, a wholly systemic account would need very strong notions of function and structure. But, since the structure shows itself only in the behavior of the units, and since functional explanations must involve purposive behavior by the units, there is no way of inferring that the units are merely dependent. Thirdly, changes within and between the units are the only plausible explanations of change in the system. Even if unit changes are influenced in their turn, they must still be allowed to matter. The case rests with Waltz's remark, cited above, that "the shaping and shoving of structures may be successfully resisted."

This case, however, does not undermine the very idea of structural causation. Waltz can still maintain that structural theories, whatever their descriptive difficulties, have explanatory power. To grant that structures cannot explain every aspect of international relations is not to grant that they explain nothing. But the case does mean that we need to consider the units as well as the system and to see what happens if we approach the system "bottom-up." To repeat a point made at the start of this chapter, however, it does not yet mean taking an interest in the internal workings of the units. Only if the level-of-analysis problem cannot be settled by showing that system behavior is the sum of unit behavior or some compromise between structural forces and unit outputs will we need to "open the box." We shall indeed do so, but not until Chapter 7. In Chapter 6 the individualist retort to holism, as represented by systems theory, is like that of an economist whose micro theory contains nothing smaller than firms which behave like "individuals" in the Theory of Games without reference to the internal organization of the firms or to the human characters of the people who work for them.

21 A DEMOCRATICALLY ORGANIZED WORLD

MIKHAIL SERGEYEVICH GORBACHEV

In this address delivered May 6, 1992, from the same platform as Churchill's "Iron Curtain" speech in 1947, former President Gorbachev advocates a "democratically organized world community."

Here we stand, before a sculpture in which the sculptor's imagination and fantasy, with remarkable expressiveness and laconism, convey the drama of the "Cold War," the irrepressible human striving to penetrate the barriers of alienation and confrontation. It is symbolic that this artist was the granddaughter of Winston Churchill and that this sculpture should be in Fulton.

More than forty-six years ago Winston Churchill spoke in Fulton and in my country this speech was singled out as the formal declaration of the "Cold War." This was indeed the first time the words, "Iron Curtain," were pronounced, and the whole Western world was challenged to close ranks against the threat of tyranny in the form of the Soviet Union and Communist expansion. Everything else in this speech, including Churchill's analysis of the postwar situation in the world, his thoughts about the possibility of preventing a third world war, the prospects for progress, and methods of reconstructing the postwar world, remained unknown to the Soviet people.

Today, in paying tribute to this promi-nent statesman, we can evaluate more quietly and objectively both the merits of his speech and the limitations of the analysis which it included, his ideas and predictions, and his strategic principles.

Since that time the world in which we live has undergone tremendous changes. Even so, however paradoxical it may sound, there is a certain similarity between the situation then and today. Then, the prewar structure of international relations had virtually collapsed, a new pattern of forces had emerged along with a new set of interests and claims.

Different trends in world development could be discerned, but their prospects were not clearly outlined. New possibilities for progress had appeared. Answers had to be found to the challenges posed by new subjects of international law. The atmosphere was heavy—not only with hope, but also with suspicion, lack of understanding, unpredictability.

In other words, a situation had emerged in which a decision with universal implications had to be taken. Churchill's greatness is seen in the fact that he was the first among leading political figures to understand that.

Indeed, the world community which had at this time already established the United Nations, was faced with a unique opportunity to change the course of world development, fundamentally altering the role in it of force and of war. And, of course, this depended to a decisive degree on the Soviet Union and the United States—here I hardly need to explain why.

So I would like to commence my remarks by noting that the USSR and the U.S. missed that chance—the chance to establish their relationship on a new basis of principle and thereby to initiate a world order different from that which existed before the war. I think it is clear that I am not suggesting that they should have established a sort of condominium over the rest of the world. The opportunity was on a different plane altogether.

If the United States and the Soviet Union had been capable of understanding their responsibility and sensibly correlating their national interests and strivings with the rights and interests of other states and peoples, the planet today would be a much more suitable and favorable place for human life. I have more than once criticized the foreign policy of the Stalinist leadership in those years. Not only was it incapable of reevaluating the historical logic of the interwar period, taking into account the experience and results of the war, and following a course which corresponded to the changed reality, it committed a major error in equating the victory of democracy over fascism with the victory of socialism and aiming to spread socialism throughout the world.

But the West, and the United States in particular, also committed an error. Its conclusion about the probability of open Soviet military aggression was unrealistic and dan-

gerous. This could never have happened, not only because Stalin, as in 1939–1941, was afraid of war, did not want war, and never would have engaged in a major war. But primarily because the country was exhausted and destroyed; it had lost tens of millions of people, and the public hated war. Having won a victory, the army and the soldiers were dying to get home and get back to a normal life.

By including the "nuclear component" in world politics, and on this basis unleashing a monstrous arms race—and here the initiator was the United States, the West—"defense sufficiency was exceeded," as the lawyers say. This was a fateful error.

So I would be so bold as to affirm that the governing circles of the victorious powers lacked an adequate strategic vision of the possibilities for world development as they emerged after the war—and, consequently, a true understanding of their own countries' national interests. Hiding behind slogans of "love for peace" and defense of their people's interests, on both sides decisions were taken which split asunder the world which had just succeeded in overcoming fascism because it was united.

And on both sides this was justified ideologically. The conflict was presented as the inevitable opposition between good and evil—all the evil, of course, being attributed to the opponent. This continued for decades until it became evident that we were approaching the abyss. I am stating this because the world community has paid dearly for the errors committed at this turning-point in world history.

In the major centers of world politics the choice, it would seem, has today been made in favor of peace, cooperation, interaction, and overall security. And in pushing forward to a new civilization we should under no circumstances again make the intellectual, and consequently political, error of interpreting victory in the "Cold War" narrowly as a victory for oneself, one's own way of life, for one's own values and merits. This was a victory over a scheme for the development of humanity which was becoming slowly congealed and leading us to destruction. It was a shattering of the vicious circle into which we had driven ourselves. This was altogether a victory for common sense, reason, democracy, and common human values. . . .

II

What has to be done is to create the necessary mechanisms. In my position it is not very appropriate to give them names. It is important that they should be authorized by the world community to deal with problems. Without that there is no point in talking about a new era or a new civilization. I will limit myself to designating the lines of activity and the competence of such mechanisms.

Nuclear and chemical weapons. Rigid controls must be instituted to prevent their dissemination, including measures of compulsion in cases of violation. An agreement must be concluded between all presently nuclear states on procedures for cutting back on such weapons and liquidating them. Finally a world convention on chemical weapons should be signed.

The peaceful use of nuclear energy. The powers of the IAEA must be strengthened, and it is imperative that all countries working in this area be included in the IAEA system. The procedures of the IAEA should be tightened up and the work performed in a more open and aboveboard manner. Under United Nations auspices a powerful consortium should be created to finance the modernization or liquidation of highly risky nuclear power stations, and also to store spent fuel. A set of world standards for nuclear power plants should be established. Work on nuclear fusion must be expanded and intensified.

The export of conventional weapons. Governmental exports of such weapons should be ended by the year 2000, and, in regions of armed conflict, it should be curtailed at once. The illegal trade in such arms must be equated with international terrorism and the drug trade. With respect to these questions the intelligence services of the states which are permanent members of the Security Council should be coordinated. And the Security Council itself must be slightly expanded, which I will mention in a moment.

Regional conflicts. Considering the impartially examined experience obtained in the Middle East, in Africa, in Southeast Asia, Korea, Yugoslavia, the Caucasus, and Afghanistan, a special body should be set up under the United Nations Security Council with the right to employ political, diplomatic, economic, and military means to settle and prevent such conflicts.

Human rights. The European process has officially recognized the universality of this common human value, i.e., the acceptability of international interference wherever human rights are being violated. This task is not easy even for states which signed the Paris Charter of 1990 and even less so for all state members of the United Nations. However, I believe that the new world order will not be fully realized unless the United Nations and its Security Council do not create structures (taking into consideration existing United Nations and regional structures) authorized to impose sanctions and to make use of other measures of compulsion.

Food, demography, economic assistance. It is no accident that these problems should be dealt with in this connection. Upon their solution depends the biological viability of the Earth's population and the minimal social stability needed for a civilized existence of states and peoples. Major scientific, finan-

cial, political, and public organizations—among them, the authoritative Club of Rome—have long been occupied with these problems. However, the newly emerging type of international interaction will make possible a breakthrough in our practical approach to them. I would propose that next year a world conference be held on this subject, one similar to the forthcoming ecological conference.

III

Ladies and Gentlemen! All of these problems demand an enhanced level of organization of the international community. However, even now, at a time of sharply increased interdependence in the world, many countries are morbidly jealous of their sovereignty, and many peoples of their national independence and identity. This is one of the newest global contradictions, one which must be overcome by joint effort. That it can, in principle, be overcome can be seen from the experience of the European communities and, although still to only a slight degree, from the European process as a whole.

Here the decisive role may and must be played by the United Nations. Of course, it must be restructured, together with its component bodies, in order to be capable of confronting the new tasks. These ideas have long been under discussion, and many proposals have been put forward. I myself have no plan of my own for reorganizing the United Nations. I will just address the basic parameters of the changes which are ready for solution.

The United Nations, which emerged from the results and the lessons of the Second World War, is still marked by the period of its creation. This is true both with respect to the makeup of its subsidiary

bodies and auxiliary institutions and with respect to its functioning. Nothing, for instance, other than the division into victors and vanquished, explains why such countries as Germany and Japan do not figure among the permanent members of the Security Council.

In general, I feel Article 53 on "hostile states" should be immediately deleted from the UN Charter. Also, the criterion of possession of nuclear weapons would be archaic in the new era before us. The great country of India should be represented in the Security Council. The authority and potential of the Council would also be enhanced by incorporation on a permanent basis of Italy, Indonesia, Canada, Poland, Brazil, Mexico, and Egypt, even if initially they do not possess the veto.

The Security Council will require better support, more effective and more numerous peace-keeping forces. Under certain circumstances it will be desirable to put certain national armed forces at the disposal of the Security Council, making them subordinate to the United Nations military command.

The proposal, which I accept, has already been made that a global observation system be established for spotting emergencies. The United Nations Secretary-General should be authorized to put it into action even before a conflict becomes violent. Closer coordination of UN organs with regional structures would only enhance its capacity to settle disputes in the world.

Of course, the UN's contemporary role, and, first and foremost, an expanded and strengthened Security Council, will require substantial funding. The method adopted for financing at the founding of the United Nations revealed its weaknesses just as soon as, some years later, it became more active and came closer to actually carrying out the tasks assigned by its founders. This method must be supplemented by some mechanism tying the UN to the world economy.

My thoughts may, at first glance, appear somewhat unrealistic. But we will count on the fact that business is becoming more humane, that a powerful process of technical and political internationalization is taking place, and that business is achieving an increasingly organic relationship with contemporary world politics into which the seeds of the "new thinking" have been cast. Today democracy must prove that it can exist not only as the antithesis of totalitarianism. This means that it must move from the national arena to the international.

On today's agenda is not just a union of democratic states, but also a democratically organized world community. Thus, we live today in a watershed era. One epoch has ended, and a second is commencing. No one yet knows how concrete it will be. Having long been orthodox Marxists, we were sure we knew. But life once again refuted those who claimed to be know-it-alls and messiahs.

It is clear that the twentieth century nurtured immense opportunities. And from it we are inheriting frightful, apocalyptic threats. But we have at our disposal a great science, one which will help us avoid crude miscalculations. Moral values have survived in this frightful century, and these will assist and support us in this, the most difficult, transition in the history of humanity—from one qualitative state to another.

In concluding I would like to return to my starting point. From this tribune Churchill issued an appeal to the United Nations to rescue peace and progress, but primarily to Anglo-Saxon unity as the nucleus to which others could adhere. In the achievement of this goal the decisive role, in his view, was to be played by force, above all, by armed force. He even entitled his speech the "Musculature of Peace."

The goal today has not changed: peace and progress for all. But now we have the capacity to approach it without paying the heavy price we have been paying these past fifty years or so, without having to resort to means which put the very goal itself in doubt, which even constitute a threat to civilization. And while continuing to recognize the outstanding role of the United States of America, and today of other rich and highly developed countries, we must not limit our appeal to the elect, but call upon the whole world community.

In a qualitatively new and different world situation the overwhelming majority of the United Nations will, I hope, be capable of organizing themselves and acting in concert on the principles of democracy, equality of rights, balance of interests, common sense, freedom of choice, and willingness to cooperate. Made wise by bitter experience, they will, I think, be capable of dispensing, when necessary, with egoistic considerations in order to arrive at the exalted goal which is man's destiny on earth.

22 NEW PATTERNS OF GLOBAL SECURITY IN THE TWENTY-FIRST CENTURY

Barry Buzan

Professor of International Studies at Warwick, University in the United Kingdom, Barry Buzan is a frequent participant in conferences on security issues on both sides of the Atlantic.

This is a speculative article. It tries to sketch the main features of the new pattern of global security relations that is emerging after the great transformations of 1989–90 and the first post-Cold War crisis in the Gulf. In particular, it tries to identify the likely effects of changes in what used to be called East-West relations on the security conditions and agenda of what used to be called the Third World.[1] Because its starting-point is the nature and impact of changes in the North, it does not pretend to offer a comprehensive picture of the South.[2]

After setting out the analytical framework, the article will identify four key changes in relationships between the major powers in the North and suggest what their consequences might be for the majority of states in the South. It goes on to examine in more detail the impact of these consequences on the security agenda of the South in terms of five sectors of security—political, military, economic, societal, and environmental.

INTO THE TWENTY-FIRST CENTURY

One immediate problem is that so many of the terms in which a discussion of this kind would normally be cast have become obsolete. It is a commonplace to observe that the term "Third World" has lost nearly all its

[1] I should like to thank Pierre Lemaitre, Morten Kelstrup, H. O. Nazareth, Barbara Allen Roberson and Ole Wæver for comments on an earlier draft of this article.

[2] In order to look ahead in a systematic fashion and to avoid being swamped by detail, some theoretical framework is necessary. The study is based on a combination of a broadly structural realist approach and a center-periphery model of the international system. However, it does not demand prior knowledge of these frameworks. See Barry Buzan, Charles Jones and Richard Little, *The Logic of Anarchy: Neorealism to Structural Realism* (New York: Columbia University Press, forthcoming in 1992); Johan Galtung, "A Structural Theory of Imperialism," *Journal of Peace Research* 8:2 (1971), pp. 81–118.

Reprinted by permission from *International Affairs* **67,** 3 (1991) 431–451. Copyright © Royal Institute of International Affairs, 1991.

content.[3] In the absence of a Second World now that the communist system has largely disintegrated, how can there be a Third? What now unites countries as diverse as South Korea, India, Malawi, and Bahrain that they should be referred to as a distinct "world"? Geographical labels are not much more helpful. What does "West" mean when it includes Japan and Australia, or "North" when it includes Albania, Romania, and the Soviet Union, or "South" when it includes Korea and excludes Australia? Although South is a better term than Third World, the best available set of terms to capture the relationships of the 1990s comes from the center–periphery approach elaborated in the dependency literature of the 1960s and 1970s.[4] "Center" here implies a globally dominant core of capitalist economies; "periphery" a set of industrially, financially, and politically weaker states operating within a set of relationships largely constructed by the center. The more robust and developed states in the periphery form a semi-periphery, whose aspiration is membership of the core. This approach captures the key elements of hierarchy that now shape international relations, without necessitating recourse to misleading geographical images.

The ending of the Cold War has created a remarkable fluidity and openness in the whole pattern and quality of international relations. Although the events of 1989 were centered in Europe, they represent changes of such magnitude that it is appropriate to talk of the end of an era for the international system as a whole. Specifically, 1989 marked the end of the postwar period. It seems likely that historians will also come to mark it as the end of the twentieth century. The two world wars, the Cold War that followed them, and the process of decolonization that accompanied all three already begin to look like a self-contained historical period. In this sense, we are already in the twenty-first century. There are quite strong indications that the new century will be like the nineteenth in having, at least among the great powers, neither a major ideological divide nor a dominating power rivalry. My question is, what security consequences this pattern of relationships among the major powers in the center will have for the states in the periphery.

The security lens used here is a broad one. Security is taken to be about the pursuit of freedom from threat and the ability of states and societies to maintain their independent identity and their functional integrity against forces of change which they see as hostile. The bottom line of security is survival, but it also reasonably includes a substantial range of concerns about the conditions of existence. Quite where this range of concern ceases to merit the urgency of the "security" label (which identifies threats as significant enough to warrant emergency action and exceptional measures, including the use of force) and becomes part of the everyday uncertainties of life is one of the difficulties of the concept.

Military security concerns the two-level interplay of the armed offensive and defensive capabilities of states, and states' perceptions of each other's intentions. Political security concerns the organizational stability of states, systems of government, and the ideologies that give them legitimacy. Economic security concerns access to the resources, finance, and markets necessary to sustain acceptable levels of welfare and state power. Societal security concerns the ability of societies to reproduce their traditional patterns of language, culture, association, and religious and national identity and custom within acceptable conditions for evolution. Environmental security concerns the

---

[3]John Ravenhill, "The North-South Balance of Power," *International Affairs* 66:4 (1990), p. 745.

[4]See special issue on "Dependence and Dependency in the Global System," *International Organization* 32:1 (1978).

maintenance of the local and the planetary biosphere as the essential support system on which all other human enterprises depend. These five sectors do not operate in isolation from each other. Each defines a focal point within the security problematique, and a way of ordering priorities, but all are woven together in a strong web of linkages.[5]

During the Cold War, international security was dominated by the highly militarized and highly polarized ideological confrontation between the superpowers. This confrontation divided the industrialized North into the First World (the West) and the Second World (the Soviet bloc). Because their rivalry was intense, the danger of war was real, and political/military concerns dominated the security agenda. This political/military emphasis was transmitted into the periphery by the use of arms transfers by both superpowers as a means of exploiting already existing hostilities within the Third World as a vehicle for pursuing their own rivalry. In the opening years of the twenty-first century there are already strong signs that the security agenda among the great powers will be much less dominated, perhaps not dominated at all, by political/military issues. The Second World has disintegrated, and as the armed confrontation between the United States and the Soviet Union is wound down, economic, societal, and environmental issues are pushing their way into the top ranks of the international security agenda.

One major question for the states in the periphery is how their own security agenda will be affected by the new patterns of relations among the major powers. Will they share the shift away from political/military priorities towards a more nonmilitary security agenda, or will echoes of the term "Third World" continue to demarcate a major divide, another *world* in which things are ordered (and disordered) in ways quite different from those of the advanced industrial countries?

There are of course some massive continuities in the international position of the ex-Third World (now periphery) that are largely unaffected by the changes in the top ranks of the great powers. The center–periphery approach captures much of what remains constant from the past and is a useful framework within which to consider the impact of changes in the core on the security of the periphery. The identity "Third World" signified an oppositional stance to the West and generated the distinctive ideologies of nonalignment and *tiers-mondisme*. But in the center–periphery perspective, the aspirations of the periphery are more collaborationist than confrontational. It is better to be the lowest member of the center than the highest of the periphery.

CHANGES IN THE CENTER

In order to understand the security consequences of being in the periphery during the first decade of the twenty-first century, one first needs some sense of the changes at the center. At this early stage in the new era one can with some confidence suggest four defining features for the new pattern of great-power relations.

1. The rise of a multipolar power structure in place of the Cold War's bipolar one. The term "superpower" has dominated the language of power politics for so many decades that one is left floundering for words to de-

[5]For a full discussion of these themes, see Barry Buzan, *People, States and Fear: An Agenda for International Security Studies in the Post-Cold War Era* (Hemel Hempstead: Harvester-Wheatsheaf, 1991); see also Ken Booth, ed, *New Thinking About Strategy and International Security* (London: Harper-Collins, 1991).

scribe the new power structure that is emerging. The precipitate economic and political decline of the Soviet Union has clearly removed it from this category, despite its still formidable military strength. The decline of the United States has been much less severe, arguably leaving it as the last superpower. But the rise of Europe, particularly the consolidation of the European Community as an economic and political entity, largely removes (and in the case of the Soviet Union inverts) the spheres of influence that were one of the key elements in the claim to superpower status.[6] It seems time to revive the term "great power." If one thinks how this term was used before 1945, Russia still qualifies. So do China and India, which might be seen as the contemporary equivalents of regional great powers such as Italy, Austria-Hungary, or the Ottoman Empire before 1914. Despite their political oddities, Japan and the EC are strong candidates, albeit still more obviously in the economic than in the military and political spheres. The United States is undoubtedly the greatest of the great powers. The term superpower, however, seems no longer appropriate in a multipolar world with so many independent centers of power and so few spheres of influence.

If one moves away from the strict realist (and neo-realist) conception of power as aggregated capabilities (i.e. military, economic, and political strength all together),[7] and towards the disaggregated view of power taken by those who think more in terms of interdependence,[8] then global multipolarity stands out even more clearly. The military inhibitions of Japan and the political looseness of Europe count for less

in relation to their standing as major poles of strength and stability in the global political economy. Although not all six great powers are within the global core, multipolarity suggests a center that is both less rigid and less sharply divided within itself than under bipolarity. A multipolar center will be more complex and more fluid, and may well allow for the development of militarily hesitant great powers. If military threats are low, such powers can afford—as Japan now does and as the United States did before 1941—to rest their military security on their ability to mobilize massive civil economies.

A multicentered core offers more competing points of contact for the periphery. At the same time, the shift from two superpowers to several great powers should mean both a reduction in the intensity of global political concerns and a reduction in the resources available for sustained intervention. This in turn points to the rise of regional politics. Because the great powers are spread across several regions and do not include a dominating ideological or power rivalry within their ranks, they will project their own conflicts into the periphery much less forcefully and systematically than under the zero-sum regime of the Cold War. Because regions are less constrained by the impact of their conflicts on the global scorecard of two rival superpowers, local rivalries and antagonisms will probably have more autonomy. Local great powers such as India, China, and perhaps Brazil should also find their regional influence increased.

2. A much lower degree of ideological division and rivalry. Complementing the structural looseness of the new center is a much reduced level of ideological conflict. The twentieth century might well go down in history as the era of wars between the great powers about industrial ideology. During this short century, wars unleashed ideological rivalries and ideological rivalries un-

---

[6]See Barry Buzan, Morten Kelstrup, Pierre Lemaitre, Elzbieta Tromer and Ole Wæver, *The European Security Order Recast: Scenarios for the Post-Cold War Era* (London: Pinter, 1990).

[7]Kenneth N. Waltz, *Theory of International Politics* (Reading, Mass.: Addison-Wesley, 1979), pp. 129–31.

[8]Buzan, Jones and Little, *The Logic of Anarchy*, section one.

leashed wars—both "hot" and "cold." The first round of war, starting in 1914, gave birth to fascist and communist state challengers to the liberal capitalist West. After some uncertainty of alignment, the second round saw the Western and communist powers combining in 1941 to eliminate fascism as a serious ideological player. The third round (of cold war) saw a long period in which the military paralysis of nuclear deterrence put the emphasis on competition in arms racing, technological innovation, economic growth, and societal attractiveness. This competition ended peacefully in 1989 with the comprehensive collapse of the communist challenge in the face of a decisively superior Western performance.

The defeat of fascism and communism as alternative ideologies for advanced industrial society has been so definitive that it is hard to imagine either of them reviving their challenge. Liberal capitalism, with all its well-known faults, now commands a broad consensus as the most effective and desirable form of political economy available. The difficult formula of political pluralism plus market economics has many critics, but no serious rivals. This development means that the center is less ideologically divided within itself than it has been since the first spread of industrialization. In conjunction with the shift to multipolarity, this further reduces political and military incentives for competitive intervention into the periphery.

3. The global dominance of a security community among the leading capitalist powers.

As the alliance structures of the Cold War dissolve into irrelevance—the Soviet ones much faster than the Western—a looming void seems to be appearing at the heart of the international security system. The declining salience of military threats among the great powers makes it unlikely that this void will be filled by new alliances, especially if the European union is viewed as a single international actor (even though it is still well short of being a single sovereign state). Indeed, the main military structure of the new era requires the viewer to put on different lenses for it to come clearly into focus, for it is inverse in form to traditional alliance structures.

The dominant feature of the post-Cold War era is a *security community* among the major centers of capitalist power. This means a group of states that do not expect, or prepare for, the use of military force in their relations with each other.[9] This is a different and in some ways more profound quality than the collective expectation and preparation to use force against someone else that is the essence of alliance relationships. During the Cold War this security community grew up within, and in its latter days it was masked by, or disguised as, the Western alliance system. The capitalist powers had good reason to form an alliance against the communist states. But equally important is that they developed independent and increasingly dominant reasons for eliminating the use of military force in their relations with each other. The fact that they were able to expunge military rivalry from their own relations was a major factor in their ability to see off the communist challenge without a "hot" war. The communist powers were conspicuously unsuccessful in establishing a similar security community within their own bloc.

The existence of this capitalist security community—in effect, Europe, North America, Japan, and Australia, standing back to back—gives the Western powers an immense advantage in the global political economy. Because they do not have to compete with each other militarily, they can meet other challengers more easily, whether

---

[9]Karl Deutsch and S. A. Burrell, *Political Community and the North Atlantic Area* (Princeton, NJ: Princeton University Press, 1957).

singly or collectively. The relative ease with which the United States was able to construct a military (and financial) coalition to take on Iraq shows both the potential of such a security structure and how it might work to meet other periphery challenges to the stability of the global political economy.

The example of the Second Gulf War suggests a model of concentric circles to complement and modify the raw center–periphery idea. In the center circle stood the United States, which was willing to lead only if followed and to fight only if given wide support and assistance. In the second circle were others prepared to fight—some members of the center (principally Britain and France),andothers of the periphery (principally Egypt and Saudi Arabia). In the third circle were those prepared to pay but not to fight, primarily Japan and Germany. In the fourth circle were those prepared to support but not to fight or pay. This group was large, and contained those prepared to vote and speak in favor of the action, some of whom (such as Denmark) also sent symbolic military forces. It also included the Soviet Union and Chinaas well as a mixture of center and peripherystates. The fifth circle contained those states satisfied to be neutral, neither supporting nor opposing the venture, but prepared to accept UN Security Council resolutions. Within thesefive circles stood the great majority of the international community, and all the major powers. In the sixth circle were those prepared to oppose, mainly verbally and by voting. This contained Cuba, Jordan, Yemen, and a number of Arab states. In the seventh circle stood those prepared to resist—Iraq.

This model does not offer a hard image of the future. It is not a permanent coalition, nor is it likely to recur. But it does suggest the general nature of security relations in a center-dominated world, the mechanisms available, and the ability of the center to isolate aggressors who threaten the recognized political order and the workings of the global economy.

The capitalist security community that underpinned this coalition acts as a major moderator to the new multipolar power structure. One danger of multipolarity (at least in its pre-1945, prenuclear manifestations) was that a shifting balance of power, driven by a plethora of antagonisms and security dilemmas, would generate unstable patterns of alliance and periodic lapses into great-power wars. But a multipolar system in which the three strongest powers are also a strong security community is something quite new, and should defuse or perhaps even eliminate most of these old hazards. In the inelegant jargon of systems theory, one could describe the new structure of power relations as multipolar in the sense that several independent great powers are in play, but unipolarized in the sense that there is a single dominant coalition governing international relations. It is the single coalition that gives force to the center–periphery model and makes the new situation unique.

4. The strengthening of international society. This last defining feature of the new center is the least certain of the four, but it is a plausible product of the other three. Hedley Bull and Adam Watson defined international society as:

> a group of states (or, more generally, a group of independent political communities) which not merely form a system, in the sense that the behavior of each is a necessary factor in the calculations of the others, but also have established by dialogue and consent common rules and institutions for the conduct of their relations, and recognize their common interest in maintaining these arrangements.[10]

[10]Hedley Bull and Adam Watson, eds., *The Expansion of International Society* (Oxford: Oxford University Press, 1984), p. 1; see also Buzan, *People, States and Fear*, ch. 4.

The distinction between system and society is central. System is the more basic and prior idea, as it is inherent in the significant interaction among states. Society can be seen as a historical response to the existence of a system. As states recognize the permanence and importance of their interdependence, they begin to work out rules for avoiding unwanted conflicts and for facilitating desired exchanges. As Bull argues, international society is thus closely associated with the idea of international order, where order means "an arrangement of social life such that it promotes certain goals or values."[11]

The foundation of modern international society is the mutual recognition by states of each other's claim to sovereignty. This establishes them as legal equals and provides the foundation for diplomatic relations. The top end of contemporary international society is the whole range of institutions and regimes with which groups of states coordinate their behavior in pursuit of common goals. Some of these institutions and regimes are already nearly universal—the United Nations, the Law of the Sea regime, the nuclear non-proliferation regime. Others, such as the European Community, have been more restricted. But the EC, though only regional in scope, has now become so deeply institutionalized that many are beginning to see it more as a single actor than as a system of states. During the Cold War the Western states established a particularly rich international societal network of institutions and regimes to facilitate the relatively open economic and societal relations that they wished to cultivate. These included the IMF, the World Bank, the OECD, the GATT, and the Group of Seven. As a rule, the development of *global* institutions and regimes was obstructed by the Cold War, almost the only exception being superpower cooperation in the promotion of nuclear nonproliferation. With the ending of the Cold War and of the systematic dominance of the West, it does not seem unreasonable to expect the extension of the Western networks towards more universal standing. Old Marxian arguments that the capitalists were kept united only by their common fear of communism seem to have been overridden by the global scale and deep interdependence of early twenty-first-century capitalism. The eagerness of the ex-Soviet-type systems to join the club is a strong pointer towards consolidation of Western regimes, as is the dramatic upgrading of the UN Security Council as a focus for global consensus-building and legitimation seen in the Gulf crisis. If this occurs, a stronger international society, largely reflecting Western norms and values, will be a powerful element in the security environment of the periphery.

These four developments at the center will reshape the way in which the center dominates the periphery. In general, they seem likely to diminish the standing and the influence of the periphery states.

IMPLICATIONS FOR THE PERIPHERY

These massive changes in security relations within the center will have both direct and indirect effects on security within the periphery. There will of course be many continuities, especially in the locally rooted dynamics of regional security, whose patterns of amity, enmity, and rivalry do not depend on input from the center.[12] But as suggested above, many aspects of relations between

[11]Hedley Bull, *The Anarchical Society* (London: Macmillan, 1977), ch. 1.

[12]See Buzan, *People, States and Fear*, ch. 5.

center and periphery will change. It is useful to look at these changes in terms of the five sectors of security sketched above.

1. Political security.   Perhaps the most obvious political impact of the end of the Cold War is the demise of both power bipolarity and ideological rivalry as central features of the center's penetration into the periphery. One immediate consequence of this is to lower the value of periphery countries as either ideological spoils or strategic assets in great-power rivalry. During the Cold War, Third World alignments were important symbols of success and failure in the global competition between the United States and the Soviet Union. This fact gave Third World governments a useful lever on the divided center, though it also exposed them to unwanted intervention in their own domestic instabilities. In the unfolding order of the twenty-first century there will be little or no ideological or strategic incentive for great powers to compete for Third World allegiance. This loss of leverage will be accompanied by the loss of nonalignment as a useful political platform for the periphery. Nonalignment was a reaction to the Cold War and provided many Third World elites with a moral and political position from which to play in the game of world politics. But with the ending of the Cold War, there is no longer a divided center to be non-aligned against.

Further, many periphery states have found the legitimacy of their one-party systems undermined by the collapse of communism. So long as the communist states sustained their challenge to the West, they opened up a political space for authoritarian Third World governments. The existence of a Soviet superpower made centralized state control a legitimate form of government elsewhere, and provided a handy complementarity for those Third World states eager to take up antiWestern,

postcolonial postures. With the conceding by the leading communist power of the virtues of pluralism and markets, this political space has narrowed sharply. AntiWesternism now has no great-power supporter and no convincing alternative political model. It remains an open question whether pluralism will fare any better than authoritarianism in the unstable and in many ways unpromising political environment of many Third World states. Theory does not tell us much about the relative virtues of democratic versus command approaches to the early stages of state-building. Experience strongly suggests that state-building is a tricky, difficult, long-term and often violent business under any circumstances—especially so for poorly placed and poorly endowed latecomers under pressure to conform to norms that have already been reached naturally by more powerful states in the international system.

A further blow to the political position of many periphery states comes from the fact that the twentieth century was also the main era of decolonization. Decolonization was a high point in the epic and ongoing struggle of the rest of the world to come to terms with the intrusion of superior Western power. A more difficult period is now in prospect in which the euphoria of independence has faded and the reality of continued inferiority has reasserted itself. As the twenty-first century unfolds, with the West in a dominant position, it will become for the periphery states the postdecolonization era. For most Afro-Asian countries decolonization now lies one or two generations in the past and is therefore beyond the personal experience of a large and rapidly growing proportion of the population. As decolonization recedes into a former era, becoming old rather than recent history, the distance of many periphery governments is increased from the event that not only defined their countries but also provided them with a convenient, and sometimes justified, excuse for the many failings in their political and economic performance. As decolonization becomes remote, many governments in the periphery will find themselves increasingly laboring under the weight of their often dismal performance record, without the support of the colonial rationalizations that might once have forgiven it. They will find it increasingly difficult to evade or parry the rising contempt of both foreigners and their own citizens. Only those few that have made it into the semiperiphery, such as Taiwan and South Korea, can escape this fate.

Particularly in Africa and the Middle East, periphery states may also find it difficult to sustain the legitimacy of the colonial boundaries that have so signally failed to define viable states. The Cold War ran in parallel with the development of a strong norm cultivated in the UN that global boundaries should remain very largely fixed in their postwar, postcolonial pattern. This norm has even been reinforced by the Organization of African Unity, a body whose membership comprises states whose colonial boundaries are among the most arbitrary in the international system. As James Mayall has noted, this attempt to freeze the political map is unprecedented, and "at least so far as the territorial division of the world is concerned, seems unlikely to be successful."[13] Although there is no clear link between the Cold War and the attempt to fix boundaries, the ending of the Cold War is opening up boundary questions in a rather major way. The two Germanies have been unified—eliminating a state, reasserting a nationalist political principle, and dissolving the most

potent boundary of the Cold War. Strong revisionist pressures exist within the Soviet Union and Eastern Europe (and especially, but not only, Yugoslavia) either to redraw boundaries or to redefine their significance. The consolidation of the EC can also be read as an exercise in changing the significance, though not the position, of boundaries.

These changes at the center have little direct consequence for the periphery, but their symbolic consequences may be large. It is notable that Saddam Hussein's attempt to eliminate Kuwait and more broadly to unify the Arab world was an explicit assault on the postcolonial boundaries. Arab nationalism and Islamic communalism make a heady antiWestern political brew that could wash away territorial boundaries strongly associated with the divisions and humiliations of colonization. If the territorial jigsaw can be extensively reshaped in the First and Second Worlds, it will become harder to resist the pressures to try to find more sensible and congenial territorial arrangements in the ex-Third World. It is not yet clear whether it is the norm of fixed boundaries that is under assault or only the practice in specific locations. But it is clear that this norm is vulnerable to the counter-norm of national self-determination, and that some of the restraints on boundary change have been weakened by the ending of the Cold War.

A further possible impact of changes in the center on the political security agenda of the periphery is the pushing of Islam to the front rank of the opposition to Western hegemony. The collapse of communism as the leading antiWestern ideology seems to propel Islam into this role by default, and many exponents of Islam will embrace the task with relish. The antiWestern credentials of Islam are well established and speak to a large and mobilized political constituency. In part this can be seen as a straight clash between secular and spiritual values,

[13]James Mayall, *Nationalism and International Society* (Cambridge: Cambridge University Press, 1990), p. 56; and Jeffrey Herbst, "Liberalization and the African State System," paper for SSRC conference on foreign policy consequences of liberalization, San Diego, CA, Mar. 1991.

albeit underpinned by an older religious antagonism between Christendom and Islam.[14] In part, however, it has to be seen as a kind of civilization resistance to the hegemony of the West. Islam is centered in the only one of the four classical areas of power and civilization that has not managed to re-establish itself as a significant world actor since the retreat of the Western empires. Both Chinese and Hindu civilizations have consolidated large and quite powerful states which give them at least an acceptable position in international society. The Middle East—which is the oldest core of civilization and which has been a major center of international power for five millennia—remains divided, fractious, and weak.

Given this combined legacy of historical frustration and ideological antagonism, Islam could become the leading carrier of antiWestern sentiment in the periphery— though it could just as easily be kept impotent by the fierceness of its own numerous internal splits and rivalries. But since the West now dominates the center, while Islam has a large constituency in Africa and Asia, this old divide may nevertheless define a major political rift between North and South in the coming decades. If it does, one result will be a security problem for Europe and the Soviet Union/Russia, for both share a huge territorial boundary with Islam, and in the case of the Soviet Union this boundary is inside the country. The security issues raised may or may not be military ones, but they will certainly be societal—an aspect to be explored further below.

2. Military security. Developments in the center can easily be read as pointing to a lowering of militarization in the periphery. A less ideologically divided and more multipolar centre will have less reason to compete

[14]See Edward Mortimer, "Christianity and Islam," *International Affairs* 67:1 (1991), pp. 7–13.

politically to supply arms to the periphery. The ending of the Cold War reduces the strategic salience of many military bases in the periphery, and lowers incentives to use arms supply as a way of currying ideological favor with local governments. The outcomes of domestic and even regional political rivalries within the periphery should, other things being equal, be of less interest to the great powers than previously. In the absence of ideological disputes among themselves, the great powers will have fewer reasons to see periphery states as assets, and more reasons to see them as liabilities. The ending of the Cold War thus largely turns off the political mechanism that so effectively pumped arms into the Third World all through the 1960s, 1970s, and 1980s. In places where great-power intervention in regional conflicts was very heavy (as in southeast Asia) or where the ideological construction of the Cold War strongly underpinned a local conflict (as in Southern Africa) the ending of the Cold War points to an easing of local military confrontations and a significant mediatory role for the great powers.

But this prospect raises an important question about whether the West will use its new preeminence to neglect the Third World, or whether it will seek to subject it to stronger collective security and regional management regimes. At the time of writing, this question is an open one. The longer-term outcome of the Gulf crisis will powerfully affect which direction is taken. If the allied intervention is eventually seen to be a success at a reasonable cost, and does not give rise to long-term chaos in the region, a precedent will have been set for a more managerial and interventionist global collective security regime. Under such conditions the sanctity of existing boundaries would be reinforced, and periphery leaderships put on notice that while broad tolerance for internal nastiness would continue, efforts to change international boundaries by force would be firmly resisted. The United Nations Security Council would become a clearinghouse and legitimator for a global collective security regime.

But if the outcome is messy, costly, and judged a failure, then the West may well take a more isolationist view of the periphery, putting up the shutters and leaving it more or less to its own devices. Under these conditions, local rivalries and power balances would come into play without even the restraint imposed by the global interventionism of the Cold War. The local roots of many regional rivalries, especially in South Asia and the Middle East, are so deep that the ending of the Cold War in the center will make little difference to them. A lowering of great-power concern and engagement would by definition give more leverage to local powers to reshape the political environment of their regions.

This scenario of neglect cannot be pushed too far. Among other things, an abiding interest in oil will keep the West engaged in the Middle East. There must also be a concern that too detached an attitude towards the periphery might eventually, perhaps even quickly, generate military threats from these countries to the center. Both these interests were at play in the response to Saddam Hussein. Whether the center attempts comprehensive or selective intervention in the periphery, two specific military security issues arise either way—control of the arms trade, and the strengthening of the nuclear nonproliferation regime.

The nuclear nonproliferation regime has attracted very wide support despite its inherent inequality as a small club of nuclear haves and a large one of have-nots. Inasmuch as one of the key tensions within it was the failure of the superpowers to make much progress towards their own nuclear disarmament, the ending of the Cold War and the consequent massive reductions in

strategic forces should point to a strengthening of the regime. The success or failure of this regime will have a big impact both on security within the periphery and on military relations between center and periphery. Iraq's obvious nuclear ambitions underline the salience of the issue, but at this juncture the fate of the nonproliferation regime is unclear.

Several things favor a consolidation of the regime as the Nonproliferation Treaty approaches its 1995 renewal conference. UN organizations generally are emerging from the Cold War twilight into sunnier times. The winding down of the nuclear arms race at the center reduces, though by no means eliminates, the tension between haves and have-nots. In Latin America, the once worried-about nuclear rivalry between Brazil and Argentina is evolving steadily towards a regional inspection regime along the lines of Euratom. In South Africa, once a key threshold state, it seems highly unlikely that the white regime either needs the reassurance of nuclear weapons any longer, or wants to take the risk of having to hand control of them over to a black-led government. Civil nuclear power remains in the doldrums, which much reduces an independent pressure for the spread of militarily significant civil technology. Even in France, which has been the most vigorous promoter of civil nuclear power, technological and economic problems are mounting alarmingly.[15] If the economic complementarity between civil and military nuclear power collapses, leaving the military sector unsupported by a civil one, the costs of maintaining large-scale military nuclear power will rise.

But there are other developments that put even the existing regime into jeopardy. In South Asia, both India and Pakistan are on the brink of going public as nuclear

[15]*The Economist*, 2 Feb. 1991, pp. 73–4.

powers, and almost no one doubts that Israel is already a nuclear-weapons state. The fiction of a closed club of five nuclear-weapons states thus cannot be maintained, but neither is it obvious how the change to eight can be incorporated into the regime without seeming to reward noncompliance and open the floodgates to other claims. Even more serious in some ways is the problem of what to do about violators within the regime. Libya's leader makes calls for an Arab nuclear weapon which Saddam Hussein was doing his best to fulfil. It is hard to imagine that Iran would not "eat grass," as Pakistan did, in order to match the nuclear capability of its main regional enemy should Saddam Hussein be able to reembark on his previous course. While Iraq is temporarily down, Algeria has become a focus of speculation as the source for an Arab bomb.[16] Meanwhile North Korea soldiers on with suspicious nuclear activities while continuing to evade its legal obligation to conclude a safeguards agreement with the IAEA. These challenges from within raise serious questions about the long-term viability of the regime in the absence of some firmer mechanisms for enforcement, either through the Security Council or unilaterally in the style of both the Israeli and Anglo-American air attacks on Iraqi nuclear facilities.

On top of these particular problems sits a more general one arising from a dispute between nonnuclear-weapons and nuclear-weapons states over moves towards a comprehensive nuclear test-ban treaty. At the 1990 Review Conference a serious split developed on this issue, with Mexico leading demands for a strong, fixed-term commitment by the nuclear-weapons states to a comprehensive test-ban treaty, and the United States and Britain arguing the need for continued underground testing. This dispute was serious enough to wreck what

would otherwise have been a productive and positive final document. If pushed too far, it could have serious consequences for the renewal of the NPT in 1995.

Greater control of the conventional arms trade between the center and the periphery is another development that might be expected from the end of the Cold War, but the likelihood is that two powerful mechanisms will continue to support a substantial flow of military capability into the periphery. The first is the arms trade, driven by an ever-increasing number of suppliers, most eager and some desperate to sell their products. In the fierce commercial competition of the post-Cold War world, arms exports will remain one of the very few industrial areas of comparative advantage for the Soviet Union and China, as well as some smaller states such as Czechoslovakia. The implications of this can already be seen in China's willingness during the 1980s to sell almost any military technology (including nuclear-capable ballistic missiles) to almost any buyer. This logic also applies in lesser degree to Britain, France, and the United States. These three struggle to compete with Japan and Germany in civil manufactures, but have an easier time in the military market, where old wartime hangovers greatly restrict Japanese and German participants. All five major arms producers face shrinking domestic demand as a result of the end of the Cold War, and so need exports to sustain their military industries. In addition, several industrializing countries including Brazil, India, South Korea, Israel, and South Africa increasingly have the means and the will to compete in the arms trade. Competition among suppliers, combined with strong demand pull and the sheer diversity of sources of supply, make any systematic control of the arms trade unlikely.

The second mechanism arises from the unbreakable link between industrializa-

---

[16]*Sunday Times*, 28 Apr. 1991.

tion and the ability to make weapons. Industrialization is spreading inexorably across the planet, and all but the most extreme Greens welcome it as an essential ingredient in the development of human civilization. But the arms industry is not separate from the civil economy: Think of how the United States transformed itself from being a largely civil economy to being the arsenal of democracy in just a few years during the 1940s. In the 1990s, many of the technologies for making weapons are now old. The knowledge and skills for making poison gas and machine guns were developed more than a century ago, and even nuclear technology dates back nearly half a century. As technologies age, they become easier to acquire even for lightly industrialized counties such as Iraq.

The overlap between civil and military technology is especially obvious in the case of the nuclear and chemical industries, but also applies to engineering, vehicles, aircraft, and shipbuilding. In all these industries, there is fierce competition to export both products and manufacturing plant. Any country possessing a full civil nuclear power industry has virtually everything it needs to make a nuclear bomb. Any country that can make basic industrial chemicals can also make poison gas. Any that can make fertilizer can make high explosives. Whoever can make trucks, bulldozers, or airliners can make armored cars, tanks, and bombers. The concern over Iraq, Libya, Israel, Pakistan, South Africa, Brazil, and other states has as much to do with their industrialization as with their direct imports of arms, and there is no way of stopping the spread of industrial-military capability into the periphery. Any attempt to do so would put the goal of arms restraint into direct opposition with that of economic development.

The combined effect of the arms trade and industrialization means that military ca-

pability *will* spread by one mechanism or the other. Attempts to block the arms trade will intensify efforts at military industrialization, as they did in South Africa, so adding to the number of arms suppliers. The industrial genie, with its military progeny, is permanently out of the bottle. As a consequence, military security will remain an elusive objective posing difficult policy choices. The ending of the Cold War should result in some diminution of the flow of arms for political motives, but there is no reason to think that it will eliminate the problem of militarization in the periphery. Any regime with access to cash will still have access to supplies of modern weapons.

3. Economic security. If economic security is about access to the resources, finance, and markets necessary to sustain acceptable levels of welfare and state power, then the massive political changes of the past few years may well make little difference to the economic security problems of the periphery. The idea of economic security is riddled with contradictions and paradoxes.[17] These are indicated in the cruel truth captured by the aphorism, "The only thing worse than being exploited is not being exploited." To the extent that it has any clear meaning in relation to periphery countries, economic security points to the persistent structural disadvantages of late development and a position in the lower ranks of wealth and industrialization. The consequences of such weakness range from inability to sustain the basic human needs of the population (as in Sudan, Bangladesh, Ethiopia, Liberia), through the disruption of fluctuating and uncertain earnings from exports of primary products (as in Zambia, Peru, Nigeria), to inability to resist the policy pressures of outside institutions in return for needed supplies of capital (as in Brazil, Argentina, Tan-

---

[17]Buzan, *People, States and Fear,* ch. 6.

zania). There seems no reason to expect any fundamental change in the overall problem of the periphery in occupying a weak position in a global market whose prices, trade, finance, and technical evolution are all controlled from the center.

The periphery, in other words, will remain the periphery. Some argue that its position will continue to deteriorate because of declining commodity prices, greater divergence of interest among the developing countries, successful strategies by the center to divide and rule, the acute vulnerability of the debt crisis, and the loss of comparative advantage from cheap labor to smart automation technology in the advanced industrial countries.[18]

The political loosening and diffusion of power within the center may evolve into a series of regional economic spheres centered on Europe, Japan, and North America. But it is not clear that being transferred from a global periphery into a regional one would make much difference either to the structural position or to the economic security of most periphery countries. It might also be argued that economic aid will dwindle as the Cold War political motives that fuelled it subside and Western capital turns to the redevelopment of the ex-Soviet-type systems. Western attitudes already point towards a future in which the allocation of aid and investment is conditional more on the rectitude of economic policy than on fading notions of strategic value. Against this, however, stand two new motives for aid. One is environmental and the other societal. The periphery will increasingly be able to call on the self-interest of the center in relation to the meeting of global environmental standards. They will also be able to threaten the center with unwanted migration unless welfare standards are maintained and develop-

ment prospects kept alive. Both these levers are discussed in more detail below, and together they may well suffice to maintain or even increase the flow of economic aid.

It is not impossible to imagine that in some parts of the periphery, notably those where both imported state structures and economic development have failed totally, there may evolve a kind of de facto institutional recolonization, though some more diplomatic term will need to be found to describe it. There are many potential candidates for this in Africa, and some in South and Southeast Asia, Central America, and the Caribbean. Given the waning of post-decolonization sensitivities about independence, the harsh realities of economic and political failure and the strengthening global institutions of a Western-dominated international society, a subtle return to "managed" status for the most hopeless periphery states may well occur. There are hints of this in the international schemes for Cambodia and in the influence of IMF and World Bank "advisers" in many places. Bangladesh, for example, depends on the IMF and foreign aid for all its development budget and some of its current consumption.[19] Even if they were successful, such efforts could at best bring the worst periphery states up to the point at which they could compete in the international economy.

4. Societal security. Societal security is likely to become a much more prominent issue between center and periphery, and within both, than it has been during the Cold War era. Societal security is about the threats and vulnerabilities that affect patterns of communal identity and culture. The two issues most prominently on its agenda at the beginning of the twenty-first century in center–periphery relations are

[18]Ravenhill, *"The North-South Balance of Power,"* pp. 731–48.

[19]*The Economist,* 2 Mar. 1991, p. 58.

migration[20] and the clash of rival civilizational identities.

Migration threatens communal identity and culture by directly altering the ethnic, cultural religious, and linguistic composition of the population. Most societies have resulted from earlier human migrations and already represent a mixture. Many welcome, up to a point, the cultural diversity that further migration brings. But beyond some point, migration becomes a question of numbers. Too great a foreign influx will threaten the ability of the existing society to reproduce itself in the old way, which can easily create a political constituency for immigration control. Uncontrolled immigration eventually swamps the existing culture. This is one way of looking at the European migrations from the sixteenth century onwards into North and South America, Australia, New Zealand, and South Africa. It is what Estonians and Kazaks fear about Russians, Palestinians fear about Jews (and vice versa), Baluchs about Punjabis, Assamese about Bengalis, and so on.

For the past five centuries it has been mostly migrating Europeans that have posed threats (and not just societal ones) to other peoples. A residuum of this remains in the cultural impact of mass tourism.[21] But at the beginning of the twenty-first century incentives are rising for more permanent mass population movements in the other direction, from periphery to center. The advanced industrial cultures of Europe and North America have low birth rates and high, often rising standards of living. Immediately to their south lie dozens of periphery countries with high birth rates and low, often falling standards of living. Substantial immigrant communities from the South already exist in the North. Transportation is not a significant barrier. The economic incentives for large numbers of young people to move in search of work are high, and the markets of the center have a demand for cheap labor. As the Vietnamese boat people demonstrated, even a substantial risk of death or an unpleasant reception are weak deterrents to determined economic migrants. High incentives to migrate are sustained by the fading of hopes that political independence would bring development and prosperity. In a few places these hopes have been fulfilled, but most face a bleak future in which they seem likely to fall ever further behind the still rapidly evolving political economies of the capitalist center. Some even face falling behind the dismal standards of their own present.

An acute migration problem between societies can hardly avoid raising barriers and tensions between them. In defending itself against unwanted human influx, a country has not only to construct legal and physical barriers to entry, but also to emphasize its differentiation from the society whose members it seeks to exclude. Questions of status and race are impossible to avoid. The treatment of migrants as a kind of criminal class creates easy ground for antagonism between the societies on both sides.

The migration problem does not exist in isolation. It occurs alongside, and mingled in with, the clash of rival civilizational identities between the West and the societies of the periphery. Here the threat travels mostly in the opposite direction, reflecting the older order of Western dominance. It is much more from the center to the periphery than the other way around, though the existence of immigrant communities within the center does mean that there is some real

---

[20]Jonas Widgren, "International migration and regional stability," *International Affairs* 66:4 (1990), pp. 749–66; François Heisbourg, "Population movements in post-Cold War Europe," *Survival* 33:1 (1991), pp. 31–43.

[21]For a graphic and penetrating account of this phenomenon see Pico Iyer, *Video Night in Kathmandu . . . and Other Reports from the Not-So-Far East* (London: Black Swan, 1989).

threat from periphery to center, and a perceived threat of "fifth column" terrorism. The clash between civilizational identities is most conspicuous between the West and Islam. As noted above, this is partly to do with secular versus religious values, partly to do with the historical rivalry between Christendom and Islam, partly to do with jealousy of Western power, partly to do with resentments over Western domination of the postcolonial political structuring of the Middle East, and partly to do with the bitterness and humiliation of the invidious comparison between the accomplishments of Islamic and Western civilization during the last two centuries.

The last point is true as between the West and all periphery societies.[22] By its conspicuous economic and technological success, the West makes all others look bad (i.e. underdeveloped, or backward or poor, or disorganized or repressive, or uncivilized or primitive) and so erodes their status and legitimacy. The tremendous energy, wealth, inventiveness, and organizational dynamism of the West, not to mention its crass materialism and hollow consumer culture, cannot help but penetrate deeply into weaker societies worldwide. As it does so, it both inserts alien styles, concepts, ideas, and aspirations—"Coca-Colaization"—and corrupts or brings into question the validity and legitimacy of local customs and identities. In the case of Islam, this threat is compounded by geographical adjacency and historical antagonism and also the overtly political role that Islam plays in the lives of its followers. Rivalry with the West is made more potent by the fact that Islam is still itself a vigorous and expanding collective identity.

In combination, migration threats and

the clash of cultures make it rather easy to draw a scenario for a kind of societal cold war between the center and at least part of the periphery, and specifically between the West and Islam, in which Europe would be in the front line. There is no certainty that this scenario will unfold, and much will depend on the performance of (and support given to) moderate governments within the Islamic world, but most of the elements necessary for it are already in place. Whatever the final outcome of the Second Gulf War, it will certainly leave behind it a vast reservoir of heated and easily mobilized antiWestern feeling among the Arab and Islamic masses. The resulting tension cannot avoid feeding into the migration issue. It will, *inter alia,* increase friction between the existing Islamic immigrant communities and their host societies and help to legitimize a tougher attitude towards immigration controls, which might otherwise be morally troubling in liberal societies.

This civilizational Cold War could feed into the massive restructuring of relations going on within the center consequent upon the ending of the East–West Cold War. It would well help European political integration, by providing a common foreign policy issue on which a strong consensus would be easy to find. To the extent that it was seen as a security issue, it would confront the European Community with a challenge which both fell within its mandate and which it could handle without much help from the United States. If there was a general heating up of the boundary between "Christendom" and Islam, it would strengthen the Europeanizing tendencies within the Soviet Union and weaken those favoring a more isolationist, Slavophile, position. A societal Cold War with Islam would serve to strengthen the European identity all round at a crucial time for the process of European union. For all these reasons and others, there may well be a substantial constituency

---

[22]Theodore von Laue, *The World Revolution of Westernization: The Twentieth Century in Global Perspective* (New York: Oxford University Press, 1987).

in the West prepared not only to support a societal Cold War with Islam, but to adopt policies that encourage it.

Such a development would put Turkey into an extremely central position. Turkey is anyway the natural insulator between Europe and the Middle East, not only geographically but also culturally (nonArab) and ideologically (Islamic, but with a strong secular state tradition). Its position on the front line of a Europe–Islam Cold War would not be without hazards, but it would fit the country's recent traditions and give it a greatly strengthened hand to play in negotiating its relationship with the European Community. A similar kind of buffer role is available for Mexico, though between North and Latin America the issue is more purely a migration one, and much less a civilizational Cold War, than is the case between Europe and the Middle East.

I have drawn particular attention to societal security problems between center and periphery, but it is important to note that such issues will also be very much on security agendas within the center and within the periphery. Both the European integration project and the breaking down of the Iron Curtain between Eastern and Western Europe will unleash considerable migration inside the continent. Within the periphery, there are already mass migrations in the Middle East and South Asia in search of work and away from conflict (both illustrated by Iraq). In Bangladesh, the Horn of Africa, and Southeast Asia, mass movements are easily stimulated by famine, war, and political repression. The clash of civilizational identities is just as strong on the other side of Islam, where it abuts Hindu civilization, as between Islam and the West.

5. Environmental security. Much of the environmental agenda falls outside the realm of security and is more appropriately seen as an economic question about how the pol-

lution costs of industrial activity are to be counted, controlled, and paid for.[23] Where environmental issues threaten to overwhelm the conditions of human existence on a large scale, as in the case of countries vulnerable to extensive inundation from modest rises in sea level, then casting such issues in security terms is appropriate. The recent flooding of Bangladesh gives a small foretaste of what could well be quite literally a rising tide of disaster. There may also be some advantage in treating as international security issues activities that may cause substantial changes in the workings of the planetary atmosphere. These might include the mass production of greenhouse gases or chemicals such as CFCs that erode the protective ozone layer, or exploitative or polluting activities that threaten to diminish the supply of oxygen to the atmosphere by killing off forests and plankton.

It seems safe to predict that this whole agenda is going to rise in importance as the density of human occupation of the planet increases. It is much harder to assess how quickly this will happen and how intense the pressures will become. If serious climatic changes begin to occur soon, this could easily become a transcendent issue. Quite a few periphery countries are vulnerable to virtual obliteration by sustained drought and desertification or by rising sea levels. Their ability to cope with such changes is small, and the mass migrations that would be triggered would quickly feed into the societal issues discussed above. Even less drastic changes that did not threaten obliteration might put such stress on weak state structures as to cause political breakdown, adding to the pressures on boundary maintenance.

Barring such dramatic developments,

[23]On the risks in the idea of environmental security, see Daniel Deudney, "The Case against Linking Environmental Degradation and National Security," *Millennium* 19:3 (1990), pp. 461–76.

environmental issues look set to become a regular feature of center–periphery dialogues and tensions. The holistic quality of the planetary environment will provide the center with reasons for wanting to intervene in the periphery in the name of environmental security. The periphery will gain some political leverage out of this interest, and will continue to blame the industrialized center for having created the problem in the first place. This exchange may well stay within the political framework of interdependence, below the threshold of security. But it could also become entangled with the broader debate about development in such a way as to trigger serious conflicts of interest. As others have pointed out, environmental issues, particularly control over water supplies, look likely to generate quite a bit of local conflict within the periphery.[24]

* * *

It is apparent from this brief survey that the security agenda of the periphery countries in the 1990s and beyond will be significantly different from the one we have been used to since 1945. The replacement of a polarized center by one dominated by the capitalist security community seems almost certain to weaken the position of the periphery in relation to the center. In this sense, the West has triumphed over both communism and *tiers-mondisme*.

The changes in the center will have a substantial impact on the periphery. They will redefine not only center–periphery relations—in both directions—but also relations within the periphery. Some aspects of the security agenda will remain familiar, albeit with some new twists. This is most obviously likely in the economic sector, though there will also be many continuities in the military one. Environmental issues will certainly increase in importance, but whether they will become a major part of the security agenda is more questionable. The biggest changes are most likely to come in the political and societal sectors. Extensive shifts both in prevailing political norms and in the nature of international political interests seem entirely plausible. It does not seem too much to say that almost the entire range of center–periphery political relations, from boundaries and bases to aid and alignment, is open for redefinition. Societal concerns also seem destined to rise to a position of prominence on the security agenda that they have not held since before the establishment of the modern European state system.

The change in terminology from "Third World" to "periphery" may look like a promotion from third rank to second, but this is only a superficial view. The deeper reality is that the center is now more dominant, and the periphery more subordinate, than at any time since decolonization began.

[24]Ravenhill, "The North-South Balance of Power," p. 748; *The Economist*, 16 Dec. 1989, p. 70.

23 THE INTERNATIONAL SECURITY SYSTEM AND THE THIRD WORLD

MOHAMMED AYOOB

Professor Ayoob, an SSRC-MacArthur Foundation Fellow of International Peace and Security at The Center for International Studies at Princeton in 1989–90, teaches at James Madison College at Michigan State.

Two major events have shaped the political contours of the postwar world. The first is the awesome destructive capability of nuclear weaponry, which, as institutionalized in the doctrine of mutual assured destruction (MAD), has prevented the outbreak of major war between the two dominant powers in the international system and, until recently, had frozen the strategic situation in Europe in a bipolar mold. The second is the entrance of unprecedented numbers of new members into the system of states as a result of the decolonization process—such that the newcomers now constitute a majority among the membership of that system. Although the latter event has had as far-reaching effects as the former on the workings of the international system, it has unfortunately not received attention in the literature on international relations commensurate with its actual and potential impact on international affairs.

Despite the moral dilemma related to the capacity of nuclear weapons for mass destruction, the existence of superpower nuclear arsenals with second strike capacities helped during the last four and a half decades to stabilize the global balance of power and make it relatively immune to transient shifts in the capabilities of the great powers. By contrast, the influx of the weak, intruder majority of Third World states into the international system[1] introduced a great deal of fluidity, and therefore instability, into that system. In strategic terms, this resulted primarily from the fact that there existed a large group of "floating" states with no alliance commitments, a group that was, in a sense, "up for grabs" by the highest bidder or the great power with the largest capability to help or harm it. Consequently, Third World regions became gray areas of the globe to which cold war energies, frustrated in Europe by the existence of MAD, were diverted. They became the primary site of the new "great game" played out by the United States and the Soviet Union. . . .

[1] For a discussion of this phenomenon, see Mohammed Ayoob, "The Third World in the System of States: Acute Schizophrenia or Growing Pains?" *International Studies Quarterly* 33 (March 1989), 67–79.

Excerpted from *World Politics* 43, 2 (January 1991), 257–83, by permission. Copyright © Princeton University Press, 1991. (Footnotes have been renumbered).

II

The term *security* as it has been traditionally used in international relations literature is based on two major assumptions: one, that threats to a state's security principally arise from outside its borders, and two, that these threats are primarily, if not exclusively, military in nature and usually need a military response if the security of the target state is to be preserved. These assumptions were best summed up in Walter Lippmann's celebrated statement that "a nation is secure to the extent to which it is not in danger of having to sacrifice core values, if it wishes to avoid war, and is able, if challenged, to maintain them by victory in such a war."[2] Lippmann's definition, according to Arnold Wolfers, "implies that security rises and falls with the ability of a nation to deter an attack, or to defeat it. This is in accord with the common usage of the term."[3]

Even those scholars who have differed from this starkly state-centered realist perspective and focused on *international* rather than *national* security have been primarily concerned with reconciling national security (in terms of reducing external threats to the security of a state, especially of a major power) with systemic security concerns. They have taken their philosophical cue from authors like Martin Wight and Hedley Bull, who have argued, to quote Wight, that

> if there is an international society, then there is an order of some kind to be maintained, or even developed. It is not fallacious to speak of a collective interest, and security acquires a broad meaning: it can be enjoyed or pursued in common.[4]

Indeed, the earliest of the twentieth-century proponents of international security—the "idealists" of the first three decades[5]—refused to distinguish the security of the parts from that of the system as a whole. The post–Second World War breed of system-centered scholars has been more discriminating than its predecessors. They have argued from the assumption that the various segments of the international system are interlinked to such an extent that their security and welfare are dependent upon each other. While much of the initial impetus for this line of argument came from the awesome concentration of nuclear weaponry in the hands of the two superpowers and the periodic crises in their relations from the Berlin blockade of 1948 to the Cuban missile crisis of 1962, the economic problems that the leading Western industrialized states faced from the early 1970s, including the two oil shocks of 1973–74 and 1978–79, led to the crystallization of the "interdependence" argument.[6]

What is most interesting for our purpose is that both these dominant strands of security thinking (in their many variations) defined the concept of security in external or outward-directed terms, that is, as external to the commonly accepted unit of analysis in international relations: the state. This definition and the process by which it was reached were understandable because both reflected a particular trajectory of historical development that could be traced back at least to the Peace of Westphalia if not earlier. Between 1648 (to use it as a symbolic date)

---

[2]Lippmann, *U.S. Foreign Policy: Shield of the Republic* (Boston: Little Brown, 1943), 51.

[3]Wolfers, *Discord and Collaboration: Essays on International Politics* (Baltimore, Md.: Johns Hopkins University Press, 1962), 150.

[4]Wight, "Western Values in International Relations," In Herbert Butterfield and Martin Wight, eds., *Diplo-*

matic Investigations (London: Allen and Unwin, 1966), 103.

[5]For a representative sample of idealist thought, see Norman Angell, *The Great Illusion*, 4th ed. (1909; New York: Putnam's, 1913).

[6]For example, see Robert O. Keohane and Joseph S. Nye, *Power and Interdependence* (Boston: Little Brown, 1977).

and 1945 the evolution of the European system of states and its interaction with the domestic political processes of state building and national consolidation within the major European powers led to the legitimation both of the system and of the individual participants (at least of those twenty-five or so that survived the processes of war and change in the European system and emerged as modern states by 1900). These two trends—of interaction among sovereign states and of greater identification of individuals with their respective states—strengthened each other and in doing so firmly laid the foundations of the intellectual tradition in which, at least in terms of the literature on diplomatic history and international relations, security became synonymous with the protection of a state's vital interests and core values from external threats.

Developments since 1945 strengthened the traditional Western notions about security. In dividing the Western world (that is, Europe and its offshoots) into two halves and in stabilizing that division until recently by means of a mutual balance of terror, the cold war (and its later manifestation, detente) froze the predominant Western connotation of security in a bipolar mold. The concept of alliance security was, therefore, superimposed on the concept of state security, while its essential, externally directed thrust remained unchanged. Moreover, by making the security of major industrial states of Europe and North America the central concern of the security of the international system as a whole, the dominant strand in Western strategic thinking increasingly obliterated even the distinction between the realist (state-centric) and idealist (system-centric) approaches to the study of international security.

The application of this historically conditioned definition of the concept of security to the analysis of Third World situations has, however, created major conceptual problems. This is so because the three major characteristics of the concept of state security as developed in the Western literature on international relations—namely, its external orientation, its strong linkage with systemic security, and its binding ties with the security of the two major alliance blocs—are, if not totally absent, at lest thoroughly diluted in the Third World. Thus, the explanatory power of the concept, as traditionally defined, is vastly reduced when applied to Third World contexts.

The first and, in a sense, the fundamental attribute of the Western concept of security (in that it is a corollary of the doctrine of state sovereignty in its pure and pristine form) is external directedness. But it is clear that in the Third World, despite the rhetoric of many of its leaders, the sense of insecurity from which states suffer emanates to a substantial degree from within their boundaries rather than from outside. This is borne out by, among other studies, the findings of a recent project on the security perceptions of leaders of Southeast Asian states. That study presents the conclusion that "most Southeast Asian leaderships, like their counterparts in the rest of the Third World, are preoccupied primarily with internal threats to the security of their state structures and to the regimes themselves."[7] While this does not mean that external threats are nonexistent, it does imply that where external threats do exist they often attain saliency primarily because of the insecurities and conflicts that abound within Third World states. Furthermore, it can be argued that these internal conflicts and insecurities frequently get transformed into in-

[7]Mohammed Ayoob and Chai-Anan Samudavanija, "Leadership and Security in Southeast Asia: Exploring General Propositions," in Ayoob and Samudavanija, eds., *Leadership Perceptions and National Security: The Southeast Asian Experience* (Singapore: Institute of Southeast Asian Studies, 1989), 256.

terstate conflicts because of their spillover effects into neighboring states that often suffer from similar domestic insecurities. Several contributions to the Azar-Moon volume, particularly those by Barry Buzan (chap. 2) and by the editors (chaps. 1 and 4), as well as the second chapter of Thomas's book, which deals with nation building and the search for security, highlight this internal dimension of the Third World states' security problems and its capacity to become enmeshed in and, not infrequently, to generate interstate conflict.

The Third World's weak linkage with the systemic security agenda further circumscribes the utility of the traditional concept of security in explaining the problem (or problems) of security that Third World states face. This reflects the remarkable difference between the respective relationships of the security concerns of the Third World states, on the one hand, and those of the developed countries, on the other, to the security and stability of the international system as a whole. The Third World's relative unimportance to the central strategic balance is, paradoxically, borne out by the fact that

> during the postwar era, the Third World has been a principal arena of East-West rivalry. From Southeast Asia to the Middle East to Southern Africa to Central America, the superpowers have found themselves on opposing sides of regional conflicts, locked in a global competition for influence. (Litwak and Wells, ix)

The very fact that the superpowers chose the Third World as the arena in which they could afford to be "locked in a global competition for influence" in the thermonuclear age demonstrates the low priority they attached to gains and losses in the Third World and the vast distance that separated their Third World concerns from their vital interests, which were, and are, protected by the nuclear balance of terror. It is no wonder then that conflicts have proliferated in the Third World, while the industrial and strategic heartland of the globe has been free of major interstate conflict since the end of the Second World War. Systemic security has therefore often contributed to insecurity in the Third World.

The close linkage between alliance security and state security that has been such a prominent feature of the postwar political landscape in Europe has been conspicuous by its absence in the Third World. While several Third World states have been allied with one or the other superpower, such alliances have been either fluid and temporary (as in the case of Egypt and Somalia) or inadequate deterrents to regional conflicts involving superpower allies (for example, Vietnam and Iraq) or incapable of preventing the dismemberment of at least one aligned state (Pakistan). The nature of alliances and of superpower commitments to their allies in the Third World are therefore vastly different from the character of alliances and of alliance commitments in the developed world. Alliance security, in contrast to the postwar situation in Europe, is not synonymous with, or even inextricably tied to, the security of even the most overtly aligned states in the Third World.[8]

[8]Israel is the only exception to this rule because of the intensity of one superpower's commitment to its security, as defined largely by Israel itself. This, in turn, is related to the fact that Israel is a domestic political issue in the United States and not merely a foreign policy concern. Moreover, Israel, in terms of its ideological origins, the organization of its society and polity, the composition of its elite, and its links with strong and important European and American constituencies is not a Third World state. In other words, Israel may be physically located *in* the Third World but, in terms of the defining characteristics of the Israeli state, is not *of* the Third World. For details of the nature and evolution of the special relationship between the United States and Israel, see Nadav Safran, *Israel: The Embattled Ally* (Cambridge, Mass.: Belknap Press, 1981).

For all the three dimensions of the traditional definition of security—its external orientation, links with systemic security, and the correspondence with alliance security—the situation in the Third World is radically different from that prevailing at the heart of the global strategic system, which includes the two superpowers, Europe and its offshoots, and Japan. The security of Third World states therefore needs to be looked at from a perspective that differs somewhat from the one that is prevalent in the Western literature on international relations.

III

This leads us to our next question: Are there any factors that inhere within Third World states that can help explain this difference in the Third World state's security problematic as compared with the paradigm of security that is dominant in the international relations and strategic studies literature?"[9] The principal problem that seems to distort a great deal of Western analysis of the security of Third World states is the tendency to compare states (that is, industrialized states with developing ones) that are unlike each other in many respects. This is especially so in relation to the crucial variable of state making, where the commonality is simply that both are in formal possession of juridical statehood. This, however, does not preclude the possibility of Third World states eventually approximating more closely the ideal type of the modern industrialized state (which is the reference point of most security analysts), given adequate time to complete the prerequisite twin processes of state making and nation building.

Time is, therefore, the crucial variable in explaining the difference in the security concerns of the two sets of states. Most security analysts tend to gloss over the fact that today's modern states—which are internally relatively cohesive, possess rational bureaucratic structures as well as a good deal of "infrastructural power,"[10] and are responsible to their people as well as responsive to the demands of their populations—were not created overnight. They went through a long period of gestation (during which most embryonic and also some not-so-embryonic states were aborted) before they acquired the functional capacities as well as the legitimacy they have today in the eyes of the populace that they encompass territorially and over which they preside institutionally.

It is worth noting in this context the testimony of two leading scholars of state making in Europe. According to Joseph Strayer:

> While the sovereign state of 1300 was stronger than any competing political form, it was still not very strong. . . . It took four to five centuries for European states to remedy their administrative deficiencies, and to bring lukewarm loyalty to the white heat of nationalism.[11]

Charles Tilly makes the same point even more forcefully:

> The seventeenth and eighteenth century focus [of his edited volume] has us dealing

---

[9]For a critique of the application (or misapplication) of the strategic studies paradigm to the Third World, see Bahgat Korany, "Strategic Studies and the Third World: A Critical Evaluation," *International Social Science Journal*, no. 110 (1986), 547–62.

[10]Michael Mann has used the term *infrastructural power* to denote "the capacity of the state actually to penetrate civil society, and to implement logistically political decisions throughout the realm"; Mann, "The Autonomous Power of the State: Its Origins, Mechanisms and Results," in John A. Hall, ed., *States in History* (Oxford: Basil Blackwell, 1986), 113.

[11]Strayer, *On the Medieval Origins of the Modern State* (Princeton: Princeton University Press, 1970), 23, 57.

with periods in which, for most of Europe, both the primacy and the ultimate form of the state were much in doubt. Perhaps that is the most important historical insight the book has to offer: as seen from 1600 or so, the development of the state was very contingent; many aspiring states crumpled and fell along the way.[12]

Most European political entities had to endure the precarious balance between success and failure for centuries before their statehood was assured; during that time their state makers were constantly preoccupied with the problem of consolidating their power and control *within* the territories they aspired to dominate. Seen in light of the European historical experience, then, the magnitude of the internal security problems faced by the new states of the Third World today is not all that astounding. These problems assume inflated dimensions only when compared with the "finished" products in Western Europe and North America. And, indeed, some of those, despite the centuries available to them, have yet to establish their unconditional legitimacy with some, and sometimes significant, segments of their populations. (Witness Northern Ireland, Quebec, and the Basque country, to mention only a few.)

Recent events have clearly demonstrated that the Soviet Union, despite its claim to be the successor state to tsarist Russia with its long history of statehood, does not even come close to the model of the cohesive nation-state or even of a multinational federation whose institutional and territorial legitimacy is accepted by the overwhelming majority of its diverse ethnic and national groups. The same applies to the states in the Balkans, created out of the debris of the Habsburg and Ottoman empires,

which generally fall midway between the model of the relatively cohesive nation-states of Western Europe and the postcolonial multiethnic, polyglot states of Asia and Africa. Yugoslavia, the most extreme example in the Balkans, betrays a classic Third World syndrome in terms of interethnic antagonism and intrastate insecurity. One suspects that here, again, the time factor, coupled with the way these states were brought into being as a result of decisions largely taken by major external powers, provides the most fruitful explanation for the predicament faced by the Balkan states.[13]

Barry Buzan's distinction between "strong" and "weak" states, which accords primary explanatory power to what he calls "the variable of sociopolitical cohesiveness" (Azar and Moon, 18), is related in important ways to this difference in the time available to different categories of states to complete the twin processes of state making and nation building. This comes through clearly in

---

[12]Tilly, "Reflections on the History of European State-Making," in Tilly, ed., *The Formation of National States in Western Europe* (Princeton: Princeton University Press, 1975), 7.

[13]For an insightful analysis of state making and nation building in the Balkans, see Najdan Pasic, "Varieties of Nation-Building in the Balkans and among the Southern Slavs," in S. N. Eisenstadt and Stein Rokkan, eds., *Building States and Nations* (Beverly Hills, Calif.: Sage, 1973), 2:117–41. Pasic refers to the Balkan experience as the "missing link" and "a transition between the way nations were formed in Europe at the beginning of the present era and the nation-building now going on in the developing countries" (p. 118). Pasic also makes another interesting comparison between the way the Balkan states were carved out and spheres of influence established among them and the way many Third World states were formed as a result of intraimperial understandings:

> From the Holy Alliance and the Congress of Berlin to the Yalta Conference, where spheres of influence in the Balkans were calculated in percentages, the Balkan peoples had their destinies carved out by others. The parceling out of political and national structures in the Balkans was in a substantial part the product of such external forces. In this respect, the historical circumstances surrounding nation-building in the Balkans bear a close resemblance to those in which nations and independent national states have taken shape in other parts of the economically underdeveloped world. (p. 130)

his conclusion: "Building stronger states is virtually the only way in which the vicious circle of unstable states and an unstable security environment can be broken" (Azar and Moon, 40). Similarly, the emphasis placed by Azar and Moon (chap. 4) on the "software" side of national security in the Third World is an acknowledgment on their part that not enough time has been available to state makers in these countries to develop the intangible ingredients of security, including the identification of the people with the state (legitimacy) and of people with each other (integration). It is also an acknowledgment of the fact that in the absence of these intangibles, the state elites in the Third World are bound to take frequent recourse to the "hardware" instruments of security, namely, military force, to meet what are essentially political challenges from disaffected groups within their populations.

It should be noted here that the Latin American case in terms of the availability of time for purposes of state building appears to be somewhat different from that of the rest of the Third World because the former colonies of Spain and Portugal in South America acquired political independence over a hundred years before the process of decolonization began in earnest in Asia. For a number of reasons, however, their processes of state making and nation building remained retarded. Prominent among these was the importation, along with Spanish and Portuguese colonists, of the economic and political culture of preindustrial Iberia, which led to the fossilization of Latin American political development. As Skidmore and Smith have pointed out, "However much Latin America struggled, it was to remain an extension . . . of the Europe that had sailed west in the fifteenth century."[14]

The era of industrial society (in terms of its demonstration effect rather than its realization) caught up with Latin America about the same time that it did with much of Asia, if not Africa. (It needs to be pointed out here that the model of the industrial society includes as its essential elements a socially mobile population, forming part of a society that is culturally relatively homogeneous, that is encompassed within a legitimate state structure with adequate "infrastructural power," and that is presided over by a representative government.) While the intervening century may have provided Latin America the time to consolidate state boundaries, its social and political structures retarded other aspects of state making, above all those of societal penetration and the achievement of political legitimacy both for state institutions and for ruling elites. Thus, the acquisition of formal political independence relatively early in the game gave Latin American states only marginal advantages over their Asian counterparts. In any case, a head start of a little over a century, especially in the absence of other elements conducive to state and nation building, was not much in relation to the length of time it took Western European states to complete their process of state making.[15] It is no wonder, therefore, that state elites in Latin America continue to put as much emphasis on the "hardware" instruments of internal security as do their counterparts in other parts of the Third World.[16]

Overall, the Azar-Moon analysis corroborates the thesis that the study of the Eu-

[15]For interesting analyses of the Latin American case, see Robert E. Scott, "Nation-Building in Latin America," in Karl W. Deutsch and William J. Foltz, eds., *Nation-Building* (New York: Atherton Press, 1966), 73–83; and Howard J. Wiarda, "Social Change, Political Development and the Latin American Tradition," in Wiarda, ed., *Politics and Social Change in Latin America*, 2d rev. ed. (Amherst: University of Massachusetts Press, 1982), 3–25.

[16]Alain Rouquie comes close to tackling this question while attempting to provide explanations for the

[14]Thomas E. Skidmore and Peter H. Smith, *Modern Latin America*, 2d ed. (New York: Oxford University Press, 1989), 16.

ropean experience of state making is very relevant to the explanation of the current security predicament of states in the Third World. This European experience, in Tilly's words,

> cost tremendously in death, suffering, loss of rights, and unwilling surrender of land, goods, or labor. . . . The fundamental reason for the high cost of European state-building was its beginning in the midst of a decentralized, largely peasant social structure. Building differentiated, autonomous, centralized organizations with effective control of territories entailed eliminating or subordinating thousands of semi-autonomous authorities. . . . Most of the European population resisted each phase of the creation of strong states.[17]

The applicability of this description to the present reality within most Third World states is too uncanny to be purely coincidental.

While this similarity between the early European and current Third World experiences of state making provides part of the explanation for the internal security problems faced by Third World states, the difference in the pace of state making and nation building and the telescoping of these two processes into a combined and drastically shortened process in the case of the Third World provides the rest of the explanation. This is the result of the fact that unlike the

centuries available to most European (especially West European) state makers to complete their process of state making, today's Third World state makers are under tremendous pressures to complete this extremely complicated and costly process in only three or four decades rather than three or four centuries. As a result, the process of "primitive central state power accumulation"[18] has to be speeded up tremendously. The various phases of state and nation building, which were undertaken and complete by and large sequentially (although with significant degrees of overlap between the phases)[19] and without any significant amount of premeditation in the case of early modern Europe, have to be undertaken and completed deliberately and simultaneously within a time-bound framework of ridiculously short duration.

This drastic shortening of the time frame and the telescoping of the various phases of state making, combined with the initially low level of state power from which state making takes place,[20] provide the primary explanation for the sharp internal

---

military's involvement in Latin American politics, but he inexplicably shies away from addressing it directly in his otherwise knowledgeable treatise *The Military and the State in Latin America*, trans. Paul E. Sigmund (Berkeley: University of California Press, 1987).

[17] Tilly (fn. 15), 71. This conclusion is also borne out by the historical evidence presented by Youssef Cohen, Brian R. Brown, and A. F. K. Organski in their article "The Paradoxical Nature of State Making: The Violent Creation of Order," *American Political Science Review* 75, no. 4 (1981), 901–10. They argue that "instead of indicating political decay, violence in these [new] states is an integral part of the process of the accumulation of power by the national state apparatus" (p. 909).

[18] "Many of the new states of today are engaged in struggles whose logic is similar to that of the European period of primitive central state power accumulation"; Cohen, Brown, and Organski (fn. 20), 902.

[19] Stein Rokkan, in a very incisive essay in which he attempted to construct a paradigm explaining the various dimensions of state formation and nation building in Europe, provided four sequential phases over which these twin processes took place and termed them penetration, standardization, participation, and redistribution. For details, see Rokkan, "Dimensions of State Formation and Nation-Building: A Possible Paradigm for Research on Variations within Europe," in Tilly (fn. 15), esp. 572–74. Rokkan analyzed the internal variations in the patterns of nation-state building in Europe and concluded that, despite these differences within the European experience, "what is important is that the Western nation-states were given a chance to solve some of the worst problems of state-building before they had to face the ordeal of mass politics" (p. 598).

[20] This point is made by Cohen, Brown, and Organski (fn. 20), who argue that "the extent to which an expansion of state power will generate collective violence depends on the level of state power prior to

challenges to the centralizing state structures in the developing countries and for the high level of violence endemic in the current phase of state making in the Third World. These challenges—whether posed in the garb of ethnicity or class or a combination of the two—and the violent responses to them are functions of the low level of legitimacy enjoyed by most Third World states within their societies; they form the core of the security problems facing these states and their regimes. Several contributions to the Azar-Moon volume as well as the second chapter of Thomas's book refer to the connection between low level of legitimacy and internal security problems in Third World states. But they do not adequately probe these linkages and do not delve into root causes that are embedded in the process of state making in the Third World. This is an area that can prove to be very fruitful in terms of further research on the interconnections between the factor of time, the process of state making, and the problem of insecurity in the countries and regions of the Third World.

IV

The security problems of Third World states are exacerbated by the fact that state making in the Third World does not take place in an international vacuum. While the internal or intrastate dimension of state making may be the primary preoccupation of state elites in the Third World, the impact of international forces, whether military, political, economic, or technological, makes a substantial and substantive difference to the fortunes of the state-making enterprise and to the larger security problematic of Third World states. This is particularly so in the contemporary era when the technologies of communication and destruction link the various parts of the world in a way that is qualitatively different from the situation prevailing in any previous historical epoch.

Moreover, as a result of the colonial experience of most Third World societies, external factors have traditionally had a predominant influence in shaping their polities and, therefore, their security environments. In fact, it would not be wrong to say that many Third World states, particularly in Africa and the Middle East but also elsewhere in Asia, emerged into the post-colonial era as sovereign entities with recognized boundaries only because they had been consolidated into separate colonial protostates by the European imperial powers in the nineteenth century.[21]

This has had two major consequences for both the internal and the external security of Third World states. First, decisions taken by colonial powers for reasons of administrative convenience or intraimperial tradeoff have been largely responsible for the ethnic mix inherited by many post-colonial states as well as for the creation of new communal identities in some instances.

that expansion . . . the lower the initial *level* of state power, the stronger the relationship between the *rate* of state expansion and collective violence" (p. 905).

[21]There is a growing literature on this subject, particularly in relation to Africa. A recent, perceptive article on the creation of colonial protostates in Africa is Jeffrey Herbst, "The Creation and Maintenance of National Boundaries in Africa," *International Organization* 43 (Autumn 1989), 673–92. For the creation of protostates in the guise of mandates in the Middle East, see Elizabeth Monroe, *Britain's Moment in the Middle East, 1914–1956* (Baltimore, Md.: Johns Hopkins University Press, 1963); and for the impact of the European division of Arab lands of the Ottoman Empire on international and regional security, see David Fromkin, *A Peace to End All Peace: Creating the Modern Middle East* (New York: Henry Holt, 1989).

The colonial inheritance thus fundamentally determined the internal cohesiveness of most Third World states during their initial and crucial stages of state building and, therefore, the intensity of internal challenges to their boundaries and institutions.[22] Second, decisions taken by colonial powers have also been responsible for creating many postcolonial interstate conflicts: (1) by dividing ethnic groups into more than one state and thereby igniting the embers of irredentism, as in the Horn of Africa; (2) by denying self-determination to certain ethnic groups like the Kurds, who possibly qualified for statehood better than many that were granted that status; and (3) by leaving behind extremely messy situations, as in Palestine and in Kashmir, that have contributed tremendously to regional tensions and conflicts in the Middle East and South Asia, respectively, during the last four decades.

Equally important, in terms of the feelings of insecurity that are very widespread among Third World state elites, is the legacy of the colonial entities' individual and collective weakness and vulnerability in relation to the metropolitan centers. This sense of insecurity has been transferred after decolonization to the sphere of the Third World's relationship with the industrialized states in general and with the superpowers in partic-

ular and has largely become a function of the glaring disparities in economic, technological, and military power between the developed states on the one hand and the Third World on the other. It has been further exacerbated by the division of the globe into a relatively secure and conflict-free zone, populated by European and North American states plus Japan, and the Third World, where conflict is endemic. As Ball has pointed out, "All interstate wars since the end of World War II have taken place in the Third World, although there have been industrialized country participants in some of these conflicts" (p. 33).[23] In fact, some analysts have argued that conflict in the Third World has until recently been encouraged by superpower policies largely aimed at testing each other's political will and power projection capabilities in those areas of the globe that are not of vital concern to either superpower and, therefore, do not threaten the maintenance of the central strategic balance.[24]

This de facto division of the globe, roughly corresponding to the core-periphery dichotomy of the world system theorists,[25] allows for the exportation of the developed world's conflicts to the Third World, while

[22]For an insightful analysis of the colonial inheritance and its impact on Third World "stateness," see Joel S. Migdal, *Strong Societies and Weak States: State-Society Relations and State Capabilities in the Third World* (Princeton: Princeton University Press, 1988). See also Crawford Young, "The African Colonial State and Its Political Legacy," in Donald Rothchild and Naomi Chazan, *The Precarious Balance: State and Society in Africa* (Boulder, Colo.: Westview Press, 1988); and Sheldon Gellar, "State-Building and Nation-Building in West Africa," in Eisenstadt and Rokkan (fn. 16), 2:384–426. For examples of the creation of "traditional" authority structures as well as the evolution of new communal identities during colonial rule, see Migdal (pp. 97–141); and Ulf Himmelstrand, "'Tribalism,' Regionalism, Nationalism, and Secession in Nigeria," in Eisenstadt and Rokkan (pp. 427–67).

[23]The high incidence of violent conflict in the Third World is borne out by a number of studies, including Mark Zacker, *International Conflicts and Collective Security* (New York: Praeger, 1979); and Nazli Choucri, *Population and Conflict: New Dimensions of Population Dynamics*, Policy Development Studies No. 8 (United Nations Fund for Population Activities, 1983). For an earlier, pioneering study of the subject, see Istvan Kende, "Twenty-five Years of Local Wars," *Journal of Peace Research* 8, no. 1 (1971), 5–22.

[24]This point was best made by Sisir Gupta two decades ago; Gupta, "Great Power Relations and the Third World," in Carsten Holbraad, ed., *Super Powers and World Order* (Canberra: Australian National University Press, 1971), 105–39.

[25]For details of the core-periphery dichotomy, see Johan Galtung, "A Structural Theory of Imperialism," *Journal of Peace Research* 8, no. 2 (1971), 81–117; and the various works of Immanuel Wallerstein.

effectively insulating the "core" of the international system from the conflicts and instabilities prevalent in the Third World. As a result, it enhances the insecurity of Third World state elites who suffer from a feeling of dual impotence. First, they are unable to prevent superpower rivalries and conflicts from penetrating their polities and regions, and second, they are equally unable to affect, except marginally and in selected cases, the global political and military equation between the two superpowers and their respective alliances. This conclusion is borne out by even a casual reading of the Litwak-Wells volume and is corroborated by Thomas's statement that "the outlook for the Third World remains bleak. While it is very far from true to suggest that everything that happens to them is a result of external factors, it is fallacious to believe that indigenous factors play the most influential role most of the time" (p. 199).

All this does not mean, however, that external threats of conflict and intervention

in relation to Third World states do not also arise from within their regions, that is, from other Third World states. Obviously, Third World regions do possess autonomous dynamics of conflict and cooperation. In fact, the predominant reality of these regional dynamics is the great propensity for conflict that inheres within them. As the various contributions to the Litwak-Wells volume demonstrate, there are reasons intrinsic to Third World regions, for example, historical mistrust, territorial disputes, ethnic overlap, and hegemonic ambitions, that provide much of the raw material for interstate conflict in the Third World. Two points are worth noting in this context, however. First, many of these intrinsic reasons for intra–Third World conflict are related to, if not the products of, external domination during the colonial era. Second, the permissive attitude on the part of the dominant global powers toward conflict in the Third World promotes and exacerbates interstate violence in the gray areas of the globe.

V

One major factor that has increased the level of violence in the developing world as well as the propensity of Third World states to indulge in interstate conflict is the transfer of modern weapons and weapons technology from the industrialized countries to various parts of the Third World. According to one specialist on the arms trade, "These transfers have resulted in a significant shift in military resources from the industrialized 'North' to the underdeveloped 'South,' producing new configurations of power and contributing to the intensity and duration of regional conflicts."[26] Certainly, weapons are mainly of instrumental value and are not in

themselves the primary cause of war; but relatively sophisticated weapon systems that provide a Third World state with temporary technological superiority over a regional rival are very often a crucial factor in the calculation of decision makers to escalate disputes to a point where war becomes a distinct possibility. To cite just one instance: Pakistan's decision to go to war against India in 1965 with the objective of changing the status quo in Kashmir was based in part on the assessment that the former's edge in sophisticated weapons over the latter was likely to be eroded over the next few years.[27]

Sophisticated weapons acquired at

---

[26]Michael T. Klare, "The Arms Trade: Changing Patterns in the 1980s," *Third World Quarterly* 9 (October 1987), 1257.

[27]Gowher Rizvi, "The Rivalry between India and Pakistan," in Barry Buzan et al., *South Asian Insecurity and the Great Powers* (Basingstoke: Macmillan, 1986), 107–8.

great cost to provide greater security can often increase prospects of conflict and, therefore, add to the insecurity of Third World states.[28] Andrew Ross's contribution to the Azar-Moon volume (chap. 7) concentrates on "the various forms of arms acquisition options available to Third World countries and the impact of alternative acquisition strategies upon national security" (p. 154) and makes the point sharply that "the acquisition of military power may itself erode rather than enhance security" (p. 153). As a result of the combination of various factors (including the escalation in military technology, the superpowers' strategy to use arms transfer as political instruments to buy the loyalties of Third World clients, the leading arms exporters' interest in using arms sales as a major booster for their economies, and the inability of even the most technologically advanced Third World states independently to manufacture more than a fraction of the sophisticated weapons they need or desire to possess), "the Third World's dependence upon arms imports from the advanced industrial countries" has become "the defining characteristic of post-colonial North-South military relations" (Ross, in Azar and Moon, 156).

The 1980s saw an appreciable increase in the capacity of certain Third World states, like India and Brazil, to produce, and even export, indigenous arms. There was also a perceptible decline in the value of arms deliveries to the Third World during most of the 1980s as a result of the fall in the price of oil, which drastically reduced the purchasing capacity of major oil-exporting countries that had been among the leading acquirers of sophisticated weaponry, and of the saturation of many Third World markets. However, these two phenomena mask a different, and growing, form of weapons transfer from developed to developing countries: the transfer of sophisticated arms production technology, now an integral part of the international arms trade.[29] The transfer of such technology has two major consequences. On the one hand, as conventional wisdom holds, given both the high rate at which weapons and weapons technologies become obsolete in the late twentieth century and the inability of Third World countries to keep up with the latest technologies, the transfer of weapons technology amounts to nothing more than the substitution of one form of dependence for another. Indeed, it might even increase the level of dependency. On the other hand, as Ross has argued in the Azar-Moon volume,

> The nature of military dependence undergoes a subtle but potentially profound transformation as developing countries turn from arms imports to arms production. . . . A static dependence relationship is inevitable when a country relies upon foreign arms suppliers. But when arms production programmes are initiated, and military production technology rather than arms are imported, a more dynamic relationship is established, one that has an inherent potential for the reduction, if not elimination, of military dependence. (pp. 169–70)[30]

---

[28]The availability of large surplus stocks of modern weaponry combined with cold war motivations on the part of superpower suppliers has contributed to regional arms races and to the instability of regional balances, which must constantly be restabilized at higher levels of technological sophistication. As Raju Thomas has pointed out in the case of South Asia, "The net result was that both India and Pakistan acquired substantially more arms than they otherwise would have thus producing less regional security for both states at a much higher price"; Thomas, "Strategies of Recipient Autonomy: The Case of India," in Kwang-Il Baek, Ronald D. McLaurin, and Chung-in Moon, eds., *The Dilemma of Third World Defense Industries: Supplier Control or Recepient Autonomy?* (Boulder, Colo.: Westview Press, 1989), 188.

[29]For a detailed discussion of this issue, see Michael T. Klare, "The Unnoticed Arms Trade: Exports of Conventional Arms-Making Technology," *International Security* 8 (Fall 1983), 68–90.

[30]Ross's contention is borne out by Raju Thomas's study (fn. 28) of Indian weapons procurement and production policy, which, according to its author, at-

The political autonomy of Third World arms recipients was further enhanced during the 1980s by the appreciable increase in the number of arms suppliers and the increasingly intense competition among them, the decline in the market share of the superpower suppliers, and the increasing transformation of the nature of the arms market from a seller's to a buyer's market. However, this should not lead us to conclude that commercial calculations alone dictate the flow of arms supply or of weapons technology from the industrialized countries to the Third World. There are a number of political and strategic considerations, many of them connected with superpower global rivalries and with the myriad of political and strategic links between the superpowers on the one hand and the leading nonsuperpower arms suppliers on the other, that have a major bearing on the pattern of arms trade and even more on the transfer of sophisticated weapons technology to Third World recipients.[31]

Either way, the net effect on the overall security of the Third World can turn out to be negative. If the transfer of weapons technology increases the dependence of Third World states on major industrial powers, then the feeling of vulnerability and insecurity among the elites of Third World states is intensified. However, any reduction in such dependence, consequent upon the transfer of technology and the diversification of sources of arms supply, increases the autonomy of decision making in relation to war and peace as far as the more developed Third World countries are concerned, and it removes important international constraints on their conflictual behavior. Transfer of weapons technology also strengthens their

war-fighting capacity by making them relatively independent of the original suppliers for spare parts and ammunition and by increasing the sophistication of the technology that their war machines can command indigenously, at least in the short run. As a result, wars in the Third World, especially among major regional actors, can now be started without the protagonists being overly concerned about supplier reactions, can be sustained for longer periods of time, and can be far more costly in human and material terms than they were in the past decades.

Nuclear proliferation in the Third World is a subset of the problems connected with the transfer of sophisticated weapons technology. It is, however, the most dramatic among this set of problems. As the only Third World security issue that ties Third World security concerns directly to those of global security, it is the only one in which the great powers have taken direct and immediate interest. They have attempted to institutionalize international controls on Third World behavior through the medium of the Nuclear Non-Proliferation Treaty (NPT). However, as Thomas has pointed out, "From the point of view of Third World states (even those that have joined the NPT), the nuclear non-proliferation regime in its present form institutionalizes inequality between nuclear-weapon states and non-nuclear-weapon states" (p. 141). This has led to a certain amount of tension between the members of the nuclear club, especially the superpowers, and the have-nots in the nuclear arena. Such leading members of the latter group as India, Pakistan, Israel, and South Africa have, in fact, attempted to circumvent the controls imposed by the nuclear club in order to expand their actual or potential nuclear capabilities. These capabilities, all shrouded in policies of deliberate ambiguity, include a substantial arsenal of small nuclear weapons (Israel), a "peaceful" underground nuclear explosion coupled with an increasingly sophisticated delivery

---

tempts "to strike an optimum balance among the three basic strategies of indigeneous production, licensed production and overseas purchases" (p. 199).

[31]For details of the latter argument, see Stephanie G. Neuman, "Arms, Aid, and the Superpowers," *Foreign Affairs* 66 (Summer 1988), 1044–66.

capability (India), a dual-track effort to manufacture nuclear warheads by uranium enrichment and/or plutonium reprocessing (Pakistan), and an atmospheric explosion that seemed suspiciously akin to an atomic test (South Africa).[32]

Such unacknowledged but nonetheless credible instances of nuclear proliferation pose problems not merely for the security of Third World states and regions but for the security of the international system as a whole. Moreover, the problems are not confined to the largely abstract ones of managing a world with a dozen or so nuclear powers. The practical problems of proliferation are far more acute because the four de facto nuclear powers mentioned above are all involved in regional conflicts and confrontations that could become overtly nuclear[33] and consequently lead to the direct involvement of one or both of the superpowers in the disputes.

It is, however, impossible to put the genie of nuclear proliferation back into the bottle, especially because possession of nuclear weapons has become the hallmark of

enhanced status within the international system. The Chinese example has very sharply driven home this lesson to Third World ruling elites, in particular those of the larger and regionally powerful states. In light of the Chinese experience, no Third World leadership aspiring to graduate to the status of a major, or even moderately influential, actor in the international system can feel comfortable about giving up its nuclear option. This factor of prestige, combined with genuine security concerns on the part of several Third World states facing potential antagonists that are nuclear or near-nuclear powers, has created a situation in which the security of a number of leading Third World states has become intertwined with the issue of nuclear proliferation. While all major Third World states on the nuclear threshold continue to abide by a policy of deliberate ambiguity for the moment, external or domestic stimuli could change this situation with dramatic suddenness in individual countries, thereby setting off chain reactions that may be difficult to control.

VI

As security cannot be bought cheaply in the late twentieth century, many Third World states spend substantial proportions of their

relatively meager resources on the security sector.[34] While expenditure on costly weapon systems and military technologies is a part of security expenditure, Ball has demonstrated that it is not the major part in the case of the overwhelming number of Third World states, which "appear to spend a very high proportion of their security budgets on operating costs, particularly salaries and emoluments for the troops" (p. 393). Appendix 1 of Ball's book (pp. 396–402) exam-

---

[32]For overviews of the four countries' nuclear capabilities, see, for Israel, Peter Pry, *Israel's Nuclear Arsenal* (Boulder, Colo.: Westview Press, 1984); for India and Pakistan, Carnegie Task Force on Non-Proliferation and South Asian Security, *Nuclear Weapons and South Asian Security* (Washington, D.C.: Carnegie Endowment for International Peace, 1988); and for South Africa, Michele A. Flournoy and Kurt M. Campbell, "South Africa's Bomb: A Military Option?" *Orbis* 32 (Summer 1988), 385–401.

[33]For a prospective scenario on the Indian subcontinent, see Leonard S. Spector, "India-Pakistan War: It Could Be Nuclear," *New York Times,* June 7, 1990, p. A23. For the Middle East, where a situation of de facto nuclear monopoly prevails, see Helena Cobban, "Israel's Nuclear Game: The U.S. Stake," *World Policy Journal* 5 (Summer 1988), 415–33.

[34]Ball has correctly pointed out that it is preferable in this context to refer to the "security" sector rather than the "military" sector, "in order to indicate the inclusion of paramilitary forces" and to reflect "the fact that Third World governments frequently use their armed forces to maintain themselves in power, that is, to promote regime security" (p. xvi n. 2).

ines the evolution of operating costs as a percentage of total security expenditure of twenty selected Third World counties for the years 1951–79 and finds that in all cases except one (Iran under the Shah) operating costs have clearly dominated in the mix of security expenditures for these countries. Ball concludes therefore that while "in the public mind, security expenditure in the Third World is firmly linked with the arms trade" (p. 107), "for most of the Third World, the arms trade and security expenditure are not synonymous: Operating costs, particularly personnel-related outlays, form a large and permanent portion of most developing countries' security budgets" (p. 111). This, Ball suggests, is connected to the fact that "the internal security role of the armed forces is considerable throughout the Third World and, in many cases, is their primary function" (p. 393).

Ball's sample leaves out such oil-rich and population-poor countries as Saudi Arabia and Kuwait, for which capital costs, including expenditure on defense infrastructure and weapons procurement, would be appreciably higher than is reflected in her data. Nevertheless, her basic point regarding high operating costs and their relationship to internal regime and state security is valid for most Third World countries. This reflects not merely the relatively low level of technology and the high level of manpower required by Third World states for the maintenance of internal control; it is also indicative of where they are along the continuum of the state-making enterprise. As the European experience has demonstrated, three areas—taxation (extraction of resources under the protection of coercive state agencies), policing (maintaining domestic order where it has already been imposed), and warfare aimed at the primitive accumulation of state power (extending and consolidating a particular political order by the use of force against potential as well as dissident subjects and fending off rival

claimants to the same territorial and demographic space)—comprise the bulk of the activities undertaken by early state makers.[35] These are all labor-intensive tasks that engage relatively large numbers of persons in the security arena and thereby raise the ratio of operating (including personnel) costs relative to the total expenditure on security. Security sector costs in the Third World are understandably linked to the performance of these essential functions in their current early stage of state making.

In this context, Ball's central question regarding the relationship between security expenditure and development seems to be of secondary concern, if not misplaced. Despite the declared commitment of Third World state elites to the goal of development (defined as economic growth plus some degree of distributive justice), as far as most of them are concerned this is an instrumental value that helps them achieve their primary objectives of political legitimacy and state and regime security. Therefore, Ball's conclusion that "available evidence does suggest that expenditure in the security sector is more likely to hinder than to promote economic growth and development in the Third World" (p. 388) misses the essential motivation behind such expenditure, even though the point may be valid.

This motivation has to do primarily with the "primitive central state power accumulation" mentioned above and secondarily with meeting threats from the regional environment. As a result, development, measured as a serious objective and not merely on the basis of the rhetoric of Third World leaders, comes a poor third in the policy priorities of most Third World elites and is hardly ever considered an autonomous goal

[35]For details, see the following essays in Tilly (fn. 12): Samuel E. Finer, "State- and Nation-Building in Europe: The Role of the Military" (chap. 2); Rudolf Braun, "Taxation, Sociopolitical Structure, and State-Building: Great Britain and Brandenburg-Prussia" (chap. 4); and David H. Bayley, "The Police and Political Development in Europe" (chap. 5).

that deserves to be fulfilled independently of security considerations. It is not surprising, therefore, that, as Ethan Kapstein has argued in chapter 6 of the Azar-Moon volume, "Third World states have allocated scarce resources to meet national security threats, and in so doing have influenced the timing and/or trajectory of economic development" (p. 138).

Furthermore, given the fragility of many Third World polities, it is no wonder that "one negative effect of security expenditure," as Ball terms it, has been "the strengthening of the armed forces at the expense of civilian groups within society" (p. 390). There is no other institution that is more important as far as the interface between issues of state making and those of internal and external security are concerned than the military. While Ball devotes the whole of chapter 1 to the discussion of the military's role in development and offers a critical evaluation of various theories that profess to explain this role, none of the four volumes under review has attempted to relate the role of the military to the process of state and nation building in the Third World. The closest one comes to it is in the last few pages of Ball's volume:

> By relying on the armed forces to remain in power or by producing political and economic conditions that provide the military with the justification for intervention, many governments have facilitated the entry of the armed forces into the political arena." (p. 391)

This generalization glosses over the fact that Third World polities are currently caught in a vicious circle that is a product of their historical circumstances. As the early modern European experience has demonstrated, the role of the coercive apparatuses of state—meaning primarily military and paramilitary institutions—in the early phase of state making is considerable. In the case of most Third World states the problem has

been compounded by the existence and combination of two additional factors. The first is the weakness of civil society and of other political institutions, which precludes the emergence of strong checks on the natural proclivity of the security apparatuses to usurp as much of the power and resources at the command of the state as possible. Second, the encapsulation of the various phases of state and nation building into one all-encompassing phase and the drastic curtailment of the time available to Third World states for the completion of these twin processes enhance the political importance of the coercive functions of the state and, therefore, of the agencies that perform such functions. Even in India, where a democratic political system has operated more successfully than elsewhere in the Third World, the important and increasingly dominant role of the security apparatuses is clearly visible in states like Punjab and Kashmir, which pose major overt challenges to the Indian state in the arena of state and nation building. It should therefore come as no surprise that the security sector in most Third World states hogs a large share of the state's disposable resources irrespective of the impact this may have on the process of economic development.

Furthermore, in terms of the allocation of scarce resources to the security sector, there seems to be very little difference between those Third World polities that are overtly dominated by the military and those that are under civilian control. This is demonstrated by Ball's own data (Figure 10-1, p. 387), which include several states under civilian rule within the category of the heaviest spenders on security. It is also corroborated by a recent study of defense spending by the member states of the Association of Southeast Asian Nations (ASEAN), which, notwithstanding several caveats and qualifications, came to the conclusion that "the countries [in ASEAN] in which the military has the largest political role (Thailand and

Indonesia) are the ones in which defence spending has grown more slowly than the ASEAN average."[36] State making and the vio-

lence that accompanies it obviously make no distinction between military-dominated and civilian-ruled polities in the Third World.

VII

Despite their divergent treatments of the subject and some of their shortfalls noted above, the four volumes reviewed in this article taken together make a substantial contribution to the study of Third World security problems by highlighting areas of analysis that have remained relatively neglected so far. These problems will remain with us for the foreseeable future in spite of the changes that seem to be underway in the superpowers' relations with each other and with the rest of the world. In fact, recent and projected changes may even contribute to the accentuation of some of the security problems faced by Third World countries and regions. The anticipated withdrawal of one superpower from the Third World arena may not turn out to be an unmixed blessing. The other superpower may feel free to act more cavalierly as far as the security and the vital interests of Third World states are concerned; it may be tempted to intervene militarily if developments in what it considers to be "strategic regions" of the Third World are not to its liking. Important Third World state elites, deprived of the presence of a balancing power that could in some measure neutralize the dominant superpower's interventionist proclivities, may therefore begin to feel more vulnerable and insecure. If this happens, such an escalation of insecurity will be reflected in their internal and external behavior patterns.

It could also happen that a genuine disentanglement on the part of both superpowers from arenas of tension and conflict

in the Third World may remove some of the restraints on the conflictual behavior of important Third World states. The aggressive potential of those states has been constrained by the apprehension that it could draw negative reactions from one or both of the superpowers and thereby end up tipping the regional balance against them. But were the superpowers to pull back, it might lead to greater assertiveness on the part of regionally preeminent powers interested in translating their preeminence into hegemony or at least into a managerial role within their respective regions. Resistance by other countries in a particular region to such hegemonic behavior might in turn, lead to situations of violent interstate conflict relatively unhindered by concerns regarding superpower intervention.

Furthermore, the prospects of conventional arms control pacts and troop reduction agreements between the superpowers, which are expected to lead to major redundancies in their arsenals, are already spurring both Washington and Moscow to increase arms sales abroad.[37] This trend can be expected to accelerate once these pacts become realities and force both superpowers to remove various categories of conventional weaponry, including tanks, artillery, aircraft, and helicopters, from their inventories. Much of this surplus hardware is expected to be sold to Third World countries to fulfill hard currency needs (a particularly important consideration for Moscow), to shore up friends and allies by making them more "self-reliant" in terms of hard-

[36]David B. H. Denoon, "Defence Spending in ASEAN: An Overview," in Chin Kin Wah, ed., *Defence Spending in Southeast Asia* (Singapore: Institute of Southeast Asian Studies, 1987), 49.

[37]For details, see Robert Pear, "Prospects of Arms Pacts Spurring Arms Sales," *New York Times*, March 25, 1990, p. 12.

ware, and to find alternative sources of profitable returns for domestic arms industries. This projected escalation in the transfer of sophisticated weaponry to the Third World in the 1990s will almost certainly reverse the trend of decreasing arms transfers to the developing countries that had been visible for most of the 1980s[38] and will further enhance the destructive potential of Third World conflicts.

In the final analysis, however, most of the deep-seated sources of conflict and violence in the Third World—sources that inhere within Third World societies and are related to their simultaneously ongoing processes of state making and nation building—cannot and will not be fundamentally determined by superpower actions and interactions, even if the latter has had the capacity to exacerbate many of them in the postwar era.[39] Therefore, although changes in su-

perpower relations may continue to affect some of these sources of conflict and insecurity in the Third World, these changes alone are not capable of transforming the basic nature of the security predicament of the Third World states. As it stands, the existing parameters of the security problematic of the Third World can be altered only if Third World states have adequate time to complete the twin tasks of the state making and nation building, plus enough political sagacity on their leaderships' part to attempt to accomplish these tasks in as humane a manner as possible. At such time the security concerns of developing states will approximate more closely those of the developed states, which in the traditional literature on international relations have constituted the model for state behavior in the security arena.

REFERENCES

Edward E. Azar and Chung-in Moon, eds., *National Security in the Third World. The Management of Internal and External Threats.* College Park, Md.: Center for International Development and Conflict Management, University of Maryland, 1988, 308 pp.

Nicole Ball, *Security and Economy in the Third World.* Princeton: Princeton University Press, 1988, 432 pp.

Robert S. Litwak and Samuel F. Wells, Jr., eds., *Superpower Competition and Security in the Third World.* Cambridge, Mass.: Ballinger, 1988, 295 pp.

Caroline Thomas, *In Search of Security: The Third World in International Relations.* Boulder, Colo.: Lynne Rienner, 1987, 228 pp.

[38]For the latest analysis of this trend, see Richard F. Grimmett, *Trends in Conventional Arms: Transfers to the Third World by Major Suppliers, 1982–1989* (Washington, D.C.: Congressional Research Service, Library of Congress, 1990), esp. 1–3.

[39]Notwithstanding the fact that the most highly visible facet of the latest Gulf crisis has been its global dimension involving the United States projection of power in the Gulf, this crisis has its origins in the internal dynamics of the region. These, in turn, are closely intertwined with issues regarding the establishment and legitimization of state boundaries, institutions, and regimes in the Middle East in general and the Persian Gulf in particular. Iraqi ambitions regarding Kuwait date back to the founding of the Iraqi state under British tutelage in the aftermath of the disintegration of the Ottoman Empire following World War I. Iraq's claims on Kuwait rest both upon Ottoman assertions of sovereignty over

Kuwait and upon the widespread feeling in the Arab world that post-Ottoman borders in the Fertile Crescent and the Gulf were arbitrarily drawn by Western colonial powers to suit their own selfish requirements and are therefore less than fully legitimate. In recent times Baghdad made two abortive attempts, in 1961 and 1973, to enforce its territorial claims on Kuwait. Viewed in its proper historical perspective, the latest crisis is therefore not exclusively an Iraqi attempt to control Kuwait's huge oil resources and dictate oil production and pricing policies within OPEC. While the American reaction to the Iraqi invasion of Kuwait in August 1990 globalized the crisis, it was basically just that—a *reaction* to a crisis that was fundamentally grounded in regional realities and intimately related to rival claims over both territorial and demographic space (and, of course, over the only major resource of the region), as well as linked to issues of state and regime legitimacy in the Arab littoral of the Persian Gulf.

CHAPTER SIX

THE RULES: THE INTERNATIONAL ORDER

A general association of nations must be formed . . . for the purpose of affording mutual guarantees of political independence and territorial integrity to great and small states alike.

Woodrow Wilson, *Address to Congress*
(The Fourteen Points), January 18, 1918.

Classical diplomatic methods developed over a long period rely more on custom than on rules, on courtesy and good sense rather than on regulations. Nevertheless, States have had to adopt certain principles and structures in an attempt to govern one another's behavior rather than merely making it easier and more gracious. More formal institutions have gradually developed, with many fits and starts, as the state system which emerged at Westphalia after the Thirty Years' War has itself taken on form. The process is far from complete, with as yet no central authority in sight. Despite all that, the United Nations has slowly grown in strength and even stature, most strikingly in the enhancement of the role of the Security Council during the Gulf crisis. Brian Urquhart gives a thoughtful delineation of the qualities needed in the Security-General which, even though Boutros-Ghali has now been chosen, still provides a most useful "inside story" of how the organization works.

Though prudent practitioners of statecraft depend more upon norms rather than binding rules, Friedrich Kratochwil observes in his recent book, *Rules, Norms, and Decisions,* that for the scholar "the place of norms in political life has always been controversial, particularly in international relations analysis."[1]

---

[1]Friedrich V. Kratochwil, *Rules, Norms, and Decisions: on the Conditions of Practical and Legal Reasoning in International Relations and Domestic Affairs,* (Cambridge: Cambridge University Press, 1989). (#2 in the "Studies in International Relations Series" of CUP in cooperation with the British International Studies Association).

The reader will recall James Lee's comments on this in his essay in the Introduction to this edition. But it would be a mistake to assume that just because there is no central authority to enforce rules, international law cannot derive some degree of effectiveness from the very existence of what Alan James calls "international society."[2] Law provides norms, the UN the forum, and diplomacy the correct way for states to behave in their relationships with one another as they seek to promote their particular set of interests in the game known as "the international system." Those who deny the efficacy of international law, as Tom Farer explains in his article, simply misunderstand the special nature, role, and need for some kind of a legal foundation in the contemporary world social environment. But it is more than that; it exists because it is in the respective national interests of all the states in the world that it exist, that it provides a norm against which their actions may be judged, and that it provides some protection for peace-loving states who would otherwise have to become armed garrisons. Yet as Robert Lieber observes in his discussion of some of the limitations built into the UN system, "globalism" is not the answer, even if there is now a basis for what could be called "collective interest." Few states have ever been very convincing in claiming to act on that basis. But as Professor Farer makes clear in his criticism of the critics of international law, it represents a compelling reality, and not merely a vague hope.

What international law is "presumed to do is communicate assumptions and predispositions about the system" among its members; indeed it actually operates "as a system of rules and norms displaying a lawlike character, yet substantially bereft of the authority needed to produce order through the agency of law. . . ."[3] True, it does not appear to control or indeed even noticeably to affect many states in their relentless pursuit of what they have unilaterally decided are their "vital national interests." For this reason, doubts are often expressed as to whether international law is really law at all. But this is not the point (except possibly a *debating* point). In the absence of a value consensus and a common power base for the entire world, international law is by its very nature qualitatively different from domestic law, and in many ways is hardly comparable to it. What is its proper basis—domestic public law or the interests of the broader global society in which newer, weaker states are struggling for recognition and protection? That doesn't make it any less a legitimate form of law, any more than it makes sense to force its definition into a mold made by the particular shape of law within any given society. The same needs exist at both levels. For purely practical, operational reasons, there is a higher degree of consensus than many realize. The consensual basis for law is just as reasonable as one based solely upon enforceability.

What is important for the student of international relations to understand

[2]*Review of International Studies*, Vol. 4, No. 2, July 1978, pp. 97–100. The first use of this term as a title for a text in IR was Philip Brown, *International Society: its Nature and Interests*, (New York: MacMillan, 1923); for a discussion of this and other early texts in the development of IR as an independent field of study, see William C. Olson and A.J.R. Groom *International Relations Then and Now: Origins and Trends in Interpretation*, (London: Harper Collins, 1991), Chapter 4, "The Period of the First Consensus: a Quest for Peace," pp. 56–78.

[3]Nicholas G. Onuf, "International Law as an Idea," *The American Journal of International Law*, 73, 2 (April 1979).

at the outset is that legal processes are at work in the international system and that that system would not work in their absence. Just as having a "cop on the corner" is not sufficient to ensure obedience to law within a local community, lacking one is not sufficient cause for denying the very existence of law. It is there, and has been for three centuries or more. Furthermore, it is growing in scope and utility with every passing year as states, particularly the newer ones, recognize that they simply cannot get along without it. Both within and between contending systems of value and of power there exists a considerable degree of consensus, simply because it is useful and without it chaos could prevail. There is nothing new about this; Percy Corbett once noted that there were even some elements of what is now termed international law as early as five thousand or more years ago.[4]

Extensive legal processes are constantly at work in the adjustment of differences and in the daily conduct of affairs among states never prepared to accept one another's basic values and norms. Diplomats are exchanged and granted immunity; transportation and communications are regulated by universally accepted legal rules; detailed agreements having the virtual force of law among most states have been reached on everything from monetary policy to nonproliferation of nuclear weapons. Copyright agreements are generally accepted, though there are "pirates" who every author regards as threatening. Yet it is certainly not universally adhered to and it would be naive to contend that it is; to recognize the reality of its existence is not to argue that international law performs as effectively as the legal systems that operate within each separate state. There is no computer or library to which one can go to "look up the rule" and be sure the behavior of others can be held to it. International law grows slowly, by precedent, by acceptance, even by convenience. It may never be codified in the way the Napoleonic Code is codified.

Having noted all that with reference to one of the principal pillars of international order, what can we now say about the other? In an effort to conduct their business with one another more conveniently, States have resorted to the creation of international organizations. Even before World War I, numerous interstate agencies, commissions, and boards had been established to manage specific functional areas of international relations—the Universal Postal Union, international fisheries commissions, shipping boards, and the like. Growing out of all that was the first international organization with a global political mandate, the League of Nations, which was designed to provide an institution through which its members, acting collectively, might identify threats to the peace and take measures such as sanctions and even military action to stop an aggressor. Unfortunately, the strength of the League was sapped from the outset by the failure of the United States and the new Soviet Union to become members, the first because it decided it didn't want to, the other because it wasn't deemed acceptable by more genteel members of the "club." This situation was greatly

[4]Percy Corbett, *The Study of International Law,* (New York: Random House, 1955), p. 11. It should be noted that he concedes later (p. 45) that "while argument in legal terms marks one stage in most conflicts of interest, it leads to settlement only when the interests involved are not valuable enough to induce one side or the other to throw power into the scale."

exacerbated later by the inability of the remaining Great Powers to act when first one (Japan) and then another (Fascist Italy), and then yet another country (Nazi Germany), committed aggression in clear isolation of the terms of the Covenant. In the end, the leaders of Britain and France decided to pursue their own national interests at the expense of world order, so the system broke down almost before it got started, although it did record some modest successes where the vital interests of the Great Powers were not compromised.

During World War II, Washington determined to take the lead this time in creating the United Nations organization.[5] The keystone was to be the Security Council, made up of the five Great Powers (the United States, the USSR, the United Kingdom, France, and China) plus several other states periodically elected by the General Assembly on a roughly rotational basis. The General Assembly itself has no veto mechanism (unlike its predecessor in the League, where the fact that everyone had one effectively hobbled the whole system). Recognizing that it would be impossible for the UN to act against any of the major states, each of the five was given a veto that could prevent any Security Council action being taken against it. Almost immediately after the cessation of hostilities against the Axis powers, a "Cold War" erupted between the Soviet Union and the West, and any action by the Council was effectively stymied by use of the veto power given by the Charter to the Moscow delegation. It was only by chance that its representative was boycotting the United Nations (for failing to admit the government of Communist China after its victory over Chiang Kai-Shek) when South Korea was invaded by North Korea. This anomaly permitted the United States to secure the endorsement of the Council for several members' armies to intervene in an effort to turn back the Communist invaders. On that occasion, the new system worked as it was designed to.

When the UN was founded in 1945, it had fifty-one members, each represented in the General Assembly. So long as the body remained small, the United States enjoyed a virtually automatic majority among the membership (principally the NATO allies and members of the Organization of American States), and the UN consistently endorsed what the United States wanted done in the Assembly. After 1956, however, the majority of the new members were either opposed to Western capitalism or determined to remain aloof from the Cold War. For years, a majority of the Assembly, usually joined by the Communist bloc, concentrated upon pressing, not only for the independence of the remaining colonial possessions throughout the world, but for massive economic development assistance. Most of the Western powers, particularly the United States through its foreign aid program, preferred to provide help by bilateral arrangement.

The growing tendency in Washington to place economic assistance in a Cold War context made it all the more likely that the Third World could count on the voting (though not yet the financial) support of Moscow and its bloc followers. The whole system was effectively turned upside down as far as the West

---

[5]For a realistic account of some of the reservations held by leading advisers at the time about such a body, consult *The Wise Men: Six Friends and the World They Made,* (New York: Simon & Schuster, 1986), the "six friends" being John J. McCloy, Charles Bohlen, Dean Acheson, Robert Lovett, Averell Harriman, and George Kennan.

was concerned, especially after the Arab states saw in UN resolutions a way to punish Israel. The Communists in turn saw in this an opportunity to isolate the United States, often even from its closest friends, because of its unwavering support for Israel. This was based upon congressional pressure, which was in turn based upon campaign contributions, though the more frequently-cited reason was a belief in helping the infant democracy get started on a firm footing. This goal held no interest for the Arab bloc, but there was then no Arab lobby. By this time, the system was not working as it was intended, though despite this the Americans continued to provide about a quarter of the organization's financial support. This policy of buttressing the concept of international order lasted until the Reagan administration, which allowed the U.S. to run up a dues arrearage of some $585 million, enough to begin to have a crippling effect upon the body's worldwide functions. The framework for action is still there, and at the very end of his years in office, President Reagan went before the Assembly and, in light of the recommended administrative improvements made by the Secretary-General, finally undertook to restore U.S. support, praising Perez de Cuellar in the process as the man who had brought about change.

The Third World voting bloc has promoted justice and development, rather than security against aggression, as the UN's primary concern. This dichotomy is reflected in the philosophy guiding different kinds of states in their whole approach to international law. The thrust from the Third World has been for more investment funds and a more equitable distribution of the world's wealth—"New International Economic Order," which has been described as an example of "universalist strategies for systematic economic reform."[6] On these issues, many Americans have felt frustrated, if not downright disillusioned. Having invested so much ideological faith in the UN as a panacea and then finding itself to be at the mercy of hostile majorities, some have even called for withdrawal, following earlier U.S. patterns in the ILO (International Labor Organization) and UNESCO (United Nations Educational, Scientific, and Cultural Organization). The UN could not act in the absence of the United States should it actually discontinue its membership. Washington was unlikely to take that step, not solely in its own "national interest," but because the UN continues to serve the international community of which the United States is a vital part. Even before its signal success in the Gulf crisis, the UN has managed to perform an effective peace-keeping function in such places as the Congo, Lebanon, the Gaza Strip, and Cyprus. On more than one occasion, during the Cold War era, its capacity to dispatch a military force drawn from member-states to enforce cease-fires and truces, and even to establish peace between the parties, kept the United States and the Soviet Union from becoming embroiled in these conflicts. This peace-keeping function should be regarded, not as a device for deterring aggression and certainly not for coercing the Great Powers, but as a means of helping those powers to contain potential threats to the peace or, to put it another way, to keep little wars from becoming big ones.

[6]David H. Blake and Robert S. Walters, *The Politics of Global Economic Relations*, 2nd ed., (Englewood Cliffs, N.J.: Prentice Hall, 1983), p. 192.

Generally speaking, two alternatives are usually put forth as models for achieving a manageable world order. As we have seen, one is the balance-of power global leadership model, taken up and popularized by successive administrations as a replacement for the now obsolete Cold War. This approach broke down badly in Vietnam as the United States proved unable to mobilize world support for its eventually failing war effort there. The balance-of-power model for order postulates that each state, by acting to preserve and enhance its own security and national capability, needs to help maintain a stable system. Under this model, no change in the values by which each state now manages its own affairs is required, each remaining the judge of its own best interest. No motivation for questioning the existing distribution of resources of wealth within and between societies is needed because disruptions will be handled by the efficacious mechanism of the balance of power. Or so goes the theory.

The other model is one that, while not advocating or promoting the abolition of the nation-state with which people are so fully conditioned to identify, calls for a modification of the values that have until now governed the conduct of states. This might be called the mutual-interest or world-society model. It stands in contrast to the traditional state system, which assumes that domestic politics, in the oft-quoted words of Senator Vandenburg when chairman of the Senate Foreign Relations Committee, "stops at the water's edge." National goals and policies are supposed to be framed exclusively with an eye to security and other so-called national interests of the state, as distinct from the individuals who live within it as well as the interests of those outside it. This view of the state as an autonomous actor is anachronistic according to the advocates of the world-society model. They argue that international relations now involve as many economic, social, ethical, ideological, and moral considerations affecting both individuals and societies as do internal politics; vice versa, the content and style of domestic policy-making and implementation have a growing impact upon international politics. One need only look at the acid rain controversy between the Canadians and the Americans to see an example of this. Political and economic values can no longer be separated. Just as order at home has required that active concern for the weak and the poor be included among the obligations of the national community, so too must they not be ignored if order is to prevail in the international community. Domestic tensions of all advanced industrialized societies, to say nothing of those now just embarking upon full industrialization, increasingly influence their dealings with one another.[7]

Under these circumstances, acting in one's exclusive self-interest is only likely to worsen any crisis. The rules of the international order, if only understood rather than being codified and enforced, are beginning to prevail, though there is plenty of evidence to the contrary in specific situations. Such an approach cannot exclusively rely upon technique to achieve international order. Nor are value-free pragmatism and neutrality possible when the nature of the

[7]An instructive and original analysis of the implications of this phenomenon is provided by Hidemi Suganami in his recent *The Domestic Analogy and World Order Proposals*, (Cambridge: Cambridge University Press, 1989), esp. Chapter seven, "The Domestic Analogy and the Establishment of the United Nations," pp. 114–128.

world system itself is in contention. For example, proving unable to contribute much to the resolution of the East-West conflict or other issues involving peace and security, a majority of UN members tended to simply use the UN as a forum for talking about solutions of their own problems of development.[8]

Meanwhile, an agreed-on definition of order in the international system seems as elusive as ever, if indeed not more so, as unilateral approaches to problem-solving are relied upon by the Powers, great and small.

DISCUSSION QUESTIONS

1. In your view, how well has the new Secretary-General, Boutros Boutros-Ghali, met the criteria set forth in Urquhart's set of particulars for the job?
2. How does Farer use the argument of convenience to support his contention that international law is a reality?
3. How does it happen that a terrorist fleeing another country to escape punishment may be better protected under the laws of political asylum than other categories of individuals?
4. Which are the only nonsovereign voting members of the United Nations General Assembly? How did they get into the Organization in the first place? How do they differ from NGOs?
6. Who are critics whom Farer says are wrong? Can you think of any arguments that indicate they may in fact be right?
7. How is the shift in emphasis in UN debates from security to development a manifestation of the development theory in international relations?
8. Since Lieber wrote his book, the UN has become a much more dynamic organization (the Gulf War, Somalia, Bosnia, etc.) Does all this undermine his view of the "limits of globalism"? or confirm them?

---

[8]What Kratochwil calls *groupings* within the UN often work together in their respective interest to produce legitimate majorities in Assembly voting, *i.e.*, not submitting to the "tyranny of the majority" against their own particular interests. *op. cit.*, p. 197.

24 *THE UN'S CRUCIAL CHOICE*

BRIAN URQUHART

BRIAN URQUHART is a scholar in residence in the International Affairs Program of the Ford Foundation. From 1974 until 1986 he was UN under secretary-general for special political affairs.

During the Persian Gulf crisis there was much talk about "defining moments," "turning points," "watersheds," and, not least, a "new world order." Beneath the usual rhetoric of an international crisis a general feeling emerged that the international system, and especially the United Nations, not only could, but should, be strengthened. There are powerful reasons, apart from the Gulf crisis, for developing an effective international system as soon as possible.

The human race reached its most important "defining moment" when it developed several ways of putting an end to the human experiment altogether. Weapons of mass destruction are the most obvious of these, but threats to the environment, to the planet's life-support system, and to our store of life-giving resources ultimately could be just as destructive. It is now urgent to agree on the strategies and to set up the mechanisms of global management to reverse the present disastrous trends. This cannot be done without a sufficient degree of peace and security for nations to scale down the vast military expenditures that now sidetrack vital resources and that create the con-

ditions for future conflict. International organization thus faces a double challenge: a reasonable degree of peace and security, and global management.

At present, the UN is the only global framework within which these twin herculean tasks can be undertaken. It is, therefore, in the interest of all governments, not to mention peoples, to strengthen the UN system and reform it as necessary for the vital tasks ahead. Much lip service has been paid to these objectives, but real commitment is less evident. At the end of 1991 a specific opportunity has arisen to demonstrate such commitment and to give substance to the wish to strengthen the UN. That occasion is the appointment of a new secretary-general to succeed Javier Pérez de Cuéllar, whose tenth year of devoted and skillful service ends on December 31, 1991.

The UN secretary-general is the world's leading international civil servant. The basic functions of the office include the administration of the world organization, worldwide negotiation and conflict resolution, coordination of the UN's twenty-nine specialized agencies, funds, and programs, and, last but

Reprinted by permission from *Foreign Policy*, 84, (1991), pp. 157–165. Copyright © 1991, Carnegie Endowment for International Peace.

not least, the provision of a last resort and hope in times of international crisis.

All this adds up to a position of great responsibility and potential. During the forty-year winter of the Cold War, when governments increasingly turned to the secretary-general in times of crisis as all other avenues were blocked, the office grew and expanded more than any other organ of the UN. Now freed of Cold War constraints, with a new generation of global problems to tackle and with many pressing challenges to multilateral diplomacy, the secretary-generalship would seem to have more purpose and importance than ever.

A great ambivalence, however, remains about the nature of the secretary-generalship. Likewise, considerable differences of opinion linger about the priorities of the office. With just a few months before Pérez de Cuéllar's second term runs out, there is little sign of any systematic search for the best possible successor or of any improvement in the haphazard, last-minute, and disorderly process by which the secretary-general was selected in previous years. This casual approach does not bode well for the future, nor does it attest to the serious concern of governments for the effective functioning of the UN.

Rhetoric to the contrary, it has never been altogether clear what governments really want from the secretary-general. Hith-

erto, the industrialized world has tended to see the UN as the guardian of the status quo, while the developing world has looked at it as the agent of change. The five permanent members of the Security Council, whose votes dominate the appointment process, have been reluctant to accept too much political independence on the part of the secretary-general, particularly in matters of special concern to themselves. Governments do not want to be upstaged or publicly opposed by the secretary-general; but as seen again in recent months, they also wish the secretary-general to take the initiative in emergencies, especially when governments themselves are unable to act. They wish the secretary-general to be the guardian of the UN Charter, while often disagreeing on the interpretation of that document. The secretary-general is universally accepted as an intermediary between states, though how and when he should step in is often a matter of controversy.

In general, the interests of the world community as a whole, as well as of its member governments, are seen as best served by an impartial, independent, and imaginative secretary-general with both the courage of his convictions and the common sense to avoid unnecessary difficulties. Yet this evaluation has not, so far at least, inspired any great effort to locate and secure the best possible candidate for the job.

AN "IMPOSSIBLE JOB"

The office's past occupants have made widely differing assessments of the secretary-general's task. Trygve Lie, the first secretary-general, called it "the most impossible job on this earth." Dag Hammarskjöld half-jokingly said that the secretary-general was a kind of secular pope and, for most of the time, a pope without a church. U Thant called the secretary-general's office "the most varied,

most interesting and most challenging political job on earth." In 1971 U Thant also described vividly the paradoxical nature of the secretary-general's political task:

In every critical situation, the Secretary-General's activity will seem to some Governments to be too much and to others too little. He must thread his way through the jungle of conflicting national policies with the Charter as his compass, and, if he is lucky, with a directive from one of the main deliberative organs as his guide. Even if such a directive exists, it is unlikely to insure him against governmental objections to his actions. . . . National sovereignty and national interest, humanitarian considerations, governmental susceptibilities and the principles of the Charter form the elements of an insoluble equation, which nonetheless the Secretary-General must continually, and in all sorts of situations, attempt to solve.

Although the political side of the job receives the most attention, the actual scope of the office is much broader. Apart from running the Secretariat, the secretary-general is responsible for representing the UN to the world and interpreting the organization to the public; for coordinating the so-called UN system; for maintaining a global watch on major developments and generating ideas and strategies; for negotiating peace and mediating crises; and for protecting and furthering human rights and humanitarian matters.

To deal effectively with such a wide and heavy agenda demands not only remarkable personal qualities but also a responsive organization and the willingness to delegate responsibility to it. At the moment, the secretary-general has to face the exigent agenda of the office with a Secretariat put together under the political constraints of the Cold War and swollen by the UN's rapid expansion in the 1960s and 1970s. The secretary-general is also supposed to coordinate a wider system of autonomous specialized agencies, funds, and programs established in the very different circumstances of 1945—a time when words like "interdependence" or "global problems" were unknown. The performance of future secretaries-general will to some extent be determined by their capacity to upgrade both of these

systems. Such reforms have the best hope of success at the outset of a new administration, before vested interests have fastened their limpet grip on the new secretary-general.

Of the two tasks, the reorganization of the Secretariat should present relatively less difficulty and resistance. Currently, some thirty top officials report, in theory at any rate, directly to the secretary-general. Such an arrangement is cumbersome and ineffective in ordinary times and crippling in times of crisis. Often, when an unexpected crisis emerges, the secretary-general virtually has to start from scratch in organizing a team to deal with it. The basic aim of reform should be to simplify the secretary-general's chain of command and group the activities of the Secretariat in mutually supporting clusters under four deputies, who would also form the secretary-general's executive and advisory cabinet. A new secretary-general with a mandate for change should be able to cut through the present disorganization and establish a more workable shape and direction for the Secretariat.

Reforming the UN "system" of specialized agencies, funds, and programs is more difficult. These autonomous or semi-autonomous organizations, most of them dating from the 1940s, are the projection on the international level of the interests of different ministries in national governments. They also reflect the then-fashionable view that the various areas of human activity—health, food, labor, etc.—are best dealt with in separate compartments by specialized agencies rigorously kept aloof from the central political body, the UN itself. This may have been a valid premise in 1945, and certainly much specialized work remains to be done. But in 1991 the challenge of great global problems and vast emergencies demands something more than a system of baronies presided over by a secretary-general to whom lip service is paid, but who does not have either the position or the constitutional power to coordinate them effectively.

The secretary-general has always been expected to provide a focal point and a sense of direction in certain complex international dealings. So far, however, there has been less emphasis on shaping the global agenda, encouraging cooperative action, and providing intellectual leadership. As global problems increasingly dominate the prospects of the future, an architect of global management systems and an advocate of vital global strategies will be needed. This requirement should be taken into account in selecting the next secretary-general.

The global problems with which the UN system must now grapple cannot, by their nature, be tackled and solved by governments alone. Public understanding and participation are needed to transform policies and strategies into successful action. A tremendous effort in communication, education, and persuasion will therefore be required, with all the variations necessitated by a global audience. It seems likely that this task will have to be shared by the international civil service and nongovernmental organizations. The need for communication on this scale adds another dimension to the secretary-general's responsibilities. Thus, to the old model of the secretary-generalship, with its emphasis on diplomacy, conflict resolution, and discreet administration, must now be added new qualities of management, advocacy, and the public articulation of large ideas, especially on economic and social issues.

If the member governments of the UN are really determined to strengthen the organization and make it more effective, what sort of secretary-general should they be looking for? It is manifestly impossible for one individual to carry out all the various functions of the office. It is therefore necessary to determine what basic and indispensable qualifications are needed. A desirable combination might be a skillful negotiator, a manager capable of delegating authority, and a communicator capable both of developing important basic ideas and explaining them to the governments and peoples of the world. The secretary-general should have the habit of authority and the capacity to exert it both directly and by delegation. Plainly, certain qualities of character are also essential. These include unquestioned moral stature and integrity, fair-mindedness, objectivity, and a sense of proportion and humor. Physical as well as mental stamina are indispensable.

To find and appoint such a person should be regarded as a major task, rather than the last-minute, chancy, and increasingly parochial scramble that has occurred in the past. No important organization in the private sector would dream of appointing its chief executive in this manner.

Article 97 of the UN Charter states that "the Secretary-General shall be appointed by the General Assembly upon the recommendation of the Security Council." This means the veto of the Security Council's permanent members applies to the secretary-generalship. It is to be hoped that this time the veto will not impose a dead hand on the search for a new secretary-general as it did during the Cold War. Restraint in applying this veto would certainly be a step in the right direction. Yet many other problems inherent in the way previous secretaries-general have been appointed persist.

No procedure exists for the orderly nomination of candidates for the office of secretary-general. As a result, self-nominated candidates, sometimes with the support of their governments, start the process, leaving the Security Council to decide which candidates are acceptable and which are not. Incredible though it may seem, there is, as yet, no methodical search process for the best possible candidate for the job.

Although the Charter says nothing about the secretary-general's term of office, a five-year renewable term has come to be accepted as normal. This tradition has many disadvantages. For a job that is relentlessly demanding and physically and mentally strenuous, 10 years or more is a very long time, while five years is a short period for carrying through important programs or reforms. An incumbent secretary-general who wishes to be reappointed may be subjected to undesirable pressures. The hope that the incumbent may be persuaded to stay on and governments' reluctance to face making a new choice combine to inhibit a properly organized and timely search for a successor. The existing process therefore tends toward staleness, stasis, and little or no effort to look for new blood. For all these reasons, a single term of seven years would be a far better arrangement for the institution itself than a renewable five-year term.

Other conventions affecting the appointment of the secretary-general may also be outdated. It has long been accepted that no national of a permanent member of the Security Council should be secretary-general. This rules out some 35 percent of the world's people as well as citizens of countries that are both major powers and major contributors to the UN. In the post-Cold War political climate, both the exclusion of nationals of the permanent members and the application of the veto to the appointment of the secretary-general should be reconsidered.

There is also supposed to be an understanding that the secretary-generalship should rotate among the main geographical regions, only one of which, Africa, has not yet provided a secretary-general. Africa, like any other region, could produce a first-rate candidate; but the paramount consideration should be to find the best possible secretary-general regardless of nationality.

The Charter commits the UN to the equality of men and women. It is the more grotesque that so far no woman has been seriously considered for the secretary-generalship.

A NEW APPOINTMENT PROCESS

It is clear that there is an urgent need to rethink and revitalize the process of appointing the secretary-general, and that many of the obstacles to a better process have now been removed. A new procedure should allow for

- serious consideration by governments of the qualities required for the job in the 1990s;
- a single seven-year term of office;
- the establishment of rules for nomination and a timetable in order to control the current practice of individuals' campaigning for the office;
- a properly organized search proce-

dure, probably conducted by the Security Council, not only to ensure the choice of the best candidate but also to locate the good candidates who are unlikely to put themselves forward, including a number of women.

It is already being argued in some quarters, with considerable success, that such a process will probably not produce better results and, more important, may create difficulty in the delicate political and diplomatic relationships and atmosphere of the UN. That a proper search process is considered not only normal but essential in great enterprises in the private world is dismissed as irrelevant to the special world of the UN. Nonetheless, the future demands of a turbulent and changing world obviously require the highest possible qualifications and stature in the world's leading civil servant. The current process seems less likely to produce such a person than would a more stringent effort to search for and select the best.

In the end the outcome will depend, as so many international issues do, on whether governments are really committed to achieving a more effective international system. If all the talk of a "new world order" has any relationship at all to the UN's future, it would seem only logical for its member governments to make a conscientious effort to find and appoint the best possible head of the international system. To do otherwise would be ridiculous and irresponsible.

Unfortunately, it is still by no means clear that governments—and especially the five permanent members that dominate the selection process—feel that this matter is sufficiently important or urgent. The old haphazard procedure has served them, with one exception, not too badly in the past, and a new, more rigorous procedure may cause embarrassments and will certainly be more work. But governments cannot have it both ways. They cannot shirk the labor of searching for, and agreeing on, the best available secretary-general, and then complain that the UN does not perform according to their expectations. The quality of their commitment to the UN will be tested in a highly visible way in the process of finding a successor for Pérez de Cuéllar.

The search for peace, justice, and equity, and for a world in which a better life in the twenty-first century will be possible, is the essence of the mission of the United Nations. Whether the world organization can fulfill that mission will be decisively affected by the quality of its appointed leaders.

25 *THE CRITICS ARE WRONG*

Tom J. Farer

Formerly head of the Human Rights Commission of the Organization of American States, Tom J. Farer is a professor of law and director of the program in law and international relations at The American University in Washington, D.C.

Not too long ago, internationalism seemed so routed that Thomas Hughes, president of the Carnegie Endowment for International Peace, penned a eulogy for it. Yet . . . President Ronald Reagan, who rode to power on the shoulders of internationalism's enemies, . . . met cordially with Soviet leader Mikhail Gorbachev, concluded the first arms control agreement eliminating a whole class of nuclear weapons and announced heady progress toward a second one that will slash the superpowers' strategic arsenals, authorized U.S. participation in a multilateral effort to limit depletion of the earth's ozone layer, and, at a moment of terrible weakness for the United Nations, enhanced its prestige by calling for Security Council action to force suspension of the Iran–Iraq war. Was news of the death of internationalism premature?

For purposes of this argument, "internationalism" is defined along the lines proposed by Hughes: a general foreign-policy orientation characterized by international cooperation, international law and institutions, economic interdependence, international development, diligence in seeking arms control, and restraint in the use of force. It is against these final aspects of internationalism—ethical and legal limitations on the exercise of coercive power to promote national interests and sensitivity toward the interests of the Third World—that the antiinternationalist coalition has aimed its principal blows.

And since these values mingle provocatively at the United Nations, it has become above all a symbolic place where conflicting wills to conserve and to destroy the postwar internationalist regime are fiercely tested. Perhaps the most powerful, or at least the most usefully concise, attack on that institution and indeed on the entire postwar internationalist order appeared in the August 24, 1987, issue of the *New Republic*. In "Let It Sink," Charles Krauthammer indicts the United Nations, suggesting that its mission is no longer in accord "either with the UN's declared purpose or with American interests." He maintains that although the UN was originally envisioned "to be the anchor of a new order" marked by the rule of law

Excerpted by permission of the publisher from *Foreign Policy* 7, (Summer 1988), pp. 22–45. Copyright © 1988, The Carnegie Endowment for International Peace. (Footnotes deleted.)

rather than the whim of the strongest, not only has it failed "to enforce norms," but it has encouraged illusions about the efficacy of multilateral enforcement that "have had the unintended, but nonetheless real, effect of weakening these norms." He goes on to refer wistfully to a past when "international norms were enforced by the great powers."

Krauthammer's invocation of a putatively lawful past is more than a little strange. What past is he talking about? The most casual student of great-power behavior during the century and a half before the UN's founding in 1945 would discover a farrago of justifications for threatening or practicing coercion against weaker political entities. Even when the great powers purported to be enforcing norms—as opposed simply to pursuing their manifest destinies—the norms were those they chose to recognize or declare.

Admittedly, out of this practice emerged among the great powers a body of formal agreements and implicit understandings designed to smooth their mutual relations. As elaborated by scholars and diplomats, the resulting normative system doubtlessly enhanced the efficiency of great-power diplomacy. With seemingly the whole non-Western world available for appropriation, and with a rough balance of strength among the major states, unbridled competition would not have best served their respective interests. Among its functions, the system mitigated the risk of conflict over materially trivial issues that, in the absence of rules of the road, could inflate into powerfully symbolic ones. For instance, by agreeing beforehand on how each country could establish title to one or another piece of nonWestern real estate, they were able to avoid the sort of petty quarrels that could agitate an increasingly literate public or compromise a monarch's dignity.

Habitual behavior, on which others rely and reciprocate, implies an informal agreement to continue until a change of conditions clearly alters the equilibrium of mutual benefits. Since the other principal source of norms was formal agreement, consent was the system's psychological linchpin. Norms not accepted, either informally or formally, did not bind—that is, they could not bind states deemed full members of the club, except in the event of war. Victory carried with it the power to legislate new norms.

The club of states powerful enough to dictate norms was white and Western until Japan fought its way to membership by defeating Russia in their war of 1904–1905. Latin American states occupied a kind of peripheral zone in that although ruled by recognizably Western elites, they were weak and inhabited largely by people unable to pass the pre-1945 world's color bar. Therefore, to almost the same degree as those communities in Africa, Asia, and the Middle East that club members had formally absorbed or subordinated, the Latins could be bound without consent. Such, at least, was the unspoken view of Western governments and their legal mandarins.

One revolutionary feature of the post-World War II international system was open admission to full membership in the club; in other words, the rule of "no obligation without consent" was globalized. The second revolutionary feature was the outlawry of force in the United Nations Charter, not only as a means of advancing selfish national goals at the expense of other states, but also as an instrument for either making or applying norms. This held true in all but two circumstances: when authorized by the UN Security Council in response to "a threat to the peace, a breach of the peace or aggression," or when used in individual or collective self-defense against aggression.

Krauthammer's implication that the old order was marked by the whim of the strongest rather than the rule of law cannot be reconciled with the additional claim that "in the past international norms were enforced by the great powers." By definition, norms are not whims. In the past, great powers secured their interests through force, a process they sometimes clothed in the word "law." If that is Krauthammer's meaning, he certainly did not find the right words to convey it.

Although the norms of the pre–World War II system were designed to serve the interests of a small segment of humanity, the host of new members subsequently admitted to the club generally found them useful. So most of the preexisting legal order— governing matters as varied as jurisdiction over ships on the high seas and the conditions for terminating treaties—was retained.

But this carry-over still does not reconcile Krauthammer's schizoid view of the past. Moreover, his indictment of the present reveals profound ambivalence about the very normative structure endangered,

according to him, by excessive reliance on multilateral enforcement mechanisms. "Institutions of international law," he writes, "create endless opportunities for avoiding [the] responsibility [to deter lawlessness]." The United Nations, Krauthammer continues, "subverts international norms more actively . . . by morally undermining the few actions that help enforce them." Here his examples are the UN votes condemning as a violation of international law the April 1986 U.S. retaliatory raid against Libya and the October 1983 invasion of Grenada.

According to Krauthammer, the November 2, 1983, UN vote on Grenada exposed yet another indictable characteristic: highly selective condemnation of "wars, invasions, and acts of terror." With this charge he confirms what might have been deduced from his strange description of the prewar normative order, namely, that although "international institutions" are his nominal target, the law itself is his real target.

CHARTER INTERPRETATIONS

Like any political system, the postwar international system has a hierarchy of values. The normative order records and elaborates that hierarchy. The value accorded highest priority by the United Nations, as indicated by the charter's language and by the subsequent practice of the UN's political organs, is preservation of the territorial integrity and the formal independence of its member states. To that end, the charter bans the actual or threatened use of force— the principal means by which stronger states have imposed their will on weaker ones— while explicitly recognizing a right of individual and collective self-defense.

The Security Council and the General Assembly have responded to indisputable violations of the ban with impressive con-

sistency. They have confirmed the ban when the United States has marshaled majorities in both bodies, and they have reconfirmed it since voting dominance passed to the Third World. Power, ideology, and bloc association have not insulated delinquents. Among countries censured have been Soviet-bloc states, including North Korea, the Soviet Union, and Vietnam; members of the Western bloc, such as France, Great Britain, Israel, Turkey, and the United States; and members of the now dominant "nonaligned" bloc, like Argentina, India, and Indonesia.

UN majorities have been equally consistent in rejecting justifications for invasion. One example was India's 1971 claim to the right to enforce the charter value of human rights in East Pakistan when it invaded that country. It is hard to imagine a stronger case for intervention on behalf of human rights than the one India made to defend the invasion, the catalyst having been the Pakistani government's campaign of extermination against the Hindu minority and the Moslem elite of what was then its exploited and rebellious eastern region. Although fully aware of the atrocities being perpetrated at the very moment of the Indian invasion, and despite the reasonable expectation that the slaughter would resume if India complied, an overwhelming UN majority voted for a resolution demanding immediate Indian withdrawal.

While reducing dramatically the discretionary use of force by states, the charter still leaves them a considerable range of unilateral options to defend and promote their interests. At least until they were confronted with the Arab oil embargo, Western states rejected even the suggestion that the charter outlawed the various forms of economic coercion, much less the many economic inducements, a country like the United States or Japan could effectively deploy as instruments of self-help. But Krauthammer and other critics of the UN obviously regard the various nonviolent means as insufficient for achieving important national ends. They in effect demand that force be treated as a legitimate instrument of diplomacy under circumstances where it is now banned. Thus in the name of law and order they appear to challenge the central postulate of the postwar system of law and order.

Probably the main objection to the charter approach to the use of force that is heard from what might be called the "proto-liberal" antagonists of the UN system—as distinguished from the hard-core rightists congenitally hostile to all the values and assumptions of internationalism—is that it does not adequately take into account new forms of aggression. The charter empha-sizes open, large-scale invasions. But in the present era, according to this argument, countries frequently employ terrorism and insurgency to undermine other countries' independence. It therefore follows that, rather than challenging the postwar normative order, violent reprisals against delinquents facilitate its defense.

Anyone making this argument might cite the General Assembly's virtually unanimous condemnation of foreign assistance to insurgents. Nevertheless, even though UN members formally agree that, with a few carefully limited exceptions, aid to rebels and terrorists is illegal, the great majority of UN members turn around and refuse to treat such aid as the equivalent of an "armed attack" justifying an attack on the source of aid to rebels by both the target state and its allies. Cases in point include General Assembly criticism of the United States for bombing Libya (retaliation for support of terrorists) and for its efforts to overthrow Nicaragua's Marxist Sandinista government (initially justified as a modest means of terminating Nicaraguan complicity with the leftist Salvadoran rebels).

UN censure of these U.S. actions cannot be attributed plausibly to an unrelenting antiAmerican or antiWestern reflex by the nonaligned states. For if it could be, the UN majority would have censured the earlier American downing of Libyan aircraft that had aggressively approached U.S. ships in the Gulf of Sidra. It did not because Libya's claim that the gulf, a 300-mile-wide indentation in its coastline, is a bay and hence as internal to Libya as the Chesapeake Bay is to the United States, is flatly inconsistent with the international consensus that only bays with mouths no wider than twenty-four miles can be treated as national waters. When American ships entered the gulf to challenge Libyan claims, they were representing the international community as well as the United States. Destroying the Libyan aircraft thus was seen as an act of legitimate self-defense.

Why, then, has the United States failed to persuade all Western governments and jurists, much less Third World legal and political elites, that the character system permits the use of force for deterring or terminating assistance to rebels and terrorists? There are several plausible reasons. One is that the great majority of states regard ward avoidance as an extraordinarily important interest in its own right, as well as an instrument for protecting national sovereignty. Since aid to rebels is a ubiquitous feature of the contemporary international system with its intensely competitive superpowers, its many porous borders and narrowly based governments, and its sectarian strife and transnational sympathies, anything other than a conspicuous barrier between a large-scale armed attack and lesser forms of intervention would make it easier for essentially local conflicts to escalate into regional or global crises. The demonstrated tendency of the two superpowers, both obsessed with their "credibility," to impute cosmic significance to minor conflicts contributes to this risk.

An attempt to reconcile the interests in protecting national sovereignty and limiting armed conflicts took place in the World Court's 1986 opinion in the Nicaraguan suit against the United States for its support of the *contras*. The majority of the court's members did so by distinguishing between even large-scale military assistance from the outside to an authentic indigenous movement—for example, the revolt in the 1970s in Zimbabwe—and situations where one state creates and directs, as well as arms and trains, it—a case typified by the Hanoi-Vietcong relationship. According to the court, the latter, if carried out on a substantial scale, is an act of aggression by the principal perpetrated through agents who happen to be citizens of the defending state.

The court's distinction does not leave governments dangerously exposed. After all, with or without external aid, most subversive movements fail. Because they control the bureaucracy and the national communications network, the principal cities and ports, the security forces, and hard-currency reserves and employment, and also because they have ready access to the international arms market, established governments begin with overwhelming advantages. Only a few states manage, by virtue of extraordinary ineptitude, to lose.

Latin America has been a graveyard for guerrillas who have failed to seize power, sometimes repeatedly, in Argentina, Bolivia, Brazil, Colombia, El Salvador, Guatemala, Haiti, Mexico, Peru, Uruguay, and Venezuela. In Asia, too, they have yet to overthrow a widely recognized regime outside of Indochina and China in the wake of World War II.

A related reason for insisting on the distinction between "armed attack," which legitimates counterattack against the delinquent state, and aid to insurgents is that it protects states when they are drawn into a neighboring insurgency against their will or preference. A number of factors may inhibit governments from preventing the use of their territory by rebels. One is military weakness. Another is political cost: The rebels may have racial, ethnic, or ideological ties with elements of the local population.

Abolish the distinction and governments that are only marginally involved in neighboring civil conflicts or are involved for reasons beyond their control become subject to legitimate attack by neighbors or powerful friends of their neighbors. Indeed, their involvement could even be fabricated to facilitate removal of an uncongenial regime. The importance most states attach to this distinction as a means of restraining the use of force by the great powers helps explain why most governments reject the right—asserted primarily by Israel, South Africa, and the United States—to cross frontiers in order to liquidate terrorists and punish states allegedly encouraging, aiding, directing, or just tolerating them.

The antiinternationalist indictment of the UN is far more popular in the United States than in any other Western democracy. The overwhelming UN vote against the United States in the Grenadian case proved this point. Why is the indictment against the UN so well received in the United States? The answer, apparently, is that the antiinternationalist movement in America has convinced many opinion leaders that the norms restraining force have burdened defense of the national interest.

Their conviction rests in part on the belief that America has in fact been restrained. That belief must be a powerful act of faith, for it has had to survive many challenges in the quotidian world of American foreign policy. U.S. policymakers have consistently resisted the majority view in regard to charter restraints in the use of force. In both the Democratic administration of Lyndon Johnson and the Republican ones of Richard Nixon and Reagan, the United States claimed a right to cross borders and attack insurgent sanctuaries or supply lines on behalf of allied states. The United States, moreover, claimed and acted upon a right to intervene on behalf of threatened nationals. This is an interpretation of international law that a majority of UN members probably do not share, in part because it, too, has served as a pretext for imperial interventions.

In addition, U.S. policymakers have construed the charter's language governing regional organizations in order to manufacture what seemed at the time novel legal justification for use of force in the Western Hemisphere. The appearance of Soviet missiles in Cuba . . . posed a real test of American legal ingenuity. How could the United

States reconcile the principle of sovereign equality with its dictating to another government the measures that country might adopt to deter U.S. efforts to overthrow it? Since a first strike against the United States could not cripple the U.S. capacity to annihilate Cuba and devastate the Soviet Union, the United States could not invoke self-defense because it did not anticipate an attack. So after declaring that, if necessary, it would act unilaterally, the United States obtained authorization from the Organization of American States to promote and maintain peace in the region. That Article 53 of the UN Charter explicitly requires Security Council authorization for peace-keeping action by regional organizations was not seen as an insuperable problem. Such authorization, State Department lawyers concluded, could be implicit. In other words, regional organizations could act unless the Security Council explicitly forbade action, a contingency subject, of course, to U.S. veto.

Since the UN members did not regard the Warsaw Pact as a "regional organization" authorized by the charter to engage in peace keeping, the precedent was pleasantly insulated from the risk of reciprocal application. Not surprisingly, therefore, it was invoked again in 1965, along with a spurious claim that U.S. nationals were endangered, to cast a modest legal veil over the U.S. occupation of the Dominican Republic. A similar story unfolded in Grenada in 1983.

The United States has not been inhibited consistently even by its own rather flexible interpretation of charter restraints, which did not prevent the United States from organizing the overthrow of the democratically elected governments of at least two countries—Iran in 1953 and Guatemala in 1954; conspiring to abort another—Chile in 1970; and encouraging a coup d'état against a fourth—Brazil in 1964. Neither did the American interpretation of UN Charter restraints inhibit the Kennedy administration from organizing an invasion of Cuba in 1961.

The United States also has not felt constrained to treat charter norms as decisive for assessing the propriety of military initiatives by U.S. competitors in the game of nations. It has, for instance, excoriated Soviet-Cuban military assistance to the Marxist government of Ethiopia. Yet even under the most rigorous interpretation of international norms, Soviet assistance to that vile but universally recognized regime in repelling a Somali invasion in 1977 and in repressing Eritrean insurgents is indisputably legitimate, regardless of the considerable moral attractions of Somali irredentism and Eritrean aspirations for autonomy.

The immediate issue is not the moral propriety or even the prudence of U.S. behavior. It is simply whether the relative decline of American influence over global events can be connected meaningfully to charter restraints on the use of force.

The more than forty years that have elapsed since the victorious allies erected the new international legal order give little evidence of cost-effective opportunities for enhancing the U.S. wealth and security that have been lost for reasons of international norm-guided restraint. But a persuasive argument can be made that the postwar system has furthered the U.S. national interest. International norms helped persuade American leaders not to attack Cuba during the 1962 missile crisis. The blockade that was adopted minimized the risk of escalation without compromising the U.S. objective of preventing Soviet missiles from being positioned in Cuba.

The extent to which the system has restrained other states from adventures inconsistent with U.S. interests is debatable. It obviously has not prevented Hanoi from forcibly unifying Vietnam nor Moscow from using force to limit change in Eastern Europe, though it may have inhibited extinc-

tion of formal sovereignty for the area's client states. But it has helped block both the Soviets and the Vietnamese from comfortably harvesting the fruits of aggression in Afghanistan and Cambodia. By continuing to condemn the Soviet invasion of Afghanistan and continuing to seat representatives of the old Pol Pot regime of Cambodia, the UN majority has prevented the clients installed by the two communist states from acquiring the trappings of legitimacy. . . . While a revived internationalism must defend the basic norms of the post–World War II system, it should simultaneously envision reform of the system's summit institution, the United Nations. Today the UN lacks the spirit, the leadership, the staff, and the structure necessary to recognize early on issues with global impact, to identify common ground, to define options, to allocate responsibility, and to coordinate and monitor the response both of national governments and subsidiary bodies like the World Health Organization.

No global institution can perform these functions unless the United States and the [Russians] are prepared to accept as partners in institutional governance not only the other permanent members of the Security Council and Japan, but also the various states that have become or are in the process of becoming important regional actors, such as India and Brazil. They must be prepared as well to accept the constraints on their freedom of action that would result from the institution's broadened mandate.

For the first time, the prospect of securing Soviet cooperation in building a strong coordinating mechanism at the global level is not utopian. In an astonishing departure from Soviet precedent, Gorbachev . . . urged increased reliance on the United Nations for peace-keeping activities and has agreed to pay arrears for earlier peace-keeping operations authorized, over Soviet objections, by the General Assembly rather than, as envisioned by the organization's founders, the Security Council. Almost immediately after his return to Moscow from the Washington summit meeting with Reagan, Gorbachev extended a modified version of the USSR's first concrete peace-keeping proposal. Having initially suggested, without much fanfare, that the UN, with U.S. and Soviet naval backing, protect Persian Gulf shipping, the Soviets urged creation of a UN-flagged naval force to provide support for any new Security Council resolution imposing an arms embargo on Iran.

The proposal offered the United States an opportunity to test Soviet willingness to cooperate in stabilizing the international system. But Washington greeted it by signaling its distaste for any initiative tending to legitimate the Soviet presence in the gulf. Its response is understandable. Ascendant states have never welcomed arrivistes, even when, as with Britain and imperial Germany before World War I, the heads of state are relatives. Even the détente of the 1970s was an effort to trade arms control agreements and financial aid for Soviet acceptance of a permanently subordinate position in global politics.

Under the changed conditions of the current international system, the United States must concede as illusory its bid for unchallenged supremacy and, instead, should take the initiative in strengthening international cooperation. For instance, Washington might propose the establishment of an informal working group . . . that would consider ways of focusing the UN's agenda, restructuring its principal organs, and resurrecting the concept of an elite and independent international civil service.

Working . . . to reform the United Nations—like sailing with the [Russians] under a UN flag—would concede to America's adversary of the past four decades a prominent place in the management of world affairs conditional on constructive behavior. Those who cannot accept any end to the long cold war other than the . . . dismemberment of the Soviet Union or the overthrow of the Soviet regime would call this a defeat. But if [the Russians help] to maintain the structure of the postwar system, the reality would be victory, victory for that peculiarly American approach to the game of nations, liberal internationalism—an idea whose time has not yet passed.

26 *LIMITS OF GLOBALISM*

ROBERT J. LIEBER

Professor Lieber is Chair of the Government Department at Georgetown University in Washington, D.C.

The embodiment of post-World War II aspirations for international order is the United Nations. Disappointment over its grave shortcomings has been all the more acute because the hopes for the institution were initially so high. As in the case of the League, this world body grew out of the ending of a worldwide conflict and was shaped by the victorious allied powers. Indeed, the term *United Nations* originally gained currency as a designation for the coalition of Allied countries battling the Axis powers in World War II.

The UN emerged from a conflict which exhibited the worst features of international anarchy and of man's inhumanity to man on a scale unprecedented in human history. The war, with its devastation of large portions of Europe and Asia, vast civilian and military casualties, and genocidal slaughter gave rise to a sense that something had to be done to provide a more durable world order, not only to prevent another such conflict, but also to combat the economic and social conditions which had contributed to the rise of fascism and the coming of war.

Initially, President Franklin D. Roosevelt and Secretary of State Cordell Hull conceived of the UN as a means by which the Big Three powers (the United States, Great Britain, and the Soviet Union—and later expanded to include China and France) could preserve the peace by acting as the policemen of the postwar world. Agreement in principle emerged from a series of wartime conferences (Moscow in October 1943, Dumbarton Oaks in August 1944, and Yalta in February 1945). Roosevelt died in April 1945, shortly before the defeat of Hitler's Germany and the subsequent August surrender by Japan. However, many of the provisions in the United Nations Charter reflected the American president's aims. The United Nations Charter itself emerged from a conference in San Francisco, in which some fifty countries took part, and was signed there on June 26, 1945.

The new organization was pledged, through the preamble to its Charter, to seek four important objectives:

1. to save future generations from the scourge of war;

Excerpted by permission of its publisher from *No Common Power: Understanding International Relations.* Glenview, Illinois: Harper Collins Publishers, 1988, pp. 259–269. © 1988 Robert J. Lieber. (Footnotes have been deleted).

2. to reaffirm faith in fundamental human rights;
3. to establish conditions under which justice and respect for international law could be maintained; and
4. to promote social progress and better living standards in larger freedom.

The organizational structure of the UN included a General Assembly, in which all member states were represented and which was to operate on the basis of majority voting (with two-thirds majorities required on important questions); the Security Council, on which the five great powers sat as permanent members, each with a right of veto, along with ten other nonpermanent members; and a Secretariat, run by a Secretary-General and charged with the day-to-day operation of the UN.

In addition, the International Court of Justice in The Hague (established as the successor to the Permanent Court of International Justice) and a wide array of specialized agencies were linked to the UN.[1] Among these agencies were such bodies as the World Health Organization, the Food and Agricultural Organization, the International Monetary Fund, and the International Bank for Reconstruction and Development (the World Bank).

While the United Nations did not represent a radical effort to restructure the international system by imposing a world authority (the Charter explicitly recognized the "sovereign equality" of all its member countries), it nonetheless aimed to provide a far greater degree of order in relations among the countries of the world. One means for doing this was to create an organization whose membership would be virtually global; that is, all countries were potentially eligible for membership. Secondly, agreement among the great powers, institutionalized through the Security Council, was to provide the means for preventing war and even for using force against aggressor nations.

This notion of preserving peace through agreement among the powers was made explicit in a memorandum by the secretary of state to President Roosevelt:

> The entire plan is based on two central assumptions:
> First, that the four major powers will pledge themselves . . . not to go to war against each other or against any other nation, and to cooperate with each other . . . in maintaining the peace; and
> Second, that each of them will maintain adequate forces and will be willing to use such forces as circumstances require to prevent or suppress all cases of aggression.

The logic of this position rested on the assumption that if the big powers were to agree, they had the capacity to halt wars or aggression. On the other hand, if any of the permanent members were not in accord, each was too powerful to be coerced into agreement. Great-power dominance was embodied in the Security Council of the UN. The Charter provided this organ with the power to act in identifying threats to the peace and in taking actions including the interruption of economic and communication links and even the use of force. Members were to keep military forces available for collective UN actions.

In fact, agreement among the major powers had become tenuous even before the end of the war. As a consequence, except in largely technical and specialized matters, the effective functioning of the United Nations was obstructed. Indeed, the problem of great-power disagreement was later exacerbated by the emergence of important regional powers. These would be increasingly difficult to coerce even in those circumstances where the United States and the Soviet Union did find themselves in accord.

---

[1]Under Chapter 14 of the UN Charter, the International Court of Justice is the "principal judicial organ" of the UN.

THE UNITED NATIONS AND THE SECURITY DILEMMA

The UN was not created as a supranational world authority meant to impose its sovereignty over a quasi-anarchic world. It cannot, therefore, be judged by the standard of an incipient world government. All the same, the UN can and should be assessed in terms of the criteria for which it was established. By this standard the record is modest in some areas and dismal in others.

War Prevention

By the single most important criterion, that of preventing aggression and war, UN performance has been weak. Since 1945, some twenty million people have died in wars. Given the need for big power unanimity, it is not surprising that the UN has been unable to act when an East-West dimension has been involved in some way. The one exception to this stalemate occurred with the outbreak of the Korean War in June 1950. Because of Soviet absence from the Security Council (their representatives having walked out earlier in a dispute with the Western countries), the United States initially succeeded in obtaining the Council's condemnation of the attack by the Communist regime of North Korea and in gaining UN support for the defense of South Korea. With the Soviets' return, American representatives managed to transfer the issue to the General Assembly, where no Soviet veto could be cast, and to obtain the necessary majority there under the "Uniting for Peace Resolution." As a result, American and other forces fought under the UN flag during the Korean War.

The shift in UN membership during the 1950s and 1960s brought a dramatic change in numbers and political composition of the UN and the General Assembly. The fifty original signatories to the Charter in June 1945 came overwhelmingly from Europe and from North and South America, and the United States enjoyed a comfortable voting majority among them. But the expansion of membership, accommodating the newly independent countries of the developing world, more than tripled the UN's membership, and with the rise in numbers came a geopolitical shift as well. Of the 159 member countries in 1984, 120 came from the developing world, ninety-nine belonged to the "nonaligned" group, fifty were from Africa, thirty-three from Latin America, and only twenty-two from Western Europe. As a result, the United States found itself regularly outvoted. According to a study released by the U.S. Mission to the UN, member countries in the General Assembly during 1985 voted with the United States only 22.5 percent of the time on issues where there was a roll call vote and which were not adopted by consensus.[2] (See Table 26-1.)

Since its inception, the UN has undertaken more than a dozen peace-keeping operations. A number of these, carried out with the support of the major powers and of the local combatants, and involving a reasonably clear demarcation of the warring parties, have been successful. The Golan Heights (Syria versus Israel) and Cyprus (Greeks and Turks) are cases in point. Roughly half the UN efforts have been in the Middle East; other noteworthy interventions have involved India and Pakistan, as well as Zaire (formerly the Congo). However, suitable conditions have not always persisted, and when one or both of the local adversaries have been bent on war, UN forces have been withdrawn (for example, the Sinai Peninsula in 1967) or have been unable to act effectively (for example, Lebanon).

---

[2]Note that countries which abstained or did not take part in the vote were treated in the study as though they had voted against the United States.

TABLE 26–1 UN VOTING PERCENTAGE IN AGREEMENT WITH THE UNITED STATES

AFRICA

Ivory Coast	27.3	Gambia	14.9
Malawi	26.9	Zambia	14.9
Liberia	23.7	Nigeria	14.7
Zaire	23.1	Zimbabwe	14.6
Mauritus	22.1	Djibouti	14.3
Swaziland	22.0	Tunisia	13.9
Equatorial Guinea	21.2	Ghana	13.2
Central Africa Rep.	20.9	Uganda	13.2
Gabon	19.7	Burkina Faso	13.1
Senegal	19.3	Guinea Bissau	12.2
Togo	19.0	Comoros	12.1
Sierra Leone	18.3	Guinea	12.1
Cameroon	18.0	Cape Verde	11.9
Chad	18.0	The Seychelles	11.9
Niger	17.6	Congo	11.3
Botswana	17.4	Tanzania	11.3
Rwanda	17.4	Mali	11.1
Kenya	16.7	Madagascar	10.6
Somalia	16.3	Sao Tome & Principe	10.3
Mauritania	16.1	Ethiopia	9.3
Lesotho	16.0	Benin	8.8
Burundi	15.9	Libya	6.9
Morocco	15.9	Mozambique	5.9
The Sudan	15.5	Algeria	5.1
Egypt	15.3	Angola	3.5

ASIA AND THE PACIFIC

Japan	66.3	Bhutan	13.9
Australia	60.2	Oman	13.6
New Zealand	55.3	Saudi Arabia	13.6
Solomons	48.1	Vanuatu	13.4
Samoa	27.4	Lebanon	13.1
Fiji	26.0	Bahrain	12.8
Singapore	23.6	Qatar	12.8
Papua New Guinea	23.1	United Arab Emirates	12.8
Thailand	22.4	Maldives	12.5
Philippines	22.3	Kuwait	12.2
Cambodia	21.4	Cyprus	11.6
Nepal	18.0	Iran	11.3
Burma	17.1	Mongolia	9.9
Sri Lanka	16.8	Yemen	9.0
Malaysia	16.3	India	8.9
Bangladesh	16.1	Iraq	8.7
Pakistan	16.1	Syria	8.1
China	15.9	Vietnam	6.5
Brunei	15.3	Afghanistan	6.2
Indonesia	14.3	Laos	5.9
Jordan	14.2	Southern Yemen	5.7

(continued)

TABLE 26–1 *(Continued)*

THE AMERICAS

Grenada	71.7	Haiti	23.8
Canada	69.8	Jamaica	22.7
St. Christopher & Nevis	50.0	Barbados	20.3
Belize	37.8	Panama	19.7
Paraguay	35.4	Venezuela	19.0
St. Vincent & Grenadines	32.7	Bahamas	18.6
Chile	31.4	Bolivia	18.5
El Salvador	30.2	Uruguay	18.1
Honduras	29.8	Trinidad & Tobago	17.9
Costa Rica	29.1	Peru	17.8
Colombia	27.9	Argentina	16.4
St. Lucia	26.2	Suriname	16.2
Guatemala	25.2	Brazil	16.0
Antingua & Barbuda	25.0	Mexico	14.5
Dominican Republic	25.0	Guyana	13.9
Ecuador	24.6	Nicaragua	8.4
Dominica	24.2	Cuba	6.2

WESTERN EUROPE

Britain	86.6	Denmark	58.3
West Germany	84.4	Spain	55.6
France	82.7	Ireland	51.0
Belgium	82.3	Sweden	42.2
Italy	81.9	Austria	40.0
Luxembourg	80.2	Finland	39.8
The Netherlands	76.3	Turkey	38.1
Portugal	75.0	Greece	33.3
Iceland	62.4	Malta	16.5
Norway	61.2		

NO AFFILIATION

Israel	91.5

EASTERN EUROPE

Poland	14.8	Czechoslovakia	12.2
Rumania	14.6	East Germany	12.2
Hungary	12.3	Soviet Union	12.2
Ukraine	12.3	Yugoslavia	11.9
Bulgaria	12.2	Albania	6.7
Byelorussia	12.2		

Source: U.S. Mission to the United Nations, as reported in *The New York Times,* July 4, 1986.

Indeed, even when Soviet-American animosity has not been intrinsic to the dispute, conflicts have frequently been beyond the reach of the UN. The bulk of post-1945 warfare has taken place in the developing world, and the conditions and views of the regional parties have often been hostile to outside intervention. Thus, to cite only a few of the more deadly cases, the United Nations has been unable to deal with warfare in Indochina, which in one form or another has been almost unending since 1946. Indeed, the UN was out of the picture altogether while the Pol Pot regime in Cambodia murdered millions of its own subjects. Nor was it in a position to act in response to the Vietnamese invasion of Cambodia, apart from refusing to seat the regime which Hanoi installed in Phnom Penh.

Another particularly murderous example concerned Uganda, which was torn by the brutality of the Idi Amin regime in the 1970s. (While the numbers remain imprecise, some 300,000 civilians are believed to have perished under Amin. An additional 200,000 persons died during the regime of Amin's successor, President Milton Obote, and in the 1985 civil war which led to Obote's ouster.)[3]

Among other cases, the UN has also been ineffective in mitigating the long and bloody Iran-Iraq war. There are important reasons for this inability to act, including the weight of military power which some of the more important of the developing countries now possess. One of the chief factors, however, is that the huge developing world voting majorities in the General Assembly have tended to avoid internally divisive controversies—no matter how grave the human cost—in order to focus on other issues and regions over which there has been less disagreement within the bloc: South Africa, Israel, and real or imagined policies of the United States.

Human Rights

Here too the UN record has fallen short of the organization's original goals. On the one hand, the UN has adopted a series of impressive declarations and conventions concerning guarantees of human rights, prevention of genocide, and opposition to

[3]In the latter period, much of the killing involved attacks on members of the large Baganda tribal group by soldiers in Obote's regime drawn from the Acholi and Langi tribes of northern Uganda. Obote had come to power as a result of a civil war and invasion by forces from the neighboring country of Tanzania.

discrimination based on race, sex, and belief. Most notable among these are the adoption by the General Assembly of the Universal Declaration of Human Rights (December 10, 1948).

In practice, however, the gap between rhetoric and practice has been immense. Countries of the Soviet bloc and a large proportion of member states from the developing world do not themselves adhere to basic human rights practices within their own borders. As a consequence, they are usually reluctant to support forceful policy standards which would be applied to all cases, rather than wielded selectively in the service of more limited political agendas. The Soviet Union, for example, frequently invokes the principle of nonintervention in internal affairs whenever its own practices are challenged.

While criticisms of grave human rights abuses in, for example, South Africa, are very much to the point, a wide array of other major cases (Afghanistan, Argentina, Cambodia, Cuba, Ethiopia, Guatemala, Iran, Syria, and Uganda, to name just a few) have been minimized or altogether ignored. Moreover, the most extensive and severe human rights violations (not only of political rights but of rights of the person to be free of physical abuse, torture, and murder) are often overlooked or cited only in passing, even while a torrent of criticism is unleashed against a handful of generally Western-oriented members. For example, Arab-Israeli and Palestinian issues have been subject to repeated and disproportionate overemphasis, culminating in the notorious November 1975 General Assembly resolution—opposed by the United States and most of the countries of Western Europe—that "Zionism is racism."

Several specific cases provide vivid illustration of the human rights problem at the United Nations. The private voluntary organization Amnesty International, which investigates and criticizes human rights abuses among all forms of political systems, and which lobbies for the release of political prisoners provided only that they have not been involved in the use of violence, has submitted large numbers of documented cases of persecution to the UN Human Rights Commission without receiving action on them. The same organization, which was later awarded a Nobel Peace Prize for its activity, actually had facilities withdrawn from its use by UNESCO (United Nations Educational, Scientific, and Cultural Organization) lest a conference concerning torture give offense to UN member governments. Shortly thereafter, the UN Human Rights Commission saw behind-the-scenes agreement reached to minimize the issue of torture in Chile in exchange for avoiding the subject of Soviet treatment of dissidents. Even requests to investigate human rights violations in Uganda, a country whose domestic polity was disintegrated to the point of anarchy, were rejected by the Commission.

Justice and Respect for International Law

The subject of international law is treated later; however, it is useful to consider here the fate of one of the key provisions of the UN Charter, Article 2(4). This provides for a particularly stringent restraint on the use of threat of force:

> All members shall refrain in their international relations from the threat or use of force against the territorial integrity or political independence of any state, or in any other manner inconsistent with the purposes of the United Nations.

In practice this stipulation has been repeatedly violated. Under the Charter, force may only be employed under one or the other of two specific circumstances. One of these is an enforcement action ordered by the UN Security Council in response to a threat to the peace. In practice, however, this does not take place because of lack of agreement among the permanent members. The other avenue is that of individual or collective self-defense, under Article 51 of the Charter:

> Nothing in the present Charter shall impair the inherent right of individual or collective self-defense if an armed attack occurs against a Member of the United Nations, until the Security Council has taken the measures necessary to maintain international peace and security. Measures taken by members . . . shall be immediately reported to the Security Council. . . .

In the absence of effective enforcement machinery, the self-defense justification becomes a blanket rationale, or else the officially sanctioned justifications are overlooked altogether in a world where much contemporary conflict (civil wars, violence in the developing world, terrorism, guerrilla wars) has little to do with the kind of formal declared wars which the framers of the UN Charter had sought to prevent.

Less dramatically, however, internationally agreed upon rules and norms are widely adhered to in a host of functional, technical, and economic spheres (such as health, aviation, and monetary affairs). Some of these matters involve the operation of specialized UN agencies; many others lie outside the UN realm altogether.

In any case, the effort to enact significant new international legal agreements has been halting. The UN Law of the Sea Conference is a case in point: After conferences in 1958 and 1960, the UN brought together a third conference, which took place from 1973 through 1982. This produced the UN Convention on the Law of the Sea, aimed at addressing not only the issues of territorial waters, freedom of transit, and coastal resource jurisdiction, but also deep seabed mining. Although signed by 159 states, only twenty-six ratified the convention within the next four years. The stumbling block concerned deep seabed matters, where the United States, backed by Britain and the Federal Republic of Germany, objected to a number of provisions for international control and refused to sign.

Clearly, the codification of accepted international law has proved difficult. Major powers have been reluctant to accede to international jurisdiction when they have believed their vital interests to be at stake. This refusal has taken the form of claiming a privileged status for internal matters—as in the frequent Soviet practice, even when this directly contravenes existing international agreements which the USSR has entered into (for example, in the case of the Helsinki Accords of 1975 or the Universal Declaration of Human Rights). It is also reflected on occasion in the actions of the United States—as in its refusal to accept the jurisdiction of the World Court in a suit brought against it by the government of Nicaragua in April 1984.

Social Progress and Better Living Standards

Here, the record of UN specialized agencies and of other bodies much more loosely associated with the United Nations reveals some areas of substantial achievement. Notable successes have been reached by the World Bank, the International Monetary Fund, the International Civil Aviation Organization, and to a lesser extent the GATT (General Agreement on Tariffs and Trade) and UNCTAD (UN Conference on Trade and Development). Other agencies have provided effective technical assistance on agriculture, the environment, and aid to refugees. The picture had been more mixed in the case of bodies such as the International Atomic Energy Agency (IAEA), while for others—UNESCO being the outstanding case in point—it has been so abysmal a record of extreme politicization and gross fiscal irresponsibility that the United States and Britain have opted to withdraw from membership.

A BALANCE SHEET ON THE UNITED NATIONS

The record of the UN is not wholly negative. Even those governments most severely critical of its failings have thus far opted to remain within the organization. The criterion of universal membership has been nearly approximated with exceptions such as Switzerland's choosing not to belong, and challenges such as the seating of Taiwan instead of the People's Republic of China during the 1950s and 1960s, as well as repeated Arab attempts to expel Israel.

In addition to the successful operation of a number of its specialized agencies, the UN provides an avenue for dispute settlement and peace-keeping in those circumstances where the parties to the conflict are willing to seek such an avenue. On occasion, it can provide a face-saving way out of a confrontation for a country which would prefer to avoid more overt entanglement or even war.

The UN also provides, however imperfectly, a forum for regular meeting and communication among widely diverse and sometimes bitterly antagonistic countries. And, despite serious abuses, its existence does force countries to justify and explain their actions in front of a wider audience than would otherwise be the case. (The Suez crisis and the Soviet invasion of Hungary in 1956, the Cuban missile crisis of 1962, and the Soviet shooting down of a Korean Airlines plane in 1983 are all cases in point.) By no means does the organization eliminate the problems of the quasi-anarchic international environment, nor of the security dilemma, but it does slightly alleviate the anarchic characteristics of the international system by creating at least a faint shadow of an international community in which countries live.

On the other hand—and it is quite a caveat—the UN exhibits severely debilitating limitations. Many of these have been enumerated above and require no repetition. In addition, the organization itself has become bloated and overstaffed, a source of international patronage and secure employment for a class of diplomats and former diplomats—many of whom prefer living in the headquarters city of New York (or in the locales of the specialized agencies, such as Geneva, Vienna, Rome, and Paris) to returning to their home countries. Less mundane is the organization's selective morality. At its worst, this results in spokesmen for countries with records of behavior which grossly contradict the most basic UN ideals arising to denounce a small group of semi-officially designated target countries in order to invoke huge bloc vote majorities. International standards are applied selectively and capriciously, with some of the worst infringements of human rights escaping condemnation altogether.

The climate of institutionalized hypocrisy is even reflected in the belated revelation that a former two-term UN Secretary-General, Dr. Kurt Waldheim, had lied about his World War II years and in fact served as intelligence officer for a notorious Nazi general. Waldheim's unit operated in Yugoslavia where it was involved in the infamous Kozara roundup and massacre of Yugoslav civilians as well as the deportation of Jews, Serbs, and others to Nazi concentration camps. Waldheim's commanding general, Alexander Lohr, was himself later executed for war crimes. That an international civil servant could serve for ten years as head of the world organization, with a claim to speak on behalf of the international community, and do so without his past coming to light—or being divulged by those individuals and countries which had some prior knowledge—testifies in some measure to the very limits of the UN itself.

In sum, although it is the one world organization with nearly global membership and the mission of addressing the widest array of international concerns, the United Nations is generally unsuited and unable to provide a major challenge to the anarchic international environment. To be sure, the causes of many of its institutional shortcomings lie far beyond the reach of the UN, and in that sense the organization's limits reflect the problem of the international system itself. All the same, the United Nations has also fallen far short of fulfilling the purposes for which it was created in the first place. . . .

CHAPTER SEVEN

THE REGIMES: A NEW TRANSNATIONAL REALITY

> *In the intense competitive atmosphere that will exist in the twenty-first century, all of the participants should remind themselves daily that they play in a competitive-cooperative game, not just a competitive game. Everyone wants to win, but cooperation is also necessary if the game is to be played at all.*
>
> Lester Thurow, *Head to Head: the Coming Economic Battle among Japan, Europe, and America,* 1991.

In the transformation of classical theory, based as it was upon the idea of the dominance of essentially monolithic nation-states relating politically with one another, few new ideas have been as significant as the growing definition of transnational forces and the recognition of their importance to international relations, both in practice and in theory. As will be seen in the selections making up this chapter, they range all the way from drugs to human rights involving all kinds of organizations, private as well as public, which carry out operations all over the world. Thanks principally to Stephen Krasner, the expression "international regimes" has now entered the lexicon of the field to describe this wide range of activities, some of which outdo states themselves, and many of which materially affect what states can do. In this new usage, "regimes" is not just another name for governments but "sets of implicit or explicit principles, norms, rules, and decision-making procedures around which actors' expectations converge in a given area of international relations."[1]

[1]Stephen Krasner, "Structural Causes and Regime Consequences," *International Organization,* Spring 1982, in which he then goes on to define what each of these terms (principles, norms, rules, decision-making) connotes, p. 186.

The term "anti-apartheid regime" has been put forth in a recent issue of *Human Rights Quarterly*[2] just as Helga Haftendorn has used the term "security regime" in her highly theoretical Presidential address to the International Studies Association.[3] The drug lords of Medellin represent a particularly threatening form of regime, as Robert Tomasek brings out in his reading, its leaders continuing to defy the entire world's efforts to bring them under control. From yet another perspective, what may be called "communications regimes" have become increasingly significant in affecting the course of world politics, as Barbie Zelizer shows in a fascinating description of the way CNN operated in the Gulf War—the reporting of events themselves *became* events. Most of the time, however, the expression tends to be used as Charles Kegely and Eugene Wittkopf use in their contribution to the chapter—to explain the role and behavior of overseas multinational corporations.

All this serves to demonstrate what a useful and indeed essential concept "regimes" has become. While the idea of regimes may have only recently entered the realm of theory, in practice it has been around for a long time. In discussing what they call "the new diplomacy" in their new book, *Rival States, Rival Firms: Competition for World Market Shares,* Susan Strange and John Henley put it this way:

> International business is an ancient feature of the world economy. . . . Indeed, the travelling merchant has been one of history's unsung heroes in providing the initial contacts among entire cultures. It is only in the last century that the multinational corporation has emerged in forms we would recognize today.[4]

Early political economists such as Richard Cobden, Friedrich List, and Karl Marx observed the behavior of the mercantile predecessors of these actors, but the influence of forces beyond the control of any given state has grown to the point where they represent significant change in the very nature of international relations. No longer does it make any sense for the IR analysts to confine their interest to the nation-state, however longer it may remain the core political unit in IR (some say that won't be very long).

These significant new actors are, as Kegley and Wittkopf recently put it in their contribution to this chapter, "the key participants in the regularized conduct of contemporary world politics . . . in such diverse areas as law of the sea, nuclear nonproliferation, the global monetary and trade system, and the global food system."[5] The behavior and strength of certain international regimes appear to even threaten to replace the state-centric approach to the study of international relations itself. The dominance of this classical outlook may—if not soon supplanted by the behavior of IGOs (intergovernmental organizations),

[2]Newell M. Stultz, "Evolution of the United Nations Anti-Apartheid Regime," *Human Rights Quarterly,* February 1991, pp. 1–23.

[3]Reproduced in the *International Studies Quarterly*, 35, 1991, pp. 3–17.

[4](Cambridge: Cambridge University Press, 1991), p. 13 (#18 in the Cambridge University Press "Studies in International Relations" Series in conjunction with the British International Studies Association).

[5]Charles W. Kegley, Jr. and Eugene R. Wittkopf, *World Politics; Trend and Transformation* 3rd ed. (New York: St. Martin's Press, 1989), p. 174.

MNCs (multinational corporations), NGOs (nongovernmental organizations), and other nonstate actors—be so influenced by them as to represent an entirely novel form of political organization. Hence, if IR consists of the relationships of states, including everything that materially affects their relations, then the student of IR can ill afford to pretend that these new forces do not exist. Traditionalists may argue that admitting that they exist does not mean that they do not make all that much difference. They do, even if perhaps not to the degree some anticipated in the 1960s and 1970s, when "multinationals" were seen to constitute a fundamental threat to the existing order. What is unmistakably clear is that the "upheavals of the international political economy during the last decade have altered, irreversibly we believe, the relationships between states and multinational enterprises."[6]

When does a so-called international regime come into play? The answer seems to be: when the policies and activities of state and nonstate actors combine—often inadvertently—in such a way as to create an entity greater than the sum of its parts. Such a regime is a player on the world stage which possesses so much economic, social, or political strength, whose operations go so far beyond the confines of any given state, that it can perform, for all practical purposes, as an independent actor. It can influence or even at times appear to control the activities and even the policies of some small states. In terms of sheer financial power and resources, several multinational corporations possess more capital, skill, contacts, and certainly entrepreneurship than most new states can possibly expect to achieve for a long period to come.

During and after the emergence and recognition of these regimes as compelling new forces, many leaders of the new countries feared that the further expansion of immense overseas conglomerates might seriously limit their own governmental freedom of action, even within their own national boundaries. So aggressive had some firms become in their zeal to acquire raw materials and other resources that they were practically able to dictate trade terms. The fear was turning into a reality. Or so it seemed.

By their very nature, MNCs have little sense of long-range purpose in terms of any commitment to the national interest or development goals of local government. Short- or middle-term profit was the objective. Unlike the colonial expansionists of an earlier generation, neither do they necessarily serve the strategic objectives of their own governments. So their interest in staying continues just so long as it is profitable. Indeed, their activities may run counter to the interest of the governments of the countries where they are based. For this reason, they in fact represented no serious long-term political threat to stability, to sovereignty, nor necessarily to economic development, though that was more coincidence than intent and often the contrary was true in the exploitative sense. At least at first, companies seemed not to care one way or the other.

Governments of most developing countries seem to have now adopted the stance that the practical way to deal with large corporations is not to oppose them but to work with them. Mutual interest dictates the rational exploitation of the natural resources that even minor states possess within their boundaries and

[6]Strange and Henley, *op cit.,* p. 1.

the building not only of factories but of more sophisticated infrastructures in the process of strengthening their own fledgling economies. Meanwhile the boards of the giant companies have either been forced by restrictive laws or persuaded by far-sighted national leaders to adapt their methods and policies to the interests of the countries within and between which they carry out their operations, so that both they and their hosts profit from their enterprise. Sometimes this works to mutual advantage, sometimes it doesn't. Companies want to go home or go elsewhere as soon as the resources they are after run out or become too costly to extract profitably. The desire for dependable stability which must characterize the leadership of a state responsible for serving the national interest and the welfare of its people does not represent any particular value for companies operating for the time being in a particular area.

What makes international regimes so vital in understanding contemporary international politics, however, goes beyond the internal concerns of specific states in the less-developed world. The movement of commerce on an international plane is determined by the flow of goods and services from one country to another, many of these movements being beyond the effective control of any given state nor indeed of any combination of states or international organizations. At the same time, as Robert Keohane and Joseph Nye pointed out in their pioneer work on structural models of international regime change, MNCs often perform as a sort of transmission belt through which one nation's policies become responsive to those of other states, their very transnational nature serving to broaden the essentially provincial outlook that often especially characterizes the new leaders working on behalf of but one country.[7] As Howard Wriggins, a Columbia professor of international relations who has served as ambassador in a developing country, has written, this creates a dilemma for a leader:

> To stay in power and effect government policies, the new leader must cope with a host of complicated problems, for which his experience gives little precedent. . . . The uncertainty of his position makes it prudent for him to tackle these problems in ways which will most likely weaken his support.[8]

The systems-level of analysis places emphasis upon the distribution of power among states and upon the effects that advances in technology and weapons (especially nuclear weapons) have in terms of the danger of war. Not only have such weapons of mass destruction made embarking upon war potentially suicidal, but they make the game of power-politics competition a peculiar mix of constraints and race. Now regime theory has taken us beyond that, for an equally profound change in the nature of interstate relations has been brought about by technology and economics. Modern states are highly dependent upon foreign trade, investment, and even tourism, as well as upon access to such vital

[7]Robert Keohane and Joseph Nye, eds. *Power and Interdependence*, (Glenview, Ill.: Scott, Foresman and Co., 1989), their first work on this subject having been the editing of "Transnational Relations and World Politics," a special edition of *International Organization*, 2, 3 (Summer 1971).

[8]W. Howard Wriggins, *The Ruler's Imperative: Strategies for Political Survival in Asia and Africa.* New York and London: Columbia University Press, 1969, p. 17. Professor Wriggins, a Ph. D in International Relations from Yale, served on the National Security Council staff in the Carter White House after representing the United States in Sri Lanka, then returned to academic life—a prime example of combining "theory and practice."

resources as oil. No longer can they secure their ends simply by imposing their will upon others. This has given rise to a condition of "interdependence" that limits even the mightiest states in their ability to determine their own actions entirely without regard to anyone else.

Some see Brazil, China, and India as future participants in an increasingly interlocking world trading and financial network. If, as it appears, the military dimension of world politics is receding and the economic is in the ascendancy, international regimes will become even more important in future years than they are now, particularly if no better means of controlling their behavior are discovered and put into place. The emergence of this new kind of actor reconfirms the value and necessity of a systems-level approach, instead of the old foreign policy/strategic perspective that has characterized so much research (largely because of ample funding) in our field. This approach also enables one to take into account the manner in which the underdeveloped states are learning to confront international systems.

The emergence in the period since 1948 of about 100 new states has had a dramatic effect upon the manner in which the system has developed. Quite apart from the sheer number and variety of societies involved, most are non-Western in religion and culture. Their struggle to make good their sovereignty and to meet the needs of their often needy populations has introduced an element of volatility and instability into almost all international systems, complicating their management in hundreds of unforeseen ways. One might ask whether rational conditions for international order any longer exist, or whether whatever order is apparent is mere convenience.

Frequently the scene of coups and revolutions, many new states exist economically on the margin of subsistence; others are driven by tribal, religious, and social conflict within their borders, often victims of proxy wars supported, if indeed not created, by larger powers to serve their own interests. Some may even deny the proposition that smaller states have any stake in preserving the existing international order. Most want to replace it, a major objective of many LDCs being to bring about a massive redistribution of global economic wealth. They have even raised a challenge to the legitimacy of many of the norms of international law. Hence no understanding of contemporary global problems would be possible without a recognition of the extent to which the Third World challenges the international system as now constituted. The challenge is partly directed at such manifestations of Western industrial and financial power as the multinational corporation, which leaders of governments which are remote from the great financial centers assume are part and parcel of the political order in the West. "How could it be otherwise?" they conclude. A major contributing source of this challenge is the reverse side of the coin, by which international regimes, whatever form they may take, in turn have undercut and usurped the authority of the emergent nation-states, not to replace them in the local power structure but merely to get them out of the way.

With the growth of communications and technology, movements linking people and activities that go beyond the nation-state and cross international boundaries—usually by simply ignoring them—have been on the increase. These are termed transnational movements and, to the extent to which they take on an institutional form having a discernible impact upon the international system or upon the behavior and values of states themselves, are called "transnational actors." Many of these have a positive effect, such as activities of environmentalists and protectors of endangered species of birds, fish, and animals. On the other hand, the growing need to condemn drug-trafficking and punish acts of terrorism against airlines reveals another face of the transnational phenomenon. However distasteful and unconventional may be the kinds of regimes Robert Tomasek describes in his contribution to this chapter, they reflect a feature of political and economic life on a world level which is to some degree out of the control of the traditional players.

With the advances, sometimes mind-boggling, in communications and technology, new kinds of relationships of interdependence are being created which political leaders can only ignore at their peril. We have already noted in Zelizer's article how the information revolution has created yet another international regime—the "communications common," as Vicki Golich has recently termed it.[9] One should not go so far as to argue that the nation-state is giving way to revolutionary new basic units in a new international order. Nor is it necessary to accept the theory that the state is becoming "functionless" and that the base for an alternative world order is already being fashioned by technicians, information managers, criminal networks, and political elites who think in extranational terms. Nevertheless, new transnational forces are imposing themselves upon the sovereignty of the state and forcing governments to adjust to a new level of activity in order to control and manage them, insofar as they are able to continue to do so at all. They are beginning to have their doubts.

This focus on transnational movements is also an aspect of the ongoing debate between the federalists who favor supranational organization at the regional or world level, and the functionalists who advocate unification through organizing international activity on a function-by-function foundation. In either case, the stunning rise of a number of novel transnational actors, whose activities seem to effectively skirt the jurisdiction of governments or force them to negotiate agreements with other states in their efforts to regulate them, has given new life to the argument that it is through such movements that basically nationalist, conservative states will simply be forced to help knit an ever-widening web of worldwide authority on some basis or other. What the argument tends to overlook is the built-in structure of nation-states and the reliance of existing international governmental organizations, such as the regional commissions of the United Nations, upon member governments to continue to support them. They certainly cannot be expected to do so if their activity threatens rather than serves the interest of the state.

The proliferation and growing strength of international regimes of all kinds already have a discernible impact on conventional international relations, whether at the system, the state, or the individual level of analysis. It is not hard to understand why some observers claim to see the emergence of a true world society or community, one in which IR conceived merely as the formal relation-

---

[9]Vicki Golich, "A Multinational Negotiation Challenge: International Management of the Communication Common," *Journal of Applied Behavioral Science*, 27, 2, June 1991.

ships between sovereign states is fast becoming something of an anachronism. Something other than chaos has to take their place. Ambitious schemes for reorganizing the entire world are probably not the answer; as the creator of the term "superpowers," William T. R. Fox, pointed out just before the end of World War II,

> Grand designs are important. They furnish analytical models for public discussion of important problems. They provide criteria by which to test the long-run consequences of various short-run alternatives. Most grand designs are, however, presented by their authors as the one best hope of avoiding a fresh descent into the maelstrom of global war.[10]

Because many of them "just happen" as firms pursue their basic export-import interests beyond the borders of their own countries, few would put international regimes in the category of "grand designs," most particularly those who manage them in terms of simply trying to meet what are often short-term objectives. As Professor Renee Marlin-Bennett has explained; "in practical terms, overlapping rules, but not universal regimes, will facilitate international cooperation."[11] Hence for the time being their significance for IR lies not in presenting some revolutionary alternative nor in some sweeping expression of moral condemnation, but in the degree to which they have an impact upon the ongoing conventional state system that still manages the planet, for better or worse.

DISCUSSION QUESTIONS

1. Just what are "regimes," and why are they important? Do you think they are replacing the state as the focus of power in the world?
2. Do you see signs that the U.S. still engages in "dollar diplomacy"? In its 1910 form, did this represent an early example of what we now call "international regimes"?
3. Like most forces in politics, regimes have their "good" and "bad" sides. How has Tomasek's contribution enhanced your understanding of this?
4. Do you think CNN is a "regime" in itself, or just part of a larger communications regime?
5. Show the limitations imposed upon international regimes (1) by their own operational goals and methods and (2) by the governments of states within which their operations take place.
6. MNCs are variously considered to be either a cure or a curse. Which position do you take on the issue?
7. Do you agree with Marlin-Bennett on the relative importance to international cooperation as between regimes and overlapping rules?
8. Differentiate between an "NGO" and an "IGO".

[10]William T. R. Fox, *The Super-Powers: The United States, Britain, and the Soviet Union: Their Responsibility for Peace* (New York: Harcourt Brace and Co., 1944), p. 159.
[11]Renee Marlin-Bennett, "Where Do Regimes Come From?," an original essay published in full in the eighth edition of this reader, pp. 212–216, and updated in this edition as Selection 33.

27 COMPLEX INTERDEPENDENCY THEORY: DRUG BARONS AS TRANSNATIONAL GROUPS

ROBERT D. TOMASEK

Professor, Department of Political Science, The University of Kansas, Lawrence, Kansas

The flow of international drugs has increased immensely in the last twenty years. The drug problem has commanded media attention and led the U.S. public and government to elevate it as a major concern. Yet it has been considered a national crisis during previous administrations, and regardless of the efforts made to solve it, the problem has only become worse. The increase in drug use has had a corresponding increase in Europe, Canada, Australia, and most of the Third World, meaning that it has become a worldwide problem. . . .

Presidential interest, though, does not mean that presidents will spend that much time in decision making on the drug issue. Instead, pressing security issues have crowded the agenda. Presidents have tended to delegate authority on the drug issue to an expert brought into the government, a departmental head, a cabinet committee, or the vice president. . . .

THE DRUG BARONS AS TRANSNATIONAL GROUPS

Complex interdependency theory has stressed the importance of transnational groups. A problem arises, though, in determining what would constitute the strongest type of transnational groups. Critics of interdependency theory have argued that the state is still the deciding factor in international politics, and that governments are still able to control transnational groups if they desire to do so. In assessing the extent to which drug barons are transnational groups, it seems necessary to first determine the power they have within a state. Are they powerful enough to be viewed as states within states, with governments unable to control their activities? Even if this situation existed, though, the drug operators would have to extend their operations to other countries, setting up processing laboratories, transportation networks, and distribution outlets. The drug barons would develop contacts with other drug operators,

Excerpted from "The International Drug Issue as an Illustration of Complex Interdependency Theory," *International Third World Studies Journal and Review*, Vol. 2, No. 1, pp. 15–28 Copyright © 1990 Media Periodicals. (Footnotes have been renumbered).

travel extensively, live abroad if hounded in their own country, and launder their profits in different overseas banks to spread the risk. With this conception in mind, different types of individuals and groups that handle drugs can be looked at.

The Golden Triangle in Asia was written about extensively in the 1960s and 1970s as a major source of opium. It interested observers because the area covered eastern Burma and northern Thailand and Laos, with drug routes crisscrossing these areas. The area was also geographically remote, inhabited by dissatisfied minority ethnic groups often fighting against their central governments, and poverty stricken. Many of the ethnic groups were involved in drugs. But did transnational drug barons develop?

The most interesting group were the 12,000 troops of Chiang Kai Shek that crossed the Chinese border into Burma in 1949 when the Nationalists lost the civil war. These troops in the 1950s were aided both by the CIA and Chiang Kai Shek from Taiwan, and carried out seven fruitless raids into southern China. In the following years the group was reduced to 6,000 due to repatriation to Taiwan and Burmese military operations. The remnants of the original army then went from Burma to Thailand and existed by raising poppies for the opium trade.[1] The characteristics of this group are quite interesting. The soldiers in reality belonged to no state, moved at will from Burma to Thailand, and became involved in the drug trade without much resistance. They did not expand their operations outside of the Golden Triangle, however, or develop strong contacts with other drug barons, and thus could not be called a transnational group in the truest sense.

The same type of analysis can be used to evaluate individual drug barons who became real power centers in the areas they operate in. Three examples will be given. The first is the sixty-year-old Shan warlord Chang Chi-fu whose drug headquarters in the Golden Triangle has its own hospital and swimming pools and whose ten heroin refineries on the Thai-Lao border are guarded by an army of 4,500 men. The second is the drug baron Roberto Suarez of Bolivia who has his own fleet of aircraft, bribes officials, makes about $600 million annually, and at one time offered a deal to the U.S. State Department in which he would pay off Bolivia's $4 billion debt in exchange for the release of his son arrested in the United States. The third example are Mexican drug barons living in fortified mansions in the hills around Tijuana who have their own bodyguards, and have bribed some 800 policemen to make sure that drugs cross the border unmolested.[2] Obviously the power of these drug barons is enormous. In regard to the transnational characteristics, though, the most that can be said is that they develop ingenious ways to move drugs outside of their countries, and in doing this they must cultivate major purchasers abroad. They do not, however, develop worldwide or even regional operations. Also, they are susceptible to arrest even though specialists feel that this would be most unlikely. Roberto Suarez was arrested by the Bolivian government in a surprise raid on his jungle headquarters, although conviction and lasting imprisonment remain an uncertainty.

A better example of a transnational drug baron is Juan Ramon Mata. A Honduran by birth, he got his start in the drug business in Colombia by cooperating with their drug barons. He considered Colombia

[1]See Catherine Lamour and Michel R. Lamberti, *The International Connection-Opium From Growers to Pushers* (New York: Pantheon Books, 1974), chapter 7 for an extensive account of their activities.

[2]See Ben Whitaker, *The Global Connection: The Crisis of Drug Addiction* (London: Jonathan Cape, 1987), pp. 333, 337, 338.

his home, and with drug profits he acquired two huge ranches and a construction outfit. He was important in developing connections in Mexico for transshipping Colombian drugs to the U.S. Later in Colombia he was arrested, and with a one million dollar bribe escaped from prison, and returned to Honduras, his country of birth. While there, he acquired two large farms and a factory, became somewhat of a celebrity in Tegucigalpa, and seemed to have good relations with some elements of the Honduran military who were profiting in drugs.[3] His demise came when the U.S. convinced the Honduran government to seize him in a surprise raid and put him on a plane for trial in the U.S. on charges that he was involved in the death of a U.S. Drug Enforcement Agency agent in Mexico. Honduran mobs, upset that his seizure violated the Honduran constitution's proper procedures on extradition, and angry about the U.S. military and the Contra's presence in the country, burned the annex of the U.S. embassy in retaliation.

The role of the Mafia in drugs in the U.S. is an excellent example of a transnational group. The older Mafia leaders had shunned drugs up to the Second World War, feeling that it would worsen their image. Later, however, the leaders could not resist the profits, and when they linked with the Italian Mafia, they used their expanding connections to transship drugs. A Mafia organization in Canada was also brought into the network. Much of the Mafia's early supply of drugs came from Turkey, but at present they do most of their business with Asian and Latin American dealers whom they do not trust and are unable to control.[4]

The best example of transnational drug barons are those operating from Co-

lombia. They consist of a loose coalition of some twenty crime families based in the city of Medellin, of which five predominate and are viewed as a cartel.[5] Drug operators are also located in Leticia and along the Caribbean coast who do not openly defy the leaders in Medellin but are not directly under their command. A more important group has surfaced in Cali which has moved into direct competition with the Medellin group. The Colombian drug barons are viewed as a state within a state, neutralizing most of the government efforts to control their activities.

The wealth of the drug barons is enormous. They at one time offered to pay off Colombia's $20 billion debt if they were all pardoned and left alone. They have built palatial mansions, hired bodyguards, bought newspapers, donated to political parties, flooded Colombian and Miami banks with drug profits, started ventures where people could purchase shares for certain specific drug operations, and bought fleets of planes to transport drugs. Bribery has been extensive, going to the military and police to ignore their operations, to judges for minimal or no sentences, and to prison wardens to help arrange escapes.[6] Their bribery has even been extended to the New York City and Miami police forces, and to southern county sheriffs to allow small planes to fly into remote airstrips.[7]

The Colombian drug barons would ideally like to gain respectability. They have

[5]See Alan Riding, "The Cocaine Cartel," *The New York Times,* January 17, 1988, p. 3E for sketches of the five.

[6]See *The Miami Herald,* February 8, 1987, pp. 1A and 16A; February 9, 1987, pp. 1A and 14A; February 10, 1987, pp. 1A and 9A; and February 11, 1987, pp. 1A and 11A for an excellent four part series on the power of the drug barons and their expanding overseas operations.

[7]See Philip Shenon, "Enemy Within: Drug Money is Corrupting the Enforcers," *The New York Times,* April 11, 1988, p. 1 for a detailed description of the problem.

[3]See Sam Dillon, "Drug King Becoming a Folk Hero," *The Miami Herald,* April 18, 1986, pp. 1A and 8A for a detailed description of his life and travels.

[4]See Whitaker, *op.cit.,* pp. 327–332.

given parties for the cream of local society, donated money to the Catholic Church and local welfare organizations, and sponsored soccer teams. One drug baron was elected to congress, and another started his own party.

The drug barons have no qualms about assassinating anybody who gets in their way. They have a permanent body of hit team squads they call upon. Their victims have included a Justice Minister, fifty judges including a Supreme Court Justice, the heads of police antidrug units, a crusading editor of the second largest newspaper, a score of journalists, the leader of a leftist party, and an informant witness about to testify in the United States. They were also responsible for the guerrilla raid on Bogota's Palace of Justice in 1985 in which half of the top justices were killed. Their drug records were burned in the fire. The drug barons have threatened to kill the head of the Drug Enforcement Agency in the United States, the U.S. Ambassador, and are believed to be behind the attempted assassination of Secretary of State, George Shultz, when he was visiting Bolivia. They have terrorized Colombia. The only thing they fear is being extradited to the United States. It was considered a big defeat for them when one of the five drug barons, Carlos Lehder Rivas, was extradited and tried. However, he was considered an outsider by the others, quickly replaced, and with the breaking down of Colombia's extradition system, it is unlikely that any of the others will go through a similar experience.

The drug barons have developed extensive transnational contacts. Ironically, this occurred mainly in 1984 when they assassinated the Justice Minister. The Colombian president became so angry at the audacity of the assassination that he put the heat on the drug barons, sequestering some of their property, raiding their processing laboratories, and threatening arrest. Previously the drug barons had brought most of the drugs from the major source centers of

Bolivia and Peru, processed them in Colombian laboratories, and then transshipped them to the United States. In 1984, they felt they had to leave Colombia at least temporarily for safety purposes and for finding contacts in other countries where they could set up processing laboratories. While abroad they also made contacts with more supply areas, and were able to work out deals with officials to help in the transshipment of drugs. Thus the Colombian network expanded into Brazil, Venezuela, Panama, Mexico, Honduras, Cuba, Haiti, the Bahamas, and the Turks and Caicos islands.[8]

The military in some of these countries was considered especially vulnerable to bribery. General Noriega, the military strongman of Panama, received $4.6 million in bribes for allowing the drug barons temporary residence, transshipment through Panamanian airports, and the laundering of drug profits in the many Panamanian banks.[9] In Haiti, Col. Jean-Claude Paul, head of an elite battalion, was given a large bribe to allow drug transshipment from Haiti's poorly policed coast, and at least ten other major officers were thought to be involved in drugs.[10] In Honduras high ranking military officers have been bribed, much to the dismay of the U.S., and the bribery has added to the many splits in the army.[11]

Civilian governments have also been vulnerable. The many isolated Bahama is-

---

[8]See Bradley Graham, "Impact of Colombian Traffickers Spreads," *The Washington Post*, February 24, 1988, pp. 1A and 22A, and Barbara Bradley, "Cracking the Drug Menace," *The Christian Science Monitor*, February 26, 1988, pp. 1 and 16 for long articles on this expanding network.

[9]See Merrill Collett, "Colombia's Drug Cartel Said To Aim at Military," *The Washington Post*, April 11, 1988, pp. 17A and 18A.

[10]See David Hancock, "Senator Told Haiti is a Drug Way Station," *The Miami Herald*, May 22, 1988, and "Colombian Drug Dealers Set Up Shop in Haiti," *The Washington Post*, July 12, 1988, p. 4A.

[11]See James LeMoyne, "Military Officers in Honduras are Linked to the Drug Trade," *The New York Times*, February 12, 1988, pp. 1 and 6.

lands were considered ideal transshipment points by the Colombian drug barons, and the Bahamian Prime Minister Lynden Pindling was bribed somewhere between $400,000 and $3 to 5 million for protection.[12] The chief minister Norman Saunder of the Turks and Caicos islands was similarly involved.[13] In Mexico the Colombian drug barons firmed up their relationship with their Mexican counterparts and also worked out deals for arms purchasing.[14] Large South American countries where the drug problem had not previously been a major problem also became involved in the network. Venezuela has been used increasingly as a transshipment point since the drug barons and Colombian guerrillas control the poorly patrolled border between the two countries.[15] In Brazil the drug barons linked up with the coca leaf growers in the Amazon, developed transshipment outlets, and tapped in on the emerging consumer market for drugs.[16]

The Colombian drug barons now account for 80 percent of the cocaine consumption in the United States. The domestic demand for drugs has been increasing in Brazil, Venezuela, and Ecuador, and the Colombian drug barons have been partially re-

sponsible for this problem as well.[17] The drug use in their own country, Colombia, has become extremely serious and added to the existing large crime rates.[18] The Colombian drug barons have developed a regional transnational network of immense importance. They have linked this with the Mafia network. If they should ever link with the Asian and the Middle Eastern drug suppliers and distributors, there would be a worldwide loosely coordinated transnational drug operation.

Drugs could also be spread by terrorists, which are already an existing loosely coordinated transnational grouping. So far it seems that only the pro-Iranian Hezbollah terrorists operating from the Bekaa Valley in Lebanon use drugs to help finance their operations and sell drugs in Europe to weaken the West.[19] It would seem that most terrorists are already financed adequately from hostage ransoms and aid from sponsoring governments. However, as one worried Israeli writer pointed out, terrorists if they so desired, could use their regular underground networks and diplomatic cover to distribute drugs worldwide, possibly linking up with criminal operators.[20]

THE INSIGNIFICANCE AND POROSITY OF NATIONAL BORDERS

Complex interdependency theorists often envisage transnational interactions that make borders less meaningful. Multinational corporations have received the most publicity. They still must receive their entry into foreign countries by legal procedures, however. This is not the situation for the worldwide movement of drugs. The drug

[12]See Robert Pear, "Drug Trade in Bahamas is Creeping Into Politics," *The New York Times*, December 23, 1984, p. 2E, section 4.

[13]See Joseph B. Treaster, "In Old Pirate Haunt, Daunting News of Drug Trade," *The New York Times*, March 13, 1985, p. 4.

[14]See Guy Gugliotta, "Mexico Drug War Becomes More Violent," *The Miami Herald*, June 15, 1988, p. 14A.

[15]See Alan Riding, "Colombian Drugs and Rebels Move in on Venezuela," *The New York Times*, January 20, 1988, p. 7.

[16]See Alan Riding, "Brazil Now a Vital Crossroad for Latin Cocaine Traffickers," *The New York Times*, August 28, 1988, pp. 1 and 8.

[17]See Clara Germani, "Abuse Rises in Coca Producing Nations," *The Christian Science Monitor*, July 21, 1986, p. 1.

[18]See Alan Riding, "Drug Abuse Catches Up to Dismayed Colombia," *The New York Times*, August 20, 1986, p. 4.

[19]See E.A. Wayne, "Militias Cooperate on Drug Trade to Pay for War-Against Each Other," *The Christian Science Monitor*, March 9, 1988, p. 1.

[20]See Luiz Simmons and Abdul Said (eds.), *Drugs, Politics and Diplomacy: The International Connection* (Beverly Hills: Sage Publication, 1974), p. 208.

barons look upon boundaries as inconveniences to be overcome. Only terrorists worldwide may outdo the drug operators in the ease which borders are crossed.

The insignificance of borders would be especially noticeable in geographic areas where governments have little control. This pertains to parts of Burma, Thailand, and Laos constituting the Golden Triangle. Large pack trains crossing the borders at will are the most common means of getting drugs out of the area. Another area is the Afghanistan and Pakistan border, controlled by fierce Afghan tribesmen who have long been involved in drugs.[21] In Latin America the coca cultivated in Bolivia and Peru has easily been flown to Colombia for processing by small planes taking off from remote airstrips often hacked from the jungle. Also, the Bolivian-Brazilian border and the Colombian-Venezuelan border present few obstacles to hinder the flow of drugs. Along many of the Third World borders the customs officials are extremely vulnerable to bribery due to their low pay.

It is not merely Third World borders that seem porous, however, for the United States has had little success in stopping drugs. Officials estimate that only 3 to 10 percent of drugs are seized on the U.S. border. The failure has not been due to lack of effort. The portion of the drug budget for interdiction rose from $399 million in 1982 to $1.3 billion in 1987, consuming almost one-third of the entire $4 billion allocation.

Much of the interdiction money went into a concerted effort to stop drugs from entering Florida. Vice-President Bush was put in charge of a South Florida Task Force. A Blue Lightning Operations Command Center was set up in Miami with great fanfare and given the latest in radar and other sophisticated equipment to track all of the

small planes and boats in the Caribbean. Added to this were three radar balloons, an AWAC plane, and twenty-four radars put on top of condominiums along the Florida coast to help detect smugglers. The patrolling of the Caribbean was beefed up. More Coast Guard cutters were used to patrol key straits and follow suspicious freighters, and the Customs Service received fast speedboats and planes to intercept drug smugglers. Yet the venture was considered a failure. The sophisticated radar equipment at times did not work and could not cover all of the many planes and boats in the Caribbean area. Drug smugglers flew under the radar network, kept shifting their transshipment locations, and devised new ways of getting drugs in by boat. Other reasons for the failure were attributed to interagency rivalry and a paucity of useful intelligence information.[22]

Many congressmen in the past have felt that bringing in the U.S. military could do the job. Yet a Defense Department report estimated that to seal the borders effectively would cost $22 billion and require 110 AWACs, ninety-six infantry battalions, fifty-three helicopter companies, 165 cruisers and destroyers, and seventeen fighter squadrons. One Rand study compared the problem to that of the U.S. attempting to interdict North Vietnamese supply routes into South Vietnam. Many congressmen in formulating the 1988 drug budget have shifted their focus from the supply side and interdiction to the demand for drugs in the U.S., realizing that successful interdiction is a virtual impossibility.

What makes drugs so hard to seize is that there are so many ways of getting drugs across the U.S. border. Normally one would

---

[21]See Lamour and Lamberti, *op.cit.,* chapter 11 for a detailed description of this area.

[22]See Jeff Leen, "Drug War Proving a Costly Failure," *The Miami Herald,* September 11, 1988, pp. 1A, 18A, and 19A and Jeff Leen, "Drug War Bedevils Blue Lightning," *The Miami Herald,* September 12, 1988, pp. 1A and 6A for an excellent two part series on this venture.

suppose that it would be the easiest to check individuals and their luggage as they go through the U.S. Customs. Yet the ways of hiding drugs have been ingenious.[23] Alert Customs Service personnel, specially trained dogs, and detection devices have led to the seizure of only a small amount of the drugs. Other ways of getting drugs in are even harder to control. Drugs have come in hidden in freighters and passenger planes, often with dock workers and airport ground crews bribed to get the drugs to their destination. Some thousands of smuggling flights a year involved the landing of small planes at hundreds of remote airstrips in Florida, other southern states, and the southwest. Another popular technique is to transfer drugs from larger boats to fast speedboats that go to remote coastal areas. The U.S.-Mexican border is especially porous. Drug smugglers have joined the wetbacks in crossing the Rio Grande River. If a major effort is made to choke off one of the ways of bringing in drugs, the smugglers will go to the other ways or think of new ideas. The supply of persons willing to take the chance of getting drugs across the border is unlimited since their payments are so high.

Drugs have also been carried across borders by diplomats in their diplomatic pouches which are immune from search under international law.[24] There have been a growing number of tourists, students, hippies, and celebrities who have taken small amounts of drugs across borders for their own personal use or to give or to sell to friends. The lengthy prison sentences and rough treatment given to those caught in many overseas countries do not seem to be much of a deterrent.[25]

If a thorough search were made of every person, plane, and ship moving across borders it could lead to a hindrance of trade and travel. There would be long waits of individuals going through customs, airport delays, and long lines of ships waiting to unload at ports. The few times the U.S. Customs Service has attempted a thorough search of cars, trucks, and individuals crossing U.S.-Mexican border cities has led to traffic snarls and strong complaints by citizens on both sides of the border.[26] Furthermore, overzealous searches of individuals could lead to complaints of violations of personal rights.

THE INSEPARABILITY OF THE DEMAND AND SUPPLY FACTORS LEADS TO INTERDEPENDENCE

The theory of complex interdependency should describe situations in which the involved participants are equally dependent upon each other. If one side is more influential than the other, it would be more useful to move toward evaluating relations according to dependency theory, so popular among scholars in Latin America and Africa. Dependency theory, most of it economic in nature, describes inequality, dominance, subordination, resentment, and accusations

[23]See Whitaker, *op.cit.*, pp. 308–312 for a description of over thirty ingenious ways. Also see Nicholas Gage, "Drug-Smuggling Logistics Bizarre and Often Total," *The New York Times*, April 22, 1975, pp. 1 and 24.

[24]See "Thorny Issue: Peeking Into a Privileged Pouch," *The New York Times*, August 1, 1988, p. 12 where the U.S. State Department opposed several congressional bills that would allow examination of pouches.
[25]The U.S. State Department attempts to warn U.S. citizens who travel of often horrible consequences of being caught, yet in 1986 some 952 Americans abroad were arrested on drug charges. See the State Department pamphlet GIST, "The Drug Problem: Americans Arrested Abroad," May 1987.
[26]See Robert Reinhold, "U.S. Drug Searches Snarl Border Traffic and Vex Businesses," *The New York Times*, February 16, 1987, pp. 1 and 8.

that the West has conspired to keep the Third World in its place. There is no possible way that dependency theory is appropriate in discussing the worldwide drug issue. The demand and supply factors make the relationship inseparable. It is not only the drug barons that prosper in the Third World but the many cultivators as well. The drug users in the West rely on the Third World for drugs. Drug addiction has caused horrendous personal, social, and criminal problems, and this paper has not attempted to belittle these problems. We may even have a situation that should be described as perverted or dysfunctional interdependence, but it is interdependence nevertheless. The Third World countries have had a great demand for drugs among its own people. Thus it is not just a Third World versus the West problem. The effect of Third World consumption is that it makes interdependence even more complex.

The demand for drugs has been increasing enormously within the last few decades. Drugs have overtaken oil and are the world's second biggest trade next to armaments, in value amounting to some 9 percent of all international merchandise. The heroin trade alone grosses more than $225 billion annually.

The demand for drugs has been publicized mainly as a U.S. problem. This is because the U.S. consumes about 60 percent of all illegal drugs in the world. Drug use has spread to all classes. The problem is prevalent in the urban slums particularly affecting Blacks and Puerto Ricans. All kinds of drugs have been used throughout the years. The latest is crack, a derivative of cocaine, which in three years has spread so rapidly in the cities of New York, Detroit, Miami, and Los Angeles that it has overwhelmed the police forces and is now considered uncontrollable.[27] The drug problem is

so prevalent, with 23 million Americans who have used drugs and millions addicted, that the old debate about whether drugs should be legalized has taken on a new urgency.[28] Drug use has been considered responsible for much of the crime in cities, and for this alone it has been taken more seriously than the problems of tobacco and alcohol.

Drug use has also spread rapidly in Western Europe. Great Britain's problem is so great that it is now considered of crisis proportions. All of the Western European countries, including France, West Germany, Italy, Austria, Switzerland, Spain, and the Netherlands have major drug problems. Canada and Australia are no better off.[29]

The Third World drug consumption has often been overlooked. Yet studies are now interested in determining whether consumption levels are approaching those of the West. Every geographic region of the world seems to have major problems except Africa where drug use is in its early stages. In Asia the addiction numbers are Thailand 500,000, Burma 48,000, Malaysia 104,000, Singapore 10,000, and Vietnam 100,000 for some of the examples.[30] In Latin America drug use has been prevalent historically among the Andean Indians in Peru and Bolivia, but has spread rapidly to other countries. Colombia alone has some estimated 3 million drug addicts out of a population of 28 million. The Middle East is another area of heavy use. Drug consumption has been so

---

[27]See Michael Wines, "Against a Tide of Drugs in New York, the Police Resort to a Holding Action," *The New York Times*, June 24, 1988, p. 12.

[28]See John Finlator, *The Drugged Nation* (New York: Simon & Schuster, 1973), chapter 9 for the different viewpoints. Also see Martin Merzer, "Latest Proposal in Drug War: Legalization," *The Miami Herald*, June 19, 1988, pp. 1A and 10A for two articles giving contending points.

[29]See Whitaker, *op.cit.*, pp. 39–49 for a detailed description of the British problem and pp. 51–59 for short descriptions of the other country problems.

[30]*Ibid*, pp. 65–70. See C.P. Spencer and V. Navaratnam, *Drug Abuse in East Asia* (New York: Oxford University Press, 1981), for a detailed description of each country in Asia in regard to the drug problem among youth and adults, the preventive and rehabilitation efforts, and law enforcement.

common historically in Pakistan, Afghanistan, and Iran that the area is often compared to the Golden Triangle in Asia. The Afghan guerrillas raised poppies even during their battles with the Russians and it will be the first crop the refugees will attend to on returning from Pakistan.[31] In Egypt, Oman, and several other countries the chewing of kat has increased.

The drug problem has even spread to the Soviet Union, which was considered to have only an alcohol crisis. The use of hashish has increased in the Moslem areas of Soviet Central Asia, and numerous Soviet soldiers became hooked on heroin and opium while serving in Afghanistan, much like the experiences of U.S. soldiers while in Vietnam.[32] Only Albania in its isolation seems to have no drug problem. Countries such as China that have drastically reduced drug consumption are few. Saudi Arabia and Iran have declared the death penalty for drug smugglers, but this measure seems too harsh for most governments.[33]

The supply of drugs seems unlimited. This is not due merely to the zealousness of drug barons. The peasant cultivators of opium and coca in most areas of the world are poor, living in harsh geographic areas, and resentful of their central government. They will go to the best cash crop to better their existence. In the Golden Triangle, for example, peasants find that opium is labor intensive and perfect for their small plots, can be grown on a variety of terrain, takes only two-thirds as much labor time as rice, is non-perishable, and easily transported. The poppy hulls can also be used in cattle feed and the stalks burned as fuel.[34] Peasants have balked at crop substitution programs whenever they have been tried, feeling that no matter how much aid is given by the central government in helping to grow something else, it will not have the same value. The peasants have been resentful of forceful cleanup operations. In the Huallaga Valley of Peru, one of the main coca producing areas in Latin America, peasants have demonstrated and threatened Peruvian police agents during raids in the past.[35]

In some countries drugs have been used by peasants themselves to the extent that it has long been accepted as part of their culture. In Bolivia and Peru almost all of the Indians chew coca as an "energizer" to alleviate hunger and to adapt better to manual labor at high altitudes. Coca leaves can be bought in any marketplace and are considered a valued gift and brought by guests at festivities.[36] In parts of the Middle East the chewing of kat is considered a way of facilitating conversation in special rooms at social functions.[37] In Iran the use of opium has been part of the country's traditional heritage and serves certain social and cultural needs.[38]

The supply of drugs is also facilitated by the value it adds to the economy of many Third World countries. Their governments are plagued by enormous debt problems and unpopular austerity programs. Most of their leaders have not been bribed to protect drugs. However, they cannot but help notice

[31]See Robert Pear, "State Department Foresees Big Increase in Opium Crops in Afghanistan," *The New York Times,* September 7, 1988, p. 6.

[32]Russia finally admitted the problem when it surprised the U.S. by requesting a formal agreement with the Drug Enforcement Agency on exchanging information on international smugglers and drug use effects. See Michal Isikoff, "Soviets Suggest Swapping Facts About Drug Use," *The Washington Post,* July 20, 1988, p. 13A.

[33]See Donna Fenn Heintzen, "Death Penalty Deters Drug Smugglers in Saudi Arabia," *The Miami Herald,* July 28, 1988, p. 2A.

[34]See Andre McNicoll, *Drug Trafficking: A North-South Perspective* (Ottawa: North-South Institute, 1983), pp. 23, 30, 36.

[35]See Tyler Bridges, "Drug Traffickers, Guerrillas Curtail Peru's Antidrug Efforts," *The Christian Science Monitor,* April 28, 1987, pp. 9 and 12.

[36]See McNicoll, *op.cit.,* pp. 44 and 47.

[37]See Whitaker, *op.cit.,* pp. 63 and 64.

[38]See Simmons and Said (eds.), *op.cit.,* the chapter by Hamid Mowlana, "The Politics of Opium in Iran: A Social-Psychological Interface," pp. 159–181.

that drugs can benefit their economies. Bolivia would be bankrupt if it were not for drugs. In the Bahamas cocaine is estimated to contribute 10 percent of the gross national product. In Jamaica drugs exceed twice the value of all exports combined.[39]

The United States itself has had a drug cultivation problem in northern California and southern Oregon that is a microcosm of the Third World. Entrepreneurs cultivated marijuana in the national forests to such a large extent that the areas were considered unsafe. Some townspeople, poorly off because of the recession in lumbering, went into business for themselves. Many of the small towns prospered. The Drug Enforcement Agency with the cooperation of state and local police carried on several raids that were able to eliminate 40 percent of the planting, but have not been able to eliminate the rest. During the raids many inhabitants of the area complained of overzealous police state tactics. Finally, environmentalists objected to the use of paraquat spraying, as they have likewise done for the Huallaga Valley of Peru, arguing that it is an environmental hazard.[40] So far no Third World leaders have goaded U.S. officials, saying that if the U.S. cannot eradicate its own problem, it should not expect superior efforts abroad.

It has often been said that Third World leaders are finally eradicating drugs because their own children have become addicts. This would be a strong motivation but so far no evidence has been given of this actually happening abroad.[41] Furthermore, the leaders or officials would have to be in the type of governmental positions where they could do something about the problem and persuade others to go along. It has also been said that the Third World leaders will make greater efforts as their own citizens become more addicted. So far, it is difficult to discern any correlation. The leaders themselves may be getting drug payoff money. Or they may feel they do not have the power to discipline important officials in the government or party or military that are taking bribes. Finally, their military and police may be both unenthusiastic about and incompetent in carrying out drug raids, knowing that they will not get a welcome reception in the rural areas they enter. Perhaps the best that can be said is that several Latin American leaders have said that they do not want their country to become another Colombia.

THE UNLIKELIHOOD AND IMPRACTICALITY OF USING JOINT MILITARY FORCES TO ERADICATE DRUGS

Complex interdependence theorists have stressed that the use of military force is completely inappropriate for resolving interde-

pendence problems. This is contrasted quite often with the older realist school which assumed that military force would be used quite often if need be to defend and further vital security interests. It seems rather obvious that military force cannot resolve pop-

---

[39]See Whitaker, *op.cit.*, p. 60.

[40]See Robert Lindsey, "Raids Reduce California Marijuana Planting Forty Percent," *The New York Times*, July 25, 1985, p. 10; Michael Isikoff, "U.S. Targets Domestic Crop of Marijuana," *The Washington Post*, July 3, 1988, pp. 1A and 22A; Michael Isikoff, "Paraquat Spraying to Resume at Suspected Marijuana Fields," *The Washington Post*, July 14, 1988, p. 3A; Michael Isikoff, "Seeds of Success or Budding 'Police State'?", *The Washington Post*, September 25, 1988, p. 3A.

[41]The past U.S. Secretary of Interior Donald Hodel had all 17,000 departmental employees tested for drugs due to the tragic death of his son. Thus, there is one U.S. example. See Judith Havemann, "Behind Hodel's Tough Antidrug Policy: The Tragic Death of a Son," *The Washington Post*, July 7, 1988, p. 3A.

ulation, food, and the environmental problems of acid rain and carbon dioxide. The drug topic, however, is more difficult to analyze. National antidrug units at times actually do use military equipment and force to stage surprise raids in the drug areas. They will rip out and burn the plants, demolish processing laboratories, arrest drug smugglers, and defend themselves with arms if necessary. All of these raids, however, have merely dented the problem. Thus the pertinent inquiry is to determine whether there could be cooperative military efforts to stage raids that would be more effective. Conceivably the cooperative military efforts would lead to better trained units that could cover many more areas with much more regularity.

Proposals have abounded from many sources during the last three years that move in this direction. The U.S. Ambassador to the Barbados recommended the creation of a multinational police force to combat drugs.[42] A U.S. Congressman submitted a bill in 1988 that called for the formation of a Latin American strike force that would be trained in the United States.[43] The Joint Chiefs of Staff recommended a more moderate plan in 1985 that would have the U.S. military train mobile drug teams from each Latin American country.[44] The Washington Post editorialized after the death of a U.S. Drug Enforcement Agency agent in Mexico that the two governments should form a joint narcotics police force that would have full legal authority to work in both countries.[45]

These proposals would seem to build on cooperative efforts that appear promising. In 1985 Peru and Colombia cooperated in a drug raid in the Leticia area, Colombia providing the helicopters for a Peruvian police force that carried out the assault, and Colombia sealing the borders to cut off escape routes.[46] In 1986 a hemispheric meeting was held under the auspices of the Organization of American States that created a new Inter-American Commission for Drug Control modeled after the Inter-American Commission on Human Rights that would help to coordinate efforts and share intelligence.[47] Finally, in 1988 the U.S. and Latin American governments coordinated plans, with the U.S. beefing up its border interdiction, Peru carrying out raids in the Huallaga Valley, and Colombia and Venezuela coordinating joint operations along their common border.[48]

In assessing the significance of these cooperative efforts, however, skepticism seems to be in order. The bilateral Latin American efforts have been few and far between. There has been little heard from the Inter-American Commission for Drug Control, implying it could well be a paper organization. The U.S. cooperation with Latin American governments was a one time affair. There has been a lack of follow through and the type of permanent concerted effort that would be necessary to be more effective.

The proposals for combined forces would be resisted in Latin America. The OAS has never had an Inter-American Army except for its emergency force in the 1965 Dominican Republic civil war episode,

[42]See Paul Russo's letter, "Multinational Police Force Should Fight Drugs," *The New York Times*, July 2, 1988, p. 14.

[43]See Carlos Harrison, "Measure Would Escalate War on Drugs," *The Miami Herald*, March 22, 1988, p. 3A.

[44]See George Wilson, "Military Urges Wider Drug War," *The Washington Post*, June 20, 1985, p. 22A.

[45]See "Why Not a Joint Force," *The Washington Post*, August 30, 1986, p. 22A.

[46]See Michael Smith, "Peru Scores a Victory In War on Drug Traffic," *The Washington Post*, August 19, 1985, p. 19A.

[47]See Alan Riding, "Latin Lands Join Anti-Drug Effort," *The New York Times*, April 27, 1986, p. 14.

[48]See Michael Isikoff, "Nations Join In Attacks on Colombian Drug Cartels," *The Washington Post*, August 31, 1988, p. 4A.

so there is no precedent for a special multi-lateral drug force. The Latin American governments have sanctified nonintervention as a guiding principle in their foreign affairs. A United Nations multinational drug police force is even more unlikely. The many UN ad hoc peacekeeping armies have worked fairly well, but their roles have been completely different from what a military trained in drug eradication would do, and the UN armies use force only in self-defense. Moreover, there have never been any UN ad hoc peacekeeping armies in Latin America, where conceivably a drug force would be the most useful. The UN has been active in the past few years on the drug issue in regard to discussion, reports, and sponsoring a 1988 treaty that would help to halt the bank laundering of drug profits and improve extradition procedures for drug barons, but there has been nothing from all of this moving toward a multilateral force.[49]

Latin American bilateral cooperation with the U.S. is also unlikely. U.S. military forces in Latin America would not be popular, leading to domestic political opposition cries of Yankee dominance. The proposal for a joint U.S. and Mexican narcotics force sounds reasonable, but would never be accepted. The political system in Mexico is already under considerable stress. Mexico is ultra-sensitive about U.S. intervention, and the state and local police forces are riddled through with drug bribery corruption, all of which are factors dooming the idea.

The U.S. cooperative experience with Bolivia in 1986 is illustrative of the problems of joint cooperation. President Paz Estenssoro, democratically elected and concerned about the enormity of the drug problem in Bolivia, invited the U.S. military to help transport his drug units to drug producing regions for raids. The U.S. military, aware of the sensitivity of the arrangement, agreed to provide six Black Hawk helicopters and 160 military personnel to operate them under the conditions that they would stay no longer than sixty days and would only transport the units. However, right and left opposition parties complained about an infringement of national sovereignty, the labor federation went on strike because of this and economic reasons, and the Bolivian peasants in the areas raided complained that they were losing their main source of income. Also, the raids were temporarily so successful that the government complained that its economy was suffering, and requested a huge loan from the U.S. . . .

Even if cooperative military ventures could be put together, one other problem remains that would make them impractical. Drug elimination in certain areas would only lead to an increase in drug cultivation in other countries of the region or other areas of the world. . . . The profitability in drugs is the main reason for this phenomenon, and there are few signs that profitability is decreasing. The drug issue is worldwide in scope and will exist for a considerable time to come.

---

[49]See Robert Pear, "World Pact Aims at Drug Financing," *The New York Times*, October 2, 1988, p. 5.

28 Multinational Corporations

CHARLES W. KEGLEY, JR., AND EUGENE R. WITTKOPF

Professors at The University of South Carolina and Louisiana State University, respectively, the authors have stressed a holistic approach to IR. Professor Kegley is President-elect of the International Studies Association.

It is clear that multinationals have become important actors in world politics in that decisions critical to nation-states (especially those in the Third World) are now made by entities over which those nations may not have control. Thus, the question of control of MNCs constitutes a significant issue in the debate about the costs and benefits of multinational corporations.

The question of control is not confined to the Third World, for the international interests of MNCs are not necessarily more compatible with the interests of their home governments than with those of their hosts. As one senior foreign policy official in the United States declared at the time of the Dresser Industries controversy, "Basically we're in an impossible situation. You don't want to get rid of the advantages of this international economic system, but if you try to exercise control for foreign policy reasons, you cut across sovereign frontiers." Furthermore, the MNCs' complex patterns of ownership and licensing arrangements mean that it is often difficult to equate the MNCs' interests with particular national jurisdictions. General Electric, for example, one of the most "American" of all American MNCs, has granted licenses for the production of energy-related equipment to Nuovo Pignone of Italy, Mitsubishi Heavy Industries and Hitachi of Japan, Mannessmann and AEG Telefunken of West Germany, John Brown Engineering of Great Britain, and Thomassen Holland of the Netherlands (U.S. Office of Technology Assessment, 1981). Controlling such a complex pattern of interrelationships, joint ventures, and shared ownership for any particular national purpose is nearly impossible. "The internationalization of the economy—which the U.S. spearheaded—has rendered obsolete old ideas of economic warfare," Richard J. Barnet, coauthor of *Global Reach*, observed in 1982. "You can't find targets any more, and if you aim at a target you often find it's yourself."

The potential long-run importance of MNCs for transforming world order is also depicted in *Global Reach:*

> The global corporation is the most powerful human organization yet devised for colonizing the future. By scanning the entire

Excerpted from *World Politics Trend and Transformation*, 3rd ed. New York: St. Martin's Press, 1989, pp. 171–5. Reprinted by permission Copyright © St. Martin's Press, 1989. (Footnotes omitted)

planet for opportunities, by shifting its resources from industry to industry and country to country, and by keeping its overriding goal simple—worldwide profit maximization—it has become an institution of unique power. The World Managers are the first to have developed a plausible model for the future that is global. . . . In making business decisions today they are creating a politics for the next generation. (Barnet and Müller, 1974:363)

Whether the corporate visionaries who manage the MNCs will contribute to the creation of a more prosperous, peaceful, and just world—as some hope, and others, whose interests are threatened by a new world political economy, fear—is questionable. "For some, the global corporation holds the promise of lifting mankind out of poverty and bringing the good life to everyone. For others, these corporations have become a law unto themselves; they are mini-empires which exploit all for the benefit of a few" (Gilpin, 1975).

Those who view the MNC favorably see national competitiveness giving way to a supranational world order in which welfare issues will be more important than narrow ideological or security contests. From this perspective, the MNC, which knows no national boundaries or national loyalties and whose profits (except for the arms manufacturers) are threatened by national aggressiveness and militarism, plays the role of a "peacemonger" in world politics (Ewing, 1974).

Those more negatively disposed toward MNCs maintain that because of their desire for political stability in order to realize maximum profits, MNCs are often prone to align with repressive political regimes and "powerfully oppose the kinds of revolutionary upheavals that in many backward areas are probably the essential precondition for a genuine modernization" (Heilbroner, 1977). Furthermore, multina-

tionals may be the agents of a worldwide dispersion of economic benefits, but the distribution of these benefits is likely to be very uneven. Hence, multinationals perpetuate and deepen global inequality; because they threaten national autonomy, the rise of independent, transnational corporations challenges to some degree the governments of all countries.

Given the global reach, economic power, and ostensible autonomy of the MNCs, efforts by nation-states to strengthen their bargaining positions vis-à-vis the MNCs are to be expected. Through the United Nations Commission on Transnational Corporations, the less-developed countries have sought a code of conduct to govern the activities of transnational corporations. In 1986 the commission put forward a proposal that sought to cope with the legitimate interests of both host countries and multinational corporations in such matters as transfer pricing, taxation, ownership and control, and environmental protection.

Other attempts to control the MNCs include the Convention on the Settlement of Investment Disputes, negotiated under the auspices of the World Bank, and the Declaration on International Investment and Multinational Enterprises, embraced by the Organization for Economic Cooperation and Development.

In recent years the developing nations have become less strident in their demands for controls on multinationals and more pragmatic in dealing with them, largely because of a more realistic recognition of the role that MNCs play as agents of investment, trade, and technology transfer in today's interdependent global political economy, and perhaps because they believe that the risks can be managed. Whether such a change in attitude will be conducive to moving those codes of conduct already devised for controlling MNCs toward an effective international regulatory regime, or whether they will sap the impetus and political will to do so, remains to be seen. In either case, contention over the role of multinational corporations in national and international affairs will remain, for states often view the costs and benefits of MNCs quite differently.

NONSTATE ACTORS, INTERNATIONAL REGIMES, AND THE TRANSFORMATION OF WORLD POLITICS

Because multinational corporations challenge the nation-state, they also challenge the very foundations of the contemporary global system. But states will not disappear quickly. Conflict between them and the MNCs is therefore to be expected. As Robert Heilbroner (1977) has argued, "what we seem to be witnessing . . . is a conflict between two modes of organizing human affairs—a 'vertical' mode that finds its ultimate expression in the pan-national flows of production of the giant international corporation, and a 'horizontal' mode expressed in the jealously guarded boundaries of the nation-state."

In the meantime, the rise of multinational corporations and the prodigious growth of other types of nonstate actors challenge the traditional state-centric theory of international politics, which holds that nation-states are the primary actors on the world's political stage. Because the state has "purposes and power," according to this view, it "is the basic unit of action; its main agents are the diplomat and soldier. The interplay of governmental politics yields the pattern of behavior that students of international politics attempt to understand and that practitioners attempt to adjust or to control" (Nye and Keohane, 1971; see also Mansbach et al., 1976).

Clearly such a view no longer adequately depicts the complexity of world politics. As described in Chapter 2, the behaviors of state and nonstate actors sometimes converge to form *international regimes*. Sovereign states are important members of international regimes. Oran R. Young (1980) argues, in fact, that "the members of international regimes are always sovereign states." Significantly, however, he quickly adds that "the parties carrying out the actions governed by international regimes are often private entities." In this sense the nonstate actors discussed in this chapter—IGOs, INGOs, MNCs, and TNBs—are often the key participants in the regularized conduct of contemporary international relations encompassed by international regimes in such diverse areas as the law of the sea, nuclear nonproliferation, the global monetary and trade systems, and the global food system.

Moving from the level of cooperative international interactions to the level of foreign policy making within nation-states, an adequate conceptualization of contemporary world politics must also acknowledge the influence of nonstate actors on a government's ability to formulate public policy and on the ties among them. Nonstate actors help build and broaden the foreign policy agendas of national decision makers by serving as transmission belts through which one nation's policies become sensitive to another's (Keohane and Nye, 1975). At the same time, some nonstate actors are capable of pursuing their interests largely outside the direct control of nation-states while simultaneously involving governments in particular problems as a result of their activities. . . .

The transformation of world politics is being played out in these complex, interdependent relationships among diverse national and transnational actors. This by no means indicates that the nation-state is dead, however. Governments still retain the capacity to influence, indeed to shape, transnational interactions. It is not accidental that supranationalism (as in Western Europe) has been confined largely to economic interactions and that matters of national security are confined largely to government-to-government interactions.

Thus it is important not to exaggerate the importance of nonstate actors and their impact on nation-states. Nation-states retain a (near) monopoly on the use of coercive force in the international system. The majority of new international governmental organizations founded in the 150-year period since the Congress of Vienna (1815) were established *after* the most warlike periods, but there is almost no association between the number of IGOs in the international system and the incidence of interstate war during the 150-year period. The nation-state cannot be lightly dismissed, therefore; it still molds the activities of nonstate actors more than its behavior is molded by them. Hence it would be premature to abandon the focus on the nation-state in international politics, just as it would be inadequate to regard the state as the only relevant actor or the sole determinant of its fate.

29 *THE COMMUNICATIONS REGIME: THE CNN-GULF WAR EXAMPLE*

BARBIE ZELIZER

Barbie Zelizer is an assistant professor in the Department of Rhetoric and Communication at Temple University, Philadelphia, PA.

The world of journalism is cluttered with practices that should generate questions about newsworkers' ability to act as authoritative reporters of events of the "real world." From news gathering to news presentation, a journalist's authority often derives from the fact that the public cannot verify what he or she has done. This situates the establishment of journalistic authority within the hands of journalists, and their authority is informed by their own decisions about how, why, and in what way they turn ordinary events into news stories. Such decisions in turn become the topic of discussions among journalists.

This is even more the case with major events, like the Gulf War. While the war's central events were unraveled in the eye of the media, their telling was accompanied by extensive discourse among journalists and news organizations about who put those events into narrative form, and in what way. This discourse particularly centered on the Cable News Network (CNN), the value of satellite-fed communication, and the advantages and disadvantages of reporting a war in "real time." In discussing the Gulf War, journalists thereby turned war stories into a forum for discussing issues of concern to the professional community.

This article considers how this took place—how journalists entwined stories about CNN, satellite-fed technology, and "real-time" war reporting with Gulf War discourse. The article uses what Glaser and Strauss (1967) call a "strategically chosen example" to track down journalistic mediated and professional discourse about covering the Gulf War. Analysis is based on systematic examination of the public discourse by which reporters discussed their part in covering the Gulf War, as it appeared in the printed press, television news, professional reviews, and trade journals.[1] In so doing, it addresses the emergence of the Gulf War as a critical incident for journalism professionals, which helped journalists redefine boundaries of appropriate practice.

[1] Discussions of Gulf War coverage appeared between January and August 1991 and were located via the *Current Guide to Periodical Literature*. The *New York Times, Philadelphia Inquirer,* and select television programs were also scanned during the same time period, as was the trade press (*Columbia Journalism Review, Washington Journalism Review, The Quill,* and *Electronic Media*) and newsletters of professional organizations (ASNE *Bulletin* and the Associated Press' *AP Log*).

Regardless of what they call them, journalists have long used critical incidents as a way to frame the hows and whys of journalistic practice. Critical incidents are what Levi-Strauss once called "hot moments," phenomena or events through which a society or culture assesses its own significance (Levi-Strauss, 1966, p. 259). Gerbner coined the term "critical incident" in his discussion of decision-making processes in media organizations (Gerbner, 1973, p. 562). He allowed that critical incidents give organizational members a way to defuse challenges to recognized authority. When employed discursively, critical incidents refer to those moments by which people air, challenge, and negotiate their own boundaries of practice. For journalists, discourse about critical incidents suggests a way of attending to events that are instrumental for the continued well-being of the journalistic community.

A number of events in journalism history can be seen as having functioned as critical incidents. Watergate—the scandal that journalists uncovered—displayed the appropriate boundaries of investigative journalism (Schudson, 1978, in press; Woodward & Bernstein, 1976). The Kennedy assassination allowed the journalistic community to negotiate its response to the ascent of television news (Zelizer, 1990, in press). The Vietnam War helped journalists rethink the hows and whys of televisual reporting and journalistic responsibility during wartime (Arlen, 1969; Braestrup, 1977). Critical incidents of different kinds illuminate different rules and conventions about journalistic practice and authority.

At the heart of critical incidents is discourse about more general topics at issue for journalism professionals. The Kennedy assassination, for example, emerged at a time when the professionalization of journalists was uppermost and the legitimation of television news questionable. Journalists used assassination stories to address both agendas (Zelizer, in press). Using discourse in this way helps journalists attend to different notions about journalistic practice by telling and retelling the stories of major public events.

Critical incidents are generally shaped by discourse about two features: technology and archetypal figures. Technology, or the devices that shape an incident into news, offers a stage for journalism professionals to experiment with new ways of achieving work-related goals. During the Vietnam War, journalists were given the opportunity to append filmed pictures to words in reporting the war on television, even if a certain time lag was involved (Braestrup, 1977). At the time of the Kennedy assassination, live television gave the American public its first live televisual experience of a major public event. The shooting of Kennedy's presumed assassin, Lee Harvey Oswald, on television prompted reporters to consider the advantages—and disadvantages—of live coverage (Zelizer, in press). Changes in technology thereby form the backdrop against which a critical incident is acted out, and made meaningful for those involved in its relay.

Archetypal figures, or the individuals who successfully use the technology of news reporting, are an instrumental part of a critical incident's development. They provide the faces behind the technological devices. The Kennedy assassination produced the Walter Cronkites and Dan Rathers, reporters who covered the story in what came to be referenced as exemplary television journalism (Zelizer, in press). Watergate generated the Bob Woodwards and Carl Bernsteins (Woodward & Bernstein, 1976), both of whom were seen as exemplar investigative journalists.

Within this context, the Gulf War can be seen as a potentially critical incident for journalism professionals. As *Time* magazine opined: "Like the Kennedy assassination or the space-shuttle disaster, the outbreak of war in the Gulf was one of those historic events destined to be remembered forever in the terms by which television defined it" (Zoglin, 1991a, p. 69). Called by one trade journal "the biggest news story in decades" (Boot, 1991, p. 23), it problematized for journalists the hows and whys of the newest dimension of news-gathering technology—the satellite-fed television news report. At the same time, it offered a forum for negotiating the response of the journalistic community to that same technology, as it was already being successfully employed by CNN.

LIVE FROM THE GULF

From the onset, the Gulf War offered a forum for journalists to discuss concerns about the profession. For most journalists, covering the Gulf War exemplified the ultimate dilemma of wartime reporting, which, in *Time*'s view, involved "how to communicate events fairly and accurately, without revealing confidential military information" (Zoglin, 1991c, p. 44). The growing availability of live satellite-fed television communication from within enemy territory made wartime reporting particularly visible to the public, in all its negative and positive aspects. It "opened up the news-gathering process to millions of people" (Osborne, 1991, p. 2), and showed them how "disorganized, sloppy and unappetizing the process can be" (Greenfield, 1991, p. 7).

It also made the war a "real-time" story. As U.S. viewers watched air raid alerts of SCUD attacks in real time, so did the Iraqis. Reporting real-time war constituted an unprecedented professional challenge for many journalists, who needed to act fast, "professionally," in unknown territory—and all in the eye of the camera. This generated the feeling that "for much of American journalism, especially broadcasting, the implications of the gulf war will be as far reaching as they are for the Middle East" (Katz, 1991, p. 29).

Yet once the war began, news organizations moved to accommodate unusually large audiences. Newsstand sales of *News-week* doubled (Diamond, 1991b), and dailies like the *Philadelphia Inquirer* and the *Boston Globe* sold up to 20,000 more copies per day (Zoglin, 1991b, p. 78). Newspapers printed second editions, supplements, and wraparound sections ("The Persian Gulf Explodes," 1991). Television offered news coverage that clarified the war effort (for example, "Meet the Press," 1991). Special issues of the trade press and proceedings of professional forums were devoted to war coverage.

Journalists' fundamental unfamiliarity with the reporting of modern wartime technology, however, gave coverage the aura of a Nintendo game. As media critic Peter Braestrup saw it:

> A new generation of journalists is learning about war and they're learning about the military . . . They're ahistorical; they can't remember any precedents for anything. They keep discovering the world anew. They either concentrate on high-tech stories or on what an ABC producer described as "boo-hoo journalism," that is, asking "How do you feel?" not "What do you know?" . . . They're yuppies in the desert (quoted in Valeriani, 1991, p. 26).

Time lamented the scarcity of "reliable, objective information about the war's progress" (Zoglin, 1991c, p. 44). Journalists were faulted for surrendering to governmental attempts at censorship (Boot, 1991), providing what Hodding Carter called "essentially phony coverage" (quoted in Valeriani, 1991, p. 28), toeing the government line (Massing, 1991; Schanberg, 1991). *U.S. News & World Report* claimed that all the press corps had to show for its coverage was "a big black eye" (Gergen, 1991, p. 57). Television addiction, said the editor, had turned into a "sour distaste for journalists." A critic for *The Progressive* went further in commenting that journalists were "on call twenty-four hours a day to report that they know nothing" (Landau, 1991, p. 26).

Perhaps as a means of compensating for insufficient reportage, reporters entwined the war story with the story of those doing the reporting. Television networks began to offer programs that concentrated on the media and the Gulf (i.e., *The Press Goes to War*, 1991; *The Media and the Military*, 1991). *TV Guide* tracked journalistic celebrities who became famous for their war coverage (Lieberman, Stein, & Collins, 1991) and relayed reporters' experiences at war, as if journalists, not soldiers, were the privileged tellers of tales from the front (Stein, 1991). As one critic wryly observed, "the United States has nearly 500,000 troops in the Gulf Region, and the only people you see in jeopardy are reporters . . . the process of reporting had become the story" (Rosenberg, 1991, pp. 17–18).

In the spring of 1991, *Newsweek* published a special commemorative war issue, which hailed reporters' cooperation with each other and their ability to overcome professional challenges like desert heat or censorship restrictions ("The Story Behind the Story," 1991, p. 3). The more innovative the activity, the more attention it received: One journalists shaved his head to spare himself the effort of grooming while reporting the war; another lost 15 pounds during his seven weeks in the region. *Newsweek*'s reporting was lauded (by the magazine's own staff) as "prescient," "heroic," and "tremen-

dous." It brought journalists "as close to writing history as journalism goes" ("The Story Behind the Story," 1991, p. 3). Because it introduced a story about Americans at war, this article placed journalists at the forefront not only of efforts to tell the story but of the war effort itself.

Television journalism provided a particularly fertile forum for reporters' war discourse. Television became the "proscenium of the theater of war," said veteran newsperson Fred Friendly (quoted in *The Media and the Military*, 1991), in that many activities took place before its cameras. The war's onset seemed to have been timed to coincide with the networks' evening news programs, and night after night Americans were treated to action that heated up as prime time neared. Television networks broke into scheduled programs with live shots of reporters under SCUD attack. Even radio borrowed or purchased television audio in order to keep up with the story (Collins, 1991, p. 29). From gas-masked reporters to teary Iraqis outside a bombed shelter to scenes of Kuwaitis hanging up American flags made of old pajamas, the war for most Americans "ended as it had begun—on television" (Diamond, 1991a, p. 26).

The war's emplottment thus favored the television journalist. One reporter offered the view that the "dearth of uncensored, firsthand information about the war [forced] the press—especially television—to focus on the few parts of the story reporters can witness" (Zoglin, 1991c, p. 45). This made the eyewitness accounts of television reporters one of the few authoritative relays of the war coverage. As one press reporter recalled, "a friend took a picture of me the other day taking notes in front of a television set. That's what being a war correspondent has come to" (quoted in Zoglin, 1991b, p. 78).

An emphasis on television news sometimes turned nonnewsworthy events into news, largely because television technology was there to report them. "To have technology is to use it," said David Halberstam, as he lamented the widening gap between the immediacy offered by satellite-fed technology and the instantaneous journalism it created, and the time needed to make reliable news judgments (Halberstam, 1991, p. 1). One bizarre recasting of events "came not when General Powell unveiled his diagrams of damaged Iraqi targets, but when CNN's Charles Jaco scrambled for his gas mask on the air in Saudi Arabia" (Zoglin, 1991c, p. 45). Called the "biggest gaffe" of the war by one account, it nonetheless was reported by nearly every news organization. The incident not only displayed the emotional toll of reporting war in real time, accompanied by a technology that superseded one's ability to gain composure, but it called on journalists to consider establishing new boundaries of appropriate behavior.

Network news organizations could not adopt the setup required of reporting the war in real time for long. The story called for reporters to be constantly on call, cramming "three years' worth of stories into three weeks (Diamond, 1991b, p. 33). The breaking story, one reporter said, was

". . . old by dinnertime. Satellite-linked stations and CNN, serving 58.9 million homes, can and do give the viewers the day's hot news well before the network newscasts crank up" (Sharbutt, 1991, p. 5D). By contrast, CNN's "ubiquity, mobility and hustle seemed to leave [its] network competitors paralyzed" (Katz, 1991, p. 29). The cost of covering breaking news had generated a situation whereby the "networks [couldn't] afford to be in the breaking news business anymore" (Katz, 1991, p. 29). As the cost of coverage rose, they were unable to continue covering the story, no longer competent to run it in its most developed technological form. *Newsweek* went so far as to claim that the night the war began was "the night the networks died" (Alter, 1991, p. 41).

From the beginning, then, journalists linked issues of professionalism with discourse about war coverage. Stories of the Gulf War raised questions about the preferred form of journalistic practice, that addressed not only long-standing concerns about censorship, editorial integrity, and economic viability but a specific issue related to the Gulf War—how to establish authority for reportage in real time.

THE ASCENDANCY OF CNN

Discussions of the Gulf War focused on CNN for its successful usage of the newest news-gathering technology, the satellite-fed communication. CNN not only distributed news by satellite but brought portable satellite uplinks, called "flyaway dishes," to the front line. This enabled journalists to collect news by satellite, introducing faster news transmission and generating a continuous stream of news copy from diverse locations. Because CNN had successfully employed this technology, the story of Gulf War coverage became entwined with the

story of CNN's technological mastery and its emergence as a viable news organization.

Network news was vividly contrasted with cable news during the initial shelling of Baghdad, when ABC, NBC, and CNN all succeeded in transmitting reports for their correspondents. Within minutes, only CNN was left with an operable line, and its three reporters provided what *Time* called "an exceptional, and perhaps unprecedented, live account of the start of war from inside an enemy capital" (Zoglin, 1991a, p. 69). Journalists and news organizations uneasily watched what CNN would do next:

> The CNN team had what every other American news organization—the old-line networks, the newspapers, and the wire services—wishes it had: implicit recognition on the part of Iraqi authorities that it is the preeminent news-gathering force in the world, a continuing and officially sanctioned presence in the Iraqi capital, and the technology that allows its reporters to get their stories out (Diamond, 1991b, p. 30).

CNN possessed the ability to present, transmit, and distribute news twenty-four hours a day, making it the sole news organization capable of "keeping up" with satellite-fed communication.

As the war progressed, other media began to notice CNN's coverage. Local stations signed on to carry CNN affiliates and bypass the other traditional networks (Mott, 1991). On one night, over 200 news directors at local affiliates abandoned their own network's feed to acquire CNN material (Cooper, 1991). NBC anchor Tom Brokaw interviewed CNN's Bernard Shaw from Shaw's hotel room in Baghdad. CNN became "the unpaid news service for papers" (Bernard Gwertzman, quoted in Colin, 1991, p. 31), which adapted traditional formats to include more graphics and visual layouts (Colin, 1991; Diamond, 1991a). Audiences also began to pay attention and CNN's ratings increased five-fold (Cooper, 1991; Kamen, 1991; Gannett Foundation, 1991).

CNN's triumph was seen by many reporters as an about-face on the part of what had been considered a second-rate news organization. In one view, CNN went from being the "Chicken Noodle Network" to having public credibility (Diamond, 1991b, p. 35). Often this was relayed through war terminology: *U.S. News & World Report* ob-

served that "January 16 will be remembered as the night [producer Bob] Furnad and his CNN colleagues carpet-bombed the competition" (Cooper, 1991, p. 44). Headlines like "CNN Wins" or "CNN Hits Its Target" were strewn across the print media, as was mention of the "collateral damage" inflicted on CBS, NBC, and ABC (Katz, 1991). War terminology suggests the extent to which CNN was originally seen as part of the opposition, a second-rate news organization, and helps explain why journalists needed to link CNN's legitimation with an event like the Gulf War. In a sense, the magnitude of events that underscored CNN's triumph softened the blow of being positioned as members of the losing side.

Thus CNN was largely hailed across media in statements that linked its ascendancy with the war. *Time* called CNN its "undisputed star," which "affirmed its credibility and worldwide clout with new authority" (Zoglin, 1991a, p. 69). *U.S. News & World Report* called CNN a network that "shows how to cover a war" (Cooper, 1991, p. 44). And *Newsweek,* applauding a "new television order," commented already in January that CNN was "changing the news business forever" (Alter, 1991, p. 41). The Gulf War offered the kind of news story that portrayed CNN's technological advantages in their best light (Diamond, 1991b, p. 35). Its coverage thus somewhat changed expectations of wartime reporting.

In the eyes of CNN insiders, however, war coverage adapted itself to the form of reportage that CNN did best. As one CNN executive said, "we handled the big story hour after hour, taking incoming materials from satellites, but that's what we do all the time" (John Baker, quoted in Diamond, 1991b, p. 34). Wartime coverage played into "CNN's traditional strengths: its unquenchable lust for the breaking story, its willingness to feed a story in contradictory fragments to an audience hooked on drama and the very ambiguities of life" (Polman, 1991, p. 27). On these grounds, CNN executives claimed to offer "a new kind of journalism," which presented "the unfolding story . . . live" (Ed Turner, quoted in Polman, 1991, p. 26).

Shortly after the war began, CNN's publicity department distributed a pamphlet entitled "War in the Gulf" (*War in the Gulf,* 1991). The pamphlet was telling for how it incorporated the Gulf War into CNN's publicity effort. Alongside a map of the Gulf region, its front cover hailed CNN as "the world's news leader." Inside, it recorded the sentiments of CNN's main players—Peter Arnett, Bernard Shaw, and John Holliman—as well as a daily accounting of the war's main events. Shaw conveyed how he, Arnett, and Holliman had "cheated death" on the first day of the war. "The world benefitted," he said, "CNN was there. History was served" (*ibid.,* p. 1). The pamphlet also recounted the praise of key public officials and media organizations throughout its twenty-three pages of text and pictures: Dick Cheney lauded CNN for the "best reporting" (*ibid.,* p. 11), while foreign newspapers praised it for being more objective than other networks (*ibid.,* p. 13). The pamphlet concluded with the following statement: "No one will ever doubt . . . that CNN is the most important network in the world. This is the most important journalism story of the decade" (*ibid.,* p. 23).

CNN's so-called "overnight success"— which *The Quill* called a "quantum leap into the broadcasting big leagues in only a mat-

ter of hours" (Mott, 1991, p. 15)—did not take place in one night. It had actually been in the making for nearly ten years. Years earlier, CNN's coverage of events like the Challenger shuttle disaster or the shooting of Ronald Reagan had already hinted at the advantages to be had in continuous live coverage, and recognition of those parameters prompted CNN executives to negotiate for the installation of an overseas telephone link in Iraq in case of emergency power failure (Mott, 1991). Even before the war there were hints of public legitimacy, such as a *Washington Journalism Review* readers' poll conducted in October that gave CNN the title of Best Network for News ("Best in the Business," 1991).

So why was CNN's ascendancy linked with the Gulf War? Such a linkage was necessary for the negotiation and successful recognition of altered parameters of journalistic professionalism. By narratively reworking the tale of CNN's legitimation via Gulf War discourse, journalists were able to couch it in terms that made its ascendancy more understandable and less threatening to existing boundaries of journalistic practice. It also gave CNN itself a marker through which it could claim its own legitimation. "New King of the Hill" was how *The Quill* pronounced CNN's newfound status (Mott, 1991), and it was a cry echoed by mediated and professional forums alike, however true a recounting it was. Journalists' discussions came to underscore the central role of CNN in mastering the technology that gave the Gulf War story its form.

THE PETER ARNETT PHENOMENON

Left unresolved in discussions of CNN's ascendancy, however, were concerns about the reporter. One professional forum offered the view that reporters were "hardly needed" in much of CNN's coverage "other

than as a relay point along the transmission line" (Haarsager, 1991, p. 3). Journalists questioned whether they had been displaced by satellite-fed communications, whether the reporter had become "less important than the satellite dish that he's standing next to" (Yaari, 1991). While CNN coverage was described by one trade journal as "technologically ingenious and dramatic" (Katz, 1991, p. 29), these were hardy adjectives favored by hard-boiled reporters. The idea that a reporter was created from one night of saturation footage did not bode well for definitions of professional activity.

Questions remained about the authority of the reporter vis-à-vis that of the portable satellite uplink, creating a need for stories that might help journalists deal with their own mastery over the satellite-fed news item. Thus, journalists used the archetypal figure as a way of negotiating their mastery of the satellite-fed story, and they positioned Peter Arnett as the archetypal figure of Gulf War discourse. Arnett was seen as the reporter who met newly-defined professional challenges despite great personal risk and hardship. By staying behind enemy lines to report the story, he exemplified what was needed of a reporter in an age of satellite-fed communication. Within these parameters, an image of him was constructed that addressed questions among journalists about their authority within such an age.

The media labelled Arnett the "last American correspondent left in Baghdad" (Zoglin, 1991c, p. 45). They likened his dispatches to the legendary reportage of Edward R. Murrow during World War II. Newspaper columns outlined his performance in Baghdad (i.e., Heller, 1991). Reporters like David Halberstam, Marvin Kalb, and Malcolm Browne went on national media to remind viewers of Arnett's reportorial competence and experience, which had won him a Pulitzer Prize for his Vietnam reportage (Browne, 1991; Granger, 1991; *The Media and the Military*, 1991). He had, said Halberstam, "an almost unique ability to operate in an environment that most reporters would have found unendurable" (quoted in Halonen, 1991, p. 6). CNN

executives praised Arnett as a "seasoned combat correspondent, who has been tested by time and in so practicing his craft received the highest honors journalism can bestow" (Ed Turner, quoted in Halberstam, 1991, p. 31).

While public figures leveled criticism at the reporter for relaying Iraqi-censored reports, for not being overtly loyal to America, for insisting on staying behind enemy lines, journalists spoke almost to a person in his defense. When Arnett reported that the allies had bombed a plant producing infant formula, and not biological weapons as the U.S. insisted, and public fears intensified that his dispatches were being used for propaganda purposes, journalists spoke out in his behalf. The *Philadelphia Inquirer* called him an "endangered species" (Heller, 1991, p. D1). At one point lawmakers pressed for control over his broadcasts (Halberstam, 1991, p. 1), and the *Washington Journalism Review* called the attempts "Malice in Wonderland" (Monroe, 1991, p. 6). Interestingly, these comments addressed the appropriateness of a reporter's actions within the expanded boundaries of coverage offered by satellite-fed communiques. In other words, discourse about Arnett explored whether adjusting the boundaries of appropriate coverage was necessary to suit the newest news-gathering technology.

Nearly all of the trade press—including *Washington Journalism Review, Columbia Journalism Review,* and *Electronic Media*—ran articles praising Arnett's performance. The *New York Times Magazine* traced his personal history under the title "If There's a War, He's There" (Prochnan, 1991, p. 30). One editorial called Arnett the "anti-hero hero of Baghdad" (Monroe, 1991, p. 6). The logistics of Arnett securing his interview with Saddam Hussein were tracked by *Electronic Media,* whose front-page headline proclaimed that "CNN's Secret Journey Ends in Exclusive Hussein Broadcast" (Shaw, 1991,

p. 1). The *Washington Journalism Review* defended Arnett with the phrase, "observe the legend taking shape—the legend of Peter Arnett, go-to-hell war correspondent" (Monroe, 1991, p. 6). He was:

> . . . the hero that journalists deserve, sent by the Lord to comfort us in our time of affliction and gross unpopularity . . . [he was] the perfect symbol of the beleaguered press in the Scudded world of February 1991. He lives and breathes the story (Monroe, 1991, p. 6).

As American forces began their pullout from the region, the *Columbia Journalism Review* ran a special article about war coverage that was simply titled "Arnett." In part, it went as follows: "By turns defiant and defensive, [Arnett] upheld his role even as he acknowledged that the sort of journalism he had practiced, or been permitted to practice, had been severely circumscribed" (Goodman, 1991, p. 29). Such remarks underscored that reporting a war in real time called for a change in reportorial practice. In many reporters' eyes, Arnett had become "the first war correspondent of the global village" (Halonen, 1991, p. 7).

The controversy surrounding Arnett's coverage did not go unnoticed by the reporter himself. In a speech to the National Press Club shortly after he returned to the U.S., he claimed that the same public figures who criticized him for being too soft on Saddam Hussein had upbraided him before the war began for being too critical (Rosenstiel, 1991). He also claimed that his ability to conduct unrehearsed question-and-answer sessions with his CNN anchors was what "saved [his] reputation"; those sessions showed that he was not simply "reading material that I was forced to write" (Rosenstiel, 1991, p. 12A). The response of the journalistic community was overwhelmingly supportive.

He was called upon to address other professional forums on the same issue, including the Knight Fellows at Stanford and the American Society of Newspaper Editors (Collins, 1991). He also signed a contract to write his memoirs.

For an understanding of appropriate boundaries of journalistic practice, Arnett's activities were instrumental in illustrating the need for a change. His response confirmed his authority as a reporter through the spontaneous and unplanned nature of reporting in real time. Casting journalistic practice in this way upheld the need for changing the boundaries of reportage in an age of satellite-fed communication. His remarks thereby not only underscored his own stature and that of CNN, but also that of the technology of satellite-fed communication that made his reportage possible. It is significant that he was a reporter who had previously proved himself in the print media, and his ascendancy as CNN's star illustrates a peculiar, but workable, wedding of the old and new in American journalism. By being filmed sitting next to the satellite, he also signified the connection between the archetypal figure and the new preferred technology of news gathering.

It is worthwhile to contrast Arnett with another journalistic personality who was central to stories about the Gulf War: CBS's Bob Simon. Simon was captured by the Iraqis when he abandoned pool arrangements and went on his own in search of a story. He spent weeks in captivity. Simon emerged as the mirror image of Arnett, the reporter who defied military restrictions to investigate the scene and was then taken captive for his efforts. Simon was portrayed as having walked away from the technology of transmission (and losing the story), while Arnett was seen as having prevailed for remaining alongside that same technology (and winning the story). In a semiotic sense, this signified the importance of remaining alongside the satellite, regardless of what one saw, did, or heard.

In this way, discourse about Arnett as the archetypal reporter underscores the journalist's mastery of satellite-fed communication. Such a pattern is found in other critical incidents. Discourse about Woodward and Bernstein constitutes a personalized way of telling the story of Watergate (Woodward & Bernstein, 1976), and stories about Edward R. Murrow mark discourse about World War II (Monroe, 1991). Stories about Arnett thus humanize Gulf War discourse, lending a human element to tales that hail the advent of satellite-fed technology.

HAS JOURNALISM CHANGED?

In response to the Gulf War, the journalistic community has adapted to altered boundaries of journalistic practice in two ways: imitation and surrender. Discourse about CNN and Peter Arnett has made clear to members of the journalistic community that altered boundaries of appropriate practice are inevitable. It has called on them to consider new ways of adapting. Certain journalists and news organizations have chosen to imitate the news as it is produced by satellite-fed technology. They in effect have "redefined themselves":

> During the opening days of the gulf war, viewers were never in need of greater cool, clear, informed reporting and analysis. . . . Yet for years now the networks have been busily tossing onto the streets the very researchers, producers, commentators and staff that could have helped carry out such a role (Katz, 1991, p. 29).

For the first days of the war, the networks expanded their evening broadcasts to one hour, providing their version of what one journalist called "saturation coverage": "expanding their evening newscasts, preempting prime-time entertainment lineups and rushing stories onto the air as soon as possible" (Lieberman, 1991, p. 14). Newspapers used eye-catching graphics, sidebars, boxes, maps and special pull-out sections—a response to the increasing centrality of the visual element in news (Colin, 1991). Even the *AP Log,* the in-house organ of the Associated Press, appended its own full page of graphics to its monthly newsletter ("The Persian Gulf Explodes," 1991).

Such practices persist today in expanded forms. Newspapers continue to favor the more visual packaging and informative graphics that many adopted during the war. On the international front, Sky News in Britain, the BBC's World Service Television, and the European Broadcasting Union's Euronews Channel offer versions of television news along lines suggested by CNN (Goodwin, 1991). Veteran CBS producer Don Hewitt called for a general television news service, much like a visual wire service, that would supply the networks with the basic visual and factual frame of each news story (Alter, 1991). A recent plane crash over a suburban Philadelphia school generated six hours of live television broadcasting, which, as one local journalist said, "we might not have necessarily done without the lessons learned from CNN" (Guttman, 1991). Imitation suggests that CNN's rendition of the news has come to be seen as a viable, and worthwhile, form of transmission.

Other news organizations have elected to surrender to the demands suggested by CNN coverage. While CNN recently said it would spend over $2 million to open new bureaus in Amman, Rio de Janeiro, and

New Delhi (Sharbutt, 1991), network news organizations are closing bureaus. One NBC executive admitted that his network is no longer able to cover breaking news: "We're not going back to covering everything that breaks. . . . We're not running after bus crashes. We're relying on our affiliates and our owned stations to cover that kind of story" (Sharbutt, 1991, p. 5D). Interestingly, this gives CNN exclusivity on breaking news, as do attempts to explain shutdowns and other moves of adaptation as a recasting of journalistic practice.

Since the war ended, journalists discussions of war coverage have taken on an increasingly critical stance. The Associated Press convened a special panel discussion on the Gulf War at its annual meeting, where it featured Peter Arnett as one of its speakers ("AP Annual Meeting," 1991). The American Society of Newspaper Editors' (ASNE) president used its monthly newsletter to ponder the effect of judging war correspondents "on the basis of how they behave on television" (Osborne, 1991, p. 2). The Association for Education in Journalism and Mass Communication published two divisional newsletters that separately pondered journalists' authority alongside ever-present television cameras and CNN's evolution as a "new genre of news" (Atwood, 1991; Haarsager, 1991). All of this suggests that journalists have begun to use discussions about the Gulf War as a critical marker of appropriate journalistic practice, much like stories about the Kennedy assassination, Watergate, and Vietnam were used in earlier decades.

Two lines of thought continue to punctuate Gulf War discourse. One line still debates long-standing journalistic concerns about the appropriate boundaries of censorship, viability of pool arrangements, and degree of appropriate opposition to governmental curbs ("AP Annual Meeting," 1991; Hentoff, 1991; Lewis, 1991; McMasters,

1991; Nathan, 1991). Such discourse might have been appended to a number of conflicts in which the United States has been involved, including Grenada, Vietnam, or Panama.

But a second line of thought is specific to the Gulf War. It addresses the potentially dangerous liaison that has formed between CNN and the Gulf War, by which the war and CNN are seen to legitimate each other (Diamond, 1991a; Malik, 1991). Characterizations of the war—"the television war" (*Meet the Press,* 1991), the "real-time war" (Kinsley, 1991, p. 80), "war in video verité" (Osborne, 1991, p. 43), or the "CNN war" (Capuzzo & Shister, 1991, p. 14A)—are conflated with labels about CNN—"news without end" (Polman, 1991, p. 26), a "new kind of journalism" (quoted in Polman, 1991, p. 26), or "instantaneous journalism" (Kamen, 1991, p. 27)—in discussions about the contemporary practices of American journalists.

CNN's role in the war has generated suggestions that its mode of news gathering signals an end to recognized journalistic practice and the beginning of a new era of journalism. While CNN insiders would certainly favor such a view, this article suggests that what is different about CNN's mode of news gathering is simply a matter of degree: CNN does not offer "new" journalism, just faster, more continuous, less polished, and less edited journalism. Journalists continue to engage in generally the same activities of news gathering, although they may emphasize and reveal different aspects of the process for public viewing.

This discussion also suggests that viewing CNN's mode of news gathering as new journalism is historically myopic. Response to CNN's modes of news gathering parallels response to the ascent of television news thirty years ago (Zelizer, 1990, in press) and to expanded boundaries of investigative journalism a decade later (Schudson, in press). This suggests a need to attend more closely to the role of technology in generating journalistic authority. While technology provides a logical extension of the appropriate practices of journalism, reporters are able to negotiate their response to it through their discussions about critical incidents, yet maintain their professional identities. This means that rather than regard the Gulf War as an end to recognized forms of journalism, we need to accept the role of the Gulf War in providing a stage for journalists to reshape their professional practices in accordance with new preferred forms of technology. The Gulf War extends, rather than deadens, journalism as we know it.

It is within such a context that the Gulf War constitutes the beginnings of a critical incident for American journalists. Discussing the Gulf War offers reporters a stage on which to evaluate, negotiate, and ultimately reconsider ideas about professional practice and appropriate boundaries of journalistic authority. The American journalistic community is thereby using the Gulf War to choreograph tales of its own adaptation to satellite-fed communication. Only time will tell the extent to which that adaptation is beneficial, or dangerous—for CNN, for network television news, and for the journalistic community.

REFERENCES

Alter, J. (1991, January 28). When CNN Hits Its Target. *Newsweek*, p. 41.

AP annual meeting. (1991, May 13). *AP Log*.

Arlen, M. (1969). *Living-room War*. New York: Viking.

Atwood R. (1991, Spring). War provides case study re "objectivity." *Clio: Among the Media* (Newsletter of History Division of AEJMC), p. 2.

Best in the Business: CNN Best Network for News. (1991, March). *Washington Journalism Review*, p. 44.

Boot, W. (1991, March/April). Covering the Gulf War: The Press Stands Alone. *Columbia Journalism Review*, pp. 23–24.

Braestrup, P. (1977). *Big story*. Boulder, CO: Westview.

Brown, M. W. (1991, March 3). The Military vs the Press. *New York Times Magazine*, pp. 27–30.

Capuzzo, M., & Shister, G. (1991, January 18). "The CNN War": Cable Underdog Scoops the Big Three. *Philadelphia Inquirer*, p. 14A.

Colin, T. J. (1991, March). As Television Glanced Off the Story, Newspapers Surrounded It. *Washington Journalism Review*, pp. 31–33.

Collins, M. (1991, March). News-hungry Turn to Radio—It's a (s)Hell of a Medium. *Washington Journalism Review*, p. 29.

Cooper, M. (1991, January 28). The Very Nervy Win of CNN. *U.S. News & World Report*, p. 44.

Diamond, E. (1991a, March 18). Who Won the Media War? *New York Magazine*, pp. 26–29.

Diamond, E. (1991b, February 11). How CNN Does It. *New York Magazine*, pp. 30–39.

Gannett Foundation. (1991, June), *The Media at War: The Press and the Persian Gulf Conflict*. New York: Gannett Foundation Media Center.

Gerbner, G. (1973). Cultural Indicators: The Third Voice. In G. Gerbner, L. Gross, & W. Melody (Eds.),

Communications Technology and Social Policy: Understanding the New "Cultural Revolution". New York: Wiley.

Gergen, D. (1991, March 11). Why America Hates the Press. *U.S. News & World Report*, p. 57.

Glaser, B., & Strauss, A. (1967). *The Discovery of Grounded Theory*. Chicago: Aldine.

Goodman, W. (1991, May/June). Arnett. *Columbia Journalism Review*, pp. 29–31.

Goodwin, P. (1991, April). News for the Taking. *TV World*, pp. 31–33.

Granger, R. (1991, February 25). Media Defend News from Iraq. *Electronic Media*, p. 1.

Greenfield, J. (1991, February 16). America Rallies Round the TV Set. *TV Guide*, pp. 4–7.

Guttman, S. (1991, April 30). [Interview with Michael Groulmin].

Haarsager, S. (1991, Summer). The Press and the Gulf War. *QS News* (Newsletter of the Qualitative Studies Division of AEJMC), p. 3.

Halberstam, D. (1991 February 21). Where's Page 2 in TV News? *New York Times*, pp. 1, 31.

Halonen, D. (1991, February 25). Cronkite Calls for Greater Access, More Censorship. *Electronic Media*, pp. 3, 6–7.

Heller, K. (1991, February 1). For CNN Reporter Peter Arnett, It's a Life on the Front Lines. *Philadelphia Inquirer*, p. D1.

Hentoff, N. (1991, May/June). When It Was Time to Challenge the Military, Where Were the "Lords of the Press"? *ASNE Bulletin*, pp. 38–39.

Kamen, J. (1991, March). CNN's Breakthrough in Baghdad: Live by Satellite (Censored). *Washington Journalism Review*, pp. 26–29.

Katz, J. (1991, March/April). Covering the Gulf War:

Collateral Damage to Network News. *Columbia Journalism Review*, p. 29.

Kinsley, M. (1991, February 25). Trusting Ourselves with the News. *Time*, p. 80.

Landau, S. (1991, March). The Real Nintendo Game. *The Progressive*, pp. 26–28.

Levi-Strauss, C. (1966). *The Savage Mind*. Chicago: University of Chicago Press.

Lewis, C. J. (1991, May/June). The "City Editor" of the Persian Gulf was a Colonel. *ASNE Bulletin*, pp. 14–23.

Lieberman, D. (1991, February 9). With its Desert Stand, CNN Charts the Course for TV News' Future. *TV Guide*, pp. 14–16.

Lieberman, D., Stein, L., & Collins, M. (1991, February 23). On the Firing Line, a Handful of Reporters Stake Their Claim to Stardom. *TV Guide*, pp. 8–11.

Malik, R. (1991, March/April). The Media's Gulf War: Notes and Issues. *Intermedia*, pp. 4–7.

Massing, M. (1991, May/June). Another Front. *Columbia Journalism Review*, pp. 23–24.

McMasters, P. (1991, March). Journalists Aren't Winning Their Gulf War. *The Quill*, p. 8.

The Media and the Military. (1991, February 21). PBS.

Meet the Press. (1991, January 27). NBC News Division.

Monroe, B. (1991, March). Peter Arnett: Anti-hero of Baghdad. *Washington Journalism Review*, p. 6.

Mott, P. (1991, March). New King of the Hill. *The Quill*, pp. 14–16.

Nathan, D. (1991, February). Just the Good News, Please. *The Progressive*, pp. 25–27.

Osborne, B. (1991, March). With Friends Like Us in the Press, the First Amendment Doesn't Need any Enemies. *ASNE Bulletin*, pp. 2, 43.

The Persian Gulf Explodes. (1991, January 21). *AP Log*.

Polman, D. (1991, March 19). News without End. *Philadelphia Inquirer Magazine*, pp. 25–30.

The Press Goes to War (with Bill Moyers). (1991, January 26). CNN Productions.

Prochnan, W. (1991, March 3). If There's a War, He's There. *New York Times Magazine*, pp. 30–34.

Rosenberg, H. (1991, March). TV and the Gulf War. *The Quill*, pp. 17–19.

Rosenstiel, T. (1991, March 20). Arnett Defends Baghdad Reporting. *Philadelphia Inquirer*, p. 12A.

Schanberg, S. H. (1991, March). Censoring for Political Reasons. *Washington Journalism Review*, pp. 23–26.

Schudson, M. (1978). *Discovering the News*. New York: Basic Books.

Schudson, M. (in press). *Watergate in American Memory: How We Remember, Forget and Reconstruct the Past*. New York: Basic Books.

Sharbutt, J. (1991, July 26). Cable News Is on the Rise, while the Networks Retrench. *Philadelphia Inquirer*, p. 5D.

Shaw, R. (1991, February 4). Secret CNN Journey Ends in Exclusive Hussein Broadcast. *Electronic Media*, p. 1.

Stein, L. (1991, February 16). Tales from the Front: The Glitches and Hitches in Bringing the War to Your Living Room. *TV Guide*, pp. 8–11.

The Story Behind the Story (1991, Spring/Summer). *Newsweek* (Special Commemorative Issue on "Americans At War"), p. 3.

Valeriani, R. (1991, March/April). Covering the Gulf War: Talking Back to the Tube. *Columbia Journalism Review*, pp. 24–28.

War in the Gulf. (1991, March). CNN promotional pamphlet, pp. 1, 11, 13, 23.

Woodward, B. and Bernstein, C. (1976). *The Final Days*. New York: Simon and Schuster.

Yaari, E. (1991, June 12). The Role of the Media in the Gulf War. Roundtable discussion at the International Symposium on the Media, Protest and Political Violence, Jerusalem, Israel.

Zelizer, B. (1990). Achieving Journalistic Authority through Narrative. *Critical Studies in Mass Communication* 7(4), 37–48.

Zelizer, B. (in press). *"Covering the Body": The Kennedy Assassination and the Establishment of Journalistic Authority*. Chicago: University of Chicago Press.

Zoglin, R. (1991a, January 28). Live from the Middle East. *Time*, pp. 69–71.

Zoglin, R. (1991b, February 11). How Dailies Cover a TV War. *Time*, p. 78.

Zoglin, R. (1991c, February 4). Volleys on the Information Front. *Time*, pp. 44–45.

CHAPTER EIGHT

SECURITY
AND THE CONTROL
OF CONFLICT

The causes of war, which are the subject of speculation in international relations over the last four centuries, remain obscure, but less obscure than previously. Modern research has still left a trail of uncertainty, partial clues, contradiction, and continued mystery.

Kalevi J. Holsti, *Peace and War: Armed Conflicts and International Order 1648–1989* (1991)

Security studies have experienced a kind of love-hate relationship with the broader field of international relations. Put differently, a post-World War I preoccupation with preventing war seemed during the Cold War to have given way to a preoccupation with war, or preparation for it. A condemnation of militarism characterized the initial phases of IR, when "military studies" remained suspect in the minds of many IR specialists, as Olson and Groom point out in "The Period of the First Consensus: the Quest for Peace."[1] Later, the popularity or even the fad of geopolitics before and during World War II nearly cost the military dimension its academic respectability. After a brief period in the shadows, the predominance of security considerations in the analysis of super-

[1] In William C. Olson and A.J.R. Groom, *International Relations Then and Now: Origins and Trends in Interpretation,* (London: HarperCollins Academic, 1991), pp. 56–78.

power relationships threatened to turn IR itself into what one writer called a "Cold war discipline." The collapse of consensus which accompanied the Vietnam war reversed the trend once more, when "peace studies" again occupied center stage, particularly among students and younger scholars. It was not until the mid-1970s that the field of security studies began what Stephen Walt of the University of Chicago calls a "dramatic resurgence."[2]

From the vantage point of the U.S. policy-maker there has never been, as there was in the corridors of power in Britain in the pacifist-influenced 1920s and 1930s, any such problem. Security, often under such catchwords as "preparedness" and later, "peace through strength," has been well serviced, as Vincent Davis has so well chronicled, by the lobbies which create and maintain heavy appropriations, especially for the Navy even during times of what was called "peace."[3] Since Pearl Harbor, the Armed Services Committees of both houses of Congress have given the Pentagon just about what it wanted, even in some cases more than it asked for (on the legislators' assumption that if one can buy so much security for so much money, you can buy even more if you spend more, a hypothesis no head of the Joint Chiefs of Staff ever argued.) The question, as Zbigniew Brzezinski, National Security Advisor to President Carter, brings out in his contribution to this chapter, is one of selectivity, of priorities, and one of relating resources to objectives in foreign policy. The United States cannot do everything, he contends, so it must take care in the commitments it makes so that it can be certain of being able to carry out those pledges. It is a powerful and timely argument, and few are so well placed to make it as Professor Brzezinski, who now teaches at the Johns Hopkins School of Advanced International Studies in Washington, because he brings to security the experience of a decision-maker combined with the perspective of an academic.

There are, according to Walt, several reasons for a "new wave" in security studies, among them the enhanced use of history, the challenge to deterrence theory, the need for a nuclear weapons policy, conventional warfare, renewed interest in the theory of a grand strategy, and the return of security studies to the "scholarly agenda among theorists of international politics."[4] The argument was that "security" represented a term which actually bridged the gap between war and peace, since the object of security studies was peace just as much as that of so-called "peace studies," which tended to treat war as a disease to be avoided. Like doctors and hospitals, the security analysts contended, the only way to combat disease is to understand it.

While it is too early to tell for sure, nothing seems to indicate that the end of the Cold War will automatically bring an end to security studies. Instead, what is being seen is a redefinition of what security is all about. Jessica Tuchman Mathews' article in *Foreign Affairs,* the quarterly journal of that bastion of traditional thought in IR, the Council on Foreign Relations in New York, is an out-

[2]Stephen Walt, "The Renaissance of Security Studies," *International Studies Quarterly,* 35, 1, 1991, p. 211.

[3]The best account of at least part of this well-organized and effective phenomenon is Vincent Davis, *The Admirals' Lobby,* (Chapel Hill: Univ. of North Carolina Press, 1967), esp. Part III.

[4]Walt, *op. cit.,* pp. 216–220.

standing example (excerpted in this chapter.) Having served on the National Security Council from 1977 to 1979, she is now the Vice President of the World Resources Institute, contending that "global developments now suggest the need" for a "broadening definition of national security to include resource, environmental and demographic issues."

What was called "deterrence theory" for many years dominated security studies, well-financed as it is by government and foundations alike, developing an elaborate methodology and even terminology of its own.[5] Yet, as Admiral Sir James Eberle put it during a debate at the Royal Institute of International Studies when he was Director there, "all deterrence really means is that if you do something or decline to do something, against the interest of the community, something unpleasant is going to happen to you."[6] Even simpler is what this is all about, for which the shortest word in the lexicon of IR suffices: war. Until well into the twentieth century, war was viewed as a more or less normal aspect of the working of the state system. "War," wrote Clausewitz around 1830, "is nothing but a duel on a larger scale," adding that

> international law and usage impose minor restrictions, which do not really weaken its power, on the use of force. . . . Philanthropic souls may imagine that there is a way to disarm or overthrow our adversary without much bloodshed, and this is what the art of war should seek to achieve. Agreeable as it may sound, this is a false idea which must be demolished.[7]

Not only was the legacy of martial valor alive in many societies, but war was accepted because all social life is marked by tension among opposing groups which could be controlled internally by governments that were helpless to act at the international level. Hence war. In the absence of any outside authority to guarantee each state's security or to resolve conflicts, war and the threat of war were acceptable means of doing so. War was so much a part of international relations that rules by which a state was justified in going to war and by which hostilities themselves should be conducted were codified under the Law of War. Even the rules for those who wanted to stay out of a fight were defined under the Law of Neutrality. In other words, war was not seen as an aberration but as an inherent feature of a system that had yet to create any viable method of regulating but especially of preventing its outbreak. International law seemed not to be designed to stop war, just to render it somewhat less horrible.

What causes war? There are as many explanations as there are types of armed conflict, political dissatisfaction, and social disorder. Consider the fol-

---

[5]Charles W. Kegley, Jr. and Eugene Wittkopf have provided a concise list of principle terms of this type, with definitions, such as balance of terror, compellence, brinkmanship, massive retaliation, countervalue, counterforce, second-strike capability, mutual assured destruction (MAD), etc., in *World Politics: Trend and Transformation,* (New York: St. Martin's, 1989), pp. 375–385. Were the Cold War still on, we would have felt compelled to devote an entire chapter to this compendium.

[6]The quote is excerpted from an informal debate at Chatham House, headquarters of the Royal Institute of International Affairs which he directed, in June 1987, while the author was a Research Fellow there.

[7]From the Collins translation of selections from *On War,* (Chicago: Henry Regnery Co., 1962), pp. 63–4.

lowing list of "proximate causes" based on a list drawn up about fifteen years ago but still very instructive:

1. power asymmetry—an unfavorable tilt in the distribution of power;
2. nationalism, separatism, and irredentism—the desire of a people to throw off foreign rule or annex nations living under foreign rules;
3. social Darwinism—the belief that societies, like biological species, evolve and advance through competition resulting in the survival of the fittest;
4. communications failure—misunderstanding and hostility due to stereotypical images and mutual misperception of intentions;
5. arms races;
6. the exploitation of a foreign war to achieve unity at home;
7. instinctual aggression—the psychological predisposition of people toward aggression;
8. economic and scientific stimulation—new economic and scientific innovations which stimulate expansionist tendencies;
9. military-industrial complexes—groups within a society, principally the military, the defense industry, and their political allies, acquiring a vested interest in maintaining a state of conflict;
10. relative deprivation—to achieve greater benefits or to relieve the frustration of denial, groups may turn to aggression and political violence;
11. overpopulation;
12. conflict resolution—war as a device for challenging and changing unacceptable conditions between two or more states.[8]

To these might be added, simply, opportunity—the chance to score a cheap victory when a neighbor is weakened by internal or external strife, as in the case of Italy's attacking France in 1940 and Iraq's invading Iran in 1981.

As one devastating war succeeded another in this century, scholars and statesmen have given increasing attention to the problem of why states continued to prepare for and to engage in war when the cost, material and physical, exceeded any possible gain that victory might bring. They concluded that political leaders appeared to be prisoners of the logic of the system itself. Which individual could challenge it? If he did, his career would come to an abrupt end. Any group considering objection to the "conventional wisdom" might immediately be branded as traitors, undermining the very security of the sacred nation. Later, psychologists discovered the phenomenon of something they call "group think," in which assumptions and even statements of fact are only accepted, never challenged, this being more true the higher up the policy ladder one goes. On the eve of World War I, responding to passion and fear, two alliance systems built up massive military machines. Each feared that an unfavorable tilt in the balance of power could be disastrous, so that when the Austrian Empire appeared threatened with disintegration as a result of an assassination,

---

[8]Stephen Rosen and Walter Jones, *The Logic of International Relations*, (Cambridge, Mass.: Winthrop, 1977), pp. 283–312.

Imperial Germany felt it had no choice but to accept war as the most viable alternative.

Now thinkers like Mathews, Zalewski, Milner, and Haftendorn (all women) are seeking to discover new ways of looking at the whole concept of what has fallen under the rubric of "security," reexamining the entire fabric of assumptions about the nature of the international system, whether it is in fact anarchistic or whether in fact war is more or less inevitable. The peacemaker understands that the assertion of influence involves a relationship of interdependence of a different order than that which was discussed concerning regime theory. To employ power effectively, one must first determine one's intent and how it will be perceived by the "target" of one's influence, as well as to others who are observing the process at work. A government that seeks peace but appears to be seeking war will find that its policy is counterproductive. Perception may not be everything in IR, but it is a great deal. Nowhere is that more evident than in peacemaking. For example, if a superpower's intent is to enhance the prospects of peace as well as its security, it is more likely to achieve both objectives at once by openly endeavoring to reach agreement on arms limitations than by striving for nuclear superiority. When he introduced "new thinking" in the Soviet system, Gorbachev understood that perhaps better than any other contemporary world leader.

An equally crucial equation derives from the necessity facing the policymaker to choose between goals and to set priorities, particularly in the implementation of policies undertaken to meet those goals. In the real world where theory is seldom the guide—at least explicitly—the problem facing the policymaker often comes down either to how to choose between two or more results, all of which have merit but nevertheless are at odds with one another, or how to move toward a desired result in a situation where one has little or no leverage. Needless to say, national and subnational interests are often, if not incompatible, not equally capable of solution. This greatly complicates the practical necessity of deciding which goal is to be pursued by policy-makers and which ones are to be sacrificed or given a lower priority. It becomes particularly acute when the threat of violence is high.

All this raises some disturbing questions. Why is it that the logic of the state system puts a premium upon readiness for war, which is almost invariably set forth as a purely defensive necessity, when the true objective is peace? It is often said that peace is more than the mere absence of war; but is war more than the mere absence of peace? Obviously not, for war must have a goal (although often this has to be created, like the "Four Freedoms" during World War II, well after war has broken out). If each combatant pursues its own interests, if necessary at the expense of others, is not its regard for the interests of others purely expedient if it concerns policy-makers at all? War and other "evil" actions have been for so long accepted as being a characteristic of the current system that international relations has become synonymous with "power politics." In other words, it is hard to demonstrate that peace is an integral component of the modern state system. It becomes merely a means to an end rather than an end in itself, if all other national goals take priority in the choice-making process. Idealists may reject *realpolitik* (a German word for the idea that wars are caused by the cynical prejudices and interests of ruling classes or militarists), convinced that if realist nationalism could just be changed or superceded by some kind of world government, war could be eliminated and a more just world order established. But does that really follow?

Many who have tried to endow the noble concept of peace with content beyond the negation of war postulate that it must be based upon law. The resort to force cannot be taken lightly in the face of constraints imposed by international legal norms, which to the smaller state is seen as a source of security when it is unable to provide it for its citizens through military means. This may be why so many of the great international lawyers since the Peace of Westphalia have come from the smaller states. The difficulty with international law as a guarantor of peace is that the Powers have to guarantee the application of law. If peace on a grand scale is ever to be achieved, it can only come about by the gradual adoption, acceptance, and general application of legal norms or rules to which all states can be expected to give their adherence.

They will only do that if it serves their interest to do so or if they are forced to do so. No mechanism yet exists that gives promise of providing the second of these, but as the great Dutch international lawyer, Hugo Grotius, wrote early in the seventeenth century:

> Just as the national, who violates the law of his country in order to obtain an immediate advantage, breaks down that by which the advantage of himself and his posterity are for all future time assured, so the state which transgresses the laws of nature and of nations cuts away also the bulwarks which safeguard his own future peace.[9]

In other words, a third reason for compliance is awareness of the long-term consequences of noncompliance. At the same time, few actions better serve the cause of peace in the short-run, limited situation than the conscious and well-publicized application of established international norms.

A country can overextend itself or confront political and strategic challenges on so many fronts that the cost of meeting its commitments exceeds its national capacity. This is essentially what happened to Britain in the period between the two great wars. Indeed, as Paul Kennedy points out in his widely read book on the shifting balance of power, the British Empire had already become so overcommitted by 1914 that the aim of its statesmen became one of maintaining its position rather than adding to its obligations.[10] This is what Brzezinski is trying to warn policy-makers to avoid today. The preservation of peace was desirable but not at the sacrifice of British prestige and power. In 1938, its position was even more precarious, which explains why Chamberlain sought "peace in our time" through an approach to peace-keeping known as

---

[9]Hugo Grotius, "Prolegomena to *The Law of War and Peace*," excerpted in John A. Vasquez, *Classics of International Relations*, (Englewood Cliffs, N.J.: Prentice-Hall, Inc., 1986), p. 329.

[10]Paul Kennedy, *The Rise and Fall of the Great Powers: Economic Change and Military Conflict from 1500 to 2000*, (London: Unwin Hyman, 1988), pp. 256ff.

"appeasement," the attempt to make concessions in order to satisfy the appetite of the Nazi aggressor. It was a failure, not only because it failed to prevent war, but because it led Britain and France to sacrifice the security of a third country—Czechoslovakia—in the process. History affords few examples of the compromise of moral principle in the name of peace so cynical, and so unsuccessful. Peace through self-abnegation is an unlikely prospect.

The catalogue of approaches to conflict resolution is a massive one, all the way from "Peace through Strength," (the American slogan of the Cold War) to such devices as requiring delegates to UN Security Council meetings to walk through a children's playground at the entrance, to the substitution of women for men in the governing of nations. More promising is what a recent National Security Advisor observed after leaving office in a book aptly entitled *Power and Principle,*

> To cope with the problem of survival in a turbulent world, American policy will have to be derived from an efficient organizational structure; it will also have to involve a sustained and even draining effort to shape a wider framework of global cooperation. . . . The vital question for the era ahead is whether the world will move haltingly toward some wider cooperative arrangements or whether it will plunge into destructive chaos.[11]

Careful readers will have noted a striking resemblance between this insight and that issued a decade later by Mikhail Gorbachev at Westminster College in Fulton, Missouri, site of Winston Churchill's famous "Iron Curtain" address in 1947.[12] They will also have noted that the other two experts whose work has made up this chapter would add that an entirely new conception of security itself needs to be introduced.

DISCUSSION QUESTIONS

1. When Brzezinski advocates *selective* global commitment, what are the kinds of alternative "selections" that could otherwise be chosen by policy-makers? Of Haftendorn's three paradigms, which most nearly fits his ideas? Or does his position contain elements of all three?
2. Is it really useful to redefine a term which has come to have a more-or-less understood meaning? Why not invent a new word?
3. How have international organizations contributed to preventing a war between the superpowers? Which has been more effective, NATO or the United Nations?
4. Were you to rewrite this chapter, how would you handle the subject of pacifism? Can you cite any evidence that it is a significant factor in contemporary world politics?

[11]Zbigniew Brzezinski, *Power and Principle,* (New York: Farrar, Straus, Giroux, 1983), pp. 538–9.
[12]Selection 3, Chapter One above. See also Gorbachev's *Perestroika: New Thinking for Our Country and the World,* New York: Harper and Row, 1987), esp. pp. 9–13 and 253–54.

5. Does the fact that both Mathews and Zalewski happen to be women have anything to do with their attitudes about war and security?

6. Is "peace" merely the absence of war? Or does it have, as the conflict resolution advocates claim, positive content of its own? In other words, does peace derive more from social and economic conditions which produce cooperation than it does from artificially constructed peace plans, such as that created by the Duc de Sully in his "Grand Design of Henry IV" in the seventeenth century?

7. Can you think of any other "causes of war" since Rosen and Jones put together their list of a dozen twenty-five years ago? Would you now eliminate any of these? What about the counter-argument that wars are no longer possible simply because they are to horrible to contemplate?

8. How would you define "deterrence theory?" With the end of the Cold War, does it still have any relevance? Or is it a kind of permanently-applicable theory, only requiring a change of names of the adversaries involved?

9. In what ways is Brzezinski's "selective commitment" idea different from the criticism so often made of the United States as "the world's policeman?"

30 DANGEROUS DYADS: CONDITIONS AFFECTING THE LIKELIHOOD OF INTERSTATE WAR

STUART A. BREMER

State University of New York, Binghamton

Clauswitz's assertion that war is "nothing but a duel on a large scale" reminds us that one of the core questions in the study of conflict is "who fights whom?" A good deal of theoretical speculation and some empirical evidence suggest that war is more likely to occur between states that are

- geographically proximate,
- roughly equal in power,
- major powers,
- allied,
- undemocratic,
- economically advanced, and/or
- militarized

than between those that are not. Some of the component propensities in this summary statement are so widely assumed to be true that they have become "stylized facts" that, to some observers, need no further verification. But a closer scrutiny of the empirical evidence on which this confidence is based reveals one or more critical deficiencies in the relevant research. The most important of these follow.[1]

[1] In stating these criticisms, it is not useful to single out individuals who are guilty of particular "sins" of

Inappropriate unit of analysis. In spite of the fact that interstate wars arise out of the interactions between states,[2] the overwhelming majority of empirical studies of war have been undertaken at the systemic or (less frequently) national level. If one is willing to make a number of critical and controversial assumptions, then some of these nondyadic studies will yield deductions that pertain to the question of who fights whom, yet the direct evidence they offer is, at best, inconclusive. My own assessment is less generous, because I view these studies as largely irrelevant to the dyadic question.

Limited spatial-temporal domain. In spite of the fact that wars are comparatively rare

research. Indeed, all war (and peace) researchers (including the author) have committed one or the other of these sins in the past.

[2] After assessing a variety of war data collections, Most and Starr conclude that all share the following definition: "A war is a particular type of outcome of the *interaction* of at least dyadic sets of specified varieties of actors in which at least one actor is willing and able to use some specified amount of military force for some specified period of time against some other resisting actor, and in which some specified minimal number of fatalities (greater than zero) occur" (1989, 73, italics in original).

Journal of Conflict Resolution, Vol. 36 No. 2, June 1992, pp. 309–341. © 1992 Sage Publications, Inc. (Some footnotes have been omitted)

events, too many empirical studies to date have used narrow spatial and/or temporal domains. The spatial domain most frequently used is typically limited to the major powers, and the favored temporal domain is the post-World War II period. And there appears to be a fairly clear inverse relationship between the spatial and temporal domains used in previous studies, that is, the longer the time period studied, the fewer the states included. I do not dispute the fact that, within a given resource constraint, there is an inevitable tradeoff between the two domains; my point is rather that, given the comparative rarity of interstate war, narrow spatial and/or temporal domains provide us with a very weak basis for drawing conclusions about who fights whom.

Faulty case selection strategy. As Most and Starr (1989) point out, there has been a tendency in previous empirical work to use research designs that exclude a control group. That is, cases are selected for analysis based on the values of the dependent or independent variables, rather than some other factor not obviously related to either of these. For example, tests of the impact of some factor on war at the dyadic level are limited to dyads that experience war. Such practices logically lead to problems in assessing necessary and/or sufficient conditions and limit the value of conclusions drawn in ways that are not always readily apparent to the casual reader.

Bivariate analytical methods. Although less true now than earlier, empirical studies of war still tend to be bivariate in nature. This by itself is not indicative of negligence, for the number of potentially important factors that are excluded from any analysis must necessarily be very large in number, but the problem of spurious and masked associations in bivariate analyses is a serious one. However, the call for multivariate analyses of interstate war is especially difficult to respond to because the basic frequency of war is small and the statistical degrees of freedom can quickly be exhausted by the addition of independent variables. Recognizing this estimation problem does not, however, obviate the need for more multivariate analyses of who fights whom.

Questionable measures of war. Many years ago Duvall (1976) pointed out that the onset and amount of war are two conceptually different phenomena (an opinion shared at the time by others, including myself), yet too often the various standard measures of war are still treated as substitutable for one another. For theoretical and methodological reasons, it is important to distinguish between the occurrence of war and the manner in which it evolves thereafter. More important for the topic under discussion here is the fact that tests with different measures of war as the dependent variable do not, with few exceptions, add up to multiple tests of the same hypothesis. On the contrary, they usually entail the testing of implicitly different hypotheses. I believe this is one key reason why it has proved so difficult to integrate the findings of empirical studies of interstate war.

All of the factors indicated above contribute to a general lack of comparability between empirical studies of interstate war. Different levels of analysis, different spatial-temporal domains, different cases, different analytical methods, and different measures of war all make it very difficult to assess the relative importance of factors that purportedly contribute to the occurrence of war. While not claiming to avoid or solve all the problems outlined above, this study does aim to rectify the more serious errors found in previous research. To discover or verify the relative importance of the seven factors listed at the outset of this article, a broad spatial-temporal domain (that is, all states,

1816–1965) is used here, and the interstate dyad is the unit of analysis. A uniform measure of war that clearly reflects the focus of this study—the onset of interstate war—is employed, and both bivariate and multivariate analyses are conducted. Given that the primary mission of this article is of a "fact finding" nature, no elaborate formal models will be presented, nor will I dwell at length on subtle theoretical issues. However, I think the results reported below do have important theoretical implications and suggest directions for future modeling work. Now, let us briefly review the theoretical arguments and empirical literature relevant to the seven predictors of war under consideration here.

SEVEN PREDICTORS OF WAR

Geographical Proximity and War

The proposition that war is more likely to occur between states that are geographically proximate than between those that are not is disputed by few, and even considered trivial by some, perhaps because of the strong geopolitical component that is inherent in the very act of war. Boxers, after all, cannot fight until they are physically able to reach one another. This analogy is somewhat misleading, however, since the proposition does not state that war is more likely if the armed forces of two states are within striking distance of one another. Rather it argues that war is more likely between states that share a common border zone, regardless of whether that border zone is a heavily fortified no-man's land or an almost forgotten boundary for which little physical evidence exists save its designation on maps.

A stronger and more interesting argument for why geographical proximity promotes war builds on the notion that proximity engenders serious conflicts of interest between states, a fraction of which are bound to lead to war. Shared access to a physical area can lead directly to interstate friction, even if the states involved agree as to where the border lies between them. A common example of this is where insurgents use the territory of an adjacent state as a basing area, and the state thus being used is unable or unwilling to suppress the insurgents' activities on its territory. A large variety of other examples of how proximity can introduce an unwelcome degree of interdependence between states can be cited. Because this enforced "common fate" breeds frustrations and rivalries between states, so the argument runs, interstate tension increases and, ceteris paribus, war is more likely.

The empirical evidence linking war and proximity is scattered but generally consistent.[3] Several studies have found an association between the number of borders states have and their foreign conflict behavior generally or war involvement specifically (Richardson 1960; Rummel 1972; Starr and Most 1976, 1978; Terrell 1977). These studies do not enable us to conclude that sharing a common border increases the likelihood of conflict and war between a given pair of states because they do not demonstrate that the increased conflict involvement of states with many neighbors is directed toward those neighbors. Thus, the evidence that these studies present for the proposition must be considered indirect.

More direct evidence is to be found in studies by Gleditsch and Singer (1975), Garnham (1976), and Gochman (1990a).[4]

[3]See Diehl (1991) for a recent review of geography and war.

[4]The work of Diehl and Goertz (e.g., Diehl and Goertz

Gleditsch and Singer found that the average intercapital distance between warring states was significantly less than the average such distance between all states over the period from 1816 to 1965. Garnham also employed an intercapital measure of distance to assess proximity, and found that the distance between warring pairs of states was significantly less than what would be expected by chance. This led him to conclude that "international war is more probable between more proximate pairs of nation-states" (p. 240). Gochman reported that about two-thirds of militarized interstate disputes occurring between 1816 and 1976 were between states that shared a common land border or were separated by 150 miles or less of water. Gochman also found that the proportion of disputes in which contiguity was present has tended to increase with the passage of time. Hence, if any trend is present in the effect of proximity on conflict, it would appear to be in the opposite direction from that commonly thought; that is, proximity may be more salient today than it was a century and a half ago.

Power Parity and War

Whether equality in power between states promotes war or peace has been hotly debated in the theoretical literature. Both sides make convincing arguments that appeal to common sense. One side argues that states that are radically different in power should not engage in war because the clearly weaker side would not be so foolish as to initiate or allow itself to be drawn into a war it cannot win. Hence, at the dyadic level, preponderance promotes peace. The other side of the debate argues that when two

1988; Goertz and Diehl 1990) which focuses upon territorial changes does not deal directly with the overall propensity for proximate states to engage in war, but the basic thrust of their work certainly supports the notion that geographical proximity is an important determinant of interstate conflict.

states are relatively equal in power, neither can be certain of victory, and they therefore deter one another from war. Ergo, power parity promotes peace between states. The first of these two views is found in more contemporary treatments of the question (for example, Organski 1968; Blainey 1973; Gilpin 1981), whereas the second prevails in the older balance of power tradition (for example, Claude 1962).

Although many empirical studies have examined the relationship between power and war, very few have looked specifically at the dyadic level. Garnham (1976) examined two-nation wars during the period from 1816 to 1965 and found that warring pairs of states were more equal with respect to several power-base measures (that is, area, population, fuel consumption, iron and steel production) than would be expected by chance. This led him to conclude that power parity is more likely to lead to war than preponderance. Weede (1976) restricted his analysis to a smaller spatial-temporal domain (that is, contiguous Asian dyads over the period from 1950 to 1969), but found essentially the same result, that is, that preponderance of power promotes peace. More recently, Gochman (1990b) found evidence to support the proposition that major powers are more likely to engage in war with other major powers when their capabilities are relatively equal. After reviewing the empirical literature on dyadic power and war, Sullivan concludes that "though the findings do not speak with one voice, a tendency seems to be, with some certain exceptions, that situations of preponderance are more likely associated with nonwar than the opposite" (1990, 129), an assessment with which I essentially agree.

Power Status and War

As with geographical proximity and war, there may be a tautological element in the proposition that major powers are more likely to engage in war than minor powers. It can be quite convincingly argued that major powers achieve and maintain their status as such because, in large measure, they pursue an active, interventionist, perhaps even aggressive, foreign policy that brings them more frequently into violent conflict with other states. The literature on war making and state making suggests that the two phenomena are intimately connected (Rasler & Thompson 1989). To the extent that this is true, it may be impossible to determine on balance whether states become major powers because they engage frequently in war or states engage frequently in war because they are major powers. A true test of the two propositions may come when and if Germany and Japan are readmitted to the major power club.

The nondyadic empirical evidence is quite clear (Bremer 1980b; Small and Singer 1982); major powers are much more likely to become involved in wars than minor powers. Ceteris paribus, dyads that contain one or more major powers should be more war prone than those that do not.

Alliance and War

In the modern era, alliances tend to be seen as defining "security communities" among their members, and, as such, it is expected that they will reduce the likelihood of war between members. In truth, this expectation may be based largely on a few durable and institutionalized alliances like NATO in the post-World War II era rather than on alliances in general. Yet the assumption that allies are more likely to resolve disputes by means other than war and, therefore, are less likely to engage in war with one another seems deeply ingrained in conventional wisdom. The older, more traditional view of alliances sees them as growing out of expediency and reflecting nothing deeper than a

temporary need of two or more states to coordinate their actions against one or more other states. In this second view, alliances are not seen as contracts but rather as bargains, wherein it is understood by all parties that each has the right to withdraw quickly should a better deal come along. Under this conception of alliances as limited, transient arrangements, war between allies should be neither more nor less frequent than between nonallied states. In theory, then, alliances may or may not reduce the chances of war between allies, but they should not increase the likelihood of war between allies.

Perhaps for this reason, Bueno de Mesquita's assertion that "war is much more likely between very close allies than between enemies" (1982, 30) was a counterintuitive, if not startling, deduction from his expected utility theory.[5] And the empirical evidence he offered (1981, 159–64) seemed to confirm this assertion. After a thoughtful review of Bueno de Mesquita's arguments and evidence, Ray concluded that "in light of the fact that it would be surprising to find that allies are even as conflict prone as unallied pairs of states, it is not unreasonable to conclude that allied dyads were disproportionately involved in international conflict with each other in the 1816–1974 time period" (Ray 1990, 86). Thus, contrary to most theoretical expectations, war appears to be more likely between allied states than between nonallied states, at least since the end of the Napoleonic era.

Democracy and War

At a time when democracy seems to be experiencing a resurgence, the argument that

---

[5]Of the 347 propositions about alliances that Holsti, Hopmann, and Sullivan (1985) gleaned from the traditional literature, not one posits that an alliance should increase the likelihood of war between member states. This may be a good indicator of just how counterintuitive Bueno de Mesquita's assertion is.

democracies are less war prone (at least vis-à-vis one another) gives some grounds for optimism about an otherwise turbulent future. The philosophical justifications for why democratic states should be less war prone than others will not be repeated here.[6] Instead, I will focus on the empirical debate that has been underway for some years.

Until recently, the prevailing appraisal of the empirical evidence regarding the linkage between democracy and war proneness supported the conclusion that democracies were neither more nor less war prone than other states. Studies by Wright (1965), Rummel (1968), Russett and Monsen (1975), and Small and Singer (1976) all reached this conclusion. Rummel (1983) challenged this conclusion and gave evidence that democracies were less war prone and especially so vis-à-vis one another. This prompted Weede (1984) to reexamine the question focusing on the period from 1960 to 1980, after which he concluded that democracies were neither more nor less likely to engage in war than other states. Chan (1984) considerably extended the analysis of Rummel's contention by examining the period from 1816 to 1980, and, although he did not dispute the proposition that democracies do not tend to fight one another, he did conclude that democracies were not less war prone in general than undemocratic states. Domke (1988) used Gurr's Polity (I) data set and failed to find any consistent association between the degree of democracy and likelihood of war. Dixon (1989) also failed to find much association between the degree of democracy and the frequency of war over a long span of time (1816–1971), but his study, like most others discussed here, was conducted at the national rather than dyadic level. Maoz and Abdolali (1989) did include a dyadic analysis as part of their larger study

[6]See Waltz (1959) and Doyle (1986).

of regime type and militarized interstate conflict. They found strong evidence that democracies tend not to go to war with one another, but little evidence that democracies tend to be less war prone overall.

Most of the studies surveyed above contain one or more serious design flaws, such as using a monadic level of analysis when a dyadic one is called for, failing to control for the number of democracies, or using an inappropriate measure of war. Nevertheless, the weight of evidence they yield clearly supports the proposition that democracies have a much lower likelihood of becoming involved in wars against other democracies than would be expected by chance. Russett has even gone so far as to assert that "this is one of the strongest nontrivial and nontautological generalizations that can be made about international relations" (1990, 123). The evidence as to whether or not democracies are less war prone overall is far less conclusive, but the absence of strong evidence to the contrary leads one to conclude that democracies have been neither more nor less war prone than nondemocracies.

Development and War

The rise of international political economy as a subfield has resensitized many to the importance of economic factors and international conflict. A central focus of much of the literature in this area is the way in which economically advanced states relate to each other and, more importantly, to states that are not economically advanced. Although war appears not to be a central concern of most of those engaged in research in this area, two propositions relating to war can be deduced from their work. The first derives from the Leninist thesis that states that are more economically advanced will tend to come into sharp conflict with one another as they compete for markets and resources in a largely zero-sum world. Of course, a critical caveat for the Leninist thesis is that these states be capitalistic in nature, and this is, no doubt, an important theoretical distinction. Unfortunately it is not a distinction that can be used meaningfully in empirical analyses because, with few exceptions over the last two centuries, all more advanced states have also been capitalistic. For this reason the proposition examined here is simply that more advanced states are more likely to start wars with one another than are other states.[7]

The second proposition that is suggested by this literature is that war is more likely between more advanced and less advanced states than between pairs of more or less advanced states. This would follow from an admittedly unsophisticated dependence theory that states that the likelihood of war increases when a more advanced economy attempts to penetrate a less advanced economy, or when a less advanced economy attempts to shake off the yoke imposed by a more advanced economy. If this pattern of conflict were widespread then one would expect to see a disproportionate amount of war between more and less advanced economies.

Efforts to uncover empirical studies that bear directly on these propositions were unsuccessful. Studies that include measures of development, as opposed to economic size, were not conducted at the dyadic level (for example, Rummel 1968), whereas dyadic studies (for example, Garnham 1976) used measures of economic size rather than development. And some (for example, Bremer 1980a) that considered the linkage between economics and war were neither dyadic nor concerned with development. It would appear, then, that we

are in virgin territory, empirically speaking, with respect to these propositions.[8]

Militarization and War

According to the old maxim, "states that seek peace should prepare for war." The questions that concern us here are whether states that devote a disproportionate share of their resources to military preparedness succeed in reducing their chances of war, as the maxim implies they should, or will such states exhibit a higher likelihood of war? I should emphasize that more militarized states are not necessarily those with the largest absolute military capability. Several countries in the Middle East, for example, maintain armed forces much larger than most other countries of comparable size and are more militarized, as I use the term here, even though their armed forces are small in a global sense.

The war-avoidance properties of militarization flow clearly from the logic of deterrence. If a state can persuade a potential attacker that the costs of war will be high relative to the expected gains, then the odds of being attacked will be lower. And this logic applies to small states as well as large since, although small states may not be able to avoid defeat in wars with large states, they can, by extensive military preparations, guarantee that victory will be costly to the large states and thereby deter attacks. Ac-

---

[7]This proposition is also broadly consistent with the lateral pressure theory (Choucri and North 1975) because it posits, ceteris paribus, that technologically advanced societies should exhibit high levels of conflict among themselves.

[8]I should note that the distinction between more and less advanced states cuts across other distinctions made in this study. Among major powers, for example, England falls into the first category throughout the nineteenth century, whereas Russia does not, and Germany moves from less advanced to more advanced during that century. Similarly, economically advanced states need not possess large capabilities, as witnessed by the existence of Austria, the Netherlands, Belgium, and so on in the contemporary system. In short, distinguishing more advanced from less advanced states should provide us with a different perspective on the possible preconditions of war.

cording to deterrence theory, then, more militarization means less war.

As is usually the case, for each maxim there is an equally convincing counter-maxim. In this instance it would be that "those who live by the sword, die by the sword." For a variety of reasons, states that prepare for war may get exactly that for which they prepare. The construction of a "garrison state" may call forth leaders that are bellicose and unyielding rather than flexible and accommodating. The militarization of a society may cause leaders and followers alike to conclude that war is inevitable rather than merely possible. Justifying the sacrifices that high degrees of military preparedness require may strengthen enemy images and even lead to collective paranoia. And, of course, other states may not see the defensive motivation behind the heightened military posture, and perceive instead a substantial threat to their own security. On balance, I find the second argument more persuasive than the first so the exact proposition under examination is stated accordingly; that is, pairs of more militarized states are more likely to begin wars than other states.

The empirical evidence on this proposition is, at best, indirect. The most germane comes from the numerous but inconclusive studies on the relationship between arms races and war. On one side of this question we find Wallace (1979, 1981, 1982, 1990) who has presented evidence that arms races do increase the likelihood of war between racing states. On the other side, we find Diehl and others (Diehl 1983, 1985; Weede 1980) who dispute this connection. To a great extent the outcome of this debate hinges on the definition of what constitutes an arms race.[9]

Even if it were shown conclusively that arms races increase the likelihood of war, this would not constitute direct confirming evidence for the proposition under consideration here for two reasons. First, the arms race thesis is dynamic while the militarization hypothesis is static. That is, continued increases in preparedness are central to the former, while high levels of preparedness are the concern of the latter. Second, the arms race thesis is not concerned with the relative defense effort of racing states, while the militarization hypothesis is. Two states could be involved in a low level arms race with neither reaching the stage of militarization referred to here, although continued, large increases in resources devoted to the military should eventually lead to that stage. . . .

IMPLICATIONS AND CONCLUSIONS

In closing I will consider some implications for theory and research, beginning with the individual factors and concluding with the overall pattern they reveal.

The importance of contiguity in accounting for the onset of interstate war argues that it should be commonly included in almost all studies of war, if only as a control variable. Whether it is only a measure of opportunity for war, or whether it taps something deeper that reflects the willingness to engage in war as well, is unclear, but its importance is not, and the argument for its inclusion applies to all levels of analysis. These results suggest that Diehl's conclusion that "although geography may not be the most important factor in international relations, its significance justifies increased and more careful attention from scholars of international conflict" (1991, 24) is true, but

[9]For a recent "recap" of this debate see Siverson and Diehl (1989).

understated, for in this competition between many purportedly important preconditions for war, contiguity finished first.

Alliances have been found to reduce significantly the likelihood of war between allies, except under the special condition where both are more militarized, in which case they have almost no impact. Thus our theoretical expectations are generally confirmed and the bivariate finding that alliances promote war between allies is shown to be essentially spurious. There is nothing in this finding inconsistent with the argument that alliances promote the spread of war, once it breaks out, however (Siverson and Starr 1990).

In the economic sphere, these results suggest that the likelihood of war starting between "have" states is considerably lower than between "have" and "have not" or between "have not" states. This could reflect a mutual recognition among advanced economies that war is, in Mueller's words "abhorrent—repulsive, immoral, and uncivilized—and methodologically ineffective—futile" (1989, 217), or, less charitably, it may indicate the presence of cartel-like collusion among richer states to avoid war between themselves in order to maintain their exalted economic positions. More conclusively, the (neo)-Leninist notion that competition between advanced economies is a major determinant of war has found little support. However, more research is certainly needed on this factor before any definitive conclusions can be drawn.

Democracy has once again shown itself to be a war-reducing factor, and its effect is readily apparent even after the effects of many other factors have been removed. It would not appear that the bivariate relationship between democracy and war is spurious, as some have contended; on the contrary, democracy is once again shown to be a quite powerful inhibitor of war. More studies are needed like that of Morgan and Campbell (1991) and Morgan and Schwebach (1991) to ascertain more precisely what it is about democracy that serves to inhibit war.

The results obtained in these analyses clearly support the position that power preponderance is more conducive to peace in a dyad than the lack thereof. Although its effect is not as strong as others considered here, and certainly weaker than hard-core realists would have us believe, the existence of overwhelming preponderance is, ceteris paribus, a "pacifying condition." It should be noted that these are precisely the dyads where one side should perceive itself to have a high probability of winning any war, based on relative capabilities. According to expected utility theory (Bueno de Mesquita 1981), the decision for war is based on this probability times the utility of victory. If we can assume that the utility of victory is independent of the probability of victory across our 200,000 dyads, then, if this theory is true, we should observe that dyads with large power differences are the more war-prone ones, precisely the opposite of what has been found here. This suggests that some reexamination of a basic premise of expected utility theory may be in order. At the very least, the way in which the probability of victory is typically operationalized should be questioned.

I have long felt that the designation of some states as major powers was an overly subjective classification and somewhat ad hoc. With respect to war, there is also the distinct possibility that the well-established propensity for major powers to engage in war is tautological (that is, states are considered major powers because they fight many wars). In view of this I would have preferred to find *no* significant association between power status and war after controlling for other factors like power difference. Yet, under this condition, the major power effect remains and is found to be about as influential as power preponderance. This suggests to me that there is another important characteristic, for which the major power designation serves as a proxy, that remains to be identified.

Perhaps the most important contribution of this study is that it provides, for the first time, a direct assessment of the relative importance of more than a few factors that are alleged to promote or inhibit the outbreak of war. In order of declining importance, the conditions that characterize a dangerous, war-prone dyad are:

1. presence of contiguity
2. absence of alliance
3. absence of more advanced economy
4. absence of democratic polity
5. absence of overwhelming preponderance
6. presence of major power.

The first four of these are each over twice as important as each of the last two. If the order of this list were compared to that of the implicit research priorities that have guided war and peace research, the correlation would not be positive. This leads to the rather sobering conclusion that our priorities may be seriously distorted.

Taken together these results give a strong endorsement to the idealist prescription for peace than to the realist one. Core components of the Wilsonian recipe for a more peaceful world were: establish collective security alliances, spread democracy, promote economic progress, and reduce armament levels. All of these save the last have been found to reduce strongly the likelihood of war at the dyadic level, and even the last factor is not discredited given that nothing in these findings suggests that high levels of military preparedness reduce the likelihood of war. In contrast, some of the primary concerns of realists, that is, relative power and power status in this analysis, have been shown to be less important than the above. Moreover, realists generally dismiss domestic factors as unimportant, yet these results suggest that they have a greater impact on the likelihood of war than others which they consider far more important. Certainly the results reported here do not constitute a head-to-head test of idealism versus realism (perhaps such a test is not possible), but they do suggest that a deeper examination of the idealist position might bring us closer to understanding the conditions that foster peace. We now have neo-realism; perhaps it's time to seriously entertain neo-idealism.

31 *SELECTIVE GLOBAL COMMITMENT*

ZBIGNIEW BRZEZINSKI

Zbigniew Brzezinski was National Security Adviser to President Jimmy Carter, 1977–81. He is now Counselor at the Center for Strategic and International Studies, and a professor of American Foreign Policy at The Johns Hopkins University.

There is a pervasive sense that the world is on the threshold of a new era. The dilemmas, passions, and especially utopias of the recent past have suddenly become irrelevant. Yet before a new world order is proudly proclaimed and majestically inaugurated, some serious geostrategic rethinking is necessary, lest global disorder comes to dominate the onset of the post-Cold War era.

The end of the Cold War marks this century's third grand transformation of the organizing structure and motivating spirit of global politics. The first two great transformations did not enhance international security. The question now is, will the third?

The catalyst for the third transformation is the success of the West and, specifically, the United States in the outcome of the Cold War. Much therefore depends on the geostrategic implications drawn from the conclusion of that era, especially by America and those nations that were its principal partners in that prolonged engagement.

I

The first transformation was generated by the collapse of Europe's balance of power and thus its decisive position in the world. That balance was sustained by several European-centered but global empires. Dominant worldwide and conservative in spirit, the European system—in existence since 1815—eventually came undone because it was able neither to assimilate the rise of German national power nor contain the centrifugal forces of rising chauvinism.

The first "world" war was in reality the last European war fought by globally significant European powers.

That war gave rise to an abortive attempt to reorganize Europe and thus, indirectly, the international system as a whole on the basis of a new principle: the supreme primacy of the nation-state, with nationalism fueling political emotions. The attainment—or enhancement—of national independence became the sacred goal of politics, and the protection—or expansion—of national frontiers was viewed as the key measure of success.

The result was massive failure. That new European order was too precarious to survive for long. With the territorial imperative igniting interstate conflicts and with weak nation-states dotting the map of the new Europe, it was only a question of time before a new eruption occurred. Germany was again the precipitator, though not entirely the root cause, of the resulting explosion.

The Second World War, in reality the first truly global war, completed Europe's historical suicide. In the course of that war Europe ceased to be the effective center of world politics and became instead the critical theater of a global competition waged by two powerful extra-European states. Both realized that geostrategic control over Europe would be tantamount to eventual control of Eurasia, and that control of Eurasia would yield global preponderance. Accordingly, throughout the resulting Cold War, Europe was for each of them the central stake.

World politics were again transformed, but for the first time in almost half a millennium they were no longer decisively affected by either the competition or the decisions of the principal European powers. Europe, instead of being the subject, now became the object of global contest.

The competition of the two superpowers was fueled not only by traditional nationalism but by a powerful new ingredient: ideology. This doctrinal imperative infused an unprecedented degree of intellectual self-righteousness into the conflict. The struggle between America and Russia thus quickly acquired a Manichaean character, with two colliding concepts, not only of social organization but ultimately even of the nature of the human being itself. Each superpower saw itself as the carrier of universalist values, and the opponent as the embodiment of evil.

This century's second great transformation of world politics—like the first—also failed to enhance genuine international security. The forty-five-year-long conflict between the two superpowers entailed, first of all, enormous risks. With ideological hostility intensifying their arms race, and with their arms possessing for the first time a lethal capacity on a globally devastating scale, the superpower rivalry was enormously costly in economic terms and potentially devastating beyond comprehension.

Ultimately the United States was successful, first, in deterring the Soviet Union from dominating Eurasia and, second, in discrediting its ideology and exhausting its economy. Belated efforts by the Soviet leadership to set in motion a process of domestic renewal created openings for intensified challenges to its control of vassal states. These challenges were fed by both nationalist resentments and an ideologically significant perception of the failure of the Soviet-style socioeconomic system to match the performance of the American-sponsored recovery of the western and eastern extremities of Eurasia. The crisis of power in the Kremlin and the sense of the historical failure of communism eventually caused the Soviet empire to disintegrate.

The Cold War thus ended without a hot war. In so doing it generated fundamental changes in two critical dimensions of world affairs: the geostrategic and the philosophical. In Eurasia Soviet power shrunk back not only to its 1940 frontiers, but it is now being challenged even within the Soviet Union. Indeed, the future survival of the Soviet system itself is now in doubt. Moreover a united Germany is now in NATO, noncommunist east European governments are craving membership not only in the European Community (EC) but in NATO as well, while a politically independent China is making steady progress in its pragmatic economic modernization. Geostrategically, far from subjugating Eurasia, the Soviet Union is now on the defensive within it.

The philosophical tenor of our time is now dominated by Western concepts of democracy and the free market. This is not to say that such concepts are being successfully implemented in the postcommunist states, but to assert that they represent today's prevailing wisdom. The competing notions of Marxism, not to speak of its Leninist-Stalinist offshoot, once so intellectually dominant, are generally discredited.

II

The end of the Cold War—and particularly its rather one-sided geostrategic and philosophical outcomes—has direct consequences for this century's third grand transformation of world politics.[1] The first transformation can be said to have been fueled by nationalist aspirations within a Europe no longer capable of dominating the world but still capable of disrupting it. The second involved an ideologically intensified global contest between two non-European superpowers. The structure and the spirit of the third are increasingly being shaped under the political and philosophical influence of the West's successful Cold War coalition.

In the course of the Cold War that coalition acquired a comprehensive institutional character, embracing not only America and western Europe but increasingly Japan as well. Considerations of security, a shared interest in economic growth based on global free trade, a commitment to democratic policymaking, and the impact of modern communications drove that coalition toward institutionalized cooperation. As a result its internal relations came to manifest a pattern of conduct motivated by what might be described broadly (if somewhat clumsily) as functionally pragmatic transnationalism.

[1]The author wishes to acknowledge arguments developed along these lines by others, notably Samuel P. Huntington, "America's Changing Strategic Interests," *Survival*, January/February 1991; and Paul H. Nitze, "America: An Honest Broker," *Foreign Affairs*, Fall 1990.

Important residues, both of nationalism and ideology, undoubtedly continue to surface in the conduct of affairs even within the coalition, and much more so in the world at large. But these impulses tend to be constrained by at least two pragmatic considerations: maximizing collective security and promoting an open international trading system. The quest for collective security stems from the realization of the vulnerability of even the major powers to weaponry of mass destruction as well as from the prohibitive cost of modern weaponry. At the same time the wealth of nations is increasingly a function of their capacity to trade without external restraints. Traditional nationalist notions of military self-sufficiency and economic autarky are thereby being rendered obsolete.

The revolution in behavior among the most advanced countries is reinforced not only by the growing interaction and personal familiarity among their governing elites, but also by a profound alteration in public values. For the average citizen the imperatives of consumption are now more important than those of territory or ideology. Neither the desire for complete national independence nor ideological self-righteousness are the overriding motivations shaping the coalition's public opinion.

It is difficult to find an average German who is politically driven by the passion to repossess Alsace-Lorraine, a Frenchman dreaming of a reconstituted empire, or even an American desperately fearful of world-wide communist takeover. As a result, functional pragmatism as well as transnational institution-building generally tend to dominate policy-making in the democratic West.

In the process the successful Western coalition—symbolized by the Group of Seven leading industrialized nations—is beginning to transform international politics into a more organic global process. This process tends to blur the distinction between domestic and foreign priorities. It also enhances the importance of internal economic and political well-being in determining the conduct and relative international importance of individual states. With nuclear weapons inhibiting the recourse to war among the leading powers, global politics are becoming in some ways similar to American urban centers: a mixture of inter-dependence and inequality, with violence concentrated in the poorer segments of society. Today, on a global scale, war has become a luxury that only poor nations can afford.

While morally unpalatable this reality nonetheless does somewhat enhance global security. So does the spread of democracy. This fact has even been recognized by once-hostile Moscow. As the thoughtful and iconoclastic minister of foreign affairs of the Russian republic, Andrei Kozyrev, has observed: "The main thing is that the Western countries are pluralistic democracies. Their governments are under the control of legal public institutions, and this practically rules out the pursuance of an aggressive foreign policy. In the system of Western states . . . the problem of war has essentially been removed."[2]

III

Threats to international security have traditionally been defined in terms of state-to-state relations. That was especially the case in an age in which the nation-state was the principal vessel of decisive political action. But in the emerging age of organic global politics, it is just as likely that major threats could originate from within states, either through civil conflicts or because of the increased technological sophistication of terrorist acts.

The character of the security challenges now facing the global community was dramatically defined by EC Commission President Jacques Delors in his important March 1991 address to the International Institute for Strategic Studies: "All around us, naked ambition, lust for power, national uprisings and underdevelopment are combining to create potentially dangerous situations, containing the seeds of destabilization and conflict, aggravated by the proliferation of weapons of mass destruction."

This general description could be amplified by a long list of specific problems, some due to the end of the Cold War, some long-lasting regional conflicts or legacies of imperialism, others likely to arise because of the emergence of new regional powers, and still others inherent in the inequality and poverty of the human condition—exacerbated by the population explosion. But all will be made potentially more lethal because of the inevitable further diffusion of weapons of mass destruction.

Accordingly, in determining when and how to address such problems the international community may have to be guided less by traditional notions of sovereignty (that is, is one state violating the sovereignty

[2]Kozyrev also boldly asserts that in contrast the totalitarian systems—among which he includes the Leninist-Stalinist—are inherently aggressive, automatically viewing any democratic system as a "mortal enemy." A. Kozyrev, "Building a Bridge—Along or Across a River: The Parameters of Our Security," *New Times*, Moscow, Oct. 23–29, 1990.

of another?) and more by the scope of the threat itself. In other words, there may develop situations in which external intervention in the seemingly internal affairs of a state—as in Yugoslavia yesterday and perhaps elsewhere tomorrow—may be necessary and justified by the potential consequences of activities that are otherwise of internal character and that do not, of themselves, involve interstate collision.

In these complex and dynamic circumstances, much depends on whether pragmatic transnationalism becomes not only the defining but also the enduring substance of this century's third transformation of global politics. A great deal thus hinges on the eventual resolution of four large structural dilemmas—each central to international security and a consequence of the Cold War's end.

First, how will Europe define itself? Will it be a truly European Europe with a supranational basis, emphasizing deeper cooperation before wider participation; or will it be a Europe of closely cooperating states, perhaps wider before deeper? Which is more likely to enhance global security, and which should America favor?

Second, how will the Soviet Union be transformed? Is its preservation in a reformed mode—for the sake of "stability"—desirable from the standpoint of international security; or is its progressive but fundamental transformation ultimately the safest path toward enhanced international security?

Third, how will the Pacific region organize itself? Should the United States remain decisively involved in the security arrangements of that region, or should Japan be encouraged to assume a preeminent role consistent with its economic power; if so, how will this impact on regional security and, notably, on China's likely posture?

Finally, how will the Middle East be pacified? Can the United States, now so deeply absorbed in the Middle East's complex problems, afford not to promote energetically a framework of security and accommodation; or are the region's problems so intractable that the wiser course dictates a policy of cautious diplomacy? Which is preferable from the standpoint of international security and America's capacity to contribute to it?

The answers to these questions will go a long way either in defining a system capable of containing and mitigating future threats to global security or in yielding to a condition of intensifying global disorder. Each area involves a series of critical and complex policy dilemmas. The positive development of each case—or at least three of the four—would represent a major contribution to the emergence of politically and economically stabilizing zones of international cooperation. This would enhance in an ink-blot fashion the scope of international security and reduce to tolerable levels the inevitable presence on the world scene of some degree of violence and conflict. . . .

32 REDEFINING SECURITY

JESSICA TUCHMAN MATHEWS

Jessica Tuchman Mathews is Vice President of the World Resources Institute. She
served on the National Security Council from 1977 to 1979 as Director of the Office
of Global Issues. The author acknowledges a great debt to colleagues at W.R.I.

The 1990s will demand redefinition of what
constitutes national security. In the 1970s
the concept was expanded to include international economics as it became clear that
the U.S. economy was no longer the independent force it had once been, but was
powerfully affected by economic policies in
dozens of other countries. Global developments now suggest the need for another
analogous, broadening definition of national security to include resource, environmental, and demographic issues.

The assumptions and institutions that
have governed international relations in the
postwar era are a poor fit with these new
realities. Environmental strains that transcend national borders are already beginning to break down the sacred boundaries
of national sovereignty, previously rendered
porous by the information and communication revolutions and the instantaneous
global movement of financial capital. The
once sharp dividing line between foreign
and domestic policy is blurred, forcing governments to grapple in international forums with issues that were contentious
enough in the domestic arena.

I

Despite the headlines of 1988—the polluted
coastlines, the climatic extremes, the accelerating deforestation, and flooding that
plagued the planet—human society has not
arrived at the brink of some absolute limit to
its growth. The planet may ultimately be
able to accommodate the additional 5 or 6
billion people projected to be living here by
the year 2100. But it seems unlikely that the
world will be able to do so unless the means
of production change dramatically. Global
economic output has quadrupled since 1950
and it must continue to grow rapidly simply
to meet basic human needs. . . .

Greenhouse change is closely linked to
stratospheric ozone depletion, which is also

Excerpted from *Foreign Affairs*, Vol. 68, No. 2. Spring, 1989, pp. 171–7. Reprinted
by permission of *Foreign Affairs*, Spring 1989. © 1989 by The Council on Foreign Relations, Inc.

caused by chlorofluorocarbons. The increased ultraviolet radiation resulting from losses in that protective layer will cause an increase in skin cancers and eye damage. It will have many still uncertain impacts on plant and animal life, and may suppress the immune systems of many species.

Serious enough in itself, ozone depletion illustrates a worrisome feature of man's newfound ability to cause global change. It is almost impossible to predict accurately the long-term impact of new chemicals or processes on the environment. Chlorofluorocarbons were thoroughly tested when first introduced, and found to be benign. Their effect on the remote stratosphere was never considered.

Not only is it difficult to anticipate all the possible consequences in a highly interdependent, complex system, the system itself is poorly understood. When British scientists announced the appearance of a continent-sized "hole" in the ozone layer over Antarctica in 1985, the discovery sent shock waves through the scientific community. Although stratospheric ozone depletion had been the subject of intense study and debate for more than a decade, no one had predicted the Antarctic hole and no theory could account for it.

The lesson is this: current knowledge of planetary mechanisms is so scanty that the possibility of surprise, perhaps quite nasty surprise, must be rated rather high. The greatest risk may well come from a completely unanticipated direction. We lack both crucial knowledge and early warning systems.

II

Absent profound change in man's relationship to his environment, the future does not look bright. Consider the planet without such change in the year 2050. Economic growth is projected to have quintupled by then. Energy use could also quintuple; or if post-1973 trends continue, it may grow more slowly, perhaps only doubling or tripling. The human species already consumes or destroys 40 percent of all the energy produced by terrestrial photosynthesis, that is, 40 percent of the food energy potentially available to living things on land. While that fraction may be sustainable, it is doubtful that it could keep pace with the expected doubling of the world's population. Human use of 80 percent of the planet's potential productivity does not seem compatible with the continued functioning of the biosphere as we know it. The expected rate of species loss would have risen from perhaps a few each day to several hundred a day. The pollution and toxic waste burden would likely prove unmanageable. Tropical forests would have largely disappeared, and arable land, a vital resource in a world of ten billion people, would be rapidly decreasing due to soil degradation. In short, sweeping change in economic production systems is not a choice but a necessity.

Happily, this grim sketch of conditions in 2050 is not a prediction, but a projection, based on current trends. Like all projections, it says more about the present and the recent past than it does about the future. The planet is not destined to a slow and painful decline into environmental chaos. There are technical, scientific, and economical solutions that are feasible to many current trends, and enough is known about promising new approaches to be confident that the right kinds of research will produce huge payoffs. Embedded in current practices are vast costs in lost opportunities and waste, which, if corrected, would bring massive benefits. Some such steps will require only a reallocation of money, while others will require sizable capital investments. None of the needed steps, however, requires globally unaffordable sums of money. What they do demand is a sizable shift in priorities.

For example, family-planning services cost about $10 per user, a tiny fraction of the cost of the basic human needs that would otherwise have to be met. Already identified opportunities for raising the efficiency of energy use in the United States cost one-half to one-seventh the cost of new energy supply. Comparable savings are available in most other countries. Agroforestry techniques, in which carefully selected combinations of trees and shrubs are planted together with crops, can not only replace the need for purchased fertilizer but also improve soil quality, make more water available to crops, hold down weeds, and provide fuelwood and higher agricultural yields all at the same time.

But if the technological opportunities are boundless, the social, political, and institutional barriers are huge. Subsidies, pricing policies, and economic discount rates encourage resource depletion in the name of economic growth, while delivering only the illusion of sustainable growth. Population control remains a controversial subject in much of the world. The traditional prerogatives of nation states are poorly matched with the needs for regional cooperation and global decision-making. And ignorance of the biological underpinning of human society blocks a clear view of where the long-term threats to global security lie.

Overcoming these economic and political barriers will require social and institutional inventions comparable in scale and vision to the new arrangements conceived in the decade following World War II. Without the sharp political turning point of a major war, and with threats that are diffuse and long-term, the task will be more difficult. But if we are to avoid irreversible damage to the planet and a heavy toll in human suffering, nothing less is likely to suffice. A partial list of the specific changes suggests how demanding a task it will be.

Achieving sustainable economic growth will require the remodeling of agriculture, energy use, and industrial production after nature's example—their reinvention, in fact. These economic systems must become circular rather than linear. Industry and manufacturing will need processes that use materials and energy with high efficiency, recycle by-products, and produce little waste. Energy demand will have to be met with the highest efficiency consistent with full economic growth. Agriculture will rely heavily upon free ecosystem services instead of nearly exclusive reliance on man-made substitutes. And all systems will have to price goods and services to reflect the environmental costs of their provision.

A vital first step, one that can and should be taken in the very near term, would be to reinvent the national income accounts by which gross national product is measured. GNP is the foundation on which national economic policies are built, yet its calculation does not take into account resource depletion. A country can consume its forests, wildlife and fisheries, its minerals, its clean water and its topsoil, without seeing a reflection of the loss in its GNP. Nor are ecosystem services—sustaining soil fertility, moderating and storing rainfall, filtering air and regulating the climate—valued, though their loss may entail great expense. The result is that economic policy-makers are profoundly misled by their chief guide.

A second step would be to invent a set of indicators by which global environmental health could be measured. Economic planning would be adrift without GNP, unemployment rates, and the like, and social planning without demographic indicators—fertility rates, infant mortality, literacy, life expectancy—would be impossible. Yet this is precisely where environmental policymaking stands today.

Development assistance also requires new tools. Bilateral and multilateral donors have found that project success rates climb when nongovernmental organizations distribute funds and direct programs. This is especially true in agriculture, forestry, and conservation projects. The reasons are not mysterious. Such projects are more decentralized, more attuned to local needs and desires, and have a much higher degree of local participation in project planning. They are usually quite small in scale, however, and not capable of handling very large amounts of development funding. Often, too, their independent status threatens the national government. Finding ways to make far greater use of the strengths of such groups without weakening national governments is another priority for institutional innovation.

Better ways must also be found to turn the scientific and engineering strengths of the industrialized world to the solution of the developing world's problems. The challenges include learning enough about local constraints and conditions to ask the right questions, making such research professionally rewarding to the individual scientist, and transferring technology more effectively. The international centers for agricultural research, a jointly managed network of thirteen institutions launched in the 1960s, might be improved upon and applied in other areas.

On the political front, the need for a new diplomacy and for new institutions and regulatory regimes to cope with the world's growing environmental interdependence is even more compelling. Put bluntly, our accepted definition of the limits of national sovereignty as coinciding with national borders is obsolete. The government of Ban-gladesh, no matter how hard it tries, cannot prevent tragic floods, such as it suffered last year. Preventing them requires active cooperation from Nepal and India. The government of Canada cannot protect its water resources from acid rain without collaboration with the United States. Eighteen diverse nations share the heavily polluted Mediterranean Sea. Even the Caribbean Islands, as physically isolated as they are, find themselves affected by others' resource management policies as locusts, inadvertently bred through generations of exposure to pesticides and now strong enough to fly all the way from Africa, infest their shores.

The majority of environmental problems demand regional solutions which encroach upon what we now think of as the prerogatives of national governments. This is because the phenomena themselves are defined by the limits of watershed, ecosystem, or atmospheric transport, not by national borders. Indeed, the costs and benefits of alternative policies cannot often be accurately judged without considering the region rather than the nation.

The developing countries especially will need to pool their efforts in the search for solutions. Three-quarters of the countries in sub-Saharan Africa, for example, have fewer people than live in New York City. National scientific and research capabilities cannot be built on such a small population base. Regional cooperation is required.

Dealing with global change will be more difficult. No one nation or even group of nations can meet these challenges, and no nation can protect itself from the actions—or inaction—of others. No existing institution matches these criteria. It will be necessary to reduce the dominance of the superpower relationship which so often encourages other countries to adopt a wait-and-see attitude (you solve your problems first, then talk to us about change).

The United States, in particular, will

have to assign a far greater prominence than it has heretofore to the practice of multilateral diplomacy. This would mean changes that range from the organization of the State Department and the language proficiency of the Foreign Service, to the definition of an international role that allows leadership without primacy, both in the slogging work of negotiation and in adherence to final outcomes. Above all, ways must soon be found to step around the deeply entrenched North-South cleavage and to replace it with a planetary sense of shared destiny. Perhaps the successes of the UN specialized agencies can be built upon for this purpose. But certainly the task of forging a global energy policy in order to control the greenhouse effect, for example, is a very long way from eradicating smallpox or sharing weather information.

The recent Soviet proposal to turn the UN Trusteeship Council, which has outlived the colonies it oversaw, into a trusteeship for managing the global commons (the oceans, the atmosphere, biological diversity and planetary climate) deserves close scrutiny. If a newly defined council could sidestep the UN's political fault lines, and incorporate, rather than supplant, the existing strengths of the United Nations Environment Programme, it might provide a useful forum for reaching global environmental decisions at a far higher political level than anything that exists now.

Today's negotiating models—the Law of the Sea Treaty, the Nuclear Nonproliferation Treaty, even the promising Convention to Protect the Ozone Layer—are inadequate. Typically, such agreements take about fifteen years to negotiate and enter into force, and perhaps another ten years before substantial changes in behavior are actually achieved. (The NPT, which required only seven years to complete these steps, is a notable exception.) Far better approaches will be needed.

Among these new approaches, perhaps the most difficult to achieve will be ways to negotiate successfully in the presence of substantial scientific uncertainty. The present model is static: years of negotiation leading to a final product. The new model will have to be fluid, allowing a rolling process of intermediate or self-adjusting agreements that respond quickly to growing scientific understanding. The recent Montreal agreement on the ozone layer supplies a useful precedent by providing that one-third of the parties can reconvene a scientific experts group to consider new evidence as it becomes available. The new model will require new economic methods for assessing risk, especially where the possible outcomes are irreversible. It will depend on a more active political role for biologists and chemists than they have been accustomed to, and far greater technical competence in the natural and planetary sciences among policy-makers. Finally, the new model may need to forge a more involved and constructive role for the private sector. Relegating the affected industries to a heel-dragging, adversarial, outsiders role almost guarantees a slow process. The ozone agreement, to cite again this recent example, would not have been reached as quickly, and perhaps not at all, had it not been for the cooperation of the chlorofluorocarbon producers.

International law, broadly speaking, has declined in influence in recent years. With leadership and commitment from the major powers it might regain its lost status. But that will not be sufficient. To be effective, future arrangements will require provisions for monitoring, enforcement, and compensation, even when damage cannot be assigned a precise monetary value. These are all areas where international law has traditionally been weak.

This is only a partial agenda for the needed decade of invention. Meanwhile, much can and must be done with existing means. Four steps are most important: prompt revision of the Montreal Treaty, to eliminate completely the production of chlorofluorocarbons no later than the year 2000; full support for and implementation of the global Tropical Forestry Action Plan developed by the World Bank, the UN's Development Programme, the Food and Agricultural Organization, and the World Resources Institute; sufficient support for family planning programs to ensure that all who want contraceptives have affordable access to them at least by the end of the decade; and, for the United States, a ten-year energy policy with the goal of increasing the energy productivity of our economy (that is, reducing the amount of energy required to produce a dollar of GNP) by about 3 percent each year. While choosing four priorities from dozens of needed initiatives is highly arbitrary, these four stand out as ambitious yet achievable goals on which a broad consensus could be developed, and whose success would bring multiple, long-term global benefits touching every major international environmental concern.

III

Reflecting on the discovery of atomic energy, Albert Einstein noted "everything changed." And indeed, nuclear fission became the dominant force—military, geopolitical, and even psychological and social— of the ensuing decades. In the same sense, the driving force of the coming decades may well be environmental change. Man is still utterly dependent on the natural world but now has for the first time the ability to alter it, rapidly and on a global scale. Because of that difference, Einstein's verdict that "we shall require a substantially new manner of thinking if mankind is to survive" still seems apt.

CHAPTER NINE

INTERNATIONAL TRADE AND THE INTERNATIONAL SYSTEM

No nation was ever ruined by trade.
Benjamin Franklin, *Thoughts on Commercial Subjects*, 1780

Free trade is not a principle, it is an expedient.
Benjamin Disreali, Speech on Import Duties, 1843

Throughout the postwar era, trade has been heralded as the "engine of growth" that has driven the world economic system. Trade liberalization in a multilateral context has continued apace until recent years, when the regional context has suddenly become the focus of economic activity. This chapter looks at the world economy through the prism of trade and how the current system has evolved.

Informal trading arrangements have taken place between individuals of differing societies for nearly as long as there have been human beings. Anthropologists excavating archaeological cave sites in southwest France, which date back at least 20,000 years, have discovered large quantities of handcrafts made of sea shells. Since the site in central France was hundreds of miles from the ocean, the researchers could only conclude that this inland people traded with a people who lived on the coast. Clearly, trading patterns over time between these peoples must have built some norms and modalities of behavior and therefore engaged in multilateral trade negotiations. These negotiations are important pieces in creating and managing any economy. Will this prehistoric system presage the future? In a following article Richard Rosecrance argues that the "territorial" wars of the past will make way for "trading" wars in the future.

But multilateral trade negotiations in the context used here imply a higher degree of coordination and rule setting than the kind of commerce which existed between prehistoric peoples. Multilateral trade negotiations began in earnest with the explosion of international trade in the 1700s. This explosion, driven both by the industrial revolution and advances in transportation, made these more formal economic arrangements necessary.

The rise of trade was also coupled with ongoing political events of the time. Adam Smith, in the 1776 landmark *Wealth of Nations,* described the need for specialization in international trade, using the example of the inherent comparative advantage in the trade of British textiles and Portuguese wine. It was only a coincidence that the American Revolution took place in the same year as the publication of Smith's seminal piece. But the notion that this refinement of capitalism was born with the movement of Western nations towards liberal democracy is inescapable.

Formal trading agreements between nations began to appear in the 1800s. In Germany, domestic trade barriers were substantially reduced by the creation of the customs union known as the Zollverein. In the years between 1820 and 1870 many European and North American states liberalized external trade policies. Britain, for example, removed prohibitions against the export of both skilled workers (labor) and machinery (capital) in this time. It followed with liberalization of international shipping by the abolishment of the Navigation Act and grain imports by revoking the infamous Corn Laws. British import tariffs, now more revenue- than protective-oriented, were down to 5.8 percent in 1880.[1]

Elsewhere, similar trends were occurring, albeit at a slower pace. Tariffs in the United States fell to 24.7 percent in the late 1850s, but rose after the Civil War—ostensibly due to the need to raise revenues. France concluded the Cobden-Chevalier treaty with Britain in 1862, which opened free trade between the two nations and spurred further tariff cuts by the Zollverein. Zollverein duties on manufactured imports were at 10 percent in 1834, but steadily increased in the 1840s.

A liberal trading environment grew in the late 1800s but withered both before and after World War One. In fact, economic nationalism, paralleling the growth of political nationalism which ultimately led to the war, reversed the fifty year trend towards freer trade. Colonial empires developed into preferential trading blocs, particularly in the case of the British Commonwealth. Germany and France abandoned free trade in agriculture in the 1880s, for the most part due to complaints about cheap American imports!

Economic nationalism became even stronger in the inter-war period. Argentina and Brazil erected substantial protective barriers. Most industrial nations, especially with the onset of the Depression, also retreated behind protectionist walls. Paramount was the Smoot-Hawley Tariff Act, passed by the United

---

[1]World Bank, *World Development Report,* 1991, pp. 40–43.

States and ultimately blamed for exacerbating the Depression. The United Kingdom and France followed suit and aligned their trading regimes more so towards their colonial empires. Germany created complex systems of exchange controls for trade with south and central Europe.

In retrospect, one can see a pattern of expansion and contraction of the world trading system.[2] Average tariff levels today for industrial countries, now in the range of 10 percent, are certainly lower than in the earlier part of this century, but are still higher for the most part than what existed under the regime of the late nineteenth century. As far as trade liberalization is concerned, the GATT has only been able to return us to a trading environment which existed some 100 years ago. In a following article, Reneé Marlin-Bennett argues that such multilateralism will soon give way to regionalism as the basis for trade relations.

In 1944, at the Bretton Woods conference, the countries of the Western Alliance agreed to set up an organization to manage the international economic system. The purpose of the organization, beyond the reconstruction of countries after the end of World War Two, was to avoid the "beggar thy neighbor" policies that emerged in the 1930s and deepened the Depression. Many also blamed these policies for the instability in Germany during this period which allowed Adolph Hitler to come to power.[3]

The organization was to be based on three pillars: the World Bank, International Monetary Fund (IMF), and International Trade Organization (ITO). The World Bank was to be responsible for reconstruction (then of Europe, now of developing countries), the IMF for managing financial matters, and the ITO for establishing international trade and commercial policy. The General Agreement of Tariffs and Trade (GATT) was to be an interim agreement pending the ratification of the ITO. That ratification never came about because the U.S. Congress refused to ratify it on the grounds that its enforcement would preempt domestic economic prerogatives. Simply speaking: the United States feared the loss of sovereignty envisioned under the broad powers of the ITO.

The GATT is a forum for discourse on the disciplines of international trade, in which the purpose of the discourse is to advance the area under its discipline (an external concern) and to resolve differences between its members when they arise (an internal concern). Joan Spero describes this dual role of the GATT as a necessary symptom of a system (the international system) which is dominated by its sub-components (nations). There are certain characteristics inherent to this type of system. "Because of the absence of central government, the central problems of international politics are the adjustment or management of conflict and the achievement of cooperation. . . . When there are effective rules, institutions, and procedures, conflict takes place within agreed limits and cooperation is facilitated."[4]

---

[2]These are not unlike long cycles of capital accumulation described by Kondratieff. Indeed, long-term capital and trading cycles seem to be linked.

[3]See World Bank, *1987 World Development Report*, p. 156.

[4]Joan Edelman Spero, *The Politics of International Economic Relations* (New York: St. Martins Press, 1977), p. 10–11.

What is the GATT? Formally, it can be regarded as an institution because it provides rules that guide behavior. Blake and Walters note that it is simply ". . . a legally binding codification of rules for the conduct of trade among its member states."[5] Yet some regard the stated claim of GATT as an institution to be dubious; it is lacking in enforcement and completely voluntary in adherence. After all, it is an interim agreement. On closer inspection, they argue, GATT appears to be more of a contract than an institution (technically, it is). Dean Acheson pushed this point: "No code of laws is worth very much without an authoritative body to interpret it and administer it."[6]

The GATT generally has followed the path of adaptive evolution, propounded through what is called the "bicycle" theory. Under this theory, "the smart way to keep freer trade going is to keep negotiating it: as with a bicycle, if you stop moving you fall off."[7] In conceiving of the GATT back in 1947, it was felt that an ongoing process of negotiations would act to fend off persistent protectionist tendencies that would undoubtedly arise. Indeed, the recent Uruguay Round was begun in part to counter growing protectionist sentiments in the U.S. Congress. As such, the trading system can be viewed as a mediative or adjustment entity: forging a middle ground between domestic and international interests.[8]

The GATT philosophy propounds economic liberalism. Blake and Walters find that:

> The classical liberal economic approach is evident in the various works of analysts such as Harry Johnson and in the basic contemporary foreign economic-policy orientations of the United States and other governments of advanced industrial societies in the West. They are evident as well in the policy orientations of key international economic institutions such as the General Agreement on Tariffs and Trade, the International Monetary Fund, and the International Bank for Reconstruction and Development.[9]

Regionalist approaches to trade relations are becoming more prominent quite often at the expense of multilateral approaches. While the Uruguay Round stalls, around the world countries are forming regional blocs. What does this mean? A student of history would point to the continuing pattern of expansion and contraction in the world trading system and conclude that today's events are but one phase of a much longer cycle.

[5]David H. Blake and Robert S. Walters, *The Politics of Global Economic Relations* (Englewood Cliffs, N.J.: Prentice Hall), p. 12.

[6]Dean Acheson, "Economic Policy and the ITO Charter," *Department of State Bulletin XX* (1949), p. 626.

[7]Jagdish Bhagwati, Anne Kreuger, and Richard Snape, "Introduction: A Symposium Issue on the Multilateral Trade Negotiations and Developing Country Interests," *The World Bank Economic Review* (September 1987) Vol. 1, No. 4, p. 540.

[8]Richard Rosecrance, *The Rise of the Trading State: Commerce and Conquest in the Modern World* (New York: Basic Books, 1986), p. 40.

[9]David H. Blake and Robert S. Walters, *The Politics of Global Economic Relations* (Englewood Cliffs, N.J.: Prentice Hall), p. 5.

The U.S.–Canada free trade has been up and running for some years and negotiations extending the area of coverage to Mexico are underway. President Bush proposed a longer-term Enterprise for the Americas Initiative to create a free trade area stretching from Nome, Alaska to Tierra del Fuego in Chile. Chile may in fact begin negotiations with the United States on a free trade area fairly soon. Cooperation is also helping to revive moribund regional economic groups such as the countries in the northern South America (the Andes Pact), the South American cone (the free trade agreement between Argentina and Brazil), and the countries of Central America (CARICOM).

In Asia, ASEAN has been in existence for some time and Australia and New Zealand have opened their economic borders to one another. South Asian countries are working more intensely together and several Middle Eastern countries have discussed economic union. Morocco and Libya have, for the moment, some sort of special economic relationship.

EC 1992 intends to unify the economies of western and southern Europe and their associations with the EFTA countries create a huge economic base. But the optimism about EC 1992 has waned ever since the Danish rejection of the treaty and the narrow victory in the French refererendum. These sentiments put the whole scope of reforms in doubt.

The growth of regionalism in economic relations is evident in the difficult Uruguay Round negotiations under the auspices of the GATT. The slowdown in the talks is said to lie at the feet of several causes, including (1) the recession in the world economy, (2) the technical problems in extending GATT discipline to cover new areas such as services trade, and (3) the EC 1992 program which diverted attention from multilateralism to regionalism.

DISCUSSION QUESTIONS

1. Is this the last GATT round? What is the likely direction in world economic relations over the next decade?
2. Sumitomo, IBM, and Siemens recently signed a cooperative deal to develop the next generation of computer chips. This unlikely alliance came about because the sheer cost of developing new technologies is so expensive. Together, these three companies have combined sales which exceed the GNPs of many countries of the world. What does the multilateral nature of today's companies mean for state sovereignty?
3. Compare the differences between multilateralism and regionalism in the world economic system.
4. Does "free trade" really exist?
5. The growth of services trade has in recent years outpaced the growth of trade in goods. Why has this occurred and what are its implications?
6. U.S. trade law allows the imposition of trade sanctions in cases of worker rights violations in other countries? Should trade policy be linked to human rights policy?
7. Is trade an antidote for war? That is to say: will extensive trade relations

create a kind of mutual dependency that will reduce the likelihood of conflict?

8. Compare the generalized benefits from trade to the specialized costs it incurs on workers in a limited number of industries. What are the political consequences of each?

9. Are trade competition and environmental protection compatible or incompatible?

10. Can trade increase cultural awareness between peoples?

33 *THE MILITARY-POLITICAL WORLD AND THE TRADING WORLD*

RICHARD ROSECRANCE

Long in the forefront of IR theory, Richard Rosecrance is now Professor of Political Science at the University of California, Los Angeles.

The choice between territorial and trading means to national advancement has always lain before states. Most often, however, nations have selected a point between extremes though nearer the territorial end. In the early years of the modern period in the sixteenth and seventeenth centuries, that point was close to the territorial and military pole; at mid-nineteenth century it briefly moved toward the trading pole. In World Wars I and II the military and territorial orientation was chosen once again. Only after 1945 did a group of trading nations emerge in world politics. Over time this group has grown and its success, at least in economic terms, has been greater than that of either the United States or the Soviet Union. Before we look at the hybrid forms that have been attempted, it may be desirable to sketch the polar or pure types: the military-political and the trading worlds.

THE MILITARY-POLITICAL WORLD

In a military-political world nations are ranged in terms of power and territory from the greatest to the weakest. States in such a world are homogeneous in form; that is, they do not have differentiated objectives or perform a variety of functions.[1] They all seek the same territorial objectives and each, at least among the major powers, strive to be

[1]There has been an important difference between those who see homogeneity as desirable and those who find it disruptive in the international system because of different definitions of the term. Raymond Aron and Hedley Bull believe a homogeneous system, that is, one without ideological differences, is more cohesive than a heterogeneous system. Kenneth Waltz contends that the state system is homogeneous, in that all states depend only on themselves. Peter Blau notes that "exchange" can only emerge in a social system when there is some differentiation in the functions performed by the parties, and therefore suggests that heterogeneity and social exchange can level power hierarchies and produce cooperation. Ideological heterogeneity (in Aron's sense) may be quite compatible with homogeneity (in Waltz's sense) for ideological disunity can be the stimulus to seek total independence. Raymond Aron, *Peace and War* (New York: Praeger,

the leading power in the system. None of the contenders wishes to depend upon any other for any vital function, from the provision of defense to economic resources. Such a world might be stable in the sense of avoiding war if one single state achieved hegemony over the others.

If one power attained total mastery, the other members of the system would finally cease resisting because no advantage could be gained. Instead, they could compete for favors from the hegemonic overlord, who would reward them from his seemingly inexhaustible political and military surplus.[2] Recognizing that opposition served no purpose, the members would return allegiance and support. Historically, only the Roman Empire attained such mastery in the Western tradition: Charlemagne, Louis XIV, Napoleon, and Hitler never achieved it. Since the decline of the Roman Empire in the third to the fifth century A.D., contending feudal or state units have been the order of the day, and anarchy has been the principle of interstate relations.

The military-political world involves a continual recourse to war because the units within it compete for primacy. None is content to accept the hegemony of one of their number if it can be prevented; each is afraid that the dominance of one power will undermine its domestic autonomy and perhaps its very existence. Hence the balance of power becomes a means of resistance to threatened hegemony. The means of constructing a balance ultimately involves a resort to force to discipline an ambitious pretender. Warfare may be stabilizing if it succeeds in restraining challenge, but it cannot be acceptable if the destruction it causes more than outweighs the evil it seeks to prevent. In addition, since every state in a political-military order seeks to be self-sufficient, each strives to grow larger in order to achieve full independence. This drive itself is a cause of war.

THE TRADING WORLD

In contrast, the trading world is not composed of states ranked in order of their power and territory, all seeking preponderance. Instead, it is composed of nations differentiated in terms of function. Each may seek to improve its position, but because nations supply different services and products, in defense as well as economics, they come to depend upon each other.[3] While some will be stronger than others, their functions give them a kind of equality of status. They may specialize in terms of particular defense functions: conventional or nuclear forces. They may offer raw materials or primary products to the international trading system as opposed to manufactured goods. Within the category of manufacturers, there may be intra-industry specialization in terms of technology. Certain industrial countries may concentrate, like Switzerland and Italy, on producing goods of very high quality and craftsmanship. Others, like Korea or Taiwan, may produce shoes, watches, textiles, steel, or ships on an efficient low-cost basis. Trading states will also normally form alliances as a precaution against sudden intrusion by military-political nations.

While trading states try to improve

1967), pp. 99–103; Hedley Bull, *The Anarchical Society* (New York: Columbia University Press, 1977), pp. 33–34, 317; Kenneth Waltz, *Theory of International Politics* (Reading, Mass: Addison-Wesley, 1979), pp. 93–97; Peter Blau, *Exchange and Power in Social Life* (New York: John Wiley & Sons, 1964), pp. 190–192.
[2] See Peter Blau, *Exchange and Power in Social Life* (New York: John Wiley & Sons, 1964), pp. 106–12.
[3] Blau, See chap. 4 and 5.

their position and their own domestic allocation of resources, they do so within a context of accepted interdependence. They recognize that the attempt to provide every service and fulfill every function of statehood on an independent and autonomous basis is extremely inefficient, and they prefer a situation which provides for specialization and division of labor among nations. One nation's attempt to improve its own access to products and resources, therefore, does not conflict with another state's attempt to do the same. The incentive to wage war is absent in such a system for war disrupts trade and the interdependence on which trade is based. Trading states recognize that they can do better through internal economic development sustained by a worldwide market for their goods and services than by trying to conquer and assimilate large tracts of land.

In general terms, the competition for power emerges in social relations wherever needs are provided for independently and without reciprocity and where resources are limited. If needs do not have to be met independently, a reciprocal division of labor may give rise to stable cooperation. If resources are in unlimited supply, self-sufficient persons or nations may gain all they need without encroaching on the wants of others. Hence in a bountiful state of nature, primitive people could have an idyllic existence free from competition and conflict. Alternatively, in a social order characterized by a degree of scarcity, conflict could still be limited by interdependence, exchange, and sharing. But where scarcity and the urge to full independence exist, government and law are needed to restrain a competition over power leading to social conflict.

In international society where government does not exist, nations will have power conflicts unless they can work out a system of interdependence to satisfy their needs. Only the reciprocal exchange and division of labor represented by the trading world can prevent conflict in such an anarchic environment. Industrial and population growth strengthen interdependence and make it harder to achieve national objectives autonomously. When technology was rudimentary and population sparse, states had little contact with one another and did not generally get in each other's way. With the commercial and industrial revolutions, however, they were brought into closer proximity. As the Industrial Revolution demanded energy resources—great quantities of food, coal, iron, water power, and petroleum—the number of states which could be fully independent declined. Those which sought complete autonomy and even autarchy had to conquer the lands which contained the materials they needed. The military-political and territorial system, then, required more war. Only a shift in direction toward an interdependent trading system, giving up autonomy in return for greater access to world resources and markets, could produce greater cooperation among nations.

The trading system does not require large, self-sufficient units. As the national objective is exchange and trade with other states, trading countries do not need large territories and populations. Like Singapore and Hong Kong, they may be small countries, little more than cities, which manufacture the raw materials of other nations into finished commodities, gaining a high return in foreign trade.

Military technology also influences the trend toward one system or the other. One theory of historical development charts an increase in the size of the state as developments in military technology make smaller predecessors vulnerable to attack. Thus the medieval castle became vulnerable to gunpowder loaded in the siege gun. Large territorial states achieved a hard-shell character for a time, but even they become permeable when economic blockade, airpower, and the intercontinental missile allowed one country to strike at the very heart of another's population.[4] Now the largest territorial state is no longer immune to attack and depends upon its opponent's decisions. Such trends make the goals of the military-political and territorial system harder and harder to achieve.

Shifts in domestic cohesion also affect the choice between trading and military-political worlds. The ramshackle feudal monarchies were hardly integrated enough to fight purposeful and continuous war against each other. They did not enjoy the loyalty of their citizens and were hard pressed to find the finances for military campaigns. As greater resources were tapped by the new administrative systems of the centralizing monarchies emerging from the Reformation, the conquest of adjacent territories became easier. Sixteenth-century Spain and eighteenth-century England proved that states with relatively efficient administrative structures could create large navies and conquer empires. The French Revolution and the Napoleonic reforms lent even greater authority to the revolutionary leader or his imperial successor. With greater discipline existing in citizen armies, soldiers fighting for their country would be more effective than the hired mercenaries of eighteenth-century monarchies. New vistas of territorial expansion beckoned. Finally, in the late nineteenth and first half of the twentieth centuries, further increases in nationalism and support for the policies of the government produced the final gusher of massive violence in World Wars I and II. The greater the obedience of an unquestioning citizenry, the more acceptable were the demands of the military-political and territorial world.

Conversely, the trading system depended on setting free the productive and trading energies of peoples and merchants who, without guidance and direction from the administrative capital of the state, would find markets for their goods overseas.[5] Governments had to loosen control of their populace in order to generate the opportunities required to establish the trading system. They had to revoke mercantilist requirements and controls, abolish monopolies and chartered companies to enlist the efforts of capitalists and bring forth the necessary investment to finance productive enterprise. In certain cases trading cities with a wide range of independence grew up inside territorial states. They served the economic and financial interests of merchants and investors in other countries as well as their own. The nineteenth-century age of laissez faire in which government moved out of domestic economic activity fostered their aims better than the old official sponsorship and control. By liberating groups engaged in commerce on the high seas, governments in fact created classes of persons who were not exclusively loyal to the national state but catered to a wider constituency. In the American Civil War, New York merchants and financiers were close to the trading cities of the confederacy and were initially tempted to secede as well.[6] In the late nineteenth century, Hamburg traders were closer to their English markets and suppliers than they were to the administrative and imperial center in Berlin. The development of such trading relations stimulated the revival of connections like those uniting the trading city-states of the Renaissance. Free from imperial supervision and control these early-modern city-states banded together, as in the Hanseatic League, to further mutual re-

[4] J. Herz, "Rise and Demise of the Territorial State" in *World Politics*, 9:4 (July 1957), pp. 473–93.

[5] Edward Whiting Fox, *History in Geographic Perspective: The Other France* (New York: W. W. Norton, 1971), pp. 33–37, 55–71. In this path-breaking book, Fox calls this system "The Commercial Society."

[6] R. G. Albion, *Rise of New York Port, 1815–1860* (New York: Charles Scribner's Sons, 1939), pp. 120–21.

lations, protection, and trade, enforcing contracts between them. In the nineteenth century although no such formal organization was established, the connections of centers of commerce were much the same. They transcended exclusive loyalties to a single political jurisdiction.

To sum up: military-political and territorial states are homogeneous competing countries. Each seeks to secure hegemony or at a minimum to gain independence and self-sufficiency from foreign control. They do not generally cooperate except when the balance of power requires opposition to a hegemonic aspirant. In the territorial system in the past, wars were continually fought to safeguard independence and prevent preponderance by any single power. Trading states, in contrast, are interdependent nations which accept equality of status on the basis of differentiation of function. Their objectives—to improve national welfare and the allocation of resources through internal development and trade—do not require preventing other states from achieving similar goals. As long as states were generally out of contact with one another and the waging of war was relatively easy, the military-political and territorial world would predominate over the trading world. When interdependence grew with large populations, industrialization, and need for resources, the military-political world faced greater difficulties. Rulers in that tradition sought to compensate by drawing more support from their people for imperial policies and war, but this solution only went so far.

HYBRID POSSIBILITIES

Despite the contradictory requirements of military-political and trading systems, states have sometimes tried to live in both worlds. The great hegemonic pretenders—Philip II of Spain, Louis XIV, the Sun King of France, and Napoleon—aimed to govern Europe. Spain used her monopoly on the gold and silver production of the mines in Mexico and Peru to build unexampled military strength in the sixteenth century. Spain's objective was to conquer new lands in Italy, Portugal, the Low Countries, France, and England, reducing the rest of Europe to subjection. But the effort involved in campaigns of such magnitude ruined her economy. Even Spain's conquest of gold had a double-edged effect. The great imports of bullion inflated Spanish domestic prices and made her goods less attractive in world markets. By 1640, the Spanish challenge had been defeated and she neared the brink of internal collapse.

In the late seventeenth century, Louis XIV wanted to dominate the states of Europe, overseas trade, and also found an empire. But his offensive policy was costlier than the Dutch fortifications which resisted it. His naval forces were no match for England or Holland, and on land his armies were checked by Austria, the German states, Holland, and England. Jean Baptiste Colbert, Louis's great finance minister, had tried to fashion a French alternative to Amsterdam's control of world trade, but he failed miserably. French culture permeated continental Europe, but the French King's territorial expansion was defeated at home and abroad.

A century later, Napoleon conquered a great deal more territory in Europe than his royal predecessors, hoping after 1805 that by concentrating upon one objective he could establish a lasting empire. Recognizing that he could not compete with British trade in the Atlantic and Pacific, he gave up colonies overseas. Instead, through the Continental System, he sought to exclude British goods and develop a self-sufficient commerce within Europe itself. The Continent ultimately rebelled against this system; and Britain was able to sell as well as to buy from Europe. Russian and German armies defeated Napoleon at Leipzig (1813) and finally with English help at Waterloo (1815).

Thus none of the historic hegemonic pretenders actually achieved his goal. Only Great Britain came close to establishing a lesser version of such a system, but she did so by avoiding commitments in Europe itself.[7] In the mid-eighteenth century she gave economic help to Prussia but otherwise abjured a role on the Continent. Against Napoleon she contributed small forces which alone never would have turned the French tide. Her success in gaining an empire overseas was partly due to her avoidance of a military role in Europe. But Britain never established hegemony over other European states, the only powers who could be real military rivals. Instead, she kept out of their way. Thus, the attempt to maximize both trading and military-political possibilities has failed throughout history, and, since Rome, hegemony has never been won by any state.

THE CHOICE BETWEEN MILITARY-POLITICAL AND TRADING WORLDS

If states cannot realistically expect to succeed at both ends of the spectrum, to be both fully developed military-political and trading countries, it is nevertheless possible to combine traits from the two systems in different ways. No nation entirely dispenses with police or military authority. Each has armed officials who can arrest evil-doers, whether they are domestic or foreign. Equally, even the most territorially oriented governments of all time, those of Nazi Germany and interwar Japan, engaged in international trade. Germany needed food, iron ore, and petroleum; Japan a variety of materials, including rubber, tin, iron ore, and oil. German and Japanese manufactures were sent abroad to pay for these goods so that the two countries could build a stockpile for war. If most states were to rely exclusively on trading methods, the few that specialized in military and territorial expansion would make great gains at the formers' expense. If most nations were to have no defense, the cost of war for others would be low and the incentive to engage in it high. Thus every state procures some defense and participates in some trade.

The difference between states is that some rely primarily on military force and only incidentally engage in trade; others make their livelihood in trade and use defense only against the most remote contingencies. For the first, trade is an economic palliative between the territorial wars that truly determine a nation's fate; for the second, trade and internal development are primary and defense a tactical measure to reduce another state's temptation to strike. Each country has to determine where it will place its emphasis in policy terms, which method it will primarily seek to use.

There is a third possibility: that nations will rely on internal economic development without resorting to trade *or* to military force. They could then remain isolated and nonparticipants in broader international politics. With the growth of interdependence among states, this alternative ulti-

[7] See Michael Howard, *The Continental Commitment* (London: Maurice Temple Smith Ltd., 1972); Paul Kennedy, *Strategy and Diplomacy, 1870–1945* (London: Fontana Paperbacks, 1984), chap. 8, esp. p. 216.

mately reduces to one of the two other choices. Once an industrial machine has been built, to what use will it be put? At the end of the nineteenth century, Imperial Germany began to rearm for the coming conflict to decide the final distribution of colonies and resources in world politics. Taking a different course, mid-Victorian England used her industrial prowess to further her trade and sought neither empire nor territory on the Continent.

In the twentieth century most developed nations have industrial capacities that are too large to be sustained entirely by the home market. Unless they can sell overseas—to other industrial countries and to states with a less developed manufacturing plant—they cannot expect to maintain employment and growth. The excess capacity must be disposed of in some way—either through arms production or through sales of manufactured goods to other nations. When they make such a choice, they elect one of the two major competing worlds.

What decides the choice they will make? What balance will the future generations choose between trading and territorial worlds? That depends upon the cost and benefit of waging war on the one hand and engaging in trade on the other. The greater the restraints on trade and the fewer its likely benefits, the more willing nations have been to seek to improve their position through military force. The higher the cost of war and the more uncertain its benefits, the more nations have sought trade as a livelihood.

34 A RULE-BASED VIEW OF INTERNATIONAL TRADE

RENEÉ MARLIN-BENNETT

Now assistant professor of International Politics and Foreign Policy at the School of International Service, the American University, Ms. Marlin-Bennett commenced her study of IR at Pomona College, taking her doctorate at M.I.T.

International regimes which order states' and non-state actors' behavior are a hot topic in international relations research. Can we identify principles, norms, rules, and procedures about proper behavior in a given issue-area? If so, then we find the silver lining in the pessimistic expectations of realism. Regimes, if they exist, make international cooperation *rational* in the economic sense. Each actor can "maximize its utility" when all agree to operate according to a set of rules. This is the premise behind international regimes theory.

Compelling and idealistically pleasing as this premise is, a serious question remains: What happened to the deep-seated political and ideological blocs that we generally think of as defining the intentional system? Do regimes transcend blocs? I think not. Regimes, I argue, should be reconceptualized to specify the principles, norms, rules, and procedures which order the behavior and expectations for *a group of actors* for a given issue-area.

In practical terms, overlapping rules, but not universal regimes, will facilitate international cooperation. The overlapping rules in and of themselves, however should not be considered a universal meta-regime. Regimes, because they embody generalized principles and norms, are generated from political ideologies. Rules simply held in common across political ideologies are not undergirded by universal principles and norms derived from a hypothetical universal political ideology.

A long-winded metaphor can illustrate my position. Regimes are basically formalized "rules of the game." The game is the issue-area. For the moment, assume that poker is the game. There are many different sets of rules which can apply to poker: Five Card Draw, Five Card Stud, Seven Card Stud, Chicago, High—Low, to name just a few. Each of these different variations on poker represents a different regime. Each has its own, independent set of rules. At the same time, each variation is identifiable as poker: The best five-card poker hand wins in the end. Some of the rules overlap. In Five Card Stud and Five Card Draw the dealer deals five cards. In Five Card Stud and Seven Card Stud the dealer deals some cards face-down and some cards face-up. If

Printed with the kind permission of the author, this article is an update of her contribution on trade regimes in the eighth edition of this book, pp. 212–216.

you stumbled into a smoke-filled room of poker players, how would you know which particular variation they were playing? You would ask the players. Who plays which game in poker is usually determined by which game or games your particular crowd likes to play.

International regimes work the same way. For any given game, distinct (but linked) sets of rules order behavior. In the international arena, who complies with which regime is determined by the political and ideological blocs that continue to define the configuration of the international system. In short, *regimes are bounded by both participants and issue-area*.

Political and ideological orientation of the participants gives a regime its character. Politics limit who joins a regime and how the costs and benefits of maintaining the regime will be distributed. Ideology informs the principles, norms, rules, and procedures. Young (1980:342) makes the point best:

> [R]egimes resting on socialist premises will encompass more extensive collections of rules as well as more explicit efforts to direct behavior toward the achievement of goals than *laissez-faire* regimes that emphasize decentralized decision making and autonomy for individual actors.

MULTIPLE TRADE REGIMES

The issue-area of international trade has been one of the most fertile for exploring regime concepts. It is also an area in which the role of political and ideological blocs has not been recognized. Four overlapping political–ideological blocs describe the membership of four identifiably distinct trade regimes. These blocs are:

- the industrialized West,
- the socialist East,
- the corporatist North, and
- the developing South.

Industrialized West

Since most regimes theorists are from the industrialized West, most analytical discussions of trade regimes focus on what goes on among the advanced capitalist economies. Regimes theorists most commonly write about some variations of a neoclassical trade regime organized around the General Agreement on Trade and Tariffs. Ruggie (1982), for example, developed a very sophisticated concept of "embedded liberalism." He argued that protectionism was part

and parcel of today's international trade regime and that, despite the contradiction, protectionism and free trade principles exist side by side.

Embedded liberalism does make a lot of sense—for describing trade behavior in the industrialized West. The United States both subsidizes some agricultural products and vigorously argues for the multilateral reduction of trade barriers. The European Community and Japan do the same. However, embedded liberalism only orders trade for certain actors and then only for certain products and commodities. Embedded liberalism is the trade regime of GATT members, but not all countries are members of the GATT and not all GATT members always trade in accordance with GATT rules. Corporatist practices, discussed below, are becoming more common among these actors.

Socialist East

In the socialist world protectionism versus free trade is not an issue. The goal has been self-sufficiency through a division of labor within the bloc. Yet this centralization and planning places a heavy burden. To encourage political solidarity, the Soviet Union had subsidized oil prices for its allies and overpaid for sugar from Cuba and Nicaragua.

Decisions about production, imports, and exports are becoming somewhat decentralized. Resistance to these changes can be partially ascribed to uncertainty about the direction and extent of regime change. Nevertheless, the bloc system still maintains a socialist character and much more planning and centralization is expected than in the industrialized West.

Corporatist North

The corporatist North presents yet another bloc with its own trading regime. Here the taxonomy is complicated because many of the members of the corporatist North are also members of the industrialized West. Actors may pursue policies complying with either bloc's trade regime depending on the actors' interests regarding the particular commodity or product being traded.

First, let's define, in a simplified way, what corporatism is, since it is not part of the usual international relations jargon. Schmitter (1979) defines corporatism as "a system of interest representation" within a country. The state, through legal mechanisms or a *de facto* process, legitimizes certain interest groups as representing particular constituencies. Policy is made when the government decides how to divide the pie among competing interest groups. Corporatism is easily recognized in the authoritarian Newly Industrialized Countries in which the government encourages and aids chosen industries at the expense of others. Corporatism also develops in the industrialized market economies, and this development decreases the power of the market.

In the international trade arena, corporatism orders trade behavior for some groups of actors for some products and commodities. Generally, these are the prod-

ucts and commodities, such as some agricultural products, which fall outside the embedded liberal regime. In contrast to the "acceptable" market-correcting protectionism of embedded liberalism, corporatism legitimates government intervention in the market for reasons other than correcting market failures. Moreover, corporatist protectionism is usually discriminatory. It is targeted against an offending state.

Under the corporatist regime, states negotiate for trade rights and market shares. Aggarwal, *et al.,* (1987) have referred to this behavioral pattern as "negotiated protectionism." The agreements arrived at through negotiated protectionism generally institutionalize asymmetries of market power.

In embedded liberalism, actors will sanctify the market. Protectionism addresses market failures and usually uses market mechanisms (e.g., tariffs) to correct the failures. The negotiated protectionism of corporatism, on the other hand, vitiates the free market and substitutes a managed market, one in which governments intervene for the sake of ordering the trading process. Quotas are more typical of corporatist behavior than tariffs.

When do actors "defect" from embedded liberalism and pursue trade policies consistent with the corporatist trade regime? The answer depends on the level of development of the actor. The Newly Industrialized Countries often adopt corporatism as part of their development strategies. In the advanced industrialized countries, however, the switch to corporatist trade usually follows the corporatization of government–industry relations when an industry is in decline (senile in economic terms) or is facing an erosion of its international market share.

Developing South

Developing countries also advocate a market-managing trade regime, although the intent of the regime is to redistribute market share rights and create market duties. Duties refer to the responsibility of richer states to help poorer states by, for example, agreeing to purchase a set amount of a specified commodity. Despite the calls for a New International Economic Order and the best efforts of United Nations organizations at promulgating a Southern trade regime, this latent regime has not succeeded in ordering behavior. The form exists: Principles, norms, rules, and procedures have all been established. Some representatives of states and international organizations continue to invoke these regime elements in international negotiations over trade. But for the day-to-day conduct of interna0 tional trade, little is ordered by a Southern regime.

Some commodity agreements under the aegis of the United Nations Integrated Program on Commodities have achieved limited success at restructuring and managing international markets. The goal of these agreements is to create a stable and profitable environment for developing country traders. However, the commodity agreements are usually plagued by the need to placate powerful industrialized country exporters. The agreements are generally watered-down compromises that break down under severe market pressures such as a glut of a particular commodity. Of course, severe conditions are exactly the time when a commodity agreement needs to function best to protect the developing countries from economic harm.

CONCLUSION

The existence of regimes is clearest when we recognize the role of political and ideological blocs in generating principles, norms, rules, and procedures. The developing countries want to reconstruct an international market that protects their income and furnishes them with essential imports at stable prices. They have developed a mostly unrealized Southern trade regime articulated in the New International Economic Order. In contrast, Newly Industrialized Countries and advanced industrialized countries sometimes find it in their interests to manage the international market to protect their shares. This corporatist behavior involves negotiated protectionism.

Embedded liberalism involves both some free trade and protectionism that is imposed without negotiation, although it may be removed through negotiation. Still, protectionism under the embedded liberal trade regime attempts to correct market failures while limiting government intervention in the market. At the other end of the spectrum, the trade regime of the socialist bloc is completely structured around government determination of the market.

Trade within blocs generally complies with the bloc's trade regime. Trade across blocs takes advantage of overlapping rules. Contracts and sovereignty, for example, are generally respected. Long-term arrangements are acceptable for socialist, corporatist North, and developing South traders. However, I argue that trade within blocs is easier than trade across blocs. The more expectations the participants hold in common, the more cooperative trade can be.

Moreover, changes in the political orientation of major international actors should signal a change in regimes. A lessening of East–West political tensions should lead to revisions of the trade regimes. This prediction is almost the reverse of the "spillover" effects expected by integration theorists (for example, Haas, 1964). In the theory of functional integration, increased cooperation in some international function such as trade was expected to produce political cooperation. A revision of regimes theory that is sensitive to the dynamics of international politics would predict that political conciliation and regime revision should go hand in hand.

Understanding the role of political and ideological blocs in international regime creation and maintenance increases the analytical power of regimes theory and links it more closely to our intuitive sense of the way the world works.

CHAPTER TEN

THE POLITICAL ECONOMY OF THE ENVIRONMENT

It has been observed, for example, that if the last 50,000 years of man's existence were divided into lifetimes of approximately sixty-two years each, there have been about 800 such lifetimes. Of these 800, fully 650 were spent in caves.

Only during the last seventy lifetimes has it been possible to communicate effectively from one lifetime to another—as writing made it possible to do. Only during the last six lifetimes did masses of men ever see a printed word. Only during the last four has it been possible to measure time with any precision. Only in the last two has anyone anywhere used an electric motor. And the overwhelming majority of all the material goods we use in daily life today have been developed within the present, the eight hundredth lifetime.

Alvin Toeffler, *Future Shock*

The material impact of human beings on the physical environment is becoming too clearly evident. Likewise, the environment and issues related to it are rapidly becoming a fixture in IR discourse. Whether the focus is power or development, economics or politics, or any of the other diverse subjects under the IR umbrella, most are creating theoretical room for the environment in research and including it in their teaching of the subject. The "environment" obviously is a very generous term but there are two specific areas in which it has come under serious discussion in IR. In the first area, the threat of overpopulation, the state is unimportant to the problem. In the second area, environmental disputes, the state is critical. A third area for discussion is now evolving: possible instances where the environment may lead to political conflict between states.

The first area of environmental concern is the growing threat of human habitation to the very planet, characterized by problems such as deforestation and global warming. On the whole, this general problem is not caused by states (rather by the collective actions of individuals) although the solution may well rest with states. At the root of the problem with respect to the global environment, say many, is simply there are too many people in it.

Are there too many people? The answer is surely a relative one: It is too much if it exceeds the resources available. Will it? That is a matter of debate, and a fierce one at that. Many scholars cannot imagine the resource requirements needed if 10 billion people had per capita incomes that equalled current average levels in industrial countries. Others, such as Julian Simon and Herman Kahn, can easily imagine such a world, and a bountiful one at that!

Predicting the number of humans is not so difficult, given we know today the approximate size of the age cohorts that will make up the next reproductive generations. In 1988 there were about 4.7 billion people in the world. By the year 2025, that total will rise to 8.0 billion and thereafter stabilize somewhere between 10 and 15 billion in the middle to latter parts of the twenty-first century.

Projections supplied by the World Bank (and made by the United Nations) offer a startling vision of the world of the future. By the year 2025, when the typical IR student of today will be middle-aged, the world's population will look as follows.[1]

- Mexico's population of 184 million will be nearly four times greater than Canada's 32 million.
- The Philippines at 139 million will surpass Japan at 131 million.
- Brazil at 303 million and Indonesia at 370 million will roughly equal that of the United States at 316 million.
- China and India will each exceed 1.8 billion, with India slightly larger.
- Nigeria will have 617 million, roughly the same as all of Europe combined.
- Ethiopia's population will climb to 471 million (from 47 million now) and Bangladesh to 346 million (from 109 million now).
- Iran will rise to 247 million, Pakistan to 556 million, and Iraq to 90 million.
- Both Italy and the former area of West Germany will see a fall of over 10 million, with smaller losses in the Netherlands, Belgium, Austria, Hungary, and Switzerland.

The simple demographic aspects of these predictions are of some interest to IR researchers. More important, however, is the implications that these numbers have for future relations between states (if they still exist then). Is it conceivable, for example, that Ethiopia could rise tenfold in population without experiencing some unrest and conflict? One would think that impossible. Likewise,

[1]World Bank, *World Development Report,* 1991.

could Nigeria remain united under a single state with 617 million people? What would it mean if Greece's population of 10 million remained the same but Turkey's population of 54 million grew to 120 million?

Read these statistics and their implications with caution. The future will probably not follow a linear progression from today. Fifty years *ago,* much of today's technology would have been unthinkable. Practical use of nuclear energy and computers were not yet invented. Who knows what other breakthroughs may change our lives in the upcoming years? Some believe that the pace of scientific breakthroughs is actually increasing and there is strong evidence to believe this to be true.

The debate over population has been one of the great overarching questions of our time. It is a question that spans borders and disciplines. No generation had ever worried about there being too many people. More often, the worry was there were too few people. By the same token, no generation ever considered accepting declining expectations as today's does because of the threat of too many people.

Because IR researchers devote their energies to understanding large-scale social phenomena the debate over population has perhaps been louder in our field than in any other. In IR, we are naturally comfortable about discussing behavior at this high level of abstraction and the fact that population presents such a multifold problem or opportunity is itself something natural to the IR researcher. Moreover, the question is often discussed in the context of development, a subfield of IR.

The second area in which the environment is being discussed in IR is how it relates to the policies of states. The idea that the environment is one element of a state's security concerns is not new. The environment holds resources such as forests, agricultural lands, and oil which have long been of importance to national security and of concern to IR. For a long time the only concern for IR was on what happened to the supply of resources. Both the Japanese in 1941 and the Iraqis in 1991 launched wars related to controlling the supply of oil. Now, for the first time we are becoming concerned with the consequences of the consumption of oil (for example, emissions, storage, and transportation), as evidenced in the Rio Summit. The relation of the environment to a state's security is indirect and of consequence mostly in the long-term. There is of course no immediate impact of the environment on the sovereignty of the state nor can it suddenly reduce a state's ability to defend itself.

How can one look at the various types of environmental issues and state policies in a coherent fashion? We can divide problems of an environmental nature into two general groups: those that involve *depleting* resources from the environment (for example, cutting down too many trees) and those that involve putting too much *pollution* back in the environment (for example, acid rain). From these two cornerstones, policy problems can also be sorted out into bilateral and multilateral fora indicating whether the problems are regional or global in scope, under the assumption that the number of participants surely changes the dynamics of cooperation between states. Thus, environmental problems in the end can be divided into four general categories:

1. bilateral pollution problems,
2. global pollution problems,
3. bilateral resource problems, and
4. multilateral resource problems.

Each type is briefly discussed.

(1) Bilateral pollution problems. When pollution crosses boundaries, states have so far had little recourse. Canada has found little action from the United States on cleaning up the facilities that bring so much acid rain from U.S. sources (this is due to the prevailing wind patterns). Likewise, Austria has no compensation from the dirty industries in Czechoslovakia and Hungary. When a recent accident dumped tons of chemicals into the Rhine River in Basel, Switzerland, the German government was in no way adequately compensated for the problems caused or by the loss of resources incurred. The costs of Chernobyl to other countries in the world, particularly neighboring countries to the old Soviet Union, easily reached billions of dollars long ago. Compensation has not been forthcoming.

(2) Multilateral pollution problems. In some cases it is not a problem of pollution migrating from one state to another but rather that the combined effects of some practice have severe environmental consequences. For example, the use of chlorofluorocarbons (CFCs) was found to cause holes in the ozone layer of the planet's atmosphere. This led countries to agree to limits contained in the Montreal Protocol. By the same token, most states agreed to a plan to limit CO_2 emissions at the Environmental Summit at Rio de Janeiro. The United States, however, while the largest emitter of CO_2, was not a party to the agreement.

(3) Bilateral depletion problems. States often share resources because the environment has no respect for the arbitrary boundary lines which governments

TABLE 1   AN ENVIRONMENTAL CONCEPTUAL FRAMEWORK

	Bilateral	
[1]		[3]
Pollution		Depletion
[2]		[4]
	Multilateral	

have drawn on the face of the earth. The United States and Canada have taken several cases to the GATT where the use of a resource was the issue. In one case, Canada accused the United States of discrimination by not allowing lobsters of a certain size to be imported. The United States maintains a minimum size to protect future lobster stocks and the Canadian version of one type matured earlier than its American counterpart, largely because it was in a more northerly location and the season was briefer. Therefore, Canada argued, the Canadian lobster should be allowed entry into the U.S. market at a smaller size than its U.S. counterpart since the real issue was not the size but the maturity of the lobster. The GATT committee ruled in favor of the United States, basing its decisions not on the environmental or biological truths to the arguments but rather on the administrative burden it would place on U.S. inspectors in determining if smaller lobsters were Canadian or not.

(4) Multilateral depletion problems. Just as the combined pollutants from many states can lead to a problem, so too can the use of a particular type of resource by a number of states lead to depletion problems. The Convention for International Trade in Endangered Species (CITES) bans trade in items such as ivory, furs, and other products made from certain animals. The Whaling Convention and other agreements limiting harvesting of animals also fall into this category.

These conventions have worked in varying degrees in differing countries. In Africa just south of the Sahel (Kenya, for example), the ban on ivory trade has only marginally slowed the taking of elephants by poachers. In the most southern part of the continent (South Africa, for example), the level of protection and regulation has always been fairly high. The result: several southern African countries including South Africa have asked to be excused from the convention rules since they now face a *surplus* of elephants. The convention body declined the request, again relying on arguments of an administrative nature rather than a theoretical nature.

The following article by Ebba Dohlman shows the links between the environment and the economy. In spite of the many instances where environmental protection is clearly justifiable and needed, in others environmental protection is merely a smokescreen for trade protection. Again, the perception of environmental regulations as being indicators of cooperation versus conflict will have a growing bearing on relations between states.

As pollution and resource issues continue to be important to the security of a state, the likelihood that the ultimate policy instrument—conflict—will be used to solve an environmental dispute will surely increase. Consider the following four scenarios that could occur in the near-term, where the environment may be a part of a political problem.

- By the end of the twentieth century most of the forests of the Philippines had been cut down. Nearby Malaysia had great forest reserves in Sabah and Sarawak that were at least in some places virtually untouched. Economic conditions in the Philippines were so bad the government in Manila did not try to stop Philippine companies from poaching on Malaysian forest land. Conflict occurred when Malaysia accused Manila of also claiming a Malay island known for its oil potential.

- Israeli and Syrian aircraft attacked dams on the Euphrates in the southeast corner of Turkey in uncoordinated but tacitly parallel missions. Turkey's huge dam and canal projects to provide water to this arid part of the Anatolian peninsula succeeded all too well. It increased local water supply to huge parts of this semiarid region but severely limited the downstream flow of water. Both Israel and Syria subsequently suffered severe water shortages, in part due to the newly increased level of Turkish water offtake.
- Korea's fishing fleet of tuna boats was decimated by terrorist attacks on the high seas, in the wake of Korea's refusal to improve its record on coincident dolphin deaths. Some attacks were direct assaults by other boats, other were incidents involving floating mines, torpedo attacks, and terrorist bombings. The terrorist groups are reputed to have links to western environmental groups (enviro-terrorists).
- Saudi Arabia began running out of both oil and water in the early part of the twenty-first century. Saudi supertankers, no longer needed given the paltry oil output, had been pressed into service hauling glaciers from the Arctic and Antarctic Oceans (depending on the season) to Saudi Arabia where they are melted and used for fresh water. Initially, Saudi glacier crews simply took Atlantic and Antarctic glacial icebergs that naturally broke away and floated in the ocean. As the enterprise grew, however, the crews started to dynamite glacial chunks and unlodge them in various ways that went beyond simply "harvesting" the glacier. International protests soon followed.

Peter H. Sand, in a following article, juxtaposes such possible cases with how, on the other hand, they have been peacefully resolved through cooperation. Sand divides the types of disputes into multinational ("reciprocal") and transnational ("collective") categories. The problem is that none of the various agreements or treaties on the environment imposes arbitration but rather allows it once the parties in dispute agree so. Thus, there is no obligation that a dispute even be settled or that it be done in a peaceful manner. Perhaps the above scenarios are not so fanciful.

DISCUSSION QUESTIONS

1. Is there a real security need associated with the environment? Should there be treaties which address these security problems?
2. Is there a real possibility of the environment being the cause (or the excuse) for conflict? Give some possible examples.
3. Could there be a series of "Green" negotiating rounds, similar to the negotiating rounds in the GATT, where global frameworks on the environment are created?

4. Many believe that free trade is good. Is free trade good for the environment?
5. Are there other examples of the four types of policy areas where the environment is important: (1) bilateral pollution, (2) multilateral pollution, (3) bilateral depletion, and (4) multilateral depletion.
6. Was the United States justified in not signing the CO_2 convention at the Rio Summit?
7. Do developing countries have the right to neglect the environment in favor of improving the lives of their citizens?
8. Is the environment an issue that should be left to the discretion of individual sovereign states?
9. Are economic growth and the protection of the environment mutually exclusive?
10. Do we live in a finite world and do limits to growth exist?

35 NEW APPROACHES TO TRANSNATIONAL ENVIRONMENTAL DISPUTES

Peter H. Sand

Principal Legal Officer, United Nations Conference on Environment and Development (UNCED), Geneva. (Views and opinions expressed are those of the author and do not necessarily reflect those of the UNCED secretariat).

One of the many myths about environmental law is the assumption—found in many legal textbooks—that international disputes in this field are settled along the lines of the 1941 *Trail Smelter* arbitration.[1] Yet over the past 50 years there have only been two intergovernmental dispute adjudications that could even remotely be compared to *Trail Smelter*—and even those cases (the 1957 *Lake Lanoux* arbitration[2] between France and Spain, and the 1968 *Gut Dam* arbitration[3] between Canada and the United States) concerned classical questions of water use and flood damage, rather than a genuine environmental problem.

So is there something wrong with our textbooks? Richard Bilder, in his pioneering Hague course on environmental disputes in 1975,[4] drew attention to the fact that "governments have tended to avoid judicial and liability-based methods of dealing with these questions." The time may indeed be ripe to compare theories and realities in this field.

A first glance at the more than 140 existing environmental treaties[5] shows no lack of provisions for dispute settlement, including references to the International Court of Justice (ICJ) and highly elaborate arbitration procedures.[6] Closer analysis reveals, how-

---

[1]*UN Reports of International Arbitral Awards*, vol. 3 (1949), p. 1905. See John E. Read, "The Trail Smelter Dispute," *Canadian Yearbook of International Law* 1 (1963): 213–229; and Marjorie Millace Whiteman, *Digest of International Law*, vol. 6 (Washington: U.S. Department of State, 1968), pp. 253–256.

[2]*UN Reports of International Arbitral Awards*, vol. 12 (1957), p. 281. See John G. Laylin and Rinaldo L. Bianchi, "The Role of Adjudication in International River Disputes: The Lake Lanoux Case," *American Journal of International Law* 53 (1959): 30–49. The reference to environmental pollution in this case was entirely hypothetical and obiter, or incidental to the proceeding.

[3]See Lambertus Erades, "The Gut Dam Arbitration," *Nederlands Tijdschrift voor International Recht* 16 (1969): 161–206.

[4]Richard B. Bilder, "The Settlement of Disputes in the Field of the International Law of the Environment," *Recueil des Cours: Collected Courses of the Hague Academy of International Law* 144 (1975 1): 139–239.

[5]See the *Register of International Treaties and Other Agreements in the Field of the Environment* (United Nations Environment Programme, Nairobi 1989; revised edition to be issued in 1991); and the 78 texts in *Selected Multilateral Treaties in the Field of the Environment*, UNEP Reference Series 3 (Alexandre Charles Kiss, ed., Nairobi: United Nations Environment Programme, 1983; revised edition by Grotius Publications, Cambridge 1991).

[6]Annex B of the 1974 Paris Convention for the Prevention of Marine Pollution from Land-based Sources

"New Approaches to Transnational Environmental Disputes," *International Environmental Affairs*, 3, 3, Summer 1991, pp. 193–206. © by the Trustees of Dartmouth College.

ever, that these provisions can usually *not* be invoked unilaterally at the request of any one state—as postulated, for example, in the legal principles proposed by the World Commission on Environment and Development (Brundtland Report)[7]—but that in most cases they make third-party adjudication dependent on "common agreement" by the parties to a dispute. Hence they require prior compromissory negotiation and clearly fall short of mandatory settlement.

This was long considered an East-Wing problem—with the USSR and other socialist countries traditionally opposing compulsory adjudication as an infringement on their sovereignty. But the change of position of the United States, when it claimed the ICJ had no jurisdiction in the dispute over the U.S. mining of Nicaragua's Managua harbor,[8] also meant a significant change in the standard clauses for dispute settlement in international environmental agreements. For example, Article 20 of the 1989 Basel Convention on the Control of Transboundary Movements of Hazardous Wastes and their Disposal[9] stipulates that disputes may only be submitted to the ICJ or to arbitration by "common agreement," unless a party has expressly waived this condition. This type of optional dispute settlement clause goes back directly to a formula introduced, at the request of the U.S. State Department, in the 1985 Vienna Convention for the Protection of the Ozone Layer[10] —in spite of strong resistance by sixteen other western countries favoring easier access to arbitration or the ICJ.[11]

It should be remembered that the first blow to the World Court's potential as a forum for environmental dispute settlement had already been dealt in 1970 when Canada reserved jurisdiction with regard to her Arctic Waters Pollution Prevention Act,[12] even though that reservation was later withdrawn,[13] and even though the idea of "environmental chambers" for the ICJ has actively been encouraged by some of its most distinguished judges.[14] Whatever the histor-

---

served as a model for many arbitration procedures in this field—though with the all-important difference that most subsequent copies (such as the arbitration annex of the 1976 Barcelona Convention for Protection of the Mediterranean Sea against Pollution; and three other regional conventions adopted under UNEP auspices for the Caribbean in 1983, the Eastern African area in 1985 and the South Pacific in 1986) made the procedure optional rather than compulsory. See texts in Peter H. Sand, *Marine Environment Law in the United Nations Environment Programme* (London: Cassell Tycooly, 1988), pp. 13, 148, 169, 207.

[7] World Commission on Environment and Development, *Our Common Future* (Oxford: Oxford, 1987), p. 351 (principle 22). See also the commentary by Robert D. Munro and Johan G. Lammers, eds., *Environmental Protection and Sustainable Development: Legal Principles and Recommendations adopted by the Experts Group on Environmental Law of the World Commission on Environment and Development* (London: Graham & Trotman, 1987).

[8] This case concerned military and paramilitary activities in and against Nicaragua (*Nicaragua vs. United States*), judgment of November 26, 1984 with regard to jurisdiction of the court and admissibility of the application, *International Legal Materials* 24 (1985):

59; and the statement of January 18, 1985 on United States withdrawal from the proceedings initiated by Nicaragua in the International Court of Justice, with observations by the U.S. State Department, *International Legal Materials* 24 (1985): 246, 249.

[9] *International Legal Materials* 28 (1989): 657.

[10] *International Legal Materials* 26 (1987): 1529.

[11] See the declaration annexed to the Final Act of the Vienna Conference of Plenipotentiaries on the Protection of the Ozone Layer, UNEP/IG.53/5/Rev. 1 (1985).

[12] Declaration of April 7, 1970, *International Legal Materials* 9 (1970): 598.

[13] Declaration of September 10, 1985, *International Legal Materials* 24 (1985): 1729.

[14] Phillip C. Jessup, "Do New Problems Need New Courts?" *Proceedings of the American Society of International Law* 65 (1971): 261–268; Manfred Lachs, "Some Reflections on the Settlement of International Disputes," *Proceedings of the American Society of International Law* 68 (1974): 323–330. See also the proposal for a new "world tribunal to enforce proper regulation in environmental matters" by the late Judge Nagendra Singh in: *The Future of the International Law of the Environment*, René-Jean Dupuy, ed. (Dordrecht: Nijhoff, 1985), p. 422.

ical reasons for this particular "Hague phobia," environmental agreements that can be enforced by compulsory international adjudication today are the exception rather than the rule.[15]

Which alternatives, then, are available for the resolution of environmental problems at the international level? Richard Bilder defined international environmental disputes as "any disagreement or conflict of views or interests between States relating to the alteration, through human intervention, of natural environmental systems."[16] In my view, this traditional limitation to intergovernmental conflicts is too narrow, and as already mentioned, would practically restrict us to the extremely rare *Trail Smelter* syndrome. It is perhaps worth recalling here that the *Trail Smelter* case, too, arose from a dispute between individual pollution victims and a nongovernmental polluter— and it was only an unfortunate deadlock of private international law remedies which prevented the case from being settled in the ordinary national courts.[17] Bilder himself, in his concluding enumeration of "principles of environmental dispute management," emphasizes the principle of the lowest-level solution,[18] which by definition includes local remedies *below* the inter-

governmental level. Similarly, the thoughtful 1977 UN Institute for Training and Research (UNITAR) study by Aida Luisa Levin[19] makes a strong plea for including private international law approaches in our spectrum of environmental dispute settlement—a point that has recently found support in the UN International Law Commission.[20] I would, therefore, prefer the term "transnational," as defined by Philip Jessup,[21] to describe not only the problems but also the various types of solutions to be considered in this context.

Another equally important question of definitions concerns the nature of the legal relationships over which transnational environmental disputes arise. It is true that the bulk of environmental conflicts occur between specific victims (for example, of pollution) and specific villains (for example, polluters). In legal terms, we may classify these as disputes over *reciprocal obligations*. On the other hand, a growing number of environmental problems are typically not concerned with obligations vis-à-vis particular states or individuals, but with *collective obligations* owed to the international community or to "mankind" as a whole.[22] This second type of dispute raises problems of its own.

---

[15]See Alexandre Charles Kiss, "Le règlement des différends dans les conventions multilaterales relatives à la protection de l'environnement," in: *The Settlement of Disputes on the New Natural Resources*, René-Jean Dupuy, ed. (The Hague: Nijhoff, 1983), pp. 119–130; and Patricia Birnie, "The Role of International Law in Solving Certain Environmental Conflicts," in: *International Environmental Diplomacy*, John E. Carroll ed. (Cambridge: Cambridge University Press, 1988), pp. 95–121.

[16]See note 4, p. 153.

[17]Under an ancient House of Lords rule (*British South Africa Co. vs. Companhia de Mocambique*, 1893 A.C. 602) as then interpreted in Canada, the local Canadian courts would have refused to take jurisdiction over suits based on damage to land situated abroad; see J. Willis, "Jurisdiction of Courts: Action to Recover Damages for Injury to Foreign Land," *Canadian Bar Review* 15 (1937): 112–115.

[18]See note 4, p. 224.

[19]Aida Luisa Levin, *Protecting the Human Environment: Procedures and Principles for Preventing and Resolving International Controversies* (New York: United Nations Institute for Training and Research, 1977).

[20]Annex 1 of the *Sixth Report on the Law of the Non-navigational Uses of International Watercourses* (by Stephen C. McCaffrey, UN document A/CN.4/427, 1990) contains draft provisions on nondiscrimination, recourse under domestic law, equal rights of access, etc. This draft annex met with considerable opposition, however, at the 42nd session of the Commission in May–July 1990.

[21]Phillip C. Jessup, *Transnational Law* (New Haven: Yale University Press, 1956), p. 2.

[22]On this distinction (sometimes expressed in Latin terms as obligations *erga aliquem* vs. obligations *erga omnes*), as applied to the international law of the marine environment, see the detailed study by Paolo Picone, "Obblighi reciproci ed obblighi *erga omnes* degli stati nel campo della protezione inter-

I. DISPUTES OVER RECIPROCAL OBLIGATIONS

The prototype of environmental disputes is a bilateral one: over transboundary issues normally arising between neighboring states or between states sharing a territorially defined natural resource or ecosystem—giving rise to obligations vis-à-vis identifiable other states and/or individuals. That does not necessarily mean that the legal basis for resolving this type of dispute must be a bilateral agreement. Primary environmental obligations to "injured" or "affected" states or individuals may well arise from multilateral treaties[23] or from reciprocal customary duties over and above a state's collective obligations to the international community.[24]

Voluminous empirical information is available on how states address this type of environmental dispute, from Karl Neumeyer's classic treatise on international administrative law[25] to well-documented recent surveys and case studies.[26] A large number of environmental disputes in post-war Europe have thus been settled—usually with little more than local publicity—at the interadministrative level among border regions, by way of direct ad hoc negotiations, or through standing transboundary commissions. Third-party mediation has played little or no role.

Another and even more significant factor explaining the virtual absence of intergovernmental environmental litigation in Europe has been the widespread and successful use of local legal remedies and private law proceedings[27]—either by recourse to domestic civil and administrative courts, or by way of insurance arrangements and out-of-court settlements with individual claimants. While in some instances, such as the Rhine chlorides case, these remedies were pursued simultaneously and interactively with diplomatic negotiations,[28] other examples show that disputes hardly even escalated to the intergovernmental level because claimants found private law settlements more effective or more expedient.[29]

nazionale dell'ambiente marino dall'inquinamento," in: *Diritto internazionale e protezione dell'ambiente marino*, Vincenzo Starace ed. (Milan: A. Giuffre, 1983), pp. 15–135.

[23] See Kamen Sachariew, "State Responsibility for Multilateral Treaty Violations: Identifying the 'Injured State' and Its Legal Status," *Netherlands International Law Review* 35 (1988): 273–289.

[24] See Brian D. Smith, *State Responsibility and the Marine Environment: The Rules of Decision* (New York: Oxford University Press, 1988), p. 97.

[25] Karl Neumeyer, *Internationales Verwaltungsrecht*, 5 vols. (Munich-Zurich 1910–1937).

[26] For example, see Joachim Grawe, "Probleme des Umweltschutzes im deutsch französischen Grenzgebiet" [Problems of environmental protection in the French-German border area], *Zeitschrift für ausländisches öffentliches Recht und Völkerrecht* 34 (1974): 299; W. Hendewerk, "Transfrontier Pollution Rules for International Settlement of Controversies," in: *Legal Protection of the Environment in Developing Countries*, Ignacio Carillo Prieto and Raul Nocedal, eds., (Mexico: Universidad Nacional Autonoma de Mexico, Instituto de Investigaciones Juridicas, 1976), pp. 267–274; Emmanuel du Pontavi, "Compensation for Transfrontier Pollution Damage," in: *Legal Aspects of Transfrontier Pollution* (Paris: Organisation for Economic Cooperation and Development,

1977), pp. 409–487; Ludwig Fröhler & Franz Zechetner, *Rechtsschutzprobleme bei grenzüberschreitenden Umweltbeeinträchtigungen* [Problems of legal remedies for transboundary environmental interference], 3 vols. (Linz: Trauner, 1979–1981); *Les problémes juridiques posés par les pollutions transfrontieres*, Michael Bothe, Michel Prieur, and Georg Ress, eds., (Berlin: E. Schmidt, 1984); *Transboundary Air Pollution: International Legal Aspects of the Co-operation of States*, Cees Flinterman, Barbara Kwiatkowska, and Johan G. Lammers, eds. (Dordrecht: Kluwer Academic Pub., 1986), pp. 191–198.

[27] Peter H. Sand, "The Role of Domestic Procedures in Transnational Environmental Disputes," in: *Legal Aspects of Transfrontier Pollution* (Paris: Organisation for Economic Cooperation and Development, 1977), pp. 146–202.

[28] See Johan G. Lammers, "The Rhine: Legal Aspects of the Management of a Transboundary Resource," in: *Nature Management and Sustainable Development*, Wil D. Verwey, ed., (Amsterdam: IOS, 1989), pp. 440–457.

[29] For a case study of the Sandoz chemical spill, see Andrew H. Darrell, "Killing the Rhine: Immoral, But Is It Illegal?" *Virginia Journal of International*

One major advantage of settling transnational environmental disputes privately between polluters and victims has to do with welfare economics and the principle of cost internalization at the source (the "polluter-pays" principle), which could virtually be defeated by public compensation arrangements. A major disadvantage, at least in the past, has been a lack of uniformity, predictability, and even enforceability of private international law remedies in transboundary situations.[30] Significant advances have, however, been made in this field over the past twenty years in terms of substantive harmonization of liability and insurance regimes (especially in the field of marine pollution,[31] and in the transportation of dangerous goods[32]), as well as in terms of procedural relief (especially the Brussels and Lugano conventions on jurisdiction and enforcement of judgments in Europe[33]). We also witness a tendency toward more flexible choice of law approaches—exemplified by the 1957 *Poro* case,[34] where a German court resolved a situation similar to *Trail Smelter* by applying the national law "most favorable to the plaintiff."

In some cases, the "transnational handicap" can even be eliminated altogether. The claims settlement procedure adopted in 1967 by the Austro-German Boundary Airport Treaty[35] provides that the German government shall substitute its own liability for the civil liability of Austrian authorities in regard to specific claims for damages or the taking of German property caused by the establishment or operation of the Salzburg airport, and shall subsequently be reimbursed by the Austrian government. This procedure actually reverses the traditional process of international claims settlement, where lump-sum deals are first transacted between governments and then distributed to individual claimants.[36] The procedural fiction of "substitution" is not a novelty in international environmental law; it has been standard practice in claims for noise and sonic-boom damage caused by NATO military aircraft in Western Europe, pursuant to Article VIII (5) of the 1951 Status of Forces Agreement (SOFA).[37] Many claims for noise damage from foreign military aircraft have been settled locally under this provision as

---

Law 29 (1989): 421–472; see also Alexandre Charles Kiss, "'Tchernobâle ou la pollution accidentelle du Rhin par les produits chimiques," *Annuaire français de droit international* 33 (1987): 719–727; and Alfred Rest, "The Sandoz Conflagration and the Rhine Pollution: Liability Issues," *German Yearbook of International Law* 30 (1987): 160–176.

[30]Said Mahmoudi, "Some Private International Law Aspects of Transboundary Environmental Disputes," *Nordic Journal of International Law* 59 (1990): 128–138.

[31]On IMO experience in particular, see Reinhard H. Ganten, *The International System of Compensation for Oil Pollution Damage* (Oslo: 1981); and Reinhard H. Ganten, "Die Regulierungspraxis des internationalen Ölschadensfonds" [Settlement practice of the international oil pollution damage fund], *Versicherungsrecht* 40 (1989): 329–334.

[32]For example, see the 1989 UNECE Convention on Civil Liability for Damage Caused During Carriage of Dangerous Goods By Road, Rail and Inland Navigation Vessels (UN doc. ECE/TRANS/79); see the explanatory report by the International Institute for the Unification of Private Law (UNIDROIT), UN doc. ECE/TRANS/84 (1990).

[33]*International Legal Materials* 8 (1969): 229, and 28 (1989): 620.

[34]W. *Poro vs. Houillères du Bassin de Lorraine*, judgment of October 22, 1957 by the Court of Appeals (Oberlandesgericht) of Saarbrucken, *Neue Juristische Wochenschrift* 11 (1958): 752; for an English summary see Sand, note 27, pp. 148–149.

[35]German *Bundesgesetzblatt* II, pp. 13 and 783; for background see Ignaz Seidl-Hohenveldern, "A propos des nuisances dues aux acroports limitrophes: le cas de Salzbourg et le traite austro allemand du 19 decembre 1967," *Annuaire français de droit international* 19 (1973): 890–894.

[36]See Richard B. Lallich and Burns H. Weston, *International Claims: Their Settlement by Lump Sum Agreements* (Charlottesville: University Press of Virginia, 1975).

[37]*United Nations Treaty Series*, vol. 199, p. 67; see Richard R. Baxter, "Jurisdiction Over Visiting Forces and the Development of International Law," *Proceedings of the American Society of International Law* 52 (1958): 174; Serge Lazareff, *Status of Military Forces*

if they contained no international elements at all.[38]

So there are ways to bypass the transnational problems of environmental disputes; and the number of legal instruments to improve the chances of dispute settlement and dispute avoidance in this field is increasing. A major breakthrough was undoubtedly the Nordic Environmental Protection Convention of 1974,[39] establishing that member states shall mutually grant the national standard of treatment in judicial and administrative proceedings both to foreign individuals and to foreign administrative authorities designated for this purpose by other member states. The 1991 UNECE Convention on Environmental Impact Assessment in a Transboundary Context[40] also aims at harmonizing procedures for environmental planning and decision-making in border regions. In addition, there are several "soft law" instruments relevant to the resolution and avoidance of environmental disputes: from the OECD Recommendations on Equal Right of Access and Nondiscrimination in Relation to Transfrontier Pollution[41] to the UNEP Principles of Conduct in the Field of the Environment for the Guidance of States in the Conservation and Harmonious Utilization of Natural Resources Shared by Two or More States.[42] I have already mentioned the ongoing work of the UN International Law Commission, which has included extensive dispute settlement provisions in its draft articles on the nonnavigational uses of international watercourses.[43] These are expected to be finalized in 1991.

II. DISPUTES OVER COLLECTIVE OBLIGATIONS

There are, however, a growing number of environmental disputes that do not fit the typical "A vs. B" case format. This development was foreshadowed in the *Nuclear Tests* cases in the International Court of Justice,[44] even though that dispute was instituted and decided under traditional rules of international law, requiring an injured party to have standing to sue. Yet most environmental obligations concerning global commons and "common heritage" resources are owed to the international community as a whole—including future generations;[45] that is, com-

---

Under Current International Law (Leyden: Sijthoft, 1971), pp. 300–327; and W. Schwenk, "Jurisdiction of the Receiving State Over Forces of the Sending State Under the NATO Status of Forces Agreement," *International Lawyer* 6 (1972): 524–540, at 537.

[38]For illustration of the compensation method in practice, see *Dame Brun veuve Ethevenard vs. French State Treasury*, judgment of December 14, 1965 by the Tribunal de grande instance of Montbeliard, *Annuaire français de droit international* 13 (1967): 858. See Alexandre C. Kiss and Claude H. Lambrechts, "Les dommages causés au sol par les vols supersoniques," *Annuaire français de droit international* 6 (1970): 771; and Peter H. Sand, "Neue internationale Aspekte des Fluglärmproblems" [New international aspects of the aircraft noise problem], in: *Nouvelles tendances du Droit Aérien* (Zurich: Association Suisse de Droit Aérien et Spatial, 1973), pp. 15–22.

[39]*United Nations Treaty Series*, vol. 1092, p. 279; see Bengt Broms, "The Nordic Convention on the Protection of the Environment," in: *Transboundary Air Pollution* (note 26 above), pp. 141–152.

[40]Adopted at Espoo (Finland) on February 25, 1991, text in UN document ENVWA/R.36 (1990).

[41]Texts in *Legal Aspects of Transfrontier Pollution* (Paris: Organisation for Economic Cooperation and Development, 1977), pp. 11–34.

[42]UNEP Governing Council Decision 6/14 of May 19, 1978; see Andronico O. Adede, "United Nations Efforts Toward the Development of an Environmental Code of Conduct for States Concerning Harmonious Utilization of Shared Natural Resources," *Albany Law Review* 43 (1979): 488–519.

[43]See Note 20; and UN document A/CN.4/427/Add. 1, Annex II: Fact-finding and Settlement of Disputes (June 1990).

[44]Australia vs. France and New Zealand vs. France, *ICJ Reports* (1974), p. 253.

[45]See Edith Brown Weiss, *In Fairness to Future Generations: International Law, Common Patrimony and Intergenerational Equity* (Tokyo: United Nations University, 1989).

munity members and pollution victims who cannot even be identified as yet. Included here are collective duties concerning a state's conduct within its own territory, with corresponding environmental rights accruing to its own citizens—a situation not unlike the international protection of human rights.[46] Complaints for noncompliance with this type of obligation (that is, the procedural opening step in a dispute between the noncomplying state and the international community, or the community of parties to a multilateral agreement) may be initiated by states other than those directly victimized. The new "noncompliance procedure" adopted by the parties to the Montreal Protocol on Substances That Deplete the Ozone Layer[47] (at their London Conference in June 1990[48]) provides that any party may (through the Secretariat) submit "reservations regarding another Party's implementation of its obligations under the Protocol" to an implementation committee reporting to the Conference of the Parties. Even though this procedure was cautiously defined by its drafters as nonjudicial and nonconfrontational,[49] its general approach

(not requiring any injury or other condition of standing for the party submitting the complaint) resembles that of a "class action" in the interest of all parties.

Probably the body with the longest experience in dispute resolution and collective compliance control with regard to international environmental obligations is the International Labor Organization (ILO). It has enacted and monitored a long line of multilateral conventions since the 1920s—ranging from bans on white lead paint and other occupational health hazards, to workplace protection from air pollution, radiation, and toxic chemicals.[50] All of these conventions contain provisions on dispute settlement allowing states to initiate complaints and ad hoc inquiries against other states for not observing the treaty. However, detailed studies of the ILO's enforcement record over more than sixty years show that this adversarial procedure was used only rarely and then mostly for political potshots.[51] Instead, ILO member states developed an entirely different procedure that turned out to be far more effective in enforcing compliance: annual or biennial reporting by governments, combined with regular auditing by an independent technical committee of experts to ascertain compliance in each member state, followed by public debate of these audited reports by the Conference Committee on the Application of Conventions and Recommendations.[52] Similar systems of mandatory re-

[46]See Brian D. Smith (note 24), pp. 100–102; see also W. Paul Gormley, *Human Rights and Environment: The Need for International Co-operation* (Leyden: Sijthoff, 1976), at pp. 146–185, for a discussion of the Nuclear Tests cases from this perspective; and W. Paul Gormley, "The Legal Obligation of the International Community to Guarantee a Pure and Decent Environment: The Expansion of Human Rights Norms," *Georgetown International Environmental Law Review* 3 (1990): 85–116.

[47]*International Legal Materials* 26 (1987): 155C; see Richard E. Benedick, *Ozone Diplomacy: New Directions in Safeguarding the Planet* (Cambridge, Mass.: Harvard University Press, 1991).

[48]Report of the second meeting of the Conference of the Parties, UN document UNEP/OzL.Pro.2/3, Annex III (1990), adopted on an interim basis.

[49]Report of the first meeting of the Ad Hoc Working Group of Legal Experts on Non-compliance with the Montreal Protocol, UN document UNEP/OzL.Pro.LG.1/3 (1989); *Environmental Policy and Law* 19 (1989): 223.

[50]For a summary of ILO conventions and recommendations on the working environment, see *Environmental Law: An In-Depth Review*, UNEP Report No. 2 (Nairobi: United Nations Environment Programme, 1981) pp. 53–64.

[51]Victor Yves Ghebali, *The International Labour Organization: A Case Study on the Evolution of UN Specialized Agencies* (Dordrecht: M. Nijhoff, 1989); see also Antony Alcock, *History of the International Labour Organization* (London: Macmillan, 1971).

[52]E. A. Landy, *The Effectiveness of International Supervision: Thirty Years of I.L.O. Experience* (London:

porting and "environmental auditing," for public review of compliance (with the active participation of nongovernmental organizations), have been adopted under other multilateral conventions in the environmental field. Examples include the Convention on International Trade in Endangered Species of Wild Fauna and Flora (CITES),[53] and the Convention on Long-Range Transboundary Air Pollution (LRTAP).[54]

A much bolder step toward collective compliance control was taken by the 1957 Treaty of Rome establishing the European Economic Community[55] Article 155 made the EC Commission the guardian of the treaty's implementation, and Article 169 empowered it to initiate proceedings against any member state in case of infringements, sanctioned if necessary by formal action in the European Court of Justice at Luxembourg.[56] Over the past ten years, this "custodial" procedure has become one of the most important means of enforcing EC environmental standards.

The EC infringement proceedings[57]

comprise three stages. As a first step, the Commission sends "letters of formal notice" to member states that fail to enact or apply a Community directive, or to report on its enactment or application. After giving the member state an opportunity to respond, the Commission can next render a "reasoned opinion" confirming the infringement in the light of all the facts gathered. If the member state still doesn't remedy the problem, the Commission may then refer the matter to the European Court of Justice. During 1988, the Commission issued ninety-three letters of formal notice, seventy-one reasoned opinions, and eleven referrals to the court concerning infringements of EC environmental directives (some seventy of which were in force at that time).[58]

What may be the most significant feature of this procedure is mentioned nowhere in the treaty and evolved only gradually during its implementation. More than half of the infringement proceedings initiated against member states were based not on the Commission's own monitoring of compliance but on citizen complaints— from private individuals, associations (such as Greenpeace and Friends of the Earth), or municipalities.[59] As a result of public information on the complaints procedure and the establishment of a "complaints registry" within the Commission secretariat in Brus-

Stevens & Sons, 1966); and Nicolas Valticos, "Contrôle," in: *A Handbook on International Organizations*, René-Jean Dupuy, ed. (Dordrecht: M. Nijhoff, 1988), pp. 332–353, at pp. 340–344.

[53]*United Nations Treaty Series*, vol. 993, p. 243; see David S. Favre, *International Trade in Endangered Species: A Guide to CITES* (Dordrecht: M. Nijhoff, 1989).

[54]*International Legal Materials* 18 (1979: 442; see Evgeny M. Chossudovsky, *"East-West" Diplomacy for Environment in the United Nations* (Geneva: United Nations Institute for Training and Research, 1988).

[55]*United Nations Treaty Series*, vol. 298, p. 3.

[56]See J. Mertens de Wilman and I. M. Verougstrate, "Proceedings against Member States for Failure to Fulfill Their Obligations," *Common Market Law Review* 7 (1970): 385–406; and H. A. H. Audretsch, *Supervision in European Community Law* (Amsterdam: North-Holland Pub. Co., 1978).

[57]See Ingolf Pernice, "Kompetenzordnung und Handlungsbefugnisse der europäischen Gemeinschaft auf dem Gebiet des Umwelt- und Technikrechts" [The European Community's system of competences and authority to act in the field of environmental and technological law], *Die Verwaltung* (22 (1989): 1–54.

[58]Sixth annual report to the European Parliament on Commission monitoring of the application of Community law–1988, *Official Journal of the European Communities*, no. C 330 (December 30, 1989), pp. 1–160. The previous (fifth) report appears in the *Official Journal*, no. C 310 (December 5, 1988); see Ludwig Kraemer, "Du contrôle de l'application des directives communautaires en matière de l'environnement," *Revue due Marché Commun* (1988) pp. 22–40. For a country-by-country table of EC environmental infringement proceedings pending as of January 1, 1990, see Peter H. Sand, *Lessons Learned in Global Environmental Governance* (Washington: World Resources Institute, 1990), p. 32.

[59]See Pernice (note 57) p. 40.

sels, the number of environmental complaints rose dramatically—from ten in 1982 to 190 in 1988, and to 460 in 1989.[60] While complaints are usually based on local noncompliance with EC standards, some have wider effects. A single complaint by a resident in one of the United Kingdom's two nonattainment areas with regard to the 1980 EC Directive on Air Quality Limit Values and Guide Values for Sulphur Dioxide and Suspended Particulates[61] thus triggered a Commission investigation that led to infringement proceedings against seven member states.[62]

Significantly, the EC has no powers of physical enforcement comparable to those of a national government. Although virtually all of the more than thirty judgments rendered by the European Court of Justice in environmental infringement proceedings since 1982 went against the defendant member states and upheld the Commission's opinion, not all led to compliance. In the 1988 case of *Commission vs. Kingdom of*

Belgium,[63] for instance, the court noted that Belgium had failed to fulfill its obligations under Article 171 of the treaty by refusing, in defiance of earlier (1982) judgments of the court, to adopt the measures necessary to implement four EC directives on waste disposal. The mere opening of EC action can, however, have internal political and economic consequences in member states. In the United Kingdom, the government's plans for privatization of local water management agencies were stalled in part because of pending EC infringement proceedings, when it turned out that some areas scheduled for privatization did not meet EC water-quality standards.[64] As a result, the custodial action procedure of the EC Commission has evolved from a three-stage to a four-stage process: the optional first stage in most cases is now a citizen complaint.[65] Some commentators already see the role of the EC Commission in this field as that of a "European environmental ombudsman."[66]

OUTLOOK

Fifty years after the *Trail Smelter* case, there have been no significant advances in intergovernmental settlement of transnational disputes over "reciprocal" environmental obligations. Governments have tended to

avoid recourse to third-party adjudication—favoring bilateral, local, and informal chan-

[60]*Commission of the European Communities,* Information Memo P/90/5 (February 8, 1990).

[61]Directive 80/779 of July 15, 1980, *Official Journal of the European Communities,* no. I. 229 (August 30, 1980); see Jan Smeets, "Air Quality Limits and Guide Values for Sulphur Dioxide and Suspended Particulates: A European Community Directive," *Environmental Monitoring and Assessment* 1 (1982): 373–382.

[62]Nigel Haigh, "Impact of the EEC Environmental Programme: The British Example," *Connecticut Journal of International Law* 4 (1989): 453–462, particularly p. 458 note 11; see also Negel Haigh, *EEC Environmental Policy and Britain,* 2nd ed. (London: Longman, 1989).

[63]Court of Justice of the European Communities, Joined Cases 227/85 to 230/85, *Reports of Cases Before the Court* (1988-I) pp. 1–12; summary in *Official Journal of the European Communities,* no. C 37 (February 9, 1988), p. 4.

[64]*The Financial Times* of April 7, 1989, p. 2; see Philippe J. Sands, "The Environment, Community and International Law," *Harvard International Law Journal* 30 (1989): 393–420, particularly p. 415, note 98. The proceedings in this case were triggered by a complaint from a non-governmental organization (Friends of the Earth).

[65]See Pernice (note 57) and Kraemer (note 58).

[66]Dieter Helmut Scheuing, "Umweltschutz auf der Grundlage der Einheitlichen Europäischen Akte" [Environmental protection on the basis of the Single European Act], *Europarecht* 24 (1989): 152–192, particularly p. 192.

nels instead. While it may be argued that this is at least partly due to the notorious lack of compulsory dispute settlement procedures in this field, a more persuasive explanation probably is the sheer inertia of formal intergovernmental proceedings. To wit, both the *Trail Smelter* case and the *Gut Dam* case took a solid fifteen years from the first claims to the final arbitral award—a time cost few environmental problems today can afford. One of the lessons of this experience therefore should be further efforts to strengthen available lower-level procedures (such as mutual access to, and mutual recognition of, local remedies), as well as procedures with noncompulsory outcomes[67] (such as agreed data collection and fact-finding mechanisms[68]).

By contrast, several truly innovative approaches have been developed regarding compliance with "collective" environmental obligations—that is, in disputes opposing the international community (or a community of contracting parties[69]) and a noncom-

plying state. The methods available range from nonadversarial collective auditing and public review of performance, to designing complaint procedures at varying levels of formality. Among the new problems emerging in this context are potential conflicts between obligations incurred under different international instruments. Examples include the prohibition of discriminatory trade barriers under the General Agreement on Tarriffs and Trade (GATT)[70] or under regional free trade agreements,[71] and the collective imposition or authorization of new trade barriers for environmental reasons under the 1973 CITES Convention[72] or under the 1987 Montreal Protocol.[73] While there is a well-established mechanism for the settlement of trade disputes under GATT,[74] only a broad general exception refers to permissible environmental restrictions.[75] There seems to be growing recognition of the need for a functional mechanism to resolve potential conflicts in the interpretation of trade restrictions based on other international agreements, environ-

---

[67]As suggested by Martti Koskenniemi, "Peaceful Settlement of Environmental Disputes," *Nordic Journal of International Law* 60 (1, forthcoming 1991); for a recent example of flexible dispute settlement provisions, see article XIII of the U.S. Canadian Air Quality Agreement of March 13, 1991. See also Robert E. Stein, "The Settlement of Environmental Disputes: Towards a System of Flexible Dispute Settlement," *Syracuse Journal of International Law and Commerce* 12 (1985): 283–298.

[68]For example, see the Inquiry Commission proposed by six countries (Austria, Czechoslovakia, Hungary, Italy, Poland, and Yugoslavia), in a draft "resolution on prevention of international disputes concerning the environment" submitted to the second session of the Preparatory Committee for the United Nations Conference on Environment and Devleopment, UN document A/CONF.151/PC/L.29 (Geneva, March 1991).

[69]Thomas Gehring, "International Environmental Regimes: Dynamic Sectoral Legal Orders," *Yearbook of International Environmental Law* 1 (forthcoming 1991), emphasizes the sectoral autonomy of dispute settlement within the ozone layer and transboundary air pollution agreements, as distinct from third-

party adjudication based on general international law.

[70]*United Nations Treaty Series*, vol. 55, p. 194.

[71]For trade-vs.-environment problems in the European Community, see Sand, note 58, pp. 12–14.

[72]See note 53.

[73]See note 47.

[74]The flexible conciliation procedures developed within GATT as (formulated in the 1979 Draft Understanding Regarding Notification, Consultation, Dispute Settlement and Surveillance) have indeed been suggested as a model for the settlement of environmental disputes; Abram and Antonia H. Chayes, "Adjustment and Compliance Processes in International Regulatory Regimes," in: *Preserving the Global Environment: The Challenge of Shared Leadership* Jessica Tuchman Mathews, ed. (New York: W.W. Norton, 1991), pp. 280–308, particularly pp. 301–304.

[75]Pursuant to GATT article XX. b (measures "necessary to protect human, animal or plant life or health"), and article 2.2 of the GATT Standards Code ("protection for human health or safety, animal or plant life or health, or the environment").

mental ones in particular.[76] To determine what constitutes bona fide environmental restrictions, then, we may expect that authoritative fact-finding and scientific/technical advice from competent international institutions established under sectoral environmental regimes will play an increasingly important role in dispute settlement and prevention.[77]

[76]The GATT "Group on Environmental Measures and Trade" established in 1971 (C/M/74, item 9) actually never met. In a ministerial statement submitted to the 46th session of the Contracting Parties in December 1990, the six EFTA countries (Austria, Finland, Iceland, Norway, Sweden and Switzerland) proposed to revive the dormant group under an updated mandate, and informal consultations on this matter were initiated in February 1991 (see the progress report and debate in C/M/248, item 8).

[77]A relevant precedent from the sector of international trade in food products is the role of the FAO/WHO *Codex Alimentarius* Commission, whose pesticide residue limits and other environmental quality standards are widely accepted as reference; see David M. Leive, *International Regulatory Regimes: Case Studies in Health Meteorology and Food* Vol. II (Lexington, Mass.: Lexington Books, 1976), pp. 375–541; and Eric Christensen, "Pesticide Regulation and International Trade," *Environment*, 32, no. 9 (November 1990): 2–3, 44–45.

36 *THE TRADE EFFECTS OF ENVIRONMENTAL REGULATION*

Ebba Dohlman

A frequent writer on ecological problems, Ebba Dohlman serves on the Trade Directorate staff of the Organization for Economic Cooperation and Development in Paris.

Measures to conserve the environment can often involve trade policy or have direct or indirect implications for trade. In the past, these spillover effects were rarely questioned since it was assumed that they were both necessary and beneficial. And in more recent years there has been a marked proliferation of national environmental regulations as well as of international agreements on environmental control.

Two main kinds of trade effects may arise from environmental regulations. The first is when trade policy measures—import or export restrictions, for example—are used directly as tools to help achieve the objectives of environmental policy. The second emerges less directly, through the setting of national or regional standards which, when different from those applied elsewhere and entailing a compliance cost, influence the international competitiveness and trade of firms subject to these standards.

The most direct relation between trade and environmental policies appears when trade policy instruments serve as a principal or complementary means for achieving environmental goals by restricting or prohibiting international trade in certain products.

Examples are numerous. Endangered species, or products from them, may be subject to export controls as provided for under the Convention on International Trade in Endangered Species of Wild Fauna and Flora (CITES), administered by the United Nations Environmental Programme (UNEP). Some countries have imposed unilateral import bans on furs, skins, leather, products of the whaling industry, and, more recently, on ivory. The "Basel Convention on the Control of Transboundary Movements of Hazardous Wastes and their Disposal," adopted in March 1989, and the "Montreal Protocol on Substances that Deplete the Ozone Layer" (1988) both include export and import restrictions affecting countries that are not party to the conventions.

In some cases, it might not be possible to achieve environmental goals without these restrictions. There would be no point, for example, in compelling domestic industry to manufacture environmentally sound products or substitutes if consumers could import the products now discouraged from

Reprinted from the *OECD Observer,* 162, Feb–Mar 1990, 28–32, Ebba Dohlman.

countries which do not implement the same strict regulations.

But the benevolence of such trade restrictions might be contested by other countries, thus giving rise to trade frictions. Certain exports restricted for environmental reasons may be essential inputs for foreign producers. For example, cutbacks in the production of chlorofluorocarbons (CFCs) for export might cause disruption in developing countries which are still modernizing their industries and which do not possess the technology to produce alternatives. And banning or regulating the trade in ivory, although a measure of literally vital importance to the African Elephant, will hurt the ivory-cutters of Japan and Hong Kong, just as wood-processing industries will be damaged by export bans of tropical timber.

Import restrictions may also be regarded, rightly or wrongly, as a disguised form of protection for domestic industries, or as discriminatory. The Danish government, for example, was taken to the European Court because it decided that all beers, soft drinks, and mineral waters should be sold in refillable containers, allegedly a restriction of free trade (the Court ruled in Denmark's favor). And some car-producing countries might perceive the stricter exhaust emission regulations of others as a disguised form of protection.

The temptation might also arise to use trade policy measures more aggressively, to penalize countries which do not accept certain product or production standards—although so far such cases are purely hypothetical. One country might, for instance, impose a border surtax on imports from a neighboring country which is a major source of atmospheric pollution. The central policy question this instance raises is, of course, how effective are trade-policy measures for achieving environmental goals? The answer obviously depends on the individual sets of circumstances and, with few precedents, is likely to be speculative.

"Global warming" has ensured that deforestation occupies the headlines with a regularity that would have astonished conservationists a decade ago. Several producers of tropical timber have already prohibited exports. In the mid-1980s the Philippines and Indonesia prohibited the export of raw logs, and in January 1989 Thailand banned logging altogether because of overcutting. Brazil has also proposed an export ban.

But export bans tend to be less easily enforceable by customs authorities than are those on imports. Indeed, it is reported that smuggling still accounts for a large amount of trade in tropical timber, especially from Borneo to Sarawak, and in the Philippines where more than a third of timber exports are reported to be contraband.[1]

FROM LOGGING TO LOGROLLING

And there are other reasons that export bans on raw materials alone might not protect the rainforests. The motivation behind these trade restrictions may be rather to develop local processing industries, thus perpetuating the massive logging. That may already have happened in Southeast Asia. Indonesia has created a successful plywood industry. Thailand is importing hardwood from Laos and Burma for its proceing. The Philippines and China have also become net importers. An export ban in Brazil, on the other hand, is unlikely to have much impact on conservation since the problem there is not so much one of commercial logging as of land clearance by potential settlers.

[1] *The Economist*, 22 April 1989.

So what would be the efficacy of import bans on tropical timber? Some might argue that a widespread ban would decrease the value of the stocks so much as to make trading unprofitable, even when illegal. They would also argue that the absence of legal trade makes it easier to suppress illegal trade.

Others contend that the effect of a ban would be to drive up the prices even faster and thus increase the incentives for smuggling. In any event, if one single importer refuses to take part in the ban, the chances of its success are substantially reduced. In-deed, to be successful, it would also have to be extended to processed goods; but since commercial logging is big business in South-east Asia, the effects of such a ban on these economies would be devastating.

With Brazil, on the other hand, an import ban by trading partners would solve very little. What would help put an end to the devastation of the Amazonian rainforest would be the stopping by the Brazilian government of its direct and indirect subsidies on land investment and agricultural development.

A MARKET FOR NATURAL RESOURCES

Indeed, are trade bans the only way to help the tropical forests to survive? Is not part of the problem the mismanagement of resources? Finding ways to improve forest management and commercialization of tropical forest products, such as fruit and rubber, or encouraging pharmaceutical companies to invest locally in the research or cultivation of plants used for healing may provide solutions. Such a far-sighted approach sees the encouragement of trade—not its suppression—as a much more effective guarantor of environmental stability.

Plans to prohibit the import of ivory have also received widespread support in recent months. In June 1989 the United States announced a ban on imports of ivory. In the same month a ban throughout the European Community, to cover raw and worked ivory, was also called for. Australia, Switzerland, and Japan have adopted total or partial bans. And Canada announced its intention to take measures to impose further restrictions on imports of raw or worked ivory from African elephants.

More recently yet, CITES, the world body controlling wildlife trade, at its meeting of October 17, 1989, approved a compromise proposal that placed the African elephant on the endangered list (thus effectively banning trade in elephant tusks) but also created a special panel of experts to consider future exemptions. Opponents of the ban argue that it would punish the countries that were managing their wildlife successfully and that proceeds from ivory sales helped to maintain this successful management.

WHAT EFFECTS ON COMPETITION?

Standards, whether imposed on product or production, may introduce distortions in the conditions of international competition. With automobiles and other motor vehicles, standards may be set on emissions of carbon monoxide, particulates, sulphur dioxide, and nitrogen oxide, all of which have respiratory consequences as well as contributing to acid rain. But at any moment more stringent standards exist in some countries than others, forcing car producers to vary the specifications of their cars depending upon the market.

The adoption of strict standards in one country clearly puts pressure on others to modify the nature or composition of their exports or even to adopt the standards themselves. The United States, Japan, Switzerland, and the Scandinavian countries have maintained strict but not identical controls on automobile emissions for some time. The European Community is introducing stricter standards over time, as is the United States. This domino effect increases the costs for producers and consumers alike. It is, for instance, expected that the introduction of catalytic converters to new cars produced in Europe will increase the cost to the consumer by 7–12 percent.

The Netherlands recently proposed a tax rebate on any car fitted with catalytic converters bought in anticipation of the introduction of mandatory EC standards. The measure would have obvious implications on sales of cars without converters. The proposal arose in the context of a long-standing dispute within the Community over standards, especially as Germany, Denmark, and Greece followed suit with similar proposals. The EC Council finally voted for the imple-

mentation of car pollution controls for small cars, to be applied throughout the Community by 1993.

The expense of developing substitutes or modifying production methods may be felt to undermine the competitive advantage of certain producers over other producers better able to absorb the costs. Moreover, the high costs incurred, combined with different national timetables for the implementation of particular environmental standards, may make the pace at which substitutes are developed very uneven, thus introducing further possibilities for the distortion of competition and trade.

Yet the market for the initially more expensive products is hard to predict. There does appear to be an increasing demand for "green" products, at least in the most environmentally conscious OECD countries. In many developing countries, nonetheless, it might be necessary to consider ways of providing incentives for them to introduce substitutes for pollution-intensive goods and production methods, even at the risk of some distortion of trade.

SPIRALLING INTERVENTION

The response of governments to the new costs will vary and therefore potentially introduce new distortions. One important question which then arises for trade policy is how to allocate the cost of compliance. When the costs are internalized (that is, born by the producing firm) and deemed to be particularly high, the government may feel the urge to step in with the provision of subsidies.

Subsidies represent one of the key areas of discussion in the Uruguay Round of trade negotiations. Current GATT rules do not proscribe production subsidies *per se,* as they do not necessarily distort trade. But if

such subsidies are large and paid to industries operating in the international market, they could very well give a competitive edge to the products of a particular firm or sector, thus causing short- or long-term trade distortions. Firms in other countries or sectors might then request similar subsidies or countervailing duties to neutralize the trade effects, thus setting off a spiral of government intervention and, very possibly, trade friction.

Might firms then be inclined to transfer production abroad in order to escape more stringent environmental regulations at home? So far there is little evidence of it. Indeed, firms which can anticipate new environmental regulations may even gain a competitive edge in producing and exporting pollution-control equipment and technology. It has been reported that the West European market for pollution-control equipment—everything from advanced waste-disposal technology to catalytic converters—is worth more than $30 billion a year and that more than a million people in the EC are employed in this market and related services.[2]

This growth may partly offset the short-term competitive disadvantage that some countries may suffer in trade in pollution-intensive goods and services. Yet not all will manage to raise the capital required to re-equip their industries. Developing countries, in particular, may find themselves at a serious disadvantage if they have to bring their environmental standards into conformity with those of OECD countries within a short period.

Finding a balance between environmental control policies and liberal trade obligations is not always easy, and is likely to become more difficult in the future. A number of issues will therefore have to be examined:

- In what circumstances are trade-related actions justified and effective in preventing damage to the environment?
- How does one determine which—indeed, whether—environmental standards are "legitimate"?
- To what extent should account be taken of the popular pressure that governments may be under in some cases to adopt standards without adequate scientific assessment of their efficiency and consultation with other trade partners?
- Once environmental actions have been taken by governments, will they not be difficult to modify, even if protectionist effects can be demonstrated?

The GATT and other international agreements may provide some guidelines on tackling these questions. For instance, the GATT Code on Technical Barriers to Trade provides disciplines for the use and harmonization of standards so they do not create unnecessary barriers to trade. In addition, the OECD in 1972 drew up a list of Guiding Principles concerning International Economic Aspects of Environmental Policies for member countries.[3] One of these principles, the "Polluter-Pays Principle" was created specifically to prevent trade distortions as a result of different methods for financing pollution abatement.

But it will take further cases to establish how effective these instruments are in ensuring a balance between environmental concerns and trade. Governments might ultimately feel they should, on the one hand, set up new instruments to generate transparency in the use of standards and, on the other, establish more accurate criteria for determining "necessity" in environmental terms. And, finally, an increase in worldwide harmonization of environmental standards would prevent the unavoidable problems created by the existence of diverse national and regional regulations.

---

[2]*Financial Times,* 21 April 1989.

[3]Published in *OECD and the Environment,* OECD Publications, Paris, 1986; available free of charge from the OECD Client Services Unit, Paris.

CHAPTER ELEVEN

DEMOCRACY AND HUMAN RIGHTS

[Decision-makers] must decide how, where and why to collect information, and what it should be. These choices are made, by and large, by men. As a result women are often absent from compendia of international statistics. . . . Decisions affecting millions of people—as in international development planning—hinge on the nature of the information used by the decision-makers.

Ann Olson and Joni Seager
Women in the World, 1986

In the introductory chapter, Marysia Zalewski defined the growing interest of women in the relationships between such decisions and the theory of IR. In this concluding chapter, selections have been chosen from four quite different perspectives. The effects of the Cold War on human rights are analyzed by a female Canadian law professor, Brenda Cossman, whose penetrating analysis assesses whether there have been gains or losses, or both. Reflecting on a two and a half year assignment to a novel overseas program mandated by the U.S. Congress, Peter Olson records some qualitatively remarkable if quantitatively modest contributions toward freedom in South Africa. From Krakow, Piotr Sztompka describes the frustrations fostered by the inability of people conditioned by a totalitarian system to break, not only habits of acting, but of thinking as well. And from Athens, a brilliant rising star in the theory of IR, Constantine Arvanitopoulos, also discusses transitions from authoritarianism to democracy, but from a more conceptual perspective.

From these writers, nationals of four distinct societies, one can see that decision-making depends even more upon attitudes than it does upon statistics. How often have the brave hopes with which emergent governments began their independence a generation ago been cruelly dashed by obstacles both domestic and external to their economic development? TV-watchers the world over witness with horror and frustration the ability of gun-toting thugs to steal food and medical supplies from shipments by many countries and prevent their ever getting to the starving and disease-ridden children of Somalia.

The causes and consequences of anarchy in the Third World, however, are clearly not limited to the developing countries themselves. Among others, the views of the new Secretary-General of the United Nations, the first African to hold that post, have been reproduced in the second chapter of this book reacting to Western pronouncements of a "new world order." Scholars are increasingly aware that the world economic system tends to keep the poor, poor and the rich, rich.[1] The very injustice of inequality shows that one does not need to adopt a Marxist interpretation to recognize that with the exception of scarce minerals, the poor countries need the products of the industrially-advanced states more than the latter need the products of developing societies. That and the limited interest which the management of multinationals have in investing in anything but the most profitable sectors of such countries limits and distorts their development. The presence in their mean docks of ships loaded with Western goods for the affluent few deepens the sense of injustice and bitterness among indigent people, who often cling to their traditional ways and religion and see in ostentation a form of sin and evil.

Despite the increase of terrorism on the world stage and alarm among globally-minded interpreters, most classical theories of international relations assume that the state actor is capable of maintaining a just domestic order and acting externally so as to preserve sovereignty and to protect its citizens abroad. As Charles Kegley has recently observed,

> These differences of opinion indicate that reasonable people can arrive at reasonable but different conclusions about something as basic as whether international terrorism is a growing, stable, or declining activity and that the picture of its occurrence and significance depends greatly on the way it is described and defined.[2]

The maintenance of equilibrium and of the presumed self-regulating nature of the state system depends upon this assumption. The state's ability to function rationally in the external realm depends in turn upon the maintenance of domestic order. Working largely independently of the interstate political system,

---

[1] See Mahbub al Huq, "The Inequities of the Old Economic Order," reproduced in the seventh edition of this book from *The Third World and the International Economic Order,* (Washington D.C.: Overseas Development Council, 1976).

[2] *International Terrorism: Characteristics, Causes, Controls,* (New York: St. Martin's Press, 1990), p. 14. A chart indicating the up-and-downs of terrorist incidents worldwide, but with a generally increasing trend during a twenty-year period up to 1988 is reproduced on p. 15 of Kegley's book.

international economic regimes may actually undermine the conditions of order essential to its smooth functioning. Newer states tend to be prone to a degree of incoherence, foreign penetration, and revolution. This throws a tremendous burden on the international political system and particularly upon the United States, which, as the status-quo power, is assumed to possess the greatest responsibility for maintaining global order. In the face of this challenge the United States government and, whether they realize it or not, the American people have been moved or driven to support those regimes (however, repressive) that promise order and to oppose those movements (however just) that threaten revolution.

The behavior of the Soviet Union, a totalitarian state, preserving its own empire by force while exploiting disorder and revolution outside was used to justify the United States', a democratic state, intervention in Iran, Guatemala, Chile, and Grenada, to say nothing of Nicaragua, El Salvador, and Iraq. The danger lies in failing to acknowledge that some disorder in the system is unavoidable, and that to oppose it everywhere for the sake of demonstrating American will and power may well be counterproductive, as was shown both in Vietnam and in the Philippines. This does not mean that all interventions are ill-advised and hence to be avoided. It does mean that great prudence must be exercised, and that justice is sometimes a better guide than strategy. An original coauthor of this series, David McLellan, has warned that

> Any adequate theory of international relations and any adequate strategy for American foreign policy must recognize the magnitude and intractability of the forces of disorder presented by the Third World and not expect to impose an American-inspired order—least of all an order inspired almost exclusively by American self-interest.[3]

It is in this context that the issue of human rights enters the picture. In a world so vulnerable to repression and barbarism, one would think that the protection of human rights should head every intelligent country's foreign policy agenda, or at least its propaganda agenda. Emphasis on human rights constitutes an implicit challenge to the legitimacy of many regimes, as Peter Olson explains below in describing the care with which a legislatively-initiated American program of human rights had to be administered in South Africa. However necessary their leaders may justify terror, torture, and murder in an attempt to ensure their survival, it is seen by the international community as an unjust violation of basic rights. Invocation of human rights by any government toward another needs to always be prudent and restrained; it also needs to be more than mere rhetoric. In her closely reasoned article in the *Harvard International Review*, Brenda Cossman issues a grim reminder that, at least in the so-called Cold War era, despite all the rhetoric and all the foreign aid, there is a real question as to

---

[3]"The International System: Inequal and Revolutionary," in William C. Olson, ed., *The Theory and Practice of International Relations*, seventh ed., (Englewood Cliffs, N.J., 1987), p. 114, an original article prepared for that edition.

whether the cause of international human rights advanced or regressed. The answer is obviously that the process was pushing in both directions at the same time, even within a given country, particularly if the internal civil rights record of that country was not well-established.

While it may be true that strategic and geopolitical issues had more to do with the failure of détente than human rights, the reality of human rights as a foreign policy issue has now been accepted, even by authoritarian regimes who cannot bring themselves to practice what they preach. Yet even Gorbachev came to understand, even accept, the legitimacy of American concern about freedom of emigration. Western democracies experience difficulty themselves in implementing inspiring principles.

In the case of the Soviet Union, the emphasis given to the issue of human rights tended to obscure other issues of friction, because of the significance of the Jewish emigration issue in U.S. domestic politics. In the case of the Shah, had he heeded the call for human rights in time he might well have saved his throne. *Realpolitik* and justice are not always at odds. At worst, emphasis on human rights exposes American policy to charges of inconsistency—continuing to provide arms and support to a regime (for example, Nicaragua's Somoza) being accused of violations of its own stated principles. Nevertheless, the relationship of human rights to international relations is a complex subject deserving to be treated as such within the broader context of the very concept of justice in IR theory.

Yet to dismiss violations of human rights by African, Latin American, Middle Eastern, and Communist governments simply on the grounds that their societies do not place the same emphasis upon the individual as does Western culture is to miss the point. Latin America is, after all, part of Western civilization, and several countries (Argentina, Uruguay, and Chile) had achieved a high level of democratic rule before the recent violations of legality and torture began and now seem to be returning to a form of democracy. Nor does it make ethical sense to ignore these violations on the basis of the right of a "sovereign" regime to do whatever it pleases to its citizenry. A society which rejects both in theory and practice the proposition that the individual has rights apart from the society, even if that society is ideologically committed to raising the material standards of the people, is caught in a fundamental contradiction. Within the twin frameworks of openness and restructuring, that system was successfully challenged. It may be too early to judge whether a viable democratic regime will emerge in Yeltsin's Russia from glasnost or perestroika, but that the impulse is present in that society is unmistakable, events in Uzbekistan or Soviet Georgia notwithstanding.

A dilemma with which the issue of democracy confronts IR is the inhibition that some say sovereignty places upon intervention by an outside power into the domestic affairs of another country. One leading expert on ethics in foreign policy once argued that "there is and should be a profound moral constraint on efforts designed to alter domestic practices, institutions and policies within other states," adding that "we cannot export human rights or respect for the rule of law,"[4] while another authority argued that human rights was "one area where the observation of moral principle would do far less damage to and far more good for American national interest than is commonly understood.[5] Thus the issue is joined.

To be sure, there are persuasive arguments against letting foreign policy become too involved with human rights concerns. For example, it was immediately apparent that when President Carter espoused human rights as a goal of American foreign policy more than one country, both of the left and of the right, regarded it as an attempt to interfere in its domestic affairs. The People's Republic of China objected when a prominent scientific dissident was given protection in the U.S. Embassy during the rebellion over democracy late in May, 1989. The ranking minority member of the Senate Foreign Relations Committee even suggested that an armed attack on the embassy should not be ruled out on the grounds of the Chinese interpretation of international law as forbidding foreign interference in its domestic affairs. Totalitarian states have an advantage in these matters in that they are able to justify repression of dissent and political rights in the name of some superior elitist insight. Ironically, Communists have thus had no qualms about exploiting the freedom of expression and assembly that exists within a democracy as a justifiable part of the class struggle for power, a struggle which, once the communists win, supposedly comes to an end. Hostility to human rights campaigns is an expression of insecurity and fear that opposition might well get out of hand and put the legitimacy of the regime itself in doubt. That is why the risk was high in the execution of Gorbachev's "new thinking" on this issue.

Sir Michael Howard, the distinguished British military historian, bridged the so-called gap between power and ethics when he set forth a basic conception of international politics that does not preclude a role for ethical values and moral judgments in the decision-making process.[6] In the first place, the state is not an end in itself; it exists as a means by which its citizens may enjoy a better life. People everywhere want a better life; not all people all of the time want to wield more power over their neighbors. Only a handful of regimes are ever ruled by "mad tyrants" for whom war and domination are exclusive goals. Admittedly conflicts over religion and other absolutes are not easily resolved when they enter into interstate politics, but they have not been the only cause of war. According to the late Arnold Wolfers, even the pursuit of security should be viewed as a matter of "more" or "less" and not as a condition to be remedied by absolute superiority. Therefore, effective political action for most leaders most of the time ought to consist of reconciling their state's interests with those of other states rather than imposing one's will upon them. That is what a just world

[4]Ernest W. Lefever, "The Trivialization of Human Rights," *Policy Review*, Winter 1978, cited in the fifth edition of this book, p. 353, which was later the subject of a reply in the form of an original article in the following edition.

[5]David S. McLellan, "Human Rights: a Rejoinder," seventh edition of this book, Prentice Hall, 1991, p. 381.

[6]"Reflections on Injustice and International Politics," *Review of International Studies*, 12, 1, January 1986, pp. 67–83.

order is all about. To reconcile the ethical and the strategic requires the statesman or stateswoman to be in touch with the human forces that constitute the taproot of actions by other governments, and to accommodate as well as to check governments hostile to one's own interests. These are not easy problems to deal with intelligently, without emotional fervor, revealing just how frustrating the exercise can be for the serious scholar endeavoring to relate ethics and politics.

A purely strategic or power-political view will be as inadequate to this task as would be a purely idealistic one. Just as the pursuit of an ethical objective at the expense of political considerations can cause one to ignore "the tedious and murky problems of how to attain it," so an obsessive emphasis upon power (and inferentially upon the emotional cliche of maintaining one's status as "Number One") can lead those in the national security apparatus to a similar sort of tunnel vision. Writing on "the moral equation" in Vietnam, Howard Zinn once asked, "How can we tell butchers from surgeons, distinguish between a healing and a destructive act of violence?"[7] Even policy-makers in a democracy can blind themselves to the fact that they are serving neither their own people nor the international community by making strategic imperatives the exclusive measure of national policy. As American policy-makers seem once again to have realized, democracy and human rights also have their place in that process. But who is going to determine, when it comes to policy, what effectively (which means lastingly) promotes a democratic society? Universally accepted standards simply do not exist, however universal the legitimate demand for justice may be. The growing demand for democracy throughout the world is a recognition that without the appropriate form of government, justice is unlikely to be either established or maintained. In identifying U.S. policy with "those on every continent who are building democracy and freedom," President Clinton made their cause "America's cause."[8]

DISCUSSION QUESTIONS

1. What are some of the frustrations one experiences in trying to convey an understanding of the role of justice in world politics? Is Poland, as Sztompka sees his own country, different from others in this regard, or are we talking about universal values?
2. In his Table I, how does Arvanitopoulos contrast revolutions and transitions?
3. Why must national power be understood as being more than merely economic and military in nature? Does Clinton's Haitian policy reflect this?
4. How do theory and practice relate (if at all) in the determination of human rights policy? If so, is the theory ethical in nature or purely political?
5. Did justice triumph over Panamanian sovereignty in the invasion by U.S.

---

[7]"Vietnam: Setting the Moral Equation," *The Nation*, January 17, 1996, cited in John A. Vasquez, *Classics of International Relations*, (Englewood Cliffs, N.J.: Prentice Hall, 1986), p. 60.
[8]Inaugural address, January 20, 1993.

forces to capture a head of state of another country? How do the "two general themes" in transitions from military to civilian rule which Arvanitopoulos delineates apply to this situation, as you see it?

6. William James wrote of "The Moral Equivalent of War." What do you think he meant by that? Was the U.S. program described by Peter Olson an example?

7. Do you feel that President Bush, Senator Moynihan, and others were too reticent to condemn Deng Zhao Peng over the issue of suppression of the student democratic uprising in the spring of 1989? Should China continue to be given what is called "most-favored nation" trade treatment in the light of continuing human rights violations in that country?

8. When Brenda Cossman writes about "international human rights", why doesn't she use the term "civil" rights? Is there any international authority which can enforce civil rights?

9. How can a national government reconcile its legitimate security interests with the genuine desire of its citizens to help those in other countries? To what extent is this "genuine desire" related to ethnic identity and/or to political pressure?

37 *Human Rights in the Post-Cold War Era*

Brenda Cossman

Dr. Cossman is an Assistant Professor at Osgoode Hall Law School. The author would like to thank James Hathaway for his comments on an earlier draft, Donna Young for her research assistance, and Christine Wright for her technical assistance.

As Europe East and West struggles to come in from the cold, international human rights must confront the implications of profound social, economic, and political change. It is a moment of both opportunity and challenge. The end of the Cold War may signal a renewed possibility for the co-operation so essential for the realization of the normative vision of international human rights. Notwithstanding such hopes, I would argue that fundamental changes in the relationship between East and West may undermine important dimensions of the discourse of international human rights. Moreover, the focus of attention on the changes in the East may have devastating effects on the relationship between North and South, and on the conception of human rights law emerging from developing countries. As the Wall is dismantled in Europe, new walls may only be going up elsewhere.

I. RIGHTS DISCOURSE AND DEMOCRATIC POSSIBILITIES

The end of the Cold War may bring renewed international commitment to human rights. From its beginnings, international human rights law has been limited by problems of enforcement. As one commentator has written, "[i]nternational remedial paths remain fragile, often illusory."[1] It has relied primarily on international cooperation, moral suasion and condemnation to ensure

[1]Henry J. Steiner, *Political Participation as a Human Right*, 1 Harv. Hum. Rts. Y.B. 77, 81 (1988). *See generally* Torkel Opsahl, *Instruments of Implementation of Human Rights*, 10 Hum. Rts. L.J. 13 (1989); Guide to International Human Rights Practice (Hurs Hannum ed. 1984); Louis Sohn, *Human Rights:*

Their Implementation and Supervision by the United Nations, 2 Human Rights in International Law: Legal and Policy Issues 369 (Theodor Meron ed. 1984): Robertson, *The Implementation System: International Measures* in The International Bill of Rights: The Covenant on Civil and Political Rights 332 (Louis Henkin ed. 1981); J.S. Watson, *Legal Theory, Efficacy and Validity in the Development of Human Rights Norms in International Law*, 1979 U. Ill. L.F. 609; Richard B. Bilder, *Rethinking International Human Rights: Some Basic Questions*, 1969 Wis. L. Rev. 171.

Reprinted by permission from *Harvard International Law Review*, Volume 32, Number 2, Spring 1991, pp. 339–352. Copyright © 1992. Quarterly.

compliance. Moreover, this cooperation was often elusive in the Cold War world, where deep political and ideological divides constrained the sanctioning of human rights abuses by the international community. In a polarized world, the discourse on human rights was often no more than a rhetorical device in a political game of legitimation and delegitimation which coexisted with superpowers turning a blind eye to the human rights abuses in their own sphere of influence.

Yet, despite the weakness of the enforcement machinery and the history of non-cooperation, there remains a strong commitment to the discourse of human rights principles. As Philip Alston wrote in 1988,

> It is now widely accepted that the characterization of a specific goal as a human right elevates it above the rank and file of competing social goals, gives it a degree of immunity from challenge and generally endows it with an aura of timelessness, absoluteness and universal validity.[2]

Human rights is a powerful political discourse—indeed, it is often the only discourse in which disadvantaged groups may claim a voice and legitimately make universal claims.[3] International, national, and grassroots organizations continue to make human rights the discourse of choice in their struggles. Despite its institutional limitations, the discourse provides an important source of political inspiration and energy through which people can be educated and mobilized.[4]

In a world no longer divided along the East/West axis, this political discourse may have heightened possibilities. A world no longer divided may better lend itself to the international cooperation so essential to the realization of the vision of international human rights. On the international level, we are witnessing the emergence of a renewed commitment to the United Nations as a forum for the resolution of international conflict.[5] Such international cooperation could assume many forms in the area of human rights. The mechanisms for enforcing and monitoring compliance with international human rights norms could be improved within both Charter-[6] and Convention-

---

[2]Philip Alston, *Making Space for New Human Rights: The Case of the Right to Development,* 1 HARV. HUM. RTS. Y.B. 3 (1988).

[3]*See* Patricia J. Williams, *Alchemical Notes: Reconstructing Ideals from Deconstructed Rights,* 22 HARV. C.R.-C.L. L. REV. 401 (1987); Elizabeth M. Schneider, *The Dialectics of Rights and Politics: Perspectives from the Women's Movement,* 61 N.Y.U. L. REV. 589 (1986).

[4]*See* Clarence J. Dias & James C.N. Paul, *Developing Legal Resources for Participatory Organizations of The Rural Poor,* 1985 THIRD WORLD LEGAL STUD. 19 (1985); James C.N. Paul & Clarence J. Dias, *Generating and Sharing Knowledge of Law for People-Centered Development,* 1987 THIRD WORLD LEGAL STUD. 17; Clarence J. Dias & James C.N. Paul, *Developing the Human Right to Food as a Legal Resource for the Rural Poor: Some Strategies for NGOs,* in THE RIGHT TO FOOD 203 (P. Alston & K. Tomasevski eds. 1984); Edel Guiza, *A Philippine Experience on Legal Resources Development by the Rural Poor,* 1987 THIRD WORLD LEGAL STUD. 93; Anisur Rahman, *The Roles and Significance of Participatory Organizations of the Rural Poor in Alternative Strategies of Development,* 1987 THIRD WORLD LEGAL STUD. 1.

[5]For a discussion of the role of the UN in the areas of peace, environment, and economic development in the aftermath of the Cold War, see Lister, *The Role of International Organizations in the 1990s and Beyond,* 1990 INT'L RELATIONS 101.

[6]The Charter of the United Nations sets out the general human rights mandate of the UN and empowers several subsidiary bodies to implement this mandate. Most notably, the General Assembly is directed to initiate studies and make recommendations to promote human rights, and the Economic and Social Council [ECOSOC] is directed to make recommendations in the promotion of human rights. See UN CHARTER arts. 1, 13, 55, 56, 62, 64, 68. *See generally* Tom J. Farer, *The United Nations and Human Rights: More Than a Whimper Less Than a Roar,* 9 HUM. RTS. Q. 550 (1987); UNITED NATIONS, THE UNITED NATIONS AND HUMAN RIGHTS (1984). In addition to the mandate for fact finding and

based procedures.[7] States which have not already done so could ratify article 41 of the International Covenant on Civil and Political Rights (ICCPR), which provides for interstate complaints to the Human Rights Committee,[8] as well as the Optional Protocol of the Covenant, which allows the Committee to hear complaints from individuals.[9] Much room exists for strengthening the procedures and remedies in the International Convention on the Elimination of All Forms of Racial Discrimination (CERD), and

making recommendations, ECOSOC in 1970 adopted the Procedure for Dealing with Communications Relating to Violations of Human Rights and Fundamental Freedoms, June 19, 1970, E.S.C. Res. 1503 (XLVIII), 48 UN ECOSOC, UN Doc. E/RES/ 1503 (XLVIII) (1970) hereinafter Procedure 1503). Procedure 1503 empowers the Human Rights Commission and its Subcommission on Prevention of Discrimination and Protection of Minorities to receive complaints which "reveal a consistent pattern of gross and reliably attested violations of human rights and fundamental freedoms." *Id.* at 1. *See generally* M.E. Tardu, *The United Nations Response to Gross Violations of Human Rights: The 1503 Procedure,* 20 SANTA CLARA L.R. 559 (1980).

[7]The International Bill of Rights, comprised of the Universal Declaration of Human Rights and two Covenants, the International Covenant on Civil and Political Rights and the International Covenant on Social, Economic and Cultural Rights, imposes a system of periodic reporting on member states. Universal Declaration of Human Rights, G.A. Res. 217A(III), 3 UN.GAOR 71; UN Doc. 810 (1948) (Universal Declaration), International Covenant on Civil and Political Rights, G.A. 2200 A, 21 UN GAOR, Supp. (No. 16) 52, UN Doc. A/16316 (1966), International Covenant on Economic, Social and Cultural Rights, G.A. Res. 2200A, 21 UN GAOR Supp. (No. 16) at 49, UN Doc A/16316 (1966) (ICESCR).

[8]The Declaration regarding article 41 of the ICCPR entered into force March 28, 1979, with 10 ratifications. As of January 1, 1989, the interstate complaints procedure had been ratified by 23 countries. Neither the United States nor the countries of Eastern Europe, with the exception of Hungary, had ratified the Declaration.

[9]The Optional Protocol of the ICCPR entered into force March 23, 1976. As of January 1, 1989, 45 countries had ratified it. Neither the U.S. nor the countries of Eastern Europe, again with the recent exception of Hungary, had ratified it.

the Convention for the Elimination of All Forms of Discrimination Against Women (CEDAW).[10] For example, many more states could ratify the Declaration regarding article 14 of CERD, allowing the Committee on the Elimination of All Forms of Racial Discrimination to receive communications from individuals.[11] A provision similar to article 14 could be added to CEDAW.[12]

Even short of precipitating formal changes in the enforcement machinery of international instruments, the end of the Cold War may open other and perhaps more significant opportunities for human rights. Improved international cooperation may facilitate the work of the various agencies, committees, and working groups engaged in monitoring compliance with human rights obligations. Until now, the operations of these groups and institutions have been severely limited by the deep and often hostile political and ideological differences of their members.

[10]The International Convention on the Elimination of All Forms of Racial Discrimination, G.A. Resolution 2106A (XX), 20 UN GAOR, Supp. (No. 4) 47, UN Doc A/6014 (1965), Convention on the Elimination of All Forms of Discrimination Against Women, G.A. Res. 34/180, 34 UN GAOR Supp. (No. 46) 193, UN Doc. A/Res 134/180 (1980), entered into force September 3, 1981. For a discussion of the weak enforcement machinery under CEDAW, see Burrows, *International Law and Human Rights: The Case of Women's Rights,* in HUMAN RIGHTS: FROM RHETORIC TO REALITY 80, (T. Campbell, D. Goldberg, S. McLean & T. Mullen eds. 1986); Margaret E. Galey, *International Enforcement of Women's Rights,* 6 HUM. RTS. Q. 463 (1984). For a comprehensive bibliography regarding CEDAW, see Rebecca J. Cook, *Bibliography: The International Right to Nondiscrimination on the Basis of Sex,* 14 YALE J. INT'L L. 161 (1989).

[11]The Declaration regarding article 14 of CERD entered into force December 3, 1982. As of January 1, 1989, only 12 countries had ratified the Declaration. Neither the U.S. nor the countries of Eastern Europe have ratified this Declaration.

[12]See THEODOR MERON, HUMAN RIGHTS LAW-MAKING IN THE UNITED NATIONS 81–82 (1986); Laura Reanda, *Human Rights and Women's Rights: The United Nations Approach,* 3(2) HUM. RTS. Q. 11, 22–23 (1981).

There is some indication that such co-operation is already emerging within the United Nations human rights forums. For example, the forty-first Session of the UN Sub-Commission on Prevention of Discrimination and Protection of Minorities in August 1989 was reportedly marked by "a new spirit of cooperation between Sub-Commission members from the United States and the Soviet Union,"[13] the 1989 Session of the UN Commission on Human Rights was reportedly "marked by a slight decrease in ideological polarization as compared with previous sessions,"[14] and the 1990 Session of the UN Commission on Human Rights reportedly "witnessed a radical shift in the positions of Eastern European Countries."[15]

The changing international climate may also enlarge the role regional organizations play in human rights enforcement. Nonbinding regional standards such as those contained in the Helsinki Final Act of the Conference on Security and Cooperation in Europe[16] may acquire new importance in the wake of the CSCE's emergence as a key vehicle for shaping the post-Cold War Europe. Despite their focus on security issues, recent meetings of the CSCE have directed considerable attention to human rights. Indeed, the Concluding Document of the Follow-Up of the CSCE in January 1989 has been described as signifying "great progress as regards human rights."[17] Under the new conditions of cooperation, nonbinding human rights standards such as those promulgated by the CSCE might be as effective as, if not more so than, binding instruments lacking cooperative context.

---

[13]Robin M. Maher & David Weissbrodt, *The 41st Session of the UN Sub-Commission on Prevention of Discrimination and Protection of Minorities,* 12 HUM. RTS. Q. 290, 297 (1990). Maher and Weissbrodt note that U.S. and USSR representatives cosponsored three resolutions on the right to fair trial, the prevention of taking hostages, and the elimination of racial discrimination, and they coauthored a working paper on revised procedures for dealing with human rights violations under Procedure 1503, *Id.* at 297–98. This increased cooperation can be seen as evidence of a transition in the Soviet approach to the enforcement of international human rights. The Soviets have long resisted an international role in the enforcement of human rights, based on the principle of nonintervention in domestic affairs. *See* Richard N. Dean, *Beyond Helsinki: The Soviet View of Human Rights in International Law,* 21 VA. J. INT'L L. 55, 77–83 (1980); Jhabvala, *The Soviet Bloc's View of the Implementation of Human Rights Accords,* 7 HUM. RTS. Q. 461 (1985). More recently, however, the Soviets appear to have recognized a role for international enforcement. For example, in September 1988, Soviet Foreign Minister Schevardnardze, speaking to the UN General Assembly, called international control in areas from arms control to human rights "an imperative of our time." *See* Opsahl, *supra* note 1, at 20.

[14]Brody & Weissbrodt, *Major Developments at the 1989 Session of the U.N. Commission on Human Rights,* 11 HUM. RTS. Q. 586, 611 (1989).

[15]Reed Brody, Penny Parker & David Weissbrodt, *Major Developments in 1990 at the U.N. Commission on Hu-*

man Rights, 12 HUM. RTS. Q. 559, 560 (1990). At the 1990 Session, Bulgaria and Hungary voted for scrutiny of China, Cuba, and Iraq (although the USSR voted against the first two resolutions and did not participate in the vote on the third, it proposed measures to increase and strengthen the role of the Human Rights Commission. *Id.* at 560). *See also* Brody & Weissbrodt, *supra* note 14, at 611.

[16]The Final Act of the Conference on Security and Cooperation in Europe of 1975 (CSCE) was signed in Helsinki on August 1, 1975 by thirty-five countries, including the countries of Eastern and Western Europe, as well as the U.S. and Canada.

[17]Hannes Tretter, *Human Rights in the Concluding Document of the Vienna Follow-Up Meeting of the Conference on Security and Co-operation in Europe of January 15, 1989: An Introduction,* 10 HUM. RTS. L.J. 257, 259 (1989). For the text of the Concluding Document, see 10 HUM. RTS. L.J. 270 (1989). These proceedings can be seen as further evidence of the transition in the Soviet approach to the enforcement of human rights. Tretter reports that the socialist countries' understanding of human rights and the concomitant focus on the basic principle of noninterference in internal affairs have "receded into the background (with the exception of Romania) and ha[ve] apparently been replaced by the recognition of international responsibility for human rights." Tretter, *supra,* at 259. *See also id.* at 261–62.

II. HUMAN RIGHTS IN TRANSITION

The transcendence of oppositions in the post-Cold War era may open possibilities for international human rights in democratic struggles. Yet, the failure to transcend the oppositions of political philosophy may limit these possibilities. The collapse of the Communist bloc has been accompanied by a radical shift to the right in the political orientation of the countries of Eastern Europe, and the post-Cold War political climate may be less one of transcendence than it is of retrenchment.

Most current international human rights norms emerged in the aftermath of World War II, a product of the competing political ideologies of that period. The three generations of human rights correspond to three different political visions: civil and political rights associated with Western liberal democracies; social and economic rights associated with Eastern socialist states; and development rights associated with post-colonial, developing countries.[18] The very

division of the International Bill of Rights into two Covenants—one dealing with civil and political rights, the other dealing with social, economic, and cultural rights—was in large part due to the political and ideological divisions of the postwar world.[19] It took almost two decades from the adoption of the Universal Declaration to the adoption of the Covenants to accommodate fundamental differences between liberal and so-

---

[18]Stephen Marks argues that the discourse of contemporary international human rights can be seen as the product of three different revolutionary movements: "first, the 'bourgeois' revolutions, particularly in France and America, in the last quarter of the eighteenth century; second, the socialist, anti-exploitation revolutions of the first two decades of this century; and third, the anticolonialist revolutions that began immediately after the Second World War and culminated in the independence of many nations around 1960." Stephen P. Marks, *Emerging Human Rights: A New Generation for the 1980s?*, 33 Rutgers L. Rev. 435, 440 (1981). *See generally* Jerome J. Shestack, *The Jurisprudence of Human Rights*, in 1 Human Rights in International Law 69 (Theodor Meron ed. 1984). Address by Kasel Vasak, Inaugural Lecture to the Tenth Study Session of the International Institute of Human Rights, in Strasbourg (July 2–27, 1979). Alston noted that "[p]erhaps the most important . . . characteristic of international human rights law is its philosophical complexity . . . [which] is the product of an ambivalent relationship to an already

discordant heritage of philosophical theories of rights." Alston, *supra* note 2, at 28.

[19]The official justification for the division of the Convention into two legal instruments was the allegedly fundamental difference between the two categories of rights and the different mechanisms required for their implementation. V. Voitto Saario & Rosemary Higgins Cass, *The United Nations and the International Protection of Human Rights: A Legal Analysis and Interpretation;* 7 Cal. W. Int'l L.J. 591, 595–97 (1977). Humphrey has noted that it is technically possible to include both categories of rights in the same instrument with different implementation systems, and that the decision to have two covenants was motivated primarily by the political and ideological divisions within the UN Humphrey, *The International Law of Human Rights in the Middle of the Twentieth Century,* in The Present State of International Law (M. Box ed. 1973). Some states—most notably the U.S.—have never accepted the validity of a covenant on social and economic rights. They argued that social and economic claims were appropriately construed as interests or aspirations, not as rights. The division of the Convention into two legal instruments allowed states to ratify one Covenant without the other. *See* Oscar Schachter, International Law in Theory and Practice: General Course in Public International Law (1985); David M. Trubek, *Economic, Social, and Cultural Rights in the Third World: Human Rights Law and Human Needs Programs,* in 1 Human Rights in International Law; Legal and Policy Issues 205 (Theodor Meron ed. 1984); David P. Forsythe, *Socioeconomic Human Rights: The United Nations, the United States, and Beyond,* 4 Hum. Rts. Q. 433 (1982). For the argument that social and economic rights are not rights, see Maurice William Cranston, What Are Human Rights? (1973). *See also* E.W. Vierdag, *The Legal Nature of the Rights Granted by the International Covenant on Economic, Social and Cultural Rights,* 9 Neth. Y.B. Int'l L. 69 (1978).

cialist conceptions of individual rights, and of the individual's relation to society.[20] While the international community has recognized the indivisibility of all human rights on several occasions,[21] contemporary international human rights discourse remains the product of a precarious balance of ideological differences.

As the East embraces laissez-faire economics, what will become of the social and economic rights the East has historically advocated? A trend away from social and economic rights towards civil and political rights is becoming increasingly visible throughout Eastern Europe.[22] Although it is important to recognize the progress that has been made within the United Nations system in advancing social and economic

rights,[23] we must consider the real possibility of a backslide on recent commitments. The countries of East and West may now agree on the priority of civil and political rights over social and economic rights. Indeed, they may even agree that the latter are not appropriately understood as rights, but only as aspirations. Paradoxically, the possibility for heightened cooperation in the promotion of human rights may be a product of the narrowing of the discourse itself.

Even within the realm of civil and political rights, we must further ask whether some rights will be more equal than others. Will all civil and political rights be given equal significance, or will the shifting ideological balance privilege individualistic, libertarian rights of freedom from state intervention over collective, egalitarian rights, such as the freedom from discrimination? Two examples, although far from conclusive, are illustrative of the political mood of Eastern Europe, and suggest reason to be concerned about the future of human rights.

The first example is the attack on ethnic minorities throughout Eastern Europe. Nationalist movements unleashed by political liberalization have engaged in widespread ethnic violence. In Romania, extremist groups are fueling hatred against ethnic Hungarians, Germans, Gypsies, and Jews. In the Soviet Union, violence erupted between Armenians and Azeris, Uzbeks and Meskhetian Turks, Georgians and Abkhazians. In Bulgaria, nationalism has been directed against the Turkish minority. In Yugoslavia, tensions between the six na-

[20] For a discussion of the fundamental differences in conceptions of the human rights, see Bloed & van Hoof, *Some Aspects of the Socialist View of Human Rights,* in ESSAYS ON HUMAN RIGHTS IN THE HELSINKI PROCESS (A. Bloed & P. van Dijk eds. 1985); Farrokh Jhabvala, *supra* note 13; Lane, *Human Rights Under State Socialism,* 32 POL. STUD. 349 (1984); Sinha, *Human Rights: A Non-Western Viewpoint,* 67 ARCHIV FÜR RECHTS- UND SOZIALPHILOSOPHIE 76 (1981); Dean, *supra* note 13, at 55; Przetacznik, *The Socialist Concept of Human Rights,* 13 REVUE BELGE DU DROIT INTERNATIONAL 238 (1977).

[21] Proclamation of Teheran, adopted by the International Conference on Human Rights in 1968, and confirmed by the General Assembly on January 13, 1969. UN Doc. A/Res/2416 (XXIII) to A/Res/2450 (XXIII), recognizing that the full realization of civil and political rights is impossible without the enjoyment of economic, social, and cultural rights. *See also* the General Assembly Resolution in 1977, "Alternative Approaches and Ways and Means Within the United Nations System for Improving the Effective Enjoyment of Human Rights and Fundamental Freedoms," Feb. 24, 1978, A/Res/32/130, para. 1(a) at 2 (recognizing that human rights are indivisible and interdependent).

[22] In recent meetings of the CSCE, the countries of Eastern Europe have not insisted on the inclusion of social and economic rights in exchange for the recognition of civil and political rights. See Tretter, *supra* note 17, at 259. The Concluding Document of the Vienna meeting did not refer to the indivisibility of human rights at all. *Id.* at 262.

[23] For a discussion of the recent developments on social and economic rights, see Philip Alston, *Out of the Abyss: The Challenges Confronting the New U.N. Committee on Economic, Social and Cultural Rights,* 9 HUM. RTS. Q. 332 (1987): Philip Alston & Bruno Simma, *First Session of the UN Committee on Economic, Social and Cultural Rights,* 81 AM. J. INT'L L. 747 (1987).

tional republics, as well as the eighteen other nationalities, are threatening to tear the country apart.[24] Throughout Eastern Europe and the Soviet Union, anti-Semitism is experiencing a tragic revival.[25]

The second example is the assault on women's rights. Women are experiencing a disproportionate impact of the inflation and unemployment that accompany the transition to free-market economies in Eastern Europe. Most East European women are in the workforce.[26] However, they are at high risk of losing their job security and their maternity benefits, as well as other benefits.[27] With rising unemployment, women are the first to be laid off and thereby forced to return to the sphere of domestic labor. Moreover, social pressure is mounting on women to return to the home voluntarily. Further, divorce and abortion rights are under attack in many Eastern European countries. In Poland, where the antiabortion movement has been the strongest, a woman must now visit

[24]*Quarrels Divide Ethnic Groups,* The Globe and Mail, Dec. 11, 1990, at B20, col. 6; Borrell, *The Bills Come Due: After a Year of Freedom, Eastern Europe Realizes that Toppling Statues of Stalin and Lenin is Easier Than Erecting Stable Democracies and Free Markets,* TIME, Dec. 3, 1990; Neier, Watching Rights, THE NATION, Sept. 17, 1990, at 263, col. 1; *The Dark Side of Nationalism,* editorial, The Globe and Mail, Mar. 31, 1990, at D6, col. 1; Deak, *Uncovering Eastern Europe's Dark History,* 10 SAIS REV. 51 (1990); Jonathan Eyal, *Eastern Europe: What About the Minorities?*, 45(12) WORLD TODAY 205–08 (Dec. 1989); Robert D. Kaplan, *Europe's Third World: Poverty and Ethnic Strife in Southeastern Europe Will Give Russia a Headache for Years to Come,* ATLANTIC MONTHLY, Jul. 1989, at 16, col. 6.

[25]Anti-Semitic incidents have been reported throughout Eastern Europe and the Soviet Union. In East Germany, members of the miniscule Jewish communities in the southern cities of Leipzig, Dresden, and Erfurt speak of vicious anonymous phone calls. In the Soviet Union, Jewish cemeteries and synagogues in Moscow and Leningrad have been desecrated, and rumors of pogroms are being spread by members of extremist groups, such as Pamiat', which blames Jews for the Communist regime. In Hungary, references to the predominance of Jews in the regime of dictator Matyas Rakosi in the 1950s are heard. In Romania, where the desecration of synagogues and cemeteries has been the most widespread, Jews are frequently accused of collaborating with the regime of Nicolae Ceausescu. For discussion of these developments, see Bierman, *New Openness, Old Hatred: Anti-Semitism Stalks Eastern Europe,* MACLEAN'S, Apr. 16, 1990, at 26, col. 1; Wilson-Smith, *The Jews: Anti-Semitism is on the Rise in the Soviet Union and Eastern Europe,* MACLEAN'S, Apr. 16, 1990, at 22, col. 4; Talbott, *Freedom's Ugly Underside: Anti-Semitism in Eastern Europe,* TIME, Nov. 27, 1989, at 53.

[26]In 1980, women constituted one-half of the labor force in Eastern Europe. Molyneux, *Women and Perestroika,* 1983 NEW LEFT REV. 23, 27 (1990).

[27]In Hungary, for example, over 80 percent of women work in the labor force. A woman is entitled to receive twenty-four week maternity leave with full pay, followed by a three-year leave at partial salary, and her position guaranteed upon return. Zsuzsa Ferge, a sociologist at Eotvos Lorand University in Budapest stated in a recent interview: "No market economy is going to guarantee a job after a three-year absence." *Democratic Revolution Brings Few Advantages to Many,* Globe and Mail, Nov. 26, 1990, at A13. In Poland, where women constituted 46% of the labor force, this right has already been rescinded. The transition to a market economy is expected to produce high unemployment, and women are expected to be disproportionately affected. According to some estimates, 80 percent of those already laid off are women. Brenan S. Bisop, *From Women's Rights to Feminist Politics: The Developing Struggle for Women's Liberation in Poland,* 42 MONTHLY REV. 13, 21 (1990). In Belgrade human rights activist Sonja Licht observes: "Already there is a tendency to think that the women must be sent home . . . . If you have to choose who is going to lose a job, then of course, you would choose women first, because, after all, they are mothers anyway." *Democratic Revolution Brings Few Advantages, supra. See also Challenge in the East: The Emerging Democracies Offer a Chance for Women to Share Real, Rather Than Cosmetic, Power,* TIME 130 (Special Issue, Fall, 1990). While reports of the impact of Perestroika on women's employment in the Soviet Union is conflicting, many Soviet commentators have argued that economic restructuring will require that women give up their jobs, and return to the sphere of the family. *See* Molyneux, *supra* note 26. As Molyneux notes, "A convenient link between increasing the population and raising productivity is thereby established. Predictably, the group of Russian patriots associated with Pamyat welcomes 'modernization' as a 'way to raise production standards and free women from involuntary emancipation and return her to the family where she fills the role of mother, keeper of the hearth and bulwark of the nation.'" *Id.* at 38–39.

three doctors and a psychologist before she can have an abortion at a publicly funded hospital.[28] Last November, a bill which proposed banning abortion passed the Polish Senate.[29]

Such discrimination, harassment, and violence directed against women and minorities constitute a clear violation of international human rights standards.[30] The attack on the rights of ethnic minorities has been identified as a serious problem at both the international and regional level. For example, in 1988, the UN Sub-Commission on Prevention of Discrimination and Protection of Minorities, after many years of sidestepping this divisive issue, decided to consider the protection of racial, ethnic, religious, and linguistic minorities.[31] Similarly, increased attention has been directed toward the rights of minorities within the CSCE, which has been called upon to meet the challenges of the anti-Semitism and ethnic hatred that is sweeping across Eastern Europe. At its recent meetings, the CSCE has directed increased attention to develop protections for the rights of ethnic minorities.[32] While some observers still argue that international instruments are inadequate for the protection of ethnic minorities,[33] some official efforts are being made to offset the rising intolerance toward ethnic minorities. There is at least some evidence that the states of Eastern Europe are resisting the assault on the rights of ethnic minorities by adopting official measures to protect them. The same, however, cannot be said of women's rights. On the contrary, official state discourse often encourages discrimi-

---

[28]Waclav Dec, head of obstetrics and gynecology at the Medical Academy in Lodz, has stated of these amendments: "These rules serve no medical purpose. It is another attempt to humiliate women. These psychologists are generally Church people who try to persuade women not to have abortions." Stephen Engelberg, *Anti-Abortion Bill Prompts Poles to Debate the Church's Influence*, N.Y. Times, Nov. 6, 1990, at A1, col. 1.

[29]The lower house postponed the vote on the bill until after the presidential election. *Id.* A similar battle is developing in the Croatian republic of Yugoslavia where the Catholic Church is also a strong political influence. In Serbia, married couples with no children are being threatened with punitive taxes. *See also Democratic Revolution Brings Few Advantages to Many, supra* note 27.

[30]The Universal Declaration, ICCPR, and the ICESR specifically recognize the right to nondiscrimination on the basis of national origin, religion, and language; CERD specifically prohibits discrimination on the basis of national or ethnic origin. ICERD art. 4 further requires that states adopt measures to eradicate hatred and incitement, and to prohibit racist organizations. *See also* ICCPR art. 27. The UN Charter, the Universal Declaration, the ICCPR, and the ICESCR each recognize the right to freedom on the basis of sex. Universal Declaration, art. 2; ICCPR art. 26, ICESCR, arts 2(2), 3. The CEDAW specifically prohibits such discrimination in the employment and family context. CEDAW, *supra* note 10.

[31]Mah & Weissbrodt, *supra* note 13, at 312.

[32]At a recent Helsinki-sponsored Conference on the Human Dimension, held in Copenhagen in June 1990, the thirty-five members of the CSCE adopted a resolution that included the need to guarantee political pluralism, the protection of minorities, and the importance of confronting anti-Semitism and racism. *See* Korey, *The CSCE and Human Rights: A New Chapter for Helsinki*, 73 The New Leader 11, 13 (1990); *Protection of Minorities Crucial, Human Rights Organization Says*, Globe and Mail, June 8, 1990, at A14. This concern was echoed at the Paris meeting in November 1990.

[33]Eyal, *supra* note 24; *see also* T.H. Bagley, General Principles and Problems in the International Protection of Minorities (1950); United Nations, Definition and Classification of Minorities, UN Public. Sales No. 1950. XIV.3; F. Capotorti, Study on the Rights of Persons Belonging to Ethnic, Religious and Linguistic Minorities, UN Public. Sales No. E.78.XIV.1, at 5–16 (1979). While considerable efforts were made by the Sub-Committee on Prevention of Discrimination and Protection of Minorities, and in turn, by the UN General Assembly, to deal with the issue of the protection of ethnic minorities, the proceedings did not progress beyond a mere definition of ethnic minorities, as well as the principle that such minorities ought to receive special rights. After the adoption of article 27 of the ICCPR, similar problems were encountered in interpreting the concepts of "minorities," "ethnic minorities," and "culture." *See generally id.*

nation against women.[34] It may be that women's rights, tied as they are to social and economic rights, will be first among the victims of retrenchment in human rights discourse.

III. RIGHTS DISCOURSE AND DEVELOPMENT

The heightened possibilities for cooperation in the promotion and substantive realization of international human rights presumes a world less divided. Yet, it is not at all clear that the end of the Cold War does signify the emergence of a world order that is in fact less divided. It may only signify a realignment of these divisions. As the divide between East and West disappears, the divide between North and South may only deepen.

Rights discourse has assumed a prominent role in the political, economic, and ideological struggles of the developing world to create a New International Economic Order. The relationship between rights and development has been recognized by the UN General Assembly in its recognition of the right to development as an inalienable human right.[35] However, this relationship between rights discourse and development has been controversial, with little support for this third generation human right forthcoming from the West. The United States is the only country to have voted against the Declaration on the Right to Development, and many other Western countries abstained from the vote.[36] The Working Group on the Right to Development was plagued by these political and ideological divisions.[37] For example, on the issue of the subjects of the right to development both socialist and developing countries were of the opinion that development should be a right of individuals, peoples, and States. Developed countries, on the other hand, tended to take the position that development is only a right of individuals.[38] The debate reflected a deeper tension in the very conception of rights between individual and collective rights, a tension that also underlies the debate regarding social and economic rights.[39] In the end, the working

[34]As Molyneux has noted, the call for women to return to the home in the Soviet Union "is not exclusively a neo-conservative and nationalist position: Gorbachev, too, has referred to the 'purely womanly mission,' investing domesticity and motherhood with an aura of the sacred and natural." Molyneux, *supra* note 26, at 38.

[35]Declaration on the Right to Development, G.A. Res. 41/128, Annex, 41 UN GAOR Supp. (No. 53) at 186, UN Doc. A/41/53 (1986). For a general discussion of the right to development, see Alston, *supra* note 2; Kiwanuka, *Developing Rights: The UN Declaration on the Right to Development*, 35 INT'L L. REV. 257 (1988); Turk, *The Human Rights to Development*, in RESTRUCTURING THE INTERNATIONAL ECONOMIC ORDER: THE ROLE OF LAW AND LAWYERS (P. Van Dijk ed. 1987); Philip Alston, *Third Generation of Solidarity Rights: Progressive Development or Obfuscation of International Human Rights Law*, 29 NETH. INT'L L. REV. 307 (1982); K. de Vey Mestdagh, *The Right to Development: From Evolving Principle to "Legal" Right*, in DEVELOPMENT, HUMAN RIGHTS AND THE RULE OF LAW 143 (1981); Marks, *supra* note 18.

[36]Denmark, Finland, the Federal Republic of Germany, Iceland, Israel, Japan, Sweden, and the United Kingdom all abstained from the vote on the Declaration. Declaration, on the Right to Development, *supra* note 35.

[37]The Working Group of Government Experts on the Right to Development was established pursuant to the Commission on Human Rights, Res. 36, para. 10, in COMMISSION ON HUMAN RIGHTS, REPORT ON THE THIRTY-SEVENTH SESSION 37, UN ESCOR Supp. (No. 5) at 237, UN Doc. E/1981/25 (1981).

[38]Kiwanuka, *supra* note 35, at 260–67. However, as Kiwanuka notes, some developed countries, notably Canada and Australia, adopted a compromise position. Despite their reluctance to recognize the collective dimension of rights, they voted in favor of the Declaration.

[39]For a review of these arguments in relation to the right to development, see generally Alston, *supra*

group achieved what Alston described as "a relatively artificial consensus" that locked the parties into a "set of very carefully negotiated compromise positions from which there can be no creative escape."[40] As a result, the working group has made very little progress since the adoption of the declaration.[41]

Furthermore, the right to development is seen to embrace both the first and second generation of rights, that is, it is based on the realization of both civil and political rights, and social and economic rights. While the right builds on the emerging international recognition of the indivisibility of these two categories of rights, it is at the same time plagued by the controversy regarding social and economic rights.

A fundamental question that must be considered is to what extent the transformation in Eastern Europe, and the concomitant realignment of political, economic, and ideological interests between East and West, will affect this precarious consensus on the right to development. Will the developing world lose the support it had garnered from the Communist bloc in support of the solidarity rights in general and the right to development in particular? As the East becomes West in economic and political orientation, what will become of these emerging rights? An evaporating commitment to collective rights, to social and economic rights, to the indivisibility of rights, and to the posi-

tive duties implied by these rights may only further undermine the tenuous international support for the third generation of solidarity rights. Moreover, to the countries of the South, the right to development represents a synthesis of all human rights, a holistic vision of the relationship between rights and development which informs their approach to all human rights. The loss of support for the right to development may thereby signify a growing divide in the human rights visions of North and South more generally. Indeed, the 1990 Session of the UN Commission on Human Rights is reported to have been "marked by a growing North-South division, both on substantive issues and on the future of the Commission itself."[42]

The implications of the basis of support for the right to development are not only symbolic. The realization of the right to development has been seen to require a fundamental restructuring of the international instruments of the international economic order, such as GATT, IMF, the World Bank, as well as bilateral treaties for the promotion and protection of foreign investment, and bilateral development assistance.[43] However, the realignment of political, economic, and ideological interests in the developed world may well represent an insurmountable obstacle to these initiatives. The transition in political orientation in Eastern Europe in many respects reflects the deeper economic transition from socialist planned economics to capitalist relations of production—a transition which requires extensive financial assistance.[44] This eco-

note 2. For arguments that human rights in general and the right to development in particular, are individual not collective rights, see Jack Donnelly. *In Search of the Unicorn: The Jurisprudence and Politics of the Rights to Development*, 15 CAL. W. INT'L L.J. 473 (1985); Jack Donnelly, *Human Rights as Natural Rights*, 4 HUM. RTS. Q. 391 (1982). For arguments that the right to development is both an individual and collective right, see Bejaoui, *Some Unorthodox Reflections on the Right to Development*, in INTERNATIONAL LAW OF DEVELOPMENT: COMPARATIVE PERSPECTIVES 87 (Francis Snyder & Peter Slinn eds. 1987).

[40]Alston, *supra* note 2, at 23.
[41]*Id.*

[42]Brody, Parker & Weissbrodt, *supra* note 15, at 587.
[43]See Turk, *supra* note 35; Khan, *International Law of Development at Edinburgh: Methodology, Content and Salient Issues*, 1986 THIRD WORLD LEGAL STUD. 15; Paul *International Development Agencies, Human Rights and Humane Development Projects*, 14 ALTERNATIVES 77 (1989).
[44]For a general discussion of the financial requirements of the economic transition of Eastern Europe, *see*

nomic transition may directly undermine the traditional alliance between Eastern Europe and the developing countries. Not only are the countries of Eastern Europe adopting economic policies that are directly antithetical to the economic changes contemplated by the NIEO, but these countries are also now in direct competition with developing countries for both bilateral and multilateral development assistance, debt alleviation, and capital investment from the West. Indeed, international development assistance is already being rerouted from the developing world to Eastern Europe and the Soviet Union.[45]

IV. CONCLUSION

The post-Cold War international order opens windows of opportunity for stronger enforcement mechanisms, more non-binding standards, and increased international and regional cooperation for the promotion of international human rights. However, it is essential that the discourse of international human rights is not itself compromised in the efforts to achieve these ends. The real challenge facing international human rights in this era lies in resisting the homogenization of human rights as civil and political rights. While regional organizations, such as the CSCE, are well-positioned to assume a prominent role in fostering new international cooperation, they cannot be expected to take the lead in prompting social and economic rights. The reorientation of human rights promotion and economic development along the East-West axis may only serve to deepen the divide between North and South. A renewed commitment to the existing discourse and fora for international human rights is required to ensure that the political changes in Eastern Europe bring about a real increase in democratic space within which rights claims can be made, rather than simply a rise in conservative ideologies within which rights claims will go largely unheard. But there may also be possibility in paradox. Perhaps the depoliticized East-West dialogue offers a possibility of political space for more substantive and less rhetorical debate on the essential meaning of human dignity.

Amy Deen & David A. Westbrook, *Return to Europe: Integrating Eastern European Economies into the European Market Through Alliance with the European Community,* 31 HARV. INT'L L.J. 660 (1990).

[45]The chairman of a disaster committee of six international relief agencies, including the League of the Red Cross and Red Crescent Societies, Oxfam and the World Council of Churches; recently announced their groups' concerns that millions of people will face starvation in Africa because of the emerging policy of the West of shifting aid to Eastern Europe and the Soviet Union. See Millions May Die in Africa, Agencies Say, The Globe and Mail, Jan. 5, 1991, at A1.

38 *CHANGE IN SOUTH AFRICA: A MODEST AMERICAN ROLE*

Peter Olson

Presently Assistant Legal Adviser for Ethics and Personnel at the U.S. Department of State, Peter Olson served as human rights coordinator at the U.S. Agency for International Development Mission in Pretoria from 1987 to 1989.

. . . Prior to the administration of Jimmy Carter, the United States devoted only limited attention to the internal situation in South Africa. While the Carter administration focused attention and heated rhetoric on South Africa, it backed its words with little more than symbolic action, and under the Reagan administration even that pressure diminished.

This relatively stable state of affairs changed with the township uprisings of 1984 through 1986 and the South African government's massive forceful repression, gripping reports of which dominated foreign news programs. These dramatic events concentrated international attention on the growing instability of the South African situation and convinced many that active intervention from abroad was necessary for a peaceful and durable resolution to South Africa's increasingly bitter and violent conflict.

In this context, there was a rapid growth in the number of those in Congress and elsewhere concluding that the Reagan administration policy of "constructive engagement," whatever its other merits, had failed to express clearly U.S. opposition to apartheid and to demonstrate that the fundamental alignment of the United States was with the majority of the people of South Africa rather than with its white minority and their government.

As evidence of strong public sentiment against apartheid, the United States had been providing assistance to black South Africans since 1981, when the first allocations of scholarship assistance for black South Africans were made. In subsequent years Congress expanded this program, most significantly for human rights purposes in fiscal years (FY) 1984 and 1985 when it earmarked substantial sums for grants to South African groups to "foster a just society and to help victims of apartheid."

Responding both to South African developments and to the growing domestic political pressure for stronger action, in September 1985 President Reagan issued an executive order on South Africa policy set-

Excerpted from an article entitled "The U.S. Human Rights Program in South Africa, 1986–1989," *Human Rights Quarterly,* Vol. 13, No. 1, February 1991, pp. 24–65. Copyright © The Johns Hopkins University Press, 1991. (Most footnotes have been deleted).

ting forth a range of sanctions and positive measures and substantially increasing funds for the existing limited program of human rights implemented through the U.S. embassy and consulates in South Africa.

Just over one year later, by a wide margin Congress overrode a presidential veto of the Comprehensive Anti-Apartheid Act of 1986 (CAAA), which, like the 1985 executive order, combined sanctions and positive measures. Among the latter were authorization of up to $40 million per year for a wide-ranging program of support for disadvantaged South Africans and expansion of the human rights grants program.

The assistance program that resulted from these executive and congressional actions was recognized from the beginning as something genuinely new. Explicitly and inescapably intended to assist political development and political activity by antigovernment groups and individuals, the program represented a departure at least in degree from previous practice of the U.S. government and AID. No other AID program had been, by law, effectively precluded from cooperation or, for the most part, even engagement with the "host" government.

The program was built around two major and related themes: promoting an end to apartheid and facilitating the emergence in South Africa of a nonracial, democratic society. Five program elements made up the great bulk of the AID program: community outreach and leadership development, labor, black private enterprise development, education (including scholarships), and human rights. Conceived as a wide-ranging, if not entirely comprehensive attack on one of the most glaring human rights violations of the late twentieth century, the entire program could plausibly be described as a "human rights" program.

All but the last of these five elements, however, were aimed at long-term social or institutional questions and approached them from an essentially developmental perspective. The human rights program alone expressly supported those directly confronting apartheid and creating or sustaining a human rights culture in South Africa. The balance of this article will accordingly focus on this element.

The significant change in the size and scope of assistance to black South Africans implicit in the September 1985 executive order required a major expansion of the AID[1] presence in South Africa. Previously, an "AID Affairs Officer," had been stationed at the embassy largely for the purpose of conducting necessary local liaison in support of the "self-help" and early human rights programs run by the embassy, and other programs run by regional AID offices outside South Africa or by Washington headquarters. There could be no doubt, however, that effective implementation of the new program would require establishment of a fully staffed AID office in South Africa.

Following a series of preliminary trips to South Africa by AID or joint AID and State Department teams, in July 1986 an AID office was established in the U.S. embassy in Pretoria. The initial staff consisted of four officers, supported by a regional legal adviser and controller and administration services based four hours' drive away in Mbabane, Swaziland. By mid-1987, the mission had outgrown its cramped quarters in the embassy and moved into its own offices several blocks away. By the end of 1989, the mission staff had grown to a total of thirteen U.S. AID and contractor officers, seven South African professional employees, and twelve U.S. and South African support personnel, in additional to legal and administrative support from Mbabane. . . .

---

[1]Editors note: Agency for International Development, a major outgrowth of "Point Four" in President Truman's inaugural address in 1949.

I. PROGRAM ISSUES

Both the content of the AID program and the environment within which it operated led to an unending series of issues that had to be addressed effectively if the program was to function smoothly and achieve its goals. Some of these—for example, whether the CAAA's goals were relevant to South Africa—went to the very conception of the program and were operationally relevant only in that mission staff and potential recipients had to believe that their work had value and merit in the South African context. Others were as mundane as the constant search for ways to minimize the inconveniences associated with being headquartered in Pretoria, such as the lengthy drive to Johannesburg and Soweto, where the great majority of recipients worked and lived. The following discussion treats some of the more difficult or operationally significant problems faced in implementing the human rights and other program elements.

A. Appropriateness of CAAA Goals

Perhaps the most basic question was whether the program should exist at all. Critics both in the United States and South Africa frequently expressed the view that the AID program was a political palliative, intended simply as a "cover" to permit the Reagan administration to continue with a preferred policy of constructive engagement with the South African government, or at least to avoid being forced to impose even tougher sanctions than those found in the CAAA.

This issue was infinitely debatable, although one's ultimate conclusion was as likely to reflect personal views of the Reagan or Bush administration as any objectively verifiable facts. For the staff of the mission, the operational reality was, of course, that the program had been created in the wisdom of the executive and legislative branches and as government employees they were charged with carrying it out; as suggested above, however, the staff would have had difficulty carrying out their duties had they harbored strong doubts about the program's essential validity.

The CAAA's goals—promoting the demise of apartheid and facilitating the emergence of a nonracial, democratic society—were very large compared to the available resources and even the theoretical capabilities of the United States. Must they then be dismissed as quixotic vaporings unrelated to South African realities? Did they, indeed, merely divert taxpayers' money from more achievable and pressing needs while fostering an inaccurate and possibly dangerous illusion that the United States was effectively contributing to resolving the South African crisis?

The CAAA was noteworthy in assessing the South African problem as an essentially *political* one: without in the least denying the urgent need for economic development for blacks, the law stated that U.S. policy toward black South Africans held "the apartheid system [to be] the root cause of their victimization." The CAAA's focus was therefore on achieving a political solution to both the immediate problem of apartheid and the longer-term challenge of creating the social and other conditions necessary for establishment and maintenance of a nonracial democracy.

South Africa is a middle-income country and, like other such countries, the attempt to deal with its economic and social problems may tax its resources to the breaking point. Those problems are exaggerated, however, and often caused by a radically distorted political system denying blacks any share in political power and by deliberate policy institutionalizing extraordinary disparities in wealth, income, and opportunities. In the absence of this unjust system, there is no reason that, over the long run, South Africa should not be as well or better positioned to solve its economic and social problems than most countries.

A high proportion of politically thoughtful South African blacks, and many whites, shared the perception that reformers could best address South Africa's problems by eliminating apartheid and substituting for it a nonracial democracy. Even if there could be no guarantee of the ultimate triumph of nonracial democratic principles, a program based on this perspective was therefore at least a potentially appropriate response to South African priorities.

While other elements of the AID program concentrated on longer-term development, the human rights element of the AID program was for the most part focused on current efforts to address current injustices—on supporting those fighting the daily fight against apartheid and seeking to vindicate human rights at every juncture. Those efforts were taking place on several fronts, including mass organization; civil disobedience; hunger strikes by detainees and other nonviolent resistance; political consciousness-raising through civic organizations, advice offices, and other groups; community resistance to enforcement of grand apartheid policies of incorporation or denationalization; and legal activity including legal defense as well as challenges to apartheid legislation.

Support was available under the human rights program for the great majority of activities covered under these headings. The statute explicitly identified several of these as appropriate for human rights grants; only one—mass organization—presented difficulties, due principally to the highly partisan nature of most such activity and the fact that it was by nature unsuited to AID's focus on defined projects. With the exception of mass organization and violent activity, then, the program could assist virtually the entire spectrum of anti-apartheid activity actually being undertaken during the period and in that sense at least was broadly appropriate to the South African situation.

One area in which the desirability of U.S. involvement evoked considerable controversy—especially in the United States—was that of supporting actions within the South African legal system. Many activists considered the legal system of South Africa to be so fatally compromised by its association with apartheid that it was not morally appropriate to engage with it. Others felt that funding lawsuits and other activity within that system was at best an irrelevant waste of money and at worst a wholly unwarranted contribution to the positive public image of a legal system that would never, in the end, make a real contribution to ending apartheid. Some felt that community groups or local advice centers providing highly practical advice on coping with an essentially arbitrary legal system could make far better and more cost-effective use of these funds.

These objections were not without merit. Apartheid was, among other things, a set of rules embodied in duly adopted legislation to which the courts gave full effect. Although certain individual judges stood against the trend of unquestioning acceptance, the South African judiciary as a whole certainly did not consistently distinguish itself in its resistance to apartheid and state action. And, of course, legal cases were very costly.

The case in favor of participating in the system, however, was even more compelling. The human rights program was intended to support anti-apartheid activity, and had therefore to focus on the opportunities which existed to do so. Particularly during the period of the 1986–1990 state of emergency, options for effective nonviolent activity were relatively few. Indeed, the widespread detentions and other actions taken under authority of the state of emergency themselves gave rise to a major increase in legal work challenging those actions and seeking the release of detained activists.

Had South Africans consulted by the mission insisted that "collaboration" with the legal system was illegitimate, a difficult problem would have been faced. In the event, however, there was widespread consensus that one's views of the courts' legitimacy or lack thereof could not be allowed to interfere with the possibility of obtaining the release of unjustly detained individuals or achieving even minor victories against the state of emergency, repression, or the apartheid system. Activists frequently made requests for assistance for action in the courts, and AID funds were involved in scores if not hundreds of cases challenging state actions under the emergency and other repressive legislation.

The possibility of winning one's case was not always illusory. The South African legal system, for all its flaws and injustices, was on occasion capable of protecting rights and dealing sharp blows to the apartheid system. There was, moreover, a long tradition in South Africa of using the courts as an instrument, however flawed, in the struggle against apartheid.

Yet another consideration was that newspapers could with few exceptions fully report events taking place in open court, including discussions of police and other action in the townships. Given the stringent media regulations, which the state of emergency added to the already strict statutory controls on publications, it was often only through such means that this information became widely known. For related reasons, mounting a vigorous defense built morale by providing persons whose other options for resistance had been foreclosed an op-

portunity to continue to fight back. The experience of insisting on their rights, and of forcing the state to make its case publicly, was by many accounts an important boost to the spirits and confidence of detainees and political prisoners.

Finally, funding legal defense work was justified by the fact that it underscored for the future the importance of having a functioning system of justice. Americans have historically felt a particularly strong obligation to uphold the rule of law and the principles of the presumption of innocence and right to counsel, and an equally strong distaste for prosecutions brought for openly political reasons (as was clearly the case when the charges derived from regulations under the state of emergency rather than the ordinary criminal laws). Supporting court action was an important way to express these values. Each case brought, and each defense offered, was a reminder to the judges and others that the people had legitimate expectations that justice would be done in accordance with the law. The unrelenting fight, and occasional victories, contributed to upholding the principle that courts are a place to find justice, and that they need not be the political instruments of an unjust system.

B. Constraints

The program labored under several critical constraints, many of which derived from the extraordinary environment in which it operated. South Africa was a remarkable—even bizarre—combination of first and third worlds, a phenomenon reflected in its society and politics.

White politics were, within distinct limits, relatively open and democratic—and yet the view that Afrikaners are best understood as a "tribe" was supported by their solidarity and disdain for those not forming part of their group. On the other hand, the frequent "third world rhetoric" and emphasis in black politics on mass mobilization and maintenance of unbroken political fronts (even at the occasional expense of democratic formalities) were often counterbalanced—notably but by no means exclusively within the Charterist camp—by a commitment in word and deed to a high degree of accountability to and consultation with their grassroots constituency that would do credit to long-established democracies.

South Africa's immensely complex and infinitely intriguing society included both such cities as Johannesburg and Soweto, home to, among others, a wealthy, well-established, and sophisticated black and white urban population whose life was at times remarkably similar to that found in a major U.S. city, and the rural homelands, where the bulk of South Africa's black population lived in grinding poverty and ignorance, and *platteland,* dominated by white farmers dedicated to "old time apartheid" and firm backers of Dr. A.P. Treurnicht's Conservative Party. Apartheid's divisive and unjust social engineering grossly distorted millions of lives, and yet the society did somehow function and even permit most people to find some satisfaction in their daily lives.

Although the unrest that had helped pass the CAAA was subsiding by the time the mission came into being, that surface calm had been achieved only through heavy and at times savage government repression. If South Africa was not the intense living hell foreign news coverage sometimes suggested, there was no denying it was a police state, albeit one where for external and domestic white consumption the iron fist was most often clothed in a velvet glove.

It was by no means clear that the human rights program could function effectively in such a climate. The question whether any anti-apartheid assistance at all

could be provided had been provisionally resolved with the initiation and conduct of some program elements in earlier years. Nevertheless, especially during the first two years following its establishment, the mission was constantly aware that the program could be terminated at any time and that it was in all likelihood the object of close South African government attention.

The reasons *why* the South African government was prepared to permit the AID program—and particularly the human rights element—to be conducted within its borders and in undisguised support of persons and groups actively opposing fundamental government policy were complex and not, perhaps, wholly understood by anyone outside the South African government. Among them, however, was surely an awareness that refusing to do so could lead to such unpalatable actions as a reduction in the level of diplomatic relations or expansion of sanctions. The psychological impact of a breach with the United States would have been enormous given South Africa's isolation and the generally positive feelings toward the United States that appeared widely held among South Africans of all races. Permitting such a program may, then, simply have been judged the lesser of two evils. The possibility that elements of the South African government saw the program as, on balance, a helpful contribution to addressing South African problems in a nonviolent manner cannot be wholly discounted.

Quite a separate issue was that of the availability of recipients. In response to the unrest, South African authorities had arrested or detained large numbers of anti-apartheid activists and decapitated or destroyed many organizations, particularly those with a strong community base in the townships. A related question was whether the authorities would subject persons or groups that entered into a relationship with

AID to greater scrutiny or repression. Over time, happily, it became clear that more than adequate numbers of well-qualified potential recipients with excellent programs were available and that harassment would not in most cases unacceptably increase as a result of their relationship with AID.

These problems gave rise to several responses. AID conducted the program openly and in accordance with the non-violent, nonpartisan principles of the FAA and CAAA. While the South African government might not have liked the program, it thus had no reason to believe that it was a covert effort to support violent activity or, indeed, anything other than what the CAAA made clear that it was: an effort to contribute constructively to the nonviolent elimination of apartheid and support the emergence of a society based on nonracial, democratic principles.

On the other political flank, perhaps the most significant operational problem that the program faced was that of "credibility." Although affecting the entire AID program, the politically highly-sensitive human rights sector often felt this problem most acutely.

Many South Africans working for change suspected that the United States' stated motivations did not tell the full story behind the AID program. As a result, many activists and anti-apartheid groups were unprepared to accept U.S. funds or, at times, even to speak with AID staff. This phenomenon was particularly characteristic of Charterist groups, and was a major impediment to AID's ability to conduct a wide-ranging and relevant program throughout the FY86–89 period.

The basis for these suspicions varied. Some saw the program as an attempt to avoid sanctions, a set of palliative measures with just enough "bite" to prevent a majority of the Congress from approving broader economic and political sanctions while continuing with constructive engagement. This sus-

picion, widely prevalent even after issuance of the executive order establishing the AID program, slowly dissipated following passage of the CAAA as activists came to realize that Congress had adopted the CAAA over the objections of the Reagan administration and that the expanded AID program had come about largely in response to concerns voiced by congressional opponents of apartheid.

Others cited more specific concerns, alluding most frequently to the real or alleged ties of the U.S. government with the UNITA rebels in Angola or RENAMO in Mozambique, but at other times to U.S. policy toward Nicaragua or Libya or simply to the foreign or domestic policies of the Reagan administration as a whole.

Other objections were less likely to be expressed directly to U.S. diplomats, but were if anything even more damaging: The United States was simply trying to "buy friends," or to advance a presumably nefarious secret agenda for influencing South African political developments. Heard less and less over time was the assertion that the AID program was "just CIA money."

AID could not directly overcome these objections for the most part, but could only establish a track record consistent with AID's rather than its doubters' explanations of its presence. AID drew up the principles and guidelines discussed below with this need strongly in mind. Key elements in the ultimately successful effort to establish AID's bona fides included the policies of wide consultation and respect for the confidentiality of recipients, and the "no strings" approach.

Another constraint was the poor education and training that the apartheid system offered to most black South Africans. Many community leaders possessed remarkable leadership skills, qualities of character and self-denial, commitment to their communities, and political beliefs and imagination. All too few, however, had the education, training, and other experience required if they were to manage organizations or administer funds effectively. One effect of these gaps was that many promising organizations and projects collapsed for reasons having nothing to do with their fundamental merit; many more suffered management, budgetary, personnel, and other problems simply as a result of inefficiency and ignorance.

A major secondary aim of the legal assistance program was to expand the corps of black lawyers offering human rights-related legal services. Despite continuing efforts to identify such lawyers, there was in the short term no escaping the fact that, in a country of over 30 million blacks, there were fewer than 700 black lawyers and a bare handful of experienced black advocates (barristers). The mission pursued a variety of initiatives designed to expand the number of black lawyers, improve the quality of their education, and support their entry into the mainstream legal profession from which they had traditionally been excluded.

Several specific restrictions in the statute governing the human rights program presented further difficulties. The scope of action for the small grants program was broad, and offered flexibility to support almost any meritorious program presented to the mission. Over time, however, the $10,000 ceiling on grants became a significant constraint on its effectiveness. One reason was that organizations that had originally made do with a grant of $10,000 outgrew that level of support. Unless their work fell within the scope of legal assistance or another AID program, the mission was forced to effectively drop them and hope other donors would be prepared to take up the slack. Inflation exacerbated this problem.

The ceiling on legal assistance grants also came to chafe as recipient organizations expanded their capabilities and spheres of operation. The mission's inability to cover the costs of both new initiatives and successful human rights programs that had grown beyond their original scale seriously hampered the ability of effective entities to expand. The greater problem under this heading, however, was the specificity with which the legislation defined anti-apartheid legal activity that could be supported under section 116(f). The requirement that legal assistance be "direct," for example, restricted use of funds to cover necessary overhead and support costs of public interest law firms; as noted above, whether the mission could support a given challenge to apartheid might well depend less on its merits than on the race or organizational affiliations of the plaintiff. A person whose case offered the possibility of an effective challenge to an apartheid-related law, for example, might be precluded from support under section 116(f) if he or she had been detained for reasons unrelated to the statutory purposes. While these restrictions reflected good-faith attempts by the Congress to ensure that the U.S. aid program was both vigorous and relevant, their impacts came to impede the mission's ability to do precisely that. The assumption of confrontation built into the statutory language also made it difficult to support initiatives by community-based organizations to negotiate with the authorities on local issues when such talks began to become possible in late 1989.

C. Bureaucratics

Interaction between the AID program and the embassy was closer than in many other situations because of the newness of the program and its sensitive political character.[2] After an initial period of working out the "rules" for that interaction, the relation-

[2]Congress had made clear from the beginning that the South Africa Human Rights program was to be conducted by AID in close cooperation with the State Department. See, e.g., the conference report on the bill enacting section 116(e)(2), S. Rep. 98–143, 98th Cong., 1st Sess. 84–85 (1983).

ship generally worked smoothly and in a manner supporting all interests involved.

A measure of tension was inevitable at the beginning. The AID program as a whole, and the expanded human rights program in particular, were bound to be the source of new stresses with the South African government, which could only complicate the embassy's already difficult relations with its government interlocutors. At the same time, AID had to overcome institutional doubts and reassure the embassy that the mission, as well as its individual staff members, would have the will, knowledge, and sophistication to conduct their program mandate with sensitivity toward both the political complexities of South Africa and overall U.S. foreign policy toward that country. . . .

Despite the executive branch's initial opposition to the CAAA law—which contained a variety of provisions, such as sanctions, which it considered unwise—it implemented the CAAA program in good faith and in a manner consistent with congressional wishes.

Involvement of AID headquarters was necessarily heavy in 1985–86 as strategies to carry out the various program elements were conceived, developed, and formally approved. While the mission initially submitted the larger proposed human rights grants to Washington for approval, it later assumed responsibility for all human rights program decisions. Thus, an informal and cooperative consultation procedure substituted for the frictions and delays that would surely have attended a requirement that Washington formally approve each proposed action. Among the benefits of this refreshingly unbureaucratic relationship was the human rights program's ability to respond quickly to newly identified needs.

D. Fundamental Operating Principles

The policy set forth in the CAAA and other legislation both gave direction to and constrained the human rights program. The CAAA mandated that the program advance the twin goals of ending apartheid and promoting development of a nonracial democratic South Africa. A central program goal was to help victims overcome the handicaps imposed by apartheid and help prepare them for their "rightful roles as full participants in the political, social, economic, and intellectual life" of post-apartheid South Africa. The law gave priority to nonracial nongovernmental organizations enjoying the support of the disadvantaged communities they sought to serve and precluded assistance to organizations that the South African government "financed or controlled." Finally, only nonviolent activities could be supported.

In addition to the CAAA, section 116(e) of the FAA broadly required that human rights program assistance "encourage or promote increased adherence to civil and political rights." The FAA also stipulated that human rights funds could not be used to influence an election.

These statutory principles and requirements lent the program its fundamental direction and tone but permitted very great leeway in how the program would be implemented. As a practical matter, however, they were not sufficient on their own to guide the mission in deciding on policies and setting priorities to govern selection among competing applications for funds. For these purposes, AID adopted certain fundamental guidelines to govern the program as a whole, and each element within its own sphere. The following discussion highlights the most important of these guidelines, which were developed jointly in extensive discussions involving all U.S. officers working at the AID mission.

1. Responding to South African priorities. However well-intentioned the embassy and AID staff, and however skillfully executive and legislative branch policymakers might have been in hearing and incorporating into the CAAA the views that South Africans expressed to them, the AID mission was nevertheless the foreign-staffed arm of a foreign government. Directed to address South African issues, the mission could understand the nature, possible solutions, and relative priority of those issues only by listening to South Africans. Limitations of staff and funds, moreover, made it imperative to focus its efforts rather than attempt to meet every funding request made. AID therefore decided early that, within the limits of the CAAA, the mission would attempt to set its priorities and program direction on the basis of discussions with as wide a range as possible of South Africans committed to change, including those with serious doubts about the U.S. program.

Consultation was a never-ending process; issues changed, the possibilities for action expanded or shrank, and the mission's circle of contacts grew as staff became more experienced and more South Africans were prepared to engage with them. South Africans widely, if not universally, agreed on certain priorities—the primacy of education as a long-term priority, for example, or the importance of expanding the availability of human rights legal services to rural communities—but disagreements were also inevitable. Differing advice could only be dealt with by further, focused consultation and, ultimately, basing decisions on the staff's development experience and personal assessments of the relative priorities and merits of proposed approaches.

The consultation process was essential to the effective functioning of the human rights program. While not required, as were some other program elements, to make a commitment to a single conceptual approach or even institution in addressing a problem, the human rights program aimed at placing itself at the "cutting edge" of change. In order even to approximate success, the program had to be in constant contact with a wide variety of activists, lawyers, academics, and others to determine what new problems were arising and how they might be addressed; at the same time, it could not become so "responsive" as to lose any sense of guiding principles.

2. Focusing on Black South Africa. Many of the most active and effective organizations fighting for human rights in South Africa were largely or wholly white, as were a high proportion of the best-educated contributors to the anti-apartheid struggle. Whites were far likelier than blacks to be in a position to develop and present the kinds of proposals and supporting materials on the basis of which organizations such as AID prefer to make their assistance judgments. The workings of apartheid meant that whites had, as a general proposition, far greater administrative and other relevant management experience and skills than blacks.

Absent a conscious effort to the contrary, therefore, the mission could have found itself with a project portfolio with racial characteristics perversely mirroring the apartheid system it was established to undermine. Consistent with the fundamental mandate of the CAAA to support black South Africans in attaining their "rightful roles as full participants" in their society, the mission made every effort to identify and support black organizations working in its areas of focus. While the basic requirements of competence and capacity remained paramount, this policy meant, in practice, that the mission was prepared to help a black group with good ideas and staff to develop its capacities through training and organizational development, and to take time to review with it its proposals to ensure its programs would be workable and productive.

A related conflict arose between directing funds in a way that would encourage development of skills, instill democratic values, found new community groups and the like, and focusing on maximizing the chances of getting results in the short term. This issue was inherently not susceptible to neat resolution; it was, indeed, built into the dual goals of fighting apartheid and building a nonracial, democratic society.

In the context of the human rights program, for example, it was far more effective in the short run to fund an experienced, rich urban—but white—law firm to take human rights cases than to fund an inexperienced, poorly equipped rural—and black—lawyer to do so. Supporting the latter, however, might well over the long term be far more effective in demonstrating to the local community that they have legal rights that could be vindicated.

Resolution of this conflict tended to differ depending on the goal of any given project, which in turn correlated loosely to whether AID provided funds under the small grants or legal assistance rubric. While the structure of the governing statutes permitted funding of most nonlegal human rights activity only under the small grants program, if at all, there was a certain inclination to focus on "process" in the small grants program, which was founded for the purpose of supporting black community, grassroots, and fledgling organizations. AID believed that such groups would by the very fact of their existence expand the awareness and practice of human rights and democracy into parts of South African society that had long been denied any rights at all.

In legal assistance, however, the effectiveness of legal counsel in a given case could make a vital difference to the client whose interests were at stake, and in this sphere there was greater readiness to ensure the defendant or other litigant the best possible legal service. These lines were not absolute; as noted above, in keeping with the section 116(f) charge to "support . . . actions of black-led community organizations to resist . . . apartheid," an important theme of legal assistance grants was to build up the cadre of black lawyers with the skills, experience, and funding required to play larger and more effective roles in human rights legal work. These lawyers, in most cases themselves township residents, were far likelier to know and be more able to relate to and serve groups and individuals in the townships than were the large, white law firms. AID made a particular, if only partly successful, effort to identify and support black lawyers operating in rural areas, where white lawyers were often flatly and openly unprepared to take black cases or cases challenging the police or other authorities.

In the case of small grants, AID sought to strike a rough balance between supporting grassroots and community initiatives and ones with a long-term or academic focus. This reflected to a degree the fact that despite all efforts to broadcast knowledge that funds were available under the small grants program, AID received far fewer grants meeting (or seeming to have the potential to meet) minimum standards from applicants in the former category; even after funding the great bulk of such applicants, as much as half of the small grants funds remained available for other uses consistent with the statute.

3. The "test of time." The temptation inevitably arose—especially before the AID program had gained relatively widespread acceptance—to make grants for short-term political advantage and thereby to improve the mission's credibility and thus acceptability. Without compromising on minimum standards of competence and capability, there were certainly occasions on which AID could have made grants to organizations the primary recommendation for which was their political connections. The mission realized early, however, that such an approach would likely backfire and that developing a reputation for playing "games" of this sort would be the surest route to marginalization or worse, and concluded that the fundamental guide for programming funds must be the mission's best assessment of which approaches and proposed projects were most likely to "stand the test of time" in making the most effective long-term contribution to achieving CAAA goals.

In an explicitly political program, however, it was by no means entirely clear where the line should be drawn between ensuring that applicants enjoyed adequate community support and improperly favoring politically attractive applicants for funds. This factor presented a special problem for the human rights program as a result of its conscious aim of addressing the most salient current human rights issues and initiatives and Congress' clear intent that it be a politically relevant program. The very test of that relevance might on occasion be the readiness of AID to fund the activities of an organization with a high political profile. The only way AID could meet this challenge was to insist that potential recipients present well-considered proposals for actions that fit within the terms of the statute, and that the mission be satisfied that they had the capacity and intent to carry out its proposals competently. If the proposal met those standards, then the fact that an applicant enjoyed the political support of its community or of a national network could only be viewed as an additional recommendation.

4. "No strings." Many South Africans were initially highly suspicious that acceptance of funds from AID would involve a series of further claims and obligations going beyond the particular project for which funds were sought. Some potential recipients feared, for example, that the United States would use its financial power to limit their freedom to take positions AID found unpalatable, to release information

unrelated to the funded project, or—whether intentionally or not—to influence improperly or take over the project by intervention into its administration and policy decisions. A final concern was that the United States would publicize the names of recipients in an effort to increase the credibility of its South Africa policy; such use of names could be embarrassing or even dangerous to recipients in the overheated political climate of South Africa.

To counter these fears, the mission adopted a strict "no strings" policy. Agreement terms were negotiated thoroughly and with care, and an agreement was not signed until project implementation details had been fully discussed and clarified in response to mission inquiries. The purpose of this close initial attention was to bring out all possible issues before either side had made a commitment or relinquished any autonomy. If the potential recipient was unprepared to work on this basis, it was free not to pursue its application and terminate the discussion at any time. AID informed applicants that, although no guarantees could be offered, the mission did not seek to publicize its activities and followed a policy of neither discussing nor identifying individual recipients publicly, to others applying or receiving funds, or indeed in any context other than internal ones.

Once the applicant signed the agreement, the only "strings" were ones expressly stated in its text. The most important of these related to financial accountability and were designed to ensure that funds were spent for the purposes described in the recipient's funding proposal, as reflected in the grant.

5. Amelioration versus change. An early and, at the time, somewhat controversial decision was that the human rights project would fund only change-oriented activities. There was in South Africa a desperate need for programs such as day care centers, schools, water, health, and feeding programs; funding such programs would have been socially highly useful and deeply appreciated. AID received innumerable applications for these purposes, and it was painful to realize that funds available under the self-help program were completely inadequate to meet the need.

The mission and embassy together concluded, however, that supporting such programs would treat only the symptoms of apartheid rather than address its causes or even attack its implementation, and that the purpose of the human rights program was to address the political problems that prevented the dedication of South African resources to these needs. From mid-1987 onward, AID provided funds for "self-help style" projects only when they served a primarily change-oriented purpose.

6. Outreach and portfolio renewal. To further strengthen the program, the human rights office constantly sought new recipients, and aimed as a rule of thumb to keep the proportion of repeat recipients in each year's small grant portfolio to between half and two-thirds of grantees. Congress' express desire that the small grants program operate as an "outreach" program, constantly expanding the sphere of South African society with which the embassy and mission were in contact, was one reason for this. AID placed a high priority on expanding the program's reach both to a wider political circle and, geographically, beyond the relatively easily handled Johannesburg/Pretoria, Cape Town, and Durban metropolitan areas into the rural areas of the northern and eastern Transvaal, Orange Free State, and northern Cape Province. The urban eastern Cape, centered on Port Elizabeth, was a particularly difficult target, because of both the intensity of repression and the

skepticism of its Charterist political organizations toward U.S. funding.

The constantly mutating nature of anti-apartheid activity and human rights violations was a second important reason for seeking new recipients. Both factors militated against establishment of a "stable" of small grant recipients. During one year, for example, mass detentions might create a need to shift resources toward legal and other support for them and their families; in another, the release of detainees might revive large numbers of community organizations that then require assistance in getting back on their feet, or a crackdown on squatters might require urgent action. The program could not fund all requests for funds, and thus had to relegate some to lower priority as circumstances changed.

The mission sought as well to avoid "competing" with other donors to shower funds on the same organizations, however meritorious. After taking an early lead in focusing on the defense of media against harassment and lawsuits, for example, the mission pulled back as entities supported or established with its assistance became known to other donors. Its status as a fully staffed, independent donor located inside South Africa gave it unique opportunities to identify potential recipients who might otherwise not come to donors' attention, and the human rights program in particular attempted to build on these strengths in developing its portfolio.

7. Risk of dependency. An additional reason for portfolio renewal was the risk of creating dependency, a danger of which both the mission and South Africans it consulted were constantly aware. Black South Africans were acutely sensitive to the fact that maintaining black material and psychological dependency was a keystone of apartheid, and many suspected that foreign donors preferred (presumably from less malign motives) to maintain a similar dependency relationship.

On the other hand, recipients desperately needed the funds; the program owed its existence to the fact that local funds for anti-apartheid activity were radically insufficient to the need. Fundraising was extremely difficult for South African anti-apartheid organizations—especially black ones, and even more rural groups or ones not affiliated with the major internal aid-distributing organizations—and the temptation to abandon time-consuming efforts to raise local funds and rely on a foreign donor to cover the costs of a group's substantive programs was understandably very great.

For small grants, the human rights office sought to address these conflicting pressures by making clear that funds were provided for only one or, at most, two years, and that renewal should not be assumed; any exception would be decided on a case-by-case basis. There was also a distinct preference for supporting discrete projects rather than providing general support to recipients. (Both rules were relaxed in the case of rural projects.) Most legal assistance grants were for the purpose of covering legal fees and related costs rather than overhead, and did not present the same risk of dependency.

A different form of dependency arose when organizations asked that AID intervene to address internal problems. This took the form most frequently of requests that individual officers help assemble documentation on the basis of which AID would certify payment of funds to the recipient. Provision of assistance during an initial learning period could, unless the officer was careful, all too easily become a pattern.

The temptation was great, particularly with fledgling community groups that had excellent ideas and community bases but limited administrative training and management experience, to "ease the burden" on both the recipient and mission staff by doing much of the financial and administrative work for the recipient; it was a small step further to offer unsolicited (or even invited) political advice or otherwise intervene in the grantee's operations. In view of the conflict between that natural urge and the program goal of increasing self-reliance and the development of recipient skills, AID sought to avoid this temptation as much as possible.

Yet another situation was presented when the recipient encountered internal political problems over use of funds or related matters. AID's wish not to become the source of division within anti-apartheid groups led the human rights office, after several unfortunate experiences, to raise explicitly the potential for such problems with each applicant with respect to which there appeared to be a danger of such a development, and to examine carefully the recipient's internal procedures on the basis of which an internal dispute would be resolved. Despite such efforts, on several occasions each year a recipient would request that the staff mediate or resolve an internal leadership or policy dispute, and on rare occasion the staff was forced to respond by chairing a reconciliation session or offering a proposed resolution of the dispute. Staff sought in such situations to play the role of neutral well-wisher and drew a firm line at imposing a solution. On one or two occasions per year, an organization would decide the potential cost was too great, and withdraw its application rather than risk such internal divisions.

39 *THE INTANGIBLES AND IMPONDERABLES OF THE TRANSITION TO DEMOCRACY*

PIOTR SZTOMPKA

A specialist on social theories and revolution, Piotr Sztompka is a Professor of Sociology at the Jagiellonian University in Krakow. His most recent book is *Society in Action: The Theory of Social Becoming* (Polity Issues, Cambridge, 1991.)

No reflection on the emerging new Europe can neglect the dramatic collapse of the communist system, and the fundamental transformations of social, political, economic, and ideological structures in the eastern and central parts of the continent. These events will probably go into the textbooks of history as the "Autumn of Nations 1989." In this article I want to draw attention to the dilemmas and challenges facing those Europeans (nearly 100 millions of them) who find themselves in the midst of this postrevolutionary transition and who are making a bid for a decent place in the European home. I will focus on the experience of Poland, but will claim a more general validity for the diagnoses and interpretations.

A prophetic joke circulating in Poland in the 1980s was: "What is real socialism?—The longest and most winding road from capitalism to . . . capitalism!" And rightly so, for in the 1990s we have started to build capitalism from scratch. We are witnessing the second birth of a market economy, democratic polity, and open society. Apart, however, from some superficial resemblances,[1] the situation in which this repetition of the capitalist experiment occurs is crucially different from that in which capitalism was originally born in Europe.

To begin with, during the more than forty years that Eastern European societies have spent on the road to nowhere, real socialism has managed to reshape them, even though not exactly in the fashion previsioned by its ideologues. Compared to the early precapitalist societies, Eastern Europe is starting anew with some assets, but mostly with *liabilities*.[2] Second, we are not only moving toward capitalism, but even more steadfastly *moving away* from real socialism, and all our efforts are strongly flavored by active rejection of that system. To put it another way, our return to Europe is primarily our

---

[1] We even have our own "Great Gatsby" syndrome among the *nouveau riche:* conspicuous consumption, amassing of property, snobbishness, vanity, and arrogance.

[2] Jerzy Jedlicki calls this "the unbearable burden of history"; see "The Revolution of 1989: The Unbearable Burden of History," *Problems of Communism* (July–August 1990) pp. 39–45.

---

escape from Asia. Third, all this occurs at a time when Western capitalism is already highly developed and provides patterns and blueprints to be imitated, as well life standards to be envied. Thus, our revolution is not in the name of some abstract preconceived ideal, but rather it attempts to *catch up with* prosperous and highly developed Western civilization, by applying what Lech Walesa has called the "normal, well-tested solutions" of private entrepreneurship, the market, pluralism, and parliamentary democracy. Fourth, we all live in a period of growing *globalization,* when the economic, political, and cultural interdependence of societies is stronger than ever. What we dare to attempt and how far we can go is highly dependent on international conditions. Finally, the present transformations are carried out in the immediate *postrevolutionary situation,* which produces its own, autonomous problems, dilemmas, and challenges. Fresh experience of revolution leaves an imprint on society which has both a positive and a negative, a functional and a dysfunctional effect on future reforms.

The radical and fundamental changes occurring embrace all domains and levels of postcommunist societies, but are most salient at the *institutional level,* both political and economic, where elections have installed noncommunist governments, communist parties have dissolved, multiple associations and political groupings have appeared, new constitutions have been drafted, centralized planning abandoned, large segments of the economy privatized, and rudimentary markets established, etc. Of course all this is only the beginning of a long process, but some achievements are uncontestable and, hopefully, irreversible. Various changes are also conspicuous at the *level of societal consciousness,* where the overwhelming, declarative rejection of real socialism and communist ideology, linked with a suspicious or even repulsing attitude against the left, take all forms

from rational critique of the past to calls for purges and forceful "decommunization".[3]

Given all this, how is it then that so many intellectuals, journalists, writers, and politicians repeatedly express the worry that the communist system is still very much alive? In Poland, this has recently become the leitmotif of public debate. Such intuitions clearly indicate that there must be some other level of social reality, below the visible surface, where the vestiges of communism hide untouched and manage to survive in spite of institutional reforms and declarative rejection.

There may be, first of all, a *level of deeper personal commitment* where the values, motivations, drives, attitudes, thought habits, and resentments are often subconscious, but are directly reflected in human conduct. It is with reference to this personality syndrome that many observers of the Polish scene apply the concept of "homo sovieticus,"[4] or "captive mind."[5] Second, however, there is an even deeper and more hidden *level of cultural code* which is typical for a given society, for example shared and objectified patterns, matrixes, or blueprints for both acting and thinking which strongly constrain or facilitate social life and societal consciousness. They are the truly "social facts" in a Durkheimian sense,[6] and the re-

[3]In April, 1989, just before the dramatic defeat of the communists in parliamentary elections, the opinion survey showed that 60.4 percent of the Polish population believed that "after all earlier experiences it is no longer worthwhile to build socialism in Poland," whereas some limited affirmation of socialism was expressed by only 28.8 percent. (See Miroslawa Marody, "Dylematy postaw politycznych i orientacji swiatopogladowych" ("The dilemmas of political attitudes and world views"), in J.J. Wiatr, ed., *Polska 1980–1990* (Warsaw: Warsaw University Press 1990)), pp. 157–174.

[4]Borrowed from the Russian logician and philosopher Zinoviev.

[5]This phrase was introduced in the title of his book *The Captive Mind* (New York: A. Knopf, 1953) by Czeslaw Milosz the Polish poet and Nobel laureate.

[6]Durkheim, *The Elementary Forms of the Religious Life* (Boston: Allen Unwin, 1905).

ality *sui generis* underlying human actions and beliefs, providing for them ready-made frames and molds. They are highly resistant to change, slow to be replaced, endowed with lasting potential, and marked with inertia.

It will be my central hypothesis that the residues of the communist system are entrenched at these two levels—most strongly at the level of the cultural codes and somewhat more loosely at the level of personal attitudes. If this is so, then their eradication from *human personalities* and also, most importantly, from the underlying *cultural structures* is the main challenge at present facing the revolution.

THE "DEEP LEVEL" OF SOCIETY: CODES AND DISCOURSES

Clearly, we are dealing here with the realm of *intangibles and imponderables,* hard to grasp in a precise way and even harder to pinpoint by empirical tools. But these epistemological or methodological difficulties should not mislead us into believing that such facts are not real in a hard ontological sense; that they are unable to exert strong causal influence on more tangible domains of thoughts and actions. Indeed, it is striking how commonly sociologists of quite diverse theoretical persuasions affirm their presence and their significance. Consider the variety of terms, some characteristically metaphorical, referring to such intangibles and imponderables. The best known are those old and somewhat discredited notions of "national character" or "modal personality." But there are others.[7] Terms like "social climate," "so-cial atmosphere," "social mood," "the soul of society," "the public mind," and "the public morale" all enter the vernacular. Precise definitions of such concepts are rare, but I will quote two examples, which attempt to avoid the notorious vagueness. Clearly indebted to some version of "depth psychology," Miroslawa Marody describes *"social subconsciousness"* as "a system of unconscious blueprints for thinking and perceiving, as well as dispositions which mediate between the structures of the outside world and active practice, or—to put it otherwise—between the level of institutions and the level of individual behavior.[8] Jeffrey Alexander, in obvious reference to Levi-Straussian structuralism, specifies the notion of the *"discourse"*: "we call these sign sets discourses if they meet two conditions. First, they must not only communicate information, structuring reality in a cognitive or expressive way: they must also perform a forceful, evalua-

[7]For example, Robert Bellah, borrowing the idiom from Alexis de Tocqueville, speaks of the "habits of the heart" (*Habits of the Heart,* Berkeley: University of California Press, 1985); Ralf Dahrendorf, (*Reflections on the Revolution in Europe,* London: Chatto and Windus, 1990) of the "frames of the mind"; and Edgar Morin of "l'esprit du temps." (*Duch czasu* Krakow: Znak, 1965). Sociologists come closest to our own focus and reflect on the contemporary situation in postcommunist countries: Lutynski speaks of the "psychological and socio-moral infrastructure of collective life" and Marody of the "social subconscious"-Jan Lutynski, *Nauka i polskie problemy: komentarz socjologa* (Science and Polish Problems: The Sociologist's Comment) (Warsaw: State Editorial Institute 1990); Miroslawa Marody, "Antynomie spolecznej swiadomosci" ("Antinomies of

Social Consciousness"), *Odra,* No. 1 (1987), pp. 4–9. Reprinted in *Studia Socjologiczne* No. 2 (1987). Social theorists have recently proposed a special technical vocabulary e.g. M. Thompson, R. Ellis, and A. Wildavsky (*Cultural Theory* Berkeley: 1989) suggest "cultural biases"; P. Bourdieu suggests "habitus," (*In Other Words,* Cambridge: Polity Press, 1990), and Jeffrey Alexander ("The Discourse of American Civil Society: A New Proposal for Cultural Studies," Los Angeles: UCLA, 1989, 74pp; "Democracy and Civil Society," Los Angeles: UCLA, 1990b, 125pp) suggests "discourses".

[8]Marody (1990), *op. cit.,* note 3, p. 17.

tive task. Binary sets do so when they are charged by the 'religious' symbology of the sacred and profane."[9]

I will follow these and similar theoretical concepts, trying to unravel the constitution of the "deep level" of postcommunist societies, where the unfortunate legacy of real socialism is still to be found. I would suggest that here resides the main mechanism through which communism is haunting postcommunist societies from the grave. Two recent commentators give supporting testimony. Edmund Mokrzycki observes: "forty years of the building of socialism has changed Polish society much more than might have been expected from observation of the constant resistance of that society to the communist authority." And adds: "In Poland, even if we disregard the economic ruin and bad psychological condition of society, the road to democracy is obstructed as it were by Polish society itself, with its inner structure."[10] And Miroslawa Marody warns against a similar danger: "The basic problem which the reformers must recognize has to do with the fact that everyday actions of individuals will be modelled by habits developed in the course of social experiences radically different from those which should fill out new institutions."[11]

Before we attempt to identify the components and the anatomy of the hypothetical *"deep level"* in postcommunist societies, two points must be made clear. The first has to do with the origins of mental patterns and the cultural codes to be found there, that is the sources from which they derive. Reasoning backwards from a present condition to its source is always risky. In particu-

lar it may be highly problematic as to which point in time the origins should be back-dated; how far backwards in history we should move. Some mental attitudes or cultural codes may have a quite distant genealogy, clearly preceding the period of real socialism.[12] They may derive from the specific national history of each separate country. In Poland, they are often traced back to the breakdown of dynastic monarchy, to the period of weakened states, to failed constitutional reforms, to the loss of sovereignty in the eighteenth century, or to the persistent struggles for independence in the nineteenth century. I will attempt to abstract from these more distant historical circumstances, and to focus exclusively on the shorter genealogy of the past forty or so years of real socialism. The rule of thumb allowing us to sift out the *heritage of national history* from the *legacy of real socialism* is to search to similarities across the former socialist countries. In all of them the socialist system was a more or less precise replica of a common pattern—the Soviet, or Stalinist model.[13] At the same time, their national histories were strikingly different. If, therefore, we discover similar patterns of thought and culture in various postcommunist countries, then their source may be expected to lie in those common socialist structures, rather than in their idiosyncratic histories.

The second question has to do with the

---

[9]Alexander (1989), *op. cit.*, note 7, p. 8.

[10]Edmund Mokrzycki, "The Legacy of Real Socialism and Western Democracy," *Studies in Comparative Communism* Vol. XXIV, No. 2 (June 1991), pp. 211–217.

[11]Marody (1990), *op. cit.*, note 3, p. 167.

[12]This is a perspective taken for example by Jedlicki, *op. cit.*, note 2.

[13]Stefan Nowak in his article "Ciaglose i zmiana tradycji kulturowych" ("Continuity and Change of Cultural Traditions") (*Polska Mlodziez* No. 2 (1986), pp. 167–194) has effectively ridiculed the reasoning used by some apologists for real socialism, who claimed that there are "universal necessary regularities of socialist development" and as a proof invoked the political and economic similarities between all socialist societies. Such regularities and similarities are due, he argued, precisely to the imposition of a common pattern from the outside to a common "matrix" applied to all of them in the area of Soviet influence and rule.

processes through which the purported legacy of real socialism becomes encoded at the "deep level." Three types of influence may be distinguished. First, and most obviously, there is the impress of socialist institutions, forms of organization, and ideological structures. Through prolonged habituation, *indoctrination,* "thought-control,"[14] and imposition of the fake "super-reality"[15] on human minds, this impress ultimately reaches the domain of unreflexive psychological and cultural codes. Second, there are the emerging *adaptive reactions,* or defense mechanisms, developed as ways of coping with socialist conditions. These adaptive arrangements and mechanisms paradoxically outlive their times, become petrified in social structures, cultural patterns, and popular consciousness, and remain fully operative in post-communist society. Third, somewhat ironically, the anticommunist revolutionary upheavals and the associated experiences of elation, enthusiasm, mobilization, raised aspirations and hopes, and released activism and participation leave their own lasting imprint on postrevolutionary society. Under some circumstances the return to normality may breed disenchantment, frustration, relative deprivation, and similar moods which effectively block further reforms and endanger the very fruits of the revolution.

Now that our theoretical assumptions and hypotheses have been expressed, we may pass to an analysis of them.

PRIVATE AND PUBLIC: THE CORE OPPOSITION

The most fundamental and lasting cultural code organizing thought and action in the conditions of real socialism is the *opposition of two spheres of life: private (personal) and public (official).* As Stefan Nowak puts it: "The life of the average Pole is lived in the two, overlapping worlds: the domain of private contacts and the institutional-official sphere."[16] This opposition appears in a number of guises, for example "society versus authorities," "nation versus state," "the people versus rulers," "we versus they." Using the Talcott Parsons terminology recently applied by Jeffrey Alexander, we may define the common core of all these phrasings as the dichotomy of "particularism versus universalism."[17] Following Alexander's theories a step further, we may also notice that the opposition has an unambiguous *evaluative and moral flavor.*[18] The private (particularistic) sphere is the domain of the good (virtue, dignity, pride), whereas the public (universalistic) sphere is the domain of the bad (vice, disdain, shame). Activities carried on in the private sphere are elevating, while any contact with the public sphere is, to use another of Alexander's terms, "polluting." There is a clear "cultural bias"[19] toward the private world, and away from the public world. Durkheim perhaps would accept treating the earlier as the domain of the "sacred," and the latter as the domain of the "profane,"[20] so that the dichotomy of the private and the public satisfies all the definitional criteria of the "*discourse*" specified earlier. This polar, binary opposition is the central organizing principle, the core cultural premise on which the

[14]Arther Koestler, *Darkness at Noon* (New York: Bantam Books, 1975 [1941]).

[15]Alain Besancon

[16]Stefan Nowak, "Spoleczenstwo polskie drugiej polowy lat 80-tych" ("Polish Society in the Second Part of the Eighties"), a report for the Polish Sociological Association. (Warsaw: 1987), mimeographed.

[17]Jeffrey Alexander, "Bringing Democracy Back In: Universalistic Solidarity and the Civil Sphere" (Los Angeles: UCLA 1990a), 59 pp.

[18]Alexander (1989), *op. cit.,* note 7; Alexander (1990b), *op. cit.,* note 7.

[19]Thompson *et al., op. cit.,* note 7.

[20]Durkheim, *op. cit.,* note 6.

whole discourse of real-socialist society is founded. If one agrees with Alexander that the affirmation of Universalism is the distinguishing trait of democratic discourse,[21] then the discourse of real-socialist society is shown, not surprisingly, to be basically anti-democratic. No wonder that we shall find it standing in the way of democratic reforms even when the institutional surface of the autocratic regime has been crushed.

It would be fascinating to trace back this core dichotomy which emerged partly as an adaptive "boomerang response" to the totalitarian wish to invade and completely subjugate the private life of the citizens, and partly as a side-effect of the regime's successful attempts to restrict and even eliminate the pluralistic network of voluntary associations, communities, social circles, and political groupings which mark the mediating buffer-zone between the authorities and atomized, isolated citizens.[22] However, we shall leave the task of such historical reconstruction for another occasion, focusing now on the empirical corroboration of our central hypothesis, documenting the presence of the *"private-public" opposition* at the "deep level" of real-socialist society and the continued, unfortunate viability of the same opposition in the period after the anticommunist revolutions. . . .

A typical form of action is moved by what has been called *"disinterested envy."* Socialist ideology, with its emphasis on primitive egalitarianism (well expressed by the slogan that "all people have equal stom-

achs") implants a kind of instinct against unusual achievement, excessive profits, and exceptional success; and a strong resentment against all kinds of elites. Hence, there appears a variety of actions taken to prevent others from reaching eminence, even if that success is not occurring in the competitive context and does not diminish anybody else's chance of the same success. A famous joke describes the "Polish inferno": in huge pots the sinners of various nationalities are boiling on an open fire, each pot guarded by armed devils. Only the pot marked "Poland" is unguarded. Why? Because if anybody climbs out to escape, his compatriots will certainly pull him down.

It might have been expected that once the institutional structures of "real socialism" are torn down, the "socialist mind" would disappear as well. Unfortunately this is not the case. As one knowledgeable researcher testifies: "What is striking when we analyze the political attitudes in 1990 is their surprising, truly structural similarity to the attitudes encountered and described in earlier periods."[23] By some irony of history, the core opposition of the public and private sphere, together with most of its psychological and behavioral expressions, has outlived the communist system, and stands in the way of postcommunist reforms. Let me enumerate some more spectacular symptoms of this surprising persistence.

In spite of constant reminders that "we are at last in our own home,"[24] people seem not to care and are quite reluctant to get involved in public actions. The continued *passivism and political apathy* is remarkable: in the first democratic elections after half a century, 38 percent of the population chose not to vote, and in the local elections (even

---

[21] Alexander (1990a), *op. cit.*, note 17.

[22] In the Polish case these influences of real socialism have been congruent with, and therefore additionally strengthened by, earlier historical experiences. For prolonged periods Polish society, living on that "God's playground" (N. Davies, *God's Playground: A History of Poland*, Oxford: Clarendon Press, 1981), have experienced foreign conquests, defeats, national dependence, loss of sovereignty, imperialist partitions, wars, and upheavals. And hence public authorities came to be defined as alien and hostile, "state" firmly opposed to "nation."

[23] Marody (1990), *op. cit.*, note 3, p. 166.

[24] There was a long campaign on Polish television when many famous actors in the country were appearing every evening trying to beat the same slogan into people's heads.

closer to "our own home") 58 percent were absent. Almost every second Pole does not think it worthwhile to cast a ballot for the first democratic president, and with a pluralistic spectrum of associations and political parties mushrooming during the last year, more than 90 percent of the population has decided not to belong to any of them.[25]

The government is still perceived as being in opposition to society, as *"them" against "us."* In the free presidential elections Tadeusz Mazowiecki, a man of impeccable credentials and undisputed achievements, turns out to be "polluted" by being in the government (as a first prime minister of postcommunist Poland) and loses to Stanislaw Tyminski, a demagogue and charlatan arriving from Canada, unknown to anybody, and precisely for that reason free from any associations with established authorities. The authorities are still treated with suspicion, and the perfectly normal situation where the political leader surrounds himself with former colleagues and supporters is blamed as the "new nomenklatura."

People continue their game of "beating the system" as if nothing has changed, as if the system was still alien, imposed, and destined to be rejected. *"Parasitic innovativeness"* flourishes in new forms made possible by privatization, the emerging capitalist market, and the uncertainties of transitory laws. Masses of people have become involved in all sorts of illicit trading, smuggling, and tax and duty evasions. New, highly organized forms of such actions appear. Within a year, two huge smuggling affairs, dealing in alcohol and tobacco, have been disclosed. People still try all kinds of adaptive, defensive tricks in attempting to outwit the authorities. Recently we observed a massive, hurried import of used cars from

the west arising from the rumor that import duties were soon to be raised. If one observes the spreading entrepreneurial activities, it is amazing how large a share of them are still based on distrust, uncertainty of the future, and traditional "grab-and-run" tactics.

"Disinterested envy" is still very much around, and in fact has more opportunities for expression and more potential targets as the population of those who "made it" (reached political office, quickly became quite rich, opened successful businesses, or attained public fame, etc.) is growing with tremendous speed. Resentments against this group easily use old egalitarian rhetorics. As an acute observer of the Eastern European scene correctly notes: "In most of these countries there is still widespread support for relatively egalitarian distribution of the wealth thus created and for a strong welfare state."[26] The mood has spread against all kinds of elites, including the intellectuals (of course called the "eggheads") and—interestingly—the Jews. The vestiges of traditional anti-Semitism are revived in a strange mixture with anti-intellectualism. There are too many Jewish intellectuals in the new governments says the conventional wisdom, and it concludes: It must be a new Jewish conspiracy. In effect, 26 percent of Poles, 17 percent of Czechs and 11 percent of Hungarians believe that Jews have too strong an influence in postcommunist politics.[27]

Among the majority who "did not make it" or who lost an earlier standard of life in the turmoil of revolutionary change (for example large segments of the working

---

[25]*Gazeta Wyborcza*, April 25, 1991.

[26]Timothy Garton Ash, "Eastern Europe: The Year of Truth," *New York Review of Books*, February 15, 1990, p. 21.

[27]*Gazeta Wyborcza*, April 26, 1991. How similar it is to the old archetype of the Jewish–Communist pact, current among some groups fighting the communists not so long ago.

class, the peasantry, and the more than a million unemployed—a phenomenon unknown during the socialist period) there is a growing nostalgia for the old arrangements of the paternalistic state, and strong revindicational demands. There is the belief that the government is obliged to provide for basic needs, free medical services, and free education, and to supply jobs, pensions, social security, and welfare benefits. Probably not so many would want to return to communism, but large masses dream of some *"third way,"* of humanitarian capitalism, or, paraphrasing the old slogans about socialism, they would like to see "capitalism with a human face," or "the Polish road to capitalism."

These are only some of the moods and sentiments resembling old ways of thinking and doing. They make up the persistent legacy of "real socialism" which haunts Eastern European societies.

There are, however, other sources of trouble and challenge which derive from the recent experience of anticommunist revolution. The eruption of mass mobilization, enthusiasm, excitement, elation, exhilaration, optimism, and hope; the feeling of might and omnipotence; the joy of activism and a regained meaning of life; skyrocketing aspirations and utopian visions of the immediate future—all of these so necessary for the revolution to win, leave a number of unintended side-effects once the victory is won. There are numerous "boomerang effects" of revolutionary experience which may endanger the fate of the revolutionary achievements. I will list the most significant of these dilemmas of the postrevolutionary period.

First, there is the *"dilemma of the morning after."* Revolutions are unusual times, and especially when bloodless (as almost all the revolutions of 1989 fortunately were) they are also happy times. They are a bit like festivals or carnivals. Making revolution is certainly more attractive than getting up at six o'clock to commute to work. Inevitably, when the revolution is over and people have to return to usually boring and mundane realities some kind of disenchantment, or "postrevolutionary hangover"[28] is apt to set in.

Second, there is the *"dilemma of the brief honeymoon."* The hopes and dreams so typical of revolutionary euphoria cannot be satisfied easily. Immediately after the revolution, the raised expectations and aspirations of the revolutionary period clash with the hard realities—economic scarcities, the burden of foreign debt, human demoralization, normative chaos, social disorganization, class dislocations, unemployment, injustice, etc. Neither the masses, nor even the intellectuals, in their utopian optimism were ready to admit that the "valley of tears"[29] lies ahead, and that before real improvements occur, severe costs will have to be paid. After a short time everybody has to agree with foreign observers that "thus far, neither capitalism, enlightenment, nor democracy has proved as pristine or as accessible as everyone wished."[30] This results in a reinforced experience of *relative deprivation*, which is even more painful because no more easy excuses can be found. In particular the system—traditional villain of all grievances —can no longer be blamed. After all, we really are "in our own home" now. Recent surveys report that 60 percent of Hungarians believe their situation is worse than before and only 8 percent notice any improvement. For Czechoslovakia, the numbers are similar: 48 percent define postrevolutionary conditions as worse, and 22

[28]This is the term by Leszek Kolakowski quoted by Zdzislaw Pietrasik, "Kac porewolucyjny" ("Postrevolutionary Hangover"), *Polityka*, April 27, 1991, pp. 1–2.

[29]Dahrendorf, op. cit., note 7, p. 77.

[30]Jeffrey Alexander, "Real Civil Society: Rethinking Democratic Capitalism in Eastern Europe." (Los Angeles: UCLA, 1991) 9pp. To be published in *The New Republic*.

percent claim some improvements. In Poland, 59 percent of the population do not perceive any change, 16 percent believe things have got worse, and 26 percent define the conditions as markedly better.[31]

Third, there is the *"dilemma of abdicated power"*. All observers agree that the revolutions of 1989 followed the volcanic model, whereby they erupted from the bottom, under the pressure of accumulated grievances, discontent, and frustrations, and were carried out by the masses. The revolutions were won on the streets and squares of Gdansk, Prague, Warsaw, Nowa Huta, and Bucharest. *"We, the people"* was the true force behind the revolutions. But as Timothy Garton Ash says in the insightful book of that title: "'We the people' can rise against an abhorrent regime of exploitation and oppression, but 'we the people' cannot govern."[32] The job of government requires quite different virtues, skills, and responsibilities than those commanded by the revolutionary crowds. Thus, soon after the revolution "the people" have to abdicate, relinquish their immediate power, and put it in the hands of representatives. Demobilization of the masses and political apathy is the predictable reaction. And the data clearly bear out that conclusion: A recent survey shows that 91 percent of Poles, 81 percent of Hungarians and 59 percent of Czechs and Slovaks have not attended any political meeting or public demonstration since the revolution.[33]

Fourth, there is the *"dilemma of innocence lost."* This refers to the revolutionary leadership. Inevitably, the move from the status of inspired, charismatic leaders to the status of public officials demands a price. What Max Weber described as "the routin-

ization of a charisma"[34] means at the same time the loss of the mythology surrounding the leaders, as well as the emergence of the official, formalized distance between them and their followers. It also means internal splits in a leadership which was originally united by the exigencies of common struggle, but soon afterwards began fighting among themselves for a share in the victory. The myth of unity breaks down, and with it much of the popular faith and trust in the leaders. The revolutionary legitimacy of the postrevolutionary powers is lost amid in-house fighting, and a new basis for legitimacy is not easily established.

Fifth, there is the *"dilemma of the delayed clock."* Revolutionary experience is a break in social continuity, marked by an unusual speed in social change. Dramatic transformations occur literally overnight: governments fall; regimes break down; social hierarchies are overturned; and old ways of life and common routines are suspended. It is easy to extrapolate the expectations born of that experience to postrevolutionary times and to become impatient with the slow, gradual, piecemeal fashion in which changes normally proceed. When the social clock returns to its usual speed, it is apt to be perceived as delayed. The obsessive calls for the acceleration of change, for the radicalization of reforms, and for the making of all kinds of short-cuts in current policies raised by powerful groups of politicians in Poland meet with quite favorable response among some segments of the public.

Sixth, there is the *"dilemma of the recurring nightmare."* In view of the inevitable difficulties and setbacks faced by postrevolutionary policies, doubts occur: is it for good, is it for real, is it really irreversible, aren't we going to wake up from the dream one day and see that nothing has changed? This apprehension is particularly likely in a society

---

[31]The data are from a survey sponsored by Freedom House and reported in *Gazeta Wyborcza*, April 25, 1991.

[32]Timothy Garton Ash, *We the People: The Revolution of 89* (Cambridge: Granta Books, 1990).

[33]As reported in *Gazeta Wyborcza*, April 25, 1991.

[34]Max Weber, *The Protestant Ethic and the Spirit of Capitalism* (New York: Scribner's, 1958 [1905]).

like Poland which has experienced repeated escalations of hopes and tragic failures in the past.[35] Staying with the post-World War II period, we had our September 1956, March 1968, December 1970, June 1976, August 1980, December 1981—almost no months left in the "Polish calender"—to signify struggles and defeats. Sociologists call the typical results of such experiences in the social consciousness a "*disaster culture*", a syndrome of disbelief, distrust, pessimism, and skepticism concerning future, similar upheavals. The obsessive anxiety that the communists may regroup their forces and return, or that the Soviets will move Westward after pacifying Lithuania, illustrates this dilemma in recent Polish debates.

Seventh, there is the "*dilemma of the bequeathed tenant*." For forty-five years the people in real-socialist societies were living like tenants in a house run by somebody else. This was certainly frustrating, and produced alienation and deprivation, but in some sense it was also convenient: One did not need to bother about the leaking roof, or broken elevator, or dirty staircase because somebody else was responsible. Now, after the revolution, people find themselves in "their own house." But they have inherited it in a very poor shape: decaying infrastructure; depleted resources; polluted environment; heavy mortgage; a bunch of ill, deviant, or demoralized residents— and they have to take care of all this themselves. The job of cleaning, restoring, and rebuilding is demanding, hard, and time-consuming, and takes a lot of fun from the

elation of regained property. Self-reliance and self responsibility do not come free.

Finally, eighth, there is the "*dilemma of the opened cage*." The revolution destroys many of the barriers and limitations that have constrained the citizens of real-socialist societies for decades. It breaks "the Walls" separating them from the West, literally and figuratively. The borders are suddenly open, censorship abolished, free expression allowed, punitiveness of laws released, and police control restricted. People break out from the cage, trying to taste all the previously forbidden fruit. This can easily take pathological forms or proportions. Just note the dramatic surge in crime and delinquency, the loosening of social discipline, and the avalanche of all the most superficial and least valuable products of Western commercial consumerism: pornography, third-rate books, lowest quality films and videos, the most primitive pop music, the cheap fashions, and the fads such as "punks" and "skins." Freedom has its price too, and former socialist societies seem to pay this price in excessive measure.

This brings to a close my rather sad diagnosis of the present conditions obtaining in the postcommunist world. The crucial questions remain: how to overcome the paralyzing psychological and behavioral legacy of real socialism, and how to overcome the tensions and dilemmas produced by the experience of revolutions and their aftermath? What is the path ahead for Eastern-Central Europe? In the closing part of this article I will attempt to make some suggestions.

THE KEY TO THE FUTURE: RESTORING "CIVIL SOCIETY"

The main hypothesis that I wished to substantiate asserted the fundamental split at the deep level of cultural codes typical of

real-socialist societies; that is the dissociation and opposition of the *public and private spheres*. All other dichotomies and dilem-

---

[35]"What if there is indeed a recurrence of historical patterns," asks Jerzy Jedlicki (*op. cit.*, note 2), "After

all how many times in the last two centuries were the Poles (or the Hungarians or the Bulgarians for

mas were seen as derivative from that basic dualism.

The past decade has seen a revival of a theoretical concept which for a long time was abandoned and even discredited, and which has suddenly proved its heuristic power in dealing with that fundamental tension of real socialism and pointed the way toward its revolutionary resolution. This is the concept of "*civil society*." The "poverty of real socialism" was founded on the decay of civil society, and the direction of the revolution on the restoration of civil society. The revolution of 1989, prepared by a decade of growing opposition against the communist system, was a revolution in the name of civil society. This was witnessed by a number of perceptive observers. Timothy Garton Ash remarks: "A concept that was central in opposition thinking during the 1980s was that of civil society. The year 1989 was the springtime of societies aspiring to be civil."[36] Jeffrey Alexander comments: "Almost single-handedly, Eastern European intellectuals reintroduced 'civil society' to contemporary social theory."[37] And looking to the future, Ralf Dahrendorf predicts: "Civil society is the key. . . . There is the great task of civil society. It is the most important of all, and of course the one which requires the greatest efforts in the countries concerned."[38]

Rebuilding civil society means closing the chasm separating the public and the private sphere, eradicating that dangerous fault-line dug by "real socialism" and which still persists, hidden under the emerging facade of postcommunist institutions. This task must proceed in three directions.

The first is the elimination of the "sociological vacuum" which Stefan Nowak defined in 1979 as the lack of intermediate forms of social bond—pluralistic network of voluntary associations, interest groups, political organizations, and local communities —between the highest level of the state, and the lowest level of the family.[39] The monocentric and autocratic system of real socialism has succeeded in contracting or eliminating that domain, and it must be restored. "There should be forms of association, national, regional, local, professional, which would be voluntary, authentic, democratic and, first and last, not controlled by the Party or Party-State."[40] It is indispensable for revitalizing that "rich and thick existence of a society beneath and outside the state."[41]

The second task is the creation of an economic market and a representative democracy as institutional arrangements permanently asserting and demonstrating the link between individual interests and the public good, personal choices and public welfare. This leads to the replacement of the antidemocratic discourse of "private versus public" by the democratic discourse of "private through public and public through private." Of course such full mutual *interpenetration and integration* of both spheres cannot stop at the level of institutions. It must go deeper, become anchored in everyday life, in cherished values and customs, habits and instincts, and reach the "*deep level*" of society.[42] Only then will the market

---

that matter) fighting, weapons or pens in hands, for their national independence? . . . Indeed if all those peoples . . . share any basic experience and any common wisdom, it boils down to this: that no victory is ever final, no peace settlement is ever final, no frontiers are secure, and each generation must begin its work anew."

[36]Ash (1990b), *op. cit.*, note 26, p. 20.
[37]Alexander (1991), *op. cit.*, note 30, p. 1.
[38]Dahrendorf, *op. cit.*, note 7, pp. 93, 153.

[39]Stefan Nowak, "System wartosci spoleczenstwa polskiego" ("The System of Values of the Polish Society"), *Studia Socjologiczne* No. 4 (1979); Nowak (1987), *op. cit.*, note 16, p. 30.
[40]Ash (1990a), *op. cit.*, note 32, p. 147.
[41]Alexander (1990a), *op. cit.*, note 17, p. 22.
[42]According to Brzezinski: "A truly operative free-market system involves not only an intricate set of economic relationships, but also the emergence of

and democracy attain "the social foundations which transform the constitution and the economy from fair-weather into all-weather institutions which can withstand the storms generated within and without."[43]

The third task is shaping knowledgeable and motivated agents, able and willing to use the new institutional framework of democracy and capitalism for their own benefit and for the benefit of society. In other words educating enlightened, informed, and committed *citizens* who are ready to push their society forward and, by the same token, are able to satisfy their personal aspirations and dreams. The emancipatory theme is present in all postcommunist societies. "The language of citizenship was important in all these revolutions. People had had enough of being mere components in a deliberately atomized society: they wanted to be citizens, individual men and women with dignity and responsibility, with rights but also with duties, freely associating in civil society."[44]

The reconstruction of civil society—in all three senses—is the key to the ultimate victory of anticommunist revolutions. But here we encounter the greatest challenge, and perhaps the most fundamental dilemma. It may be called—following the reasoning of Ralf Dahrendorf—"*the dilemma of three clocks.*"[45] The point is that successful transformations at various levels of post-revolutionary society require various spans of time. The deeper we move, the longer is the requisite time. At the top, there are the reforms of laws and political institutions, culminating in the enactment of new consti-

tutions. The "hour of the lawyer" (as Dahrendorf calls it) may be over in six months. Then, at a little deeper level, there are the reforms of the economic system. They take much longer. Dahrendorf estimates that "the hour of the economist" may last at least six years. Finally, at the deepest and most important level, there is the rebuilding of the cultural codes, discourses, and underlying social life. Most important here is the *reconstitution of civil society*. This takes longest and meets the strongest, even if unwitting, resistance. "The hour of the citizen" may take sixty years. The main challenge is not so much that we shall have to wait so long, but rather that at every moment we shall encounter mutually unsynchronized changes, with politics running ahead at the quickest speed, the economy following more slowly, and civil society lagging decades and generations behind. Only at the distant, but hopefully attainable moment when all three levels coincide, will the revolution be completed.[46]

The central theme of anticommunist revolutions and postcommunist reforms is "returning to Europe." An informed observer notes that "In all the lands, the phrase people use to sum up what is happening is the return to Europe."[47] But rarely is it recognized that this goal may mean two different things, and may signify more superficial or further reaching ambitions. Zbigniew Brzezinski has introduced a very insightful distinction: the European *house* is not the same as the European *home*. "House has architectural implications. Home has relational implications. The first implies a structure; the second implies a family."[48] Or to put it in a language closer to our discussion, the first implies "hard" institutional and or-

---

an effective entrepreneurial culture. It involves a change in psychology and not just a change in objective economic conditions. This is difficult to achieve." Zbigniew Brzezinski, "Toward a Common European Home," *Problems of Communism* (November–December 1989), pp. 1–10.

[43]Dahrendorf, *op. cit.*, note 7, p. 3.

[44]Ash (1990b), *op. cit.*, note 26, p. 3.

[45]Dahrendorf, *op. cit.*, note 7, p. 93.

[46]As Dahrendorf (*op. cit.* note 7) puts it: "The hour of the lawyer and the hour of the politician mean little without the hour of the citizen."

[47]Ash (1990b), *op. cit.*, note 26, p. 22.

[48]Brzezinski, *op. cit.*, note 42, p. 2.

ganizational frameworks, while the second implies soft "intangibles and imponderables." Accordingly, to reenter the European house is not the same as being accepted into the European home. The former is easier and quicker: It only requires legal, institutional, and constitutional changes and the coordination of the political and economic system with that prevailing in Western Europe. The latter is much more demanding; it requires fundamental transformations of mentality, spirit, and cultural and civilizational codes.[49] To be already in Europe, in a political and even an economic sense, is not yet the same as becoming a fully-fledged European citizen. Joining the realm of European states and markets is not the same as *entering European civil societies*. Only the latter will signify a true and ultimate return to Europe.

---

[49]"We cannot return to Europe as long as our towns are dirty, our telephones do not work, our political parties are reactionary and parochial, and our mentality Sovietized. Europe, then is a measure, a goal, a dream" (Jedlicki, *op. cit.*, note 2, p. 41).

40 FROM AUTHORITARIANISM TO DEMOCRACY: CONCEPTS AND INTELLECTUAL TRENDS

CONSTANTINE ARVANITOPOULOS

This article is part of a forthcoming book on transitions written while the author was in residence at the Center for European Studies at Harvard University. The author is now Assistant Professor of Government and Politics at George Mason University.

A useful way to conceptualize transitions is by juxtaposing them to revolutions. As summarized in Table 1, transition is a gradual process of political and/or economic change negotiated among a few actors. Instead, revolution is upwelling from below and brings about rapid political and socioeconomic change.

A common problem facing the students of transition is defining its chronological parameters. The inherent difficulty lies in the impossibility of precisely defining the exact moment of any political transition (that is, its beginning or its end). We could overcome this problem by delimiting transitions, on the one side, by the authoritarian regime's actual withdrawal and, on the other, by the installation of the democratic regime signified by the first free elections.[1]

During the process of transition the rules of the political game are in flux and they are usually arduously contested. According to O'Donnell and Schmitter:

> Actors struggle not just to satisfy their immediate interests and/or the interests of those whom they represent, but also to define rules and procedures whose configuration will determine likely winners and losers in the future.[2]

Transitions ought not to be confused with liberalizations. *Liberalization* is the process identified with measures taken by an authoritarian regime in the direction of providing more secure guarantees for the rights of individuals and groups.[3] Liberalization can be a sign that the process of transition is about to begin, but it should not be confused with transition or democratization. O'Donnell and Schmitter argue that:

[1]Authoritarian regimes as systems of government usually share the following characteristics: Political participation and mobilization is restricted or abolished (absence of a democratically elected parliament, political parties, civil rights, and an independent judiciary), and the political arena is restricted to members of the state apparatus, who exercise power within formally ill-defined limits but actually quite predictable ones. See Juan Linz, "An Authoritarian Regime: Spain," in Erik Allard and Yrjo Llittunen

(eds.), *Cleavages, Ideologies and Party Systems,* (Helsinki: Academic Bookstore, 1964).

[2]Guillermo O'Donnell and Philippe C. Schmitter, "Defining Some Concepts," in O'Donnell, Schmitter, Whitehead, *Transitions from Authoritarian Rule: Prospects for Democracy* (Baltimore: The Johns Hopkins Press, 1986), vol. IV, p. 6.

[3]Ibid, p. 6.

Reprinted by permission of the author.

TABLE 1 REVOLUTIONS VS. TRANSITIONS

Revolutions	Transitions
From below:	From above:
Rapid;	Negotiational-gradual;
Uncontrolled;	Political and economic changes negotiated
Socioeconomic changes of state and class	among few elites without class conflict;
structure carried through by class conflict;	Military subordinate to civilians
Coincidence of societal change and class	
upheaval;	
Coincidence of political and social	
transformation	
Civil-military relations fused	

Authoritarian rulers may tolerate or even promote liberalization in belief that by opening up certain spaces for individual and group action, they can relieve various pressures and obtain needed information and support without altering the structure of authority, that is, without becoming accountable to the citizenry for their actions or subjecting their claim to rule to fair and competitive elections.[4]

Although in most cases liberalization has a multiplier effect leading to increasing demands for more rights, the process could be reversed by the authoritarian rulers.

Regime installation, which is the outcome of a transition to democracy, occurs when accidental arrangements, prudential norms, and contingent solutions that have emerged during the struggles of transition are transformed into structures, that is, into relationships that are reliably known, regularly practiced, and habitually accepted by those persons or collectivities defined as participants, citizens, or subjects of such structures. When rules and patterns of interactions between groups are sufficiently entrenched, then consolidation is a reality.[5] In that sense, most scholars have used a relatively narrow and easy to operationalize definition of democracy, one that provides for: free and contested elections for the selection of political representatives; basic civil rights; and clearly established "rules of the game" that protect these democratic liberties.[6] This definition of democracy involves two dimensions, contestation and participation, which Dahl and Joseph A. Schumpeter see as critical to democracy.[7]

LITERATURE ON TRANSITIONS

During the 1950s and 1960s, scholars were optimistic that decolonization and economic development would lead to the multiplication of democratic regimes. Most American political scientists and sociologists, writing on democracy, had focused on examining data about functioning democracies, perhaps with badly functioning democracies and nondemocratic regimes thrown in for contrast. This functional orientation was natural for scholars of a country that took its

[4]Ibid, p. 9.

[5]Ibid, pp. 6–14.
[6]Donald Share, "Transitions to Democracy and Transition Through Transaction," *Comparative Political Studies*, January 1987, p. 527.
[7]Robert A. Dahl, *Polyarchy: Participation and Opposition* (New Haven: Yale University Press, 1971), pp. 4–9; Joseph A. Schumpeter, *Capitalism, Socialism, and Democracy* (New York: Harper and Row, 1947), p. 269:

crucial steps toward democracy in the previous century. It also accorded with the characteristic trends in American social science towards "systematic equilibria, quantitative correlations, and survey data engendered by the researcher's own questions. Above all, it accorded with a deep-seated prejudice against causality,"[8] eloquently described by Herbert A. Simon:

> [W]e are wary, in the social sciences, of asymmetrical relations. They remind us of pre-Humeian and pre-Newtonian notions of causality. By whip and sword we have been converted to the doctrine that there is no causation, only functional interrelation, and that functional relations are perfectly symmetrical. We may even have taken over, as a very persuasive analogy, the proposition "for every action, there is an equal and opposite reaction."[9]

In that fashion, American sociologists and political scientists like Seymour Martin Lipset connected stable democracies with certain economic and social background conditions, such as high per capita income, widespread literacy, and prevalent urban residence.[10] Almond and Verba suggested that the ideal "civic culture" of a democracy presupposes the existence of certain beliefs or psychological attitudes among the citizens.[11] Others looked at certain features of the social and political structure. In contrast to the prevailing consensus theory, Carl J.

Friedrich, Ralf Dahrendorf, and Arend Lijphart insisted that conflict and reconciliation are essential to democracy.[12] Robert A. Dahl proposed that polyarchy is based on a broad range of majority consensus.[13] These authors' main point of reference was not their preoccupation with the genesis of a democratic system, but rather how a democracy, assumed to be already in existence, can best preserve or enhance its health and stability.

The history of the next decade proved otherwise, however, and many scholars started inquiring into the nature and causes of the breakdown of civilian rule in the developing world. Subsequently, the persistence of military regimes shifted the attention of the academic community from the causes of military intervention to its consequences. Scholars focused on authoritarian regimes as systems of government and explored their differences from and similarities with democratic regimes.

In 1970, Dankwart Rustow published a highly critical article in which he argued for the need of a conceptual shift in the study of democracy.[14] All these studies, Rustow argued, focused on preconditions to democracy and often jumped from the correlation between democracy and other factors, to the conclusion that those other factors are responsible for democracy. They also tended to look for the preconditions for democracy primarily in economic, social, cultural, and psychological, but not political factors.[15] Rustow argued that if all scientific inquiry starts with the conscious or unconscious perception of a puzzle, then the puzzle

---

"the democratic method is that institutional arrangement for arriving at political decisions in which individuals acquire the power to decide by means of a competitive struggle for the people's vote."

[8]Dankwart A. Rustow, "Transitions to Democracy," *Comparative Politics*, (1970), p. 340.

[9]Herbert A. Simon, *Models of Man: Social and Rational* (New York, 1957), p. 65.

[10]Seymour Martin Lipset, "Some Social Requisites of Democracy: Economic Development and Political Legitimacy," *American Political Science Review*, LIII, (March 1959).

[11]Gabriel Almond and Sidney Verba, *The Civil Culture* (Princeton: Princeton University Press, 1963).

[12]Carl J. Friedrich, *The New Belief in the Common Man* (Boston: Little and Brown, 1942); Ralf Dahrendorf, *Class and Class Conflict in Industrial Society,* (Stanford: Stanford University Press, 1959); Arend Lijphart, *The Politics of Accommodation* (Berkeley: University of California Press, 1968).

[13]Robert A. Dahl, *A Preface to Democratic Theory,* (Chicago: Chicago University Press: 1956).

[14]Rustow, "Transitions to Democracy," p. 340.

[15]Ibid, p. 337.

for students of the developing nations is the genetic question of how a democracy comes into being in the first place. The shift from a functional to genetic inquiry implies that scholars would have to inquire into causes. That would not mean a return to old-fashioned or simple-minded causality, whereby every effect has but one cause and every cause but one effect. Rustow argued that we need not assume that the transition is a world-wide uniform process, that it always involves the same social actors, the same types of political issues, or even methods of solution. Nor does a model of transition need to maintain a temporal continuity and presumably a linear correlation. It may also not be socially uniform. Even in the same country and during the same phase of the process, political attitudes are not likely to be spread evenly through the population.

The need for such a conceptual shift in the study of democracy, as articulated by Rustow, became increasingly evident by the developments of the 1970s and 1980s. The transition from authoritarianism to democracy in Southern Europe in the 1970s and Latin America in the 1980s, made scholars realize that authoritarian regimes are ever present but not everlasting. On a global level they seem always to be with us, but as individual units they emerge and disintegrate. Moreover, the recent dissolution of authoritarianism in the former Soviet Union and Eastern Europe, and the undergoing transitions, underlined the need for the development of an analytic framework which will account for the prospects of peaceful change from authoritarianism to democracy. Consequently, scholarly interest has shifted from the functional analysis of democratic or authoritarian regimes to the genetic question of how a transition can successfully lead to the creation and consolidation of a democratic regime.

Reviewing the empirical material and the theoretical guidelines on transitions from military to civilian rule, one can discern two general themes. The first general and shared theme is normative, namely, that the transition from authoritarianism to some form of democratic regime, which will eventually establish certain rules of regular, formalized political competition, constitutes per se a desirable goal and deserves the attention of scholars and practitioners. The second theme involves an effort to capture the extraordinary uncertainty of the transitional process. These efforts have been mainly descriptive and empirical. There has been little effort to develop a typology of transitions from military to civilian rule, or to formulate a theory of such processes. Theoretical efforts have been frustrated by the lack of information regarding these processes and also the nature of the process itself. In their influential volume on transitions, O'Donnell and Schmitter argued that:

> When studying an established political regime, one can rely on relatively stable economic, social, cultural, and partisan categories to identify, analyze, and evaluate the identities and strategies of those defending the status quo and those struggling to reform or transform it. . . . During these transitions, in many cases and around many themes, it is almost impossible to specify exactly which classes, sectors, institutions, and other groups will take what role, opt for what issues, or support what alternative.[16]

Even if we share O'Donnell's and Schmitter's frustration with the nature of the transitional process, we should still place our emphasis on actors as opposed to structures and institutions, during this process, for the following reasons: Democratic insti-

[16]Guillermo O'Donnell and Phillipe C. Schmitter, "Introducing Uncertainty," in O'Donnell, Schmitter, and Whitehead, *Transitions from Authoritarian Rule,* vol. IV, p. 4.

tutions and other structures that could channel popular demands into the process of transitions have either been destroyed or are in disarray as a result of authoritarian rule. Moreover, the transition presupposes the collapse of authoritarian rule and institutions. Therefore, authoritarian and democratic leaders operate almost in an institutional vacuum. As a result, we can best explain the transitional process if we model it as a set of strategic interactions among a few specific actors, whereby each actor has limited choices and makes those choices rationally, that is, in an interest-maximizing way.

Although many forms of strategic interaction involving individual actors or organized social groups have been conceived in game-theoretic terms, such a framework has not been used to date to model transitions from authoritarianism to democracy. There have been no studies contemplating transitional paths and outcomes as products of strategic interaction, strategies, and simultaneous or sequential moves between authoritarians and democrats. The use of game theory as a heuristic device could be enormously beneficial to better understand the preferences of the actors, their strategies, and their payoffs, during the process of transition. The deductive apparatus of game theory leads to a clarity that illuminates social phenomena, and could allow us to infer new understandings about the process.[17]

Two dimensions can serve as explanations of cooperation and as targets of longer-term strategies to promote cooperation in authoritarian-democratic games during transitional processes.[18] The first regards the payoffs and how they affect the prospect for cooperation. More narrowly, when is cooperation, defined in terms of conscious policy coordination, necessary for the realization of mutual benefits? Actors must prefer mutual cooperation (CC) to mutual defection (DD). Yet, unilateral defection (DC) is preferred to unilateral cooperation (CD). There is an incentive to defect, yet mutual cooperation has a higher payoff than mutual defection. These preference orderings are consistent with the familiar games of Prisoner's Dilemma, and Chicken.

If the payoff structure in authoritarian-democratic games is the aforementioned, then cooperation between authoritarian and democratic actors will be more likely and the transition will be successful. In contrast, in transitions where at least one actor prefers mutual defection (DD) to mutual cooperation (CC) the term cooperation becomes inapplicable and the transition is unsuccessful. If payoff structure affects the likelihood of cooperation, actors can alter situations by modifying payoff structures, and thereby increase the long-term likelihood of cooperation. For example, in the Greek case, following the sentence of the dictators to death in 1974, Karamanlis, then prime minister, immediately changed it to life sentences thereby reducing a defensive defection by the armed forces. So, unilateral or bilateral strategies may be used to alter

---

[17]The use of game theory in the empirical study of international politics has been extensive. For an extended discussion see Duncan Snidal, "The Game Theory of International Politics," *World Politics* 1, (October 1985), pp. 25. Examples of its application include: Bruce Bueno de Mesquita, "The Costs of War: A Rational Expectations Approach," *American Political Science Review* vol. 77, (June 1983), pp. 347–357; Robert Jervis, "Rational Deterrence: Theory and Evidence," *World Politics* vol. 41, (January 1989), pp. 169–207; Christopher Achen and Duncan Snidal, "Rational Deterrence Theory and Comparative

Case Studies," *World Politics* vol. 41, (January 1989), pp. 143–169; George Tsebelis, "The Abuse of Probability in Political Analysis: the Robinson Crusoe Fallacy," *American Political Science Review* vol. 83, (March 1989), pp. 77–92.

[18]These dimensions have been borrowed from Kenneth A. Oye, "Explaining Cooperation under Anarchy: Hypotheses and Strategies," *World Politics*, 1, October 1985, pp. 1–24. They have been adapted to fit my theoretical framework.

payoff structures and secure long-term co-operation.

The second dimension that serves for cooperation is the expectation of future interaction. Iterated conditions decrease the temptation of immediate gains from unilateral defection, or fear of immediate losses from unrequited cooperation.[19] In transitions, if authoritarian and democratic actors place high value on future payoffs, since they are expected to continue dealing with each other, then the situation has many characteristics of an iterated game and cooperation is more likely. An iterated environment permits resort to strategies of reciprocity that may improve the prospects of cooperation in a Chicken or in Prisoner's Dilemma. Reciprocity underscores the future consequences of present cooperation and defection. The argument rests on the assumption that defection in the present will decrease the likelihood of cooperation in the future.

Strategic interactions between authoritarians and democrats can evolve along a continuum of possibilities. At one end, relations can become increasingly more stable through a series of negotiated compromises. Neither side is powerful enough to impose an ideal preference, and so each agrees to solutions where second best alternatives prevail. Moreover, and especially with regard to political pacts which are one form of negotiated compromise, actors agree to forgo or underutilize their capacity to harm each other by extending guarantees not to threaten each other's corporate autonomies or vital interests. Opponents are convinced that mutual gain is possible in this "nonzero-sum" environment. They regard each other as adversaries but not implacable enemies, and thus agree to keep their conflict within manageable limits.

At the other end, relations between authoritarian and democratic elites may deteriorate and may prove to be counterproductive for the consolidation process. Opponents cannot agree to place limits on their use of power nor to refrain from harming one another. Both sides disagree on what constitutes an appropriate purview for themselves and their adversaries. Consequently, they do not respect corporate or institutional boundaries and prerogatives. Each side tries to "move the marker" which defines the border between the respective spheres of influence until conflict gets out of hand and one party prevails.

Along the continuum interactions may change, with confrontational episodes yielding forms of cooperation, or cooperative ventures breaking down. It should be stressed that in the process of transition the nature of the game may change. The results of a single interaction can set the boundaries of action for the next game, which may or may not be the same as its predecessor.

By using rational choice and game theory as our analytical tools and by placing our emphasis on actors, their preference orderings, strategies, and choices, we could shed additional light on the transitional processes, and make suggestions for generalization regarding the process of transition from authoritarianism to democracy.

[19]Ibid, p. 12.